POLITICS, U.S.A.

Andrew M. Scott and Earle Wallace

PROFESSORS OF POLITICAL SCIENCE
THE UNIVERSITY OF NORTH CAROLINA

Third Edition

POLITICS, U.S.A.

Cases on the American Democratic Process

THE MACMILLAN COMPANY / COLLIER-MACMILLAN LIMITED, LONDON

PREFACE

This volume of "cases" on politics and the American political system has been designed specifically for use in the introductory course on the American political system. The case approach has much to recommend it. A good case will engage the student's interest—a prerequisite for effective learning. A good case makes it clear that "government is people" —men and women thinking, calculating, torn by conflicting desires, occupying offices of greater or lesser importance, making decisions, playing out the roles they have defined for themselves. Because of its basic purpose, it is difficult for a textbook to convey to the student a full understanding of the human element in politics and government.

A case often provides an excellent way of bringing out basic issues. If it concerns a conflict situation, words and arguments come from the mouths of the protagonists. The student may identify with one (or both) sides in the dispute and in so doing improve his understanding of what is involved. Students sometimes identify so thoroughly with one side or the other that they engage in "role playing" during the discussions. The ability of students to project themselves imaginatively into situations and to learn from this experience often increases markedly over a period of time. The knowledge that an actual situation is involved, and not merely a hypothetical one, causes even the skeptical student to be willing to project himself to at least some extent.

The case approach also encourages thought and discrimination. The analysis of one situation after another helps a student learn how to think about government and politics. (With luck, the habit of analysis might carry over into other areas of activity as well.) Because the student is thinking and perceiving for himself, and not simply accepting authority, knowledge and understanding gained are more likely to be retained beyond the next examination.

The case approach, moreover, has the advantage of allowing the student greater freedom in developing his own perceptions about politics and government. A case provides data against which he can check his ideas or ideas expressed by his textbook or instructor. Although the instructor may not find his task eased by the use of a case book, he will certainly find it made more exciting. The student will be thoroughly engaged and the instructor will not need to fight to maintain interest. He will also find it more effective to draw issues and "principles" directly from the case under discussion rather than from a body of anonymous data with which the student is not familiar and the existence of which he must take on faith.

Although the case approach is an extremely useful teaching tool, there are certain problems connected with it. If it provides an unsurpassed means of giving students a feeling for the processes and problems of government and politics, it leaves much to be desired in presenting a discussion of governmental structure. Textbook and case book, therefore, bear a complementary relationship, each providing what the other cannot.

A second limitation of this approach is that, as historians have been accustomed to note, there is no such thing as getting "all the facts." Even if this were a possibility, the ensuing account would be too boring and trivial to read or think about. In the preparation of any case, some of the facts will be included and a great many more left out. Which are to be included and which excluded will depend upon the skill, perceptions, purposes, and viewpoint of the individual preparing the case. Sometimes the author will try to give a balanced presentation, other times this will be no part of his purpose. If a case is written by a participant in the events described, one must expect him to try to justify the role that he played in those events. This by no means destroys the value of the case, and may increase it, for the case will then provide insight into the actor's motivation and his interpretation of the events in which he played a part. If a case is thoroughly one-sided, students can usually be relied on to see this. Not infrequently they may argue that the hero in a case is really the villain of the piece, or vice versa.

In preparing this book, the editors discovered that the total volume of case material available was substantial. They also discovered that it was uneven in its coverage, some areas having been dealt with quite often in cases, others having been virtually ignored. This has influenced our selections.

A good deal of frankly partisan material has been included and we have not worried very much about immediately offsetting one such piece by a selection representing the opposite view. We have tried, instead, to achieve a balance when the volume is taken as a whole. It is in the nature of things that not everyone will agree that we have succeeded. It is our experience, however, that the critical faculties of students develop very quickly to the point where they no longer need to be solemnly warned before they read a selection that it may be slanted one way or another.

We have tried to find cases that were vivid, that would give the volume variety, and that would make their point without being unduly long. While we have not regarded it as an iron-bound rule, most of the cases used in this volume deal with matters that are fairly recent. Exceptions have been made only for cases where the personalities are particularly interesting or well known and where the events involved are of historical significance.

Because of the interest of the editors in using timely material, the third edition of *Politics, U.S.A.* contains little that was included in the second edition. All but one of the cases are new. In addition, the organization of the volume has been changed in response to changing political priorities in the United States. For example, a chapter has been included dealing with the politics of violence. This chapter includes material on the riots, including a summary of the Report of the Commission on Civil Disorders. A chapter on poverty has been added as has a chapter on the crisis of the cities. In response to requests, we have added a chapter on the constitutional background of the American political system. That chapter incorporates material drawn directly from the debates in the Constitutional Convention in 1787. The student can listen to Hamilton, Madison, Franklin, and others and watch the emergence, for the first time in history, of ideas that were destined to shape the future development of the country.

It goes without saying that our search for case materials has taken us into some unlikely places. There are a good many items included that were not regarded as "cases" by their authors, but which serve our purposes very well.

Also, we have concentrated on materials available from sources easily accessible to the student, now and in the future. We know that most students in the introductory course in American government will not become professional political scientists and will have neither the interest nor the easy access to professional journals; therefore, the experience of analyzing cases drawn from popular sources which they will continue to read after graduation should be of lasting value.

Most of our selections carry their original titles. In some instances, however, we have taken the liberty of providing titles of our own devising, either because the selection was an untitled excerpt from a larger work or because the original title was less suitable for the purposes of this volume.

Members of the editorial and production departments at The Macmillan Company have assisted us in many ways in the production of this volume and we would like to express our gratitude to them.

Chapel Hill, North Carolina

A. M. S.   E. W.

CONTENTS

Chapter Five

INTEREST GROUPS

Chapter Six

POLITICAL PARTIES

Chapter Seven

THE ELECTORAL PROCESS

Chapter Eight

THE CONGRESS

Chapter Thirteen

THE POLITICS OF VIOLENCE

Chapter Fourteen

THE MAKING OF FOREIGN AND MILITARY POLICY

THE CONTEXT OF AMERICAN POLITICS

This book is concerned with the American political system. It asks: What is that system and how does it work? What is it that makes it "democratic"? A political system does not exist in isolation, however. It is always embedded in a culture. An important element of that culture, and the element that this chapter is concerned with, is the political element. The political culture of a nation consists of that set of ideas, traditions, assumptions, and accepted rules-of-the-game that go to make up the framework within which the political system functions. Unless one understands the political culture in which a political system is set, one cannot understand the system itself.

The context of American politics is a confused one at present. Rules-of-the-game that seemed unchallengeable a few years ago are now challenged. Assumptions that seemed firm appear to have come adrift. The selections in this chapter illuminate some of the ideological cross currents. They suggest the need for consensus—and the vital role of dissent. They suggest the need for distinguishing legitimate dissent from an outright attack on the social fabric.

The Democratic Process

Clinton Rossiter

The quickening debate over the public agenda of the next decade has given rise, happily and yet not surprisingly, to more unity than dissension among the American people. In this favored country we have almost always found more things on which to agree than to disagree, and the early 1960's appear to be a time of broad consensus on fundamentals.

The core of this consensus is a continuing commitment to democracy as the best of all possible ways of managing the affairs of men. The style of America has been democratic for more than a century, and it is hard for us to listen respectfully to those who argue that we must change that style radically in the next decade or begin the long decline to mediocrity and, beyond that, to extinction. Although we have never been more soberly aware of the faults of democracy, we have also never been more impressed by its strengths. All attempts to improve the quality of American life must, we think, be made in the manner and spirit of a free people.

WHAT IS DEMOCRACY?

One of the special strengths of democracy is that it encourages men to think for themselves, and experience proves that every thinking American can be counted on to have his own definition of this famous word. Yet amid the infinite diversity of our definitions there is a hard core of unity. When we say that America has been a democracy, and expect it to remain one, we mean it in each and all of several senses.

Our democracy has been, first of all, a process—a set of techniques for making decisions and managing affairs at every level of social organization. While our chief concern has been to practice democracy in the government of the nation, the process has also flourished, and given a special flavor to American life, in public communities and private associations throughout the land. Whether in operation in the Congress at Washington or in a school board in Palo Alto or in a service club in Keokuk, the democratic process has been a method of arriving openly, through discussion and compromise, at decisions in keeping with the reasonable wishes of the majority, and then of pursuing these decisions with the fullest possible respect for the legitimate rights of the minority.

The essence of the democratic process has been respect for the rules; the guaranty of this respect in the public arena has been the spirit and practices of constitutionalism. Constitutionalism is the generic label for all those arrangements and techniques—separation of powers, checks and balances, due process, bills of rights, the rule of law—that force our governors to think, talk, bargain, and explain before they act, and that institutionalize the procedures through which public policy is made, administered, and enforced. Although the rule of the majority is, in Jefferson's

"The Democratic Process" from *Goals for Americans* © 1960 by The American Assembly, Columbia University, New York, New York. Reprinted by permission of Prentice-Hall, Inc., Englewood Cliffs, New Jersey.

words, the "vital principle" of the American republic, constitutionalism seeks to assure us that the majority will be clear-cut and cool-headed on all occasions, extraordinary on extraordinary occasions, and powerless on occasions when the consciences of men are at issue. Above all, it seeks to assure us that the consent of the governed will not be given lightly to decisions of great moment. This is why Americans have always believed stoutly that, while a government can be constitutional without being democratic, it cannot be democratic without being constitutional.

If democracy is procedures, it is also results; if it is a way of doing things, it is also things done. America has been a democracy not merely because our public and private governments have made many decisions openly, carefully, and in response to clearly-voiced popular demands, but because the decisions themselves were intrinsically hopeful and humane. While not every decision or activity of a government can be judged in these largely ethical terms, certainly in such fields as education and welfare the people of a democracy have a right to expect that policies will strengthen the fabric of civilized existence. A democracy, in this view, is a system of government that acts, whenever it does act, to foster justice, preserve liberty, erase inequality, promote morality, and expand opportunity; and such a democracy we have tried to be.

Finally, our democracy has been a spirit that has pervaded the thoughts and directed the actions of governors and governed alike. The essence of the democratic spirit is a belief in liberty and justice; the aspiration, a commitment to liberty and justice for all; and both essence and aspiration have pervaded the American temper. Enough Americans, it would seem, have had the instinctive preference for freedom and the reasoned respect for popular government that together make it possible for a nation to make the democratic gamble. The spirit of these men has been made real in a code of public and personal behavior that has governed our strivings for generations. It would be hard to overestimate the importance of this code to the proper working of the democratic process. Without the oil of the democratic spirit, in which humility and courage are mixed liberally with the belief in liberty and justice, the wheels of constitutional compromise would clog with the rust of fear and envy, or at best grind out results designed to serve only the vested interests of those men already in favor. And it is, after all, the presence of this spirit alone that gives a "democratic" quality to many acts of leadership in a system of government in which experts play an increasingly important part.

In all these ways—in process, in result (and thus in continuing purpose) and in spirit—America has long been a working democracy. More than a few men in power have corrupted the process and turned it to evil uses; more than a few laws and policies have served narrowly selfish ends; more than a few of us, thanks to our powers of self-delusion, have engaged comfortably in practices that flout accepted standards of humanity and fair dealing. Yet all this is simply to say that Madison was right when he reminded us of the universality of "the infirmities and depravities of the human character." None of it is to say that we could have wrought half so effectively or benevolently under the terms of any other system.

We have had, to be sure, many forces working in our favor. Democracy is a somewhat less weedlike plant than anarchy or autocracy; it will flourish only when conditions are favorable. We who live in modern America are blessed more than any other nation with the social and material conditions of freedom, for we have inherited a well-structured society, a productive economy, a bold and encompassing system of education, a civilized and equitable pattern of private property, and all the political and social tools of self-government. We are blessed more than most nations with the intellectual and spiritual conditions, for we have inherited a great tradition, a humane religion, a clear-cut moralty, and a tested faith—faith, in particular, in the dignity of the person and in the fairness and competence of democracy. And surely we were favored in the days of our youth by the timetable of history, which gave us our major blessings in the right order: economic viability before political liberty, constitutionalism before democracy, a morality of self-control before a morality of self-expression.

Yet some of our blessings are the fruits as well as the fertilizer of democracy, and no one can say that we have failed to put both the process and the spirit to severe tests. We were the first to make the democratic gamble on a large scale; we made it with a thoroughly mixed bag of humanity, with men of every creed and national origin. It was not an easy experiment, despite all our good fortunes. At least once, in the decade before the Civil War, democracy failed us and we failed democracy. Yet in the grand perspective of history, which we should take more often than we do, it will surely be judged that over the years of their rise to greatness the American people were well served by American democracy.

Time of Trial

The question before us is how well it can be made to serve the American people in the years to come, particularly in the short span of years for which men in an age of disorder and innovation can reasonably plan. Although our answer to the question may be confident, it must not be offhanded, for plainly democracy is about to be put to a series of tests that will go beyond those of the past in profusion, severity, and perversity. The situation at home and abroad is hardly as favorable to the flourishing of democracy as it was, let us say, in 1900.

At home we are just learning to live with certain unforeseen consequences of our successful experiments in democracy and technology: urbanization and suburbanization, complexity and interdependence, the standardization of tastes and attitudes, the centralization of communications, the hypertrophy of organization, the institutionalization of self-indulgence. While it may comfort us to think that most of these consequences were inevitable as well as unforeseen, it cannot be denied that their cumulative tendency is to crowd the individual, place much of the responsibility for his well-being in the hands of men he cannot know or control, drown him with information he cannot digest or even understand, and thus push him, in his role as citizen, by way of impotence into apathy.

Abroad we are dealing with a world in which opportunity and danger, progress and decay, old order and new chaos are so explosively mixed that we must face this world, and thus face ourselves within, in a posture of defense far more elaborate than we have ever wanted to strike. More than that, it has not been easy for us to watch the rise of new societies whose methods are a vicious reproach to all that we cherish, and to recognize that these societies can do many of the things we have found worth doing—for example, produce steel or train doctors or eliminate illiteracy—and do them, apparently, with enviable success.

The result of all these developments is that American democracy is laboring under strains for which it was not entirely prepared. In the first place, it should be plain to see that, in operating the machinery, we no longer enjoy the margin for error of past years. The democratic process is grounded on common agreement to proceed slowly through techniques of compromise and to avoid steps that cannot be retraced. In order to work at its best it needs time and space—time in which to consider all points of view, to consult all interests, to build up a clear majority, and to reassure the reluctant minority; space in which to make mistakes and yet not do irreparable damage to the public weal or to private liberties. But time and space are both closing in on us. More and more decisions must be made quickly or go by default, be made correctly the first time on the assumption that there may be no second.

Another strain arises out of the sheer number of problems we face, a situation that has accelerated sharply the long-range trend in our public and private governments from smallness to bigness, frugality to costliness, and simplicity to complexity. The decisions to be made and executed each year are multiplying so rapidly that it is becoming harder to anticipate or coordinate them. We are certainly placing a load on the Constitution for which it was not designed by its framers; we are placing a load on many of its operators—for example, on our representatives in Congress—which compels them to be either dray horses or dilettantes.

And a third arises out of the nature of these problems. The tasks of government are qualitatively as well as quantitatively different from those of the past. The decisions to be made are more than numerous; they are also tougher. Those of the next decade may cut more deeply into the lives of the people than did all the decisions of the previous generation put together.

Numerous and tough though these decisions may be, they will have to be made. Once we could solve many of our problems by waiting for them to solve themselves, but those we face today seem to be of a different order. They will not disappear but only grow worse if approached in a spirit of careless or calculated negligence. Democracy, which has always counted heavily on the loose ways of spontaneity, must now make use of firm techniques of planning. It must think ahead as it has never had to think ahead before.

What we are up against, in short, is a shift from easiness to urgency in the circumstances under which American democracy must operate, and thus a shift from quiescence to activity in the style of American democracy itself. The quiet times are gone forever; forethought, decision, and energy are the order of the day.

And so the fateful question is put to us directly: Can democracy be active, at times even breathlessly active, and remain democracy? Can it be tough without being cruel, alert without being officious, effective without being overbearing, authoritative without being authoritarian?

Our answer, let it be repeated, should be a confident and yet measured "yes." It should be confident because we ought to have learned by now to respect the toughness and resilience of democracy. Experience, reason, instinct, and tradition cry out in unison against the judgment of despairing men that democracy is unequal to the tasks of a great nation in a revolutionary world, and against their advice that radically different techniques of decision-making and administering must be invented or imported wholesale. Democracy has proved its adaptability many times in our past; there is no convincing reason to believe that it cannot bear up under the strains of the future. Certainly no other form of government that has been developed or imagined can claim exemption from these strains. They are the growing burden of all governments everywhere in the world, and this burden will be borne most successfully by governments that make full allowance for the complexity and perversity of human events. The most thoroughly tested of such governments is constitutional democracy, which has unique resources for dealing with the problems common to all advanced societies.

At the same time, our answer should be measured because we ought also to have learned that democracy, perhaps more exigently than other systems, needs loving care if it is to perform at its best. We who are charged with such care—the active citizens of the United States—must do everything we can to strengthen the process, the conditions, and the spirit for the hard pull ahead. Of these three fundamental aspects of democracy, it is the process that most requires and best repays discussion. Let us therefore descend from the general to the specific and see what might be done to strengthen each of the major instruments and relationships of the American system of government. While no plausible case has yet been advanced (or is likely even to be listened to by the American people) for basic changes in this system, there are many small repairs and adjustments that could be made in an effort to tune it up for the heavy loads of the next decade.

The Basic Institutions

To begin at the beginning, which is with the Presidency, our chief concern must be to keep this great office in effective command of the executive branch, especially of the agents of diplomacy and national security. All things considered, the health of the Presidency is good, and we can expect it to flourish indefinitely as a reassuring example of the capacity of democracy to adapt itself to the pressures of new conditions.

Yet there is always danger of the job getting out of hand. We have given the President so many tasks that he can do only a few of them thoroughly; we have made so many men responsible to him that he can control only a few of them directly. Our chief solution to this problem has been to create that amazing collection of agencies and officials known as the Executive Office, but this solution has in turn given rise to still another problem: the danger that the President may be made a prisoner in his own house.

The answer to this and to most other difficulties of the Presidency is clearly more personal than institutional. We should be extremely suspicious of such easy panaceas as the proposed creation of a supersecretary for national security to stand between the President and his principal heads of department. It is for the President himself, through the force of his will and candid assertion of his eminence, to keep his auxiliary machinery in good working order and thus to coordinate and dominate the protean activities for which he is constitutionally responsible to the people. This means, of course, the hardest kind of work. The President must insist that he be spared routine but not thought and decision; he must leave channels open to political and social pressures that express the realities of American life; he must remind his personal agents that they serve him and the nation poorly when they commit the prestige of his office to decisions he has not really made for himself. Only thus can the institutionalized Presidency display the steady show of leadership essential to alert and energetic government in a giant democracy.

The one sure sign of a healthy democracy is a vigilant, intelligent, self-disciplined legislature, and we may therefore take satisfaction in the determination of Congress to go on playing a vital role in the process of American democracy, no matter how accelerated the pace of that process may become. Capability must match and support determination, however, and there are plainly several steps that can be taken to make Congress a more effective body than it is today.

The road to improvement in this instance is partly institutional, partly personal. If Congress is to be an active partner in an active government— that is to say, a forceful instrument for legislating and appropriating—it must sooner or later move to reduce the power of its obstructionists to more seemly proportions. It must simplify its rules of procedure, confine the House Rules Committee to its proper sphere of action, place a reasonable check on the filibuster, and find some substitute for the traditional method of selecting committee chairmen. There are merits, to be sure, in the rule of seniority, which spares Congress an infinite amount of energy, intrigue, and rancor. Yet the rigid application of this rule has brought too many men to positions of power who are out of harmony, if not indeed out of touch, with the developing sentiments of their political parties and thus of the nation. The problem is a nasty one, yet surely the American political genius can find a workable solution to it.

If Congress is to be a responsible partner—that is to say, a prudent instrument for investigating and overseeing—it must be filled with men who are masters of their craft, respecters of the imperatives of organization, takers of the long view, loyal though not servile sons of their party. It must be filled, moreover, with men who have a knack for communicating essential information about the issues of the day to their constituents. All these considerations, to be sure, throw much of the burden of an improved Congress back upon the people. They might be helped to carry it a little more thoughtfully if they were asked by the Constitution to elect Representatives every four years instead of every two.

None of these changes would be expected to alter drastically the sensible relationship worked out by the Constitution and history between the Presi-

dent and Congress, nor, for that matter, would at least one useful addition
to the President's arsenal of legislative and administrative leadership—
the power to veto separate items in appropriations bills presented for his
approval. In the interests of efficiency and economy, Congress might well
experiment with an occasional bill authorizing the President to eliminate
or reduce specific items subject to reversal by concurrent resolution. If
we learn through these experiments that the power is one he ought to have
and is unlikely to abuse, we could then catch up with forty states—and,
for that matter, with the Confederacy—by writing it into the Constitution.

   Despite the crossfire in which it finds itself today, the federal judiciary
is probably the best prepared of all our institutions to meet the challenges
of the next decade. We need more courts, and more judges on some of the
courts we already have; we should demand of the President that his
appointments be the most distinguished he can make. Further than that
we should not go with attempts to influence the character of the judiciary
and most particularly of the Supreme Court. If it is performing the tasks
staked out for it in our system with any kind of courage and foresight,
it is sure to be stirring the anger of more than one important group or
section. That is the burden the Court must bear, and we should not permit
angry men to make the burden intolerable. We must all learn to respect
its independence even when we cannot agree with some of its judgments.
We must understand why in making these judgments it cannot avoid
making policy—as it has done throughout American history. Above all,
we must remember that an upright and independent judiciary is a bulwark
of constitutional democracy, and that the true test of such a judiciary is
the manner in which it renders justice to men who are unpopular and
helpless.

THE CONDUCT OF GOVERNMENT

   The processes of modern government are in large part administrative.
Democracy must therefore be judged in terms of how efficiently it inspects
meat and collects statistics and delivers the mail as well as how forcefully
it makes foreign policy. If government is now the biggest business of all,
we have a right to expect it to be run as well as the best—frugally,
efficiently, responsibly, and ethically. While the President and Congress
can do much with their techniques of control to raise the level of administrative performance, there is no substitute for a system of recruitment
that brings men of talent and imagination into every rank of the public
service and for a code of responsible behavior that gives them pride in
their tasks.

   One notable arm of the public service has always presented a special
problem for democracy, and now, in a time of fierce and persistent stress,
it must be managed carefully lest it weaken the process and deaden the
spirit. This arm is, of course, the military, which has become so vast and
costly an enterprise that its influence is felt powerfully in almost every
corner of American life—and in almost every decision in foreign affairs.
No easy solution exists for the problem of the military, not least because
this influence, to the extent that it is unhealthy, is exerted unwittingly
by men of good will rather than consciously by men of evil intent.

There are, however, several major points to have in mind as we go about the continuing task of keeping the military in its proper place. One is that the responsibility for civilian control be placed always in the hands of civilians who are in fact able to exercise control. This means, for one example, that the Secretary of Defense should be a man of quality who operates from a solid base of prestige and political power, and acts consciously as the strong arm of the President. Another point is that pluralism in the armed forces is not an entirely unhealthy phenomenon. A rigidly unified military arm might well present far more of a threat to the democratic process than does the present loose and yet honestly competitive pattern of command. And third, the real solution to this problem, as it is to most problems of civilized existence, is education. We must see to it assiduously that the wielders of our military might are infected early and often with respect for the democratic process and are trained to understand its methods.

The condition of our state and local governments, the distribution of responsibilities among the three major levels of government, and the coordination of activities in which all three levels have a hand are problems to which another chapter in this book is directed. It should be enough for present purposes to take note of the overriding need for more active and efficient governments at both the state and local levels. A strengthening of these governments would take us far toward solving the social problems that now beset us, and would do more to quiet fears of centralization than would any other program of action. The way to reverse the flow of power toward Washington, to the extent that it can or should be reversed, is not to weaken the national government but to bolster state and local governments. The states in particular have too important a part to play in the American system to be permitted the outworn luxuries of absurdly detailed constitutions, hog-tied governors, shamefully gerrymandered electoral districts, pressure-ridden legislatures, and chaotic administrations.

Parties and Interest Groups

The democratic process is something more than a collection of offices and of men to fill them. It incorporates all those people outside government who have an active interest in the things it does and in the way it does them; and that, in a healthy democracy, is a large part of the adult citizenry. The process must therefore provide techniques that encourage citizens to gather and digest information, to form and exchange opinions, to debate issues, to communicate needs, and, in those areas where direct participation is possible and advisable, to hear the questions of their public servants and return their sovereign answers—and perhaps to put a few questions of their own. To accomplish these essential tasks of giant democracy we have created an amazing network of organizations. Three categories in particular are vital parts of the democratic process and deserve at least as much attention as we have given to the Presidency or Congress or the military: political parties, interest groups, and the media of communication.

The two-party system has served the needs of American democracy so long and, all things considered, so well that recommendations for its radical reform or total abandonment have a ring of unreality. Without the help of active political parties we could never hope to bring the eternal struggle for power into the open and under control; and we should be more understanding of the ways in which our two great parties have filled the largest gap in the Constitution by performing their vital functions as managers of elections, personnel agencies, sources of public policy, operators and yet also guardians of the machinery of decision and administration, schools of politics, and skilled buffers between individuals and society. Our parties are far from perfect in virtue, but that is only to say that they are managed by real men and women. They are far from high-minded in interest, but that is only to say that the interests they represent are substantial. And if they are not as clearly-divided, principled, disciplined, and responsible as some critics would like them to be, that is largely because they operate in a system in which power is divided vertically between nation and states and horizontally between executive and legislature, and because they seek to build majorities in a society of minorities. At the price of doctrine, and of at least some of their reputation, the parties have brought a vast measure of unity to a diverse nation. Few thinking Americans would want to argue that "the price of union" has been too high.

One could construct in fancy, to be sure, a party system better suited to direct the active government we can expect in the next decade, yet the one we have is the one we are going to have, especially because it is so remarkable a reflection of the realities of American life. When those realities demand action, action will follow. Critics who doubt the capacity of our major parties to make hard decisions would do well to recall two facts about the pattern of American politics. First, it is designed to check but not to frustrate indefinitely the will of the majority. When a majority shows itself clearly and persistently, it will push through the restraints of the party system just as surely as it pushes through those of the Constitution, which are also designed to delay but not to paralyze. And second, the rules of American democracy do not demand that every political decision be first of all a party decision. Partisanship must have a large place in the making of the great decisions before us, yet so, too, must bipartisanship and nonpartisanship. In the American system there are many ways to form and express majority sentiment, and even the best friends of parties would not presume to assert a monopoly of the democratic process.

This leads us naturally to consider the thousands of interest groups, known less fondly as pressure groups or lobbies, and more fondly as civic groups, that form one of the continuing wonders of American life. Whatever we call these groups, we are aware that they swing a sizable amount of persuasive power over the men who make and execute policy in all governments in all parts of the land, and that the democratic process would be very different without them. They do not have a high standing in the mythology of American democracy. Indeed, they are often represented as the worst enemies of democracy. Yet they are natural products of an open, plural, energetic society, serving effectively to institutionalize two of our most precious liberties: freedom of association and the right of petition. They, like the parties, can be no better, no more honest, no more broad-minded than the men who direct or support them. Laws that seek to regulate them can reach only a small way; most hopes for cleansing their methods and raising their sights begin and end with educating the active citizenry.

The one large objective that we might keep in view as we strive to make the interest groups a healthier feature of American democracy is to give a broader, more democratic character to the influence they exert. The serious doubts we have about these groups arise out of contemplation of their purposes as well as of their methods. Too many of them have too much energy to burn, money to spend, and thus influence to peddle in behalf of highly special and selfish interests. What the democratic process needs is the strengthening of existing organizations (and perhaps creation of new ones) that are broad rather than narrow in scope, general rather than particular in interest, public rather than private in operation. We need interest groups that speak out persuasively for majorities as well as for minorities—for consumers of natural gas as well as for producers, for parents of children as well as for teachers, for people who ride railroads as well as for those who run and man them. We need interest groups, too, that are not afraid of stimulating and ventilating intramural discussions, that make specific provision, to cite one intriguing possibility, for minority reports at annual conventions.

COMMUNICATIONS: CIRCUS OR FORUM?

Democracy is at bottom an agreement to hold civilized discussion of issues that count, and those who cherish it must find and cultivate the techniques of reason. Giant democracy has found most of its own techniques in the wondrous media we have created—newspapers, journals, books, radio, television, polls, advertising, and the mails—to inform, educate, and entertain ourselves.

The trouble is, of course, that entertainment has almost swallowed up information and education in the operation of the mass media. Television, for example, is fast becoming the Circus Maximus rather than the Forum of American democracy, and we are missing out consistently on a rare opportunity to hold popular discussions of a range and influence unmatched in all history. While the Nixon-Kennedy confrontations were a welcome departure, they only scratched the surface of the democratic potentialities of this medium. A few brave spirits have done something to inform and educate the public on controversial issues, but for the most part television has not even come within hailing distance of the press as a device by which Americans can communicate sensibly with one another —not that the press is very far down the road to perfection.

Once again the fault lies with ourselves as well as with our trustees, who in this instance are the owners and managers of the mass media. Just as there is no panacea for the sensationalism of some of the press, for the vulgarity of much of radio, and for the presumptuousness of many of the polls, so there is none for the scarcity and sterility of public programming on television. This whole problem forms a jungle of doubt and unforeseen consequences in which we will have to feel our way along toward higher ground. It is possible, of course, that a stout-hearted Federal Communications Commission could compel the television stations of America to pay for the privileges they have been accorded in the coin of genuine public service, for example, by requiring them to set aside a sizable block of "prime" hours in each week for the use of civic groups anxious to communicate their ideas to the people and to men in power. There are also great opportunities for networks of non-profit public service stations.

Sooner or later we are going to have to face up to the harsh fact that the democratic dialogue is in real danger of being smothered. Plainly we are in need of new rules and techniques for keeping this dialogue alive as an active ingredient of the democratic process. Plainly the mass media offer us a splendid opportunity, which we will lose at peril of losing democracy.

Private Governments

This inquiry has concentrated of necessity on democracy in the public arena. We must not forget, however, that it is no less right and viable a force, whether as process or purpose or spirit, in the private activities of men. If democracy is a good way to conduct the affairs of nation and states, it should also be a good way to conduct the affairs of trade and professional associations, churches, unions, community projects, and perhaps even corporations and universities. Indeed, we could hardly expect the democratic process to function in the public arena if it were not also the standard pattern of action in the private. Where, for example, would most men be trained for the public offices of democracy if private organizations did not exist in profusion and perform many of their tasks as miniature democracies?

The affairs of these organizations are labeled "private," of course, only to distinguish them from those that are strictly governmental. Their decisions have far too profound an influence on the public at large to be thought of as something generically different from the decisions of a court or legislature. When a union decides to strike or a church to eliminate segregation or a corporation to close down the only plant in a New England town, it acts in the capacity of a private government, and we should expect it to act as deliberately and responsibly—that is to say, with as much concern for due process—as if it were in fact an arm of the state. We should also expect it, whenever the situation permits, to act openly. While the citizens of that New England town may have no right to override the decision of the directors of the departing corporation, they do have a right to present their views and to hear those of the directors.

We must not make a fetish of the democratic process and ask the impossible of these private governments. There are obvious difficulties in the way of running a corporation like a checked-and-balanced government; in the affairs of a large union the techniques of the town meeting may be as unworkable as they are in the affairs of a large city. For example, much of the clamor for "union democracy" overlooks the blunt fact that a massive infusion of populism into the operations of many of our big unions would either cripple them for the ongoing struggle with management or turn them into jungles of instability. Democracy is participation, but it is also responsibility; it is the play of opinion but also the prudent management of affairs. In private and public governments alike it is an attempt to maintain a pragmatic balance between the urges of populism and the imperatives of organization, between the rights of the individual and the claims of the community, between the wishes of the led and duties of the leaders. The widely differing circumstances of the countless private governments in America must, of course, alter cases considerably, yet all such governments should be expected, within the limits of reason and strategy, to make provision in their operations for the techniques of constitutional democracy. Due process, publicity, open discussion, representation of the public interest, and accountability can be as good for General Motors—and for the United Automobile Workers—as they are for the country.

The Pursuit of Democratic Goals

Democracy as results and goals rather than as procedures, as things done and still to be done rather than as methods of doing them, is the central concern of most chapters in this book. In them one reads of the goals of American democracy in the next decade; in them one discovers a many-sided program designed to preserve our liberties, expand our opportunities, and improve the quality of our lives. The pursuit of these goals will repay us twice-over for our efforts, for in winning them we will make even stronger the social, economic, cultural, and spiritual conditions under which the democratic process can operate.

The pursuit will prove futile unless it is made for and by all Americans. The goals of this book are goals for every citizen; the complicated process of deciding on priorities among these goals and then of working imaginatively toward them is one in which every citizen should be invited and indeed encouraged to join. Democracy, let us remember, has a fundamental commitment to equality, in the best and most realistic senses of that word: to equality before the law, equality of political voice, equality in constitutional rights, equality of opportunity, and equality of consideration. Somehow we must push farther and faster than we have in the past— through education, persuasion, example, and, where clearly necessary, force of law—to honor this commitment. Somehow we must eliminate the sordid or timid techniques of unequal treatment that still leave millions outside the circle of first-class citizenship in which most Americans are privileged to go about their affairs. While America is not a guaranty of success, it is a promise of opportunity; and we have no more pressing task in the decade before us than to see that the promise is made in good faith to all who live among us.

If this means that some men must renounce old privileges in order that other men may enjoy new liberties, then that is the way the knife of democratic aspiration will have to cut. It would be happier for all, to be sure, and far healthier for American democracy, if those who now deny other men their rights and opportunities as Americans could be persuaded to suppress their fears and to let democracy take its natural course. One way or another, however, the goals of the next decade, and of every decade after that, must be conceived and pursued as goals for all Americans.

The Imperative of Responsibility

In the end, of course, the fate of American democracy rests in the minds and hearts of men rather than in political machinery or social conditions. If enough minds in this country were to work rationally and enough hearts to beat kindly, the machinery of freedom could be far more rusty and conditions far less propitious than they are today—and still America would face the world as a proud, secure, confident democracy. Again and again we have had cause to note that the solution to most problems of American democracy is personal rather than institutional. Surely many of our techniques of decision and administration are about as soundly constructed as nature and art permit; they are simply waiting patiently for better men to operate them. To enlist, train, support, and instruct such men is a major task of American democracy in the years ahead. This task, in turn, calls for better men throughout the land.

Better men in government (or, more exactly, in the seats of power everywhere) means men who are upright, fair-minded, imaginative, and reliable, who practice the fine art of democratic leadership with skill and prudence, who summon up strengths rather than pander to weaknesses in the people with whom they must deal. Above all, it means men who are responsible, who act judiciously, openly, unselfishly, and correctly, who can bear the inspection of their constituencies with credit and await the judgments of posterity with confidence. There was a time—and not so long ago—when we could put up with large amounts of demagoguery, chicanery, and just plain bungling in our public and private governments. That time is long gone; the margin for political error, let it be repeated, has been reduced drastically by the revolution at home and abroad, most of all by the prodigious growth in the capacity of men to help and, by the same token, to harm one another. The great new dimension of industrial civilization is power for good and evil over the lives of men, and in this power we all share—the doctor with his antibiotics, the farmer with his pesticides, the pilot with his cargo of humanity, the manager with his plans to step up or step down production, the worker with his strategic place in the automated factory, the union official with his authority to call a strike, even the least of men who, dwelling in a great city, can flick a switch or mumble a few words into a telephone and bring discomfort if not indeed danger into the lives of thousands of persons on whose faces he has never looked.

This fact of power puts a new strain on all Americans, but especially on those who hold public responsibilities. We need only think, for the most persuasive example, of the challenge to the democratic process that arises out of the instantaneous and all-destroying nature of modern weapons. The men to whom we assign control of these weapons have none of the room in which to be silly or vainglorious or pig-headed that was furnished warriors of the past. Nor, for that matter, do the men to whom we assign control of our finances, public services, and schools, of our factories, fields, and facilities of transportation. They, too, hold far too much power over the lives of other men to be exempted from the growing demand for decision-makers and administrators who are first of all mature and prudent. What we might call the "imperative of responsibility" must pervade and stiffen the whole spirit of democracy.

So, too, must the "imperative of anticipation," for these same decision-makers and administrators must have a perception of the future, a grasp of the predictable and an instinct for the unpredictable, that managers of the democratic process have not found quite so necessary to cultivate in the past. The stumbling reaction of our government to the immense legal and administrative problems raised by the swift advance toward practical exploitation of outer space is example enough of the need for a new order of imagination all through the structure of democracy.

THE ROLE OF THE CITIZEN

Better men throughout the land means men who cherish liberty, who enjoy it themselves and respect it in others. Of such men, the democrats of the spirit, we can never have enough. Unless tens of millions of Americans are determined to be free themselves and to support other men in freedom, democracy is doomed to disorder and sorrow. The price of liberty, today as through all history, is self-reliance and self-discipline. Nothing has happened in this revolutionary age to relieve each of us of the prime responsibility for the state of his own freedom. Rather, the shift from independence toward power within the equation of personal liberty, and from untrammeled individualism toward a sense of community in the public philosophy, makes the practice of self-discipline more essential than ever before.

To say this is not in the least to deny the immense influence of social environment. But we cannot permit ourselves to become so bewitched by the new truth that liberty is socially influenced as to forget the old truth that it must also be personally cultivated. Liberty is offered by the good society, but it is achieved and practiced by the person. It is most securely achieved and practiced by men who submit themselves to the demanding self-disciplines of faith, knowledge, effort, virtue, and purpose. We have no more challenging task ahead of us than to strengthen old ways and create new ones in which men can be encouraged to choose liberty over sloth or surrender.

These considerations raise the familiar question of popular participation in public affairs. Whether for their own ends or for those of the community, whether at the polls or on public platforms or in private meetings, the citizens of a democracy are expected to take an active interest and role in the political process. Yet many citizens of American democracy do not participate persistently and enthusiastically, and many do not participate at all. The statistics of participation, whether measured in the total vote cast in presidential elections or in contributions to political parties or in attendance at annual meetings of school districts, are distressingly low. The statistics of voting are especially distressing because in a big democracy, which must count heavily on techniques of representation for expressing the wishes of the people, the choosing of leaders becomes the critical opportunity for participation. What are we to think of an enlightened community in which something up to 40 per cent of the eligible public will not vote in a presidential election and up to 60 per cent in a congressional election?

One thing we can think is that the community is not so enlightened after all, a thought that may encourage us to redouble our efforts at political education. Another is that millions of Americans find it difficult and often impossible to vote, a thought that may encourage us to move forcefully to clear away disabilities and discriminations. A third is that the remarkable "coolness" of American politics is, paradoxically, a sign of our confidence in the durability of democracy. And a fourth, perhaps the most important, is that the American future rests rather on the quality of our votes—and of our participation of every kind—than it does on the quantity. What America needs is not more voters, but more good voters, men and women who are informed, understanding, and reasonable. To produce such men and women in ever larger numbers should be a major goal of all labors to preserve American democracy.

WE ACT FOR ALL MANKIND

Will the process and substance and spirit of democracy prove equal to the hard pull ahead? That is a large question to which history, not this or any other essay or prophecy, must make final answer. The most that we can do is to remember that democracy has always been a gamble, that few nations have ever been in a position to make the gamble, and that we, because we have been uniquely privileged to make it, have a responsibility for making it successfully that transcends our own fortunes. What Jefferson said of us in 1802 is every bit as true in 1960: We are "acting for all mankind" as well as for ourselves and our posterity. The failure of American democracy would bring democracy everywhere down into ruins. That is a thought to sober and inspire all Americans, and to stiffen them for the substantial sacrifices that lie ahead.

It may be, of course, that democracy as we have known it will have no place in the fantastic world—automatic, antiseptic, abundant, and presumably painless—that has been promised by the seers into the twenty-fifth century. So far as the eye of reality can stretch, however, it is the way of life best designed to serve the needs of the American people. As it serves our needs, so it expresses our traditions, without which we would be simply a mass of people occupying a large plot of land. Even if it could be proved that some other way of life might be more efficient in handling the problems common to all advanced societies, we would be foolish and dishonorable even to think of adopting it.

For what shall it profit a nation if it shall solve all its social problems and lose the character that made it a nation in the first place? Whatever we do, we must do as democrats—or perhaps not bother to do at all.

The Righteous Rightists

Ira S. Rohter

The Watts riots have been traced directly to plans laid down by Lenin in Moscow. (The Los Angeles Communists, who organized the riots, cleverly blew up their own headquarters in order to appear as innocent martyrs.)

Progressive education (a term including most modern educational methods) was inaugurated by a Columbia University professor on his return from Moscow; it is a deliberate design to expedite the Red take-over by turning our children into un-Christian, un-American, mindless, and will-less robots. For proof of success, we have only to look at Berkeley.

The two stories above—much more heavily elaborated and "documented" —are typical of the items that appear in radical right publications. They illustrate well the characteristic that distinguishes radical rightists from other Americans.

Radical rightists are not merely conservatives or even arch-conservatives. What occupies them full time, what gives them their unique voltage and drive, is not their reverence for old-fashioned fiscal policies and morals, but what Richard Hofstadter calls their "paranoid style"—the overriding and galvanizing belief in a gigantic, insidious Communist conspiracy that has infiltrated and infected all levels of American government and most of its social institutions. The calm conservative who would merely like to see a balanced budget and less welfare is not really a rightist, and they both know it.

Another distinct characteristic by which the rightist (I shall call him that for brevity) may be known is his dedication to *action*. When the enemy is already within the gates attacking all that we hold dear, the true patriot does not sit idly by discussing the income tax or civil rights—he mounts the counterattack.

For the purposes of this study, therefore, (and because membership lists and other identifications are often secret) I have used these two characteristics—belief in Communist conspiracy and in direct action—to define and describe rightists, and I have drawn my samples accordingly.

WHO'S RIGHT?

How do people get to be rightists? A major thesis of this article is that rightists are the victims of *status frustration*. That is, for some reason they are dissatisfied or insecure about their places in society and feel that others do not esteem them sufficiently; further, they express their frustration, and compensate for it, by political and social acts which give them emotional identity and support as well as real influence.

Many psychologists regard the striving for self-regard as an essential

"The Righteous Rightists," from *Right Wing Extremism,* New York, Basic Books, in press. Reprinted by permission of the author.

social and psychological need. To a large extent self-regard must depend on how others regard us. Nobody can really tolerate feeling downgraded or ignored; he must make some defense. The rightist chooses the path of radical right ideology and action, which pinpoints and personifies his enemy as a horrendous evil (and the rightist, therefore, as a kind of St. George) and gives him a means to combat it—not merely for himself but as a champion for all decent mankind.

The rightist becomes loudly superpatriotic—which makes anyone disagreeing suspect of un-Americanism. Those who are higher or richer than he (as the Communist-infiltrated world sees them) or who possess different values can be pulled down to their true levels—below the rightist on the scale of virtue—by being exposed as "Communist."

DUEL WITH THE DEVIL

Of course, such an orientation—and such action—depend heavily on a highly charged emotionalism and a closed system of paranoid-like logic that is impervious to objective facts that happen to differ. For instance, Communism cannot be considered primarily a political, social, and economic movement and system of thought capable of objective study. Such an idea horrifies the rightist. Communism is Satan personified; it can be faced only in a fight to the death, and only by those properly armed and inoculated.

People who undergo status frustration generally fall into three categories: the *decliners,* the *new arrivals,* and the *value keepers.*

THE DECLINERS. These are the people in our modern, changing society who are going down in the social scale—undeservedly, as they see it.

Modern technology and modern organizations increasingly require new skills, new orientations, more education. Those trained under different and outmoded disciplines (small farmers, for instance) and those with insufficient or outdated educations must feel their positions becoming more and more insecure.

Also threatened are the old professional and entrepreneur classes, especially from the smaller communities: the small-town general practitioner in medicine, the small home builder, gas station owner, neighborhood grocer—in fact most independent operators trying to survive in the shadows of the great corporations, large labor unions, and big government agencies. The well-educated professionals and corporate executives are taking over the small businessman's role in the community. He is being shoved aside; the hard work and independence on which he had built his self-esteem and his concept of the good and righteous life become increasingly worthless and irrelevant. He begins to ask *why?* Who is doing this to me?

A similar process affects workers, both white and blue collar, displaced by new methods and machinery. They find themselves useless, and their self-regard wavers. The elderly without funds are in an even worse situation—our society no longer respects age, especially when it pulls no economic weight.

As these groups decline, their consciousness of rejection is made even more acute by the rise of those formerly considered low-class or rejected.

An Irish Catholic, grandson of an immigrant, is elected President; a Negro "agitator" receives many honors and confers frequently at the White House. Jews are everywhere in prominent places. Again the decliner—often of old white stock—asks *why*?

THE NEW ARRIVALS. Status frustration occurs not only on the way down, but on the way up. There is almost always a lag between the time the gauche new arrival achieves success and the time those who got there first accept him as an equal. Like the decliner he can easily feel that he has come into a closed and unfriendly society that will not recognize virtue. He is especially upset since he earned it himself in the good old American way instead of being handed prestige on a silver platter.

To the newly arrived, radical rightism can be a potent weapon to destroy their mighty enemies—those who had the opportunity to be better educated, better mannered, more cosmopolitan, and, obviously, more prone to liberal ideas and "bohemian" behavior and immoralities. The charge of "Communism" is a great leveler, and the newly rich can often be counted upon to be twice as narrowly patriotic as anybody.

THE VALUE KEEPERS. Those moving up or down the ladder of success are bound to find themselves, temporarily at least, among aliens who know not the Lord, but so should those who merely stand still long enough in a society that changes as fast as ours.

A person of any conviction or integrity has social and moral values and beliefs that help determine his behavior, his self-definition, and his place in the community. But let the community begin to re-examine those values critically or displace them with others, and the foundation of his whole universe begins to turn to sand.

For the great majority of us, many of the traditional rural or small town ways or virtues are no longer useful or true. Modern society needs education and expertise more than hard work and self-denial; an expanding economy rather than thrift; organized community welfare programs rather than primary reliance on savings, personal charity, relatives, and contemplation of the sufferings of Job.

Moreover, the preponderance of political and economic power, for good or ill, has definitely shifted from the country with its white settlers to the metropolis with its combinations of minority populations. Those whose beliefs and behavior were shaped by older traditions—who, as they see it, settled and built this country—now find themselves, in effect, increasingly disinherited.

Even more important than the objective loss of power and prestige are the *subjective* feelings of loss, of being displaced and discredited. God and the devil, good and evil, are absolutes and do not change; therefore, the change that discredits and displaces the old morality must be evil triumphing over good. Only by such rationalization can true believers retain their orientation and self-regard.

The values defended include hard work, saving, prudent investment, and self-discipline—the Protestant ethic. As the name implies, these values are not only economic but moral, with deep psychological meaning. They are supposed to result in independence and individualism, as the rightist sees them. An apparent attack on them—such as increased government control or taxes—becomes not only an economic change but an immorality and must be answered.

Therefore, as experience demonstrates daily, those most closely identified with older traditional values reduce and discuss almost all social problems to moralistic terms: If the wayward society or individual would only cease transgression and return to the old tried-and-true paths of religion, decency, and family virtue, all would in time be well.

This accounts for much of the intense and emotional opposition to social change by rightists—the counterattack, often blind, to government controls, integration, religious secularism, welfare, the United Nations, foreign aid, Supreme Court decisions, modern education, and even such apparently non-controversial scientific and health advances as fluoridation and mental health programs.

Fundamentalism is an important source of rightist fervor. In fact, from their titles and rhetoric, it is hard to distinguish between a rightist political rally and an evangelistic campaign—note the Rev. Carl McIntire's "Twentieth Century Reformation" and Dr. Fred Schwarz's "Christian Anti-Communist Crusade." Communism, a twentieth century abomination, becomes the catch-all for everything that seems evil and unacceptable in the easygoing, affluent, sophisticated, urban twentieth century.

These then are the theses advanced about the rightist which I tested in this study:

Rightists are people undergoing status frustration. They feel they do not have the prestige and power they should have if the world were just—and their enemies have too much. They are on the move as far as status is concerned—either they are going down in a changing world (which should be true of most of them), they are standing still as the world passes them by, or they are rising more rapidly in economic position than in social recognition.

They identify themselves with the older, traditional (Protestant ethic) values of work, religion, and morality, so that their fight for status recognition also becomes a crusade for truth, justice, decency, God, and America.

They believe that their troubles—and therefore also the attack against Christianity and America—are caused by an all-pervasive conspiracy, wholly evil and implacable, called Communism.

They relieve their anxieties and feelings of resentment and inadequacy by radical right belief and activity. This gives them an effective explanation and compensation for their difficulties, a means of bringing their enemies down, and a method of gaining power, prestige, and mutual support.

Do these hypotheses survive empirical examination?

To start with objective findings first: Are the rightists of our sample actually undergoing status mobility and frustration?

The data show that there are only 10 percent of rightists in the highest occupations, such as executives and professionals, compared to 24 percent of non-rightists; and that rightists are over-represented among the lower-middle class (such as clerical and salesworkers)—15 to 4 percent.

Further, nearly twice as many rightists as others are retired—removed, for most practical purposes, from economic importance to society altogether. Rightists also tend to be older (median age 54 compared to 45) and are more often self-employed (although at lower levels)—if business-men, they tend to run smaller businesses; if professionals, their standing is lower.

In profile, therefore, the radical rightist is older, less secure financially, and less often an important part of a major modern industrial enterprise; he more often has a low prestige white collar job or is thrown on his own resources—retired or operator of a marginal "independent" business. Such a picture is quite consistent with the status frustration hypothesis; such a person, especially if he identifies with an older tradition that was once dominant, could hardly help feeling frustrated.

Occupation alone, however, is not enough to measure social standing. What of education? In our increasingly sophisticated society, education is not only a necessity but a mark of prestige, especially in the middle and upper classes. But even in these occupational strata the rightists have less education than their non-rightist equivalents. In the highest levels (high executives, proprietors, major professionals, etc.) almost twice as many non-rightists as rightists have graduate degrees (64 percent to 33 percent), while three times as many rightists (12 percent to 4 percent) never went beyond high school. In the middle levels over twice as many non-rightists got college degrees (27 percent to 12 percent) while over twice as many rightists (54 percent to 24) never went beyond high school.

DOWN AND TO THE RIGHT

What about mobility? Comparing a male rightist's (or a female rightist's husband's) occupation and education with those of his father (this is called "inter-generational status mobility"), we found, as hypothesized, that the rightist did undergo much more status mobility than non-rightists, most often downward.

In the *lowest* occupations (typically, unskilled blue collar) the rightists had fallen farther and more consistently than non-rightists had done any-where. Thirty-eight percent of rightist men compared to 6 percent non-rightist had declined sharply. Rightist laborers were quite apt to have had middle class or farm-owning fathers.

In the *middle* groups (white collar, small business) rightists were more mobile, both up and down, than non-rightists. Relatively few had stayed at the same occupational and educational level as their fathers (14 to 29 percent). There tended to be a few more losers than winners.

In the *highest status*, however, rightists on the way up surpass not only those on the way down but even the relatively static non-rightists. This fits in very well with the thesis that the "newly arrived" undergo status frus-tration.

As predicted, therefore, the rightists had significantly greater mobility, especially downward, and less education where it counted most.

Another way to measure mobility should be by length of residence in a neighborhood. The old fundamentalist morality is closely associated with a rural and small town past; many people from that background, who cling to the old standards, have moved to a faceless Babylon of a city where they have few skills they can use. Those on the way down—or in from the farm—must move into poorer neighborhoods; those on the way up, though they take their values and their accents with them, are most likely, as soon as possible, to move to higher status suburbs or neighborhoods. Those who stay the shortest time should therefore be the most mobile.

Studying length of residence of people under 50, we found two basic groups of rightists. One seems to be primarily composed of people new to the community who seem unable to accept or be accepted by that community; also, they are declining in status more rapidly than a similar group of equally mobile non-rightists.

The other rightist cluster is composed of old-timers who have lived in their communities most of their adult lives; they are considerably older than their neighbors, and many more turn up in the 50 and 60 age brackets. Their neighborhoods have gone down, and they have declined in status with them. Here too, therefore, there seems a clear association between decline (whether in new or old residency) and radical rightism.

THAT OLD TIME RELIGION

Are rightists to any significant extent fundamentalists? Belief in traditional values, along with many rightist attitudes, was earlier related to religious fundamentalism. Empirically, this is true. Rightists very much subscribe to fundamentalist tenets and belong to these churches; nearly half the rightists (44 percent compared to 17 percent of the non-rightists) are affiliated with fundamentalist denominations. Rightists were also more often raised in rural areas or small towns, environments most likely to produce traditionalism and hostility toward modernity.

So much for objective factors. How do the people themselves view their plights?

Fewer rightists than non-rightists actually belong to the upper class; but more of them *rated themselves* "upper class." When asked, "How hard do you think it is for people today to move upward from one social class to another?" their answers revealed a view of society as essentially closed, dominated by personalities, controlled by the wrong kinds of people:

> Not much opportunity anymore; it's getting harder; depends on having money, knowing the right people.

The views of the non-rightists were much more objective and impersonal:

> Depends on education; must work hard and have abilities to get it; special skills; hard to change direction of early life. . . .

We asked, "Do you think that people . . . influential in this community are, in *general*, friendly . . . or cliquish?" Rightists answered "cliquish and unfriendly" more often than non-rightists. When those answering "cliquish" were asked to give reasons, rightists more often indicated belief in a closed structure run by a small group:

> Old residents tend to look on new people as outsiders; certain families run things here; segregated groups want their own way; all have common political views.

The rightist, then, more often sees himself as the outsider, discriminated against in a closed society run by an elite.

What about the predicted concern with the Protestant ethic? We asked, "Are there any differences between what you believe should be the American way of life, and the way things are done in the country nowadays?" "In what way are things different?" Typically, from the rightists:

> Morality and standards are going bad; the American way of life is deteriorating because of a suppression of morality; we need a moral and spiritual revival among our leaders; we need to follow the Ten Commandments more.

RUGGED INDIVIDUALISTS
What about individual initiative, self-reliance, respect for authority?

> I am worried about the drift of the country; the amount of crime and disrespect for authority shows things are going the other way; we must instill more emphasis on respect, integrity, and individual responsibility; parents aren't teaching their children the right things anymore.

Traditional morality and values dominate many rightists' perception of everything. No matter what the topic—what things they worried about, what community concerns they had, what qualities they admired, what things Communists actually believed in, whatever—sooner or later they indicated that if we would only return to the old morality every problem would be solved.

Our findings are clear: The rightists are more dissatisfied with the values of contemporary American society; they adhere to the "old truths" and believe everyone else should "return" to them. They suffer severe frustration because of this, a frustration heavily reinforced by a religious righteousness expressed in absolute and positive terms.

"In your own case . . . do you think that *everyone* gives you as much respect as *you feel you* deserve? This question was deliberately worded to emphasize extremes—yet rightists answered "no" more frequently than non-rightists. This is true both of rightists who are on the way up and those on the way down; but the decliners say "no" *twice* as often as those on the rise—emphasizing that it is the losers who are most impelled to seek radical rightism. (Presumably, once those on the rise secure recognition, they will cease attacking high-status people and changing times.)

Rightists felt more unaccepted than non-rightists, and rightists on the decline more unaccepted than anybody.

Does joining radical right organizations and causes help the rightist combat his anxieties successfully? By being more patriotic and anti-Communist than anybody else, the rightist seems to wrap himself in greatness and goodness, in importance, righteousness, and self-satisfaction. He is a savior carrying out a holy crusade. As the *John Birch Society Bulletin* (November, 1964) points out, if you join their society ". . . you feel a tremendous satisfaction . . . to save for our children and their children the glorious country and humane civilization which we ourselves inherited."

We asked them to select "two great Americans" and describe what is admirable about them. Later, we asked them to describe "the typical member of an anti-Communist group"—that is, in effect, an idealized version of themselves. Their great people, they said, were "true" Americans and "very" patriotic; 75 percent found the same things true of themselves (compared to 22 percent of non-rightists, who tended to use less extravagant terms). Courage, strength, and "guts" were likewise qualities they shared with the great, as was deep Christian faith and high moral standards. And 50 percent further saw the great to be honest, truthful, and sincere—like themselves.

Non-rightists, however, viewed rightists very differently—"dishonest," "hypocrites," "no integrity," "use character assassination."

This tactic of rightists to acquire status and importance by associating themselves closely with the great and the good is perhaps best illustrated by their emphasis on "self-education." They are, in fact, less well-educated than the non-rightists. But the world of radical rightism is full of parades of quasi-experts, study groups, monographs, footnotes, and bibliographies —almost all with no standing among scholars. But the rightists study them avidly, mention intelligence and education highly among those things they admire in the great, and give themselves strong ratings as "intellectuals, very brilliant," "well informed," "people with sound judgment, good reasoning," and "lots of sense." Needless to add, non-rightists hold almost precisely the opposite view of them.

THE RIGHTIST PERSONALITY

The need to relieve status anxiety and to attack values that do not conform to their beliefs are not enough to explain why some people become radical rightists and others, in like circumstances, do not. The rightist tends also to have certain personality characteristics—to be, in effect, a particular kind of human being.

SIMPLISM. Psychologists say that a basic need of man is his desire for meaning, to understand what is happening to him. In an important sense the rightist, a traditionalist in changing times, is adrift in frightening darkness—he needs landmarks, he needs simple guidelines, before he loses direction altogether. Radical rightism gives him this "understanding"—and this security. All becomes clear and very simple. It is all a conspiracy. Nothing is really changed—God is still in His heaven; but He needs help.

Extremely simple explanations have great attractions for the confused. They are a necessity for those personalities who have what psychologists call "simplistic cognitive structure"—who have a strong need for simple, firm, stereotyped views of people and events, with no place for ambivalence or ambiguity. Such persons reject unbelievers, need external authorities, and, for emotional reasons, hold their beliefs so rigidly that compromise is intolerable.

Testing for this rigidity of belief, using statements on Communism and Russia ("Communism is a total evil." "The Soviet Union is 'mellowing.'"), on intolerance of ambiguity ("There is usually only one right way to do anything."), on anti-compromise and closed-minded stances ("The compromise of principles leads to nothing but destruction." "A group which tolerates too much difference of opinion cannot exist for long."), we found the rightist to fit this description. He is intolerant of ambiguity, opposed to compromise, and closed-minded.

EXTRA-PUNITIVENESS. It is difficult not to be struck by the strident negativism and combativeness of rightist writings, thought, and speech. Terrible things exist all about, the future is steeped in gloom; everything is in strong blacks and whites—the forces of light are locked in mortal combat with the forces of darkness. It is not only necessary, therefore, but moral and virtuous to be resentful, discontented, belligerent, and full of hate. While the rightist justifies his behavior in the name of Americanism and anti-Communism, the actual thrust of his attacks are against the political, social, and intellectual leaders of the community—those who have the respect and influence he does not.

This vehement scapegoating is characteristic of a psychological defense mechanism called "extra-punitiveness." The extra-punitive have a great deal of free-floating hate and aggression they project outward, blaming others or the world for their personal or social failures. Their view of the world is paranoid.

We tested for extra-punitiveness by asking what measures they would take against "Communists" and, in later questions, against other "safe" scapegoats (those with few defenders, such as delinquents, sex deviants, homosexuals, and "disrespectful persons"). Rightists were more in favor of strong measures against Communists (sample statement with high response: "Take them out and hang them"); but their *generalized* hostility showed up even more clearly in their attitudes toward nonpolitical deviants. (Sample statements: "There is hardly anything lower than a person who does not feel a great love, gratitude, and respect for his parents." "Homosexuals are hardly better than criminals and ought to be severely punished.")

Rightists not only condemn Communists but define them so differently that it is sometimes hard to believe they are talking about real people. There is a heavy emphasis on religion and black-or-white morality: To believe that we can live with Communism is to be a dupe or worse. Communism is the anti-Christ, it is evil incarnate. This allows for convenient projection of personal hatreds. Rightists often find the highly educated—including professors—to be Communists. "From what racial or religious groups are Communists most likely to come?" Rightists frequently mentioned "atheists," "Jews," "Methodists," "Unitarians," and "modernistic religious groups." (Non-rightists denied more frequently and more vigorously that race or religion was involved.)

POWERLESSNESS. It is a basic tenet of rightism that individual freedom —as they define it—is being lost and that the ordinary citizen (meaning themselves) is being ignored. Is "the federal government . . . extending too much . . . power into . . . everyday life?" Nearly 70 percent of the rightists "agreed very much." "Are there any groups . . . that you think have too much power or influence?" "Yes," the rightists said, significantly more often than non-rightists, and listed labor (and its leaders), Communists, big government, and such groups as the ADA, ACLU, and Council on Foreign Relations. Who has *too little* power? They mentioned twice as many groups as the non-rightists, most often the two surrogates for themselves: the individual "common man" and "conservative" organizations.

Do rightists, as hypothesized, feel maligned and persecuted? They pointed out with considerable heat that their idealized "great men," with whom they identify, were mistreated: "Got a raw deal; treated badly by others, his country; a victim of injustice."

ALIENATION. We found our rightists to be significantly more alienated politically than the non-rightists, to feel that their elected public officials do not actually represent them, that local officials avoid or ignore them, responding only to special interests. On referenda on community issues—such as new bond issues or taxes—they more consistently than others vote "no."

Do they trust other people? (A person who feels lost, who has little sense of personal competence, often lives in a jungle of suspicion and distrust.) We found a significant association between radical rightism and low trust in others. Generally, the rightists in our sample were less often involved in social and community organizations.

Finally, the rightist *feels* that by joining other rightists he can overcome his own powerlessness and estrangement.

Extra-punitiveness, a paranoid view of society, a great deal of free-floating hostility and aggression, desire for direct action, a rigid devotion to absolutes in religion and morality and to black-or-white standards—all these characteristics describe particular kinds of closed-minded, insecure, authoritarian persons undergoing particular kinds of status crises. And that is who the radical rightists are.

A NOTE ON THE STUDY

Radical rightists generally keep their membership lists secret. Therefore, for the purposes of this study they were defined in terms of their characteristic activities and beliefs.

Radical rightists were defined as those people who believed, to a large degree, in the existence of an internal Communist conspiracy infiltrating all levels of government and most social institutions in the United States and who were deeply involved in action to counter this Communist threat.

The sample was selected from lists of people who, through such activity and through their expressions, had made their rightist orientations matters of public record. Specifically, names were taken from a newspaper article listing members of the John Birch Society and the Liberty Amendment Committee in a northwestern city; others were found through published "letters to the editor." Fifty-six came from a list of contributors and subscribers to a radical right organization and publication. Similarly, the sample of non-rightists was selected through content analysis of other "letters to the editor" and from referenda petitions. The final sample from which the analysis was made contained 169 rightists and 167 non-rightists.

Liberals and Radicals

William P. Gerberding

One of the recurrent problems for liberals in the United States is what their relationship with radicals should be. If liberals are defined roughly as those who accept the basic characteristics of the existing political and economic systems and who believe that the government should be an active instrument for improving the lot of our citizenry and perhaps of mankind as a whole; and if radicals are defined as those who seek fundamental changes in the political, social, and economic systems—some adhering to democratic norms and some not—then it is obvious that the relationship between liberals and radicals will usually be strained and often nonexistent. Only in periods of great stress and loss of confidence will liberals be drawn toward radical prescriptions and personalities. The 1930's are the classic example of how alluring this temptation can become at such times.

The distemper and division in the nation today are so intense that many liberals are receptive to radical analyses and conclusions, and therefore to radical politics. Many liberals, including this one, believe that the decision to intervene in Vietnam with American combat troops was a grave strategic mistake; but whether the original intervention was wise or unwise, our massive presence there changes the situation entirely and renders it infinitely more difficult to try to answer the question of what should be done *now*.

In such agonizing times, it becomes more difficult to distinguish between legitimate and illegitimate dissent, between constructive opposition and destructive adventuring, between those who honor humane and democratic values and those who do not. That there are anti-democratic extremists seeking to exploit the disaffection of the anti-Vietnam liberals and of the aroused Negro Americans should surprise no one. What is surprising and dangerous is the extent to which disaffected liberals have been willing to associate their names and activities with the extremists.

NO COMPROMISE

In the opinion of this writer it is wrong and destructive to embrace or even to adopt a tolerant attitude toward the radical politics of, for example, the New Left or the black racists. It is wrong—morally and intellectually —because these radicals, whatever may be their personal motives and however real and profound their grievances, do not offer liberal democrats an acceptable alternative, nor are they acceptable allies. They detest compromise, conciliation, and accommodation, the necessary elements of a democratic, tolerant, and humane policy; they accept violence as an appropriate means to whatever ends they happen to be pursuing at any given time; abjuring any serious moral or political calculations about which ends justify which means under what circumstances; they preach racial hatred and intolerance; their style is full of cant, hypocrisy, and self-righteousness; and their ultimate purposes are at best shrouded in mystery and riddled with naïve utopianism, and are at worst coercive and illiberal. Many of them have explicitly rejected liberal democracy as a sham and a fraud.

The ability to make basic distinctions is a cardinal virtue in politics. Liberals have long and properly been contemptuous of the frequent inability or unwillingness of those in this country who call themselves conservatives to dissociate themselves from the radical Right, i.e., those whose techniques and purposes are essentially and occasionally explicitly anti-democratic. Most men of the Right condemn the Klan, the Minutemen, and the Nazis; but too many of them have not been willing to repudiate the many other wild men, whether Birchers or local vendors of related poison. And so we watch with amusement as, say, William F. Buckley, Jr. —McCarthy apologist and, more lately, clever spokesman for a kind of sophisticated and somewhat housebroken rightist viewpoint—attacks Robert Welch but defends the John Birch Society, and finds himself the object of bitter attacks from his erstwhile admirers. How, we ask ourselves, can experienced, knowledgeable, and apparently reasonably decent people like Buckley put themselves into such absurd and demeaning postures?

Although perceiving this moral and intellectual fuzziness in others, many liberals have not been as alive to the related dangers among themselves. Thus it was a rare treat to learn recently that the Northern California regional officers of the National Committee for a Sane Nuclear Policy (SANE) resigned en masse because the national board of SANE rejected their request that it purge itself of what the Northern California officers called "anti-democratic and anti-American elements." Silence or an attitude of indulgence has been a more typical response of liberals to the excesses of some of the radicals. When, for example, an officer of Students for a Democratic Society (SDS) was recently reported as having said that "When an institution is without legitimacy, it is without rights, it is without the right of free speech," how many liberals view this as the blatantly illiberal pronouncement that it most certainly is?

In addition to these basic questions about who is morally and intellectually an acceptable ally in an emergency, there is the practical question of the likely consequences of co-operation with or even of an indulgent attitude toward the New Left and the black racists. It seems obvious to me that association with these elements is a political liability and, therefore, destructive of the very purposes for which I think liberal democrats ought pre-eminently to be striving, i.e., a satisfactory termination of the war and an imaginative, creative, and unprecedentedly costly attack upon the unacceptable realities of Negro life in this country. (There are, of course, many other problems that need attention, but they do not at least currently involve the explosive force and immense tragedy of the two mentioned.) Among liberals, there is always tension between those who are willing and able to look the hard facts in the face and those to whom moral posturing and denigration of the political processes are the more comfortable responses. It is the latter who, despite their adherence to democratic norms, are the most susceptible to sentimentality and confusion about such phenomena as the New Left and the black racists.

THE BENEFICIARIES

What "facts" am I suggesting need to be faced? The following discussion includes some with an uncontestable status as fact, while others are more arguable. My only claims are that where I have substituted opinion for fact it is because the facts are not conclusively known and that these opinions deserve to be taken seriously.

First and foremost, an overwhelming majority of the body politic rejects violence as a permissible method of altering policies and conditions in this country. It is fashionable these days to point out that violence has always been a conspicuous element in American life; that a case can be made—and I agree—for its legitimacy under extreme conditions; that many Negroes have despaired of achieving their rightful aspirations through nonviolent methods; that violence has indeed "worked" in alerting many more people to such realities as Negro deprivations and the depths of dissatisfaction with the administration's policies in Vietnam. All this is true, but it is a beguiling non sequitur to conclude that therefore liberals will profit politically from an attitude that condones or even encourages violence. Anyone who believes that is fooling himself and, more importantly, helping sow the seeds for an illiberal reaction of incalculable proportions.

I live in California. The New Left has been shrewd enough to understand that its activities were and are a political asset for Ronald Reagan both as candidate and governor. They welcome this development for all of the usual foolish and incompatible reasons: "Things must get much worse before they can get better"; "It's time for a showdown, a confrontation, between bourgeois America and 'the prophetic minority' "; "Reagan is the incarnation of the true American spirit"; "We pursue principle, not expediency"; and on and on. These slogans and rationalizations are attractive to the totally alienated, to the hysterical, and to utopians. But they are dangerous doctrine for democratic liberals and they will continue to weaken the political power of liberals while strengthening that of the Ronald Reagans and the George Wallaces. The New Left and the black racists do not make distinctions among such categories, except perhaps that they reserve a special contempt for liberals while saluting the "honesty" of the others mentioned. Liberals, suffering from the weaknesses of their virtues, too often receive such abuse with forgiveness, understanding, and even—among those obsessed with guilt—agreement. A more fitting response is to make the contempt mutual, because what divides liberals from the anti-democratic radicals is fundamental and not negotiable.

There is also the problem of the relationship between liberals and the police. I admit that the ritualistic "anti-cop" attitude of many liberals is sophomoric and escapist. I trust that no one is prepared to argue that we can do without police forces. A good beginning—and only a beginning—is to tell the whole truth about police activities and responsibilities. This has not by any means been automatic among liberals. Much of the liberal reporting and commentary on, for example, the riots outside the Century Plaza Hotel in Los Angeles while President Johnson was there last June was shockingly one-sided. No doubt the police acted too harshly once they moved on the crowd of anti-Vietnam demonstrators; perhaps they should not have moved at all. But why was it so seldom pointed out that both the parade permit and a court order prohibited stopping in front of the hotel, and that the police warned the marchers about their responsibility to disperse? Do liberals want to live in a society where court orders and parade permits are routinely violated? It is no answer to say that some laws and regulations are manifestly unjust or unconstitutional and that breaking them is a moral right, perhaps a duty. The questions are: which laws and where and when? Is a California court order the same as a Mississippi sheriff's decree? An inability or unwillingness to make such distinctions is intellectually inexcusable and politically risky.

It's too bad there aren't more liberals on police forces, but what would a liberal police chief have done if he had had the responsibility of guarding the President of the United States, if there had been rumors of an attempt to storm the hotel, if the marchers had stopped in front of the hotel in violation of a court order and their parade permit? Is anyone prepared to argue that Presidents of the United States are immune from physical danger?

Or is there perhaps a conviction among some liberals—as there assuredly is among many radicals—that this particular President does not merit protection?

THE BIG LIES

This brings another issue into view. The unremitting efforts to defame President Johnson are repugnant and unfair. They are, relatedly, politically disadvantageous. Liberals have generally understood that the conspiratorial and devil interpretations of American history so common on the radical Right are bizarre and absurd. Roosevelt may have misjudged Stalin, but he did not willfully betray the interests of this country. Yet many of these same people are now prepared to believe that Lyndon Johnson is a moral monster, a man who actually loves war and hates Negroes, and whose alleged concern for education and for the poor is a gigantic hoax. Consider the success of the play *MacBird*. A portion of the liberal community enthusiastically embraced this sick imagery, some of them arguing evasively that of course they didn't believe Johnson had killed Kennedy but that the play contained a "larger truth." Compare the response of these same people to Robert Welch's charge that Dwight Eisenhower was a conscious agent of the Communist conspiracy. From the radical Right, this kind of nonsense is immediately perceived and properly denounced. From the radical Left, it is too often taken with great seriousness and, if not altogether accepted, then justified in terms of some larger and usually murky purpose.

This will not do. It is morally and intellectually unacceptable for liberals —or anyone else, for that matter—to manufacture Big Lies in order to combat the very real problems that beset us as a nation. We must be able to make the elementary kinds of distinctions that extremists are incapable of making, or we shall lose our integrity and our claim to seriousness.

Moreover, the consequences of such cynicism (or, to give it the benefit of the doubt, such naïveté) are not pleasant to contemplate. The fund of decency and mutual respect upon which a democratic society depends for its survival is not available on demand in this or any other society. If some liberals join those who debase political discourse for short-run gains, they are playing with fire and are adding strength to those very forces in our society whose loyalty to democratic norms is most suspect. They poison the well.

Although I am over thirty, I will also say something about young people and about the relationship between generations. I teach in a university and am familiar with and appreciative of the idealism and altruism that inspire some of the most visible elements of this generation of youth. What most of the more sensational and publicized among them do not deserve is to have their sweeping socio-economic-political pronouncements taken so seriously. The solemnity with which adults treat such things as the anarchic demands of many student radicals, or the social analyses of the Students for a Democratic Society, or the pronouncements of the black racists about history would be laughable if it weren't so consequential.

The first responsibility toward youth is to tell the truth and to refute error. The sins of omission and commission of the over-thirty generation (if it makes any sense to speak in such general terms) are many and serious; so it has always been and so it will always be. But unless one is willing to compare reality only with utopia, then the nation into which these young people are entering as adults cannot be simply or reasonably characterized as a "sick society." It is, among many other things, a nation that enjoys and has always enjoyed more political, cultural, and religious freedom than any—or almost any—other society, past or present; it is a nation with an economy of almost unbelievable productivity; and it is a nation that has, since having leadership thrust upon it, generally played an honorable role in international affairs.

I know all the arguments against such positive and optimistic statements, and I know how many qualifications and disclaimers need to be added. Especially it must be said that the unemployed and the Negroes do not share appropriately in wealth and status and that American foreign policy has its darker side. That there is plenty of room for improvement is all too obvious.

It is a measure of our loss of confidence and a sign of the super-sophisticated fashion of our time that few liberals say such things today. Anyone who deviates from an unremittingly hypercritical and gloomy line about institutions, policies, and people is regarded as square, pompous, and flag-waving, an evader of ugly truths. We are in danger of becoming a generation of cranks. Surely it is a derangement of the critical faculties when a nation as diverse and complicated and comparatively successful as this one is perceived exclusively in negative terms.

THE ANTI-INTELLECTUAL RAMPAGE

Liberals should not be ashamed to make positive claims about American society and politics, not only because they are true but also because today's youth is being told so many other and contradicting things. The view of reality that the radicals of the Left are trying to peddle to today's youth includes the following ingredients, among others: the United States started and has perpetuated the cold war; the policies associated with the containment doctrine could have been designed to promote U.S. economic and political imperialism, and the anti-Communist rhetoric, especially regarding Vietnam, is a cynical mask; genuine democracies can only be found in Communist and underdeveloped countries, not in the West; the Johnson administration is determined to exploit and suppress the Negro population, as is "the establishment" in general, and all talk of the search for assistance and co-operation with legitimate Negro aspirations is deceitful; the War on Poverty is not only unsuccessful, it was designed to be so; there are no important differences in attitudes, purposes, or policies among the leading political figures in this country, from George Wallace to Nelson Rockefeller; and our great universities and colleges are really nothing more than willing and corrupt instruments of the guardians of the status quo.

There are grains of truth in this chamber of horrors, but they are trivial alongside the immense distortions and crass falsehoods. Much of what passes for a redeeming and healthy idealism among today's youth is based on these and related grotesque distortions of truth and on a virulent anti-intellectual and anti-rational bias. For liberals to indulge these fantasies, to congratulate every adolescent rebel on his (fictitious) moral superiority, to applaud each new millennial prescription or apocalyptic vision, to deny or ignore the positive aspects of American politics and society, is to become what the radicals claimed we were all along, i.e., dishonest, cowering, sentimental, irresponsible, hollow men.

Decency and self-respect require that liberals avoid such a craven role, but so too do political considerations. For better or for worse, the American public is not amused by guilt-ridden, hand-wringing displays of self-flagellation by liberal adults. The radicals at Berkeley sought and deserved greater student freedom; they got it. Then they went on and sought other goals, intra- and extra-mural. A vacillating administration—unimpeachably liberal, tolerant to a fault—hesitated, fumbled, and lost its nerve. It was not Governor Edmund G. Brown who profited from this prolonged debacle; it was Ronald Reagan. And so it will continue to be. I find it difficult to blame only the students for failing to distinguish between legitimate demands (which were met) and genuinely liberal leaders on the one hand, and radical extremists who pursued unreasonable goals for their own illiberal reasons on the other. They were encouraged to do so by blindly permissive, intellectually sloppy, and morally confused professors, administrators, and politicians, most of whom were liberals. Most of these people have continued to congratulate themselves on their "principled" position, and they will probably continue to do so if their past and future actions help to elevate the lucky Reagan into the Presidency.

It will be said that an attack on a liberal-radical coalition is a call for inaction. It is no such thing. There is plenty for liberals to do, as there always has been, and the generous spirit of democratic liberalism will continue to motivate people to action, as it always has. But condoning or co-operating with the anti-democratic elements of the radical Left is morally insupportable and politically disastrous.

Dissent or Destruction?

Eric Sevareid

THESE ARE ODD TIMES. Tens of thousands of Americans of every age, color, sex, and economic and intellectual condition are daily and hotly invoking every right and privilege mentioned in the Constitution, the Bible and Bartlett's *Familiar Quotations*. Others are busy invoking self-serving "higher laws" to supersede the national rulebook. None of them seems familiar with the words "duty" or "obligation."

The production curve on putative saints and martyrs has been rising rapidly—possibly in direct proportion to the availability of press and TV cameras. The country bears the aspect of one vast wailing wall, washed down daily with the tears of the self-pitying.

The general import of their varying messages, taken as a whole, seems to be that: all American policemen have joyfully renounced their days off in order to bludgeon Negroes as a wholesome exercise; the armed services of the United States, drunk with bloodlust, eagerly notch their guns for every Vietnamese civilian they kill; administrators burn the midnight oil in order to conceive new ways to coerce, threaten, silence and otherwise "alienate" that oppressed *lumpen-proletariat*, American college students.

And all the while, a mysterious group known as the "Power Elite" or the "Establishment" sits in Washington, New York, Chicago and Los Angeles, fat cigars in one hand, telephones in the other, engaged in a round-robin conversation featured by chortling remarks, such as "Hi, fella, how many of the downtrodden did you trod on today?"

As a result of all this, the familiar quotation that comes first to mind for an increasing number of other Americans is one of the opening lines of *The Man Who Came to Dinner*—"I may vomit."

Still others who believe firmly in free speech can no longer find the strength even to murmur Voltaire's celebrated remark that while he disapproved of what you say, he would defend to the death your right to say it, because they are already half-dead—with boredom.

When we reach the point, which we have, where an organization is formed, called "Proxy Pickets," to rent out picketers for any cause at so much an hour, then we know that the fine, careless rapture of this era of protest is all over and that the corruption of faddism has begun to set in. Every movement becomes an organization sooner or later, then a kind of business, often a racket. This is becoming the age of the cause Cause. Kids will soon be hanging around back lots trading causes the way they used to trade aggies.

One of the oddest things about the period, no doubt, is that anyone like me should feel moved to say these things. I have always believed in the Negro "revolution," if that's the right word. I have not believed, for some time now, in the Vietnamese war because to me the official rationale for

it simply does not add up, and as a college kid in the thirties, I was a
hollering "activist" and even voted for that Oxford oath—"I will not fight
for flag or country" (though I couldn't sleep that night for doubts about it,
which will merely prove to today's hip set that I had the seeds of square-
dom in me at an early age).

But it seems clear to me now that a high percentage of today's protests,
in these three areas of civil rights, the Vietnam war and college life—all
of which commingle at various points—have gone so far as to be sense-
lessly harming the causes themselves, corroding the reputations of the
most active leaders and loosening some of the cement that holds this
American society together. There never was any real danger that this
country would find itself groaning under Fascist oppression, but there
is a measure of real danger that freedom can turn into nationwide
license until the national spirit is truly darkened and freedom endangered.

The notion is abroad that if dissent is good, as it is, then the more
dissent the better, a most dubious proposition. The notion has taken hold
of many that the manner and content of their dissent are sacred, whereas
it is only the *right* of dissent that is sacred. Reactions of many dissenters
reveal a touch of paranoia. When strong exception is taken to what they
say by the President or by a General Westmoreland, the dissenters cry
out immediately that free speech is about to be suppressed, and a reign
of enforced silence is beginning.

What is more disturbing is that a considerable number of liberal Left
activists, including educated ones, are exhibiting exactly the spirit of the
right-wing McCarthyites 15 years ago, which the liberal Left fought so
passionately against in the name of our liberties. For the life of me, I
cannot see the difference in morality between the right-wing woman in
Texas who struck Ambassador Adlai Stevenson and the left-wing students
and off-campus characters at Dartmouth College who howled down ex-
Governor Wallace of Alabama and tried to smash his car.

The use of force to express a conviction, even if it takes so relatively
mild a form as a college sit-in that blocks an administration building,
is intolerable. When Dr. Martin Luther King, who may well be one of the
noblest Americans of the century, deliberately defies a court order, then
he ought to go to jail. Laws and ordinances can be changed, and are
constantly being changed, but they cannot be rewritten in the streets
where other citizens also have their rights.

I must say that, kooky as we may have been in that first real American
student movement in the thirties, we never, to my memory, even dreamed
of using force. We thought of the university, much as we often hated its
official guts, as the one sanctuary where persuasion by reason must rule
alone and supreme, if the university itself were to be preserved from the
outside hands of force and unreason. What makes today's college activists
think they can take the campus forcibly into national politics without
national politics—in the form of police or legislature or troops—forcibly
coming onto the campus? (Some of the activists, of course, are pure nihi-
lists and *want* this to happen, but that's another story.)

The wild riots that have exploded in the Negro areas of American cities the last few summers should not be confused with protest movements. Most of them do not even deserve the designation of race riot. We had genuine race riots in Chicago, Detroit and Tulsa nearly half a century ago, whites against Negroes, and mass murders occurred. Nearly all the recent summer-night riots have chiefly involved Negro kids smashing and looting the nearest property, most of which was owned by other Negroes. This is sheer hoodlumism, involved as its psychological and sociological origins may be. It is a problem for sociologists, psychologists and economists only in the second instance. In the first instance, it is a police problem, as are the episodes of mass vandalism staged by prosperous white kids on the beaches of New Hampshire or Florida. Majorities have a right to protection quite as much as minorities, heretical as this may sound.

If there were no protests at all about the Vietnamese war, the American society would really be in sad shape. We were in this war very deeply almost before the average busy citizen grasped what had happened, and there was no serious congressional debate on the issue until the winter of 1966. The present national disunion, including the disaffection of so much of the "intellectual community," is just what happened in the War of 1812, the Mexican War of 1846–1848, the Spanish-American War and the war in the Philippines that followed. As historian Henry Steele Commager has pointed out, the only wars during which the President had all but universal support were the two world wars, and both were debated and discussed all over the nation for many long months before we got into action.

So the present protests about Vietnam are entirely within the American tradition. Even so, the law, public necessity and human reason must impose certain limitations.

It is outrageous and insupportable for anyone to desecrate the flag, the one symbol of nationhood that reminds all citizens of the country's meaning. It is disgusting for paraders to chant, "Hey, hey, LBJ, how many kids did you kill today?" These deaths in battle are eating at his soul, too, and vulgarities can help no high-minded cause.

It is a crime for rioters to terrorize cities as they did in the disgraceful upheavals in Newark and Detroit.

It is silly for a group of American artists to ask Pablo Picasso to withdraw his famous Spanish Civil War painting, *Guernica*, from the Museum of Modern Art in protest against our bombings in Vietnam.

It is unreasonable to become indignant about the civilian casualties our forces accidentally cause in Vietnam while remaining silent about the thousands of assassinations of civilian leaders by the Vietcong's "murder committees." The President rightly calls this "moral double bookkeeping."

It is unfair to say that some members of Congress don't mind the war because it helps defense industries in their districts, as Senator Fulbright did say—and then apologized.

It is damaging to the national awareness of reality, and to his own name and cause, for Dr. King to declare that the U.S. "is the greatest purveyor of violence in the world," and that "we may have killed a million [Vietnamese civilians]—mostly children." These statements are untrue. The first is a subjective generalization. The second bears no relationship to what civilian casualty figures we have been able to gather.

It is unreasonable to maintain that President Johnson does not *want* a negotiated peace and is intent on a military victory, because to say that is to say he has deliberately and repeatedly lied to the people, and for that, there is no convincing evidence.

If some of the war protesters go out-of-bounds, so do some of the war supporters and counterprotesters.

It is unfair for them to charge that the protesters are "letting the boys down." Serious protesters want to save the boys entirely by getting the war ended, and in the meantime will insist they have every bullet and article of use they require.

For the same kind of reason, it is unfair for the President to imply, as he did, that a Medal of Honor winner died by an enemy weapon shipped down during one of the bombing pauses. Rightly or wrongly, those calling for a pause in the bombing believe it may lead to an armistice saving the lives of *all* our heroes in Vietnam, and while they can only ask for the pause, it is the President who decides it.

It is grossly self-serving for Administration spokesmen to imply repeatedly that our domestic disunion over Vietnam keeps Hanoi fighting on in expectation that we will quit the war. Of course, Ho Chi Minh's regime *hopes* our will is going to break; but the overwhelming American reality they see before their eyes and that surely governs their reactions is our ever-increasing land force and our continuous bombing of the North. I am persuaded that were there no debate whatsoever in this country, Ho's regime and the Vietcong would be fighting just as relentlessly as they are today.

It was pettifogging, and indeed illegal, for General Hershey to support the drafting of young protesters by deliberately reclassifying them 1-A. The draft is not a punitive instrument.

It was pettifogging for state boxing commissions to strip Casius Clay of his title—even before his conviction—because he refused to accept the draft. If he can lick any man in the world, he's still champion of the world. These silly irrelevancies are counterproductive.

It is wrongheaded for any maritime union to refuse to load or unload a foreign ship because they disapprove of that nation's philosophy or actions. It is hard enough for the Government to conduct foreign policy, without such presumptuous handicaps.

I happen to feel that the experience of American Negroes these many generations is the one deep stain in the American national soul. I cannot help a greater readiness to condone their excesses than those of prosperous white college students (though the law cannot be morally choosy). But there are some basic misconceptions about both.

One is that youths of both colors have been driven to action because their conditions of oppression were becoming intolerably miserable. The reverse is the truth. The barriers to Negro equality were beginning to fall before the period of mass physical action set in; this, in fact, is *why* mass action swept the nation. It is a commonplace now among social historians that change produces revolution before revolutions add to and institutionalize change. Basically, it has not been the street orators and marchers who have been bringing desegration, for example; the marchers were set in motion by the fundamental changes of principle and law won in the courts by the quiet work of leaders like Roy Wilkins and Thurgood Marshall.

Totally oppressed people, here or in Africa or Asia, do not go into action. It is when the chains have been loosened, when they see some light at the end of the tunnel, that is, when *hope* is aroused, that the people arouse themselves.

In a certain sense, this pattern also applies to white college students protesting their "alienation" and the "establishments" they feel oppress them. Youth in any generation feels alienated because youth is the precarious, emotionally uprooted stage between childhood and maturity. But while individual youths of any generation are self-conscious because of this biochemical transition, today's collective self-consciousness of the young was not generated by them. The great American "youth cult" was generated by older people concerned with youth, from popular psychologists to advertising writers who realized that youth for the first time had sizable spending money, to publishers of girlie magazines who realized old moral barriers were giving way—and not, incidentally, from pressure by the young.

It is easy to sympathize with students in the massive institutions who feel they are treated as index-card numbers, not as individual souls, and various forms of decentralization must come about. But these youths will never persuade the graduating classes of the thirties, who faced the quiet desperations of the jobless Depression *and* the unmistakable imminence of a vast world war, that their lot is a tragic one. From my own life experience and travels, I would happily hazard the conjecture that to be young and to be a student in the United States of today is to enjoy the most favored condition that exists for any large, identifiable group anywhere in this world.

But experience, as every parent knows, is scarcely transferable. That hilarious slogan—"you can't trust anybody over thirty"—is, indeed, the explicit denial of the validity of experience.

When I listen to the young vigorously suggesting that if *they* had the governing influence, peace, love, beauty and sweet reason would spread o'er the world, I am tempted to remind them of the barbarities of the Hitler *Jugend,* the Mussolini Youth, the Chinese Red Guards, the Simbas of the Congo—but perhaps that would be over-egging the pudding, as the English say.

When I hear the passionate arrogances of a Mario Savio (the Berkeley fellow) or read about hundreds of University of Wisconsin students smashing windows and stopping traffic because they're sore about a bus-route schedule (or was it the price of textbooks?), I mutter to myself a private remark of Winston Churchill's: "I admire a manly man and a womanly woman, but I cannot abide a boyly boy."

If youth were complacent, devoid of the spirit of innovation and challenge, we would be in a bad way because some of the source springs of the American genius would dry up. Yet I think the "generational gap" in viewpoint will always be with us, for this reason: Youth can measure society only in one direction—forward, from things as they are, to their ideals. Older people, by the imperatives of experience, must add two other equally valid directions—backward, to things as they used to be, and sideways, to the other societies in the world they know.

Older people know something else: that the Savios, the Adam Clayton Powells and the Stokely Carmichaels are not, despite appearances, genuine leaders. Because they are not the strong men but the weak ones. They have not the moral stamina for the long haul with its inevitable routines and periods of boredom. Eloquence, brilliance and perhaps even physical bravery are not what count in the end. What counts is the quality the Romans defined and respected above all others—*gravitas*, meaning patience, solidity, weight of judgment. As Eric Hoffer puts it, "people in a hurry can neither grow nor decay; they are preserved in a state of perpetual puerility."

Furthermore, it is usually true that the habitual protester, the man with a vested emotional interest in protest, unconsciously does not *want* his goals to be realized. Success would leave him psychically bereft. Many successful revolutionaries in other lands had to be replaced as leaders when the new order of life was installed, partly because of their practical incompetence, partly because they continued in one way or another as protesters, as their nature obliged them to do.

There is a great deal wrong with American society of mid-twentieth century. There are some very ugly areas in our life; but never have they been so thoroughly exposed, researched and organized against. Never in our history have we seen an assault on these evils mounted on the level of Federal action to compare with the legislation and programs started under the Kennedy and Johnson Administrations, particularly the latter. Were it not for the creeping calamity of the Vietnam war, Mr. Johnson would, I think, stand revealed to everyone as one of the most vigorously humanitarian Presidents America has had, in spite of those personal crudities that upset the fastidious.

America has never been a frozen, rigid society, caught in conformity. At times we may seem becalmed, but as the Frenchman Jacques Maritain wrote, "Wait a moment, another current will appear and bring the first one to naught. A great country, with as many windshifts as the sea." We are not repeating the experience of Europe, whatever the Marxists and other doctrinists may think. America has eloped with history and run away with it, says Eric Hoffer.

Conformity, mass-mindedness? Go to the totalitarian or to the primitive societies if you wish to see them. Not here. If we live in a web of conforming laws and regulations, it is *because* we are so individualistic, so infinitely varied in our ideas, desires, ambitions and fears, and so very free to express them and to act upon them. Those who despair of getting public action on, let's say, our fearful urban problems, are wrong in thinking this is because "people don't take enough interest in public affairs." It is for the opposite reason; it is because so many groups, interests, points of view conflict. Ask any mayor. Ask any congressman whose desk is daily heaped with windrows of petitions, complaints, suggestions or denunciations.

It is not our freedom that is in peril, in the first instance. We have never had more freedom to speak out, to organize, to read what we choose, to question authority, whether political or cultural, to write, to film, to stage what would have been impermissible years ago. Never has the police authority been more restricted, never have defendants been so girded with legal protections.

Our freedom will be imperiled only if it turns into license, seriously imperiling order. There can be no freedom in the absence of order. There can be no personal or collective life worth living in the absence of moderation. Repeatedly, since the ancient Greeks, people have had to relearn this. Aristotle expressed it no better than Edmund Burke, the Anglo-Irish statesman, who said:

"Men are qualified for civil liberties in exact proportion to their disposition to put moral chains upon their own appetites . . . society cannot exist unless a controlling power upon will and appetite be placed somewhere, and the less of it there is within, the more there must be without. It is ordained in the eternal constitution of things that men of intemperate minds cannot be free. Their passions forge their fetters."

Chapter One

SUGGESTED TOPICS FOR CLASS DISCUSSION.

1. Do you think Professor Rossiter's description of consensus and unity on the fundamentals of American democracy in the early 1960's applies today?
2. The democratic process, grounded as it is on common agreement to proceed slowly through compromise, to consider all points of view, to consult all interests, to build up a clear majority, and to reassure a reluctant, and sometimes violently opposed minority may be having trouble adapting to today's necessity for quick decisions. Is there a danger of losing our traditional emphasis on protection of individual rights in the process of adaptation?
3. Does the high level of political apathy on the part of most of our people really present an opportunity for extremists groups to spread their views and win converts, or are they dismissed as cranks?
4. Radical groups exert great strains on a system which depends heavily on patterns of behavior which reflect consensus and on the simple democratic principle that every person has an equal right to his own opinion and to make his own choice as to when and how to express them. At the same time the government has the right and obligation to protect both itself and others who have different views. What, then, are "tolerable levels of dissent"? How far can objectors to the draft, for example, be permitted to go? What steps can government take to control the propaganda of "hate" groups? Can and should the private sector attempt to control such propaganda? Would control further alienate such groups? If so, what might be the consequences?

THE CONSTITUTIONAL BACKGROUND: THE POLITICS OF THE "MORE PERFECT UNION"

On June 7, 1776, Richard Henry Lee of Virginia, offered in the Second Continental Congress the following resolution:

> *Resolved, that these United Colonies are, and of a right ought to be, free and independent States, that they are absolved from all allegiance to the British Crown, and that all political connection between them and the State of Great Britain is, and ought to be, totally dissolved.* *

Thomas Jefferson was appointed Chairman of a committee, which included John Adams, Benjamin Franklin, Robert Livingston, and Roger Sherman, to draft an appropriate document. On June 28, 1776, the Declaration of Independence was offered to the Congress.

Not all of the delegates representing the colonies were ready to take this irrevocable step. New England leaders were restless and impatient, and Virginia was ready to support the break; but New York and Pennsylvania were lukewarm and there were controversies in other colonies. In general, the conservatives, the well-to-do, who had most to lose from a revolution— whether successful or not—were fearful of the "mob" and opposed the more radical leadership. After considerable debate the Declaration was adopted on July 4.

It would be difficult to overstate the importance of the Declaration to American constitutionalism. It expressed the beliefs of the American people in the natural and inalienable rights of man, a philosophy that justified

---

* *The Federal Convention and the Formation of the Union of the American States,* Winton U. Solberg (ed.) (New York: Liberal Arts Press, 1958), p. 32.

rebellion against tyranny and announced that governments were possessed of derived authority only and that such authority could spring only from the consent of the governed.

THE CONSTITUTIONAL BACKGROUND

It is no service to the members of the Constitutional Convention who gathered in Philadelphia in May, 1787, to make their work little more than a triumphal procession. Their achievement was magnificent because they faced staggering problems. When they gathered for the first session, it was not even clear that representative government was a viable concept when applied to a nation of so great an extent. The decisions and arrangements that are now so well known to every schoolboy lay hidden in the shadowed future.

> "All was doubtful and uncertain. It was clear that Americans would now go their way independent of England, but it was not clear which way the path would lead. Would they successfully assume the "separate and equal station to which the Laws of Nature and of Nature's God" entitled them, or would they be absorbed by a foreign power, be torn apart by internal strife, or sink into impotence and thence into despotism—the ideal of self-government proving unattainable? Did Shay's Rebellion represent the handwriting on the wall? Could several million people, with varying interests, spread over a vast territory, actually govern themselves on Republican principles? Could the proud and independent state governments be combined with a central government and, if so, how? *

In a time of troubles, such as the present, it is helpful to see how the events of an earlier era appeared to the men of the time. As late as July 10, George Washington, President of the Convention, was moved to write, "I almost despair of seeing a favourable issue to the proceedings of the Convention and do therefore repent having had any agency in the business. . . . " † Yet patience, reason, tolerance, and a willingness to compromise, eventually resulted in the document known as the Constitution.

This chapter contains selections from the notes James Madison took during the Constitutional Convention. In them, the reader can find the differences that divided the men in the Convention and he can trace the gradual emergence of agreement on some issues. On the final day of the Convention, Benjamin Franklin urged the members who still had objections to the instrument to doubt a little of their own infallibility and join with him in signing it.

---

* Andrew M. Scott, *Political Thought in America* (New York: Rinehart and Company, 1959), p. 93.

† Max Farrand, *Records of the Constitutional Convention* (New Haven, Conn.; Yale University Press, 1911), III, 56.

The Federal Convention and the Formation of the Union of the American States, Winton U. Solberg (ed.) (New York: Liberal Arts Press, 1958), p. 344.

Declaration of Independence-1776

THE DECLARATION OF INDEPENDENCE

IN CONGRESS, JULY 4, 1776.

The unanimous Declaration of the thirteen united States of America,

When in the Course of human events, it becomes necessary for one people to dissolve the political bands which have connected them with another, and to assume among the Powers of the earth, the separate and equal station to which the Laws of Nature and of Nature's God entitle them, a decent respect to the opinions of mankind requires that they should declare the causes which impel them to the separation.

We hold these truths to be self-evident, that all men are created equal, that they are endowed by their Creator with certain inalienable Rights, that among these are Life, Liberty, and the pursuit of Happiness. That to secure these rights, Governments are instituted among Men, deriving their just powers from the consent of the governed, That whenever any Form of Government becomes destructive of these ends, it is the Right of the People to alter or to abolish it, and to institute new Government, laying its foundation on such principles and organizing its powers in such form, as to them shall seem most likely to effect their Safety and Happiness. Prudence, indeed, will dictate that Governments long established should not be changed for light and transient causes; and accordingly all experience hath shown, that mankind are more disposed to suffer, while evils are sufferable, than to right themselves by abolishing the forms to which they are accustomed. But when a long train of abuses and usurpations, pursuing invariably the same Object evinces a design to reduce them under absolute Despotism, it is their right, it is their duty, to throw off such Government, and to provide new Guards for their future security.— Such has been the patient sufferance of these Colonies; and such is now the necessity which constrains them to alter their former Systems of Government. The history of the present King of Great Britain is a history of repeated injuries and usurpations, all having in direct object the establishment of an absolute Tyranny over these States. To prove this, let Facts be submitted to a candid world.

He has refused his Assent to Laws, the most wholesome and necessary for the public good.

He has forbidden his Governors to pass Laws of immediate and pressing importance, unless suspended in their operation till his Assent should be obtained; and when so suspended, he has utterly neglected to attend to them.

He has refused to pass other Laws for the accommodation of large districts of people, unless those people would relinquish the right of

Poore, ed. *The Federal and State Constitutions*, Pt. I, pp. 1–6.
The Federal Convention and the Formation of the Union of the American States, Winton U. Solberg (ed.) (New York: Liberal Arts Press, 1958), 34–38.

Representation in the Legislature, a right inestimable to them and formidable to tyrants only.

He has called together legislative bodies at places unusual, uncomfortable, and distant from the depository of their Public Records, for the sole purpose of fatiguing them into compliance with his measures.

He has dissolved Representative Houses repeatedly, for opposing with manly firmness his invasions on the rights of the people.

He has refused for a long time, after such dissolutions, to cause others to be elected; whereby the Legislative Powers, incapable of Annihilation, have returned to the People at large for their exercise; the State remaining in the mean time exposed to all the dangers of invasion from without, and convulsions within.

He has endeavoured to prevent the population of these States: for that purpose obstructing the Laws for Naturalization of Foreigners; refusing to pass others to encourage their migration hither, and raising the conditions of new Appropriations of Lands.

He has obstructed the Administration of Justice, by refusing his Assent to Laws for establishing Judiciary Powers.

He has made Judges dependent on his Will alone, for the tenure of their offices, and the amount and payment of their salaries.

He has erected a multitude of New Offices, and sent hither swarms of Officers to harass our People, and eat out their substance.

He has kept among us, in times of peace, Standing Armies without the Consent of our legislature.

He has affected to render the Military independent of and superior to the Civil Power.

He has combined with others to subject us to a jurisdiction foreign to our constitution, and unacknowledged by our laws; giving his Assent to their Acts of pretended Legislation:

For quartering large bodies of armed troops among us:

For protecting them, by a mock Trial, from Punishment for any Murders which they should commit on the Inhabitants of these States:

For cutting off our Trade with all parts of the world:

For imposing taxes on us without our Consent:

For depriving us in many cases, of the benefits of Trial by Jury:

For transporting us beyond Seas to be tried for pretended offences:

For abolishing the free System of English Laws in a neighbouring Province, establishing therein an Arbitrary government, and enlarging its Boundaries so as to render it at once an example and fit instrument for introducing the same absolute rule into these Colonies:

For taking away our Charters, abolishing our most valuable Laws, and altering fundamentally the Forms of our Governments:

For suspending our own Legislatures, and declaring themselves invested with Power to legislate for us in all cases whatsoever.

He has abdicated Government here, by declaring us out of his Protection and waging War against us.

He has plundered our seas, ravaged our Coasts, burnt our towns, and destroyed the lives of our people.

He is at this time transporting large armies of foreign mercenaries to compleat the works of death, desolation and tyranny, already begun with circumstances of Cruelty & perfidy scarcely paralleled in the most barbarous ages, and totally unworthy the Head of a civilized nation.

He has constrained our fellow Citizens taken Captive on the high Seas to bear Arms against their Country, to become the executioners of their friends and Brethren, or to fall themselves by their Hands.

He has excited domestic insurrections amongst us, and has endeavoured to bring on the inhabitants of our frontiers, the merciless Indian Savages, whose known rule of warfare, is an undistinguished destruction of all ages, sexes and conditions.

In every stage of these Oppressions We have Petitioned for Redress in the most humble terms: Our repeated Petitions have been answered only by repeated injury. A Prince, whose character is thus marked by every act which may define a Tyrant, is unfit to be the ruler of a free People.

Nor have We been wanting in attention to our Brittish brethren. We have warned them from time to time of attempts by their legislature to extend an unwarrantable jurisdiction over us. We have reminded them of the circumstances of our emigration and settlement here. We have appealed to their native justice and magnanimity, and we have conjured them by the ties of our common kindred to disavow these usurpations, which would inevitably interrupt our connections and correspondence. They too have been deaf to the voice of justice and of consanguinity. We must, therefore, acquiesce in the necessity, which denounces our Separation, and hold them, as we hold the rest of mankind, Enemies in War, in Peace Friends.

We, therefore, the Representatives of the united States of America, in General Congress, Assembled, appealing to the Supreme Judge of the world for the rectitude or our intentions, do, in the Name, and by Authority of the good People of these Colonies, solemnly publish and declare, That these United Colonies are, and of Right ought to be Free and Independent States; that they are Absolved from all Allegiance to the British Crown, and that all political connection between them and the State of Great Britain, is and ought to be totally dissolved; and that as Free and Independent States, they have full Power to levy War, conclude Peace, contract Alliances, establish Commerce, and to do all other Acts and Things which Independent States may of right do. And for the support of this Declaration, with a firm reliance on the Protection of Divine Providence, we mutually pledge to each other our Lives, our Fortunes and our sacred Honor.

JOHN HANCOCK.

(and Delegates of New Hampshire, Massachusetts Bay, Rhode Island, Connecticut, New York, New Jersey, Pennsylvania, Delaware, Maryland, Virginia, North Carolina, South Carolina, Georgia)

The Federal Convention

James Madison's Notes on the Debates *

Mr. Randolph then opened the main business.

He expressed his regret, that it should fall to him, rather than those, who were of longer standing in life and political experience, to open the great subject of their mission. But, as the convention had originated from Virginia, and his colleagues supposed that some proposition was expected from them, they had imposed this task on him.

He then commented on the difficulty of the crisis, and the necessity of preventing the fulfilment of the prophecies of the American downfal.

He observed that in revising the fœderal system we ought to inquire 1. into the properties, which such a government ought to possess, 2. the defects of the confederations, 3. the danger of our situation & 4. the remedy.

1. The Character of such a government ought to secure 1. against foreign invasion: 2. against dissentions between members of the Union, or seditions in particular states: 3. to procure to the several States various blessings, of which an isolated situation was incapable: 4. to be able to defend itself against incroachment: & 5. to be paramount to the state constitutions.

2. In speaking of the defects of the confederation he professed a high respect for its authors, and considered them, as having done all that patriots could do, in the then infancy of the science, of constitutions, & of confederacies,—when the inefficiency of requisitions was unknown— no commercial discord had arisen among any states—no rebellion had appeared as in Massts.—foreign debts had not become urgent—the havoc of paper money had not been foreseen—treaties had not been violated— and perhaps nothing better could be obtained from the jealousy of the states with regard to their sovereignty.

He then proceeded to enumerate the defects: 1. that the confederation produced no security against foreign invasion; congress not being permitted to prevent a war nor to support it by their own authority—Of this he cited many examples; most of which tended to shew that they could not cause infractions of treaties or of the law of nations, to be punished: that particular states might by their conduct provoke war without controul; and that neither militia nor draughts being fit for defence on such occasions, inlistments only could be successful, and these could not be executed without money.

2. that the fœderal government could not check the quarrels between states, nor a rebellion in any, not having constitutional power nor means to interpose according to the exigency:

3. that there were many advantages, which the U. S. might acquire,

* *The Federal Convention and the Formation of the Union of the American States,* Winton U. Solberg (ed.) (New York: Liberal Arts Press, 1958).

which were not attainable under the confederation—such as a productive impost—counteraction of the commercial regulations of other nations—pushing of commerce ad libitum—&c &c.

4. that the fœderal government could not defend itself against the incroachments from the states.

5. that it was not even paramount to the state constitutions, ratified, as it was in ma[n]y of the states.

3. He next reviewed the danger of our situation, appealed to the sense of the best friends of the U. S.—the prospect of anarchy from the laxity of government every where; and to other considerations.

4. He then proceeded to the remedy; the basis of which he said must be the republican principle

He proposed as conformable to his ideas the following resolutions, which he explained one by one. . . .

1. Resolved that the Articles of Confederation ought to be so corrected & enlarged as to accomplish the objects proposed by their institution; namely, "common defence, security of liberty, and general warfare."

2. Resd. therefore that the rights of suffrage in the National Legislature ought to be proportioned to the Quotas of contribution, or to the number of free inhabitants, as the one or the other rule may seem best in different cases.

3. Resd. that the National Legislature ought to consist of two branches.

4. Resd. that the members of the first branch of the National Legislature ought to be elected by the people of the several States every   for the term of   ; to be of the age of   years at least, to receive liberal stipends by which they may be compensated for the devotion of their time to public service; to be ineligible to any office established by a particular State, or under the authority of the United States, except those peculiarly belonging to the functions of the first branch, during the term of service, and for the space of   after its expiration; to be incapable of reelection for the space of   after the expiration of their term of service, and to be subject to recall.

5. Resold. that the members of the second branch of the National Legislature ought to be elected by those of the first, out of a proper number of persons nominated by the individual Legislatures, to be of the age of   years at least; to hold their offices for a term sufficient to ensure their independency; to receive liberal stipends, by which they may be compensated for the devotion of their time to public service; and to be ineligible to any office established by a particular State, or under the authority of the United States, except those peculiarly belonging to the functions of the second branch, during the term of service, and for the space of   after the expiration thereof.

6. Resolved that each branch ought to possess the right of originating Acts; that the National Legislature ought to be impowered to enjoy the Legislative Rights vested in Congress by the Confederation & moreover to legislate in all cases to which the separate States are incompetent, or in which the harmony of the United States may be interrupted by the exercise of individual Legislation; to negative all laws passed by the several States, contravening in the opinion of the National Legislature the articles

of Union; and to call forth the force of the Union agst. any member of the Union failing to fulfill its duty under the articles thereof.

7. Resd. that a National Executive be instituted; to be chosen by the National Legislature for the term of   years, to receive punctually at stated times, a fixed compensation for the services rendered, in which no increase or diminution shall be made so as to affect the Magistracy, existing at the time of increase or diminution, and to be ineligible a second time; and that besides a general authority to execute the National laws; it ought to enjoy the Executive rights vested in Congress by the Confederation.

8. Resd. that the Executive and a convenient number of the National Judiciary, ought to compose a Council of revision with authority to examine every act of the National Legislature before it shall operate, & every act of a particular Legislature before a Negative thereon shall be final; and that the dissent of the said Council shall amount to a rejection, unless the Act of the National Legislature be again passed, or that of a particular Legislature be again negatived by   of the members of each branch.

9. Resd. that a National Judiciary be established to consist of one or more supreme tribunals, and of inferior tribunals to be chosen by the National Legislature, to hold their offices during good behaviour; and to receive punctually at stated times fixed compensation for their services, in which no increase or diminution shall be made so as to affect the persons actually in office at the time of such increase or diminution; that the jurisdiction of the inferior tribunals shall be to hear & determine in the first instance, and of the supreme tribunal to hear and determine in the dernier resort, all piracies & felonies on the high seas, captures from an enemy, cases in which foreigners or citizens of other States applying to such jurisdictions may be interested, or which respect the collection of the National revenue; impeachments of any National officers, and questions which may involve the national peace and harmony.

10. Resolvd. that provision ought to be made for the admission of States lawfully arising within the limits of the United States, whether from a voluntary junction of Government & Territory or otherwise, with the consent of a number of voices in the National legislature less than the whole.

11. Resd. that a Republican Government & the territory of each State, except in the instance of a voluntary junction of Government & territory, ought to be guarantied by the United States to each State

12. Resd. that provision ought to be made for the continuance of Congress and their authorities and privileges, until a given day after the reform of the articles of Union shall be adopted, and for the completion of all their engagements.

13. Resd. that provision ought to be made for the amendment of the Articles of Union whensoever it shall seem necessary, and that the assent of the National Legislature ought not to be required thereto.

14. Resd. that the Legislative Executive & Judiciary powers within the several States ought to be bound by oath to support the articles of Union.

15. Resd. that the amendments which shall be offered to the Confederation, by the Convention ought at a proper time, or times, after the approbation of Congress to be submitted to an assembly or assemblies of

Representatives, recommended by the several Legislatures to be expressly chosen by the people, to consider & decide thereon.

He concluded with an exhortation, not to suffer the present opportunity of establishing general peace, harmony, happiness and liberty in the U. S. to pass away unimproved.

It was then Resolved—That the House will tomorrow resolve itself into a Committee of the Whole House to consider of the state of the American Union.—and that the propositions moved by Mr. Randolph be referred to the said Committee. . . .

.   .   .

Wednesday, May 30

Roger Sherman (from Connecticut) took his seat.

The House went into Committee of the Whole on the State of the Union. Mr. Gorham was elected to the Chair by Ballot.

The propositions of Mr. Randolph which had been referred to the Committee being taken up. He moved on the suggestion of Mr. G. Morris, that the first of his propositions to wit "Resolved that the articles of Confederation ought to be so corrected & enlarged, as to accomplish the objects proposed by their institution; namely, common defence, security of liberty & general welfare:—should be postponed, in order to consider the 3 following:

1. that a Union of the States merely federal will not accomplish the objects proposed by the articles of Confederation, namely common defence, security of liberty, & genl. welfare.

2. that no treaty or treaties among the whole or part of the States, as individual Sovereignties, would be sufficient.

3. that a *national* Government ought to be established consisting of a *supreme* Legislative, Executive & Judiciary.

The motion for postponing was seconded by Mr. Govr. Morris and unanimously agreed to.

Some verbal criticisms were raised agst. the first proposition, and it was agreed on motion of Mr. Butler, seconded by Mr. Randolph, to pass on to the third, which underwent a discussion, less however on its general merits than on the force and extent of the particular terms *national* & *supreme.*

Mr. Charles Pinkney wished to know of Mr. Randolph whether he meant to abolish the State Governts. altogether. Mr. R. replied that he meant by these general propositions merely to introduce the particular ones which explained the outlines of the system he had in view.

Mr. Butler said he had not made up his mind on the subject, and was open to the light which discussion might throw on it. After some general observations he concluded with saying that he had opposed the grant of powers to Congs. heretofore, because the whole power was vested in one body. The proposed distribution of the powers into different bodies changed the case, and would induce him to go great lengths.

Genl. Pinkney expressed a doubt whether the act of Congs. recommending the Convention, or the Commissions of the Deputies to it, could authorise a discussion of a System founded on different principles from the federal Constitution.

Mr. Gerry seemed to entertain the same doubt.

Mr. Govr. Morris explained the distinction between a *federal* and *national, supreme*, Govt.; the former being a mere compact resting on the good faith of the parties; the latter having a compleat and *compulsive* operation. He contended that in all Communities there must be one supreme power, and one only.

Mr. Mason observed that the present confederation was not only deficient in not providing for coercion & punishment agst. delinquent States; but argued very cogently that punishment could not in the nature of things be executed on the States collectively, and therefore that such a Govt. was necessary as could directly operate on individuals, and would punish those only whose guilt required it.

Mr. Sherman . . . admitted that the Confederation had not given sufficient power to Congs. and that additional powers were necessary; particularly that of raising money, which he said would involve many other powers. He admitted also that the General & particular jurisdictions ought in no case to be concurrent. He seemed however not be disposed to make too great inroads on the existing system; intimating as one reason that it would be wrong to lose every amendment, by inserting such as would not be agreed to by the States. . . .

. . .

Thursday, May 31

William Pierce from Georgia took his seat.

In Committee of the whole on Mr. Randolph's propositions.

The 3d. Resolution "that the national Legislature ought to consist of two branches" was agreed to without debate or dissent, except that of Pennsylvania, given probably from complaisance to Docr. Franklin who was understood to be partial to a single House of Legislation.

Resol: 4. first clause "that the members of the first branch of the National Legislature ought to be elected by the people of the several States" being taken up,

Mr. Sherman opposed the election by the people, insisting that it ought to be by the State Legislatures. The people he said, immediately should have as little to do as may be about the Government. They want information and are constantly liable to be misled.

Mr. Gerry. The evils we experience flow from the excess of democracy. The people do not want virtue, but are the dupes of pretended patriots. In Massts. it had been fully confirmed by experience that they are daily misled into the most baneful measures and opinions by the false reports circulated by designing men, and which no one on the spot can refute. One principal evil arises from the want of due provision for those employed in the administration of Governmt. It would seem to be a maxim of democracy to starve the public servants. He mentioned the popular clamour in Massts. for the reduction of salaries and the attack made on that of the Govr. though secured by the spirit of the Constitution itself. He had he said been too republican heretofore: he was still however republican, but had been taught by experience the danger of the levelling spirit.

Mr. Mason argued strongly for an election of the larger branch by the people. It was to be the grand depository of the democratic principle of the Govtt. It was, so to speak, to be our House of Commons—It ought to know & sympathise with every part of the community; and ought therefore to be taken not only from different parts of the whole republic, but also from different districts of the larger members of it, which had in several instances particularly in Virga., different interests and views arising from difference of produce, of habits &c &c. He admitted that we had been too democratic, but was afraid we sd. incautiously run into the opposite extreme. We ought to attend to the rights of every class of the people. He had often wondered at the indifference of the superior classes of society to this dictate of humanity & policy; considering that however affluent their circumstances, or elevated their situations, might be, the course of a few years, not only might but certainly would, distribute their posterity throughout the lowest classes of Society. Every selfish motive therefore, every family attachment, ought to recommend such a system of policy as would provide no less carefully for the rights and happiness of the lowest than of the highest orders of Citizens.

Mr. Wilson contended strenuously for drawing the most numerous branch of the Legislature immediately from the people. He was for raising the federal pyramid to a considerable altitude, and for that reason wished to give it as broad a basis as possible. No government could long subsist without the confidence of the people. In a republican Government this confidence was peculiarly essential. He also thought it wrong to increase the weight of the State Legislatures by making them the electors of the national Legislature. All interference between the general and local Governmts. should be obviated as much as possible. On examination it would be found that the opposition of States to federal measures had proceded much more from the officers of the States, than from the people at large.

Mr. Madison considered the popular election of one branch of the National Legislature as essential to every plan of free Government. He observed that in some of the States one branch of the Legislature was composed of men already removed from the people by an intervening body of electors. That if the first branch of the general legislature should be elected by the State Legislatures, the second branch elected by the first—the Executive by the second together with the first; and other appointments again made for subordinate purposes by the Executive, the people would be lost sight of altogether; and the necessary sympathy between them and their rulers and officers, too little felt. He was an advocate for the policy of refining the popular appointments by successive filtrations, but thought it might be pushed too far. He wished the expedient to be resorted to only in the appointment of the second branch of the Legislature, and in the Executive & judiciary branches of the Government. He thought too that the great fabric to be raised would be more stable and durable, if it should rest on the solid foundation of the people themselves, than if it should stand merely on the pillars of the Legislatures.

Mr. Gerry did not like the election by the people. The maxims taken from the British constitution were often fallacious when applied to our situation, which was extremely different. Experience he said had shewn that the State legislatures drawn immediately from the people did not

always possess their confidence. He had no objection however to an election by the people if it were so qualified that men of honor & character might not be unwilling to be joined in the appointments. He seemed to think the people might nominate a certain number out of which the State legislatures should be bound to choose.

.   .   .

The Committee proceeded to Resolution 5. "that the second (or senatorial) branch of the National Legislature ought to be chosen by the first branch out of persons nominated by the State Legislatures."

.   .   .

Mr. Spaight contended that the 2d. branch ought to be chosen by the State Legislatures and moved an amendment to that effect.

Mr. Butler apprehended that the taking so many powers out of the hands of the States as was proposed, tended to destroy all that balance and security of interests among the States which it was necessary to preserve; and called on Mr. Randolph . . . to explain the extent of his ideas, and particularly the number of members he meant to assign to this second branch.

Mr. Rand[olph] observed that he had at the time of offering his propositions stated his ideas as far as the nature of general propositions required; that details made no part of the plan, and could not perhaps with propriety have been introduced. If he was to give an opinion as to the number of the second branch, he should say that it ought to be much smaller than that of the first; so small as to be exempt from the passionate proceedings to which numerous assemblies are liable. He observed that the general object was to provide a cure for the evils under which the U. S. laboured; that in tracing these evils to their origin every man had found it in the turbulence and follies of democracy: that some check therefore was to be sought for agst. this tendency of our Governments: and that a good Senate seemed most likely to answer the purpose.

.   .   .

Friday, June 1

William Houston from Georgia took his seat.

The Committee of the whole proceeded to Resolution 7. "that a national Executive be instituted, to be chosen by the national Legislature—for the term of   years &c to be ineligible thereafter, to possess the executive powers of Congress &c."

Mr. Pinkney was for a vigorous Executive but was afraid the Executive powers of the existing Congress might extend to peace & war &c., which would render the Executive a monarchy, of the worst kind, to wit an elective one.

Mr. Wilson moved that the Executive consist of a single person. Mr. C. Pinkney seconded the motion, so as to read "that a National Ex. to consist of a single person, be instituted.

A considerable pause ensuing and the Chairman asking if he should put the question, Docr. Franklin observed that it was a point of great importance and wished that the gentlemen would deliver their sentiments on it before the question was put.

Mr. Rutlidge animadverted on the shyness of gentlemen on this and other subjects. He said it looked as if they supposed themselves precluded by having frankly disclosed their opinions from afterwards changing them, which he did not take to be at all the case. He said he was for vesting the Executive power in a single person, tho' he was not for giving him the power of war and peace. A single man would feel the greatest responsibility and administer the public affairs best.

Mr. Sherman said he considered the Executive magistracy as nothing more than an institution for carrying the will of the Legislature into effect, that the person or persons ought to be appointed by and accountable to the Legislature only, which was the depositary of the supreme will of the Society. As they were the best judges of the business which ought to be done by the Executive department, and consequently of the number necessary from time to time for doing it, he wished the number might not be fixed but that the legislature should be at liberty to appoint one or more as experience might dictate.

Mr. Wilson preferred a single magistrate, as giving most energy dispatch and responsibility to the office. He did not consider the Prerogatives of the British Monarch as a proper guide in defining the Executive powers. Some of these prerogatives were of Legislative nature. Among others that of war & peace &c. The only powers he conceived strictly Executive were those of executing the laws, and appointing officers, not appertaining to and appointed by the Legislature.

. . .

Mr. Randolph strenuously opposed a unity in the Executive magistracy. He regarded it as the fœtus of monarchy. We had, he said no motive to be governed by the British Governmt. as our prototype. He did not mean however to throw censure on that Excellent fabric. If we were in a situation to copy it he did not know that he should be opposed to it; but the fixt genius of the people of America required a different form of Government. He could not see why the great requisites for the Executive department, vigor, despatch & responsibility could not be found in three men, as well as in one man. The Executive ought to be independent. It ought therefore in order to support its independence to consist of more than one.

Mr. Wilson said that unity in the Executive, instead of being the fetus of monarchy would be the best safeguard against tyranny. He repeated that he was not governed by the British Model which was inapplicable to the situation of this Country; the extent of which was so great, and the manners so republican, that nothing but a great confederated Republic would do for it.

Mr. Wilson's motion for a single magistrate was postponed by common consent, the Committee seeming unprepared for any decision on it; and the first part of the clause agreed to, viz—"that a National Executive be instituted."

Mr. Madison thought it would be proper, before a choice shd. be made between a unity and a plurality in the Executive, to fix the extent of the Executive authority; that, as certain powers were in their nature Executive and must be given to that departmt. whether administered by one or more persons, a definition of their extent would assist the judgment in

determining how far they might be safely entrusted to a single officer. . . .

The next clause in Resolution 7, relating to the mode of appointing, & the duration of, the Executive being under consideration,

Mr. Wilson said he was almost unwilling to declare the mode which he wished to take place, being apprehensive that it might appear chimerical. He would say, however, at least that in theory he was for an election by the people. Experience, particularly in N. York & Massts., shewed that an election of the first magistrate by the people at large, was both a convenient & successful mode. The objects of choice in such cases must be persons whose merits have general notoriety.

Mr. Sherman was for the appointment by the Legislature, and for making him absolutely dependent on that body, as it was the will of that which was to be executed. An independence of the Executive on the supreme Legislature, was in his opinion the very essence of tyranny if there was any such thing. . . .

Saturday, June 2. In Committee of the whole

Mr. Wilson repeated his arguments in favor of an election without the intervention of the States. He supposed too that this mode would produce more confidence among the people in the first magistrate, than an election by the national Legislature.

Mr. Gerry opposed the election by the national legislature. There would be a constant intrigue kept up for the appointment. The Legislature & the candidates wd. bargain & play into one another's hands, votes would be given by the former under promises or expectations from the latter, of recompensing them by services to members of the Legislature or to their friends. He liked the principle of Mr. Wilson's motion, but fears it would alarm & give a handle to the State partisans, as tending to supersede altogether the State authorities. He thought the Community not yet ripe for stripping the States of their powers, even such as might not be requisite for local purposes. He was for waiting till people should feel more the necessity of it. He seemed to prefer the taking the suffrages of the States instead of Electors, or letting the Legislatures nominate, and the electors appoint. He was not clear that the people ought to act directly even in the choice of electors, being too little informed of personal characters in large districts, and liable to deceptions.

Mr. Dickenson moved "that the Executive be made removeable by the National Legislature on the request of a majority of the Legislatures of individual States." It was necessary he said to place the power of removing somewhere. He had no idea of abolishing the State Governments as some gentlemen seemed inclined to do. The happiness of this Country in his opinion required considerable powers to be left in the hands of the States. . . .

Mr. Mason. Some mode of displacing an unfit magistrate is rendered indispensable by the fallibility of those who choose, as well as by the corruptibility of the man chosen. He opposed decidedly the making the Executive the mere creature of the Legislature as a violation of the fundamental principle of good Government.

Mr. Madison & Mr. Wilson observed that it would leave an equality of agency in the small with the great States; that it would enable a minority of the people to prevent ye. removal of an officer who had rendered himself justly criminal in the eyes of a majority; that it would open a door for intrigues agst. him in States where his administration tho' just might be unpopular, and might tempt him to pay court to particular States whose leading partizans he might fear, or wish to engage as his partizans. They both thought it bad policy to introduce such a mixture of the State authorities, where their agency could be otherwise supplied.

Mr. Dickenson considered the business as so important that no man ought to be silent or reserved. He went into a discourse of some length, the sum of which was, that the Legislative, Executive, & Judiciary departments ought to be made as independent as possible; but that such an Executive as some seemed to have in contemplation was not consistent with a republic: that a firm Executive could only exist in a limited monarchy. In the British Govt. itself the weight of the Executive arises from the attachments which the Crown draws to itself, & not merely from the force of its prerogatives. In place of these attachments we must look out for something else. One source of stability is the double branch of the Legislature. The division of the Country into distinct States formed the other principal source of stability. This division ought therefore to be maintained, and considerable powers to be left with the States. This was the ground of his consolation for the future fate of his Country. Without this, and in case of a consolidation of the States into one great Republic, we might read its fate in the history of smaller ones. A limited Monarchy he considered as *one* of the best Governments in the world. It was not *certain* that the same blessings were derivable from any other form. It was certain that equal blessings had never yet been derived from any of the republican form. A limited Monarchy however was out of the question. The spirit of the times—the state of our affairs, forbade the experiment, if it were desireable. Was it possible, moreover, in the nature of things to introduce it even if these obstacles were less insuperable. . . . No. They were the growth of ages, and could only arise under a complication of circumstances none of which existed in this Country. But though a form the most perfect *perhaps* in itself be unattainable, we must not despair. If antient republics have been found to flourish for a moment only & then vanish forever, it only proves that they were badly constituted; and that we ought to seek for every remedy for their diseases. One of these remedies he conceived to be the accidental lucky division of this Country into distinct States; a division which some seemed desirous to abolish altogether. As to the point of representation in the national Legislature as it might affect States of different sizes, he said it must probably end in mutual concession. He hoped that each State would retain an equal voice at least in one branch of the National Legislature, and supposed the sums paid within each State would form a better ratio for the other branch than either the number of inhabitants or the quantum of property.

On Mr. Dickenson's motion for making Executive removeable by Natl.

Legislature at request of majority of State Legislatures was . . . rejected
—all the States being in the negative Except Delaware. . . .

Mr. Rutledge & Mr. C. Pinkney moved that the blank for the no. of
persons in the Executive be filled with the words "one person." He supposed the reasons to be so obvious & conclusive in favor of one that no
member would oppose the motion.

Mr. Randolph opposed it with great earnestness, declaring that he
should not do justice to the Country which sent him if he were silently
to suffer the establishmt. of a Unity in the Executive department. He
felt an opposition to it which he believed he should continue to feel as
long as he lived. He urged 1. that the permanent temper of the people
was adverse to the very semblance of Monarchy. 2. that a unity was
unnecessary, a plurality being equally competent to all the objects of
the department. 3. that the necessary confidence would never be reposed
in a single Magistrate. 4. that the appointments would generally be in
favor of some inhabitant near the center of the Community, and consequently the remote parts would not be on an equal footing. He was in
favor of three members of the Executive, to be drawn from different portions of the Country.

Mr. Butler contended strongly for a single magistrate as most likely to
answer the purpose of the remote parts. If one man should be appointed
he would be responsible to the whole, and would be impartial to its interests. If three or more should be taken from as many districts, there
would be a constant struggle for local advantages. In Military matters
this would be particularly mischievous. . . .

Wednesday, June 6. In Committee of the whole

Mr. Pinkney . . . moved "that the first branch of the national Legislature be elected by the State Legislatures, and not by the people." con-
tending that the people were less fit Judges in such a case, and that the
Legislatures would be less likely to promote the adoption of the new
Government, if they were to be excluded from all share in it.

Mr. Rutlidge 2ded. the motion.

Mr. Gerry. Much depends on the mode of election. In England, the
people will probably lose their liberty from the smallness of the proportion
having a right of suffrage. Our danger arises from the opposite extreme:
hence in Massts. the worst men get into the Legislature. Several members
of that Body had lately been convicted of infamous crimes. Men of in-
digence, ignorance & baseness, spare no pains, however dirty to carry
their point agst. men who are superior to the artifices practised. He was
not disposed to run into extremes. He was as much principled as ever
agst. aristocracy and monarchy. It was necessary on the one hand that
the people should appoint one branch of the Govt. in order to inspire
them with the necessary confidence. But he wished the election on the
other to be so modified as to secure more effectually a just preference of
merit. His idea was that the people should nominate certain persons in
certain districts, out of whom the State Legislatures shd. make the appointment.

.   .   .

Mr. Read. Too much attachment is betrayed to the State Governts. We must look beyond their continuance. A national Govt. must soon of necessity swallow all of them up. . . . The confederation was founded on temporary principles. It cannot last: it cannot be amended. If we do not establish a good Govt. on new principles, we must either go to ruin, or have the work to do over again. The people at large are wrongly suspected of being averse to a Genl. Govt. The aversion lies among interested men who possess their confidence.

.   .   .

Mr. Wilson, would not have spoken again, but for what had fallen from Mr. Read; namely, that the idea of preserving the State Govts. ought to be abandoned. He saw no incompatibility between the National & State Govts. provided the latter were restrained to certain local purposes; nor any probability of their being devoured by the former. In all confederated Systems antient & modern the reverse had happened; the Generality being destroyed gradually by the usurpations of the parts composing it.

On the question for electing the 1st. branch by the State Legislatures as moved by Mr. Pinkney: it was negatived:

.   .   .

Friday, June 15

Mr. Patterson, laid before the Convention the plan which he said several of the deputations wished to be substituted in place of that proposed by Mr. Randolph. After some little discussion of the most proper mode of giving it a fair deliberation it was agreed that it should be referred to a Committee of the whole, and that in order to place the two plans in due comparison, the other should be recommitted. At the earnest desire of Mr. Lansing & some other gentlemen, it was also agreed that the Convention should not go into Committee of the whole on the subject till tomorrow, by which delay the friends of the plan proposed by Mr. Patterson wd. be better prepared to explain & support it, and all would have an opportuy. of taking copies.

The propositions from N. Jersey moved by Mr. Patterson were in the words following.

1. Resd. that the articles of Confederation ought to be so revised, corrected & enlarged, as to render the federal Constitution adequate to the exigencies of Government, & the preservation of the Union.

2. Resd. that in addition to the powers vested in the U. States in Congress, by the present existing articles of Confederation, they be authorized to pass acts for raising a revenue, by levying a duty or duties on all goods or merchandizes of foreign growth or manufacture, imported into any part of the U. States, by Stamps on paper, vellum or parchment, and by a postage on all letters or packages passing through the general post-office, to be applied to such federal purposes as they shall deem proper & expedient; to make rules & regulations for the collection thereof; and the same from time to time, to alter & amend in such manner as they shall think proper: to pass Acts for the regulation of trade & commerce as well with foreign nations as with each other: provided that all punishments, fines, forfeitures & penalties to be incurred for contravening such

acts rules and regulations shall be adjudged by the Common law Judiciaries of the State in which any offence contrary to the true intent & meaning of such Acts rules & regulations shall have been committed or perpetrated, with liberty of commencing in the first instance all suits & prosecutions for that purpose in the superior common law Judiciary in such State, subject nevertheless, for the correction of all errors, both in law & fact in rendering Judgment, to an appeal to the Judiciary of the U. States.

3. Resd. that whenever requisitions shall be necessary, instead of the rule for making requisitions mentioned in the articles of Confederation, the United States in Congs. be authorized to make such requisitions in proportion to the whole number of white & other free citizens & inhabitants of every age sex and condition including those bound to servitude for a term of years & three fifths of all other persons not comprehended in the foregoing description, except Indians not paying taxes; that if such requisitions be not complied with, in the time specified therein, to direct the collection thereof in the non complying States & for that purpose to devise and pass acts directing & authorizing the same; provided that none of the powers hereby vested in the U. States in Congs. shall be exercised without the consent of at least   States, and in that proportion if the number of Confederated States should hereafter be increased or diminished.

4. Resd. that the U. States in Congs. be authorized to elect a federal Executive to consist of   persons, to continue in office for the term of   years, to receive punctually at stated times a fixed compensation for their services, in which no increase or diminution shall be made so as to affect the persons composing the Executive at the time of such increase or diminution, to be paid out of the federal treasury; to be incapable of holding any other office or appointment during their time of service and for   years thereafter; to be ineligible a second time, & removeable by Congs. on application by a majority of the Executives of the several States; that the Executives besides their general authority to execute the federal acts ought to appoint all federal officers not otherwise provided for, & to direct all military operations; provided that none of the persons composing the federal Executive shall on any occasion take command of any troops, so as personally to conduct any enterprise as General or in other capacity.

5. Resd. that a federal Judiciary be established to consist of a supreme Tribunal the Judges of which to be appointed by the Executive, & to hold their offices during good behaviour, to receive punctually at stated times a fixed compensation for their services in which no increase or diminution shall be made, so as to affect the persons actually in office at the time of such increase or diminution; that the Judiciary so established shall have authority to hear & determine in the first instance on all impeachments of federal officers, & by way of appeal in the dernier resort in all cases touching the rights of Ambassadors, in all cases of captures from an enemy, in all cases of piracies & felonies on the high Seas, in all cases in which foreigners may be interested, in the construction of any treaty or treaties, or which may arise on any of the Acts for regulation of trade, or the collection of the federal Revenue: that none of the Judiciary shall

during the time they remain in office be capable of receiving or holding any other office or appointment during their time of service, or for thereafter.

6. Resd. that all Acts of the U. States in Congs. made by virtue & in pursuance of the powers hereby & by the articles of Confederation vested in them, and all Treaties made & ratified under the authority of the U. States shall be the supreme law of the respective States so far forth as those Acts or Treaties shall relate to the said States or their Citizens, and that the Judiciary of the several States shall be bound thereby in their decisions, any thing in the respective laws of the Individual States to the contrary notwithstanding; and that if any State, or any body of men in any State shall oppose or prevent ye. carrying into execution such acts or treaties, the federal Executive shall be authorized to call forth ye. power of the Confederated States, or so much thereof as may be necessary to enforce and compel an obedience to such Acts, or an observance of such Treaties.

7. Resd. that provision be made for the admission of new States into the Union.

8. Resd. the rule for naturalization ought to be the same in every State.

9. Resd. that a Citizen of one State committing an offense in another State of the Union, shall be deemed guilty of the same offense as if it had been committed by a Citizen of the State in which the offense was committed.

Adjourned.

.   .   .

Mr. Wilson entered into a contrast of the principal points of the two plans so far he said as there had been time to examine the one last proposed. These points were 1. in the Virga. plan there are 2 & in some degree 3 branches in the Legislature: in the plan from N. J. there is to be a *single* legislature only—2. Representation of the people at large is the basis of the one:—the State Legislatures, the pillars of the other—3. proportional representation prevails in one:—equality of suffrage in the other—4. A single Executive Magistrate is at the head of the one:—a plurality is held out in the other.—5. in the one the majority of the people of the U. S. must prevail:—in the other a minority may prevail. 6. the Natl. Legislature is to make laws in all cases to which the separate States are incompetent &—:—in place of this Congs. are to have additional power in a few cases only—7. A negative on the laws of the States: —in place of this coertion to be substituted—8. The Executive to be removeable on impeachment & conviction;—in one plan: in the other to be removeable at the instance of majority of the Executives of the States— 9. Revision of the laws provided for in one:—no such check in the other— 10. inferior national tribunals in one:—none such in the other. 11. In ye. one jurisdiction of Natl. tribunals to extend &c—; an appellate jurisdiction only allowed in the other. 12. Here the jurisdiction is to extend to all cases affecting the Nationl. peace & harmony: there, a few cases only are marked out. 13. finally ye. ratification is in this to be by the people themselves:—in that by the legislative authorities according to the 13 art: of Confederation.

With regard to the *power of the Convention,* he conceived himself authorized to *conclude nothing,* but to be at liberty to *propose any thing.* In this particular he felt himself perfectly indifferent to the two plans.

With *regard to the sentiments of the people,* he conceived it difficult to know precisely what they are. Those of the particular circle in which one moved, were commonly mistaken for the general voice. He could not persuade himself that the State Govts. & Sovereignties were so much the idols of the people, nor a Natl. Govt. so obnoxious to them, as some supposed. Why sd. a Natl. Govt. be unpopular? Has it less dignity? will each Citizen enjoy under it less liberty or protection? Will a Citizen of *Delaware* be degraded by becoming a Citizen of the *United States?* Where do the people look at present for relief from the evils of which they complain? Is it from an internal reform of their Govts.? no, Sir. It is from the Natl. Councils that relief is expected. For these reasons he did not fear, that the people would not follow us into a national Govt. and it will be a further recommendation of Mr. R.'s plan that it is to be submitted to *them,* and not to the *Legislatures,* for ratification.

. . .

Monday, June 18. In Committee of the whole

. . .

Mr. Hamilton, had been hitherto silent on the business before the Convention, partly from respect to others whose superior abilities age & experience rendered him unwilling to bring forward ideas dissimilar to theirs, and partly from his delicate situation with respect to his own State, to whose sentiments as expressed by his Colleagues, he could by no means accede. The crisis however which now marked our affairs, was too serious to permit any scruples whatever to prevail over the duty imposed on every man to contribute his efforts for the public safety & happiness. He was obliged therefore to declare himself unfriendly to both plans. He was particularly opposed to that from N. Jersey, being fully convinced, that no amendment of the Confederation, leaving the States in possession of their Sovereignty could possibly answer the purpose. . . .

. . .

. . . Two Sovereignties can not co-exist within the same limits. Giving powers to Congs. must eventuate in a bad Govt. or in no Govt. The plan of N. Jersey therefore will not do. What then is to be done? Here he was embarrassed. The extent of the Country to be governed, discouraged him. The expence of a general Govt. was also formidable; unless there were such a diminution of expence on the side of the State Govts. as the case would admit. If they were extinguished, he was persuaded that great œconomy might be obtained by sustaining a general Govt. He did not mean however to shock the public opinion by proposing such a measure. On the other hand he saw no *other* necessity for declining it. They are not necessary for any of the great purposes of commerce, revenue, or agriculture. Subordinate authorities he was aware would be necessary. There must be district tribunals: corporations for local purposes. But cui bono, the vast & expensive apparatus now appertaining to the States.

The only difficulty of a serious nature which occurred to him, was that of drawing representatives from the extremes to the center of the Community. What inducements can be offered that will suffice? The moderate wages for the 1st. branch would only be a bait to little demagogues. Three dollars or thereabouts he supposed would be the utmost. The Senate he feared from a similar cause, would be filled by certain undertakers who wish for particular offices under the Govt. This view of the subject almost led him to despair that a Republican Govt. could be established over so great an extent. He was sensible at the same time that it would be unwise to propose one of any other form. In his private opinion he had no scruple in declaring, supported as he was by the opinions of so many of the wise & good, that the British Govt. was the best in the world: and that he doubted much whether any thing short of it would do in America. He hoped Gentlemen of different opinions would bear with him in this, and begged them to recollect the change of opinion on this subject which had taken place and was still going on. It was once thought that the power of Congs. was amply sufficient to secure the end of their institution. The error was now seen by every one. The members most tenacious of republicanism, he observed, were as loud as any in declaiming agst. the vices of democracy. This progress of the public mind led him to anticipate the time, when others as well as himself would join in the praise bestowed by Mr. Neckar on the British Constitution, namely, that it is the only Govt. in the world "which unites public strength with individual security."—In every community where industry is encouraged, there will be a division of it into the few & the many. Hence separate interests will arise. There will be debtors & creditors &c. Give all power to the many, they will oppress the few. Give all power to the few, they will oppress the many. Both therefore ought to have power, that each may defend itself agst. the other. To the want of this check we owe our paper money, instalment laws &c. To the proper adjustment of it the British owe the excellence of their Constitution. Their house of Lords is a most noble institution. Having nothing to hope for by a change, and a sufficient interest by means of their property, in being faithful to the national interest, they form a permanent barrier agst. every pernicious innovation, whether attempted on the part of the Crown or of the Commons. No temporary Senate will have firmness eno' to answer the purpose. . . . Gentlemen differ in their opinions concerning the necessary checks, from the different estimates they form of the human passions. They suppose seven years a sufficient period to give the senate an adequate firmness, from not duly considering the amazing violence & turbulence of the democratic spirit. When a great object of Govt. is pursued, which seizes the popular passions, they spread like wild fire, and become irresistable. He appealed to the gentlemen from the N. England States whether experience had not there verified the remark.—As to the Executive, it seemed to be admitted that no good one could be established on Republican principles. Was not this giving up the merits of the question: for can there be a good Govt. without a good Executive. The English model was the only good one on this subject. The Hereditary interest of the King was so interwoven with that of the Nation, and his personal emoluments so great, that he was placed above the danger of being corrupted from abroad—and at the same time was both sufficiently independent and sufficiently controuled, to answer the purpose of the institution at home. one of the weak sides of Republics was their being liable to foreign influence & corruption. Men of little character, acquiring great power become easily the tools of intermedling Neibours. . . . What is the inference from all these observations? That we ought to go as far in order to attain stability and permanency, as republican principles will admit. Let one branch of the Legislature hold their places for life or at least during good behaviour. Let the Executive also be for life. He appealed to the feelings of the members present whether a term of seven years, would induce the sacrifices of private affairs which an acceptance of public trust would require, so so as to ensure the services of the best Citizens. On this plan we should have in the Senate a permanent will, a weighty interest, which would answer essential purposes. But is this a Republican Govt., it will be asked? Yes if all the Magistrates are appointed, and vacancies are filled, by the people, or a process of election originating with the people. He was sensible that an Executive constituted as he proposed would have in fact but little of the power and independence that might be necessary. On the other plan of appointing him for 7 years, he thought the Executive ought to have but little power. He would be ambitious, with the means of making creatures; and as the object of his ambition wd. be to *prolong* his power, it is probable that in case of a war, he would avail himself of the emergence, to evade or refuse a degradation from his place. An Executive for life has not this motive for forgetting his fidelity, and will therefore be a safer depository of power. . . .

Thursday, June 21. In Convention

Mr. Jonathan Dayton from N. Jersey took his seat.

Docr. Johnson. On a comparison of the two plans which had been proposed from Virginia & N. Jersey, it appeared that the peculiarity which characterized the latter was its being calculated to preserve the individuality of the States. The plan from Va. did not profess to destroy this individuality altogether, but was charged with such a tendency. One Gentleman alone (Col. Hamilton) in his animadversions on the plan of N. Jersey, boldly and decisively contended for an abolition of the State Govts. Mr. Wilson & the gentlemen from Virga. who also were adversaries of the plan of N. Jersey held a different language. They wished to leave the States in possession of a considerable, tho' a subordinate jurisdiction. They had not yet however shewn how this cd. consist with, or be secured agst. the general sovereignty & jurisdiction, which they proposed to give to the national Government. If this could be shewn in such a manner as to satisfy the patrons of the N. Jersey propositions, that the individuality of the States would not be endangered, many of their objections would no doubt be removed. If this could not be shewn their objections would have their full force. He wished it therefore to be well considered whether in case the States, as was proposed, shd. retain some portion of sovereignty at least, this portion could be preserved, without allowing them to participate effectually in the Genl. Govt., without giving them each a distinct and equal vote for the purpose of defending themselves in the general Councils.

Mr. Wilson's respect for Docr. Johnson, added to the importance of the subject led him to attempt, unprepared as he was, to solve the difficulty which had been started. It was asked how the Genl. Govt. and individuality of the particular States could be reconciled to each other; and how the latter could be secured agst. the former? Might it not, on the other side be asked how the former was to be secured agst. the latter? It was generally admitted that a jealousy & rivalship would be felt between the Genl. & particular Govts. As the plan now stood, tho' indeed contrary to his opinion, one branch of the Genl. Govt. (the Senate or second branch) was to be appointed by the State Legislatures. The State Legislatures, therefore, by this participation in the Genl. Govt. would have an opportunity of defending their rights. Ought not a reciprocal opportunity to be given to the Genl. Govt. of defending itself by having an appointment of some one constituent branch of the State Govts. If a security be necessary on one side, it wd. seem reasonable to demand it on the other. But taking the matter in a more general view, he saw no danger to the States from the Genl. Govt. In case a combination should be made by the large ones it wd. produce a general alarm among the rest; and the project wd. be frustrated. But there was no temptation to such a project. The States having in general a similar interest, in case of any proposition in the National Legislature to encroach on the State Legislatures, he conceived a general alarm wd. take place in the National Legislature itself, that it would communicate itself to the State Legislatures, and wd. finally spread among the people at large. The Genl. Govt. will be as ready to preserve the rights of the States as the latter are to preserve the rights of individuals; all the members of the former, having a common interest, as representatives of all the people of the latter, to leave the State Govts. in possession of what the people wish them to retain. He could not discover, therefore any danger whatever on the side from which it had been apprehended. On the contrary, he conceived that in spite of every precaution the general Govt. would be in perpetual danger of encroachments from the State Govts.

Mr. Madison was of the opinion that there was 1. less danger of encroachment from the Genl. Govt. than from the State Govts. 2. that the mischief from encroachments would be less fatal if made by the former, than if made by the latter. . . .

Thursday, July 5. In Convention

Mr. Govr. Morris. thought the form as well as the matter of the Report objectionable. . . . He conceived the whole aspect of it to be wrong. He came here as a Representative of America; he flattered himself he came here in some degree as a Representative of the whole human race; for the whole human race will be affected by the proceedings of this Convention. He wished gentlemen to extend their views beyond the present moment of time; beyond the narrow limits of place from which they derive their political origin. If he were to believe some things which he had heard, he should suppose that we were assembled to truck and bargain for our particular States. . . . Much has been said of the sentiments of the people. They were unknown. They could not be known. All that we can infer is that if the plan we recommend be reasonable & right; all who have reasonable minds and sound intentions will embrace it, notwithstanding what had been said by some gentlemen. Let us suppose that the larger States shall agree; and that the smaller refuse: and let us trace the consequences. The opponents of the system in the smaller States will no doubt make a party, and a noise for a time, but the ties of interest, of kindred & of common habits which connect them with the other States will be too strong to be easily broken. In N. Jersey particularly he was sure a great many would follow the sentiments of Pena. & N. York. This Country must be united. If persuasion does not unite it, the sword will. He begged that this consideration might have its due weight. The scenes of horror attending civil commotion can not be described, and the conclusion of them will be worse than the term of their continuance. The stronger party will then make traytors of the weaker; and the Gallows & Halter will finish the work of the sword. How far foreign powers would be ready to take part in the confusions he would not say. Threats that they will be invited have it seems been thrown out. . . . But returning to the Report he could not think it in any respect calculated for the public good. . . . State attachments, and State importance have been the bane of this Country. We can not annihilate; but we may perhaps take out the teeth of the serpents. He wished our ideas to be enlarged to the true interest of man, instead of being circumscribed within the narrow compass of a particular Spot. And after all how little can be the motive yielded by selfishness for such a policy. Who can say whether he himself, much less whether his children, will the next year be an inhabitant of this or that State. . . .

Mr. Patterson . . . complained of the manner in which Mr. M[adison] & Mr. Govr. Morris had treated the small States.

Mr. Gerry. Tho' he had assented to the Report in the Committee, he had very material objections to it. We were however in a peculiar situation. We were neither the same Nation nor different Nations. We ought not therefore to pursue the one or the other of these ideas too closely. If no compromise should take place what will be the consequence. A secession he foresaw would take place; for some gentlemen seem decided on it; two different plans will be proposed; and the result no man could foresee. If we do not come to some agreement among ourselves some foreign sword will probably do the work for us.

Mr. Mason. The Report was meant not as specific propositions to be adopted; but merely as a general ground of accomodation. There must be some accomodation on this point, or we shall make little further progress in the work. Accomodation was the object of the House in the appointment of the Committee; and of the Committee in the Report they had made. And however liable the Report might be to objections, he thought it preferable to an appeal to the world by the different sides, as had been talked of by some Gentlemen. It could not be more inconvenient to any gentleman to remain absent from his private affairs, than it was for him: but he would bury his bones in this City rather than expose his Country to the Consequences of a dissolution of the Convention without any thing being done.

The 1st. proposition in the report for fixing the representation in the 1st. branch, one member for every 40,000 inhabitants, being taken up.

Mr. Govr. Morris objected to that scale of apportionment. He thought property ought to be taken into the estimate as well as the number of inhabitants. Life & liberty were generally said to be of more value, than property. An accurate view of the matter would nevertheless prove that property was the main object of Society. The savage State was more favorable to liberty than the Civilized; and sufficiently so to life. It was preferred by all men who had not acquired a taste for property; it was only renounced for the sake of property which could only be secured by the restraints of regular Government. These ideas might appear to some new, but they were nevertheless just. If property then was the main object of Govt. certainly it ought to be one measure of the influence due to those who were to be affected by the Governmt. He looked forward also to that range of New States which wd. soon be formed in the West. He thought the rule of representation ought to be so fixed as to secure to the Atlantic States a prevalence in the National Councils. . . .

.   .   .

Monday, September 17. In Convention

The engrossed Constitution being read,

Docr. Franklin rose with a speech in his hand, which he had reduced to writing for his own conveniency, and which Mr. Wilson read in the words following.

Mr. President

I confess that there are several parts of this constitution which I do not at present approve, but I am not sure I shall never approve them: For having lived long, I have experienced many instances of being obliged by better information, or fuller consideration, to change opinions even on important subjects, which I once thought right, but found to be otherwise. It is therefore that the older I grow, the more apt I am to doubt my own judgment, and to pay more respect to the judgment of others. Most men indeed as well as most sects in Religion, think themselves in possession of all truth, and that wherever others differ from them it is so far error. . . . But though many private persons think almost as highly of their own infallibility as of that of their sect, few express it so naturally as a certain french lady, who in a dispute with her sister, said "I don't know how it happens, Sister but I meet with no body but myself, that's always in the right—*Il n'y a que moi qui a toujours raison.*"

In these sentiments, Sir, I agree to this Constitution with all its faults, if they are such; because I think a general Government necessary for us, and there is no form of Government but what may be a blessing to the people if well administered, and believe farther that this is likely to be well administered for a course of years, and can only end in Despotism, as other forms have done before it, when the people shall become so corrupted as to need despotic Government, being incapable of any other.

I doubt too whether any other Convention we can obtain, may be able to make a better Constitution. For when you assemble a number of men to have the advantage of their joint wisdom, you inevitably assemble with those men, all their prejudices, their passions, their errors of opinion, their local interests, and their selfish views. From such an assembly can a perfect production be expected? It therefore astonishes me, Sir, to find this system approaching so near to perfection as it does; and I think it will astonish our enemies, who are waiting with confidence to hear that our councils are confounded like those of the Builders of Babel; and that our States are on the point of separation, only to meet hereafter for the purpose of cutting one another's throats. Thus I consent, Sir, to this Constitution because I expect no better, and because I am not sure, that it is not the best. The opinions I have had of its errors, I sacrifice to the public good. I have never whispered a syllable of them abroad. Within these walls they were born, and here they shall die. If every one of us in returning to our Constituents were to report the objections he has had to it, and endeavor to gain partizans in support of them, we might prevent its being generally received, and thereby lose all the salutary effects & great advantages resulting naturally in our favor among foreign Nations as well as among ourselves, from our real or apparent unanimity. Much of the strength & efficiency of any Government in procuring and securing happiness to the people, depends, on opinion, on the general opinion of the goodness of the Government, as well as of the wisdom and integrity of its Governors. I hope therefore that for our own sakes as a part of the people, and for the sake of posterity, we shall act heartily and unanimously in recommending this Constitution (if approved by Congress & confirmed by the Conventions) wherever our influence may extend, and turn our future thoughts & endeavors to the means of having it well administered.

On the whole, Sir, I can not help expressing a wish that every member of the Convention who may still have objections to it, would with me, on this occasion doubt a little of his own infallibility, and to make manifest our unanimity, put his name to this instrument.—

He then moved that the Constitution be signed by the members and offered the following as a convenient form viz. "Done in Convention by the unanimous consent of *the States* present the 17th. of Septr. &c—In Witness whereof we have hereunto subscribed our names. . . ."

The members then proceeded to sign the instrument.

Whilst the last members were signing it Doctr. Franklin looking towards the Presidents Chair, at the back of which a rising sun happened to be painted, observed to a few members near him, that Painters had found it difficult to distinguish in their art a rising from a setting sun. I have said he, often and often in the course of the Session, and the vicisitudes of my hopes and fears as to its issue, looked at that behind the President without being able to tell whether it was rising or setting: But now at length I have the happiness to know that it is a rising and not a setting Sun.

The Constitution being signed by all the members except Mr. Randolph,

Mr. Mason, and Mr. Gerry who declined giving it the sanction of their names, the Convention dissolved itself by an Adjournment sine die—

Chapter Two

SUGGESTED QUESTIONS FOR CLASS DISCUSSION.

1. What basic ideas concerning the nature of both government and society are expressed in the Declaration of Independence?
2. Why does the Declaration of Independence go to such great lengths to make revolution appear to be a *legal* action?
3. Could the Declaration of Independence be classed a radical and dangerous document? It insists that when men differ with their government they have not only the *right* but the *duty* to revolt. Could any society exist if these ideas were widely held? Does this mean that Americans never really subscribed to the doctrines that are so frequently quoted as the foundations for American liberty?
4. The debates of the convention are presented as part of the "politics of nation-building." What kinds of interests were being protected during these debates? Are the reasons advanced generally convincing? How were the demands of the major interest groups adjusted? Do the debates support the contentions sometimes made that the Constitution was produced by a conspiracy of urban financial and mercantile interests?

Chapter Three

THE URBAN CRISIS: A NEW CHALLENGE FOR FEDERALISM

Any city is a complex and delicate organism. Like other complex organisms, its processes are easily disrupted. Goods and services flow through intricate interlocking networks, and blockage at any of a large number of points will affect the system as a whole. It is at the mercy of a variety of groups of men who perform special services for it. These men, with no ill will toward their neighbors, can bring the city to its knees if they choose. The governing of a metropolis involves a succession of crises or threatened crises—too much snow, too little rain, too much traffic, too few jobs, too much air pollution, too little sense of community, too many riots and strikes, and on and on.

How are men to live in the cities they have built? How are they to gain assured control over them? Where is the point at which leverage should be applied if the problems of the city are to be solved? Or is there any such point? What are the resources that are needed? A trillion dollars? Where are resources of that magnitude to be found? How much time is there in which to find a solution? Are the cities in a race with time, and are its problems growing faster than man's capacity to find solutions? How are the governments of the cities to work with state governments and the federal government in a cooperative attack on the cluster of problems that is the modern city?

Can the Big Cities Ever Come Back?

U.S. News & World Report

Riots, skyrocketing crime, tax problems that multiply raise this question:
Can the big cities of this country ever stage a comeback?

Trends now accelerating do not suggest a strongly affirmative answer.

Despite all the remedies tried, all the billions spent, problems keep
growing in central cities across the nation.

Migrants, mostly untrained, keep pouring in from rural areas. Middle
and upper-income whites, more and more, live in suburbs.

Result: School problems mount. Relief costs keep soaring. Crime tends
to get out of hand, adding to the cost of trying to police the cities.

At the same time, the tax base—income and property from which
money can be drawn to pay the mounting bills—often stagnates or de-
clines in relation to the expanding size of the problems.

Now, adding to all the difficulties, signs grow that business is becoming
somewhat less interested than before in centering expansion within the
central cities. Costs there are seen as growing too high, labor problems
too great, uncertainties too discouraging.

LAYING PLANS. On August 24, nearly 1,000 city officials, businessmen
and other community leaders met in Washington, D.C., to establish some
long-range goals for the rebuilding of the nation's big cities.

Out of this meeting is expected to come a detailed study of just what
it will cost to rebuild two or three specific cities as a means of finding out
what can be done.

Already big-city mayors have told Congress it will take at least 1 trillion
dollars—1,000 billion—to overcome problems they face.

Yet Congress, responsive to interests of suburbs, smaller cities and
countryside, seems not inclined to vote the massive sums and tax increases
needed to give large-scale help to big cities.

It is this situation that is giving rise to other possibilities—slowing
migration of low-income people into cities, decentralizing city administration, or developing new approaches to be used by metropolitan areas.

DRAMATIC EXAMPLES. The plight of the cities, generally, is dramatized
by what is happening in those that have been hit by spectacular and costly
riots.

In Detroit, considered by many to be a model of racial peace and "progressive" leadership, race rioting was the worst in the nation's history.

Today, suburban real estate operators in the Detroit area forecast a
renewed flow of whites from the city. And conversely, the slow trickle of
whites back into the city from the suburbs has stopped, at least for the
time being. One apartment-house developer said gloomily: "I don't know
how long it will take for business to pick up—or even if it will."

Many of the stores in Negro areas that were destroyed or closed down during the "insurrection" are not expected to reopen. Public schools are forced to provide portable classrooms for 3,500 displaced youngsters. The superintendent of schools said he foresaw even more difficulty than before in finding teachers for Detroit's public schools.

In Newark, N.J., scene of another big riot this summer, forecasts are that half the small businesses in Negro areas and perhaps as many as a fourth of the larger ones will not reopen. Racial tension between whites and Negroes continues to run high. Recovery in such cities, the experts say, is not likely to come soon.

Rioting in Chicago last year was not "major." Yet officials noticed a decline in business in the Negro area directly west of the Loop because businessmen cannot get insurance coverage at the normal rates. A number of stores are boarded up still, and apparently will remain that way.

In Los Angeles, where the Watts riot of 1965 took 34 lives and caused about 50 million dollars' worth of property damage over an area of 46 square miles, only three of the 40 businesses destroyed have been rebuilt. Insurance rates have gone up three to five times since the riots. One druggist said he is now paying monthly for insurance what he paid in one year before the rioting. A white grocer said:

"I wouldn't open a branch in Watts even if the Government guaranteed me a healthy net profit and posted a couple dozen armed guards around the clock. The way things are going these days, you never know when things will break wide open again."

In the riot area itself, Negro discontent persists.

OPTIMISTIC TALK, THEN—. Just after the riots, city officials were talking optimistically of upgrading the Negro neighborhoods. Mentioned were tree-shaded malls, new apartment buildings, spacious parks and new business and industry.

Today, however, a federal estimate is that one out of three persons in the riot area remains jobless or underemployed. Negro spokesmen say that median income is down, while relief rolls have gone up 34 per cent— largely because a number of organizations have been created to inform people of their "welfare rights."

Negroes who have benefited from job training are moving to better neighborhoods. Left behind, as a nucleus for future trouble, are the castoffs along with new and unskilled migrants from other parts of the country.

What city planners in Los Angeles and other big cities are discovering is this painful fact:

No longer can they count on a big drop in the tide of ill-prepared people from the South. Developing in that part of the nation, they find, is a virtually inexhaustible reservoir of migration for future years.

CENSUS CLUES. A few figures explain why city planners are increasingly alarmed.

The huge flow of Negroes out of the South in recent times has reduced that region's share of the Negro population in America from 77 per cent in 1940 to about 54 per cent at present.

In absolute numbers, however, the Negro population of the South has gone up, in that period of time, from 9.9 million to 11.2 million.

Furthermore, about 38 per cent of Negroes now living in the South are under 14 years of age. Another 11 per cent are aged 14 to 19. As these youngsters enter the labor force, many will be moving to cities in the North and West where jobs are more plentiful—and welfare more generous. Negro migration from the South, which amounted to 1.5 million during the 1950s, is expected by some authorities to reach 2 million during the 1960s.

Nor does the problem for cities end there.

Nonwhite children accounted for one third of the increase of children under 14 in metropolitan areas between 1960 and 1966. They are increasing at a rate three times as fast as that for whites.

Accordingly, one estimate is that 14 cities will have Negro populations of 40 per cent or more by 1970. Today, Washington and Newark, N.J., are the only big cities with Negro majorities, but population experts are saying that 20 or more cities will share that distinction by the 1980s.

If these projections turn out to be true, cities today are getting a foretaste of even bigger problems in the offing.

WELFARE, CRIME AND SCHOOLS. In city after city, welfare costs are going up. Police try to stem a rising tide of crime flowing out of Negro slums. Public schools are under pressure from courts to integrate across neighborhood boundaries—thereby spurring the exodus of middle-class taxpayers from the city.

This is what some cities are up against:

• In New York City, which has 1.25 million Negroes, welfare rolls have more than doubled since 1958. Negroes and Puerto Ricans make up more than 80 per cent of all welfare recipients.

• In Cleveland, where the Negro share of population has gone up from 28 to 35 per cent since 1960, police costs over those years have almost tripled. Murders increased from 84 in 1960 to 139 last year, forcible rapes are up from 79 to 159, and aggravated assaults up from 530 to 1,137.

• In Los Angeles, school officials have prepared a record budget of 663.5 million dollars for 1967–68. A big item in that outlay consists of special services aimed primarily at "disadvantaged" Negro and Mexican-American children. These include smaller classes in slum schools, remedial teaching—and a school for pregnant girls aged 13 to 15.

A SHATTERED HOPE. Over the years, city officials hoped, social problems spilling out from the slums would diminish as raw migrants picked up job skills and education. The growing number of Negroes entering the professions and skilled occupations each year was seen as an important solution to the social problems of the slums.

Now, evidence grows that the untutored migrant is only the beginning of those problems.

One bit of evidence: a sampling of arrested rioters in Los Angeles in 1965 found many who were not ignorant newcomers or teen-age hoodlums. Forty-one per cent were married, 32 per cent were high-school graduates, 38 per cent were in skilled and semiskilled jobs, 22 per cent earned $400 or more a month, and 75 per cent had lived in Los Angeles for at least five years.

Said Dr. Seymour Martin Lipset, professor of sociology and government at Harvard:

"What you are getting in the big cities is a situation quite similar to that in newly independent countries—where the situation of people, in this case Negroes, has not changed enough to match their expectations. Revolutions tend to come when things are getting better—but not fast enough."

REVOLUTION ASIDE—. Finding a way to stave off revolution comes at a time when cities are trying to cope with a multitude of other woes.

Streets are snarled in traffic. Air pollution becomes worse each year. Water and power shortages are becoming critical in some places.

What is making the dilemma of cities acute is a basic fact: Tax resources are lagging further and further behind skyrocketing costs.

Personal income and property values in cities declined as middle-class people moved out—followed by a large chunk of downtown business. Now industries are shifting to suburbs and small towns to find cheaper land and a labor pool of skilled workers and technicians.

Recently a congressional hearing on open housing was told that employment in U.S. manufacturing has increased by nearly 2 million jobs since 1961—but almost all of the increase has been outside areas of Negro concentration.

In New York, Leonard Yaseen, chairman of a firm specializing in industrial relocation, said: "I look for New York to lose 100,000 industrial jobs in the next three or four years—and I think this reflects what is going on in most of the big cities."

High-speed roads, once seen as making it easier for suburbanites to commute downtown, are making it easier for jobs to move to the suburbs. One engineering study predicted recently that the Capital Beltway around Washington, D.C., will lure about 10,000 jobs from the city by 1976—lopping about 9 per cent from the city's expected growth in jobs during the next nine years.

Result is that tax bases in big cities are only growing slowly or, in some cases, actually shrinking. From John Shannon, assistant director of the U.S. Advisory Commission on Intergovernmental Relations, came this summary of the problem:

In the mid-1950s, tax experts assumed that city tax bases would show a 5 per cent increase annually. Today, average gains are running well below that figure.

PROPOSALS FOR COMEBACK. It is against that broad background of trouble that suggestions are made of what it will take for cities to make a comeback.

One widely publicized estimate is that it will cost at least 1 trillion dollars—30 per cent of it in public spending—over the next 12 years to renovate metropolitan areas and bring the central cities back to health.

Some proposals call for spending of 10 billion dollars a year or more to help Negro slum dwellers. Vice President Hubert H. Humphrey recently suggested the equivalent of the Marshall Plan for helping Negroes.

Being explored is the idea that perhaps it is time to discourage the flow of Negro migration to cities of the North and West. Recently Secretary of Agriculture Orville L. Freeman proposed a national policy aimed at providing more opportunities in smaller towns and cities in order to stem the flow of people out of rural areas.

On August 23, the Republican Coordinating Committee—pointing to problems raised by migration to the cities—urged a drive to locate new industries in rural regions by offering tax inducements, channeling Government contracts to such industries and stepping up aid to rural education and road building.

AN "UNDERCLASS." Another thought comes from Daniel P. Moynihan, former Assistant Secretary of Labor and now director of the Joint Center for Urban Studies operated by Harvard University and Massachusetts Institute of Technology.

Dr. Moynihan finds the cities' social problems centering in an "urban underclass" of aimless and unstable Negroes who are the products of widespread disorganization of families in the slums.

These figures are cited:

Nationwide, 6 out of every 10 Negroes reaching the age of 18 have at some time been supported by federal aid to dependent children. Probably not more than one third of low-income Negro children reaching 18 have lived their entire lives with both parents.

Also cited is the high rate of illegitimacy among low-income Negroes— as in Detroit, where a 1965 study showed that one quarter of low-income Negro households reported children of illegitimate birth.

It is Dr. Moynihan's contention that cities can solve their central problem of Negro slums only with aid from federal programs aimed at reinforcing Negro family ties. Among them would be family allowances and federally supported jobs for the unemployed.

ONE JUDGE'S SUGGESTION. Some planners would like to disperse Negroes from central cities to the suburbs. Recently U.S. District Judge J. Skelly Wright, in a decision involving the 90 per cent Negro enrollment in public schools of Washington, D.C., suggested that school officials explore the possibility of large-scale exchange of pupils between city and suburbs on a voluntary basis.

Few suburbs, however, seem eager to take on the central city's problems —nor is it likely that Congress would countenance forced dispersal of Negroes from the central cities.

Changes in the structure of city governments to handle the broad range of their problems are also under discussion.

One such proposal is to decentralize urban government somewhat, setting up "little city halls" in neighborhoods to provide a closer relationship between officials and people. Presumably this would bring a greater measure of public support for laws and policies aimed at improving cities.

One possibility suggested recently by Police Commissioner Howard R. Leary of New York City was that some police precinct houses should become centers where slum dwellers could get advice on health, housing and welfare problems. This, he thought, would be one way of "humanizing" the police department.

Others are suggesting that schools serve as neighborhood centers, remaining open at night for adult-education classes and neighborhood meetings.

Said Dr. Stephen K. Bailey, dean of the Maxwell Graduate School of Citizenship and Public Affairs at Syracuse University:

"We're caught in a paradox where the necessities of living together in cities impose the need for certain controls, yet those controls could cut into the fabric of our values—individual rights, equality and all the rest."

This is becoming clear:

The crisis of the big cities, coming to a head in recent years, continues without letup. And no real solution appears in the immediate future.

Baker v. Carr and the Political Thicket

The Constitution of Tennessee provides that the representatives in the state legislature shall be based upon the number of qualified voters residing in each county. It also requires a reapportionment of the legislators every ten years in accordance with the federal census. Despite this constitutional requirement, by 1962 the state legislature had not reapportioned representatives since 1901. During this sixty-one year period the population of Tennessee had increased by 75 per cent and the growth had been accompanied by a significant movement from rural to urban areas resulting in extreme disparities in voting districts. Voters in districts having only 40 per cent of the voting population could elect nearly 64 per cent of the lower house, and 37 per cent could elect 60 per cent of the senate. All efforts to force the legislature to reapportion had failed.

In 1959 Baker and others brought suit against Secretary of State Carr, and other state officials, seeking reapportionment under the equal protection clause of the Fourteenth Amendment. A federal district court, relying on Colegrove v. Green *(1946) dismissed the complaint, and the case was appealed to the United States Supreme Court. This case is obviously of great importance because it calls upon the Court to sit in judgment on the possession and distribution of political power.*

Mr. Justice Brennan delivered the opinion of the Court.

I. . . . THE DISTRICT COURT'S OPINION AND ORDER OF DISMISSAL

Because we deal with this case on appeal from an order of dismissal granted on appellees' motions, precise identification of the issues presently confronting us demands clear exposition of the grounds upon which the District Court rested in dismissing the case. The dismissal order recited that the court sustained the appellees' grounds "(1) that the Court lacks

Baker v. Carr, 369 U.S. 186; 82 Sup. Ct. 691; 7 L. Ed. 633 (1962).

jurisdiction of the subject matter, and (2) that the complaint fails to state a claim upon which relief can be granted. . . ."

The District Court's dismissal order . . . rested . . . upon lack of subject-matter jurisdiction and lack of justiciable cause of action without attempting to distinguish between these grounds. . . .

The court proceeded to explain its action as turning on the case's presenting a "question of the distribution of political strength for legislative purposes." For,

> from a review of [*numerous Supreme Court*] . . . decisions there can be no doubt that the federal rule, as enunciated and applied by the Supreme Court, is that the federal courts, whether from a lack of jurisdiction or from the inappropriateness of the subject matter for judicial consideration, will not intervene in cases of this type to compel legislative reapportionment. . . .

The court went on to express doubts as to the feasibility of the various possible remedies sought by the plaintiffs. . . . Then it made clear that its dismissal reflected a view not of doubt that violation of constitutional rights was alleged, but of a court's impotence to correct that violation:

> With the plaintiffs' argument that the legislature of Tennessee is guilty of a clear violation of the state constitution and of the rights of the plaintiffs the Court entirely agrees. It also agrees that the evil is a serious one which should be corrected without further delay. But even so the remedy in this situation clearly does not lie with the courts. It has long been recognized and is accepted doctrine that there are indeed some rights guaranteed by the Constitution for the violation of which the courts cannot give redress. . . .

In light of the District Court's treatment of the case, we hold today only (a) that the court possessed jurisdiction of the subject matter; (b) that a justiciable cause of action is stated upon which appellants would be entitled to appropriate relief; and (c) because appellees raise the issue before this Court, that the appellants have standing to challenge the Tennessee apportionment statutes. Beyond noting that we have no cause at this stage to doubt the District Court will be able to fashion relief if violations of constitutional rights are found, it is improper now to consider what remedy would be most appropriate if appellants prevail at the trial.

II. JURISDICTION OF THE SUBJECT MATTER

The District Court was uncertain whether our cases withholding federal judicial relief rested upon a lack of federal jurisdiction or upon the inappropriateness of the subject matter for judicial consideration—what we have designated "nonjusticiability." The distinction between the two grounds is significant. In the instance of nonjusticiability, consideration of the cause is not wholly and immediately foreclosed; rather, the Court's inquiry necessarily proceeds to the point of deciding whether the duty asserted can be judicially identified and its breach judicially determined, and whether protection for the right asserted can be judicially molded. In the instance of lack of jurisdiction the cause either does not "arise under" the Federal Constitution, laws or treaties (or fall within one of the other enumerated categories of Art. III, Section 2), or is not a "case or controversy" within the meaning of that section; or the cause is not one described by any jurisdictional statute. Our conclusion . . . that this cause presents no nonjusticiable "political question" settles the only possible doubt that it is a case or controversy. Under the present heading of "Jurisdiction of the Subject Matter" we hold only that the matter set forth in the compaint does arise under the Constitution. . . .

An unbroken line of our precedents sustains the federal courts' jurisdiction of the subject matter of federal constitutional claims of this nature. The first cases involved the redistricting of States for the purpose of electing Representatives to the Federal Congress. . . . When the Minnesota Supreme Court affirmed the dismissal of a suit to enjoin the Secretary of State of Minnesota from acting under Minnesota redistricting legislation, we reviewed the constitutional merits of the legislation and reversed the State Supreme Court. . . . When a three-judge District Court . . . permanently enjoined officers of the State of Mississippi from conducting an election of Representatives under a Mississippi redistricting act, we reviewed the federal questions on the merits and reversed the District Court.

The appellees refer to *Colegrove* v. *Green* . . . as authority that the District Court lacked jurisdiction of the subject matter. Appellees misconceive the holding of that case. The holding was precisely contrary to their reading of it. Seven members of the Court participated in the decision. Unlike many other cases in this field which have assumed without discussion that there was jurisdiction, all three opinions filed in Colegrove discussed the question. Two of the opinions expressing the views of four of the Justices, a majority, flatly held that there was jurisdiction of the subject matter. Mr. Justice Black joined by Mr. Justice Douglas and Mr. Justice Murphy stated: "It is my judgment that the District Court had jurisdiction. . . ." Mr. Justice Rutledge, writing separately, expressed agreement with this conclusion. . . . Indeed, it is even questionable that the opinion of Mr. Justice Frankfurter, joined by Justices Reed and Burton, doubted jurisdiction of the subject matter. . . .

Several subsequent cases similar to Colegrove have been decided by the Court in summary per curiam statements. None was dismissed for want of jurisdiction of the subject. . . .

Two cases decided with opinions after Colegrove likewise plainly imply that the subject matter of this suit is within District Court jurisdiction.

We hold that the District Court has jurisdiction of the subject matter of the federal constitutional claim asserted in the complaint.

III. STANDING

A federal court cannot "pronounce any statute, either of a State or of the United States, void, because irreconcilable with the Constitution, except as it is called upon to adjudge the legal rights of litigants in actual controversies. . . ." Have the appellants alleged such a personal stake in the outcome of the controversy as to assure that concrete adverseness which sharpens the presentation of issues upon which the court so largely depends for illumination of difficult constitutional questions? This is the gist of the question of standing. It is, of course, a question of federal law. . . .

We hold that the appellants do have standing to maintain this suit. Our decisions plainly support this conclusion. Many of the cases have assumed rather than articulated the premise in deciding the merits of similar claims. And *Colegrove* v. *Green* . . . squarely held that voters who allege facts showing disadvantage to themselves as individuals have standing to sue. A number of cases decided after Colegrove recognized the standing of the voters there involved to bring those actions.

These appellants seek relief in order to protect or vindicate an interest of their own, and of those similarly situated. Their constitutional claim is, in substance, that the 1901 statute constitutes arbitrary and capricious state action, offensive to the Fourteenth Amendment in its irrational disregard of the standard of apportionment prescribed by the State's Constitution or of any standard, effecting a gross disproportion of representation to voting population. The injury which appellants assert is that this classification disfavors the voters in the counties in which they reside, placing them in a position of constitutionally unjustifiable inequality vis-à-vis voters in irrationally favored counties. . . .

It would not be necessary to decide whether appellants' allegations of impairment of their votes by the 1901 apportionment will, ultimately, entitle them to any relief, in order to hold that they have standing to seek it. If such impairment does produce a legally cognizable injury, they are among those who have sustained it. They are asserting "a plain, direct and adequate interest in maintaining the effectiveness of their votes" . . . not merely a claim of "the right, possessed by every citizen, to require that the Government be administered according to law. . . ."

IV. JUSTICIABILITY

In holding that the subject matter of this suit was not justiciable, the District Court relied on *Colegrove* v. *Green* . . . and subsequent per curiam cases. . . . We understand the District Court to have read the cited cases as compelling the conclusion that since the appellants sought to have a legislative apportionment held unconstitutional, their suit presented a "political question" and was therefore nonjusticiable. We hold that this challenge to an apportionment presents no nonjusticiable "political question." The cited cases do not hold the contrary.

Of course the mere fact that the suit seeks protection of a political right does not mean it presents a political question. Such an objection "is little more than a play upon words. . . ." Rather, it is argued that apportionment cases, whatever the actual wording of the complaint, can involve no federal constitutional right except one resting on the guaranty of a republican form of government, and that complaints based on the clause have been held to present political questions which are nonjusticiable.

We hold that the claim pleaded here neither rests upon nor implicates the Guaranty Clause and that its justiciability is therefore not foreclosed by our decisions of cases involving that clause. The District Court misinterpreted *Colegrove* v. *Green* and other decisions of this Court on which it relied. Appellants' claim that they are being denied equal protection is justiciable, and if "discrimination is sufficiently shown, the right to relief under the equal protection clause is not diminished by the fact that the discrimination relates to political rights. . . ." To show why we reject the argument based on the Guaranty Clause . . . we deem it necessary first to consider the contours of the "political question" doctrine.

Our discussion . . . requires review of a number of political question cases, in order to expose the attributes of the doctrine. . . . That review reveals that in the Guaranty Clause cases and in the other "political question" cases, it is the relationship between the judiciary and the coordinate branches of the Federal Government, and not the federal judiciary's relationship to the States, which gives rise to the "political question. . . ."

The nonjusticiability of a political question is primarily a function of the separation of powers. Much confusion results from the capacity of the "political question" label to obscure the need for case-by-case inquiry. Deciding whether a matter has in any measure been committed by the Constitution to another branch of government, or whether the action of that branch exceeds whatever authority has been committed, is itself a delicate exercise in constitutional interpretation, and is a responsibility of this Court as ultimate interpreter of the Constitution. . . .

Prominent on the surface of any case held to involve a political question is found a textually demonstrable constitutional commitment of the issue to a coordinate political department; or a lack of judicially discoverable and manageable standards for resolving it; or the impossibility of deciding without an initial policy determination of a kind clearly for nonjudicial discretion; or the impossibility of a court's undertaking independent resolution without expressing lack of the respect due coordinate branches of government; or an unusual need for unquestioning adherence to a political decision already made; or the potentiality of embarrassment from multifarious pronouncements by various departments on one question.

Unless one of these formulations is inextricable from the case at bar, there should be no dismissal for nonjusticiability on the ground of a political question's presence. The doctrine of which we treat is one of "political questions," not one of "political cases." The courts cannot reject as "no law suit" a bona fide controversy as to whether some action denominated "political" exceeds constitutional authority. . . .

But it is argued that this case shares the characteristics of decisions that constitute a category not yet considered, cases concerning the Constitution's guaranty, in Art. IV, Section 4, of a republican form of government. . . . [The Court then discusses, at great length, *Luther* v. *Borden* and numerous other cases holding that the republican guaranty provision is judicially unenforceable.]

We conclude . . . that the nonjusticiability of claims resting on the Guaranty Clause which arises from their embodiment of questions that were thought "political," can have no bearing upon the justiciability of the equal protection claim presented in this case. . . . [W]e emphasize that it is the involvement in Guaranty Clause claims of the elements thought to define "political questions," and no other feature, which could render them nonjusticiable. Specifically, we have said that such claims are not held nonjusticiable because they touch matters of state governmental organization. . . .

[O]nly last Term, in *Gomillion* v. *Lightfoot* . . . we applied the Fifteenth Amendment to strike down a redrafting of municipal boundaries which effected a discriminatory impairment of voting rights, in the face of what a majority of the Court of Appeals thought to be a sweeping commitment to state legislatures of the power to draw and redraw such boundaries. . . .

We conclude that the complaint's allegations of a denial of equal protection present a justiciable constitutional cause of action upon which appellants are entitled to a trial and a decision. The right asserted is within the reach of judicial protection under the Fourteenth Amendment.

The judgment of the District Court is reversed and the cause is remanded for further proceedings consistent with this opinion.

Reversed and remanded.

MR. JUSTICE WHITTAKER did not participate in the decision of this case.

Mr. Justice Douglas, concurring.

While I join the opinion of the Court and, like the Court, do not reach the merits, a word of explanation is necessary. I put to one side the problems of "political" questions involving the distribution of power between this Court, the Congress, and the Chief Executive. We have here a phase of the recurring problem of the relation of the federal courts to state agencies. More particularly, the question is the extent to which a State may weight one person's vote more heavily than it does another's. . . .

The traditional test under the Equal Protection Clause has been whether a State has made "an invidious discrimination," as it does when it selects "a particular race or nationality for oppressive treatment. . . ." Universal equality is not the test; there is room for weighting. As we stated in *Williamson* v. *Lee Optical Co.*, 348 U.S. 483 . . . "The prohibition of the Equal Protection Clause goes no further than the invidious discrimination."

I agree with my Brother Clark that if the allegations in the complaint can be sustained a case for relief is established. We are told that a single vote in Moore County, Tennessee, is worth 19 votes in Hamilton County, that one vote in Stewart or in Chester County is worth nearly eight times a single vote in Shelby or Knox County. The opportunity to prove that an "invidious discrimination" exists should therefore be given the appellants. . . .

The justiciability of the present claims being established, any relief accorded can be fashioned in the light of well-known principles of equity.

Mr. Justice Clark, concurring.

. . . The Court holds that the appellants have alleged a cause of action. However, it refuses to award relief here—although the facts are undisputed—and fails to give the District Court any guidance whatever. One dissenting opinion, bursting with words that go through so much and conclude with so little, contemns the majority action as "a massive repudiation of the experience of our whole past." Another describes the complaint as merely asserting conclusory allegations that Tennessee's apportionment is "incorrect," "arbitrary," "obsolete," and "unconstitutional." I believe it can be shown that this case is distinguishable from earlier cases dealing with the distribution of politcal power by a State, that a patent violation of the Equal Protection Clause of the United States Constitution has been shown, and that an appropriate remedy may be formulated. . . .

II

The controlling facts cannot be disputed. It appears from the record that 37% of the voters of Tennessee elect 20 of the 33 senators while 40% of the voters elect 63 of the 99 members of the House. But this might not on its fact be an 'invidious discrimination" . . . for a "statutory discrimination will not be set aside if any state of facts reasonably may be conceived to justify it."

It is true that the apportionment policy incorporated in Tennessee's Constitution, i.e., state-wide numerical equality of representation with certain minor qualifications, is a rational one. On a county-by-county comparison a districting plan based thereon naturally will have disparities in representation due to the qualifications. But this to my mind does not raise constitutional problems, for the overall policy is reasonable. However, the root of the trouble is not in Tennessee's Constitution, for admittedly its policy has not been followed. The discrimination lies in the action of Tennessee's Assembly in allocating legislative seats to counties or districts created by it. Try as one may, Tennessee's apportionment just cannot be made to fit the pattern cut by its Constitution. . . .

. . . Tennessee's apportionment is a crazy quilt without rational basis. . . .

No one—except the dissenters advocating the Harlan "adjusted 'total representation' " formula—contends that mathematical equality among voters is required by the Equal Protection Clause. But certainly there must be some rational design to a State's districting. The discrimination here does not fit any pattern—as I have said, it is but a crazy quilt. My Brother Harlan contends that other proposed apportionment plans contain disparities. Instead of chasing those rabbits he should first pause long enough to meet appellants' proof of discrimination by showing that in fact the present plan follows a rational policy. Not being able to do this, he merely counters with such generalities as "classic legislative judgment," no "significant discrepancy," and "de minimis departures." I submit that even a casual glance at the present apportionment picture shows these conclusions to be entirely fanciful. If present representation has a policy at all, it is to maintain the status quo of invidious discrimination at any cost. . . .

III

Although I find the Tennessee apportionment statute offends the Equal Protection Clause, I would not consider intervention by this Court into so delicate a field if there were any other relief available to the people of Tennessee. But the majority of the people of Tennessee have no "practical opportunities for exerting their political weight at the polls" to correct the existing "invidious discrimination." Tennessee has no initiative and referendum. I have searched diligently for other "practical opportunities" present under the law. I find none other than through the federal courts. . . .

This is because the legislative policy has riveted the present seats in the Assembly to their respective constituencies, and by the votes of their incumbents a reapportionment of any kind is prevented. The people have been rebuffed at the hands of the Assembly; they have tried the constitutional convention route, but since the call must originate in the Assembly it, too, has been fruitless. They have tried Tennessee courts with the same result, and Governors have fought the tide only to flounder. It is said that there is recourse in Congress and perhaps that may be, but from a practical standpoint this is without substance. To date Congress has never undertaken such a task in any State. We therefore must conclude that the people of Tennessee are stymied and without judicial intervention will be saddled with the present discrimination in the affairs of their state government. . . .

Mr. Justice Frankfurter, whom Mr. Justice Harlan joins, dissenting.

The Court today reverses a uniform course of decision established by a dozen cases, including one by which the very claim now sustained was unanimously rejected only five years ago. The impressive body of rulings thus cast aside reflected the equally uniform course of our political history regarding the relationship between population and legislative representation—a wholly different matter from denial of the franchise to individuals because of race, color, religion or sex. Such a massive repudiation of the experience of our whole past in asserting destructively novel judicial power demands a detailed analysis of the role of this Court in our constitutional scheme. Disregard of inherent limits in the effective exercise of the Court's "judicial Power" not only presages the futility of judicial intervention in the essentially political conflict of forces by which the relation between population and representation has time out of mind been and now is determined. It may well impair the Court's position as the ultimate organ of "the supreme Law of the Land" in that vast range of legal problems, often strongly entangled in popular feeling, on which this Court must pronounce. The Court's authority—possessed neither of the purse nor the sword—ultimately rests on sustained public confidence in its moral sanction. Such feeling must be nourished by the Court's complete detachment, in fact in appearance, from political entanglements and by abstention from injecting itself into the clash of political forces in political settlements. . . .

Recent legislation, creating a district appropriately described as "an atrocity of ingenuity," is not unique. Considering the gross inequality among legislative electoral units within almost every State, the Court naturally shrinks from asserting that in districting at least substantial equality is a constitutional requirement enforceable by courts. Room continues to be allowed for weighting. This of course implies that geography, economics, urban-rural conflict, and all the other non-legal factors which have throughout our history entered into political districting are to some extent not to be ruled out in the undefined vista now opened up by review in the federal courts of state reapportionments. To some extent—aye, there's the rub. In effect, today's decision empowers the courts of the country to devise what should constitute the proper composition of the legislatures of the fifty States. If state courts should for one reason or another find themselves unable to discharge this task, the duty of doing so is put on the federal courts or on this Court, if State views do not satisfy this Court's notion of what is proper districting.

We were soothingly told at the bar of this Court that we need not worry about the kind of remedy a court could effectively fashion once the abstract constitutional right to have courts pass on a state-wide system of electoral districting is recognized as a matter of judicial rhetoric, because legislatures would heed the Court's admonition. This is not only an euphoric hope. It implies a sorry confession of judicial impotence in place of a frank acknowledgment that there is not under our Constitution a judicial remedy for every political mischief, for every undesirable exercise of legislative power. The Framers carefully and with deliberate forethought refused so to enthrone the judiciary. In this situation, as in others of like nature, appeal for relief does not belong here. Appeal must be to informed, civically militant electorate. In a democratic society like ours, relief must come through an aroused popular conscience that sears the conscience of the people's representatives. In any event there is nothing judicially more unseemly nor more self-defeating than for this Court to make in terrorem pronouncements, to indulge in merely empty rhetoric, sounding a word of promise to the ear, sure to be disappointing to the hope. . . .

Dissenting opinion of Mr. Justice Harlan, whom Mr. Justice Frankfurter joins.

The dissenting opinion of Mr. Justice Frankfurter, in which I join, demonstrates the abrupt departure the majority makes from judicial history by putting the federal courts into this area of state concerns—an area which, in this instance, the Tennessee state courts themselves have refused to enter. . . .

It is at once essential to recognize this case for what it is. The issue here relates not to a method of state electoral apportionment by which seats in the federal House of Representatives are allocated, but solely to the right of a State to fix the basis of representation in its own legislature. Until it is first decided to what extent that right is limited by the Federal Constitution, and whether what Tennessee has done or failed to do in this instance runs afoul of any such limitation, we need not reach the issues of "justiciability" or "political question" or any of the other considerations which in such cases as *Colegrove* v. *Green* . . . led the Court to decline to adjudicate a challenge to a state apportionment affecting seats in the federal House of Representatives, in the absence of a controlling Act of Congress. . . .

The appellants' claim in this case ultimately rests entirely on the Equal Protection Clause of the Fourteenth Amendment. It is asserted that Tennessee has violated the Equal Protection Clause by maintaining in effect a system of apportionment that grossly favors in legislative representation the rural sections of the State as against its urban communities. Stripped to its essentials the complaint purports to set forth three constitutional claims of varying breadth:

(1) The Equal Protection Clause requires that each vote case in state legislative elections be given approximately equal weight.

(2) Short of this, the existing apportionment of state legislators is so unreasonable as to amount to an arbitrary and capricious act of classification on the part of Tennessee Legislature, which is offensive to the Equal Protection Clause.

(3) In any event, the existing apportionment is rendered invalid under the Fourteenth Amendment because it flies in the face of the Tennessee Constitution. . . .

I

I can find nothing in the Equal Protection Clause or elsewhere in the Federal Constitution which expressly or impliedly supports the view that state legislatures must be so structured as to reflect with approximate equality the voice of every voter. Not only is that proposition refuted by history, as shown by my Brother Frankfurter, but it strikes deep into the heart of our federal system. Its acceptance would require us to turn our backs on the regard which this Court has always shown for the judgment of state legislatures and courts on matters of basically local concern.

In the last analysis, what lies at the core of this controversy is a difference of opinion as to the function of representative government. It is surely beyond argument that those who have the responsibility for devising a system of representation may permissibly consider that factors other than bare numbers should be taken into account. The existence of the United States Senate is proof enough of that. To consider that we may ignore the Tennessee Legislature's judgment in this instance because that body was the product of an asymmetrical electoral apportionment would in effect be to assume the very conclusion here disputed. Hence we must accept the present form of the Tennessee Legislature as the embodiment of the State's choice, or, more realistically, its compromise, between competing political philosophies. The federal courts have not been empowered by the Equal Protection Clause to judge whether this resolution of the State's internal political conflict is desirable or undesirable, wise or unwise. . . .

A State's choice to distribute electoral strength among geographical units, rather than according to a census of population, is certainly no less a rational decision of policy than would be its choice to levy a tax on property rather than a tax on income. Both are legislative judgments entitled to equal respect from this Court.

II

The claim that Tennessee's system of apportionment is so unreasonable as to amount to a capricious classification of voting strength stands up no better under dispassionate analysis.

The Court has said time and again that the Equal Protection Clause does not demand of state enactments either mathematical identity or rigid equality. . . . All that is prohibited is "invidious discrimination" bearing no rational relation to any permissible policy of the State. . . .

What then is the basis for the claim in this case that the distribution of state senators and representatives is the product of capriciousness or of some constitutionally prohibited policy? It is not that Tennessee has arranged its electoral districts with a deliberate purpose to dilute the voting strength of one race . . . or that some religious group is intentionally underrepresented. Nor is it a charge that the legislature has indulged in sheer caprice by allotting representatives to each county on the basis of a throw of the dice, or of some other determinant bearing no rational relation to the question of apportionment. Rather, the claim is that the State Legislature has unreasonably retained substantially the same allocation of senators and representatives as was established by statute in 1901, refusing to recognize the great shift in the population balance between urban and rural communities that has occurred in the meantime. . . .

A Federal District Court is asked to say that the passage of time has rendered the 1901 apportionment obsolete to the point where its continuance becomes vulnerable under the Fourteenth Amendment. But is not this matter one that involves a classic legislative judgment? Surely it lies within the province of a state legislature to conclude that an existing allocation of senators and representatives constitutes a desirable balance of geographical and demographical representation, or that in the interest of stability of government it would be best to defer for some further time the redistribution of seats in the state legislature.

Indeed, I would hardly think it unconstitutional if a state legislature's expressed reason for establishing or maintaining an electoral imbalance between its rural and urban population were to protect the State's agricultural interests from the sheer weight of numbers of those residing in its cities. . . . These are matters of local policy, on the wisdom of which the federal judiciary is neither permitted nor qualified to sit in judgment. . . .

It is my view that the majority opinion has failed to point to any recognizable constitutional claim alleged in this complaint. Indeed, it is interesting to note that my Brother Stewart is at pains to disclaim for himself, and to point out that the majority opinion does not suggest, that the Federal Constitution requires of the States any particular kind of electoral apportionment, still less that they must accord to each voter approximately equal voting strength. . . . But that being so, what, may it be asked, is left of this complaint? Surely the bare allegations that the existing Tennessee apportionment is "incorrect," "arbitrary," "obsolete" and "unconstitutional"—amounting to nothing more than legal conclusions—do not themselves save the complaint from dismissal. . . .

From a reading of the majority and concurring opinions one will not find it difficult to catch the premises that underlie this decision. The fact that the appellants have been unable to obtain political redress of their asserted grievances appears to be regarded as a matter which should lead the Court to stretch to find some basis for judicial intervention. While the Equal Protection Clause is invoked, the opinion for the Court notably eschews explaining how, consonant with past decisions, the undisputed facts in this case can be considered to show a violation of that constitutional provision. The majority seems to have accepted the argument, pressed at the bar, that if this Court merely asserts authority in this field, Tennessee and other "malapportioning" States will quickly respond with appropriate political action, so that this Court need not be greatly concerned about the federal courts becoming further involved in these matters. At the same time the majority has wholly failed to reckon with what the future may hold in store if this optimistic prediction is not fulfilled. Thus, what the Court is doing reflects more an adventure in judicial experimentation than a solid piece of constitutional adjudication. . . .

In conclusion, it is appropriate to say that one need not agree, as a citizen, with what Tennessee has done or failed to do, in order to deprecate, as a judge, what the majority is doing today. Those observers of the Court who see it primarily as the last refuge for the correction of all inequality or injustice, no matter what its nature of source, will no doubt applaud this decision and its break with the past. Those who consider that continuing national respect for the Court's authority depends in large measure upon its wise exercise of self-restraint and discipline in constitutional adjudication, will view the decision with deep concern.

I would affirm.

One Man, One Vote— So What?

David Brady
Douglas Edmonds

For at least three decades political reformers have cited *malapportionment* in state legislatures as the major obstacle to solving the problems that beset our big cities. The reformers' case for *reapportionment*, briefly, has been this:

—Rural areas are over-represented in most states;

—Rural areas, and thus rural legislators, are traditionally and environmentally conservative;

—Therefore, state legislatures, because they are apportioned in favor of rural areas, are not responsive to the needs of the urban majority in the state.

As far back as 1938, H. L. Mencken was complaining bitterly about the "barnyard government" of his own state of Maryland:

> The vote of a malarious peasant on the lower Eastern Shore counts as much as the votes of 12 Baltimoreans. But that can't last. It is not only unjust and undemocratic; it is absurd.

Mr. Mencken, as it turned out, was overly optimistic. It lasted until the 1960's, when a man named Charles W. Baker got together with some of his fellow Tennesseans to sue Joe C. Carr, the Secretary of State of Tennessee, in protest over a state legislature that hadn't been reapportioned since 1901. Baker and his companions claimed that the legislature that resulted from this antique districting system was so unrepresentative that it deprived them of the equal protection of the laws guaranteed by the fourteenth amendment. In 1962 the Supreme Court felt bolder than it had in 1946, when Justice Frankfurter and the court had declined to enter "this political thicket," and the justices declared in *Baker vs. Carr* that the federal judiciary does have jurisdiction in malapportionment cases. So flagrant were the injustices involved all over the country that within two years of *Baker vs. Carr*, the court had ordered reapportionment in 15 states.

The day will soon be here when all reapportionment suits have been heard and all the state legislatures have gone through the convulsions of reapportionment. The urban political millennium should be just around the corner. But somehow, we have our doubts. Our study leads us to believe that reapportionment is not the cure-all many people expect.

We are not equipped as political scientists to test for the imminence of the millennium; but we can pick out some of the specific consequences that have been alleged to flow from malapportionment, and see whether they are indeed at their worst in the worst apportioned states. To do that, we need a standard of measurement for malapportionment, and we need to examine a list of specific state issues.

Choosing the Issues

Using a measure of malapportionment developed by Glendon Schubert and Charles Press, we then tested the effects of the apportionment situation on specific issues.

The first area of state policy we investigated concerned expenditures to see if there was any significant relationship between the way a state is apportioned and the way it spent money. If the reformist critics have a case, the conservative legislatures of malapportioned states would be less likely to spend money on education and public welfare measures than the legislatures of well apportioned states. Expenditure categories were chosen to mirror basic state policies and to be comparable for all states. Deliberately excluded were all programs heavily influenced or dominated by federal grants. (Our data is from 1962 or earlier, prior to the *Baker vs. Carr* decision.)

Did the worst apportioned states spend least on the selected items? To find out we tested each program against the apportionment score for each state. Our basic measurement is called a *coefficient of correlation*. When a correlation coefficient turns out to be *zero*, there is *no relationship between the two factors being considered*. If we got a *perfect positive correlation* (*plus one*) it would mean that there is a direct relationship—the worse the apportionment, the less the state spends on welfare and education. If we got a *perfect negative correlation* (*minus one*), we would know that a relationship existed, but it ran opposite to the one the reformers predicted, so that the badly apportioned states were the most generous with welfare and education.

Here is how the correlations came out on some specific state expenditures:

Teachers' salaries	.025
Amount spent on local schools for each person living in the state	.023
Per cent of state spending that goes to schools	.105
Amount spent on higher education for each person in the state	−.132
Per cent of state spending that goes for higher education	−.138
Amount spent on each pupil	.124
Weekly unemployment compensation benefit	.127
Maximum unemployment benefit	.093
Amount spent on public welfare for each person living in the state	−.212
Percentage of state spending that goes for public welfare	−.130
Amount spent on health for each person living in the state	−.088
Percentage of state spending that goes for health	−.119

Clearly, *none of these variables is strongly related to the extent of malapportionment.* (To doublecheck, we ran all these variables against another index of malapportionment, the David and Eisenberg index; by this measure too, we found no strong relationship between any of the variables and malapportionment.)

State policies in all these areas vary a great deal, but our analysis shows that the variations can't be explained by the extent of malapportionment. In fact, we tested three other socio-economic variables that go much further than the apportionment scores in explaining the variation:
—the per capita income in the state,
—the percentage of the state population living in cities,
—and the percentage of the population that has at least a high school education.

For instance, while the correlation between teachers' salaries and apportionment scores was very low (.025), the correlation between those salaries and the three socio-economic variables was quite high (.876). For weekly unemployment compensation, the apportionment correlation was insignificant (.127) but the relationship to the three variables was strong (.811); for per capita spending on health, the apportionment correlation was very weakly negative (−.088), but the relationship with the three variables was strong (.515).

This kind of analysis is not as precise as we would like. We would have preferred to examine much narrower aspects of state policy, but the data we need is not readily available. However, we are convinced that our analysis shows there is not much substance in the reformers' case.

This is not to deny that a poorly apportioned state might be located where serious policy consequences result from inequality in the legislature. But the general pattern, throughout all the states, does not show such a relationship. And it seems unlikely, on the basis of this evidence, that more equal apportionment will bring any noticeable changes in the levels of spending for education or public welfare. Quite clearly, most of the badly apportioned states are performing as adequately (or inadequately) as the well apportioned states.

City Slickers or Country Slickers

The most vociferous complaints about malapportionment have always come from big city people. They resent the cavalier attitude that a legislature dominated by rural counties often takes to city problems. Does the city really suffer at the hands of the farmers? Or is this also part of the reformers' myth?

MEASURING MALAPPORTIONMENT

The measuring device we have chosen was developed by Glendon Schubert and Charles Press. It is a somewhat complicated index, but the situation it is intended to describe is complex too. Schubert and Press reasoned that an adequate measurement of apportionment should have these characteristics:

It must be a figure that is comparable from one state to another.

It should sum up the extent of malapportionment in both houses of the legislature in one figure.

It should reflect the political fact that the senate is the more powerful chamber in a bicameral legislature.

It should make use of the best techniques statisticians have developed for measuring normal distributions and deviations from the normal.

To compute an apportionment score, Schubert and Press assume that the goal of the apportionment, the norm for the system, is that *each state legislator should represent as many constituents as every other legislator* serving in the same chamber. If you take a state like California, for instance, you will see that the situation until recently was very far from this norm; in 1959 the population of state senatorial districts in California ranged from a low of 14,294 to a high of 6,038,771. That was because some senatorial districts in California were populated mainly by sheep and cows, and others—like the one that included Los Angeles county—mostly by people.

If you list the population of every district in the state, only simple mathematics are required to find out the average population per district in the state and whether most districts are close to the average, or whether there is a great deal of deviation from it. If it turns out that there is a great deal of deviation, you can also find out whether many districts have *more* population than the average, or whether many districts have *less*. So we must calculate three factors:

—the *mean* (average population),

—the *standard deviation* (range on either side of the mean),

—and *skewness* (which side the deviations pile up on).

How do we put number values on these factors? In a perfectly apportioned house all districts contain the same number of people, so none of the districts deviates from the mean; the score for deviation is zero. Because in their measurement system low scores mean good apportionment and high scores indicate malapportionment, Schubert and Press simply turned the deviation score upside down. With the measure inverted, a perfectly apportioned state would be scored 1. Since there are no deviations in a perfectly apportioned state, there is also no skewness, so the skewness score is zero. However, in the usual malapportionment situation, most of the districts are thinly populated and a few units with big cities in them contain most of the population of the state, so there will be a positive skewness score.

The way to get a single score for each state is simply to add together the house and senate scores. While they were at it, Schubert and Press also multiplied each of these scores by a constant in order to get them into a more familiar range of numbers. To indicate the greater importance of the senate, they used a larger constant for the senate than for the house. The final equation looks like this: apportionment score = 60 (senate score) + 40 (house score).

In a perfectly apportioned state, this would mean that the apportionment score = 60 (1 deviation score plus zero skewness) + 40 (1 deviation score plus zero skewness) or *100*. Here are a few samples of the apportionment score for various states:

Ohio	90.3	Mississippi	42.4
Tennessee	71.8	California	20.2
New York	69.2	Minnesota	1.8
Illinois	47.2	Georgia	− 4.9

Brady and Edmonds

To get more specific about it, let us pose this question: Is it true that the larger urban areas (places with a population of 100,000 or more) in malapportioned states get a smaller proportion of state revenue than the large urban areas of well apportioned states? We know from the *Compendium of Government Finances* (1962) what percentage of the population lives in counties of various size (rural areas, towns, cities) in each state; we also know what percentage of state funds goes to each type of county. If, for example, *one-third* of a state's people live in big cities (counties with a population of 250,000 or more) but only *one-fourth* of the state's revenue goes to those counties, we could say that people who live in the big cities of that state are not getting a fair deal from the state government. (We don't know, from this data, whether or not the city's plight is compensated by federal aid.)

This particular situation would show in our computations as a score of less than 100; how much less would depend on how great the discrepancy between the percentage of revenue going to those counties and the percentage of the population living in them. For those counties that were getting more than their fair share of state revenue, the score will be greater than 100. Thus we can see whether or not the cities are really getting the short end.

Apportionment categories	County Population Size					
	250,000 and above	100,000 to 249,999	50,000 to 99,999	25,000 to 49,999	10,000 to 24,999	Under 9,999
Well-apportioned states	94.3	98.6	100.7	101.8	102.2	101.6
Medium	93.7	98.7	100.1	101.5	102.8	101.2
Poorly apportioned	94.9	98.6	99.3	100.7	103.8	106.8

But to prove the reformers' argument, we would also have to show that this discrimination against cities is worse in poorly apportioned states than in well apportioned states. To decide that question, we divided our states into three apportionment categories—well apportioned, medium, and poorly apportioned—and compared the discrimination scores in each category. (See table above.)

As the table shows, all the heavily populated counties are getting less than their fair share of state revenue. *But this situation is just as common in well apportioned states as in poorly apportioned ones.* We got a very similar result when we tried this with the David and Eisenberg index of malapportionment, and so we are inclined to argue that malapportionment has little or no effect on the share of revenue that counties of different size receive.

Policy Output

If apportionment is of crucial importance to the way state governments are run, as so many critics of older apportionment schemes contend, then surely there should be differences in the kind of policy made by well apportioned and poorly apportioned legislatures.

Reformers have argued that policy in the malapportioned states has a conservative bias, reflecting the dominant political outlook in rural constituencies. There are a number of policy issues that divide liberals and conservatives, and some of them fall into the yes/no category that we need to analyze relationships. For instance, it is a reasonable assumption that a conservative legislature is less likely to provide government-paid health care for its indigent citizens, and that such a state would turn down the opportunity to be a part of the Kerr-Mills program that provides such aid. The specific hypothesis we tested was that malapportioned states:

—would not have Kerr-Mills programs as often,

—would have right-to-work laws (opposed by organized labor and liberal politicians generally) more often,

—and would not have state income taxes (generally considered to have the effect of redistributing income in favor of poorer people) as often.

We found no significant differences between well apportioned, medium, and poorly apportioned states in their likelihood of having a Kerr-Mills program, a state right-to-work law, or an income tax. These are, of course, a very limited number of policy issues, and we can draw only tentative conclusions from the analysis. Nevertheless we believe that, at best, malapportionment is not the most significant way to explain policy outcomes.

"All those farmers in Albany are Republicans."

As we've just indicated, most commentators are inclined to believe that malapportionment leads to conservative domination of the legislature. That proposition can be tested quite directly. Since to most people conservative control means Republican control, we simply asked whether the Republican party did in fact have control of the legislature more often in poorly apportioned states. We left the old states of the Confederacy out of this examination, because their history of one-party Democratic domination confuses this particular issue. By our count, Republicans controlled a legislative chamber if they held at least 51 per cent of the seats for two out of the three terms of 1957, 1959, and 1961. For the 35 states in the analysis (leaving out the 11 states of the Confederacy, the unicameral legislature of Nebraska, Minnesota where the strength of the Democratic-Farmer-Labor party confuses the picture, and Alaska and Hawaii which were not states throughout the period we were considering) the legislatures looked this way:

House Control	Democratic	Republican
Well apportioned	5	5
Medium	7	7
Poorly apportioned	7	4
Senate Control		
Well apportioned	3	7
Medium	7	7
Poorly apportioned	7	4

When we computed the averages of the total legislative seats held by each party over the six year period from 1957 to 1961, we got a similar result:

Party	Well apportioned states	Medium	Poorly apportioned states
House			
Republican	53.9%	49.4%	40.0%
Democratic	46.1	50.6	60.0
Senate			
Republican	50.7	49.0	39.1
Democratic	49.3	51.0	60.9

These results show very minor differences, except in the malapportioned category, where it turns out that the Democrats had a sizable advantage in both houses and senates. The usual complaint of rural Republican domination in malapportioned states simply does not hold up.

We believe this study shows clearly that big city dwellers who expect reapportionment to bring about a revolution in the way their problems are handled at the state capital are going to be disappointed. The policy consequences of malapportionment do not appear nearly so important as most of us had thought. Malapportionment, in fact, shares the sad fate of most single factor explanations of social phenomena. Life is rarely that simple.

If we persist in looking for a single factor that explains more than other factors do about state policies, we suggest that *per capita income* would probably be the better choice. States that *have* money are the ones that spend it—on education, welfare, health, or highways. Our study found significant relationships between per capita income and

—average weekly unemployment compensation benefits,
—the maximum weekly benefit under unemployment compensation,
—average annual teachers' salaries,
—per capita expenditures on local schools,
—expenditures per pupil in local schools,
—and per capita expenditures on health and hospitals.

Also, expenditures on higher education are significantly related to the percentage of the state's population which has completed at least four years of high school. There seems to be a natural willingness in those states with a higher proportion of high school and college educated people to support higher education. States with a more highly educated population also tend to support higher levels of spending for highways.

In other areas, like public welfare, a wider range of factors—the percentage of the population that is more than 65 years old, the percentage that is nonwhite, the percentage of city dwellers, the level of education, and degree of industrialization—together or in various combinations may offer a far more adequate explanation for policy than malapportionment does.

Finally, there are factors which cannot be analyzed quantitatively at the present time that probably have some impact on policy:
—the activity of pressure groups;
—the expertise of state administrators;
—how well the governor gets along with the legislature;
—constitutional provisions that hamstring certain policies;
—the degree of party discipline and ideological orientation among legislators.

Gerrymandering of legislative districts may be relevant, but difficult to measure.

We hope this study does not lead anyone to the conclusion that malapportionment is not worth discussing. Quite the contrary. We are convinced that the philosophical case against malapportionment is valid. "One man, one vote" is surely the democratic ideal—an ideal that has not yet been reached in this country and one that is worth pursuing. We do argue that the whole Pandora's box of evil consequences which supposedly result from malapportionment—from right-to-work laws to not spending enough money on school children—really has very little to do with malapportionment. To use these arguments for reapportionment serves only to weaken a case that is strong enough to stand on its own merits.

STATE RANKINGS ON APPORTIONMENT AND EXPENDITURES

	Apportionment Rank	Average Weekly Unemployment Benefits	Average Annual Teachers Salaries	Per Capita Expenditures Local Schools	Per Capita Expenditures Higher Education	Expenditures Per Pupil	Per Capita Expenditures Public Welfare	Per Capita Expenditures Health and Hospitals	Child Welfare Visits Per 10,000	Per Capita Expenditures Highways	Percent Revenue from Property Tax	Percent Revenue from Sales Tax
Ohio	1	5	19	27	37	23	39	45	15	30	11	19
Oregon	2	18	15	7	11	6	14	21	10	11	23	46
New Hampshire	3	30	34	39	34	25	29*	30	7*	8	4	34
Nebraska	4	27*	40	33	27	33	40	35	35	17	3	39
Massachusetts	5	12	14	25	50	14	4	6	36*	47	2	44
Utah	6	16	28	4	3	35	30	44	28	19	25	25
Maine	7	45*	39	34	29	36	17	40	3	14	9*	15*
Tennessee	8	43	43	45	45	44	38*	29	30	22	31	9
Pennsylvania	9	21	22	26	49	17	26	32	24	40	29	14
Indiana	10	26	12	15	13	20*	44	17	17	31	7	16
New York	11	8	3	10	47	1	11	2	19	49	16	45
Arkansas	12	45*	48	49	39	43	16	38	36*	26	40	6
West Virginia	13	46	42	40	31	40	7	47	7*	21	39	2
So. Dakota	14	31	47	28	22	29	29*	50	29*	5	15	30
Hawaii	15	7	18	24	19	28	46	5	33	50	47	4
Washington	16	20	10	5	7	9	6	22	16	23	32	1
Wyoming	17	2	24	1	6	5	32	3	38	1	28	36
New Jersey	18	6	7	20	44	3	42	18	31	48	1	38
Wisconsin	19	4	23	19	23	11	23	14	9	34	5	41
No. Carolina	20	47	35	38	33	39	38*	34	8	44	36	10*

So. Carolina	21	40	45	47	41	45	45	28	21*	43	42	3
Colorado	22	3	21	11	4	20*	3	13	20*	35	18	32
Delaware	23	11	13	14*	17	8	37	25	18	13	43	37
Alaska	24	13	1	2	2	2	35	1	6	2	48	15*
Illinois	25	10	6	22	32	15*	10	31	39	42	6*	17*
Vermont	26	28	37	30	9	31	33	42	5	3	27	35
Montana	27	27*	31	23	10	16	28	43	32*	6	12	40
Missouri	28	19	27	32	46	26	8	26	26	38	24	27*
Idaho	29	14	38	31	28	38	27	24	41*	7	21	43
Michigan	30	17	4	14*	15	18	25	8	41*	15	14	13
Virginia	31	39	36	41	40	38	47	36	13	33	30	31
Mississippi	32	44	49	48	25	47	19	23	4	36	38	8
Rhode Island	33	29	16	42	36	10	13	19	21*	45	10	7*
Louisiana	34	32	32	36	26	30	2	20	20*	20	44	24
Texas	35	36	26	29	35	32	34	41	40	41	20	26
Arizona	36	24	9	6	12	21	31	48	22	12	17	18
No. Dakota	37	22	44*	17	8	27	22*	49	2	10	19	33
Maryland	38	25	11	16	38	13	43	11	12	29	22	20
Connecticut	39	13	5	13	48	4	21	16	11	18	6*	17*
Nevada	40	9	8	8	16	15*	36	4	32*	4	33	11
New Mexico	41	34	17	12	5	24	15	39	21*	25	45	23
California	42	1	2	3	1	7	5	7	29*	32	13	28
Florida	43	38	25	35	43	34	41	10	37	46	26	12
Iowa	44	33	29	18	20	19	18	27	23	16	6*	29
Kentucky	45	23	44*	44	24	42	22*	46	27	9	35	10*
Alabama	46	42	46	46	30	46	12	33	14	39	46	7*
Oklahoma	47	41	30	37	21	37	1	37	25	24	37	22
Kansas	48	15	33	21	14	22	20	15	29*	28	8	27*
Minnesota	49	35	20	9	18	12	9	12	1	27	9*	42
Georgia	50	37	41	43	42	41	24	9	34	37	34	5

* Indicates ties

Lindsay and Rockefeller at Odds

Walter Lippmann

Living in a big city like New York fits G. K. Chesterton's description of modern civilization. We are, he said, like men at the bottom of the ocean. They get their air and everything else they need through tubes that can easily become tangled and fouled up.

Robinson Crusoe, the self-sufficient man, could not have lived in New York City. These last few weeks the garbage piled up in the streets, and if the snowstorm that was threatened had come, the traffic would have been impossible. In recent months we have nearly had a standstill of transportation, both horizontal and vertical. The schools have been closed by a teachers' strike, and there have been threats by the police and the firemen.

New York is a dramatic and conspicuous example of the vulnerability of urban living. Certain services are indispensable to city dwellers. In the past they have been more or less taken for granted. But in our time such services as collecting garbage and operating subways and buses are performed by men who have learned to organize. These men read that this is an affluent society. They hear about the goods and services of affluent people. They realize that by striking they can come nearer to a glittering, affluent good life. They know they have power, and they have not yet tested the limits of that power.

MANAGEABLE PROBLEM. Two of the best men in public life, Mayor Lindsay and Governor Rockefeller, are struggling with this problem. It is, I believe, inherently insoluble. Under prevailing standards the problem cannot be solved if it is reduced to an issue of abstract principle. The problem can only be *managed*. Thus it is quite true that there ought to be no such thing as a strike against the public security and welfare. But in fact there are such strikes and if garbage men organize and strike, there is no clearly accepted method of preventing them from doing it.

This was the dilemma which Mayor Lindsay found himself facing when, having come to the end of his own resources, he asked the governor of the state to call out the National Guard. This was not a solution. The National Guard cannot collect the garbage and operate the subways and teach school. If the National Guard had tried to break the garbage strike by collecting the garbage, there would probably have been something like a general strike by city employees.

The city has been caught between the intolerable and the impossible. It has had to choose between letting the garbage pile up and trying to make the militia collect it. This abstract issue was unrealistic. The issue could not be resolved by a showdown on principle. Governor Rockefeller took the unheroic and unpopular but realistic view of the situation. He by-passed the legal principle at issue and tried to manage the problem by buying his way out of an illegal but most effective strike.

FATEFUL QUESTION. What he did was not according to the law. It was not noble and it was not heroic. But the fact of the matter is that a great modern city has no means of enforcing a law against powerful unions. There is no way of evading the fact that in a city as big as New York only the garbage men can collect the garbage. This is their power. The individual citizen does not have his own incinerator. The police and the firemen cannot collect garbage. The courts cannot put in jail or levy fines on thousands of garbage men.

This ultimate defenselessness of modern cities is ominous. If the unions keep on exploiting it there will certainly be a reaction, and the reaction will be some American variant of Fascism, that is to say a counter-revolution of the victims, themselves for the most part poor and unprivileged, against organized minorities. We already have such a reaction against militant Negroes. It is called the white backlash. But there is developing also a backlash against the insecurity of modern living brought on by other minorities.

Modern living is dangerous. We are confronted with a fateful question —can we remain a free society and still provide the great urban masses with the vital services they must have?

We must remind ourselves that it is not written in any book or enshrined in any law that American democracy will master the problem of modern living. The American way of life was formed in a simple environment when the mass of the people had not yet become dependent, as they are today, upon the restraint and the goodwill and cooperation of the people of their communities.

The future is in doubt. For it is not certain that the indispensable virtues of a free life are now being generated in sufficient force and quantity amidst the violence and nihilism of the modern age.

A Trillion Dollars to Save the Cities?

U.S. News & World Report

Seven out of 10 Americans—nearly 140 million out of 197 million—are crowded into just 1 per cent of this nation's land.

Three out of 10—or some 57 million—enjoy the remaining 99 per cent of the diverse and beautiful U.S. countryside.

Now it's predicted that in the next 25 years, 100 million additional

Americans will try to pile in on top of the 140 million already in the cities and their suburbs.

If that happens it would mean nearly a quarter of a billion people crowded into areas already staggering under their problems.

So what to do? A Senate subcommittee, headed by Abraham Ribicoff (Dem.), of Connecticut, is trying to find some answers.

From a conference of experts on city problems, just held, have come other ideas.

A first suggestion: Spend 1 trillion dollars—1,000 billion—trying to save present cities by reorganizing, redesigning, rebuilding. One trillion dollars, it's explained, would give a "good start" toward bringing order out of impending chaos.

A second suggestion: Create as many as 1,000 "new cities" all across the country—modern cities designed for a modern kind of America, not those built for the horse-and-buggy age.

New cities would be built from scratch in parts of the nation where people could enjoy living. These cities would grow around the needs and desires of people for recreation, as well as for work; for beauty as well as for utility; for easy access to all means of communication.

The cost? Nobody is suggesting a figure, but all agree it would be staggering.

How financed? By expanding industry, just as some "new towns" already are being financed, and by use of some forms of subsidy from the Federal Government.

A NEW ERA. America is seen as moving steadily toward the era when it must provide for half a billion people. Those studying city needs insist there is no time to waste and that the nation must begin soon in earnest to deal with the problems of its big cities and its expanding population.

A dream? Far from it, say those who see problems even today overwhelming city and State governments.

New York City's Mayor John V. Lindsay told the Senate Subcommittee on Executive Reorganization that his city alone needs 50 billion dollars to try to cope with its local problems.

Jerome P. Cavanagh, mayor of Detroit, put a price tag of 15 billions on the needs of his city, and one of 250 billions, over the next 10 years, to help out all major cities of the U.S.

The veteran mayor of New Haven, Conn., Richard C. Lee, said that it is "impossible" to put a price tag on what it is going to cost to save the cities.

When Robert F. Kennedy, New York Senator, added up suggested costs of federal aid for cities, he concluded that, if figures for major cities were extended to all, the total for the next 10 years would be 1.1 trillion dollars.

From the National Planning Association, a private research organization backed by business and labor, comes the prediction that it will take 2.1 trillion dollars, spent over a 20-year period, to make cities "viable."

"I admit that the figure is a very staggering one," says Detroit's Mayor Cavanagh.

Others, however, see in the vast spending that city officials regard as necessary not only a great expense but a tremendous opportunity.

Building on the scale now being talked about, as they see it, could keep the people of the nation—and their industries—fully occupied for as far ahead as anyone would try to look.

Costs of a war on the scale of Korea or Vietnam, by comparison, appear almost trivial.

And what would the country get in return for the trillion dollars paid out to save the cities?

The Constitution Plaza in Hartford, Conn., is referred to as one example of what can be done when a city faces up to a problem.

An older downtown area of Hartford now is restored into a beautiful pedestrian plaza with hotels and shops and an expressway close by, and with parking underground. This development, in turn, is generating adjacent renewal projects, opening more of the downtown area to new business and residential facilities.

Philadelphia showed earlier what could be done by moving rail yards out and reclaiming large areas for redevelopment. In Pittsburgh, one of the pioneers in urban renewal, the Pennsylvania Railroad is planning a 40-square-block "business and residential park" where rail yards now stand, next to the city's famed Golden Triangle.

SLUMS WIPED OUT. In Washington, D.C., a blighted area in the Southwest section is being reclaimed. Where there had been slums are now apartments and hotels, office buildings, Government buildings, a theater and plans for a refurbished waterfront with restaurants. Private and Government capital is involved.

The Rosslyn area in nearby Arlington County, Virginia, is cited as a spectacular example of redevelopment with private capital.

Not all of the plans for larger cities now being discussed as essential call for wiping out old areas and starting over.

In many neighborhoods, it is pointed out, if an investment would be made to get parked cars off the streets, really tidy up those streets and add benches and trees, a much more attractive appearance would result.

Georgetown, in Washington, D.C., and some areas of Philadelphia and San Francisco are referred to as examples of what can be done to bring back decaying areas through renovation rather than large-scale rebuilding.

Those who look ahead say that population densities in some sections of the major cities probably will have to be lowered, or at least prevented from growing more dense. This would be true of Manhattan. Space in present cities is described as often poorly used.

More than downtown areas will have to be redeveloped. Those areas between the central business district and the suburbs, as planners see it, will also have to be rebuilt in many cases to wipe out slums, build new schools, provide open space and recreation areas.

Plans to do just that are under way already in Detroit, Baltimore, St. Louis, Boston and many other cities.

In New York City, State and local officials are thinking of locating government buildings and encouraging a large private business complex in the heart of Harlem, the famed Negro area, as a way of "bringing the jobs to where the workers are," as one official put it.

BETTER TRANSIT. Subways and other forms of rapid transit are coming to be accepted as a necessary supplement to autos and highways to beat rising traffic congestion in big cities.

These transit systems, in turn, are expected to touch off a boom in new office and apartment building, reshaping the living patterns of city dwellers.

Edgardo Contini, partner in Victor Gruen Associates, a Los Angeles land-planning firm, looks for stores, restaurants and other commercial facilities to be built right into subway terminals and thus help turn decaying areas into new business centers.

An official of an economic-research organization had this to say:

"We are trying to get along with a completely obsolete idea of how we can live, an obsolete structure of Government and obsolete methods of planning.

"The remedy lies in taking a national view of our urban problems, in developing regional and metropolitan organizations of government that are capable of planning and executing development programs.

"That means, whether we like it or not, more controls on where buildings are established, on where homes are built or autos can drive.

"It also means revising the structure of Government so that people do not flee from the cities with their tax money and then expect to come back during the day to earn their living—leaving the poorer people in the cities without the tax base needed to correct the city's deficiencies."

"IF WE REBUILD. . . ." From Wilfred Owen, economist and senior staff member of Brookings Institution:

"If we are going to rebuild existing cities to standards that will provide for the kind of life our wealth and increasing leisure permit, then we will be forced to put a limit on the extent to which the city sprawls and extends to meet with contiguous cities.

"We are going to be forced to limit densities of people, because, when we bring in trees and open space and more recreational facilities, we are going to have a looser fabric.

"So there will be an overflow of people from the renewal of existing cities. On top of that, we are told that there will be another 100 million more Americans to provide for in the not too distant future.

"This new population and the overflow from cities will require us to think about new urban centers—and these should be planned communities."

It is from this analysis that the idea of 1,000 new cities springs.

NEW-CITY SYMBOLS. Is the vision of new cities on that scale taken seriously? Those who are thinking of the problem ahead say that it is a very serious proposal. They say that two communities growing near Washington, D.C., are symbols of what can be expected on an expanding scale.

These cities are Reston, 25 miles west of the nation's capital, and Columbia, midway between Washington and Baltimore to the northeast. One is designed for about 75,000 people; the other for about 100,000.

Already scores of towns, on roughly the same scale as Reston and Columbia, are being planned on land that only yesterday was farmland. Urban planners say new cities of even larger size will be needed to meet the mounting pressure of urban growth.

The maximum size suggested for new cities is set by many planners at about 300,000. Beyond that figure, according to an urban economist, "the cost of providing public services for each inhabitant tends to rise quickly while the standard of living may drop."

Cities to be created would not, in most cases, be around the metropolitan areas of today. Instead, they would be located in open areas of the country that meet peoples' tastes with respect to climate, recreation or geography.

In fact, says Joseph Timan, head of the Committee for National Land Development Policy, Chicago-based group of builders, bankers and real estate men, new cities are going to have to be hundreds of miles from present population centers or they will be overwhelmed as the big cities spread outward.

"WONDERFUL PLACES." Ian C. McHarg, urban expert at the University of Pennsylvania, says:

"There is no difficulty at all about finding wonderful places where you could put a thousand new cities."

Mentioned were places near the Cascade Range in the Northwestern U.S.; sparsely settled areas in Hawaii and Minnesota, in Texas and other parts of the Southwest.

New England, with its opportunities for summer and winter sports, is frequently cited as an ideal place for new cities. So are areas in Utah, Idaho and Wyoming, where people could enjoy the mountains or fishing and yet be within easy reach of business centers in San Francisco or Los Angeles by high-speed air transportation.

Says Mr. Owen: "We are reaching the point where we can locate new cities wherever we please. New developments in highway and air transport and in communications, here and on the way, make it no longer necessary for cities to be located in specific places, such as the confluence of a river or a railroad junction or a deep seaport.

"What we now have the opportunity to do is to take advantage of this country and the space that is one of our big assets. Every part of the U.S. is going to be on the main stream."

SELF-CONTAINED. Talk to urban planners and other authorities on new cities and you find broad agreement on what these place will be like.

Most will be self-contained. Some residents might still commute to other cities, but the idea is to have people live, work and play all in one area— "to close the gap between home and work, as in the preautomobile age," one architect explained.

Housing, business and industry, schools, churches, recreation all would be within walking distance or only a short, enjoyable trip away. Around these cities, land would be preserved for farming, forests and recreation.

New cities, as now visualized, would be architecturally pleasing and orderly, with far more open space, trees and greenery than found in present cities. The pedestrian would be king.

Traffic ways would be made less obvious. Main routes, for example, would be run around a community or be depressed or tunneled under it. Human traffic would be separated from motorized traffic as much as possible.

"Separate rights of way for pedestrians" is the idea of C. McKim Norton, president of the New York Regional Plan Association. Pedestrian under-passes might be built at potentially busy corners when the city is laid out.

UNDERGROUND PARKING. Businesses would be centered around pedes-trian plazas, an outgrowth of today's shopping centers, but with parking underground. The same would apply to industrial parks on new-city out-skirts.

Small electric carts that create no air-pollution problem, according to Mr. Contini, would be ideal for daily trips too far for walking.

Special roads, in addition, would be reserved for public transportation, with nearly everybody within minutes' walk of a bus stop.

The kinds of industry now growing fastest in the U.S.—research and light industry—are expected to be attracted to new cities. The promise of greater efficiency in modern new plants with a good deal of space, it is claimed, will make such a move by industry economical in the long run.

In some cases, new cities may turn out to be "college towns," built around large universities. Right now, for example, the new town of Irvine is going up near Los Angeles around a branch of the University of Cali-fornia.

Private funds—from builders, bankers, big corporations—are expected to finance these new cities in major part. Yet there is general agreement among urban authorities that Government aid, of one sort or another, will be needed to get new urban settlements under way.

State and local governments, it is said, will have to take over and assem-ble large tracts of land. Tax concessions by federal and State governments will have to be made to lure the first industries. There may be need for federal "seed money" and for other financial aid to developers of new communities.

One suggestion often made, in the words of an economist for a major research organization: "Let the Federal Government, in distributing money for education, hospitals and highways or in putting up federal buildings, focus on those places where the new cities of tomorrow will be built."

An example cited is the decision to move the headquarters of the U.S. Geological Survey, with its 4,000 workers, from downtown Washington to Reston.

Many specific moves of this kind will be taken in coming years, special-ists in urban problems are convinced.

TIME IS SHORT. Their basic point is that time is running out. People have been talking about the plight of the city for decades, but doing little.

But doing nothing, these authorities say, can be costly too—in terms of congestion, noise, pollution, traffic snarls, slums, crime, welfare loads.

Now Congress is showing signs of concern. Money is beginning to pour out to stimulate mass transit. There are proposals by President Johnson for money to remake "demonstration cities" and for new towns.

Planners see changes ahead for urban America in the coming decades—changes that will be vast and costly.

Tax Sharing with States: Plan That's in Trouble

U.S. News & World Report

A plan for the Government in Washington to share its huge revenues with the 50 State governments is running into serious trouble.

Vigorous attacks are suddenly being mounted against the idea by people in influential positions.

The country's mayors are lining up against it. The chairman of the tax-writing Ways and Means Committee of the House has just gone out of his way to list objections to the proposal.

This reaction comes just at the moment when Republican leaders in Congress have moved to stamp their party's label on tax sharing.

On February 12, Representative Melvin R. Laird (Rep.), of Wisconsin, chairman of the House Republican Conference, declared that tax sharing would be the "keystone" of his party's strategy in Congress.

On February 15, Mr. Laird followed up by introducing a bill calling for 5 per cent of the revenue from the federal tax on personal incomes to be distributed to the States "with no strings attached."

Mr. Laird said the Government's 200 or more grant-in-aid programs, passing out 15 billions a year, have gotten States snarled up in federal red tape and taken away much of the States' independence.

Even before that, about 35 tax-sharing bills had been introduced in the House, most of them by Republicans.

Governors, too, have gone on record for tax sharing. They say the States face massive problems at a time when the Federal Government has pre-empted most big revenue sources.

Many big-city mayors, testifying before a committee of Congress, have spoken up to denounce the plan. They fear a fresh flood of funds from Washington will dwindle to a trickle for the cities as it passes through the State capitols.

Mayor John F. Collins of Boston called tax sharing "the most dangerous idea in America today." Mayor Harold Tollefson of Tacoma, who spoke for the National League of Cities, said past experience has given urban communities little reason to look to the States for help in solving their overwhelming problems.

Tax sharing has drawn strong criticism, too, from Representative Wilbur D. Mills (Dem.), of Arkansas, chairman of the Ways and Means Committee.

In a February 12 speech, Mr. Mills raised many objections to, and questions about, tax sharing. While he said, "I take no position on this particular issue," he made little effort to hide his distaste for the whole idea.

Later, Mr. Mills amplified his views in an interview with "U.S. News & World Report."

The "big danger" in tax sharing, in the view of Mr. Mills, is that "State and local governments would become more and more dependent on Washington, which is just the opposite of the direction we should be moving."

CONSTITUTIONAL ISSUE? The tax chairman also has serious doubts about the "propriety" and even the constitutionality of any plan by which the Government would distribute revenues without supervising their expenditures or even specifying the purposes for which they are to be spent.

Would tax sharing affect discipline in State-local spending?

"I have always felt," said Mr. Mills, "that more discipline could be exercised over the spending by a governmental unit if that unit had the responsibility, or some measure of responsibility, for collecting the revenues to provide the money for expenditures."

Mr. Mills has other doubts. "One might well ask," he said, "whether the State governments are in a worse position than the Federal Government with regard to production of revenues."

Under the Constitution, Mr. Mills notes, States have virtually unlimited taxing authority. He raises a question about "the extent to which the Federal Government should provide funds from its federal income tax collections to States which have not attempted to formulate and impose any type of income tax upon their own citizens."

A HOST OF PROBLEMS. In addition, said Mr. Mills, "a whole host of problems" are involved in allocating tax-sharing funds among the States and between States and localities.

A new boost for tax sharing came from Arthur F. Burns, Chairman of the Council of Economic Advisers under President Eisenhower. He said total government spending was bound to rise, but he would like to see the rise at the State and local level, with a cut in federal outlays. While favoring tax sharing, he said this was not the year to vote it.

Privately, Republican leaders agree tax sharing cannot be started any time soon, if for no other reason than the strain of war costs on the budget.

In that situation, Republicans have adopted a temporary strategy to attack the present grant-in-aid programs. Most of these grants require some State matching and nearly all of them are for limited and highly detailed programs operated under federal supervision.

As these programs come up for renewal this year, Republicans say, attempts will be made to replace them with "block grants," or funds for broad purposes to be spent with less or no federal supervision.

The block-grant approach, however, is also expected to run into heavy opposition from big-city mayors, labor unions and many Democrats.

Chapter Three

SUGGESTED TOPICS FOR CLASS DISCUSSION.

1. Do the problems of urbanism indicate that American society is becoming more or less pluralistic? Are the problems more regionally diverse or tending to become more alike regardless of region?
2. What is the basic weakness today in the contention that the states pro-

vide fifty laboratories for experimentations with new ideas in providing services for their people?

3. Do the problems of contemporary America render discussion about reserved powers v. delegated powers "academic"? Can a meaningful distinction be made between the provision for general welfare by the states and general welfare by the national government?

4. Does the concept of "creative federalism," an even stronger partnership between federal and state governments, pose an increased threat to state governments?

5. Will the requirement of fair apportionment in the state and federal legislative bodies reduce or increase the level of dependence by the states upon federal funds?

PUBLIC RELATIONS
AND PUBLIC OPINION

The importance of public opinion in a democracy is obvious, since "the public" makes its choices of candidates and policies in accordance with its opinions. Furthermore, political opinions, expressed in terms of support, or at the least apathy, is the ultimate foundation for any system of government. Those who influence public opinion, therefore, may be very powerful indeed.

In recent years the professional public-relations expert has become an important figure on the political scene. He possesses skills that help him manipulate public attitudes toward anything from soap flakes and automobiles to presidential candidates. Political campaigns are being directed less by the candidates for office and more by the professional propagandist who decides what the candidate should say and do and what issues he should stress. What implications does this development have for the relationship between voter and candidate? Does an election still serve the purpose it is supposed to when it becomes a contest between rival public-relations agents?

Are professional pollsters reflecting political opinion or are they, too, helping to mold it? What influence do the polls have on voting behavior? On the acceptance or rejection of public policy?

The cases included in this section illustrate the operating techniques of public-relations men and raise a number of questions concerning the proper role of communications experts in politics.

The Perfect Candidate

Robert Wernick

At intervals through the winter and early spring, variations on the following small ad appeared in a Los Angeles newspaper: "Leading public relations firm with top-flight experience in state-wide campaigns wants state senator candidate."

A number of interested parties made their way to the headquarters of the Public Relations Center on Wilshire Boulevard and subsequently into the office of the Center's boss, a swarthy, jowly, bubbly 50-year-old gentleman named Hal Evry. With the brisk dynamism of his trade, Evry then explained the modern scientific techniques for getting elected to public office. To be sure, an unknown like Pennsylvania's Milton Shapp may still manage to win a gubernatorial primary (LIFE, May 27) with the help of hard work, speeches and taped TV spots, but Evry considers such methods to be both obsolete and—worse—risky. For next week's California primaries he has masterminded the campaigns of a half dozen candidates—both local and statewide, including one for state senator. Evry is confident that all six of his men will win.

Other P.R. men start with a candidate and an Issue, then try to sell them to the people. Hal Evry starts with the people, and 90 or more per cent of the time he ends up with a winner. (He says he has elected 35 out of the 39 clients whom he has represented in the past 10 years.) He has persuaded dozens of southern California towns to incorporate as cities, and he has persuaded dozens of others not to incorporate. He has pushed through dozens of school bond issues, and he could have beaten an equal number except that what he calls "a certain emotional immaturity" keeps him from ever taking the anti-school side. Evry and his Center have been so successful that already they are branching out to run campaigns this year in Newark, in Baltimore and in Alaska. They also hold $100-a-day seminars for would-be candidates and their managers to expound their techniques for winning elections.

If it's so easy, why can't you or I be elected to some high office?

Well, we can. Hal Evry will do it with pleasure. All he asks from us in return are these three things:

First, enough cash to pay for a campaign: $60,000 for state senator; $100,000 for a seat in the U.S. Congress; and so on. The Center's fee is a flat 20%. The operative word is *cash*.

Prospective clients are always coming in to the Center and saying, "I've just seen my important old friend Joe Bonanza and he's 100% for me. Isn't that great?" Hal Evry doesn't believe in dream worlds. "Gee, that's great, it really is," he answers. "Now, would you mind telling me to just what extent Old Joe is 100% behind you? Fifty thousand dollars worth? Two thousand? Two hundred? Oh, I see."

Second, we must present a character, or at least the appearance of a

"The Perfect Candidate," *Life*, June 10, 1966. Copyright © 1966 by Robert Wernick. Reprinted by permission of the author.

105

character, which fits into what Evry calls the "code of the great middle cluster of normality."

Presumably there has to be some sort of reality behind the appearance, but it's the appearance that counts. After all, Evry says, people voted for Eisenhower because he looked like a typical benign American father, and for Kennedy because he looked like a typical virile American young man; but no one outside of their immediate families and circle of close acquaintances could have known for sure whether these public images corresponded in any way to reality.

The other day a man came into the Center waving large sums of money and insisting that he had to beat Pat Brown and become governor of California this year because having all the money in the world didn't mean anything any more in modern society; you needed political power, and he had to start getting power right away because he didn't want to run against Bobby—he wanted to run against Humphrey. Evry could not help being impressed by the scope of these ambitions, not to speak of the millions of dollars the man claimed to have made. But Evry turned him down: "When it comes to the public taste, you have to avoid anything that's too different. Goldwater tried to be different, and look what happened to *him*."

And third, we must take an intelligence test and score at least 120 on the Stanford-Binet scale.

The reason for this last is not any residual puritanism in Evry's nature. He is not a nut on the subject of improving the quality of our public servants. In fact, he is fond of repeating the maxim, "You can't upgrade society." The reason is simply that people with only an average I.Q. or less find it difficult to understand Evry's approach, and it takes so much effort to argue with them that it isn't worth the time and money. And yet his approach, as it applies to the conduct of the individual candidate, is simple indeed. It can be summed up in the single adjuratory phrase: Shut up.

According to Evry, all candidates talk too much. From the magic moment when first they feel that shaft of light from heaven, that ghostly finger touching their shoulder and summoning them to a life of public service, they also feel a compulsion to get out and bend the ears of their fellow-citizens—with messages, with arguments, with Issues; and their fellow-citizens couldn't care less.

"Have you ever noticed the audience at a political speech?" asks Evry. "Reporters are always looking at the candidate, but the interesting part of the scene is the audience. Have you seen them when the man gets to Point Five of his eleven-point program for reforming the world? How they're all fidgeting and sneaking looks at their watches?

"Hell, we had a lunch the other day for one of our candidates. I wouldn't let him show up. Some of his friends insisted on making speeches, so I let five of them do it—for one and a half minutes each. That's the absolute maximum anyone will pay attention to a speech."

Evry may stretch a point in a particular case. At present he is running Ivy Baker Priest, ex-treasurer of the U.S. for treasurer of California, and since she is, as he says, "a glib, eloquent person," he lets her prowl a bit on the lecture circuit. But fundamentally he considers all such speeches a waste of time.

The object of Mrs. Priest's campaign, according to Evry, is not to put across theories of high finance but simply to get people to know that there is such a person as Ivy Baker Priest and such an office as treasurer of California.

The goal of recognition can be reached more easily with less expense and worry by taking a big ad in the local paper saying I LIKE IVY than by sending her off to make a speech, even a good speech before a couple of hundred people who would probably vote for her anyway. Furthermore, Evry points out, after even the best speech in the world—a one-and-a-half minute knockout—what is to prevent some kook in the audience from getting up and asking a question like, "Should we impeach Earl Warren?" The candidate has to answer the question, and *then* where is he—or she?

As Evry says, there are three ways of answering a question: Yes, No, or something in between. Whatever answer you give is going to irritate the people holding the other two positions, so in the long run if you keep on answering all sorts of questions you may end up alienating two-thirds of the voters. That is why Evry candidates are urged to spend a maximum amount of time at the bowling alley, or in Disneyland.

"The ideal campaign," says Evry, "is like Teddy Kennedy's. Where was he? Flat on his back in a hospital. No speeches, and he gets the biggest majority in the history of Massachusetts. Or Lodge winning those primaries. Where was he? In Saigon.

"Whereas you look at the people who have thrown it away because they couldn't keep their big mouths shut. Why did Nixon have to let himself get murdered in those debates with Kennedy? You say the people would have disapproved if he ducked out? What people? How many people? How many people cared when Johnson wouldn't debate Goldwater? Just look at Goldwater! Oh, he learned his lesson finally—he wouldn't talk to anybody. But by that time it was too late."

But aren't there some candidates associated in the voters' minds with intellectual brilliance? Who would have heard of Stevenson if he hadn't made all those stirring speeches?

"Stirring speeches?" says Evry. "What did he stir with them—soup? Sure, millions of people loved his speeches. They loved William Jennings Bryan's speeches. But how many elections did those boys win? If Stevenson had consulted me, I'd have told him: Get rid of Schlesinger and all those guys. I would have run him as 'Old Joe' Stevenson, with that hole in his shoe. He would have had a chance that way."

It isn't just speeches that Evry wants to get rid of, it's the whole standards of the past, it should be a safe seat for Mr. Beilenson.

But here comes Alex Campbell. "He is one of the finest men I ever met," says Evry. "A pioneer oil developer. Quiet, mild-mannered, utterly objective—he makes me look biased, he's so objective—48 years old. What I'd call an average American, a typical Presbyterian Scotsman. He was hanging around the Joe Shell headquarters—remember, Shell was running against Nixon for the Republican nomination for governor a few years back—and he saw all these party workers scurrying around, and got to wondering what they really did. He came to me and said, 'Do they really do anything?' I said, 'No.' So a little later he said, 'Why don't I run for state senator—just for the heck of it? I've done everything else, just about. It would be sort of nice.'

"So now we're running him. He can't lose. IN THE LINCOLN TRADITION, we call it.

"First we win the primary next week. Alex is registered as a Republican. At first he didn't know which party he wanted to run in, but we told him he was registered and he couldn't switch. There's a publisher of some sort running against him, and it will look good when we beat him.

"Then, by November, we'll have had time to really work on the voters. They'll be going for Lincoln or for Campbell's soup, or both. You can't beat the combination."

To observers who charge that this type of campaign degrades the level of politics by making possible the election of unqualified candidates, Evry replies that unqualified candidates are being elected all the time under the old methods, and the new methods may actually improve the level of politics by bringing in candidates who would not have run in the old unsophisticated days. And, he adds, the way things are now, only noisy boisterous types are apt to run for public office—people who love to press the flesh of thousands of their sweaty countrymen and who love to talk at the top of their voices. But under Evry's methods of candidacy—or noncandidacy, if you prefer—refined introverted types as well can run and win: they certainly won't wear themselves out by trying. All they have to do is have the courage of Evry's convictions and pay no attention to critics.

"In the long run," reads a document prepared by the Center, "only he will achieve basic results in influencing public opinion who is able to reduce problems and issues to the simplest terms and who has the courage to keep forever repeating them in this simplified form despite the objection of the intellectuals."

Let doubters chew over the story of the 1964 elections. An unknown named Jerry Pettis came to Evry and Dresser, and asked for help in running for Congress in the 33rd District. They were willing, and they ran a campaign based entirely on cartoons of a little boy and a little girl lying on their backs with warm folksy words ballooning out of their mouths on the order of: "I like Jerry Pettis. He likes us kids."

Jerry Pettis outdrew every single candidate of both parties in the primaries. Then he got cold feet, called in a bigger, fancier public-relations outfit, which outfitted him with a good deal of ponderous material about Issues. Pettis compounded *that* sin by making speeches—and he was defeated in November.

Though the lesson should be plain for all to see, prospective candidates still come forward and run on tired old slogans like, IT'S TIME FOR A CHANGE. But the computers at the Center have conclusively proved that this is one of the worst of all possible slogans: the average person doesn't like change. (On the other hand, if you simply want to *improve* things, he'll buy that.) The computers also indicate that politicians are out of their minds when they insist on making their positions clear on offshore oil, balance of payments, water pollution and all that esoteric jazz. What the voters really worry about is bound to be closer to home. As a matter of fact, the thing that most voters of California worry about most is Parking Meters. Evry is looking for a man brave enough to run the Evry way for Attorney General of the State. The campaign would cost a quarter of a million dollars and would consist of one giant slogan: END THE PARKING-METER RACKET! It would be a shoo-in.

Hal Evry does not want power or even glory for himself. He is just an unassuming, politically unambitious, horse-playing, average American. But his brown eyes light up when he talks of that day—coming soon, he says, perhaps not precisely in 1984 but thereabouts—when the techniques of motivational analysis and sampling and polling will be so refined that, instead of going through the sweat and strain of a national election, a flick of an IBM machine will poll a cross-section of American voters. They will be intensively questioned on just what they want their President to be: dark or fair, tall or short, paternally benign or youthfully virile, grandiloquent or soft-spoken, hawk or dove. Their answers will be tabulated and constructed into a profile of the ideal President the people want.

Then, all the people who want to be President will have their characteristics coded and fed into a machine. *Whir! Clack!*—and the one candidate whose card most closely corresponds to the ideal will be chosen. Finally, a guaranteed-typical, central cluster of 1,000 All-American voters will vote. The peoples' choice—the Evry Man—wins again.

Were the Polls Wrong?

Elmo Roper

Political polls have probably never been used more abundantly than they are in America today. They play a major role in pre-nomination scrambles and pre-election campaigns. They are quoted in newspapers, leaked to reporters by candidates, and closely watched by those in high office. Yet they have probably never contributed less to public understanding of elections. What is the reason for this odd state of affairs?

Take November's election. Discussion before the election centered on how great a loss the Democrats would sustain in Congress. Opinion seemed to vary as to whether the loss would be below forty seats (the expectation of President Johnson) or about forty (the prediction of former Vice President Nixon), or twenty-nine, which was *The New York Times's* estimate of the probable results. The day of the election the *Times* also mentioned, in passing, the latest Gallup Poll results, which recorded a national percentage increase in support for the Republicans since 1964 of 5.5 points, indicating to the Gallup organization a probable Republican

"Were the Polls Wrong?" *Saturday Review*, December 10, 1966. Reprinted by permission of the author.

gain of from thirty-five to fifty-five seats. Apparently this was considered an odd statistic, strangely out of joint with what "most analysts" had forecast. It was mentioned simply as one opinion among many. As a result of this prevalent expectation that the Republican gain would be forty House seats or considerably less, there was general surprise the next day when the GOP picked up forty-seven House seats and sent three new members to the Senate. (*The New York Times* headlined: REPUBLICANS STRONGER THAN EXPECTED IN OFF-YEAR VOTE.)

"Stronger than expected" by whom? This shouldn't have been a surprise to anyone. It was certainly not a surprise to me. A week before the election I concluded that the probable GOP gain in the House and Senate combined would be between forty-five and fifty-five seats, and I so stated publicly in a speech on November 2. Let me hasten to say that my prediction was not based on results of surveys done by our firm, since we have never done national polls in off-year elections. It was based on my own analysis of the Gallup figures, which required no mastery of advanced calculus, but simply an awareness of the relationship between those figures and past Congressional election results—and a respect for George Gallup.

Nothing is more publicly available than the Gallup figures, and nothing has been more reliable over the years. There is, naturally, no perfect correlation between the percentage of voters in the nation planning to vote Democratic for Congress and the actual seats gained or lost, but the relationship is remarkably close and remarkably predictable. The Gallup Poll's published interpretation of its figures was slightly on the conservative side, but the basic message was clear, and a telephone call to Dr. Gallup convinced me he agreed with my forty-five to fifty-five seat gain: Republicans would do considerably better than most out-of-power parties in most off-year elections, and certainly better than most political "analysts" expected this year.

Then there were the individual election contests. In the same speech I gave a week before the election, I also made rather flat predictions of victory on twenty-one races for governor and senator, including not only such widely expected victories as those by Reagan in California, Percy in Illinois, Cooper in Kentucky, and Case in New Jersey, but also such "close" races as those involving Nelson and Winthrop Rockefeller, Edward Brooke, and Shafer, Tower, Metcalf, Hatfield, and Levander. A really close race cannot be predicted, but none of these races was as close as the newspapers had believed they would be. Again, the accuracy of these predictions is no credit to the research of our own organization, which polled none of the races I have mentioned. It is simply a question of getting the best available information from *reliable* public polls, such as the California, Iowa, Minnesota, and Denver *Post* polls, and from reputable private polls (when available), such as those by John Kraft (except in New York this year) and Archibald Crossley. When polls give conflicting readings on a contest—and this election was no exception—it is simply a question of believing the one with the better reputation for accuracy and integrity.

Why do the newspapers—and I should add, the television networks as well—fail to take full advantage of this expert and reliable information when they make their pre-election analyses? I can only speculate. I suspect that the central reason is an inability or an unwillingness to discriminate between the available polls. To too many members of the press, a poll is a poll is a poll. Such an attitude leads, for example, to the publishing—on page 1—of a poll of a Congressman's constituents conducted by mail, while the usually reliable Gallup results are buried in the back pages. It leads to treating such polls as that run by the New York *Daily News* as seriously as polls that are much more highly thought of by professionals. And it also leads to a general skepticism toward polls, which are often assumed to be as likely to miss as to hit election results on the nose.

If the record of all polls of all types done over the years is examined, it is likely to confirm this skepticism. But the record of the scientifically conducted polls done by the organizations generally respected in the field is another thing entirely. Such polls have a record of high and consistent accuracy, and are the best available source of pre-election prescience.

It is not really necessary to predict elections at all. Election forecasts have no particular social utility, although an understanding of the mood and movement of the electorate is valuable both to candidates and to elected officials. But such forecasting is clearly here to stay. And if the press is going to continue to devote considerable time and space and money to analyzing the voters' intentions, it has an intellectual responsibility to do it with the best tools available. What is needed is a more sophisticated understanding of the polls, which will enable the press to discriminate between polls and between pollsters—learning which to trust and which to disregard—and so to be in a position to better inform the public.

How the Polls Fared

William C. Selover

For the public opinion polltaker, the day of reckoning comes after the election. To hedge their predictions, polling specialists have learned to choose their words carefully, guard their hunches, and spell out qualifying conditions.

Before listing his findings, George Gallup protects himself with this standard phrase: "If elections were held today." And Samuel Lubell, among others, only interprets trends, without citing precise figures.

But whether they like it or not, pollsters are judged by the most obvious of criteria: Election-Day statistics.

Alfred M. Landon's erroneously predicted election victory in 1936 spelled extinction for the Literary Digest poll.

ACCEPTABLE MARGIN MAINTAINED

And in 1948, the faulty prediction of Thomas E. Dewey's victory meant a serious blow to the prestige of the Gallup poll, the Crossley poll, and the Roper poll.

But in the presidential election this year, the polling organizations had very little trouble: All of the nationwide polls and most of the statewide polls were remarkably accurate, to within 5 per cent of the actual vote—a figure generally cited as the acceptable margin of polling error.

Two factors account for the accuracy of this year's polls:

The methods of sampling have been improved and interviewing has become greatly refined.

And pollsters were careful to interview up until the last possible time before the election, generally detecting any last-minute trends.

UNDECIDED FACTOR ALLOCATED

To find how accurate the polls were The Christian Science Monitor surveyed more than 20 polls across the country. Each was put to the ultimate test: its success on Election Day.

For the nationwide election results, the percentage is figured on the basis of total popular votes of the two major candidates. The figure is: for the Johnson-Humphrey ticket, 61.4 per cent; for the Goldwater-Miller, 38.6 per cent. This is the actual result.

The Gallup poll preelection survey gave Mr. Johnson 61 per cent of the vote and Senator Goldwater 32 per cent, with 7 per cent undecided. With the undecided vote allocated on the basis of the voter's position on the issues, the Gallup poll gave Mr. Johnson a 64–36 per cent margin of victory. Here, the margin of difference is about 2½ per cent—safely within the 5 per cent margin. Thus, the Gallup poll passes the test.

And so does the Harris poll.

Its final preelection poll gave Mr. Johnson a 62 to 33 per cent lead, with 5 per cent undecided. And when the Harris poll allocated the undecided vote, the result was the same as the Gallup findings: Johnson, 64 to 36.

The Samuel Lubell poll also passes. Its final nationwide findings predicted a "landslide victory" for President Johnson. Lubell did not give figures. But the generally accepted margin for an election to be a "landslide" is 60 per cent of the popular vote and over.

'HIDDEN VOTE' DISSOLVES

From the analysis of these nationwide polls and from most of the statewide polls, one basic factor of this election emerges clearly: there was no "hidden vote" of any consequence; there was no "unknown factor"—something which had worried the pollsters before the election. In short, there were no surprises.

The undecided vote did not hide a great number of voters for one side or the other: In many cases, outside the South, voters who told pollsters they were undecided were roughly equally divided between the candidates in actual voting.

In the South, Senator Goldwater gained slightly in the allocation of undecided voters. But this can be attributed to the natural reluctance of the

	Johnson	Goldwater	Undecided or not saying	Actual popular vote percentages John-son	Gold-water
Nationwide Polls					
Gallup poll	61	32	7	61.4	38.6
Gallup poll (after allocating undecided vote)	64	36	—		
Harris poll	62	33	5	61.4	38.6
Harris poll (after allocating undecided vote)	64	36	—		
Statewide Polls					
Hal Dunleavy poll (California)	58	37	5	59.8	40.2
California poll by Mervin D. Field (California)	60	34	6	59.8	40.2
Arizona poll for the Phoenix Gazette (Arizona)	46	45	9	49.7	50.3
Albuquerque Journal by Univ. of New Mexico (New Mexico)	51.5	25.4	23.1	59.1	40.9
Tennessee poll by John Kraft for the Democratic Party (Tennessee)	49	35	16	55.5	44.5
United Press poll (Oklahoma)	53.1	32.2	15.7	55.8	44.2
Texas poll by Joe Belden (Texas)	61	34	5	62.9	37.1
Chicago Sun-Times poll (Illinois)	62.63	37.37	—	59.5	40.5
Indianapolis Star poll (Indiana)	51.5	38.1	10.4	56.1	43.9
Oliver Quayle poll for the Democratic Party (Indiana)	51	36	13	56.1	43.9
Minnesota poll by the Minneapolis Star and Tribune (Minnesota)	67	29	4	64	36
Detroit News poll (Michigan)	68	23	9	67.7	32.3
Iowa poll by the Des Moines Sunday Register (Iowa)	57	37	6	61.9	38.1
Denver Post poll (Colorado)	64	31	5	61.5	38.5
Denver Post poll after allotting the undecided vote	66.2	33.8	—	61.5	38.5
Denver Post poll (Wyoming)	68	31	1	56.4	43.5
The South Dakota poll by the Sioux Falls Argus-Leader, Aberdeen American News, and Watertown Public Opinion (South Dakota)	45	49	6	55.7	44.3
New York Daily News poll (New York)	74.5	25.5	—	68.2	31.8
Portland Sunday Telegram poll (Maine)	56	18	26	68.8	31.2

* Chart prepared by Russell H. Lenz.

traditionally solidly Democratic Southerners to express open preference for a Republican. The Goldwater gains in undecided votes were not enough to change the final results in any except in his own state of Arizona.

LAST-MINUTE TRENDS

In the detailed breakdown of statewide polls which follows, there is one further factor to watch for. That is, how successfully did the polls indicate last-minute trends.

Notable examples of such success were found in the Iowa and the Minnesota polls, each of which disclosed a late trend toward Senator Goldwater.

In all of the statewide polls, except two, the survey predicted the winner accurately. The failures were the South Dakota poll, which predicted a Goldwater victory, and the Arizona poll, a non-partisan survey, which showed President Johnson leading that state.

But aside from these, the final results of the statewide polls, with few exceptions, were within the allowable 5 per cent error.

Chapter Four

SUGGESTED QUESTIONS FOR CLASS DISCUSSION.

1. Does the question posed by Professor Irish and Prothro, "will Madison Avenue inherit the earth?" really pose a threat to our electoral system? Could the "merchandizing" of candidates lead us to elect incompetent and even dishonest officeholders through the device of "image building"? Is there anything that can be done to prevent this?
2. No major candidate for major office would undertake a campaign today without considerable reliance on polls. Do these polls have an effect on molding opinion before the election? Do the voters take them as seriously as the candidates?
3. Should public opinion polls be used to guide those responsible for making public policy? Should the President, Congress, public agencies, use them?

Chapter Five

INTEREST GROUPS

The right to organize is valued and protected in the United States. It is natural, therefore, for those having common attitudes and interests to associate. It is also natural for the members of an association to use their organization for the pursuit of ends they hold in common, including political ends. One of the noteworthy features of the American scene is the way the landscape is dotted with "pressure groups" and "interest groups" hard at work trying to influence policy in one respect or another.

How concerned should one be about the role of interest groups in the governmental process? Do those that are effectively organized have undue weight?

Should interest groups have free rein in their activities, or should they be subjected to certain kinds of regulation?

Should the "public interest" be considered to be whatever emerges from the conflict and competition of political groups, or is there a public interest separate from this outcome that ought to be sought? If the latter, where does that interest lie and how can it be known for certain?

The cases offered in this section show a number of interest groups at work and raise some of the questions mentioned above and others.

The Company's Man in Washington

Richard Austin Smith

The Washington vice president of a leading aerospace company recently rocked back in his throne-like swivel chair and declared with aplomb: "I look on myself as the corporation's ambassador here in the capital." A few blocks away, in a similarly resplendent suite of offices, the Washington representative of one of the nation's biggest oil companies described himself less grandly, though with equal justification, as "a glorified errand boy."

These two disparate opinions of the same assignment go a long way toward pointing up the problem confronting major U.S. corporations: how to make effective use of that time-honored capital fixture, the Washington representative. Few companies would be willing to settle for "errand boys" and most would balk at setting up corporate "ambassadors," yet the need for some sort of individualized representation grows more pressing every day. American business is still learning how to live with Lyndon Johnson's Washington, and it is a perplexing, sometimes painful process. The President may wine and dine corporate executives at the White House and talk as if he believed free enterprise were the paramount force in the economy, but that hasn't deterred his Administration from reaching further and further into areas that used to belong exclusively to corporate decision making. Management policies dealing with prices, wages, labor relations, mergers, are all under some kind of stricture or surveillance. The flow of U.S. investment overseas has been restricted by "voluntary" controls while at home the biggest budget in history seems to offer both glittering opportunities and proliferating federal influence in the private sector. Almost everything the government does, no matter how seemingly irrelevant, has come to have an impact on business.

More than 300 companies now have their own Washington representatives to meet government on its own terms or its own ground—and sometimes with important grants of corporate authority. Harvey Gaylord, executive vice president and a director of Textron, runs the company's entire aerospace operation out of Washington; the corporate policy-making and sales groups for Bell Aerosystems, Bell Helicopter, and Hydraulic Research & Manufacturing and other divisions have been put under his control at a central headquarters there.

While this has worked well for Textron, it is naturally impractical for other companies, with totally different problems, to approach Washington the same way. To begin with, they vary in their areas of concentration, depending on the areas of government their companies are particularly concerned with. The men from the aerospace and arms companies obviously concentrate on the Defense Department and NASA. Corning Glass

"The Company's Man in Washington," *Fortune,* April 1966. Reprinted by permission of the publisher.

Works is mainly interested in legislative developments that may affect its business, so its Washington man, Charles Francik, whose title is director of government services, spends most of his time around Capitol Hill. Because of the diversity of their interests, corporate giants like Standard Oil (New Jersey) and American Telephone & Telegraph split up their representation. Jersey Standard has one office that watches international affairs, while its subsidiary, Humble, has a staff that limits operations to domestic matters. A.T. & T.'s resident vice president, Lloyd Miller, instructs his staff to keep in as close touch as possible with government—both to report what's going on (it acts as an intelligence service for the entire Bell System) and to determine how the company can do a better job for its principal customers: the Post Office, the Weather Bureau, the private-line network of the General Services Administration, etc. A.T. & T.'s manufacturing subsidiary, Western Electric, has an entirely different concern. Though 14 per cent of its sales come from government, and it has regularly ranked among the first ten in this regard, it is not interested in taking any more federal business if it can help it. When Western Electric's Washington man, O. M. Green, takes an official to lunch, his usual aim is to persuade the government *not* to give W.E. another contract.

THREE FOR THE MONEY

Whatever company he works for, the Washington rep is likely to be burdened with a number of housekeeping chores: making appointments for visiting brass, seeing that top management is invited to prestige functions, setting up the right kind of golf match or intimate little dinner for the right kind of people. These things take a lot of time but, properly handled, they can contribute to his general effectiveness in his main activities, which usually involve, in one degree or another, selling, information gathering, and politicking.

For many companies the main reason for having a man in Washington is to have a salesman permanently on the doorstep of the biggest customer of them all. He is an unusual kind of salesman, for he rarely, if ever, nails the sale by himself. The Washington rep can't know enough about the present enormously complicated products or systems to sell them single-handedly—and isn't supposed to. What he does, essentially, is to have such an intimate knowledge of his company's capabilities and such a close association with the customer's (the government's) present and anticipated needs that he can bring the two together.

Sometimes those needs might be satisfied by an existing piece of hardware, sometimes by a research-and-development proposal, shrewdly tailored to his company's capabilities, and thus of invaluable help in gaining the expertise that would put the company ahead of the pack in bidding on any eventual contract for prototypes. Characteristically the actual sale is made by men sent to Washington from corporate or divisional headquarters, or sent to a decentralized "command"—e.g., Ballistic Systems Division of the Air Force—with the Washington rep helping to coordinate selling at both field and Pentagon levels.

This kind of indirect salesmanship makes up the daily routine of Robert Davis, Washington vice president of Thiokol. On one recent typical day,

Davis set off on a round of "selling calls" on people at Andrews Air Force Base and the Pentagon. His objective was to keep alive a research-and-development test program for the 156-inch solid-propellant rocket motor. The program had begun with $5,700,000 in fiscal 1963, but this stood at only $6 million by fiscal 1966 because neither the military nor NASA had a visible need for such a motor. The Pentagon's attitude was simply: why not put the program on the shelf until a requirement materializes, then start afresh? Davis' strategy was to try to prove that there were many important technological areas still to be investigated; as added bait, he intended to re-emphasize some ideas on reducing the cost of nozzle materials from the present $30 to $35 a pound to $1 a pound.

The net of his efforts, some six hours of patient, friendly, intelligent, very low-pressure selling, was extremely hard to evaluate. Davis walked away with nothing concrete, no assurance beyond a sympathetic and receptive attitude on the part of the men he saw. Nor was there much comfort to be found in the speculation that the new budget when it finally emerged would probably show only $2 million to $3 million set aside for the program. But the chances are that if Davis hadn't slogged around from one office to another pressing his case, the demands of Vietnam would have squeezed the program out of consideration altogether. The cardinal sin in Washington selling is not losing a "sale" but failing to make the kind of dogged effort that keeps your company in the running.

THE MAN IN THE KNOW

In another major area of operation—information—the Washington rep has a dual function. He operates a listening post, feeding his company valuable intelligence picked up from friends in government, helpful newsmen, staff members of congressional committees, other company representatives. But he is also a source of information, supplying facts and figures about his own company's operations to Congressmen and government officials.

For information gathering, the Washington office is often set up something like a news bureau; members of the staff work on regular "beats" or assignments, covering Capitol Hill, the Pentagon, the Treasury, Commerce, the FTC, the ICC, etc., depending on the company's main concerns. Where the Washington rep must do the job all by himself, he may seek the help of the N.A.M., the U.S. Chamber of Commerce, or others of the many associations in Washington that keep their own staffs busy seeking information about forthcoming legislation and impending investigations. Most Washington reps file reports of their gleanings to top management on a weekly basis, supplementing these with telephoned intelligence as the occasion demands. But some major corporations operate on a daily basis—e.g., U.S. Steel's incisive five- or six-page Washington report goes to 1,000 executives every workday.

In his role of providing information *from* his company, the Washington rep serves not only his own interests; his contribution can be little short of indispensable to the workings of government. Committee staffs, as well as individual Congressmen, depend heavily on the technical data he can supply. This is particularly true in complicated fields like atomic energy, defense, aerospace, urban development, and economic forecasting, where both Congress and the executive branch need precise, rapid, and complete information from private industry. Often the material is tangential to whatever product or service the company might be trying to sell the government. "If there is something major that involves taxes or labor, housing starts, population growth, economic projections, social legislation—you name it—these committees are apt to want statistical information from us," says Lloyd Miller of A.T. & T. His company generates a great volume of statistics both to do its job and to handle its responsibilities as the nation's largest single private employer of labor. "I think 20 per cent of our time is spent answering congressional requests; perhaps more than 50 per cent would be a good estimate for both Congress and the executive branch."

Washington reps have learned to handle this sort of information—even when there may be a sales pitch behind it—with a high degree of probity. Not only must the data be sound, it must also be objective to the point of apprising the receiver of any frailties in the donor's position or project. Washington has no fury like the bureaucrat or Congressman who has been humiliated because he was given misleading or inaccurate information. Once doors are slammed shut under those circumstances, Washington reps can spend years trying to get them reopened. On the other hand, few of the reps would hesitate to supply a friendly Congressman with an arsenal of half-truths or distorted facts with which to demolish an adversary, so long as the Congressman knew what he was getting. Many a Washington rep has drawn up lists of questions for a congressional-committee member either to illuminate the good points of his company's position or to expose the flaws of a counterproposition.

OLD FRIENDS AND NEW MONEY

Getting Congressmen to see things his way is part of the Washington rep's third major function—politicking. Here his objective is plainly to influence the processes of government so as to achieve something of benefit to his company. This may mean beating the drums for an investigation, smoothing the way for desirable bills, keeping tabs on shifting power alliances, and using the folks back home to the best advantage. The rep's effectiveness in politicking is likely to be governed by the worn Washington adage: don't try to make a friend when you need one, have him on your side long before that. Money helps to make friends on Capitol Hill, not in the form of anything as crude as a bribe (the *Congressional Quarterly* reports only one prosecution involving allegations of bribes offered Congressmen to influence their votes—no conviction—since 1945), but as campaign contributions. These are sometimes made through law firms or advertising agencies and decorously concealed in padded billings.

Politicking, of course, can be defensive as well as offensive—in which case it takes on such negative aspects as sidetracking unfavorable legislation, forestalling investigations, or thwarting attempts to clobber the company. Here the successful Washington rep's trail is difficult to follow, but Chad Calhoun, for over twenty years Kaiser's Washington vice president, illustrates how things get done. At the height of the bitter fight between

Kaiser Aluminum and a competitor over a government-owned extrusion plant back in the middle Fifties, Calhoun heard via the grapevine that the competitor had prepared a speech blasting Kaiser, and that a certain New England Senator was primed and ready to deliver it. Calhoun managed to secure a photocopy of a draft of the speech along with a copy of a secretary's notebook full of revisions. With this impressive detail in his possession, he then went to see a close friend of the Senator's. The friend was aware, Calhoun began, that the press had suspected the Senator of improprieties and had been waiting for an opportunity to pin one on him. Well, the occasion may have presented itself: he had just heard at a party that the Senator had been induced by Kaiser's competitor to make an anti-Kaiser speech on the floor. When the Senator made his speech, the scheme was going to be publicly exposed. Calhoun then mentioned some of the changes in the secretary's notebook to show how much he knew about the situation. The speech was never delivered. In fact, the Senator, grateful for the tip, sent Calhoun his "regards."

THREE WORDS: $35 MILLION

In 1952, Rod Markley, Ford Motor Co.'s Washington managing director, found himself involved in a similarly defensive situation. A competitor of Ford's had persuaded the ranking minority member of the House Banking and Currency Committee to introduce a three-word change in the Defense Production Act; it was adopted on the floor of the House as an amendment. Markley, who had left the gallery for a telephone call just before the member's action, only learned of it from the *Congressional Record* the following morning. The amendment, in essence, gave the other company an advantage by changing the historical base period from which allowable production was calculated; at the same time it deprived Ford of production that could have represented a loss in income of about $35 million. Unfortunately for Markley, by then it was very late in the day to do much about the change. The Senate had already passed that year's amendments to the Defense Production Act and the House had passed the Senate version with additional amendments of its own, including this one. A House-Senate conference was imminent. Markley did point out the insidious nature of the amendment to its sponsor (who had apparently been unaware of its significance), then immediately set about cranking up grass-roots opposition. Ford's field sales offices were alerted and they in turn got in touch with dealers whose "back home" opinions would probably carry weight with the legislators concerned. The amendment was dropped three days later in the small hours of a conference that lasted until five in the morning.

How effectively a Washington rep performs all these functions, of course, is likely to vary from one Administration to another. Each new chief executive brings about a subtle sea change in government, and this affects the whole range of government relationships. Many of the reps find that under Lyndon Johnson, as under Kennedy, there is some suspiciousness of business, but that now it takes a different form. "I find this outfit deeply suspicious of anybody they don't know," explained one White House habitué. "Those Washington reps who try to get through via the executive branch may scuttle themselves; Johnson is too ornery. If anything comes from a source he doesn't know, his eyes narrow." The view of another old Washington hand, vice president of a major communications company, was that Johnson seems "more accessible to businessmen than his predecessor—he opens the doors of the executive mansion to lots of them, calls them up, invites them over—but actually is not as accessible in a meaningful way. When you go in to see Johnson you don't talk, you listen. Under Kennedy and the people around him you could present your problem or proposition and they'd take it all in and maybe decide 'this fellow has a point.' Johnson is fond of quoting Isaiah—'Come now, and let us reason together'—chapter 1, verse 18. But did you ever read the full passage, verses 18, 19, and 20? It says to me: If you cooperate, you'll be O.K.; if you don't you'll be devoured."

EVERYTHING IS "GRANDMA"

There's an occasional opportunity for Washington reps in the President's well-known dislike of being anticipated on federal appointments. A public-relations firm employed by a pipeline company, for example, believes it killed the chances of a man its client didn't want appointed to the Federal Power Commission by initiating a story that he was the President's certain choice. But for most Washington reps the fundamental change between the Johnson and the Kennedy administrations is the new necessity to go deep into the middle and lower echelons of the executive branch. One reason for this is to avoid arousing the Johnsonian ire by openly opposing him in the Congress. "He says he doesn't want to be opposed on 'grandma' [i.e., on major items]," explained one company representative, "but everything is 'grandma' with him and he doesn't forget who was doing the opposing. It's a lot safer to register your opposition deep down in the bowels of government, where the problem of the presidential image is not a factor." A second reason for the new approach to the executive branch has to do with the situation on Capitol Hill. Until recently, at least, the President has had an unmatched success in getting what he wants from Congress; once his proposals have got out of committee they have been almost certain of passage. The best place for a Washington rep to do some good for his company, accordingly, has been within the operating departments in the Administration, while the future proposal is still just a gleam in some bureaucrat's eye.

"You have to take your case to the Administration first," said a resident automobile executive. "We are interested in the Treasury for many reasons—all the way from international finance and export restrictions to corporate taxes. The taxes may start in the excise section at the Treasury, which is quite a way from the Secretary's office. International problems start in the monetary control office and a half-dozen other places. You have to get into these operations to be effective. We try to project what the important problems will be, the kinds of things that will be coming down the pike. Individual staff members make themselves available because in preparing a document they like to say we have discussed this with industry and their attitude is such and such. But after a recommendation is ready and clears a department to go to the Bureau of the

Budget, the secrecy lid is clamped on. Still, we go after the Bureau of the Budget regularly if not intensively. This is new—going to Budget—but we still want to shape things before they emerge."

THE DEFENSIVE POSTURE

The effectiveness of a Washington rep depends heavily on the attitude of his top management toward government and politics. Many corporations still seem only marginally concerned about their legislative interests and responsibilities. They prefer to remain anonymous in the current political atmosphere and let the N.A.M. or the U.S. Chamber express their collective point of view—even though these organizations are so big and diffuse that it is virtually impossible to get them to pull in the precise direction an individual company might want. The managements of such companies are essentially defensive about politics. If something threatens their freedom of movement or menaces them economically, they will try to head it off, but very few of them have long-range programs designed to establish a better climate in foreign or fiscal policy, taxation, antitrust, etc. The front office generally refuses to be concerned about anything save matters of immediate dollars-and-cents impact. Instead, it is conditioned by the credo that "the business of business is business" and it is chary of spending time on politics when a rival may be giving all his attention to something "fundamental" like sales.

Such attitudes on the part of top management have a double-barreled impact on the Washington rep. His job becomes less important than it might otherwise be, for he must go along with the boss and limit himself to short-range, highly practical objectives. Beyond that he often finds he's cut off from the decision-making process. He is not an ambassador pleni-potentiary to the seat of government, but only a specialized minister with no policy-recommending function, useful primarily as a bridge between government and company specialists.

Of the companies that take their roles in Washington more seriously, Texaco and Lockheed are prime examples. Their local representatives have a part in shaping the decisions of top management. Texaco's Washington man, Executive Vice President James H. Pipkin, is a regular participant in the weekly management meetings of the corporation's top twenty-two executives. As for Lockheed, its principal problem as the nation's No. 1 government contractor ($1.7 billion worth of orders were on the books at the end of the last fiscal year) has been to coordinate the marketing activities of its several divisions in a way that will serve the interests of the corporation as a whole. Some divisions have had to be held back lest they queer the chances of another; others are encouraged to push as hard as they're able. Lockheed's vice president in Washington, Vern Johnson, has been given responsibility for recommending changes in the direction or scope of divisional activity. The recommendations have to be handled with tact, for they may cut across the natural interest of a divisional president in getting all the business he can. But this partial transplantation of power from California to Washington has maximized the company's over-all effectiveness with the government.

There are signs that other corporations are changing their attitudes toward Washington representation. William E. MacKay, vice president and general counsel of National Biscuit Co., recently took to the rostrum in an effort to get more corporations interested in government affairs. "I am convinced," he told the Associated Industries of New York State, "that the emergence of the profession of the 'business legislative diplomat' within the business community, as opposed to the lobbyist, constitutes one of the most important developments on the American political horizon. . . . The dollars-and-cents benefits from a government-relations program can be just as great as those flowing from any effective cost-cutting program and it is high time that more and more companies realize that government decisions play a dominant role in establishing the cost structure of an industry. . . . We [i.e., National Biscuit] will not hesitate to take a position on controversial issues, and we will defend this position in a manner consistent with the public interest."

Plainly the prospects are strong for expanded business representation in Washington by companies already there, and for an influx of newcomers too. The prospects would appear to be equally good for an expansion of the role of the Washington rep. Not that vice presidents won't come winging in to take over on occasion, or that high-powered Washington law firms won't be sought out for their advice in tough situations. Government, after all, is too complex and too important for top management not to enlist all the help available. But for this very reason the Washington rep is certain to come into his own, recognized as a strong new element of management.

Industry Still Has Something to Learn About Congress

Jeremy Main

For Senator Philip Hart, the gentlemanly Democrat from Michigan, it started at the breakfast table. The Harts and their eight children all like to eat Nabisco Shredded Wheat in the morning. But in 1961 they discovered that the old, familiar box had changed; it had become taller and narrower. Inside, there were still twelve biscuits, each apparently the same size as before. But a close reading of the new label indicated that here, too, something curious had happened. The net weight of the contents had been reduced from twelve ounces to ten and one-quarter. The Harts concluded that they were paying the same price for less cereal and more package.

The Harts didn't stop buying shredded wheat, but the incident helped convince the Senator that the shopper in an American supermarket doesn't always get what the package makes him think he is getting. Thereupon Hart set off on a minor crusade that ended last fall, after five years of

"Industry Still Has Something to Learn About Congress," *Fortune,* February 1967. Reprinted by permission of the publisher.

lobbying and legislating, with the passage of the Fair Packaging and Labeling Act, commonly called the "truth-in-packaging" law.

The law that finally emerged from Congress will not seriously disrupt
industry. Many of its provisions are actually already contained in a series
of food and drug laws enacted since the beginning of the century. But
industry is concerned, for, as the National Association of Manufacturers
Report puts it, the law "gives the consumerists the start they need." Hart
himself has stated, not entirely accurately, that "this is the first time Congress legislated to protect the economic—rather than the health or safety
—interests of the consumer."

One alarmed food maker claims "consumerism is rampant." And there
is evidence to support his statement. There have been three presidential
messages on consumer interests in the last five years and, in 1964, President Johnson appointed Mrs. Esther Peterson, a persuasive lady of attractive Scandinavian wholesomeness, the nation's first Special Assistant to
the President for Consumer Affairs. The Senate Commerce Committee
has a new subcommittee on consumer affairs, which will doubtless produce new consumer laws. A "truth-in-lending" bill is already before Congress. Another bill regulating warranties and guarantees on consumer
goods is a possibility. And the N.A.M. is warning its members to watch
out for still other forms of consumer legislation that will affect manufacturers.

Relations between the consumer-products industry and the government
are plainly entering a new phase. And the lobbying against the Hart bill—
at first petulant and clumsy, later more skillful and to the point, but never
really well organized—showed how much industry has to learn about the
delicate art of dealing with Congress. The old kind of lobbying that gave
the trade such a bad name never appeared during the truth-in-packaging
battle. "There was no hanky-panky, no slush funds, no political contributions," claims one of the lobbyists, and there's no evidence to the contrary
in Congress. But the companies concerned were surprisingly backward in
the more sophisticated kind of lobbying: presenting sound arguments attuned to political reality in all the right places.

"TOO BUSY OR TOO TIRED OR TOO HARASSED"

Industry's strategic mistake in battling truth in packaging was to adopt
an attitude of intransigent opposition. The companies concerned denied
any need for the bill, challenged the right of the federal government to
interfere, and attempted to kill the legislation. They thereby lost a number
of opportunities to come to terms with Congress on an early compromise.
Five years of lengthy public hearings gave consumerists a public forum
for publicizing their cause and complaints. If "consumerism" really is
"rampant," then the companies that stock the nation's supermarkets helped
make it that way.

The long series of hearings held before Senate and House committees
between 1961 and 1966 offered plenty of evidence that food and soap
companies were, at times, guilty of deceptive packaging. Proponents of
the bill exhibited "giant economy size" cans of coffee selling for more per
ounce than the smaller jars; complained of "packaging to price" (reducing

the contents of a package without reducing the price or package size); described "cents-off" sales that went on for years and, in fact, did not always represent a saving; and criticized the confusing proliferation of odd-sized packages of the same product. (Potato chips were being sold in seventy-one different-sized bags, boxes, and cans.) One Senate witness, magazine writer and critic Marya Mannes, summed up the frustrations of many consumers when she said, "Most of us are simply too busy or too tired or too harassed to take a computer, a slide rule, and an M.I.T. graduate to market and figure out what we're buying."

The companies concerned did a poor job of meeting such complaints. In most cases they talked in generalities and argued that the bill was an attack on free enterprise. The market, said industry witnesses, was self-policing: the housewife is smart enough not to buy a deceptively labeled item twice. But evidence disproved this. The industry also claimed that existing laws and regulations were adequate to deal with deception. The bill's supporters didn't agree. Moreover, the critics were no longer satisfied with case-by-case action against deception by the Federal Trade Commission and the Food and Drug Administration, which is what the existing laws allowed. They wanted the government to set standards for packaging and labeling so the housewife would know exactly what she was buying.

PRESSURING THE PRESS

At times, industry witnesses were inept as well as vague. D. Beryl Manischewitz, chairman of the N.A.M.'s marketing committee, rose to a high cumulus of nonsense when he tried to explain the need for fancy containers. "These examples of individual taste are difficult to explain," he said. "But no more difficult than why more than half a million persons gathered in the city of Washington recently to view the four-hundred-year-old masterpiece portrait, *Mona Lisa*. Those who cannot understand this will not be able to understand why millions of American women find an urn-shaped container of toiletry with a golden stopper more appealing than a standard jug or bottle."

Senators were bored with the industry's witnesses. In fact, they were bored with the bill. During the five years that it dawdled in the Senate, only Hart himself and Oregon's Senator Maurine Neuberger consistently supported the bill. Industry, in turn, was offended by the Senate's lack of interest and apparent lack of understanding. Top executives were insulted when they traveled across the country and found themselves testifying before only one or two Senators (which is quite normal to those who know the Senate). Senators were put off by industry's refusal to consider any alternative to killing the bill. Lobbyists were disappointed when they found it difficult to see Senators (which is also normal) and then found it even harder to get them interested in the bill. "These were among the least constructive hearings in my experience," said one Senate staffer.

With the Senate unreceptive, industry turned to the press, a perfectly legitimate maneuver, but in this case badly handled. In 1962, Paul Willis, president of the Grocery Manufacturers of America, boasted in a speech to a television-industry group how he had enlisted the help of national magazines. "We suggested to the publishers that the day was here when their editorial department and business department might better understand their interdependency relationships as they affect the operating results of their company. . . . We invited them to consider publishing some favorable articles about the food industry instead of only singling out isolated cases of criticism." He pointed out that G.M.A.'s members were spending $1.2 billion on advertising that year and said threateningly, "We are not aware of any great amount of cooperation that television extended to us."

Willis' remarks set off protests in Congress and the press that delighted supporters of the Hart bill, but the speech apparently had some effect. Hart complained later that several TV appearances he had scheduled were canceled; he says, "I was told off the record that advertisers had objected." It isn't likely, however, that this crude pressure won the grocery manufacturers any close friends.

In any case, industry did not seem to have much to worry about until the beginning of 1965. The bill was blocked in the Senate Judiciary Committee. Although Esther Peterson had been traveling around the country arousing consumers, the Administration, which had never offered any truth-in-packaging bill of its own, gave the Hart bill only tepid support. But then Hart got his bill transferred to the more sympathetic Senate Commerce Committee. At first its chairman, Washington's Senator Warren Magnuson, was not convinced that there was enough support in Congress or the White House to carry the bill. However, in early 1966, President Johnson, having got approval for his priority Great Society legislation, turned to consumerism as a cause—because, say the cynics, he needed a new victory that wouldn't add to the budget. The President told Magnuson that he wanted the Hart law. In a message on consumer interests last March, the President asked Congress to pass a truth-in-packaging law because "there are instances of deception in labeling. Practices have arisen that cause confusion and conceal information even when there is no deliberate intention to deceive. The housewife often needs a scale, a yardstick, and a slide rule to make a rational choice."

By now it was clear that much of the bill was acceptable to a majority in the Senate committee. The acceptable parts included a ban on meaningless adjectives attached to statements of the quantity of contents such as "giant quart," the establishment of standards for the prominent statement of net quantity on packages, and a requirement that net weights in packages under four pounds be expressed either completely in ounces or in whole pounds.

However, a majority of Magnuson's committee—and all of the industry —were firmly opposed to a section of the bill giving the government the right to standardize package sizes and prohibit odd shapes. Opponents of the bill contended, with some reason, that setting such standards would put an end to competitive, attractive packaging; this section, they said, had to be amended if they were to vote the bill out of committee.

After beating off Republican attempts to strike the standardization section, Magnuson and Hart worked out a compromise that provided for a complicated way of establishing standards with industry participation. Basically, the government could still establish package size standards, but only after allowing industry eighteen months to formulate voluntary standards. This compromise concluded an unusually long series of executive sessions (thirteen in all) and won over the doubtful members of the committee. The bill was reported out of committee fourteen to three last May. After another unsuccessful Republican attempt on the floor to extract the standardization section, the Senate passed the bill seventy-two to nine.

The bill was weaker than Hart had intended it to be. But industry could take little credit for the change. Lobbyists did manage to get specific product exemptions written into the law's provisions. However, they had refused offers by Hart and others to discuss compromises on the main parts of the bill. Senate sources say that before the bill picked up political steam in the Senate industry could have negotiated half of it away. Instead, the industry stuck to its determination to kill the bill outright in fear that if any of its representatives helped draft a truth-in-packaging law, they would be maneuvered into supporting it. As a result, the major surgery on the legislation was performed by the Senators with little industry guidance. And it was performed not to adjust the law to industry arguments, but as a maneuver to win the support of doubters in the Senate.

Industry continued intransigent until the end. However, by the time the House Interstate and Foreign Commerce Committee opened its hearings on truth in packaging last July, the lobbyists were far better organized than they had been in the early years of the battle.

Back in 1963, an *ad hoc* committee of some fifty companies and trade associations had been formed in Washington to oppose Hart's bill. The committee limited itself to arousing industry opposition and made no effort to direct lobbying. In early 1966, however, the most active members of the group formed an executive committee, consisting principally of representatives of Proctor & Gamble, National Biscuit, the National Canners Association, the N.A.M., General Foods, the Soap and Detergent Association, Colgate-Palmolive, and Kellogg. The "excom" began coordinating lobbying chores so all of the key people on Capitol Hill would be plied with arguments.

The "excom" had a forceful ally: forty-year-old George Koch, the Sears, Roebuck representative in Washington, who had become president of the Grocery Manufacturers of America. Koch, who knows how to get people to listen to him on Capitol Hill, is credited with being the most effective industry lobbyist in the truth-in-packaging battle. "Who did I see?" Koch says. "Every living soul I could. It was important to get the facts across and important to do it person to person."

A GOOD IDEA BACKFIRES

Koch also helped to organize "district teams" of businessmen in the constituencies of the members of the House committee. The idea that Congressmen would be more likely to listen to businessmen in their own districts than to lobbyists in Washington was a sound one. In practice, it was only a partial success. The lobbyists discovered that it is difficult to arouse local businessmen except with an issue that hits the current year's balance sheet. Congressmen were contacted at home only on a haphazard and occasional basis.

One local effort backfired when the Staten Island Chamber of Commerce passed out leaflets to ferryboat commuters asking them to tell their Congressman, Democrat John Murphy, that they were against the bill. Murphy got a lot of mail on truth in packaging—as much, he says, as on the war in Vietnam—but it ran two to one in favor of the bill. To the chamber's chagrin, many of the letters were written on the back of its leaflets.

For the House hearings the industry selected its witnesses more skillfully than it had during the Senate hearings. The executives who testified had more facts and, especially on the question of standardization of packages, they had better arguments. Arthur Larkin, executive vice president of General Foods, for example, explained why his company's thirteen regular cake mixes come in different and odd sizes. The mixes have different densities. But the housewife can take any one of them, add two eggs, and produce a cake of a standard size. "If we were bound by a standard requiring all cake mixes to have the same net weight, conceivably the recipe might call for 1¾ eggs," Larkin said. "Poor a cook as I am, I know that might be difficult to accomplish in the kitchen." With such arguments presented to attentive and probing Congressmen, and with lukewarm testimony from government witnesses, several of the House committee members became uneasy about the bill.

At this point the bill's fate was focused by circumstances on a freshman Congressman from Ohio, John Gilligan, forty-five. Gilligan was a member of the committee; he represented Cincinnati, headquarters for one of the biggest lobbyists against the bill, Proctor & Gamble; and he was engaged in a difficult campaign for re-election (which he eventually lost).

As a liberal Democrat, Gilligan was expected to support the Hart bill down the line. But he and four other Democrats on the thirty-three-man committee were not convinced by the government witnesses, and became the key swing group. Gilligan decided the government had not made a good case for being given sweeping authority to standardize packages.

A VISIT AT HOME

Before the hearings began, a delegation of about eight local businessmen had called on Gilligan during one of his visits to Cincinnati. "They didn't know much about the legislation," says Gilligan, "but they knew what they were afraid of. When local people come to see you, you tend to give them more attention than you do the professional in Washington." Then, just before Proctor & Gamble was scheduled to testify, P. & G. Chairman Neil McElroy and Gilligan spent an hour chatting about the bill at McElroy's invitation. McElroy said he did not want a bill, but if there had to be one he felt something had to be done about the standardization section. Despite the "district team" idea, the two meetings were the only efforts to influence Gilligan in Cincinnati. But, in Washington, Gilligan—and the other swing men—were approached time and again by industry lobbyists as well as supporters of the bill, especially labor representatives.

When the hearings ended and the committee went into executive sessions, the problem facing Chairman Harley Staggers of West Virginia was similar to the one faced by Magnuson and Hart in the Senate: a majority of the committee would oppose the bill unless the standardization section was weakened even more than it had been in the Senate.

By this time Gilligan had decided that a compromise was possible if standardization were made purely voluntary. While campaigning at home one weekend in mid-September, he got a call from Wilbur Cohen, Under Secretary of Health, Education and Welfare. Cohen asked Gilligan why he couldn't support the bill. Gilligan explained his doubts about standardization and proposed his compromise. Cohen talked to the other swing men, to the White House, and to the Commerce Department. Before the weekend was over, he called Gilligan back to tell him the Administration would back a compromise.

With the Administration and the swing men behind it, an amended bill was easily reported out of committee on September 22. Eleven days later, it passed the House by a vote of 300 to eight. That close to Election Day, only the most adamant opponents were willing to vote against a bill with the built-in voter appeal of "truth in packaging."

"CONSUMERISM" WON'T GO AWAY

Hart claims that 90 per cent of his original bill is contained in the final act. Other "consumerists" say it was eviscerated when standardization of package sizes was made purely voluntary. Certainly industry was delighted to see this happen. The act says that when the Secretary of Commerce determines "there is undue proliferation of weights, measures, or quantities" that "impairs the reasonable ability of consumers to make value comparisons," then he can ask industry to develop voluntary standards. If industry fails to do so within a year, he can ask Congress for further legislation.

The rest of the act contains much of what Hart wanted—and much that the industry didn't want. The contents of a package, if it is less than four pounds or one gallon, must be stated in total ounces as well as pounds or quarts. Contents must be printed on the main display panel, in a color that contrasts with the background and in type sizes to be established by government agencies. When the number of servings is given, their size must be given. Exaggerations, such as "giant quart," are prohibited. Government can control "nonfunctional slack fill" and "cents-off" sales.

The law is one that industry can live with. It requires no more than changes in most labels, which are frequently revised in any case. But since much depends on future regulations and since Congress has invited future amendments, the battle over truth in packaging is not necessarily finished. Moreover, Congress will be considering other such laws.

In this time of "consumerism," the experience with truth in packaging offers some simple, important lessons: straight, factual testimony is more effective than oratory; the most telling lobbying begins at home, but an astute Washington representative is also a great asset to a company; cooperation among the companies concerned can be useful even if it is difficult and perhaps undesirable to present a united front that looks like a superlobby; legitimate complaints against industry cannot be shrugged off as attacks on free enterprise.

Most of all, the consumer-goods industry is going to have to face up to the fact that "consumerism" has become politically popular. As industry learned when it tried to kill truth in packaging, "consumerism" cannot be killed. It is part of the Democrats' legislative program; it is strongly supported by organized labor and other groups; and consumers themselves have become more aggressive and articulate.

Truth in packaging was signed into law by President Johnson last November. At the ceremony he handed out several hundred pens. With each was a statement that said, in part: "One of the pens used by the President in signing S. 985, An Act to regulate interstate and foreign commerce by preventing the use of unfair or deceptive methods of packaging and labeling." In fact, only a dozen or so of the pens had been used. It was a clear case of deceptive labeling.

The University Lobbyists

Mark Levy

In the past three years a new kind of lobbyist has appeared in Washington—the agent of a college or university. About a dozen such university lobbyists are working in the capital now, representing institutions as diverse as the vast University of California and tiny Elmira College in upstate New York. They all seek Federal money for education and research, a prize that is expected to total about $5 billion by next year.

Until recently the universities relied on a combination of institutional prestige, informal contacts, and administrators' shuttle flights to Washington to get Federal funds. The attitude of the big universities was best expressed by a spokesman for Harvard who said that it "does not have a full-time representative in Washington for grant procurement and Federal liaison work, nor have we ever considered nor are we considering a Washington office for such work."

Even now, of the top ten institutions receiving grants, only the University of California has a full-time man in Washington. But as the number and complexity of Federal programs has increased, so has the number of university lobbyists.

Some universities have found that a Washington lawyer alumnus can supply the required services. For example, Douglas Whitlock, a partner in Whitlock, Markey & Tait, whose clients include Firestone Tire & Rubber and the Automatic Canteen Company of America, acts as a representative of his alma mater, Indiana, in Washington. Sometimes faculty members studying the national government or "interning" with public officials develop useful knowledge and contacts. Others come to this new profession with a variety of backgrounds. James C. Messersmith, who represents the College Center of the Finger Lakes of New York (an association of six small colleges in upstate New York), once worked for the Office of Education. Mark Ferber of the University of California holds a Ph.D. in political science and was a professor at Rutgers. Rowan A. Wakefield of the State University of New York served in State Department and AID education programs. Most have spent time on the campus as faculty members or as administrators.

The university lobbyist reports on his Washington activities to a university bureaucrat. That official, sometimes called Vice-President for Research and Advanced Studies, Vice-President for Educational Development, or Vice-President for Research Administration, is the campus co-ordinator of Federal funds. Research proposals and grant applications filter through the academic and administrative hierarchies to his office. There the routine paper work is handled. Rarely is the university lobbyist involved directly in processing those papers.

Instead the lobbyist's function on the campus is to inform the researchers and administrators about the latest Federal programs and regulations. "My job is largely one of keeping tabs on the Federal scene and making sure my people at the university know what is going on," one university agent said. But because some fifty agencies and major administrative subdivisions dispense funds for education and research, knowing what is going on is a full-time job. Often the university agent seeks friendships and informal working relations with the men who administer the funds.

One lobbyist tells how a friendship with a high civil servant led to a rich contract. "I knew that he was drawing up guidelines for the proposals, and I also knew that his agency was in a hurry to get the project under way. The guy and I had worked together before. I was able to discuss the guidelines with him before they were published, and because we were first with the proposal, we got the contract."

But for the most part, the university lobbyists are reluctant to discuss such intimate techniques of their trade. Few will disclose the exact amounts that their efforts yield in Federal dollars for their universities. Even California's Ferber, representative of an institution that receives more than $300 million annually in Federal funds, tries to play down his role as a money broker. "I don't think any one man can take complete credit for any single grant," he said. But when pressed to reveal his accomplishments for California, Ferber conceded that a recent grant of $6.9 million for a building program for California's eight undergraduate schools was the result of his "understanding the way the Federal program worked and putting the right people in touch with each other."

Not all of the university lobbyist's time is spent seeking or administering Federal funds. Sometimes he must carry out delicate negotiations involving controversial public policies. Recently, Mark Ferber raised a complaint of several University of California faculty scientists that is having repercussions at the highest levels of the State Department. The scientists at the university's San Diego campus had invited a group of their Eastern European colleagues to visit in order to discuss common research problems. But because of the large naval installations nearby, the government refused the foreign scientists permission to travel to San Diego. Ferber discussed California's problem with the National Academy of Science, which has long been concerned with the problem of travel restrictions. As a result, the Academy informally brought the matter to the attention of the office of State Department Under Secretary George Ball. There are indications that some loosening of such restrictions is imminent.

MAKING SURE THEY KNOW

Sometimes a representative of a university must spend much time explaining the very existence of his school. Rowan Wakefield of the State University of New York said, "I have a very difficult time convincing people that we are not the City University of New York and not even New York University." Institutional identity is important for SUNY because its more than eleven thousand teachers and administrators desire a share of Federal research and training funds. It is not enough for it to buy a ready-made reputation by hiring, say, Nobel Prize physicist C. N. Yang. The people in Washington who put together research advisory panels and award one-of-a-kind research contracts must know about the school. Part of Wakefield's job is to make sure that they do know.

Sometimes the man in Washington may ask for help from the campus. For example, recently Health, Education and Welfare changed the language in its standard research contract to provide for pre-publication "clearance" of research reports financed by the agency. The changed contract was noticed by several university lobbyists, and high-ranking administrators of four schools affected were rushed to Washington to object to the department's attempted censorship. After a meeting between the university officials and Francis Keppel, then Commissioner of Education, the clearance requirement was dropped. That meeting had been arranged, of course, by the university lobbyists.

Most university lobbyists prefer not to call themselves by that name. None of those interviewed by this writer were registered under the Federal Regulation of Lobbying Act of 1946 and not one knew of any other university representative who might be. The 1946 act in effect requires registration and reporting of lobbying activities by individuals or groups who raise money for the principal purpose of influencing legislation. As one said, "We spend most of our time working with the Executive branch of government, not in trying to influence legislation." So far there is no evidence that the Justice Department would disagree.

But in fact university lobbyists do spend some time with and presumably do attempt to influence members of Congress. Legislators in Washington take great pride in announcing contracts awarded in their home districts, and there are strong political pressures to distribute existing funds more widely. Midwestern colleges, backed by state political leaders, are now making a concerted drive to get more of the Federal dollar. It is no accident that three of the final six sites now under consideration for the multi-million-dollar bevatron atom smasher are in the Midwest. Few Congressmen, however, have the time or the staff to go after the grants. The university lobbyist can provide the Congressman with expert knowledge, not only of what is needed but of the grant-getting machinery that will do the job.

By aiding Congressmen, the university lobbyist builds up political credits that can be cashed in later for legislative favors. For instance, Representative John V. Tunney, whose district includes the Riverside campus of the University of California, was asked recently to sponsor a bill to exempt a costly piece of scientific equipment, purchased by the school in Japan, from the twelve per cent import duty. Tunney has introduced the bill and if it is approved, his law will save the university nearly $10,000. (Such private bills may soon be unnecessary; Congress is considering legislation that would make the importation of all such educational and cultural materials duty-free.)

Certainly the most important legislative favor an education lobbyist can ask is a vote in support of higher education. But here the role of the individual university representative is limited. As one lobbyist said, "I think we can help our friends and reinforce their convictions, but its just about impossible to change the minds of our enemies."

And even though the university lobbyist can solicit votes from some members of the home-state Congressional delegation, he is in no position to influence all of Congress. Instead, groups such as the American Council on Education, a federation of education associations and universities, attempt to present a united higher-education front to the entire Congress. As John Morse, Federal liaison man for ACE, said, "I cannot imagine that an individual school would make a pitch directly to Congress without clearing it first with us."

Another limit on the value of accumulated political credits is self-imposed by the lobbyists, for many are reluctant to ask a Congressman to put pressure on the bureaucrats. Routine Congressional letters of inquiry asking about the status of a project carry little weight, and the bureaucrat may be annoyed by the "unprofessionalism" of such an inquiry from a non-academic source. One respected lobbyist said, "I've been in Washington long enough to know not to ask a Congressman to put the screws on. If he did, I might never be able to work informally with the agency again."

Depending upon how you want to cut the pie, you get different estimates of how much money is tagged for higher education and research. For fiscal 1965, the Office of Education reports that a total of $3.7 billion in Federal funds went to the support of higher education. Included in that figure are $1.2 billion in research and development funds from agencies such as the National Institutes of Health, the Atomic Energy Commission, and the National Science Foundation; $712 million for student loans and scholarships; $1.2 billion for construction of new buildings and equipment; $427 million for Federal schools and employee training; $101 million for institutional grants; and $28 million for veterans' education. In fiscal 1967 there will be even more for the university lobbyist to seek. President Johnson's budget calls for $10.2 billion for all education programs, and it is estimated that $4.7 billion of that sum will go to higher education. This does not include Federal funds for university-managed research centers such as the University of California's Los Alamos Scientific Laboratory. These funds are expected to amount to some $600 million in 1967.

Now that the war on poverty is an accepted part of American life, the Office of Economic Opportunity is a sizable source of funds. For example, two universities, Oregon and Northern Michigan College, are principal contractors for Job Corps centers, and six other colleges and universities are subcontractors. This summer more than two hundred universities and preparatory schools are receiving more than $20 million to run "Upward Bound" programs to prepare high-school-age students for college admission.

In the midst of all this bounty, some university lobbyists privately express concern that poverty funds will bring a new insecurity into academic life. They fear pressures from poverty officials who want the universities to take on more projects.

At a recent conference to discuss university training of Community Action workers, the participating universities were exhorted by the government officials to increase the universities' role in the social experiment. One university lobbyist who was present said later, "They wanted us to drop all our other research and enlist completely in their war on poverty."

Poverty programs and Federally sponsored activities generally put a severe strain on scarce university resources. As Clark Kerr, president of the University of California, said in *The Uses of the University*, "[Federal funds] in turn commit some of the university's own funds; they influence the assignment of space; they determine the distribution of time between teaching and research; to a large extent they establish the areas in which the university grows the fastest. Almost imperceptibly, a university is changed." Unfortunately, the universities themselves are often blind to these dangers as they rush to share the available billions.

THE AGENTS

In addition to the lobbyists, at least five privately published education newsletters and a score sponsored by associations attempt to fill the universities' hunger for information about sources of Federal dollars. The *College and University Reporter*, published by Commerce Clearing House, a tax-law information service, is generally considered to be the most authoritative. Another newsletter, edited by a former wire-service correspondent named Dallas Halverstadt, offers to keep the subscriber attuned to "the thinking of those who make policies and laws and administer the federal government."

One unusual organization, Bell Educational Services, Inc., acts as an agent for about twenty colleges and universities. Founded by Marjorie Bell, a former Senior Counselor for Women's Affairs at Indiana University, Bell Educational Services is a team of twelve Federal education-aid experts. The Staff, a self-styled "group of academic idealists," work on an annual retainer fee equal "to about what the university would pay a top-notch research administrator." One education lobbyist, commenting on the retainer fee, said, "But they're in education for a profit!" Marjorie Bell's only reply is, "We are doing a good job for our schools. Why should a small profit disqualify us?"

A former Bell associate, Ida Wallace, has recently been appointed to head the office of the Associated Colleges of the Midwest, a group of ten small schools, including Grinnell of Iowa and Carleton of Minnesota. It was formed after their presidents, meeting to discuss football schedules, found that they shared problems of fund raising.

According to Ida Wallace, Associated Colleges is not looking for massive Federal projects. Instead the schools want funds that will allow them to continue and supplement several small projects of their own. For example, student teachers in the co-operating schools may now elect to do their practice teaching in Chicago, spending half of the semester in a middle-class school and the other half in a slum school. With that training, the student teachers prepare for teaching in an urban setting. Through Federal funds for this and other projects, Associated Colleges hopes to have the best of two worlds—good small-college education and the helping hand of Uncle Sam.

If the planned increase in Federal spending is approved, more and more universities will seek to get a cut of those funds. If, on the other hand, there is a forced cutback in education and research spending, universities will turn to lobbyists to get a share. Either way, there may well be a struggle between academic institutions—a struggle in which their lobbyists are the combatants and Federal funds are the prize. And, either way, an increase in university lobbyists seems inevitable.

Corps of Engineers: The Pork-barrel Soldiers

Robert G. Sherrill

Three brave and perhaps quixotic Senators will attempt in this session of Congress to disrupt the oldest established permanent floating boondoggle in American politics—that carried on between a number of their fellow legislators and the Army Corps of Engineers. Senators Frank Moss of Utah, Lee Metcalf of Montana and Joseph Clark of Pennsylvania will push a bill that would turn the Department of the Interior into a Department of Natural Resources, with the new cabinet office absorbing several scattered agencies and bureaus including the civil engineering dictatorship of the Corps.

Just another bill in a bill-laden Congress would have no significance, but this one is said to enjoy the support of Interior Secretary Stewart Udall, a man who is not unwelcome around the White House; and the rearrangement would be in keeping with the President's apparent desire to regroup cabinet responsibilities.

This isn't the first time a Department of Natural Resources has been proposed, nor is it the first time an effort has been made to cut the mighty Corps down to proper size. The Hoover Commission tried to do it thirteen years ago but, after scaring the pants off the Corps and its allies, it ultimately lost. Moss and colleagues may lose, too, but they've already got a good scare going. Braxton B. Carr, president of the American Waterways Operators, the largest and most influential organization of tugboat, towboat and barge owners, recently sent out an agony memo to his 225 member companies warning that "the future of navigation in the United States will be dim indeed if the Corps of Engineers loses its responsibility for

"The Pork-barrel Soldiers," *The Nation*, February 14, 1966. Reprinted by permission of the publisher.

civil works to a catchall Department of Natural Resources." Carr reported that while Udall would be working behind the scenes to shackle the Corps, Secretary of Defense Robert McNamara is not expected to help the engineers, with the result that "the Corps' hands will be effectively tied." He urged members to "get into the fight."

If, as Carr predicts, the Corps' hands are tied, it will be the first time. When this recommendation was previously before Congress, ex-President Hoover complained that the corridors of the Capitol were thick with engineering generals and colonels, lobbying like mad against the proposal.

Moss has carefully couched his appeal for reorganization in the phrases of efficiency, and there is certainly that to consider. Responsibility for the development of water resources is presently scattered among at least forty bureaus, departments and agencies of the government. Four cabinet offices share control at the top. Within the Interior Department alone, ten agencies meddle with the water. Federal land management is almost as splintered, and there is no unity of power development. Moss would also gather such control groups as the Forest Service (now in the Department of Agriculture), the Federal Power Commission and the Tennessee Valley Authority into the new department. They are not expected to go willingly.

The real fight will develop over the jurisdiction of the Corps of Engineers. Why should that venerable fraternity of specialists—which West Point was specifically established to perpetuate—be deprived of its civil functions? Because, some say, it has in recent decades become merely a political arm of Congress. One Texas Congressman, complaining about the public's suspicious nature, said recently: "You never heard of an Army Engineer program yet that has not been criticized as pork barrel." If the Department of Interior has not been entirely free of favoritism and the taint of pork, its reputation is still better in that regard than the Corps'.

The boondoggle routine is perfectly balanced. The Corps justifies the projects, and Congress appropriates the money. On the one hand the Corps gets bigger and more influential—two conditions dearly prized by generals—and on the other hand public-works money is doled out to civilian contractors "back home" with Congress getting credit for spreading the happiness. And the largess is booming. During its 150-year life the Corps-Congress cornucopia has put, or is now putting, $22 billion into the contractors' pockets; another $35 billion is programed for the next fifteen years.

Everyone gets fatter all the time, and with no fuss and usually little debate. No special hearing was held in the Senate, for example, on the St. John River hydroelectric project in Maine, although it is expected to cost at least $300 million. Most of the nation's greatly needed flood-control dams have been built by the Corps and most of the navigable streams and harbors have been shaped and improved by the Corps. It has 222 flood-control dams, 603 local-protection levees, and 19,000 miles of improved inland waterways to its credit, and many of these are worth while. But others are merely worth boodle, and now that the Corps appears to be running out of ready sites for dams and dredgings, it seeks desperately to maintain its powerful position with Congress by sponsoring some projects that verge on the scatterbrained.

It has pushed through dam projects on the west fork of a river when it was the east fork that presented the flood problem. It has scooped out harbors to give better access for tankers carrying fuel to utility plants that are converting to natural gas. It has proposed recreational reservoirs on rivers too polluted to support fish life. It has built dams to protect less farm acreage than is flooded by the resulting reservoir.

Fearing that some day it may run out of projects, the Corps authorizes far more than it can handle. Some untouched backlog projects are fifteen years old, and the longer they lie on the shelf, the more ridiculous becomes the original price tag attached to them. Sometimes, such is its haste to get business, the Corps just plain goofs in its estimates. On several projects in the Southeast, actual costs ran 257 per cent higher than the estimates. Even Louisiana Sen. Allen Ellender, who appears to think that money grows on hatracks, was heard to whimper when the cost of one project went up 600 per cent in a year. Discrepancies of 200 and 300 per cent between original estimates and final costs are not uncommon.

Obedient to Congressional whim, the Corps justifies building longer and longer waterways into the bald spots of America. It approved the notorious 516-mile channel connecting Tulsa with the Mississippi—a $1.2 billion project which inspired the observation from economist Cecil Haver that, considering the cost of maintenance, the nation would be better off if it abstained from using the canal after it was built.

Now the Corps is ready, and Congress seems more than willing, to build a canal from the Gulf to connect with the Trinity River at Fort Worth and Dallas. This Trinity River project has been proposed, off and on, for a generation, but it used to be considered a joke. Will Rogers is usually given credit for being the first to suggest that the best thing they could do with the Trinity was to pave it—an allusion to the fact that in the Fort Worth-Dallas area the Trinity is often a reluctant trickle, shallow enough to wade across. The cost of this project will be such that one critical Congressman allowed as how it would be cheaper to move Fort Worth to the Gulf. Nevertheless, such projects emanating from Texas are no longer a joking matter; San Antonio now seriously proposes that it have its own canal to the Gulf—125 miles as the crow flies. Give the Corps enough time to study the matter, and it is sure to come up with a positive response to San Antonio's dream ditch. The Corps is famous for rationalizing fantastic proposals.

The idea of building a canal from Lake Erie to Pittsburgh has been kicking around since the old canal days of the last century. Although it was revived again in the 1930s, nothing ever came of it because, except for the fact that the canal might readjust the commercial traffic pattern to benefit Youngstown, Ohio, other possible gains were hard to envisage. However, Rep. Mike Kirwan of Youngstown is fond of this project, and the Corps is expected eventually to come up with a study that justifies digging. Kirwan is a big man in water-resources development.

The Water Valley Dam on Eleven Point River down in Arkansas is another good illustration of the Corps' research bounce. Just about everybody but the Corps and a group of influential Arkansas politicians has agreed that putting a dam on Eleven Point River is a poor idea. The state of

Missouri, the Interior Department, the Bureau of Fish and Wildlife, the U.S. Forestry Service, many conservation organizations—all oppose it. The Corps gamely started out with the argument that the dam was needed for, of course, flood control. But inasmuch as the last serious flood on that river occurred in 1915, nobody took that seriously. Next, the Corps proposed to build the dam for power development, but could find nobody who wanted to buy the power. Then it tried to sell the idea of a dam to impound a "recreational" lake—although there are seven other man-made lakes in the area and fourteen in the state, and although to build this superfluous dead-water reservoir they would have to destroy one of the last free-flowing rivers in the Ozarks. The lake would ruin $28 million worth of farmland and businesses, and force 500 families to move.

Last April the Corps which, when left alone is not always unreasonable, agreed that the idea for a dam should be scrapped. But Arkansas Congressmen howled in protest and demanded a new study. So the Corps took another look and said, well, the dam might be a good idea after all.

Then there is the Cape Fear River development in North Carolina. Thirty-two years ago the Corps made a study and reported that flood control is not justified in the lower Cape Fear basin. Nineteen years ago, after that area's worst flood of modern times, it again studied the situation and again could not justify a dam. But today the Corps—with a joyous background chorus of most Congressmen from North Carolina—says flood control is essential. The Corps' estimate of potential flood damage is about 40 per cent higher than the estimate of the Soil Conservation Service. Even if flood control isn't needed, says the Corps, see the fine recreational reservoir we shall make for the people of North Carolina!

Into this reservoir will feed the Haw River, the most polluted stream in North Carolina, and the New Hope River, which the National Park Service says carries moderate to severe pollution. One knowledgeable critic forecasts the result to be an expenditure of $72 million to create a "gigantic cesspool for raw sewage from towns and cities and for discharged chemicals from industrial plants" upstream. To achieve this, the Corps will drown 35,000 acres, and drive 150 families off farms that have come down to them through seven and eight generations.

A resident of New Hope Valley, which will be at the bottom of the reservoir, appeared before the House Public Works subcommittee to beg Congress to leave them alone. When he was asked, "What is an average price of the land in the valley?," he answered proudly: "I would say that there is much land in the valley that is of such value to the people that it would take as much to buy it as it would to buy the Capitol in Washington." (His neighbors who had come to Washington with him, and who filled the committee chamber, applauded.) "I do not mean to be disrespectful but I mean that many of those are not to be sold. They have been handed down from generation to generation as an asset, something that has been looked forward to." The committee was unmoved.

Back in 1942, Congress revived an old idea of a canal across north Florida as a way to out-fox enemy submarines lurking offshore. Those were desperate days when cost didn't matter, but even under such conditions Congress gulped when the Corps reported that the benefit-cost ratio would be a wretched 0.19—that is, the cost would be more than five times greater than the benefit. Defense officials said to forget it. Taking a second look at the project, they decided that ships going around the tip of Florida would not be nearly the sitting ducks that barges emerging from the canal would be.

And so forget it most of the nation did. But not Florida land speculators, or politicians, or pulpwood and phosphate companies with stuff to barge. They wanted that canal. The Corps eventually obliged with the right benefit-cost ratio, although it did take some time. The year the war ended they squeezed here and squeezed there and managed to come up with a benefit level of 1.05, still not good enough. In 1958, they tried again, and again decided the benefit level wasn't high enough to move.

But five years later, with some superb juggling, the Corps had a respectable figure. It took some doing. Although construction costs had risen nationally 36 per cent since the 1945 estimate, and though the project plan had been expanded, the estimated cost was mysteriously slashed 13.5 per cent. As for the forecast benefits, they now included half a million dollars a year in "land enhancement"—something nobody had thought to consider before. It wasn't pointed out until some time later that the Corps had forgotten to place on the minus side the permanent flooding of the Oklawaha River Valley—a river which *The New York Times* has properly called "one of this country's most beautiful free-flowing streams"—and the disenhancement of the lands that will be covered by the canal.

Raymond W. Stuck, who was for four years chief of the Corps' civil works division but is now retired and can speak frankly, calls it a nice piece of "hocus-pocus." The sleight of hand would probably not have been successful if President Kennedy had not needed the support of Florida Congressmen to liberalize the House Rules Committee. Getting their support, he personally asked that the barge canal be put into the 1963 budget.

The Cross-Florida Barge Canal—which Senator Ellender calls a "little work," costing only $145 million—at least illustrates with what a free hand the Corps is permitted to maneuver. In 1964 the Corps asked for, and got, $200,000 to start Rodman Dam on that canal project. The politicians put on their best suits and trooped out to the site and made speeches and set off some dynamite. Last year, the Corps was back, asking $350,000 for Rodman Dam. To continue work on it? No, to *start* work. Even such great and good friends of the Corps as Ellender and Florida's senior Senator, Spessard Holland, were embarrassed by the fast shuffle. Said Ellender to the Corps' General Welling: "Last year you asked for $200,000 to initiate Rodman Dam. Today you are asking for $350,000 to initiate the Rodman Dam. What happened?" And Holland chimed in: "I went there when they supposedly started that project and you all put on quite a good show of blowing up a lot of soil a year ago. Now you mean to tell me you have not been able to go ahead and award this contract?"

That, said General Welling, was exactly what he meant to tell him: "We applied it to other contracts."

That seemed to end the discussion, because Ellender and Holland do not mean to be critical by such questioning. When Florida's Governor Haydon Burns appeared before the Senate Public Works committee to beg that the government continue with the canal, he complained that some people were writing about it as being a "pork-barrel outrage." Tut tut, soothed Ellender, "we get such blasts as that every now and then. Don't pay any attention to such articles."

And then Ellender made a point that is basic to the leapfrog philosophy by which Congress and the Corps cooperate: that is, spend a little money and then you can argue it would be wasted unless you spend a lot more. Up to now the government has put $5 million into the Cross-Florida Barge Canal, leaving a minimum of $140 million to go. Said Ellender, "We have invested quite a bit of money up to now in that project and once a project of that kind is started—"

GOVERNOR BURNS: "It is no time to stop."

ELLENDER: "That is right. This criticism is just so much chaff."

Chaff or not, it irritates. When Arthur Maas of Harvard wrote his book *Muddy Waters*, criticizing the Corps for highhandedly ignoring the President, Lt. Gen. Lewis A. Pick, then chief of the engineers, explained publicly that Maas was simply "trying to get more centralized power in government" (and you know what *that* means). *Life* magazine's recent editorial, "The Seductive Odor of Pork," suggested that there might be something other than logic behind the proposed canal from Fort Worth-Dallas to the Gulf. Gen. John L. Person (Ret.), executive vice president of the National Rivers and Harbors Congress, flared back that the editorial was "ridiculous . . . superficial, inaccurate and cynical . . . using innuendo and false implications."

Maj. Gen. Jackson Graham, currently director of the Engineers' civil works program, is really showing a thin skin. In two recent speeches he complained of "a downpour of the 'pork barrel' and 'boondoggle' type of criticism" and "the current fad of castigating water-resource engineers and highway engineers and other engineers on this subject of beauty. 'Despoilers' and 'uglifiers' are typical of the epithets. We try to put these brickbats in perspective. . . ."

The Corps and its allies have a way of handling their critics. Chief among these critics is Senator Proxmire of Wisconsin. It may be only accidental, of course, but while every neighboring state is receiving several millions of dollars from last year's rivers-and-harbors budget, Wisconsin will receive nothing. It may be only coincidental, too, that Utah, Moss's home state, is left out of the budget.

Leslie A. Miller, ex-Governor of Wyoming and chairman of the Hoover Commission's task force on natural resources, once gave this appraisal:

> The Corps of Engineers, one of the oldest of government services, has become undoubtedly the most powerful lobbying and pressure group in the government today.
>
> By various grants of authority from Congress, it has extended its power and influence into many fields of civilian services, including the plum-rich areas of river-and-harbor improvements and flood control.
>
> Theoretically, the Corps is responsible to the Secretary of the Army, and through him, to the President. In practice, it has worked out that the engineers deal directly with Congress itself, often arrogantly ignoring, as has been demonstrated in many instances, the expressed wishes of the

Commander-in-Chief. It has become hard to tell now who is the master—Congress or the Corps of Engineers—for, though Congress provides the appropriations for these rich and often wasteful engineering projects, the Corps provides the *modus operandi* and the excuse for the spending of billions on the project that brings such joy to the home districts of the rivers-and-harbors-bloc Congressmen.

Miller wrote that thirteen years ago. He could have written it today. Nothing has changed.

Last year, in a further effort to by-pass the executive branch and make as many arrangements as they can just between themselves, Congress voted to allow the Corps to proceed with any project costing not more than $10 million that the Corps and the two Congressional Public Works Committees agreed on, without going to the full Congress for approval and without even looking for a nod from the White House.

President Johnson, properly jealous of his powers in this instance, said they wouldn't get away with it. He is likely to remember this attempted slight and act accordingly in the coming Department of Natural Resources fight.

The opposing camps are already assembling. On the one side will be such groups as:

¶ The National Farmers Union and the Grange and other rural blocs that are tired of the Corps coming in with its grandiose schemes and, without consulting local farmers, flooding them with another reservoir on which city folk can water-ski on weekends. The Interior Department's Bureau of Reclamation is not guiltless in this regard, but the Corps is much more high-handed.

¶ The National Audubon Society and all lovers of wild retreats, to whom the Corps is The Great Destroyer. Speaking for these opponents, one columnist wrote recently that to the Army Engineers "a vast sheet of water apparently is the most coveted thing in the world—another great artificial lake to attract tourists, swimmers, boat riders, fishermen, hot-dog peddlers, motel operators, all to 'up the economy' of the area. If there is anything that challenges, even nauseates, the Army Engineers, it is a free-flowing stream."

¶ The Soil Conservation Service, which is constantly being badgered by the Corps. The SCS was the first government agency to challenge the Corps' total domination over flood-control matters. Nine years ago it won the right to build small dams upstream, mostly for the protection of farmers (this arrangement with the Corps is quite properly called a "treaty"). But even these dams have to be approved by the Corps and it loves to quibble over the SCS's plans. One soil conservation official told me recently: "We spend more damn time rebutting the Corps than we do in planning our projects. We have 707 watershed projects going today, and we had to rebut the Corps on 20 per cent of those."

On the other side, standing four-square with the Corps and almost indistinguishable from it, will be that fascinating organization called the National Rivers and Harbors Congress. In the previous furor—the one thirteen years ago—a House member charged that the National Rivers and Harbors Congress was attacking the Hoover proposal because members of the NRHC were tied up with contractors' lobbies who feared a slump if the work was taken away from the Corps. The same charges will no doubt be heard again, because the same old National Rivers and Harbors Congress, with a few new faces, is still around.

The NRHC is an undisguised lobbying organization, and its most important members are Congressmen and Senators. In a brochure distributed by the NRHC, it describes itself as "non-official in nature" but "unique" in its "long tradition of close cooperation with top officials in the legislative and executive branches of the government."

It should indeed have uniquely close cooperation with the legislative branch, since *all* members of Congress are ex officio members of the NRHC, *all* eleven of its national vice presidents are Senators or Congressmen, as are the chairman of the board and *all* chairmen of the standing committees.

Here are found such names as Sen. John McClellan of Arkansas, chairman emeritus of the NRHC. (He is also chairman of the Senate Committee on Government Operations, where the Moss bill perilously lies.) Senator Ellender is a national director of NRHC; he is also chairman of the Senate Appropriations subcommittee which decides on the Corps' budget. Other vice presidents are Sen. Everett Dirksen of Illinois, Rep. Joseph Martin of Massachusetts, Sen. Spessard Holland of Florida, Rep. Robert Sikes of Florida, Sen. Ralph Yarborough of Texas, Sen. John Sherman Cooper of Kentucky, Rep. Mike Kirwan of Ohio, Rep. Robert Jones of Alabama, Rep. Ed Edmondson of Oklahoma and Rep. John Blatnik of Minnesota.

Once a year the NRHC gets together and decides which rivers and harbors projects it should present to Congress. Then its Congressional members change hats, go back to the Capitol, and start lobbying one another. This past session the NRHC approved projects that would cost $1,936,542,000. Congress turned out a bill costing $1,985,785,000. That's what those Congressmen-lobbyists call "close cooperation."

More of it will be seen when Moss, Metcalf and Clark come over the barricades.

Chapter Five

SUGGESTED TOPICS FOR CLASS DISCUSSION.

1. Interest groups, are generally described as shared-attitude groups that are able to influence greatly the shaping of public policy. Do the cases in this chapter sustain this view?
2. The formal organization of government, which provides numerous points of access for interest groups, is usually listed among the factors that make it possible for such groups to be effective. How important a factor is this in the cases in this chapter?
3. Were the methods used by the interest groups in these cases effective? Which group was the most successful?
4. Recognizing the interlocking interests supporting the Corps of Engineers, would you predict that the transfer of this group, which would drastically reduce its effectiveness as a lobby, will be successful?

POLITICAL PARTIES

Political parties play an indispensable role in the American political system. Indeed, it could almost be said that the American political system is what political parties make it.

In his Gettysburg Address, Lincoln may speak of government "by" the people, but the people cannot "govern themselves," in a strict sense of that term, in a society of any size. There must be a division of labor and the creation of political and governmental machinery. Government by the people is not possible, but the people must be able to choose who is to govern them, to influence those persons while in office, and to oust them, by legal means, when they see fit. This implies the existence of organized groups competing for office, by legal and nonviolent means, with the voter free to choose from among them—that is to say, political parties.

An impressive list of functions are performed by political parties. They select candidates for elective office. They pose the issues to be examined and help to educate voters on those issues. Because they are national structures, though loose ones, they help give politics a national flavor. When a party is in office, its leaders exercise many of the powers of government and exert a strong influence on foreign and domestic policy. The party that is out of office serves as the loyal opposition and, with greater or less success, plays the role of critic. It serves as an alternative to the party in power and stands ready to assume official responsibility if voted into power. Political parties also help overcome the obstacle to effective government that is represented by the principle of separation of powers written into the Constitution. They also provide the practical, if unexpected, means by which an overriding objective of the Founding Fathers is achieved —the checking of power by power.

The dominance of the two major parties has been a salient characteristic of the American political system for over a century and a half. Third parties have appeared briefly but have usually died or been absorbed into the major parties. The stability of the political order is due, in large measure, to the ability of the two major parties to draw together a variety of social, economic, ethnic, religious, and sectional interests. These amalgams of diverse interests have little unity and a low level of maneuverability. Obliged to appeal to large numbers of voters in order to achieve victory, the major parties must avoid doctrinaire positions. This leads to the charges, sometimes made, that neither party adheres to "principle" and that they are so much alike there is little real choice.

The cases in this chapter have been selected to give a picture of the differences between the parties and the kinds of conflict and struggle between them.

How to Rebuild the Two-party System

Seymour Martin Lipset

Much concern has been expressed since last November's election about the future of American politics now that reactionary conservative forces seem to have control of one of the major parties. In assessing the long-range consequences, several fundamental truths must be borne in mind.

The first is that the actual mobilizable supporters of political reaction are in the minority in most communities outside of the South, as was established statistically by the vote for Goldwater. And that vote, cast by 39 per cent of the electorate, considerably exaggerates the support for the Senator's beliefs; for in this election, as in previous ones, most voters cast a ballot for their traditional party. Evidence from a variety of opinion surveys indicates that no more than one third of Republican voters agrees with Senator Goldwater on most issues, and support for Radical Rightist groups such as the John Birch Society is much smaller than that.

The second fact is that "backlash" politics have been a recurrent phenomenon in America; the White Citizens' Councils, the John Birch Society, the Minutemen, and the Goldwater nomination itself are but the most recent examples. For more than a century, as formerly powerful groups declined in influence, they have lashed out with enough vigor to overwhelm the political process. And by espousing various emotional issues they have sought to find a mass appeal for what has been inherently a minority cause.

Third, the survival of the two-party system in this country probably depends more upon the future policies and performance of the nation's Democrats than upon the outcome of the factional disputes now raging in Republican ranks. I shall try in due course to explain why this is so.

At the outset, it is essential to understand what caused the GOP's shift to the right in 1964. To this end, it is helpful to examine the behavior of American conservative parties from the Federalists down through the Whigs and Republicans. Each of these parties drew its chief support from the higher-status, more well-to-do WASPish (white Anglo-Saxon Protestant) segments of the population. (The principal exception was the allegiance of Negroes to the Republican party before the New Deal.) However, to be identified as the representative of the privileged class has been a continuing electoral disadvantage, since American political values stemming from the Revolution and the frontier have always glorified the common man rather than elites, whether based on money, family, or intellect.

The Federalists and their Whig successors became grudgingly aware of this fact and of the corollary need to play down obviously class-linked issues and find positions which would attract the lower strata, including

"How to Rebuild the Two-party System," *Harper's Magazine*, January 1965. Reprinted by permission of the author.

the large lower-middle class. They tried to do this by appealing to traditional religious values; by attacking recent immigrant groups; and by selecting as candidates military heroes who could be represented as standing above the narrowly partisan, interest-linked battle waged by other parties.

Thus, for example, Alexander Hamilton proposed the formation of a Christian Constitutional Society which would oppose the Jeffersonians while promoting Christianity. Again in the 1830s and 1840s, the Whigs presented themselves as the party of Protestant religion fighting the irreligious and immoral Democrats and the subversive plots of Masons and Catholics. However, it was only by nominating military heroes that the Whigs were able to defeat the party of the "demagogues" in 1840 and 1848. One historian reports that the Whigs chose Zachary Taylor, the hero of the Mexican War in 1848, before it "was . . . known to what party he professed to belong," a practice which their equally desperate Republican descendants were to repeat a little more than a century later.

As many historians have noted, anti-Catholic nativism, prohibition, and abolition were backed strongly by middle-class evangelical Protestant groups in the North. The issues of abolition and prohibition, however, had little lower-class support. So nativism became the one cause which enabled the Republican party to reach into the ranks of lower-status, normally Democratic voters. (Many Republican leaders, particularly Abraham Lincoln, tried to dissociate the party from Know-Nothing doctrines.)

After the Civil War, the Republicans, as the party which preserved the Union, freed the slaves, and passed the Homestead Act, acquired a reservoir of mass support never available to its Federalist-Whig predecessors. The organization of Union veterans, the Grand Army of the Republic, was practically a Republican "front-organization." With their families, these veterans constituted an enormous bloc of voters.

In the years that followed, the party became increasingly identified with the interests of expanding industrial capitalism. At the same time, however, it maintained its anti-Catholic and nativist positions. President Ulysses S. Grant publicly suggested that the country might face a new civil war between the forces of patriotism and intelligence on the one hand and those of superstition and ignorance (the Catholics) on the other. And when the anti-Catholic American Protective Association arose in the late 1880s, it operated with some success within the Republican party.

Thus by espousing issues which concerned moralistic puritanical voters and those fearful of foreign inroads on their jobs, status, and culture, the GOP attracted people who had little in common socially or economically with the elite which strongly influenced Republican policy.

Through the late nineteenth and early twentieth centuries, however, Republican expressions of moralistic intolerance and ethnic bigotry were confined largely to campaign oratory. Immigration remained open and almost totally unrestricted; and prohibition, though enacted in a number of states, could not pass Congress.

Suddenly, however, within a few years after the end of World War I, the Eighteenth—prohibition—Amendment was adopted; restrictive immigration laws were passed, severely limiting the total number of immigrants and applying national quotas biased against Catholics and Jews; in a number of states, mainly in the South, the teaching of evolutionary doctrines was outlawed; and the anti-Catholic, anti-Semitic, anti-Negro Ku Klux Klan rose to prominence with millions of supporters in the North as well as the South.

THE POLITICS OF NOSTALGIA

Why had success so abruptly come to these crusades, which had made little legislative progress for well over a century? I believe the explanation lies chiefly in the declining relative size of the groups favoring evangelical Protestant values and their dwindling influence in major spheres of the nation's life. Broad demographic changes resulting from urban growth and the influx of millions of European Catholic and Jewish immigrants from 1890 to 1920 had brought this about. Traditional Protestantism was well on the way to becoming a *minority* instead of a majority culture. The ideal typical Republican Protestant—God-fearing, deeply religious, moral, middle-class, living in a stable, nonurban community—was losing control of the society which his father had dominated and which he had learned to expect to dominate as his birthright.

As metropolitan areas became the actual and symbolic centers of Jewish and Catholic influence, white Protestants were rapidly shrinking to a numerical minority in the cities. The evangelical Protestants were not only losing power to outgroups. The very concepts of right and wrong seemed to be changing. The result was a striking outburst of backlash politics in the 1920s, as evidenced in prohibition, the growth of the Ku Klux Klan, and the other similar phenomena I have mentioned.

The election of 1928 was perhaps the last victory of aggressive Protestantism over a symbol of the urban, nonpuritanical groups which were taking over the country. In the years that followed, the klan formed a bridge between the traditional and the newer forms of nativist politics, for it was not only anti-immigrant, but also anti-radical and specifically anti-Communist. It operated largely within the Southern Democratic and Northern Republican parties. And in the North it served as a means of winning over normally Democratic segments of the electorate to the Republicans.

The continued strain between the values of the evangelical Protestants and the majority of the country has been documented in various opinion surveys. Recent Gallup polls show that a declining but large minority of the population still favors a national prohibition law (in 1948, about one third did; today, about one quarter). One third of the country's Protestants are prohibitionists, in contrast with less than a tenth of the Catholics. Sixty per cent of Protestant farmers still favor prohibition, as do 42 per cent of Protestants living in communities with less than 10,000 people. On the other hand, among Protestants residing in metropolitan areas with more than 500,000 people, only 12 per cent support prohibition. Obviously the traditional Protestant sects and their historic strongholds, the small towns and rural areas, still support a religious-political culture which is out of date with the twentieth-century American reality.

Protestant values have declined not only in the cultural sense. There has also been a transfer of power in other vital areas. In politics, long before Kennedy became President, Catholic influence was visibly mounting, particularly in the Democratic party. In the communications field, Jews have had a highly publicized (though somewhat exaggerated) influence, first in motion pictures and later in radio and television. Protestants have remained predominant in the business community, but this, curiously, is the least useful power base for influencing cultural or moral values. Economic strength may be very significant in the overall power structure, but in terms of ethics and values, politics and communications are much more important.

As they have been driven out of urban politics by the various minority ethnic groups, the WASPs have concentrated their activities in private associations and in community-chest drives, the symphony, the opera, and other forms of community culture. Sociologists, politicians, the press, and the entertainment industry think in terms of "minority" ethnic-religious categories. Political parties and the communications media feel it is safer to discriminate in *favor* of the minorities than against them. But the residual WASPs need not be dealt with in this fashion since they do not react as a group.

BATTLE LINES REVERSED

The resentful fundamentalists have, in recent years, been joined by economic strata outraged by the growth of the welfare state and the trade-union movement. Lately, these sources of backlash politics have been augmented by the reaction of many whites against the increasingly victorious efforts of Negroes to gain equal access to public accommodations, schools, neighborhoods, and jobs previously restricted largely to whites. Each of these tendencies has fortified the right-wing crusade which has been trying for decades to convert the Republican party into a vehicle for the politics of alienation and nostalgia. Perhaps the most galling defeat suffered by the fundamentalists in the past three decades was their loss of leadership within Protestantism as a whole. No longer is the church dominated by the puritanical forces which could mount a major crusade behind the Anti-Saloon League. Instead the voice of Protestantism is the very liberal National Council of Churches, run by the metropolitan-centered denominations which retain little of that old-time religion or belief in the struggle between God and Satan.

For much of its history the Republican party has been the scene of internal conflict among its middle-class and big-business backers, a conflict sometimes linked to regional diversity. For example, in the late nineteenth and early twentieth centuries, scions of old wealth and business leaders heading moderate-sized companies in the Midwest were the chief supporters of the Progressive faction of the GOP against the reactionary Eastern wing dominated by large business, the trusts, and the monopolies. The rural, small-town Progressives also found some leaders and followers in the big cities. These people were mainly migrants from, or socially comparable to, the Protestant upper-middle class of non-metropolitan America, in that they too came from the once-powerful class who formerly had had a sense of being in control of their party and country.

The Progressivism of these relatively well-to-do men, like that of their lower-middle-class counterparts, consisted in seeking to restrain the large corporations which were stifling individual initiative. Progressivism was linked with Protestant moralism, as was shown in Congressional action on prohibition. For example, in an early test vote on the Webb-Kenyon Law of 1913, most Progressive Republican Senators voted for it, while most conservatives were opposed.

This class and regional cleavage within the Republican party has, of course, continued down to the present, but the ideological battle lines have changed drastically. The Progressive Midwestern trust-busters advocated a fairly advanced welfare-state program. Their descendants are now ardent supporters of laissez-faire, while the executives of large Eastern corporations—inheritors of the trusts and monopolies—now accept the welfare state. Before World War I the Eastern states sent conservative Republican "stalwarts" to the Senate. But in 1954 Republican Senators from these same states voted to censure Senator McCarthy and at the 1964 convention their delegates supported Governor Scranton. Conversley, the very regions which were once the backbone of Republican Progressivism supplied the Senatorial votes for McCarthy and lined up almost solidly for Goldwater at the convention.

Today the small and middle-sized businessmen and independent professionals, perhaps more than any other groups, feel constrained by progressive social legislation and the rise of labor unions. The competitive position of the small firm makes it more difficult to pay increased wages, and such governmental measures as Social Security, business taxes, and various regulatory laws tend to complicate and raise the costs of a small business in ways that little disturb the large corporations. Threats to bring the government into medicine, to regulate employee recruitment through Fair Employment Practices legislation, or to control the rental and sale of property or public accommodations, all frighten small entrepreneurs, who foresee the loss of their cherished independence.

The newly wealthy also tend to favor as little government as possible, for the man who has made his own money feels more possessive and less secure than do the members of an educated, established upper class inculcated with some of the noblesse-oblige values of aristocratic conservatism. The large, established bureaucratic corporation tends to run an internal "planned economy" of its own and is involved in continuous relations with government agencies.

In recent decades college-educated men and the scions of established wealth have moved into control of most large corporations. The result has been an alliance of economic power and traditional status in the moderate wing of the GOP, while small businessmen and the newly wealthy have backed the more conservative, laissez-faire faction.

DECISION IN CALIFORNIA

These differences were manifest in the fight for the 1964 nomination and came through most clearly in the decisive California primary. Senator Goldwater carried the southern California counties in and around Los Angeles by a large majority, while Governor Rockefeller did well in the San Francisco area.

This pattern can be explained by the nature of the community and business structures of the two Californias. Centered around San Francisco in the north is the old, established part of the state. The city's population has grown little for some decades. Located in the Bay Area are many old, wealthy, and economically powerful families whose ancestors made their money in mining, commerce, or railroads in the first decades after statehood. To back Goldwater against Rockefeller in northern California involved challenging the opinions of the social and economic Establishments.

In the Los Angeles area, on the other hand—where population has mushroomed since the 1940s—wealth is largely nouveau riche, and a politically and culturally sophisticated elite has been slow to develop. Typically, in new, rapidly expanding centers of population there is no responsible leadership accustomed to running community institutions, reducing tensions, and protecting the rights of diverse groups.

Los Angeles also contains a large concentration of fundamentalist Protestant migrants from farms and small towns who have gathered together in fundamentalist churches to resist the corrupting influence of the big city, particularly the Sodom and Gomorrah of Hollywood. Right-wing extremism and presumably Goldwater Republicanism have been fostered by the tensions of population growth, weak community integration, and lack of an established upper-class leadership group. A disproportionate number of Birch Society supporters are to be found among those who have migrated to the state within the past fifteen years. (Studies of Birch Society urban membership in other parts of the country also find that it is comprised disproportionately of migrants from smaller communities.)

MINORITY VICTORY

Goldwater Republicanism makes a powerful appeal to people who long for the Protestant small-town and rural nineteenth-century laissez-faire America. But they are not numerous enough to nominate a Republican Presidential candidate in an open national primary election. A variety of opinion surveys indicates that more than two-thirds of all Americans accept the welfare state and favor an internationalist foreign policy. As a result, the two major parties have been in substantial agreement on these fundamental issues during the past two decades. However, the secondary local leadership of the Republican party has long been out of step with the majority of its supporters. For example, in a national survey just before the 1964 Republican convention Gallup found 60 per cent of Republicans for Scranton with only 34 per cent for Goldwater.

The explanation for Goldwater's convention strength is to be found in the fact that the Republican party is run largely by men who are active because of a very conservative ideology and who can afford the time for politics. Occupationally, such people are most likely to be automobile dealers, realtors, lawyers who serve small and medium-size business, and other self-employed devotees of laissez-faire. On the other hand, the backbone of "moderate" Republicanism is among the employees and executives of the large, urban-based corporations. These men are less active in the Republican party, in part because they *are* moderate and thus much less passionately concerned about the consequences of Democratic rule. Furthermore, their bureaucratic and executive jobs make it hard for them to take time off from work for politics.

If the Republican convention delegates had voted in past years according to their convictions rather than their electoral hopes, they would have nominated men like Bricker and Taft, not Willkie, Dewey, and Eisenhower. In 1964, however, the result was different. This was due in part to the incredible stupidity of the moderate Republicans, who failed to join forces behind one candidate. Several other factors also contributed to the fiasco. Rockefeller—the one moderate who sought the nomination through the state primaries—alienated many Protestant Republicans by his divorce and remarriage. At the same time, many wealthy moderate Republicans were reasonably satisfied with Johnson's Presidential performance, felt he would win anyhow, and hence saw little reason to contribute to a losing and not very important cause. On the opposite side, the groups who felt displaced in power and prestige expressed their cumulative frustration with a tenacity and force that were nearly irresistible, much as similar groups had made an equally desperate last stand for the Lord in the 1920s. The Goldwater supporters were committed to a degree which far outweighed the fervor of their less involved adversaries.

IN SEARCH OF AN ISSUE

Though they were able to nominate Goldwater, it was obvious to the conservative Republicans that they would not win the election if they limited their appeal to the self-employed and the culturally alienated. They were thus faced with the recurring problem of conservatives in an egalitarian, mass-suffrage society: how to attract enough lower-class votes to get elected. This time they lacked a military hero standing above the fray. One available tactic was the repeated leveling of the "soft on communism" charge against the Democrats. McCarthy had demonstrated that many lower-status Democrats would respond to such an appeal. His success, however, occurred during wartime; the end of the Korean war saw the end of McCarthyism. Although Goldwater tried to exploit the Vietnamese war, it clearly did not provide him with a comparable opportunity.

What tactics remained? The racial issue and white backlash seemed the most convenient alternative, much as nativism attracted nineteenth-century conservative politicians. The Goldwater camp certainly encouraged racist support. The promise to do something to make the streets of our large cities safer was a clear-cut appeal to white anxieties about the racial issue. For the candidates who decry any interference by the federal government with "states' rights" to suggest that the problems of municipal policing would be affected by a change in the Presidency was somewhat startling, except in the context of the effort to deliver a message to the prejudiced.

THE EDGE

Four years ago many argued that the votes which Kennedy would gain *because* he was a Catholic would outweigh those he would lose. Long before the 1964 election it was evident that one should not ignore the pressure making for what Johnson called the "frontlash"—*i.e.*, the votes which he would gain from normally Republican groups. Referenda which showed Democratic white working-class districts voting against civil-rights proposals also revealed middle-class Republican areas as much more positive toward civil rights. The higher-status Protestant churches affiliated with the anti-fundamentalist National Council of Churches badgered their members to treat civil rights as a matter of conscience. Thus the Protestant weekly, *Christianity and Crisis,* editorialized early in the 1964 campaign:

> The mantle of religion is being used to support what we regard as an immoral nationalism, an immoral nuclear recklessness, an immoral racism (though the candidate is not a racist he promises the racists what they want—protection from the federal government), and an immoral economic individualism that fails to take account of the needs of the people who inhabit our cities. . . .

The more fundamentalist Protestant groups doubtless saw such expressions as further evidence of the corruption of Protestantism from within. But the fact remains that the National Council of Churches, not the much smaller conservative National Association of Evangelicals, represents the large majority of Prtoestants today, and that the weight of its influence was thrown directly or indirectly against Goldwater Republicanism.

The moderate Republican newspapers which are read by the college-educated corporation employees and executives also provided strong arguments for opposing the party ticket in 1964, and an extraordinary number endorsed Johnson. Their Republican readers are a knowledgeable group, interested in politics, and the views presented by the metropolitan pro-Johnson papers were close to their own.

On the other hand, outside of the South, Democratic defections by the racially prejudiced had to be drawn largely from the ranks of the least educated, most of whom vote regularly for the Democratic slate regardless of candidates or issues. They do not read political news, nor do they listen to campaign talks on television. There is little Republican campaign activity in their neighborhoods, and at work they were told repeatedly that Goldwater was antilabor, a union buster, and a man who would take away their Social Security. From the beginning it was doubtful that many normally Democratic workers, no matter how bigoted, would vote Republican. And in fact, Northern working-class districts—including those in Milwaukee and Gary which had given Governor Wallace a large vote in the primaries—voted overwhelmingly for Johnson.

An added handicap for Goldwater was the fact that the role of the Presidency has so increased during this century as to lift its incumbent to a stature far above anyone who is not President. Lyndon Johnson had the advantages of incumbency without some of its disadvantages. He had held office long enough to be perceived as an effective President, but not long enough to have antagonized many groups or individuals. Besides noting these assets, one must recognize that Johnson is the most consummate politician to have held the Presidency since Lincoln, with the possible exception of the two Roosevelts. Thus, for example, his proposals for saving money in the operation of the White House and in the government agencies generally did no damage to his liberal programs, but had strong appeal to the middle class; similarly, the use of the socialist slogan "war on poverty" for a program which proposes to change the attributes of poor people as individuals rather than the attributes of the economic system won support from Socialists and corporate executives alike. Both Norman Thomas and Henry Ford campaigned actively for Johnson and Humphrey.

Finally, it cannot be stressed too strongly that the active support in 1964 for the Goldwater politics of the "backlash," whether religious-cultural, economic, or racially motivated, reflect the fact that the United States is becoming more liberal. The groups which reacted with such desperation that they captured the Republican Presidential nomination are desperate precisely because they are growing less influential and less numerous. They can see no conventional means to sustain their values or interests. The Republican party itself has become the major victim of this decline. In 1940, almost as many voters said they were Republicans (38 per cent) as Democrats (42 per cent). By 1960, the proportion of Democrats had grown to 47 per cent, while the Republicans had declined to only 30 per cent (the other 23 per cent were Independent). And in 1964, before the nominating conventions and after four years of Kennedy and Johnson, those who identified themselves as Democrats were for the first time over half the electorate (53 per cent), while the Republicans were down to a mere 25 per cent.

Public attitudes toward international issues and civil rights show comparable liberal trends. For example, surveys by the National Opinion Research Center of the University of Chicago over the past two decades indicate that "support of residential integration rose from 35 per cent in 1942 to 64 per cent at the end of last year (1963) among all whites." Support for school integration in the nation as a whole jumped from 30 per cent in 1942 to 49 per cent in 1956, and to 62 per cent at the end of 1963.

Thus there is simply no evidence that the Goldwater nomination or the twenty-six million votes he received means that dogmatic conservatism, racial bigotry, or xenophobic nationalism have become popular in this country. The efforts of increasingly desperate minorities to compensate for their loss of influence by heightened political activity within the Republican party is not evidence of an increase in their numbers. Even within conservative ranks generally, the popular strength of the organized Radical Right is quite small. A variety of national surveys conducted by Gallup, Harris, and the Opinion Research Corporation have inquired about attitudes toward the Birch Society. None of these have ever reported more than 8 per cent in favor of the Society. In a preconvention investigation conducted by the Opinion Research Corporation, people in a national sample were asked whether knowledge that a Presidential candidate had been endorsed by the Birch Society would make them "more likely to vote for" him; only 4 per cent said that it would, while 47 per cent said they would be *less* likely to vote for a candidate if they knew he had the Society's endorsement.

The revival of conservative laissez-faire Republicanism in 1964 was the backlash of declining forces in American life. As electoral forces, they should not be any more durable than the sociologically comparable tendencies represented in the movements of the early 1920s. The real danger in the right-wing take-over of the Republican party is the threat it poses to the viability of the GOP. There is considerable evidence that many moderate or liberal Republicans have left the party. Both official registration records and opinion-poll data indicate that a significant number of voters have ceased their identification with the GOP during the past year. And perhaps even more important for the long run, Republican strength is lowest by far among young voters, those under thirty. These facts bode ill for the future of the party generally.

In spite of the defections from Republican ranks of many liberals and moderates, opinion-poll data and the difference between the vote Goldwater received and that secured by Republican moderates such as Keating, Scott, and Romney indicate that the efforts of the liberal GOP Governors and Congressmen to regain control of the party machinery and national nominations should be successful. There can be no assurance, however, that victories by the moderates in party primaries and conventions in the next four years will result in victories in November 1968. Bitter factional fights are not conducive to electoral triumph. There are many in the party who are more concerned with eliminating the influence of the other faction than with defeating the Democrats. To gain an effective position nationally, the Republican party must return to moderate leadership, while at the same time retaining the active support of the ideologically committed right-wingers, a task which is clearly difficult.

PRESCRIPTION FOR DEMOCRATS

To a considerable extent also, the electoral and ideological future of the GOP is in the hands of the Democratic majority. If the Democrats continue to occupy the broad center, to seek to retain major support among all strata—from the corporation presidents and Wall Street bankers to trade-unionists and impoverished Negroes—they will force the GOP to remain on the far right. However, if the overwhelming Democratic Congressional majority which constitutes the most liberal Congress elected since 1936 presses for major social reforms along the lines presented by Harry Truman in 1948, the Republican party can move back to a position slightly right of center. To have a moderate Republican party, we need a Democratic party which is perceived by many voters as being on the left, much as was the party of Franklin Roosevelt and Harry Truman. It is of some importance, therefore, to the future of the American two-party system that we do not enter a period of "good feeling," that Lyndon Johnson and the liberals in Congress should press for major social reforms even if fostering such issues helps return to the GOP some of the center support which it now so badly needs.

No politician will consciously seek to give votes to the opposition party, no matter how fervently he praises the virtues of a genuinely competitive two-party system. However, if a President desires to be viewed by history as more than a successful mediator among the diverse interest groups of the country, he must seek remedies for the problems of his day. If Lyndon Johnson's image of "The Great Society" really includes a drive on poverty, on unemployment, on slums, on the inequitable distribution of medical-care facilities, on inadequate urban transportation, on mediocre education, on the lack of facilities to meet the growing challenge of increased leisure in the age of automation, he will not only be positively responding to the challenges of the second part of this century, he will return to the Republican party the legitimate role of the conservative party. The party can concentrate on constructive criticism, modification and administration of the often over-enthusiastically fostered and sometimes not well designed reforms of the left.

Great nations in modern complex society must constantly adjust their institutions and practices to the changing needs imposed by technological advances, population growth, new ideas, external developments, and the like. And in a stable democracy, it is the role of the liberal or left groups to propose reforms which seek to bring the society ever closer to the dream of a more free society in which the disadvantages imposed on many by birth on the wrong side of the class or color lines are reduced as far as is humanly possible, and in which the American and democratic dream of complete equality of opportunity is approximated. In the ideal competitive democracy, the role of the conservative is to help make certain that the reformer does not destroy the good in the existing institutions, particularly the safeguards for individual and community freedom. The conservative points out the price which must be paid for any given reform, a price which frequently outweighs the gain which the reform is designed to achieve.

The United States currently faces the danger that both roles, that of the reformer and the conservative, will be performed badly by its two parties during the next decade. If the Democrats remain in the center and the Republicans on the far right, we may be in for a prolonged period of one-party, or more accurately one-and-one-half-party, politics, much like the situation which existed during the first quarter of the nineteenth century, when the Federalists declined and finally disappeared. Such politics, today, can only be those of the dead center, without significant choice or progress.

The New Right: What Does It Seek?

James J. Kilpatrick

Two years ago, after the bloody rites of the San Francisco convention, some of the leaders of the liberal movement took the pragmatic view that perhaps the nomination of Barry Goldwater was all for the best. If con-

"The New Right: What Does It Seek?" *Saturday Review*, October 8, 1966. Reprinted by permission of the author and publisher.

servatism, so embodied, had its chance to win, and sank instead, that would be the end of this pernicious and persistent philosophy. And when Mr. Goldwater went down by twenty-seven million votes to Mr. Johnson's forty-three million, there ensued a considerable rubbing of hands amid the gnashing of teeth. Dean Burch fled to exterior darkness; Ray Bliss sat down at the head of the surviving angels. The GOP's liberals, at once triumphant and resentful, filled the winter air with wild honks of "I told you so!" and "Never again!"

In recent months, a strangely lugubrious silence has settled upon these jubilation singers. They have discovered that American conservatism was not drowned—it was not even badly waterlogged—when our eloquent leader sank out of sight. The funeral rites were premature. At this writing, it is a fair guess that the Republicans will claim an additional thirty seats in the coming Congress, and that two-thirds of these will be occupied by men of conservative instincts. If this happy prospect materializes, the flood tides of regressive liberalism that swept the 89th Congress will be controlled by new levees in the 90th, for twenty conservative votes in the House will make a world of difference.

Now, a kind of Gresham's Law operates in the field of semantics. Bad meanings tend to drive good meanings from the marketplace of ideas. We are talking here of liberalism and conservatism. The exponents of American conservatism insist, however futilely, that they themselves are the true liberals, in the historic sense of the term. Those who today identify themselves as "liberals," in the conservative view, have inherited nothing from the liberalism of the ages; they have merely kidnapped the label, and perverted it to their own illiberal uses. But one is stuck with the lexicography of his own time. For my own partisan and probably nefarious purposes, let me define contemporary liberalism as a political philosophy that manifests itself by and large, in aggrandizement of the central state, and also manifests itself, in a benevolent contempt for the individual man. My colleagues in this symposium doubtless will have different views and different definitions.

These past few years, plainly enough, have been years of ascendant liberalism. Our brisk and busy masters, operating with a sort of spring-cleaning efficiency, have relegated old precepts of federalism to the attic of outworn doctrines. They have reduced the sovereign states to murmuring dependencies. As a structure of government, little remains of the Constitution but an empty shell; the house of our fathers is a vacant house, stripped of locks, bolts, interior walls. The theory that the central government is a government of delegated and enumerated powers is as dead as Madison; it is as dead as Calhoun. The General Welfare clause, like a soft cocoon, produces the metamorphosis that so enchants the liberal eye. Burke once observed that "the forms of a free, and the ends of an arbitrary government, are things not altogether incompatible." These past four years have proved it so.

The federal plan, summed up in the Tenth Amendment, was one of two principal safeguards devised by the founding fathers against the abuses of excessive power. The other safeguard was the doctrine of separation of powers. The new tenants of our constitutional house, whisking their energetic brooms, have junked this old doctrine, too. The two elected branches of our legislature still sit in domed splendor on the Hill, but just across the street, in its white marbled mausoleum, there sits a third. The Supreme Court of the United States, as Harlan and Stewart so often complain, is not content with interpreting law; it is affirmatively enacting law. And all around town, in a hundred executive agencies, the bureaucracy grinds out a mass of legislative rules and regulations.

The resulting aggrandizement of the central government scarcely requires documentation, but it is like a mountain seen from afar—its magnitude is not yet fully grasped. More is involved than the mere proliferation of federal programs of grants-in-aid; more is involved than the tens of thousands of rules and regulations that turn up in the *Federal Register.* What we are witnessing is a steady centralization of power too vast for the easy-going American to comprehend. He sees its tangible benefits; he is blind to its subtle perils. The cities, especially, lie as contentedly as Titania to receive the drop of federal nectar on their drowsy eyes. They awake to sweet fantasies of urban renewal, of mass transit, of slum removal, and all for free!

But the trick is that Lyndon B. Oberon's spell is no more than a midsummer's dream. The goodies that come with these prodigious federal grants are not free. They carry a heavy price in the gradual transfer of the essential policy-making responsibility from those who are most intimately affected to those who are scarcely affected at all. The tool devised by today's liberals to accomplish this transfer is a relatively new tool, not yet fully tested, but it promises to exert incredible power: It is the threat to withhold the federal grant.

Those who dwell in the South already have felt this federal crowbar wrenching at their public institutions. Under Title VI of the Civil Rights Act of 1964, power was vested in the head of every department administering a program of federal aid to withhold the grant of federal funds until a satisfactory level of desegregation had been reached. Two and a half years ago, when the bill was pending, a few voices attempted to warn of the sweeping power concealed in Title VI, but these voices had Southern accents; they went unheard. The power to withhold was delegated; and now the power is being put to work.

In the process, both manifestations of contemporary liberalism are emerging: Federal authority is exalted, and the individual is disdained. Southern hospitals have been put on notice that federal funds will be suspended—for research grants, for construction aid, for Medicare, for the payment of indigents' bills—unless white and Negro patients are placed deliberately in the same semiprivate rooms. The wishes of the patients, and their emotional well-being, are deemed immaterial. It does not matter that a Negro patient might be happier and more at ease in a room with a member of his own race. Roll him down the hall! Or roll a white patient to the Negro's room!

The same implacable power may be seen most vividly in the case of the public schools. In the days when federal aid was largely confined to vocational grants and the school hot lunch, a threat to withhold might have been serious; it would not have been disastrous. It is a different matter today. In North Carolina, federal funds now constitute one-fifth of the educational budget. In many Southern counties, federal aid represents one-third of all spending on schools. Money talks, as it has been so aptly said, and when money talks, people listen.

But what Southern school officials have been hearing from Education Commissioner Harold Howe is shrill unreason. Dr. Howe is one of the new breed of federal administrators: tough, brilliant, doctrinaire, ruthless. He is fond of saying, "If I had my way," and he now has discretionary power over enough billions to buy his way pretty well. Over most of the South, obedient to what they understood to be the commissioner's decree, local school officials dutifully set in motion enrollment plans based upon "freedom of choice." All pupils, white and Negro alike, were to be left free, within reason, to choose the school they wished to attend. But when Commissioner Howe began to impose his own coercions upon "freedom of choice," it turned out that the children's freedom was like the animals' equality in George Orwell's famous fable: Some were less free than others.

Under the commissioner's edict, if Negro pupils did not exercise their freedom to choose a predominately white school, they had to be given a second chance, or a third, until they got the point. If a locality failed to attain some arbitrary percentage of integration, off with its federal aid! Here, too, as in the case of the hospital patients, the wishes of the children and their parents have been rejected out of hand. Respected local school officials—men and women who have devoted their professional lives to developing good local systems—have been treated with insolence and contempt. During August, review teams of first- and second-year law students, possessed of a cocksure, know-it-all arrogance that had to be experienced to be believed, went roaming through the South as the commissioner's proconsuls. They demanded wholesale reorganizations. In one North Carolina county, these emissaries from Dr. Howe were dissatisfied with the progress of school desegregation. They issued peremptory commands. And they were not at all abashed when it developed that their reorganization plan would have required the construction of two entirely new school buildings in ten days.

Doubtless it will be said, by men of superior virtue, that the recalcitrant South deserves this crowbar treatment. Liberalism has taken a curious turn in such matters. A new racism is to be imposed upon the old: We are not to be color-blind, after all; we are to be intensely color-conscious, and when noses are counted we must count by black noses and white noses, and calculate the proper percentage by slide rule. This is the new liberalism. In another time it was called the old bigotry. But we learn; we learn. And what we of the South have learned is that we accept this born-again racism, or we lose the grant-in-aid. It is the Christian point of view.

Yet it is not only in the South, and it is not only in areas of racial integration, that our new masters propose to employ their handy-dandy, all-purpose tool. The threat to withhold federal funds now is embodied in every area of grant administration. Plans for local airports must conform —or no money. Plans for local sewerage must conform—or no money. Plans for local welfare must conform—or no money. Under the highway beautification program, highways must be brought to new federal standards of esthetics—or no money.

How strange it is, meditating upon these things, that liberals should have made such a fight for their Demonstration Cities Bill. In theory, at least, though the theory is as full of air as a blow-toad, contemporary liberals favor "variety" and "non-conformity." Behold their scraggly beards. The bill adopted by the Senate and vociferously supported by liberals in the House, is a total denial of these professed aims. Under the Demonstration Cities Bill, the high priest of housing, Dr. Robert Weaver, and his *éminence grise* from MIT, Under Secretary Robert C. Wood, would be given an absolute veto over the "substantive laws," whatever these may be, of every participating city. These local laws would have to be revised to the secretary's notions of sociology—or no money. Certainly, the aims of the demonstration cities program are attractive, but in the end, as the bill makes clear, these aims must be defined, shaped, and imposed by the Secretary of Housing and Urban Development. They must "satisfy the secretary"—God bless the virtuous man—or no money.

Yet the magnitude of this gentle liberalism would be misunderstood if it were interpreted merely in terms of the power to affirm or to deny a local application for federal funds. This is an awesome power—and in the area of grants for local schools, and local sewers, and for the control of air and water pollution, it sooner or later will destroy the political boundaries fixed by the people themselves—but it is only half of the power that is beloved in the liberal view. The corollary power is a power to make the original, affirmative grant.

Thus we are witnessing, especially in the fields of education and welfare, the use of discretionary grants and fellowships to reward particular social and political points of view, and to make certain that these points of view prevail in the marketing of ideas. Commissioner Howe was the first witness to be summoned recently before some hearings of an ad hoc subcommittee of the House Education and Labor Committee. The gentleman rolled his eyes to the heavens; he hoisted three fingers in a Boy Scout oath; he asked all men to witness his renunciation of any faint desire to control the content of textbooks.

And when these renunciations were neatly disposed of, he spit on his hands. Yes, he told the committee, he had quite a few millions of dollars here and there; and yes, he was seeing to it that grants for the writing of textbooks went into properly certified hands; he was consulting with counsel to determine if federal funds might yet be denied to a school district that bought a vile segregationist book for its library; and he felt certain these matters could be taken care of. He thought it would be dreadful if any one person ever should control the content of textbooks; and no, sir, he had no idea of doing this himself, and besides, any such action would be prohibited by the present state of the Elementary and Secondary Education Act; but yes, sir, Mr. Powell, and yes, sir, Mr. Daniels, he thought much could be done to see that the right sort of textbooks were encouraged and the wrong sort of textbooks were discouraged. Dr. Howe was what is known on the Hill as a friendly witness. He witnessed for liberalism, 1966.

My second point is that what passes for "liberalism," 1966, in our own Looking-Glass World, is manifested not only in the aggrandizement of the central government, but also in a bland contempt for the individual man. My liberal friends despise him.

In certain areas of civil rights, for example, the ultimate questions that are asked under Title VI are not: Is the child getting a good education? Or, is the patient comfortable? Or, is the teacher qualified? The questions are rather: How many Negro noses? How many Negro supervisors? What is their percentage of the whole? Under the new theories of public housing, families are perceived as guinea pigs in neighborhood cages. They are consumer units. Their window boxes sprout wax daffodils; these are hosed free of soot and the daffodils grow on forever. Only the human spirit withers.

This contempt for the individual is masked by a suffocating concern for his welfare. Or perhaps this is no mask; the concern may be real, but the concern is misdirected. Now pending for adoption by the Food and Drug Administration are scores of new regulations intended to inhibit the sale of vitamins. Are supplementary vitamins bad for us? Not at all, says young Dr. Goddard, who heads the FDA; but supplementary vitamins are unnecessary. The administration's truth-in-packaging bill would vest in bureaucratic hands a new power to standardize the package sizes of potato chips. Is this to prevent fraud? No, indeed, as the bill's sponsors concede, fraud is covered by existing statutes. The idea is to make things more convenient for the shopper.

Under the Job Corps and Manpower Training programs, an ambitious young man might be given a chance to submit himself to discipline, to learn a trade, to pull himself up by work and sacrifice; but this is not the way of men who measure the human soul on bar charts. The trainee is therefore given the rush-week persuasion; he is garbed in a free blue blazer, brass-buttoned; he is handsomely paid for his bodily presence. Such programs dry up the very juices of ambition, and cultivate a feeble dependency on the state.

The false values of today's liberalism, rooted in a secular materialism, do not admit any other approach to the needs of the people. Money is seen as the great mustard plaster, sucking the ill humors forth. Are they rioting tonight in Harlem? Then pay the savages not to riot. Are libraries undernourished? Let us buy socially enriched books to fill them. Is the Merchant Marine running down? Money will fuel it up. Are poorly skilled workers underpaid? A higher minimum wage will put more 50-cent dollars in their pockets. This folly applies abroad as well as at home: If the United States cannot command respect, or win it, or earn it, the United States will buy it by the billions in foreign aid.

In this kindly and loving and profligate fashion, today's liberals advance along their munificent way, oozing rectitude from every pore. They *know* that fluoride is good for our teeth; so they would compel all men to drink it. They *know* that supplementary vitamins are unnecessary; so they would make it inconvenient to buy them. They *know* that racial integration is a good thing, right down to the semi-private hospital room; so they will swing the crowbar. They *know* that local building codes are obsolete; so they will compel the codes' revision, willy-nilly, to meet their own ideas of what is best. They *know* that the mountain people of Appalachia are unhappy, so they will impose a program to make them happy even if it makes them miserable.

And the curious thing—the really curious thing—is that these compulsions are sold to a gullible people as manifestations of what the President is pleased to call a "voluntary society." It is part of the Newspeak vocabulary of the Sixties. Secretary of Defense McNamara, operating by press gang, would swear all boys and girls into uniforms of their choice. The President, signing a Peace Corps bill, longs for the day when "some form" of voluntary service is as common as going to school," but the President does not reflect that going to school is rarely a voluntary act. It is imposed upon children by law or by custom because it is good for them.

Just as the meaning of "voluntary" has been corrupted, so the meaning of "property" has been corrupted. The administration proclaims "equality" as a primary goal, but this is the equality invented by Procrustes. The Great Society promises "benefits," so long as it may shape and define what these benefits are. The states are reduced to imbecility and the cities to mendicancy, and this is "Creative Federalism." The liberal Left professes a love of freedom, right down to the repeal of Taft-Hartley's section 14(b). These people love the worker's freedom in terms of making him join a union.

In this block-by-block demolition of old values, it is small wonder that respect for law has declined with a respect for divine power. One of the most penetrating comments on the "New People" of our campuses and slums came from Roger Price, editor of *Grump*: "In rejecting the theology of Christianity, they have also, to a large extent, rejected its ethics. Many of them have concluded that if Jonah wasn't swallowed by the whale, it's okay to steal."

The American conservative holds fast to the conviction that there is something better than all this.

If our cities are to be made genuinely beautiful, and not merely plastered over, the beauty must come from within. It must be achieved primarily by the cities themselves—by the people who dwell within them, exerting their own leadership, pursuing their own dreams, acting within their own inheritance. The wounds of our cities cannot be healed by busy little federal surgeons operating with great whacks of their carving knives, and leaving a Band-Aid of rent supplements behind.

If the problems of the Negro people are ever to be solved, these, too, must be solved primarily by the Negro people themselves, and on their own terms, in their own way. In this sense of the rallying cry, "Black Power" is absolutely sound. As the Reverend Martin Luther King, Jr., remarked in his famed "Letter from the Birmingham Jail," it is the white moderate who has become "the Negro's great stumbling block in his stride toward freedom." James Farmer, in the book *Freedom—When?* repeatedly makes the point that "the Negro community must get to work on itself." When the white power structure attempts to impose its solutions upon the colored community, as Farmer says, the Negro resents it to the depth of his soul.

It is a false approach. The conservative would hope to provide genuine opportunities for the Negro, to make training available to those with gumption enough to struggle up, and then to leave integration to find its own natural level. And the conservative, in opposing the unfair provisions of "fair housing" laws, would insist that two equal and very human rights are involved in the right of free contract—the right to buy, and the right not to sell.

The conservative would insist that the principles of a wise and constructive federalism be returned from the liberals' attic. There still is a great role for the states and cities to play in creating and experimenting with new forms of government and new areas of local responsibility. The conservative would urge that the old doctrine of separation of powers also be revived, and propped up in bed, and given a transfusion, toward the end that the regulatory powers of the executive agencies be kept strictly within the surveillance of the legislative branch.

In every applicable policy of government, the conservative would seek to preserve the individual's right to be left alone—to buy potato chips as he pleases, to take vitamin pills as he pleases, to enjoy his private property as he pleases, so long as he causes no harm to his neighbor. Acting upon Jefferson's skeptical view of public magistrates, the conservative, in questions of power, would "speak no more of confidence in Man, but bind him down from mischief by the chains of the Constitution."

Barry Goldwater sought to espouse most of these views in his ill-fated campaign two years ago. The shock of the Kennedy assassination still lay upon the land. Lyndon Johnson still held the sympathy of a people instinctively unwilling to opt at the time for further change. For a number of reasons, the time for these ideas was not right. But Victor Hugo's remark still holds much truth: No force can withstand the power of an idea whose time has come. In a nation that is beginning to ache for a return to law and order, for a renewed respect for property rights, and for a greater measure of personal freedom, the time for these ideas moves steadily toward the striking hour.

"Black Power" and Coalition Politics

Bayard Rustin

There are two Americas—black and white—and nothing has more clearly revealed the divisions between them than the debate currently raging around the slogan of "black power." Despite—or perhaps because of—the fact that this slogan lacks any clear definition, it has succeeded in galvanizing emotions on all sides, with many whites seeing it as the expression of a new racism and many Negroes taking it as a warning to white people that Negroes will no longer tolerate brutality and violence. But even within the Negro community itself, "black power" has touched off a major debate—the most bitter the community has experienced since the days of Booker T. Washington and W. E. B. Du Bois, and one which threatens to ravage the entire civil-rights movement. Indeed, a serious split has already developed between advocates of "black power" like Floyd McKissick of CORE and Stokely Carmichael of SNCC on the one hand, and Dr. Martin Luther King of SCLC, Roy Wilkins of the NAACP, and Whitney Young of the Urban League on the other.

There is no question, then, that great passions are involved in the debate over the idea of "black power"; nor, as we shall see, is there any question that these passions have their roots in the psychological and political frustrations of the Negro community. Nevertheless, I would contend that "black power" not only lacks any real value for the civil-rights movement, but that its propagation is positively harmful. It diverts the movement from a meaningful debate over strategy and tactics, it isolates the Negro community, and it encourages the growth of anti-Negro forces.

In its simplest and most innocent guise, "black power" merely means the effort to elect Negroes to office in proportion to Negro strength within the population. There is, of course, nothing wrong with such an objective in itself, and nothing inherently radical in the idea of pursuing it. But in Stokely Carmichael's extravagant rhetoric about "taking over" in districts of the South where Negroes are in the majority, it is important to recognize that Southern Negroes are only in a position to win a maximum of two congressional seats and control of eight local counties. (Carmichael, incidentally, is in the paradoxical position of screaming at liberals—wanting only to "get whitey off my back"—and simultaneously needing their support: after all, he can talk about Negroes taking over Lowndes County only because there is a fairly liberal federal government to protect him should Governor Wallace decide to eliminate this pocket of black power.) Now there might be a certain value in having two Negro congressmen from the South, but obviously they could do nothing by themselves to reconstruct the face of America. Eighty sheriffs, eighty tax assessors, and eighty school-board members might ease the tension for a while in their communities, but they alone could not create jobs and build low-cost housing; they alone could not supply quality integrated education.

The relevant question, moreover, is not whether a politician is black or white, but what forces he represents. Manhattan has had a succession of Negro borough presidents, and yet the schools are increasingly segregated. Adam Clayton Powell and William Dawson have both been in Congress for many years; the former is responsible for a rider on school integration that never gets passed, and the latter is responsible for keeping the Negroes of Chicago tied to a mayor who had to see riots and death before he would put eight-dollar sprinklers on water hydrants in the summer. I am not for one minute arguing that Powell, Dawson, and Mrs. Motley should be impeached. What I am saying is that if a politician is elected because he is black and is deemed to be entitled to a "slice of the pie," he will behave in one way; if he is elected by a constituency pressing for social reform, he will, whether he is white or black, behave in another way.

Southern Negroes, despite exhortations from SNCC to organize themselves into a Black Panther party, are going to stay in the Democratic party—to them it is the party of progress, the New Deal, the New Frontier, and the Great Society—and they are right to stay. For SNCC's Black Panther perspective is simultaneously utopian and reactionary—the former for the by now obvious reason that one-tenth of the population cannot accomplish much by itself, the latter because such a party would remove Negroes from the main area of political struggle in this country (particularly in the one-party South, where the decisive battles are fought out in Democratic primaries), and would give priority to the issue of race precisely at a time when the fundamental questions facing the Negro and American society alike are economic and social. It is no accident that the two main proponents of "black power," Carmichael and McKissick, should now be co-sponsoring a conference with Adam Clayton Powell and Elijah Muhammad, and that the leaders of New York CORE should recently have supported the machine candidate for Surrogate—because he was the choice of a Negro boss—rather than the candidate of the reform movement. By contrast, Martin Luther King is working in Chicago with the Industrial Union Department of the AFL-CIO and with religious groups in a coalition which, if successful, will mean the end or at least the weakening of the Daley-Dawson machine.

The winning of the right of Negroes to vote in the South insures the eventual transformation of the Democratic party, now controlled primarily by Northern machine politicians and Southern Dixiecrats. The Negro vote will eliminate the Dixiecrats from the party and from Congress, which means that the crucial question facing us today is who will replace them in the South. Unless civil-rights leaders (in such towns as Jackson, Mississippi; Birmingham, Alabama; and even to a certain extent Atlanta) can organize grass-roots clubs whose members will have a genuine political voice, the Dixiecrats might well be succeeded by black moderates and black Southern-style machine politicians, who would do little to push for needed legislation in Congress and little to improve local conditions in the South. While I myself would prefer Negro machines to a situation in which Negroes have no power at all, it seems to me that there is a better alternative today—a liberal-labor-civil rights coalition which would work to make the Democratic party truly responsive to the aspirations of the poor, and which would develop support for programs (specifically those outlined in A. Philip Randolph's $100 billion Freedom Budget) aimed at the reconstruction of American society in the interests of greater social justice. The advocates of "black power" have no such programs in mind; what they are in fact arguing for (perhaps unconsciously) is the creation of a *new black establishment*.

Nor, it might be added, are they leading the Negro people along the same road which they imagine immigrant groups traveled so successfully in the past. Proponents of "black power"—accepting a historical myth perpetrated by moderates—like to say that the Irish and the Jews and the Italians, by sticking together and demanding their share, finally won enough power to overcome their initial disabilities. But the truth is that it was through alliances with other groups (in political machines or as part of the trade-union movement) that the Irish and the Jews and the Italians acquired the power to win their rightful place in American society. They did not "pull themselves up by their own bootstraps"—no group in American society has ever done so; and they most certainly did not make isolation their primary tactic.

In some quarters, "black power" connotes not an effort to increase the number of Negroes in elective office but rather a repudiation of non-violence in favor of Negro "self-defense." Actually this is a false issue, since no one has ever argued that Negroes should not defend themselves as individuals from attack. Non-violence has been advocated as a *tactic* for organized demonstrations in a society where Negroes are a minority and where the majority controls the police. Proponents of non-violence do not, for example, deny that James Meredith has the right to carry a gun for protection when he visits his mother in Mississippi; what they question is the wisdom of his carrying a gun while participating in a demonstration.

There is, as well, a tactical side to the new emphasis on "self-defense" and the suggestion that non-violence be abandoned. The reasoning here is that turning the other cheek is not the way to win respect, and that only if the Negro succeeds in frightening the white man will the white man begin taking him seriously. The trouble with this reasoning is that it fails to recognize that fear is more likely to bring hostility to the surface than respect; and far from prodding the "white power structure" into action, the new militant leadership, by raising the slogan of black power and lowering the banner of non-violence, has obscured the moral issue facing this nation and permitted the President and Vice President to lecture us about "racism in reverse" instead of proposing more meaningful programs for dealing with the problems of unemployment, housing, and education.

"Black power" is, of course, a somewhat nationalistic slogan and its sudden rise to popularity among Negroes signifies a concomitant rise in nationalist sentiment (Malcolm X's autobiography is quoted nowadays in Grenada, Mississippi as well as in Harlem). We have seen such nationalistic turns and withdrawals back into the ghetto before, and when we look at the conditions which brought them about, we find that they have much in common with the conditions of Negro life at the present moment: conditions which lead to despair over the goal of integration and to the belief that the ghetto will last forever.

It may, in the light of the many juridical and legislative victories which have been achieved in the past few years, seem strange that despair should be so widespread among Negroes today. But anyone to whom it seems strange should reflect on the fact that despite these victories *Negroes today are in worse economic shape, live in worse slums, and attend more highly segregated schools than in 1954.* Thus—to recite the appalling, and appallingly familiar, statistical litany once again—more Negroes are unemployed today than in 1954; the gap between the wages of the Negro worker and the white worker is wider; while the unemployment rate among white youths is decreasing, the rate among Negro youths has increased to *32 per cent* (and among Negro girls the rise is even more startling). Even the one gain which has been registered, a decrease in the unemployment rate among Negro adults, is deceptive, for it represents men who have been called back to work after a period of being laid off. In any event, unemployment among Negro men is still twice that of whites, and no new jobs have been created.

So too with housing, which is deteriorating in the North (and yet the housing provisions of the 1966 civil-rights bill are weaker than the anti-discrimination laws in several states which contain the worst ghettos even with these laws on their books). And so too with schools: according to figures issued recently by the Department of Health, Education and Welfare, 65 per cent of first-grade Negro students in this country attend schools that are from 90 to 100 per cent black. (If in 1954, when the Supreme Court handed down the desegregation decision, you had been the Negro parent of a first-grade child, the chances are that this past June you would have attended that child's graduation from a segregated high school.)

To put all this in the simplest and most concrete terms: the day-to-day lot of the ghetto Negro has not been improved by the various judicial and legislative measures of the past decade.

Negroes are thus in a situation similar to that of the turn of the century, when Booker T. Washington advised them to "cast down their buckets" (that is to say, accommodate to segregation and disenfranchisement) and when even his leading opponent, W. E. B. Du Bois, was forced to advocate the development of a group economy in place of the direct-action boycotts, general strikes, and protest techniques which had been used in the 1880's, before the enactment of the Jim Crow laws. For all their differences, both Washington and Du Bois then found it impossible to believe that Negroes could ever be integrated into American society, and each in his own way therefore counseled withdrawal into the ghetto, self-help, and economic self-determination.

World War I aroused new hope in Negroes that the rights removed at the turn of the century would be restored. More than 360,000 Negroes entered military service and went overseas; many left the South seeking the good life in the North and hoping to share in the temporary prosperity created by the war. But all these hopes were quickly smashed at the end of the fighting. In the first year following the war, more than seventy Negroes were lynched, and during the last six months of the year, there were some twenty-four riots throughout America. White mobs took over whole cities, flogging, burning, shooting, and torturing at will, and when Negroes tried to defend themselves, the violence only increased. Along with this, Negroes were excluded from unions and pushed out of jobs they had won during the war, including federal jobs.

In the course of this period of dashed hope and spreading segregation—the same period, incidentally, when a reorganized Ku Klux Klan was achieving a membership which was to reach into the millions—the largest mass movement ever to take root among working-class Negroes, Marcus Garvey's "Back to Africa" movement, was born. "Buy Black" became a slogan in the ghettos; faith in integration was virtually snuffed out in the Negro community until the 1930's when the CIO reawakened the old dream of a Negro-labor alliance by announcing a policy of non-discrimination and when the New Deal admitted Negroes into relief programs, WPA jobs, and public housing. No sooner did jobs begin to open up and Negroes begin to be welcomed into mainstream organizations than "Buy Black" campaigns gave way to "Don't Buy Where You Can't Work" movements. A. Philip Randolph was able to organize a massive March on Washington demanding a wartime FEPC; CORE was born and with it the non-violent sit-in technique; the NAACP succeeded in putting an end to the white primaries in 1944. Altogether, World War II was a period of hope for Negroes, and the economic progress they made through wartime industry continued steadily until about 1948 and remained stable for a time. Meanwhile, the non-violent movement of the 1950's and 60's achieved the desegregation of public accommodations and established the right to vote.

Yet at the end of this long fight, the Southern Negro is too poor to use those integrated facilities and too intimidated and disorganized to use the vote to maximum advantage, while the economic position of the Northern Negro deteriorates rapidly.

The promise of meaningful work and decent wages once held out by the anti-poverty programs has not been fulfilled. Because there has been a lack of the necessary funds, the program has in many cases been reduced to wrangling for positions on boards or for lucrative staff jobs. Negro professionals working for the program have earned handsome salaries—ranging from $14- to $25,000—while young boys have been asked to plant trees at $1.25 an hour. Nor have the Job Corps camps made a significant dent in unemployment among Negro youths; indeed, the main beneficiaries of this program seem to be the private companies who are contracted to set up the camps.

Then there is the war in Vietnam, which poses many ironies for the Negro community. On the one hand, Negroes are bitterly aware of the fact that more and more money is being spent on the war, while the anti-poverty program is being cut; on the other hand, Negro youths are enlisting in great numbers, as though to say that it is worth the risk of being killed to learn a trade, to leave a dead-end situation, and to join the only institution in this society which seems really to be integrated.

The youths who rioted in Watts, Cleveland, Omaha, Chicago, and Portland are the members of a truly hopeless and lost generation. They can see the alien world of affluence unfold before them on the TV screen. But they have already failed in their inferior segregated schools. Their grandfathers were sharecroppers, their grandmothers were domestics, and their mothers are domestics too. Many have never met their fathers. Mistreated by the local storekeeper, suspected by the policeman on the beat, disliked by their teachers, they cannot stand more failures and would rather retreat into the world of heroin than risk looking for a job downtown or having their friends see them push a rack in the garment district. Floyd McKissick and Stokely Carmichael may accuse Roy Wilkins of being out of touch with the Negro ghetto, but nothing more clearly demonstrates their own alienation from ghetto youth than their repeated exhortations to these young men to oppose the Vietnam war when so many of them tragically see it as their only way out. Yet there is no need to labor the significance of the fact that the rice fields of Vietnam and the Green Berets have more to offer a Negro boy than the streets of Mississippi or the towns of Alabama or 125th Street in New York.

The Vietnam war is also partly responsible for the growing disillusion with non-violence among Negroes. The ghetto Negro does not in general ask whether the United States is right or wrong to be in Southeast Asia. He does, however, wonder why he is exhorted to non-violence when the United States has been waging a fantastically brutal war, and it puzzles him to be told that he must turn the other cheek in our own South while we must fight for freedom in South Vietnam.

Thus, as in roughly similar circumstances in the past—circumstances, I repeat, which in the aggregate foster the belief that the ghetto is destined to last forever—Negroes are once again turning to nationalistic slogans, with "black power" affording the same emotional release as "Back to Africa" and "Buy Black" did in earlier periods of frustration and hopelessness. This is not only the case with the ordinary Negro in the ghetto; it is also the case with leaders like McKissick and Carmichael, neither of whom began as a nationalist or was at first cynical about the possibilities of integration. It took countless beatings and 24 jailings—that, and the absence of strong and continual support from the liberal community—to persuade Carmichael that his earlier faith in coalition politics was mistaken, that nothing was to be gained from working with whites, and that an alliance with the black nationalists was desirable. In the areas of the South where SNCC has been working so nobly, implementation of the Civil Rights Acts of 1964 and 1965 has been slow and ineffective. Negroes in many rural areas cannot walk into the courthouse and register to vote. Despite the voting-rights bill, they must file complaints and the Justice Department must be called to send federal registrars. Nor do children attend integrated schools as a matter of course. There, too, complaints must be filed and the Department of Health, Education and Welfare must be notified. Neither department has been doing an effective job of enforcing the bills. The feeling of isolation increases among SNCC workers as each legislative victory turns out to be only a token victory—significant on the national level, but not affecting the day-to-day lives of Negroes. Carmichael and his colleagues are wrong in refusing to support the 1966 bill, but one can understand why they feel as they do.

It is, in short, the growing conviction that the Negroes cannot win—a conviction with much grounding in experience—which accounts for the new popularity of "black power." So far as the ghetto Negro is concerned, this conviction expresses itself in hostility first toward the people closest to him who have held out the most promise and failed to deliver (Martin Luther King, Roy Wilkins, etc.), then toward those who have proclaimed themselves his friends (the liberals and the labor movement), and finally toward the only oppressors he can see (the local storekeeper and the policeman on the corner). On the leadership level, the conviction that the Negroes cannot win takes other forms, principally the adoption of what I have called a "no-win" policy. Why bother with programs when their enactment results only in "sham"? Why concern ourselves with the image of the movement when nothing significant has been gained for all the sacrifices made by SNCC and CORE? Why compromise with reluctant white allies when nothing of consequence can be achieved anyway? Why indeed have anything to do with whites at all?

On this last point, it is extremely important for white liberals to understand—as, one gathers from their references to "racism in reverse," the President and the Vice President of the United States do not—that there is all the difference in the world between saying, "If you don't want me, I don't want you" (which is what some proponents of "black power" have in effect been saying) and the statement, "Whatever you do, I don't want you" (which is what racism declares). It is, in other words, both absurd and immoral to equate the despairing response of the victim with the contemptuous assertion of the oppressor. It would, moreover, be tragic if white liberals allowed verbal hostility on the part of Negroes to drive them out of the movement or to curtail their support for civil rights. The issue was injustice before "black power" became popular, and the issue is still injustice.

In any event, even if "black power" had not emerged as a slogan, problems would have arisen in the relation between whites and Negroes in the civil-rights movement. In the North, it was inevitable that Negroes would eventually wish to run their own movement and would rebel against the presence of whites in positions of leadership as yet another sign of white supremacy. In the South, the well-intentioned white volunteer had the cards stacked against him from the beginning. Not only could he leave the struggle any time he chose to do so, but a higher value was set on his safety by the press and the government—apparent in the differing degrees of excitement generated by the imprisonment or murder of whites and Negroes. The white person's importance to the movement in the South was thus an ironic outgrowth of racism and was therefore bound to create resentment.

But again: however understandable all this may be as a response to objective conditions and to the seeming irrelevance of so many hard-won victories to the day-to-day life of the mass of Negroes, the fact remains that the quasi-nationalist sentiments and "no-win" policy lying behind the slogan of "black power" do no service to the Negro. Some nationalist emotion is, of course, inevitable, and "black power" must be seen as part of the psychological rejection of white supremacy, part of the rebellion against the stereotypes which have been ascribed to Negroes for three hundred years. Nevertheless, pride, confidence, and a new identity cannot be won by glorifying blackness or attacking whites; they can only come from meaningful action, from good jobs, and from real victories such as were achieved on the streets of Montgomery, Birmingham, and Selma. When SNCC and CORE went into the South, they awakened the country, but now they emerge isolated and demoralized, shouting a slogan that may afford a momentary satisfaction but that is calculated to destroy them and their movement. Already their frustrated call is being answered with counter-demands for law and order and with opposition to police-review boards. Already they have diverted the entire civil-rights movement from the hard task of developing strategies to realign the major parties of this country, and embroiled it in a debate that can only lead more and more to politics by frustration.

On the other side, however—the more important side, let it be said—it is the business of those who reject the negative aspects of "black power" not to preach but to act. Some weeks ago President Johnson, speaking at Fort Campbell, Kentucky, asserted that riots impeded reform, created fear, and antagonized the Negro's traditional friends. Mr. Johnson, according to the New York *Times,* expressed sympathy for the plight of the poor, the jobless, and the ill-housed. The government, he noted, has been working to relieve their circumstances, but "all this takes time."

One cannot argue with the President's position that riots are destructive or that they frighten away allies. Nor can one find fault with his sympathy for the plight of the poor; surely the poor need sympathy. But one can question whether the government has been working seriously enough to eliminate the conditions which lead to frustration-politics and riots. The President's very words, "all this takes time," will be understood by the poor for precisely what they are—an excuse instead of a real program, a cover-up for the failure to establish real priorities, and an indication that the administration has no real commitment to create new jobs, better housing, and integrated schools.

For the truth is that it need only take ten years to eliminate poverty— ten years and the $100 billion Freedom Budget recently proposed by A. Philip Randoph. In his introduction to the budget (which was drawn up in consultation with the nation's leading economists, and which will be published later this month), Mr. Randolph points out: "The programs urged in the Freedom Budget attack all of the major causes of poverty— unemployment and underemployment, substandard pay, inadequate social insurance and welfare payments to those who cannot or should not be employed; bad housing; deficiencies in health services, education, and training; and fiscal and monetary policies which tend to redistribute income regressively rather than progressively. The Freedom Budget leaves no room for discrimination in any form because its programs are addressed to all who need more opportunity and improved incomes and living standards, not to just some of them.

The legislative precedent Mr. Randolph has in mind is the 1945 Full Employment bill. This bill—conceived in its original form by Roosevelt to prevent a postwar depression—would have made it public policy for the government to step in if the private economy could not provide enough employment. As passed finally by Congress in 1946, with many of its teeth removed, the bill had the result of preventing the Negro worker, who had finally reached a pay level about 55 per cent that of the white wage, from making any further progress in closing that discriminatory gap; and instead, he was pushed back by the chronically high unemployment rates of the 50's. Had the original bill been passed, the public sector of our economy would have been able to insure fair and full employment. Today, with the spiralling thrust of automation, it is even more imperative that we have a legally binding commitment to this goal.

Let me interject a word here to those who say that Negroes are asking for another handout and are refusing to help themselves. From the end of the 19th century up to the last generation, the United States absorbed and provided economic opportunity for tens of millions of immigrants.

These people were usually uneducated and a good many could not speak English. They had nothing but their hard work to offer and they labored long hours, often in miserable sweatshops and unsafe mines. Yet in a burgeoning economy with a need for unskilled labor, they were able to find jobs, and as industrialization proceeded, they were gradually able to move up the ladder to greater skills. Negroes who have been driven off the farm into a city life for which they are not prepared and who have entered an economy in which there is less and less need for unskilled labor, cannot be compared with these immigrants of old. The tenements which were jammed by newcomers were way-stations of hope; the ghettos of today have become dead-ends of despair. Yet just as the older generation of immigrants—in its most decisive act of self-help—organized the trade-union movement and then in alliance with many middle-class elements went on to improve its own lot and the condition of American society generally, so the Negro of today is struggling to go beyond the gains of the past and, in alliance with liberals and labor, to guarantee full and fair employment to all Americans.

Mr. Randolph's Freedom Budget not only rests on the Employment Act of 1946, but on a precedent set by Harry Truman when he believed freedom was threatened in Europe. In 1947, the Marshall Plan was put into effect and 3 per cent of the gross national product was spent in foreign aid. If we were to allocate a similar proportion of our GNP to destroy the economic and social consequences of racism and poverty at home today, it might mean spending more than 20 billion dollars a year, although I think it quite possible that we can fulfill these goals with a much smaller sum. It would be intolerable, however, if our plan for domestic social reform were less audacious and less far-reaching than our international programs of a generation ago.

We must see, therefore, in the current debate over "black power," a fantastic challenge to American society to live up to its proclaimed principles in the area of race by transforming itself so that all men may live equally and under justice. We must see to it that in rejecting "black power," we do not also reject the principle of Negro equality. Those people who would use the current debate and/or the riots to abandon the civil-rights movement leave us no choice but to question their original motivation.

If anything, the next period will be more serious and difficult than the preceding ones. It is much easier to establish the Negro's right to sit at a Woolworth's counter than to fight for an integrated community. It takes very little imagination to understand that the Negro should have the right to vote, but it demands much creativity, patience, and political stamina to plan, develop, and implement programs and priorities. It is one thing to organize sentiment behind laws that do not disturb consensus politics, and quite another to win battles for the redistribution of wealth. Many people who marched in Selma are not prepared to support a bill for a $2.00 minimum wage, to say nothing of supporting a redefinition of work or a guaranteed annual income.

It is here that we who advocate coalitions and integration and who object to the "black-power" concept have a massive job to do. We must see to it that the liberal-labor-civil rights coalition is maintained and, indeed, strengthened so that it can fight effectively for a Freedom Budget. We are responsible for the growth of the "black-power" concept because we have not used our own power to insure the full implementation of the bills whose passage we were strong enough to win, and we have not mounted the necessary campaign for winning a decent minimum wage and extended benefits. "Black power" is a slogan directed primarily against liberals by those who once counted liberals among their closest friends. It is up to the liberal movement to prove that coalition and integration are better alternatives.

How Are Parties Organized?

Plan of Organization of the Democratic Party in North Carolina *

ARTICLE I. PRECINCT ORGANIZATION

Section 1. Precinct Committee:

The unit of the Democratic Party organization in the State of North Carolina shall be the voting precinct. In each precinct there shall be an executive committee consisting of ten registered and active Democrats, who reside full time in the precinct, five of whom shall be women and five of whom shall be men, who should be present when elected by the Democratic voters of said precinct at the precinct meeting called by the Chairman of the County Executive Committee as provided in this plan of organization. The precinct committee so elected shall elect from its membership a Chairman and Vice Chairman, one of whom shall be a woman and the other of whom shall be a man, and a Secretary-Treasurer, provided, however, the Chairman and Vice Chairman shall not be from the same immediate family.

Section 2. Precinct Meeting:

The precinct meetings shall be presided over by the chairman of the precinct committee, but in his absence, the vice chairman of the committee shall preside, and in the absence of both the chairman and the vice chairman, any member of the committee may preside.

Section 3. Quorum:

A quorum for any precinct meeting shall consist of not less than ten registered Democrats in such precinct. In the event a quorum is not present the precinct chairman shall notify the Chairman of the County Executive Committee who shall call a second meeting. If the second meeting shall fail for lack of a quorum, the officers of the County Executive Committee

* Although there are variations in party organizations from state to state, the organization of the Democratic Party in North Carolina is typical of the vast majority of both parties.

shall fill all vacancies. Provided that in precincts having fewer than 20 registered and active Democrats, ½ of such registered active Democrats shall be sufficient to comprise the precinct committee and to constitute a quorum at the precinct meeting.

Section 4. Election of Delegates:

At the precinct meeting called for that purpose the Democratic voters in attendance shall elect delegates and alternates to represent the precinct in the county convention; and said delegates or alternates, or such of them as shall attend the county convention, shall be entitled to vote the full strength of their precinct upon all questions, nominations, or elections which may come before the county convention. The chairman, or presiding officer, and the secretary of the precinct meeting shall certify to the county convention the names of the delegates and alternates selected at the meeting.

Section 5. Business Permitted:

At every precinct meeting, if requested, a vote shall be taken on the different questions, nominations, and elections anticipated to come before the country convention, and in that event, the chairman or presiding officer and the secretary of the precinct meeting shall certify to the county convention the vote so cast, and the relative vote as fixed in the precinct meeting shall not be changed in the county convention, except by two-thirds vote of the entire unit of delegates desiring to change its vote.

Section 6. Failure to Hold Meeting:

In case there shall be a failure to hold a precinct meeting in pursuance of the call of the chaiman of the county executive committee, or if at any meeting there shall be a failure to elect delegates to the county convention, in either event, the precinct executive committee shall appoint the delegates and alternates from the Democratic voters of the precinct. In the event there shall be a failure to elect a precinct committee prior to the day of the County Convention the County Executive Committee at its meeting on the day of the County Convention may appoint both the precinct committee and the delegates to the said convention.

Section 7. Representation:

Each precinct shall be entitled to cast in the county convention one vote for every 50 Democratic votes or major fraction thereof cast by the precinct for the Democratic gubernatorial candidate at the last preceding gubernatorial election; provided that each precinct shall be entitled to cast at least two votes in the county convention.

The County Executive Committee may, by resolution duly adopted, require each Precinct to appoint two delegates and two alternates for each vote to which said precinct may be entitled in the County Convention.

Section 8. Removal of Officers and Committeemen:

Any precinct Chairman, Vice Chairman or Committeeman, or Committeewoman who gives support to, aids, or helps any opposing political party or candidate of any other political party, or who refuses or fails to perform his duties in organizing his precinct, or who is convicted of a crime involving moral turpitude, shall be removed from office in the following manner:

(1). A complaint setting forth full details and duly verified shall be filed with the Chairman of the County Executive Committee by three active Democrats as defined in this Plan of Organization registered in the county of the said officer or committeemember. The Chairman of the County Executive Committee shall upon approval of the other committee officers and after giving 5 days notice thereof, call a meeting of the County Executive Committee to hear the complaintant, the alleged offender and any other interested parties or witnesses. A two-third vote of those members present and voting shall be necessary to remove a precinct officer or committeemember. The decision of the County Executive Committee shall be final.

(2). When a vacancy exists because of removal for cause, the vacancy shall be filled by the remaining members of the precinct executive committee at a duly called meeting by the Chairman of the County Executive Committee. Notice of the filling of such vacancy shall be given to the chairman of the County Executive Committee. If the vacancy is not filled within ten days, the Chairman of the County Executive Committee within ten days thereafter shall call a meeting of the officers of the County Executive Committee who shall fill the vacancy. The Chairman of the County Executive Committee shall cause a full detailed account of any removal and replacement to be filed with the Chairman of the State Executive Committee.

ARTICLE II. COUNTY ORGANIZATION
Section 1. County Executive Committee:
The Chairman and the Vice Chairman of the several precinct committees, the President of the duly organized Democratic Women's Club within a county and the President of the duly organized county Young Democratic Club within the county shall compose the County Executive Committee; provided that the North Carolina Young Democratic Club Executive Committee shall determine what shall constitute a duly organized Young Democratic Club and shall certify the proper Young Democratic Club officers to the County Chairman, whose names shall be furnished to the President of the North Carolina Young Democratic Club by the State Party Chairman, and that the Vice Chairman of the North Carolina Democratic Executive Committee shall determine what shall constitute a duly organized county Democratic Women's Club and certify the name of the member who is to serve on the County Democratic Executive Committee to the Chairman of that body, and further that the presidents of the several Young Democratic Clubs shall together have one vote on the Executive Committee with each club having a portion of said vote "in proportion to the ratio of its membership to the total membership of the combined clubs," and further that the presidents of the several Democratic Women's Club shall together have one vote on the Executive Committee with each club having a portion of said vote in proportion to the ratio of its membership to the total membership of the combined clubs.

The county Executive Committee shall meet on the same day as the county convention first held in each election year, the meeting to be held either before or after the convention at an hour and place to be designated in the call therefor. At said meeting a chairman of said county executive committee shall be elected. Immediately after the election of the chairman, the committee shall elect one or more, but not exceeding three, vice chairmen, a secretary and a treasurer. If more than one vice chairman shall be elected the order of their succession shall be designated by title, e.g., first vice chairman, second vice chairman, third vice chairman. Either the chairman or the first vice chairman shall be a woman, and the other shall be a man. The chairman, vice chairman or vice chairmen, secretary and treasurer need not be members of the County Executive Committee, but all of said officers shall be ex-officio members of the committee, with the power to vote; however, at any organizational meeting of said County Executive Committee said ex-officio members shall not have the power to vote. Should any precinct official be elected to any county organizational office or other office entitling him or her to membership on the county Executive Committee, he or she automatically vacates the precinct office.

If for any reason there should occur any vacancy in the chairmanship of the County Executive Committee, by death, resignation, or removal, or if such chairman should be incapacitated, then upon a written notice to such chairman signed by the remaining officers of the County Executive Committee, the vice chairman or vice chairmen, in their order of succession, and thereafter the secretary, shall, in such order of succession, be vested with full authority and power of the chairman until such time as said County Executive Committee has met and duly elected a successor to such chairman.

When the County Executive Committee is not in session, the officers of the County Executive Committee, presided over by the Chairman, shall act in the place of the County Executive Committee on all matters; unless this plan of organization states that action is to be by the entire County Executive Committee.

Section 2. *Additional Precinct Meetings:*

In addition to the common day fixed by the State Executive Committee during election years, the Chairman of any County Executive Committee, may issue a call between October 1st of any non-election year and March 1st in any election year for a meeting of the County Executive Committee and, in addition to any other business specified in the call, the said committee may adopt a resolution fixing a common day, times and places for the holding of precinct meetings for the purpose of electing precinct committees; and fix the day, time and place for the organization meeting of the newly elected County Executive Committee for the purpose of electing a chairman and other county officers. The County Chairman shall immediately issue a call in writing at least 10 days before the day set for the said precinct meetings. This call shall be posted at the courthouse door of the county and copies thereof shall be sent as a news item to each news media published in the county.

Any precinct meeting provided in this section shall be held more than two weeks before the common day fixed by the State Executive Committee.

Section 3. Duties of Officers:

The duties of the County Executive Officers shall be:

(1). The chairman shall be responsible for the organization of the county on all levels, including calling of all meetings, holding of political instruction classes for precinct executive committees, obtaining all materials necessary for the proper function of his duties and doing all other things necessary for the proper carrying out of the best interest of the party.

(2). One of the vice chairmen shall be responsible for the organization and activities of the women members of the County Executive Committee and the women's activities in behalf of the Democratic Party in the said county, subject to the direction of the chairman of the County Executive Committee.

(3). The other vice chairman of the County Executive Committee shall have such duties and responsibilities as may be assigned by the chairman.

(4). The secretary shall have the duty and responsbility of keeping all records of the County Executive Committee, including attendance at all meetings, of issuing all notices, preparing all correspondence, and any other duties that may be assigned to him by the said chairman.

(5). The treasurer shall have the duty of raising all money required for the operation of the activities of the Democratic Party, keep records of all money received and expended in behalf of the Party and forward a list of all donors and expenses to the Chairman of the State Executive Committee. The treasurer shall also submit any and all reports as required by the law of the finances of the County Executive Committee.

Section 4. Board of Elections:

The chairman of the Executive Committee in each county shall, before submitting to the State Chairman recommendations for the Democratic members of the County Board of Elections in such county, call a meeting of the County Executive Committee and submit such recommendations for the approval of the executive committee and only when such recommendations are approved by a majority of the committee members present shall same be submitted to the State Chairman by the county chairman. The time of such meeting of the respective county executive committees for the purpose of passing on such recommendations shall be fixed by the State Chairman.

No member or officer of a County Executive Committee shall be eligible to serve as a member of a County Board of Elections, nor as a precinct registrar or judge of elections.

Section 5. Rules:

The county executive committee shall have power to make any rules with regard to the holding of precinct meetings which it may deem proper, not inconsistent with the rules prescribed in this plan; it shall be the duty of said committee to prepare and furnish all forms and blanks needed in making the returns from said precinct meetings, and any reported challenges and appeals therefrom; and it shall have the power to raise the funds necessary to pay for the expenses thereof.

The secretary of the County Executive Committee shall forward a copy of each precinct organization and the officers of the County Organization to the chairman of the State Executive Committee.

Section 6. Removal of County Officers:

Any officer of the County Democratic Executive Committee who gives support to, aids, or helps any opposing political party or candidate of any other political party, or who refuses or fails to perform his duties in organizing his county, or who is convicted of a crime involving moral turpitude, shall be removed from office in the following manner:

(1). A complaint setting forth full details and duly verified shall be filed with the Chairman of the State Executive Committee by three active Democrats as defined by this Plan of Organization registered in the county. The chairman of the State Executive Committee shall upon the approval of the other committee officers, after giving five days notice thereof, call a meeting of the State Executive Committee to hear the complaintant, the alleged offender and any other interested parties or witnesses. A two-thirds vote of those members present and voting shall be necessary to remove a county officer. The decision of the State Executive Committee shall be final.

(2). When a vacancy exists because of removal for cause, the vacancy shall be filled by the remaining members of the County Executive Committee at a duly called meeting of that committee.

ARTICLE III. SECTIONAL ORGANIZATION
Section 1. Congressional District Executive Committees:

The Congressional District Executive Committee for each congressional district in the State shall consist of two members from each county in said district who shall be elected at the preliminary meeting of delegates from the congressional districts held on the morning of the State Convention; provided, however, that in any congressional district embracing less than five counties, the committee shall consist of three members from each county in the district.

Section 2. Judicial District Executive Committees:

The Judicial District Executive Committee for each judicial district in the State shall consist of two members from each county in said district, who shall be elected at the preliminary meetings of delegates from the congressional districts held on the morning of the State Convention; provided, however, that in any judicial district embracing less than five counties, the committee shall consist of three members from each county in the district.

Section 3. Solicitorial District Executive Committee:

The Solicitorial District Executive Committee for each solicitorial district in the State shall consist of two members from each county in said district, who shall be elected at the preliminary meetings of delegates from the congressional districts held on the morning of the State Convention; provided, however, that in any solicitorial district embracing less than five counties, the committee shall consist of three members from each county in the district.

Section 4. State Senatorial District Executive Committee:

The State Senatorial District Executive Committee for each senatorial district in the State which comprises more than one county shall consist of one member from each county in said district, who shall be elected at the preliminary meetings of delegates from the congressional districts held on the morning of the State Convention. In districts composed of only one county, the County Executive Committee of said county shall have jurisdiction as in the matter of county candidates.

Section 5. Appointment of Chairmen and Secretaries:

It shall be the duty of the Chairman of the State Executive Committee, as soon as practicable after the State Convention, to appoint one member as chairman and one member as secretary of each of the committees provided in each of the foregoing four sections and fill by appointment any vacancies in the chairmanship or secretaryship thereof as may occur.

Section 6. One County Districts:

Should any Judicial, Solicitorial or State Senatorial District be composed of only one county then the County Executive Committee of said county shall be the Judicial, Solicitorial or State Senatorial District Committee for the respective district.

Section 7. Rotation of State Senators:

In all State Senatorial Districts composed of more than one county which it has been the custom to concede the right to nominate a senator to one county of the district by a plan of rotation or otherwise, the same shall remain in full force and effect until terminated as herein provided.

The executive committees of the several counties composing such Senatorial District may hereafter adopt a plan for the nomination of candidates for the State Senate by one or more counties composing such district, but such plan shall not be effective until the executive committee of each of the counties composing the district shall, by a majority vote, approve such plan and file with the chairman of the State Executive Committee a copy of the resolution approving the same. The agreement in any senatorial district composed of only two counties may be terminated by a majority vote of the county executive committee of any one of the counties and in districts of more than two counties by a majority vote of each of the executive committees of at least two counties, provided that notice of the termination of such agreement must be filed with the chairman of the State Exectuive Committee at least 120 days in advance of the date of the primary election at which the candidates for the General Assembly are to be nominated. The chairman of the State Executive Committee shall promptly notify the State Board of Elections of all such agreements and of the termination thereof.

ARTICLE IV. STATE ORGANIZATION
Section 1. State Executive Committee:

The State Democratic Executive Committee shall consist of ten men and ten women from each congressional district in the State, who shall be elected at the preliminary meetings of delegates from the congressional districts, held on the morning of the State Convention as provided in Section 2, Article VI, provided, however, that each county shall have at least one member on the Committee.

Section 2. Election of Officers:

As early as is practical after each State Convention herein provided, the Chairman shall call the State Executive Committee to meet for the purpose of electing a Chairman and Vice Chairman, one of whom shall be a woman and the other a man, and each of whom shall serve for a term of two years, or until his or her successor shall be elected.

Section 3. Appointive Officers and Committees:

The Chairman of the State Executive Committees, as early as practicable after his election shall appoint to serve at his pleasure a full time Executive Director, a Secretary, a Financial Director and a Treasurer. The chairman may combine any of two of the above officers into one.

Section 4. Ex-Officio Members:

The officers of the State Executive Committee, the National Committeeman, the National Committeewoman and the President, National Committeeman and National Committeewoman of the Young Democratic Clubs of the State shall be ex-officio members with the power to vote, provided, however, the Executive Director shall have no vote at any Executive Committee Meeting.

Section 5. Convention Calls:

In each election year the chairman of the State Executive Committee shall convene said Committee in the City of Raleigh on or before the 15th day of January and at said meeting the following business shall be transacted:

(1). The time and place of holding the State Convention shall be determined and duly published.

(2). A common day shall be fixed, on which all precinct meetings shall be held for the election of delegates to the county conventions.

(3). A common day shall be fixed for the holding of a county convention in each county in the State for the purpose of electing delegates to the State Convention.

(4). Elect one member from each Congressional District to the Resolutions and Platform Committee. It shall be the duty of the Chairman of the State Executive Committee to designate one member of said Committee as Chairman and one member as Secretary. The Committee upon call of the Chairman shall organize and prepare the Party's proposed platform and consider all proposed resolutions addressed to the convention.

Section 6. Notices:

Immediately after the adjournment of the above mentioned meeting of the State Executive Committees, it shall be the duty of the chairman to publish the proceedings of the same and it shall be the duty of the secretary of the committee to notify, in writing, the several chairmen of the County Executive Committees in the State of the respective dates so fixed for the holding of precinct meetings and county conventions. Directly after receipt of such notice it shall be the duty of each chairman of a County Executive Committee in the State to fix the hour and places for holding the precinct meetings in his county, the hour and place for holding the meeting of the County Executive Committee required to be held on the date of the county convention; and thereupon the said chairman shall issue a call for the precinct meetings, the county convention, and the meeting of the County Executive Committee. The call shall be in writing and, at least ten days before the day set for the precinct meetings. It shall be posted at the courthouse door of the county and copies thereof shall be sent to the chairmen of all precinct committees in the county for conspicuous posting in each precinct; a copy of the call also shall be sent as a news item to each news media published in the county.

Section 7. State Campaign Committee:

As soon as is practical after each State Convention, the State Chairman shall call the County Chairmen and First Vice Chairmen in each of the Congressional Districts to meet for the purpose of electing two members of a State Campaign Committee from such Congressional District, one of whom shall be a man and one of whom shall be a woman; provided, however, no member of this committee shall hold any other party office.

Section 8. Duties of State Campaign Committee:

The State Chairman shall be a member ex-officio of this committee, shall serve as its chairman, and this committee shall promulgate and co-ordinate party activities in all counties and districts with State Headquarters under the direction of and in co-operation with the State Chairman.

Section 9. Audit Committee:

The State Executive Committee shall appoint a committee of three whose duty it shall be to audit not less frequently than biennially, the financial accounts and balances of the Committee.

Section 10. Council of Review:

There is hereby established a Council of Review for the purpose of hearing and rendering fair and impartial decisions on such disputes and controversies which have arisen or which may hereafter arise within the Party when the same are referred to said Council by the Chairman of the State Democratic Executive Committee or by the State Democratic Executive Committee.

(A) COUNCIL MEMBERSHIP. The Council of Review shall consist of three (3) members, appointed by the Chairman of the State Democratic Executive Committee; provided, that one person shall be appointed from the geographical areas of the East, the Piedmont and the West to serve for a term of two, four and six years as may be initially designated by the State Chairman. Thereafter, the three members shall be appointed for six-year terms.

Provided further, the Chairman of the Council of Review shall be designated by and shall serve at the pleasure of, the State Chairman.

(B) ADMINISTRATIVE RULES. The Council of Review is hereby empowered to adopt necessary and appropriate rules to assure that each dispute is settled impartially, equitably and according to the rules of justice and fairness. All decisions concurred in by a majority of the Council of Review shall be final until appealed to and overruled by a majority vote of the State Democratic Executive Committee or by a majority vote of the delegates assembled at the next ensuing State Democratic Convention. The State Chairman shall treat such decision as final and is hereby directed to issue such further and supplemental directives as may be necessary and proper to implement any decision of the Council, pending the determination of any appeal that may be taken.

(C) RIGHTS RESERVED TO THE STATE DEMOCRATIC EXECUTIVE COMMITTEE. The State Democratic Executive Committee reserves the right to remove from office any member of the Council of Review upon a majority of said committee being satisfied that the Council member has been disloyal to the Party or guilty of any misconduct which is not in keeping with this high position of honor in the Democratic Party.

(D) VACANCIES. The Chairman of the State Democratic Executive Committee shall fill any vacancies occurring during the term of his office; provided, however, when a vacancy shall occur among the geographical membership of the Council, as defined in sub-paragraph (A), the vacancy shall be filled by an appointment from the same geographical area.

(E) THE CHAIRMAN OF THE COUNCIL OF REVIEW is hereby directed to assume jurisdiction of all matters and disputes pending and hereafter brought to his attention by the Chairman of the State Democratic Executive Committee.

ARTICLE V. COUNTY CONVENTIONS
Section 1. Meeting:
All county conventions shall be called to order by the chairman of the executive committee of such county, and in his absence, by the vice chairman or by one of the vice chairmen in the order of succession and in his or their absence, by any member of the county executive committee who may be present at the convention, and in case none of the foregoing persons shall be present, then by any delegate to the convention, and he shall preside until a permanent chairman is elected by the convention.

Section 2. Rules:
(1). The chairman shall provide the convention with a sufficient number of secretaries or accountants, who shall reduce the votes to decimals and tabulate the same, disregarding all fractions after second or hundreths column.

(2). Nothing herein contained shall prevent the convention from making nomination by viva voce or acclamation where a vote by township or precinct is not demanded by any delegate present.

(3). The County Executive Committee shall have the power to make such other rules and regulations for the holding of county conventions not inconsistent herewith, as may be deemed necessary or expedient.

Section 3. Voting:

Each precinct shall be entitled to cast in the county convention one vote for every 50 Democratic votes or major fraction thereof cast by the precinct for Governor at the last preceding gubernatorial election; provided that every precinct shall be entitled to cast at least 2 votes in the county convention, and each precinct may appoint as many delegates to said convention as it may see fit, not exceeding three delegates and three alternates for each vote to which said precinct may be entitled in the county convention.

The County Executive Committee may, by resolution duly adopted, require each Precinct to appoint two delegates and two alternates for each vote to which said precinct may be entitled in the County Convention.

Section 4. Nomination Convention Where County Not Under Primary Law:

In all counties in which the selection of candidates for members of the General Assembly and county and township offices is not provided for by the primary law, nominations shall be made in the following manner:

(1). The county executive committee shall meet and set a time and place for holding a county convention for the nomination of candidates for the aforesaid offices, and shall also set the time and places for holding the necessary preliminary precinct meetings, and thereupon the chairman of the county executive committee shall issue a call for the precinct meetings and the county convention,. notice of which call shall be sent to the precinct officials and published in such manner and form as shall be directed by the said county executive committee.

(2). At the meeting held in each precinct in pursuance of said notice, delegates and alternates to represent it in the county convention shall be elected from the body of the Democratic voters of the precinct; and said delegates or alternates, or such of them as shall attend the county convention shall be entitled to vote the full Democratic strength of their precinct in the nomination of candidates and upon all questions which may come before said county convention.

If there is a failure to hold a precinct meeting in pursuance of said notice, or if said meeting shall fail to elect delegates to represent it in said convention, the precinct executive committee shall appoint delegates and alternates from the Democratic voters of the precinct.

(3). Each precinct shall be entitled to cast in the county convention one vote for every 50 Democratic votes, or a major fraction thereof cast by the precinct for Governor at the last preceding gubernatorial election; provided that every precinct shall be entitled to cast at least 2 votes in the county convention, and each precinct may appoint as many delegates to said convention as it may see fit, not exceeding three delegates and three alternates for each vote to which said precinct may be entitled in the county convention.

The County Executive Committee may, by resolution duly adopted, require each Precinct to appoint two delegates and two alternates for each vote to which said precinct may be entitled in the County Convention.

(4). The precinct meetings shall be presided over by the chairman of the precinct committee, but in his absence, the vice chairman of the committee shall preside, and in the absence of both the chairman and vice chairman, any member of the committee may preside.

(5). The county executive committee shall have power to make any rules with regard to holding precinct meetings which it may deem proper, not inconsistent with the rules prescribed in this plan; it shall be the duty of said committee to prepare and furnish all forms and blanks needed in making the returns from said precinct meetings, and any reported challenges and appeals therefrom.

ARTICLE VI. STATE CONVENTIONS
Section 1. Delegates:

The state convention shall be composed of delegates appointed by the several county conventions. Each county in the State shall be entitled to elect to the State Convention one delegate and one alternate for every 300 Democratic votes or major fraction thereof cast therein for Governor of the last preceding gubernatorial election.

Section 2. Congressional District Meetings:

A preliminary meeting of the delegates shall be held by each congressional district on the morning of the State Convention, at rooms, to be designated by the State Executive Committee, for the purpose of selecting the following:

(1). Elect one member of the committee on Permanent Organization, Rules, and Order of Business, which committee will nominate a permanent president and secretary of the convention.

(2). Elect one vice president of the convention.

(3). Elect one district assistant secretary.

(4). Elect one member of the committee on Credentials and Appeals.

(5). Elect nine men and nine women as members of the State Executive Committee, with at least one member being selected from each county.

(6). Elect two members from each county for the Congressional, Judicial, and Solicitorial District Executive Committees; provided, however, in districts embracing less than five counties, three members of each said committee shall be elected from each county in said district.

(7). Elect one member for each county of the State Senatorial Executive Commtitee where the district embraces more than one county.

(8). In each Presidential election year nominate the number of delegates and alternates allotted by the National Committee to each Congressional District.

(9). In each Presidential Election Year nominate one Presidential Elector for each Congressional District.

Section 3. Delegates to National Convention and Presidential Electors:

(1). The State Convention shall elect the delegates to the National Convention who shall convene promptly at the call of the National Committeeman after their election and nominate the National Committee representatives and such other officers as are required by the Democratic National Committee.

(2). The State Convention shall confirm the nominations for Presidential Electors certified by the several districts and, in addition thereto, shall nominate two Presidential Electors at Large.

Section 4. Rules:

(1). Such delegates (or alternates of absent delegates), as may be present at any State Convention shall be allowed to cast the whole vote to which their county may be entitled.

(2). In all conventions provided for by this plan, after a vote is cast, there shall be no change in such vote until after the roll call is completed and before the final result of the ballot shall be announced by the chairman of said convention.

(3). The chairman of the different county conventions shall certify the list of delegates and alternates to the State Convention, and a certified list of said delegates and alternates to the secretary of the State Executive Committee.

(4). The secretary of the State Executive Committee shall make up a roll of all delegates and alternates from the several counties and transmit the same to the chairman of the State Convention.

(5). In all conventions an election or a nomination may be made by any majority, even though it be a fraction of a vote.

(6). In all State Conventions it shall be the duty of the delegates from the several counties to choose one of their number chairman, whose name shall be reported to the president of such convention, and whose duty it shall be to cast the vote of his county as directed, and the vote as announced by him shall be recorded unless some delegate from that county shall challenge its accuracy, in which event it shall be the duty of the president of the convention to cause the roll of delegates from that county to be called, when the vote of such county shall be tabulated and recorded according to the response of its delegates; but in no event shall the vote of one county be challenged by a delegate from another county.

ARTICLE VII. MISCELLANEOUS
Section 1. Committee Meetings:

All committees shall meet at such times and places as the chairman of the respective committee may from time to time appoint and designate in the call.

Section 2. Quorum:

Thirty (30) per cent of the entire membership of any committee shall constitute a quorum.

Section 3. Voting:

A member of the State Executive Committee may designate a Democrat in good standing from within his county to serve as his alternate for a particular Executive Committee meeting by notifying the party chairman, secretary or executive director of such designation in writing prior to the call to order of any such meeting, provided however, that no one person may serve as an alternate for more than one member at any meeting and no member or alternate may be entitled to more than one vote.

A member of the County Executive Committee may designate a Democrat in good standing from within his precinct to serve as his alternate for a particular County Executvie Committee meeting by notifying the party county chairman or county secretary of such designation in writing prior to the call to order of any such meeting provided, however, that no one person may serve as an alternate for more than one member at any meeting and no member or alternate may be entitled to more than one vote.

Section 4. Vacanies:

Vacancies occurring in any Executive Committee above the precinct level shall be filled by the executive committee of the county in which such vacancies occur. Vacancies occurring in any precinct committee shall be filled by the remaining members of the precinct committee.

Section 5. Candidacies in Primary:

Any member of any Executive Committee, precinct, county, or state, or any officer thereof, who announces his candidacy for an elective office in the primary shall resign immediately his party office, and the vacancy shall be filled within 15 days as heretofore provided. Any officer of a County or State Executive Committee who manages a campaign for a candidate in a primary shall resign immediately his party office and the vacancy shall be as provided for in the Plan of Organization.

Section 6. Subcommittees:

All executive committees shall have the power to appoint subcommittees or special committees for such purposes and with such powers in their respective jurisdictions, as may be deemed necessary or desirable.

Section 7. Filling Vacancies Among Candidates:

Vacancies shall be filled among candidates, and the selection of candidates shall be as prescribed by statute.

Section 8. Municipal Committee:

In the nomination of candidates for municipal offices to be voted for in any town or city election, where the same is not controlled by charter or legislative enactment, a municipal executive committee may be created for the purpose of facilitating the orderly selection of such candidates. The committee shall be composed of five residents of the municipality, at least two of whom shall be men and two of whom shall be women, to be elected biennially at a meeting of all members of the regular executive committee or committees who reside in the municipality, the meeting to be called and presided over by the chairman of the county executive committee. It shall be the sole function of any municipal executive committee created under the provisions of this section to supervise and direct the selection of candidates for municipal offices, and to that end, the committee may formulate such rules and regulations as may be deemed necessary, or practicable. The committee shall elect from its membership a chairman and vice chairman, one of whom shall be a woman and one of whom shall be a man; and all vacancies in membership shall be filled by the committee.

Section 9. Appeals:

Unless the Council of Review has assumed jurisdiction of the controversy, the right of appeal shall lie from any subordinate committee or convention to the committee or convention next superior thereto, and in all county or state conventions appeals shall first be referred to the Committee on Credentials and Appeals, or a special committee provided by the convention, and the findings and reports of such committee had before action thereon by the convention.

Section 10. Reports:

It shall be the duty of the county executive committees and their chairmen to make such reports and furnish such information to the chairman of the State Executive Committee and chairmen of the several district committees as the said State and district chairmen may desire.

Section 11. Definition:

An "Active Democrat" is defined to mean a person who is registered to vote as a Democrat, and who, as a volunteer, takes part in party affairs, giving of his time and/or means to further the interest and efforts of the Democratic Party.

Section 12. Plan-Vs-Law:

In the several counties of the State where primaries are provided for by law, whether optional or mandatory, this plan or organization shall nevertheless be followed in all matters not inconsistent with such laws.

Section 13. General Rules:

Procedural or parliamentary questions not specifically covered by this plan or rules adopted pursuant to authority granted herein shall be governed by the provisions of Roberts Rules of Order.

ARTICLE VIII. AMENDMENTS
Section 1. Power to Amend:

The State Executive Committee, shall, at any regularly called meeting duly held, have power to amend this plan of organization.

Any amendment adopted by the State Executive Committee including those herein contained shall be effective immediately and remain in effect until the same shall be repealed or amended by action of the next State Convention. Any change in this plan of organization adopted by the State Executive Committee shall be presented to the next State Convention by the State Chairman for its action thereon.

.   .   .

The foregoing is the plan of organization of the Democratic Party as amended and adopted by the State Democratic Executive Committee at a meeting held in the City of Raleigh on the 17th day of January, 1968.

I. T. Valentine, Jr.
Chairman

ORGANIZATION
DEMOCRATIC PARTY OF NORTH CAROLINA

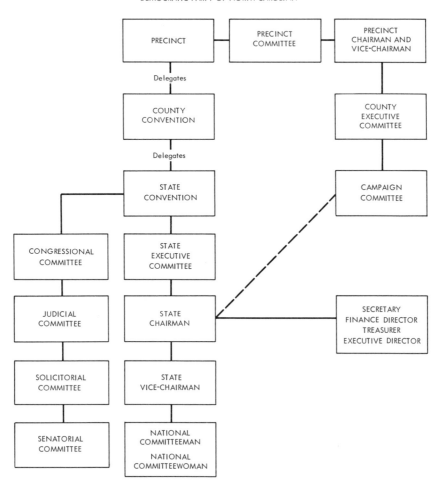

Chapter Six

SUGGESTED QUESTIONS FOR CLASS DISCUSSION.

1. The charge is frequently made that the two major parties are so alike that Lord Bryce could describe them as two "empty bottles on which are painted different labels." Do you agree?
2. Another charge sometimes made is that both major parties are such a complex of vested interests that they cannot respond to the changes of a dynamic society. Do you agree?
3. Have political ideologies and interests in this country become sufficiently identifiable that parties can become more distinctly different in terms of liberalism and conservatism? Do a majority of those who identify themselves as Republicans, Independents, and new voters, subscribe to the idea of Mr. Kilpatrick's New Right?
4. Could the present Democratic Party absorb the Black Power movement and retain its present characteristics? Is this movement too radical for the party?

THE ELECTORAL PROCESS

No political system deserves to be called "democratic" unless it incorporates substantially free elections. It is the election rite that gives to an electorate that power without which a democracy ceases to be a democracy —the capacity of the ruled to cast out the rulers and install an alternative set of governmental officials. Because of the central role of elections in a democracy, anything that has an important influence upon the electoral process is important to the functioning of the political system as a whole: the characteristics and backgrounds of candidates; the nominating system in general, including presidential primaries and national conventions; the tactics and strategy of campaigning; the matter of who bears the high cost of campaigning and what their impact may possibly be upon elected officials; the nature of the polling process, its capabilities and its limitations, and its impact upon the election; finally, the election itself, both in the states and in the electoral college. The cases selected for inclusion in this chapter illustrate a number of different aspects of the overall electoral process.

Will We Elect the President We Vote for in 1968?

Ed Gossett

For more than 150 years, our Electoral College system for choosing a President has been recognized as faulty, in need of overhaul. Today the issue is more pressing than ever, since the 1968 Presidential election promises to be—like that of 1948—a close race between relatively unpopular candidates, complicated by "splinter" candidacies on the right and on the left. There is a serious possibility that neither major-party candidate will get a majority of the electoral vote, and decision will go to the House of Representatives—a procedure which in the past has meant confusion and discord.

We condemn totalitarian forms of government because they permit voting for only one slate of candidates. Yet a somewhat similar thing occurs in each state every four years when, under our "winner take all" system of electing a President, all of a state's Electoral College votes must go to just one candidate. Unless the electors for whom you vote get a plurality within your state, your vote is not only canceled at this intermediate stage; it is counted for the candidate *against* whom you voted. Such built-in inequities led the American Bar Association's nonpartisan Commission on Electoral College Reform to report unanimously last January:

"The present method of electing a President of the United States is archaic, undemocratic, complex, ambiguous, indirect and dangerous. It gives too much weight to some voters and too little to others; gives excessive power to organized groups in states where the parties are evenly matched; places an undue premium on the effects of fraud, accident and other factors; and allows for possible abuse and frustration of the popular will."

GROWING ABSURDITIES. How to choose a Chief Executive was the most bitterly debated provision of the Constitution. The Founding Fathers discussed several proposals—election by the national legislature, by the Senate alone, by the state governors, by the state legislatures. As for the proposition that the *people* elect Presidents by direct voting, the consensus was that they simply would not have the necessary "information and discernment."

Finally, by way of compromise, a plan was adopted which provided that each state choose well-informed electors, equal in number to its U.S. Senators and Representatives, who would then get together and elect a President by majority vote.

The plan never worked as intended. Voters wanted no independent body of wise men making the crucial decision for them: they insisted on doing it themselves, using the electors, pledged in advance to a particular candidate, as mere agents. Even so, the system soon evidenced absurdities and incongruities, which have continued to grow.

In the very first contested Presidential election, in 1796, some historians claim, three electors chosen to vote for Thomas Jefferson voted instead for John Adams—the latter won 71 to 68. (But electors are still free agents, unless bound by the convention that selects them.)

In 1824, Andrew Jackson led his nearest opponent in both the popular and electoral vote; but since he lacked an absolute majority of the electoral vote, the election was thrown into the House of Representatives—where, presumably as a result of maneuvers by fourth-runner Henry Clay, second-place John Quincy Adams was chosen instead. (Adams made Clay his Secretary of State.)

In 1876, Samuel J. Tilden had 247,448 more popular votes than did Rutherford B. Hayes. But through manipulation of the Electoral College, and of a commission set up to look into election disputes, second-runner Hayes was named President. Emotions flared. Only by a real exercise of patriotism and statesmanship did Tilden dissuade his ardent supporters from starting a civil war. During the dispute, Hayes wrote in his diary: "This whole subject of the Presidential election ought to be thoroughly considered, and a radical change made. Something ought to be done immediately."

In 1888, Grover Cleveland had a plurality of almost 100,000 votes over Benjamin Harrison. Yet it was Harrison who won the Presidency—by an electoral vote of 233 to 168.

"Every reason which induced the Constitutional Convention to institute electors has failed," declared Sen. Thomas Hart Benton of Missouri as early as 1823. "At its best," said the late Justice Robert H. Jackson of the U.S. Supreme Court, "the whole electoral system is a mystifying and distorting factor. At its worst it is open to local corruption and manipulation, once so flagrant as to threaten the stability of the country."

Look at some of the more serious flaws of the present system:

1. ACCENT ON GEOGRAPHY. The Electoral College gives great advantage to candidates from pivotal states which have big electoral votes. Indeed it largely confines nominees—and campaigns—to those states.

2. THE SWING VOTE. It happens that in the five states with the most electoral votes—New York, California, Pennsylvania, Illinois and Ohio— the two major parties are closely divided. The prospect, therefore, of tipping the balance and capturing a big chunk of electoral votes by a small change in popular vote heightens the organizing of economic, religious, racial and ethnic blocs within these critical "swing" states. It gives great power to local political bosses.

Vito Marcantonio, for example, seven times a Congressman from New York City between 1935 and 1951, had easy access to President Roosevelt because his influence on Italian-Americans and other minority groups in one city could, in a close election, tip his state's electoral vote—and decide the national outcome.

During the 1960 election campaign, on October 19, the Rev. Martin Luther King was arrested at a restaurant "sit-in" in Atlanta. At the suggestion of a staff assistant, candidate John Kennedy telephoned Mrs. King to assure her of his concern. (Richard Nixon had received a similar suggestion, but did not act on it.) Robert Kennedy followed up with another call. King was released on bond.

Kennedy's action made a deep impression. Scores of Negro leaders publicly switched their stand. A million pamphlets were quickly printed, and on the Sunday before election were distributed outside Negro churches. Many expert observers believe that this single incident was decisive in enabling Kennedy to carry Illinois, Michigan and South Carolina—in a very close race where each candidate got 49 plus per cent of the popular vote.

3. SOLID STATES. The winner-take-all rule aggravates sectionalism. In the so-called solid states, many minority-party voters, knowing their votes would be wasted, stay home. And the Electoral College further distorts the picture because it fails to reflect voter turnout. A state's electoral vote remains the same whether ten people or ten million actually go to the polls.

4. ONE MAN, ONE VOTE. Supreme Court Chief Justice Earl Warren has declared: "Weighting votes according to where citizens happen to reside is discriminatory." Yet our system of choosing Presidents does far more violence to the one-voter-one-vote principle than does malapportionment of legislative districts in any state. Alaska, for example, casts one electoral vote for every 75,000 residents; Pennsylvania, one for every 390,000. Thus a vote in Philadelphia carries· less than one fifth the weight it would in Anchorage.

Popular vote and electoral vote are often wildly disproportionate. Alfred Landon in 1936 got 37 per cent of the popular vote, but only 2 per cent of the electoral vote. Woodrow Wilson, with 42 per cent of the popular vote, got 82 per cent of the electoral vote in 1912. In 1944, Thomas Dewey received 2,996,655 popular votes in ten states, for which he got 62 electoral votes. Meanwhile, in New York he won 2,987,647 popular votes— for which he got *no* electoral votes.

A candidate could carry just 12 states by a thin margin and win the Presidency, with less than 25 per cent of the nation's popular vote.

5. SPLINTER-PARTY EFFECT. It is argued that the Electoral College helps the two-party system by inhibiting growth of splinter parties, but there is evidence that our present system actually gives these parties exaggerated bargaining power. If George Wallace of Alabama and a "peace" candidate run for President in 1968, they may confuse the issue as much as did Henry Wallace and J. Strom Thurmond in 1948. Under the winner-take-all system, siphoning off a small number of votes can be enough to defeat majority opinion.

CHANCES FOR REFORM? In three decades, George Gallup has conducted 14 polls on the subject. Each time the people, in every section of the country, have indicated big majorities for a change in our Presidential election system. A poll of 254 heads of political-science departments showed that 90 per cent favored making some change.

Over the years many amendments for this purpose have been introduced in Congress. Today there are pending four different, major amendments:

1. THE ADMINISTRATION PROPOSAL TO REMOVE ELECTORAL DISCRETION. This would retain the present system but do away with—disembody—the

electors. Thus it would prevent the risk of one or a few individuals' taking it upon themselves to frustrate the public will.

2. THE DISTRICT PLAN. This provides that electors be chosen as members of Congress are—two statewide, and the others by districts—and that they be legally bound to vote for the person for whom they are chosen to vote.

3. THE PROPORTIONAL PLAN. This would abolish electors. Everyone would vote directly for President, and his vote would be counted as cast. The electoral vote of each state would be retained, but instead of going as a unit it would be divided *according to the popular vote*. (For example, in 1964, Texas' electoral votes would have gone 15.87 for Johnson and 9.13 for Goldwater, instead of all 25 for Johnson.) In 1950, with Sen. Henry Cabot Lodge, I introduced an amendment that would have established this proportional plan. It was widely endorsed, and the Senate passed it by a vote of 64 to 27. But the House failed to pass it.

4. THE POPULAR-VOTE PLAN. This would do away entirely with the Electoral College. It would base the elections of the President and Vice President on a nationwide popular vote. The American Bar Association endorses this proposal, and it has been gaining rapidly in acceptance.

Most Presidents, including Harry Truman, Dwight Eisenhower, John Kennedy and Lyndon Johnson, have urged electoral reform, and today there is strong growing support in both parties. A Senate subcommittee headed by Sen. Birch Bayh (D., Ind.) is holding hearings on the various proposals. It would be difficult to amend the Constitution in time for the 1968 election but, with concern mounting over the prospects, the time for initiating reform is *now*.

Abolition of the Electoral College would mean markedly less opportunity and incentive for fraud or chicanery. Campaigns would be less sectional, statesmanship would count for more. The Electoral College is the taproot from which many political evils grow. It must go.

Nixon's Second Chance

Richard L. Tobin

MIAMI BEACH

The Democratic party holds one distinct advantage in this quadrennial year. The Republican convention came first. Next week in Chicago the majority party will know what it's up against, or should know. If it dismisses Richard Nixon's second chance and the doings at Miami Beach as something Mark Sullivan called a mixture of oratory, grand opera, and hog-calling, the Democratic party is in for a shock and already in deep trouble. For the naked truth is that the Democrats are up against a deter-

Saturday Review, August 24, 1968, pages 19, 20, 21.

mined and thoroughly organized machine, its wheels purring smoothly and efficiently, its campaign issues ready-made, its money available, its candidates for President and Vice President convinced of their rectitude and power to win despite the fact that Governor Agnew is scarcely known outside of Maryland and despite the brief floor fight by urban and Northern liberals to replace Agnew on the ticket.

From the outset at Miami Beach, where the Republicans held their first Southern convention—and not by chance—one peak of truth stood out from the mountains of rumor and fact. The Republican party had nowhere to go but to the Right. The Left had been blocked long since by Lyndon Johnson and his predecessor. To the Right was a powerful political vacuum created by urban riots, by the national concern about "law and order," by teen-age delinquency and obstreperous college students, and by an ever-inflated federal budget that threatens the dollar. Into this vacuum had stepped George Wallace of Alabama. The Republicans had to do something drastic to stop him, to retain what had been the beginnings of a two-party system in the South, and to take advantage of what appears to be a mood of frustration and reaction.

There was nothing to be gained by trying to pretend that Republicans were more liberal and permissive than Democrats, and that is why progressives like Mayor Lindsay and Senator Percy simply would not do as the Nixon running mate. From the beginning, Richard Milhous Nixon felt by instinct that for his party to be in tune with the electorate the Republicans had to campaign for return to ways and principles he considered old-fashioned American, which is to say Right, not Left. From the beginning, too, the Southern states put pressure on Nixon to pick a conservative as his running mate. And the former Vice President went to Maryland and the man who had placed him in nomination, a "safe" partner acceptable to all factions, including the South. Men like Lindsay and Percy might help the ticket in the cities, but not enough.

The whole convention had the air of a benign dictatorship. Miami Beach itself is as close to Roman America as any place in the United States. For one thing, the high summer humidity and temperature, which varies little night or day, are far from invigorating or conducive to creative political action. The Republicans usually run a tidier convention than the Democrats anyway, neater and quieter and better organized, but nowhere near as dynamic. Only in the Eisenhower years have Republican conventions been contentious and lively. This one along the soft salt water was conventional and benign.

Republicans have almost always been on the defensive and it has been wisely said that they usually react rather than act. They reacted in Miami Beach—to Vietnam, to lawlessness, to race relations, to the high cost of living, to the uprising of the poor, to every current problem. They were against most everything that is going on in today's America, though they offered precious few concrete solutions of their own. And they may well be right in the stand they took, for the latest Gallup Poll shows that 52 per cent of the American electorate believe that the Republicans can best deal with these issues now; 48 per cent believe the Democrats can. Naturally, these figures are subject to change. Change and what happens at Chicago.

Take one issue alone—civil violence. The basic difference between the two parties was never more pronounced along the steamy gold coast of Florida. The GOP honestly believes that the nation is alarmed by and angered at the rioting and the violence, the lack of respect for law and order. The Democrats believe, and will say in Chicago, that the rioters riot because they have been unfairly deprived of votes, jobs, decent housing, equal protection by the law, and hope. The Republicans are convinced, and the Democrats had better believe it, that though they are by no means the majority party (they have less than 30 per cent of the registered voters) they are once again a broad-based party of accommodation. Bursting with self-confidence, the GOP seemed certain to a man that this is their year. There has not been so much arrogant confidence in the Center and Right since 1952, though a good many reporters at Miami Beach were less sanguine of Republican chances in November.

Since Richard Nixon is convinced that an alarmed and angered nation would applaud and support a conservative platform and since Richard Nixon is by nature a conservative man with incredibly sensitive political antennae, the party's firm stand on the side of "law and order" was not entirely unforeseen. It will be the basic slogan of the Nixon-Agnew autumn campaign, we may be sure. Vietnam will be there too, of course, and so will inflation and degeneracy. But a fundamentalist movement for "law and order" is going to be the keynote, the reiterated cry, and the Democrats had better have some good answers ready. At this twenty-ninth national convention of the GOP, the first big hand went to actor John Wayne and, from the reaction around the networks, he had plenty of sympathetic viewers. Barry Goldwater likewise seemed impressive, a far different Goldwater from the campaign bungler of 1964. In a nutshell, the Kennedy-Johnson administrations and the vagaries of historic timing have handed the minority party gold-and-silver issues that will be extremely difficult to outbid. Senator Dirksen's mellifluous plea at Miami was the first salvo.

Here are some of the things the vigorous new Republican party will talk about during the campaign, besides "law and order," the mess in Vietnam, and a degeneracy of the American moral. Since 1900 the Democrats have been in the White House for thirty-six years to the Republicans' thirty-two and the Democrats will have balanced the budget in only six of these thirty-six years, the Republicans twenty-one of their thirty-two. The cumulative deficit under Democratic Presidents exceeds $300 billion, under Republican Presidents just over $20 billion. Income taxes have been increased thirteen times as often under Democratic Presidents as under Republicans, and when it comes to wars the Democratic Presidents are way out in front, something like four to nothing. Above and beyond all this is the weight of almost eight years of decisions, and decisions mean mistakes, to the distress of the party in power, against whom there is natural political reaction. Coupled with urban riots beyond anything in our history and the most unpopular war this nation has been involved in since 1846, these GOP campaign arguments are telling and powerful, and the Democrats had better acknowledge what they're up against and plan accordingly at Chicago.

Another formidable truth that may emerge from the November vote is that the two party system is at long last being realigned through a link between Southern conservatives and Northern whigs. The unbelievable popularity of Governor Wallace everywhere, but particularly in his native South, can be transferred to the Republican cause if the GOP can prove to the average conservative voter that Nixon and Spiro Agnew have a real chance of winning it all and that a vote for Wallace is a lost vote or, even worse, a vote insuring more of the same. That the Republican party is growing in the South no one who was in Miami Beach could doubt for a moment. The realignment is not only here to stay, it is a national fact which may in the end destroy what the Democrats have always counted on to pull them through close national elections—the Solid South.

As to the candidates themselves, Richard Milhous Nixon has several things going for him in this second run and not the least of these is his family. Nixon was the only one of the three major candidates for the Republican nomination who had not been divorced. Rockefeller has had two wives and so has Reagan. Nixon is still married to Thelma Catherine Patricia Ryan, who at fifty-five is only three months youger than her husband. They became a family on June 21, 1940, and few in political life are closer knit. Their daughter Patricia, better known as Trish, twenty-two, was recently described by former Ambassador John Lodge as "demure" and that is a word seldom said of any young lady these days. Julie, twenty, is engaged to David Eisenhower, the former President's grandson. This young couple, with Patricia and her mother, are campaigners nonpareil, especially in a year that would have the voter believe that a President Nixon can return the country to old-fashioned ways of decency and order.

Besides his enormous experience in national government going back one whole generation, Richard Nixon's appeal to the conservatives of the country in both parties ought not be discounted, particularly by the Democrats in Chicago. Every street riot, every broken window, every incidence of looting, every trap set for a policeman, every student explosion, every Molotov cocktail exploded on an urban sidewalk gives a man like Nixon more votes. If violence flares in Chicago during the Democratic convention this fact will help the man the Republicans have just nominated.

Nixon is conservative and peace-loving by nature. It isn't a pose—he believes it, as he believes in what Senator Dirksen calls the old American values. Nixon is a Quaker by birth, by choice, by habit. He eats little, drinks almost nothing, doesn't smoke, and detests dirty stories to such a degree that he'll leave the room if one is told. These qualities some Democrats will attribute to the Boy Scout in Nixon and deride him for them, but in the South and in many a small town in the East, West, and North as well, the things Nixon truly believes and stands for still count and count heavily. In Nebraska, for instance, the farm community has long considered RMN the savior of America. He'll do well wherever old-fashioned people vote and that's just about everywhere in rural America, especially in the South. Whether this sort of appeal will be sufficient to displace George Wallace below the Mason-Dixon Line—or whether there is enough rural America left—no sensible person would attempt to guess at this point.

Although Nixon has identification with the Eisenhower administrations of 1952 and 1956 when he was Ike's Vice President, Nixon the man has never had real rapport with the Eastern establishment. General Lucius Clay and Sidney Weinberg were lukewarm about him in 1956 and, among others, sought elsewhere for a Vice Presidential candidate to go with Eisenhower's re-election. They tried a great many on for size and Governor Christian Herter of Massachusetts came about as close as any, but in the end the professionals won and Nixon was renominated. It was one of Nixon's greatest moments of triumph when National Citizens for Eisenhower became National Citizens for Eisenhower and Nixon in the summer of 1956.

Though he has been a corporation lawyer in New York for several years, lives on Fifth Avenue, now has an income in six figures, and considers himself an Easterner, Nixon and the international Eastern establishment are still oddly estranged. But not so Nixon and the county chairmen from coast to coast. One of the reasons RMN's nomination was secure from the first was the number of political IOUs he had piled up in fund-raising dinners, local election rallies, personal political favors, and friendships since the California disaster of 1962. Nixon is a professional, which is one reason the Eastern establishment has never quite taken to him and why the grass roots professionals have. Nixon is a living example of what persistence and road work can accomplish. Written off completely after his debacle against Governor Edmund G. "Pat" Brown in California, the man whose father was a streetcar motorman and who grew up in rented rooms over a store in one of the poorest sections of Los Angeles has through sheer pertinacity come back to pre-eminent position in his own party. Republicans at Miami Beach told me over and over again that if it had not been for Nixon's vigorous campaigning in 1966 the Republicans would not have come anywhere near gaining the forty-seven seats they picked up in the House or the eight new governorships which brought them even with the Democrats in state control. These are things pros remember. In such a context, men like Rockefeller and Reagan never really had a chance. In this respect, too, Nixon and Vice President Humphrey bear startling professional resemblance.

Just the same, and in spite of Republican optimism and solidarity, the Miami Beach convention of 1968 had an aura of unreality about it difficult to describe and even more difficult to comprehend. Collins Avenue bore no connection with the world as it really is and the convention seemed to be held in thrall by its lush Roman setting and an indefinable isolation from the rest of humanity. Starving children in Biafra? Nobody mentioned them in my hearing. The rights of ghetto blacks, their uncertain future and pathetic world? Practically the only Negroes I saw in Miami were watering palm trees and carrying trays: the few inside Convention Hall were given little or no exposure and less air time. Vietnam? The platform dealt with this overriding cloud in general terms but no electrifying Eugene McCarthy came to the rostrum to say what a lot of Americans want to hear—that the Vietnam war has to stop, one way or another. Only Richard Nixon seemed to face the Communist issue. Most delegates were still talking in pre-Tito, pre-Czech terms. Nixon told his press conference that today the Communist world is a split world, schizophrenic, with very great diversity, particularly in Eastern Europe, and whoever is President after November must proceed on the assumption that negotiations with the leaders of the Soviet world and Communist China must begin to take place. As Nixon said it: "This is a change that has come about. Therefore, our policy must change." It was the only moment of reality in the whole week along the soft salt ocean. But, then, the 1932 Republican convention platform never once mentioned the Depression.

As to the Vice Presidential nominee, he is the son of a Greek immigrant who changed his name from Anagnostopoulous and at forty-nine is one of Maryland's youngest governors and the first of Greek descent. Despite a Democratic registration four-to-one stronger than the Republican, Agnew handily won the governship in 1966 on the strength of America's first public accommodations law passed under his term as chief executive of Baltimore County. At his nomination for Vice President, Governor Agnew told the press that his name was not exactly a household word but he hoped it would be by the end of the campaign. Backing Governor Rockefeller at first, Agnew switched to Nixon in Miami Beach and delivered the chief nominating speech Wednesday night.

Will the fact that Agnew is a comparative nonentity hurt the ticket's chances? The historic fact is that Vice Presidential candidates are rarely well known men. At the time of their first federal nomination the public reaction, as in Agnew's case, is: "Who the hell is that?" The public often feels let down because the Reagans and Lindsays and Rockefellers and Percys and Hatfields are not instantly selected as running mates. But that is not the way politics works and, to be candid about it, not everyone will take the job even if offered it. Throttlebottom is still very much with us despite Nixon's own concern with the post he filled so actively.

Just the same, the floor fight against Agnew and the conservatives represented fear among the big-city and Northern delegates that Richard Nixon had made his first campaign mistake. One delegate put it this way: "He won it in Oregon and blew it in Maryland." The floor battle to replace Agnew was, of course, doomed from the start, and Mayor Lindsay, who was the first choice of the urban liberals, had the intelligence to remove himself quickly from any part in it. Lindsay, incidentally, has been acting more like a professional politician and a Republican in recent months and his impeccable conduct at Miami Beach, including his seconding of Agnew, won't hurt him a bit in the months and years ahead. If indeed Nixon blew this one by appointing Agnew, the Mayor of New York will emerge on Wednesday, November 6, as his party's brightest prospect for 1972. Already the handsome, intelligent New Yorker is in greater demand as a Republican rally speaker from coast to coast than the 1968 candidate for President.

The easiest thing in the world is to knock the great national conventions, but they are, usually, pure democracy at work and as such they represent the best and the worst in the land. Yet the Republican National Convention of 1968 seemed to be conducted in the aura of a benevolent autocracy, the quietest national convention of either political party in the last two decades. Quiet conventions do little or nothing to advance political evolution, and since this is so the Democrats at Chicago have been given a major opportunity. They know what they are up against because the Republicans met first and played it supersafe. If the Chicago conclave next week seizes the opportunity to look unpleasant truths squarely in the eye and comes up with forthright candidates and viable solutions they will stay the majority party. If they remain overconfident and sterile they will have the fight of this century on their hands from a conservative coalition bursting with optimism and loaded with cash. Nixon is a pro and his campaign will be a professional campaign using all of the latest and the oldest techniques to persuade the American voter that we must return to a safe and sane nation and that the Republicans alone are capable of achieving this. The delegates and leadership at Chicago dare not underestimate the vigor and cunning of a Nixon given a second chance.

From Chicago to November

Peter Schrag

CHICAGO

Most political conventions are party exercises composed of varying degrees of strife, hoopla, ritual, and serious debate. They exist to nominate candidates, or to ratify candidates that are already all but nominated. Most are forgotten before the election takes place. The Democratic convention in Chicago, on the other hand, may well prove to be a watershed for the party and perhaps for the nation. It produced no major surprises in the candidates that were nominated; but it revealed and probably reinforced divisions, changes, and disturbances in the very foundations of American political society. There probably hasn't been a convention like Chicago since the Civil War, and there may never be another.

"A lot was lost in Chicago," said a young Congressional candidate after the Democratic convention. "I lost my voice shouting, Mayor Daley lost his image, and the Democrats may well have lost the election." In a week of political acrimony, police violence, and, for some, unspeakable rage and frustration, many people lost their voices, their composure, and—in at least a few instances—their complacency. "I never knew it could be like this," said a delegate from Wisconsin. "This is unbelievable."

This. It meant everything—the clubbings inflicted by police on demonstrators and bystanders; the capricious harassment called "security" at the International Amphitheater; the domination of the proceedings by a big-city boss; the deep divisions in the Democratic party itself. *This.* It was a word for events and feelings that still wanted words, and that had yet to achieve an authentic voice, inside or outside political conventions. *This* is the legacy of Chicago that the Democrats carry into the 1968 campaign.

Any convention—with its confusion, its uncertainty, and its brokerage-in-power—can produce paranoia. This one, under Mayor Daley's manage-

Saturday Review, September 21, 1968, pages 19, 20, 21, 22; 54.

ment, his cops, and his propaganda, was a psychopath's dream. Learned professors went about the hall talking about "them" like so many Birchites ferreting out a Communist plot; television reporters declared they were being followed by unidentified men; and delegates remained in a state of near-rebellion against almost every aspect of the proceedings from schedule to security. Even the winners—the members of Hubert Humphrey's staff—acknowledged that the convention had exacerbated rather than resolved the fissures in the party, that the street demonstrations—and the resulting brutality by police—had not helped their man, and that the Republicans' powerful instinct for losing was more than offset by the demonstrations and the tactics of the mayor of Chicago. (The McCarthy people regarded Lyndon Johnson, of course, as the lone figure in the smoke-filled room of 1968. Nonetheless, it may be that Daley rendered Humphrey—and party unity—the greatest of services by replacing LBJ as the central figure of the convention. He made it easier for Humphrey to become his own man.)

Humphrey now faces the problem of giving his liberal constituents and supporters the voice they lost in Chicago: Immediately after the nomination nearly 1,000 people—many of them McCarthy kids—attended an organizational meeting for Marcus Raskin's New Party. (Several hundred more, while remaining in the party, declared that—at least for the moment —they would not support the Humphrey-Muskie ticket.) Most of them were not delegates or—even in the remotest sense—politicians. They were college students, housewives, academics, and a host of other newcomers to political activism.

Nonetheless, they did represent much of what was new and exciting and hopeful on the fringes of the Democratic party, and many of them spoke and acted as if they were never going to have anything to do with Democrats again. "The Democratic party," said a young man who was still carrying his walkie-talkie, "is dead." It was not so much that they felt betrayed by the party bosses—by *them*—or that they despaired in defeat after nine months of hard campaigning, but that they were convinced that the party as a system, an institution, was no longer viable, no matter who controlled it. In their view, Hubert Humphrey was nominated not because the conventional processes had failed, but because they had functioned too well. "None of those people on the National Committee is under seventy," said an angry Congressman from California. "The institutions have prevailed —the unions, the politicians—the goddamn institutions. Now the kids will quit."

In fact, the McCarthy campaign and the challenge to the Administration position on Vietnam came a lot further in nine months of campaigning than anyone could have anticipated in the days when Allard K. Lowenstein, a young New York Democrat, first suggested that Lyndon Johnson should, and could, be dropped from the 1968 ticket, and even further since Eugene McCarthy took his kiddie corps into New Hampshire. The dovish Vietnam challenge, which called for an immediate bombing halt, lost, but not until after 40 per cent of the convention delegates had voted against the Administration, and not until the convention—and the nation—had been allowed to hear two hours of debate on the issue.

More significant for the future of the party is the abolition of the unit rule, which had made it possible for men such as Governor John Connally of Texas to control large delegations and deliver them en masse (in this instance) to the Johnson Vietnam plank. No member of the so-called Texas challenge delegation—which included a substantial number of Negroes and Mexican-Americans, which had the support of Senator Ralph Yarborough, and which represented some 40 per cent of the Texas electorate —was seated in Chicago. Under the new rule, which covers county and precinct conventions as well as the state convention, that sort of mis-representation should be a thing of the past. Even this year, it was Lester Maddox who went home and Julian Bond, the young Negro legislator from Atlanta, who stayed. Mississippi was represented by Fannie Lou Hamer, and by a group of liberals—black and white—and not by Senator James O. Eastland. Negroes, to be certain, were under-represented—though not nearly to the extent they were at the Republican convention in Miami —yet there were enough of them to hold the first black caucus to take place at any national political convention.

And yet, Hubert Humphrey and the Democrats will still have trouble speaking for hundreds of thousands, if not millions, of disaffected Americans who regard him (and Richard Nixon) as a voice of the past and as a representative of a compromising, unimaginative political style. For all his charm and power, Humphrey has become the anti-hero to many young Democrats—bland, somewhat out of date, a sort of pre-modern man. As they speak of him, he is tainted not only by service in the Johnson Administration, but by twenty years in public office. Perhaps he has been around too long. The excessive exposure of television may tend to shorten the public life of any public man.

More than anything, however, Humphrey still bears the stigma of Vietnam and of association with the party in power, and he therefore becomes a target for public frustration with existing policies. "The American people are deeply discontented with the direction of the country," said Richard Goodwin, who had worked for McCarthy. "The issue is whether they'll turn to people like McCarthy or to the Max Raffertys and George Wallaces." Humphrey's liability, the party's liability, is that they still stand—by and large—for a liberalism that is, at least for the moment, on the decline. Without doubt Humphrey will be, as he claims, his own man, "the captain of the team." In his acceptance speech and in subsequent statements he has already indicated that he will not be inflexibly bound by the policies of the past. There is little doubt, moreover, that in regard to Vietnam he came close to a break with President Johnson. It was only by direct inter-vention—through people such as John Connally and through personal emissaries in Chicago—that Johnson blocked the adoption of a compro-mise plank in the platform.

Yet even if Humphrey is his own man, can he be President, too? In an ironic way, Humphrey was the Eugene McCarthy of 1948, the man who took up unpopular causes and developed a reputation for political courage when his liberalism was radical, when it stood clearly to the left of the mainstream. What remains of it now seems pallid by comparison because the Humphreys have won their battles and the lonely men speak a different language. Humphrey spoke well—to the Indiana delegation, for example—of his record in reforming the city of Minneapolis, and of his civil rights battles in the Senate, but no one under thirty seemed interested. "Who cares about things that happened twenty years ago," said a young reporter who stood in the room.

If Humphrey has trouble rallying the supporters of Senator McCarthy, who has indicated that he will not support the national ticket, he may have even more difficulty in reassembling the coalition of ethnic and labor groups which have, since 1932, been the backbone of the Democratic party. The real splits in the party, despite the rhetoric of the McCarthy forces, are not only those between liberals and bosses, or between Johnson hawks and McCarthy doves, but between lower-middle-class populism and a liberal middle-class vision that divides the nation into "slums and suburbs."

When Richard Nixon and George Wallace appeal to the "forgotten man," they are speaking to several million whites—garage mechanics, taxi drivers, stevedores, shopkeepers, cops, firemen, and trade union members—many of them former Democrats, who are caught in an inflationary financial squeeze between affluence and welfare, who have neither the amenities of wealth nor the benefits of new social programs. Until Wallace began his campaign, these were, without doubt, the most alienated and disregarded people in America. For nearly a decade they have not had a psychic home in national politics. Most social commentators and politicians saw the nation as either affluent or black; the lower-middle-class white was left out altogether, or was simply labeled a bigot when he opposed integration. The various civil rights laws, the poverty program, and the general concern about Negroes did not apply to him, excepting only those instances when suburbanites demanded that he integrate *his* schools and *his* neighborhood.

When Mayor Daley's cops beat and gassed the peace demonstrators and the hippies in Chicago, they were doing the work of the lower-middle-class white; for him, at least, Daley is not merely a boss, but a man with a constituency of working men and white ethnic groups. For every hippie in Chicago there are twenty, or perhaps a hundred, local citizens who proclaim their love for the Mayor. When Nixon and Wallace—and now Humphrey—call for law and order, they are, at least in part, appealing to them, and articulating their demands. Despite the liberal protests about the Chicago police—despite Senator Abraham Ribicoff's courageous remarks about Gestapo tactics in the streets of Chicago—one of the biggest cheers at the convention went to Congressman Wayne Hays of Ohio when he attacked those who substituted "beards for brains" and when he congratulated Daley and the Chicago police. In their shouting vengeful enthusiasm, the delegates who whooped it up for Hays and Daley may have been the most violent people in town. The majority in Chicago may have been out of touch with the young, but they were in touch with the mood of America.

The mood is new, and there appear to be new constituencies and groups to express it. It is not merely the Democratic party that is split; what is breaking apart is the great New Deal consensus that has given American politics its order since 1932. The professionals in both parties declare that when November comes most of those now supporting Wallace or Mc-Carthy will return to one of the major parties. In the South, Nixon is campaigning with a slogan that a vote for Wallace is a wasted vote. Humphrey, reading the signs—and perhaps his own heart—has declared at least qualified support for Daley: Most Americans, despite the televised police brutality, appear to side with the Chicago police, not with the demonstrators. This is not the year, say the Humphrey people (and also the Nixon people) for new programs in social welfare, for a New Deal or a New Frontier or a Great Society. It is the year of law and order.

Perhaps most of the disaffected American voters will come back to one of the major parties, if not in November, then in 1970 or 1972, yet the signs, at this moment, are inconclusive. Wallace will not only capture several states in the Deep South (the Humphrey forces have already given up Alabama, Mississippi, Louisiana, and Georgia—though they still have hopes for Texas, North Carolina, and Florida), but he will also receive a visible minority of the Northern labor vote. In some unions, according to incomplete polls, he has 30 per cent of the vote. Union leaders deny the accuracy of the polls, but they are undoubtedly worried. George Meany marched with Humphrey, both in Chicago and in the Labor Day parade in New York, but he may well be looking around to see who will follow in November.

Wallace will probably cost Nixon more votes than he takes from Humphrey. There are California liberals, for example, who feel that the only hope for Humphrey in that state state is the damage Wallace does to Nixon among Southern California conservatives. More important, however, is what Wallace takes from both major candidates. Even if the election does not go to the House, a large Wallace vote will make a powerful impact on American politics, just as Wallace's campaign has already begun to make an impact on the major parties. To many voters, both Nixon and Humphrey are men of an older establishment—comfortable, somewhat elitist, detached. Wallace is clearly a candidate of the Right. But he is also a carrier of a populist impulse that was once a segment of the New Deal mainstream, part egalitarianism, part socialism, part cussedness, part bigotry. If Wallace does well, he will send both parties on a frantic courtship of his constituents. The forgotten man (white) now has, or feels he has, a national voice.

Humphrey, of course, has barely begun to fight. He has always been an effective campaigner. Unlike Nixon, he has not lost a partisan election in twenty years. His supporters in Chicago and his own staff acknowledge that he has run behind in the polls, but those polls, they say, were taken when no candidate was definite, when "the situation was unsettled and explosive." The liberals, said a member of the staff, have no quarrel with him on domestic policy; he is, after all, a vocal advocate and supporter of Great Society programs. On Vietnam, according to members of his staff, Humphrey will make a clear break with the established policy if he is not spared the problem by events in Paris. "Now that Hanoi knows that there's no point in waiting for the election," said a member of the campaign staff, "the North Vietnamese may be more willing to negotiate. He may lose some of those kids but the kids can't vote anyway."

Nonetheless, the enthusiasm of the delegates was mixed. "A lot of people in my delegation," said a Texan, "are going home to vote for Nixon." Politicians such as Daley would have preferred Edward Kennedy because they are doubtful that Humphrey can win, but most will support Humphrey because he is their candidate, and party loyalty demands it. "He'll be just as strong as Nixon for law and order," said a member of the Massachusetts delegation. "I prefer Humphrey because he's a Democrat."

Once Humphrey begins to campaign—concentrating on the cities of the North, on California, and on labor—he can make it a good, tough partisan fight, running not only against Nixon but also against Spiro Agnew and Strom Thurmond. "Nixon's running against the Negroes," said a Texas liberal, a view that can be reinforced without ever saying it in public. Humphrey, given time, can get away from the embarrassment of his convention. Perhaps Humphrey's major problem will be to find an effective response to Nixon's simplistic call for law and order. Humphrey missed an opportunity—at least with the liberals in the party—when he failed to denounce the brutality of the Chicago cops, a brutality that was unwarranted under any standard of security or order. There were plans, he said, to assassinate the major candidates, and burn down the Hilton Hotel. Yet, as the leaders of the demonstration pointed out, arsonists and assassins don't do their work chanting peace slogans and singing songs in the park.

There is hardly a question that the Democratic party will survive its wounds from Chicago—will even survive the divisions in American society, divisions between hawks and doves, between young and old, between black and white, even between those who still believe in the efficacy of established political institutions and those who do not and who have taken to the streets. (The Republicans survived Goldwater and the disaffections he produced, and they seem now to be stronger than ever.) The question is: In what form will the Democratic party survive and with what justification?

During the week of the convention, Chicago became not only a meeting place for politicians of every stripe and persuasion, it became a microcosm of American society at large—the ugly, the commonplace, the magnificent. In the lobbies of the hotels, and in the streets outside, McCarthy kids argued with peace marchers, demonstrators with national guardsmen, black militants with white liberals. Alongside the placards and buttons of the politicians were the peace posters, broadsides proclaiming BUSTS BEGIN, signs headed THE PEOPLE VS. HUMPHREY, and chants of "Dump the Hump." Within a hundred yards of the Conrad Hilton one could hear soul music sponsored by Humphrey; see Dick Gregory and Ralph Abernathy speaking to the demonstrators in Grant Park, and listen to residents of South Chicago declaring that the demonstrators were not real American kids, that they were uncouth and unattractive.

Every one of these groups and individuals is making claims on the party; every one must either be accommodated or be relegated to the streets. What angered the liberal elements most was the fact that this theater of the absurd—demonstrations, police, delegates, hippies, convention security —that all this was held together by Mayor Daley. Because Daley was the bridge between the convention and the streets, and because he played a major role in both, it was his political and personal style that colored the proceedings.

Still another style and other possibilities were clearly visible. The very fact that there was so much confrontation, and that several hundred delegates from every part of America saw things they had never believed possible—that they saw *this*—and that they marched in protest, indicates that other forces are being heard and felt. The line between the best and the worst in Chicago was relatively narrow. Under other circumstances, this might have been Robert Kennedy's or even Hubert Humphrey's convention —not Daley's—and the proceedings might have been held together by optimism rather than despair or fear.

No one knows how much difference leadership and rhetoric make, yet it is clear that many of the disaffected—from Vietnam doves to Wallace populists—regarded Bobby Kennedy as the best alternative. The appeal of Robert Kennedy—and perhaps ultimately of Edward Kennedy, who was an omnipresent offstage figure—transcended rational political calculations. The appeal was on personality; surely death and hindsight augmented that appeal, yet it was there, and it manifested itself in a brief boom for Edward Kennedy. Within two days several hundred delegates had signed petitions urging the young Kennedy to run—despite the fact that he has virtually no experience on record worthy of a serious Presidential candidate. Within two days scores and perhaps hundreds of young men and women appeared at the Sherman House to hand-letter posters and canvass delegates on behalf of a man who had, at that moment, only the slimmest chance of nomination.

Most of those who came to Chicago are going to remain somewhere in or around the Democratic party, even if they don't support Humphrey with great enthusiasm. Some will work for local candidates, others will wait for someone like Edward Kennedy in 1972. The anger of people like Lowenstein, Senate candidate Paul O'Dwyer of New York, and Congressman Philip Burton of California derives not from cynicism about the party but from frustrated optimism. They have a sense that the parliamentary rigidity of the party and its convention—and their unwillingness to bend for a moderate Vietnam plank—were unnecessary stupidities. They couldn't get their literature on the floor, although the Humphrey forces did, couldn't get recognition from the chair, which deferred to Daley when the crucial parliamentary decisions were made. Daley even controlled the band, and ordered it to play over the protesting "We Shall Overcome" that was sung by some of the New York delegates.

Humphrey was going to be nominated anyway, the liberals said. Through moderation and tolerance toward views and ideas from a wide spectrum of American politics, the party might gain at least some of the strength and enthusiasm offered by the new people in Chicago. They were, in short, reformers-from-within: They didn't want to drive people into the streets, were not trying to prove conventional politics corrupt and hopeless. They wanted the party to extend itself, and to grow. But this was not their year, either in Chicago or—if Chicago reflected anything at all—in America. It might have been difficult even for a Kennedy to turn the convention around.

And yet—despite all the furor, despite the bosses, the brawls, despite the police and Mayor Daley—America went to Chicago, and not Miami. David Dellinger and the other organizers of the peace demonstrations said they came here—rather than going to Miami—because the Democrats are the party in power and therefore have the major responsibility for Vietnam and the war machine. Yet clearly they also came to Chicago because, in some sense, the Democrats are their party, because historically, and perhaps emotionally, they belonged or once subscribed to the Democratic position. They are not about to return to the party or to any conventional form of politics, yet undoubtedly they felt that they were more likely to be heard and respected here than in Miami and that, at least, they had a better claim on this party than on the other.

Given the situation in contemporary politics, a similar phenomenon at the Republican convention would have been all but inconceivable. It is even more inconceivable—in 1968—to think of a Republican Eugene McCarthy. Vietnam is, after all, Lyndon Johnson's War. And it was Lyndon Johnson's Party and not the Republicans that came within a respectable distance of disavowing it before the world.

The point is simply that the choice for political reform is still between the Democratic party, a totally new and still unimagined set of institutions, and the streets. For the Democratic candidates this is both an opportunity and a frightful responsibility. Much of what happened in Chicago justified and verified what the radicals among the peace demonstrators claimed: that the Democrats could only nominate a candidate in the setting of a police state, that the existing political processes are decadent, that the police are brutal, and that new institutions (or no institutions) are in order. What Chicago did was cut some more ground from the middle: It strengthened the radicals and the repressors, weakened the moderates, and heightened the frustrations. It made the campaign even harder for Humphrey and Muskie because they are middle-ground liberals and it is that shrinking middle ground on which they must run. It will be a long, and probably an ugly, campaign. Wherever the politicians go, the demonstrators will be out. And there are undoubtedly places to which they can no longer go at all.

Wallace and His Folks

Newsweek

He came squalling out of the black-belt boondocks of Alabama, a slicked-down, bent-nosed, roistering imp set unpredictably at play in the more or less fine-tuned machinery of American politics. His message was segregation smoothed down to the respectable language of "law and order," his

Newsweek, September 16, 1968, pages 25, 26, 27, 28.

following a silent, aggrieved multitude he thinks of as The Folks, his politics an audacious gamble on a single calculation that recurs in all his
changeless, numberless speeches: "There's more of us than there is of
them." Only in his most quixotic moments does George Corley Wallace
imagine that his great adventure will really carry him to the White House.
Yet he has already had his victory: he has called up impulses out of a dark,
demonic side of the American spirit, brought them into acceptable political
discourse—and in the process helped to alter the terms by which the next
President of the United States will be chosen.

For thanks to George Wallace, the next President, Hubert Humphrey or
Richard Nixon, will have to calculate how many of "us" and how many of
"them" there are—and make his own strategic decisions accordingly. The
conventional wisdom of the pollsters today gives Wallace something more
than a one-sixth share of the Presidential vote, most of it predictably rooted
in the South, more of it pirated from Nixon than from Humphrey. But the
blood and the tears spilled during Democratic convention week in Chicago
—and the prospect of a turbulent autumn in the cities and on the campuses—have left the political pros far less certain and far more nervous
about the impact of Wallace and the greivances he represents. His presence in the race has thus already figured in escalating law and order to
campaign Topic A. It could as well tip the selection of a President into the
House of Representatives for the first time in 144 years—with Wallace in
a position to bargain out and perhaps even to decide the outcome.

How well will Wallace run? Full of a deep faith that the forces of light
will somehow prevail, some of his disciples seem even to believe that he
will win—that he will sweep the South and the Border States and pick up
enough stray electoral votes elsewhere to carry the day. Last week, they
persuaded Wallace to take a week's breather at the gaudy Fontainebleau in
Miami Beach in preparation for a planned 48-state blitz in the eight weeks
left till the election. This week alone, he will speak at the American Legion
convention in New Orleans, stump rallies in eight states spraddled from
South Carolina to Wisconsin and name his choice for Vice President. (The
betting favorite: former Kentucky Gov. Albert [Happy] Chandler.)

"We gonna shake 'em up good in November," crows Wallace everywhere
he goes, which is his way of betting that—after five summers of rioting and
radicalism—America has at last caught up with Alabama. There is indeed
compelling evidence to suggest that law and order, even more than Viet-
nam, is now the pivotal issue of Presidential 1968. A new Louis Harris poll,
completed before Chicago, showed an overwhelming 81–14 majority of
Americans persuaded that law and order has simply broken down, and
their villains are precisely Wallace's: black agitators, Communists, the
courts, youthful demonstrators of all persuasions and the Establishment
itself.

'PHENOMENA'. All candidates are acutely aware of the law-and-order
mood: Nixon seized on it, Humphrey waffled it—and Wallace, with some
justice, behaved as though he invented it. "People been reading about your
phenomena, the Wallace phenomena, the people's phenomena," he tells
The Folks. "They say I'm only popular 'cause I'm sayin' what the people
want to hear. Well, what's wrong with that?"

The answer, in pragmatic political terms, is nothing at all; Wallace has already nailed down a chapter in history with his extraordinary venture in the politics of participation. A cross-country petition campaign, aptly dubbed "Mission: Impossible" when it started less than a year ago, was sure to put Wallace's burgeoning third-party movement on the ballot in 45 states by this week and will probably reach at least 49—everywhere but Ohio and the District of Columbia—by Election Day. The Alabama ex-governor's candidacy has cowed Southern pols of both major parties (Mississippi's Democratic Gov. John Bell Williams and five North Carolina GOP hierarchs all plumped for George last week) and set temblors rippling through the urban North. "I'm scared," says a Humphrey worker in San Francisco. "There's a fervor about the Wallace campaign that has to scare you. It's as if by punching the right lever in the voting booth, you can erase all the problems we're all so tired of in one stroke."

'WHITE TIGERS'. Wallace has forged a new coalition of the discontent and the disaffected—a coalition, in his familiar roll call, of "the steel-worker, the autoworker and the textileworker, the policeman and the fire-man, the taxicab driver, the beautician and the barber and the little-business man." And nowhere has he found more fervent support, North as well as South, than among local police—a pre-eminence he cemented by leaping to the defense of Chicago's cops in the lopsided Battle of Michigan Avenue. The feeling increasingly is mutual. In a Brooklyn courthouse corridor last week, a mob of 150 whites—many of them off-duty cops who proclaimed themselves "white tigers"—fell upon a dozen Black Panther ultra-militants with police-issue blackjacks until uniformed officers separated them. Some of the belligerents wore Wallace buttons and some chanted "Wallace! Wallace! Wallace!" as they waded in.

The assault, of course, was their own idea, yet it is equally so that little in Wallace's rhetoric would discourage them. "Nigger" and "nigra" have dropped out of his public vocabulary—the new Wallace is careful to say "Knee-grow" or even "black people"—and he blandly insists that he has always been against "the kind of discrimination that offends anyone." But there remains a violent strain in his rhetoric, a tendency to reduce the most subtle issues to the glandular metaphor of physical combat. His best punch lines tend to wind up with some "beatnik" or "bureaucrat" or "pointy-headed guideline writer" getting punched, run over, hauled off by the hair, or tossed *under* a jail. He needs only to rail darkly against "the trends of pseudo-intellectual government" to set the faithful whooping; they understand quite well what trends he means. "These people are listening to a candidate who is saying what they've been thinking for some time," says Wallace's Detroit area chairman, Larry Lee, a 27-year-old insurance salesman. "You don't have to stop and think about what he says —he says it right out."

What he says in his furious sallies across the country is that The Folks have been too long misused by the Federal government, the great national parties, the press—in short by the whole American Establishment—and that the time has come to rebel. The crowds—and the response—have been stunning. Plunking down aboard his chartered campaign DC-6 for a late-August trip to Hammond, Ind., he gazed out the window into a blinding morning, chomped down on his cigar and announced, altogether accurately, "They're not laughin' at us any more."

'I LIKE HIM.' The trip proved a classic of the running rite of communion between Wallace and The Folks. They came to the airport, stood patiently waiting for the plane to set down, then pressed forward around the candidate—old ladies in Sears cotton, hardhanded millworkers, girls in frocks that start at the throat and end at the knee. "God bless you, gov'nor, God bless you . . . We'll get 'em, gov'nor, you bet we'll get 'em . . ." The litany never changes; neither does Wallace's winking, grinning, handshaking, head-bobbing response: "Hi sweetie, how are you honey, hey young fella how ya doin' . . . 'Preciate you comin' out, hear?" Newsmen cornered him for a press conference, a hostile, jabbing affair that Wallace—hands jammed deep in his coat pockets—turned to his own uses. "Now Mr. Humphrey is sayin' we need law and order but a few months ago he was sayin' we needed a revolution . . . We've tried all the sissy-britches way, now we ought to try enforcin' the law." A local cop stood watching. Wallace threw him a choppy, cupped-hand salute. "I like him," said the cop. "We all do."

His speeches that night to 400 of the righteous at St. Michael's Ukrainian Hall (at $25 a head) and 4,500 more at Hammond's Civic Auditorium (no charge) were similarly ritualized. The speech is added to, subtracted from and tinkered with from time to time but it does not really change. Only modest amendments of style, indeed, distinguish it from the rhetoric that elected first George, then Lurleen, governor of Alabama. The wheedly, sequined gospel singers are gone; there is a twelve-piece brass band from Troy (Ala.) State College now, and it plays "Yankee Doodle" as well as "Dixie" as Wallace bounds on stage and takes his position behind the big bulletproof lectern. But George never changes. He stands a shade smaller than life, his head just poking over the podium, his blunt fingers fidgeting over the thicketed mikes, his monologue pinwheeling from one brassy applause line to the next.

'WE HATE 'EM.' "Some *bureau*crats tellin' the steelworkers, 'You don't know where to send your child to school so we gonna write some guidelines for you' . . . Well, when *I* get to be President, I'm gonna call in a bunch of *bureau*crats and take away their briefcases and throw 'em in the Potomac River . . ." There are screams, shouts, whistles. "If you folks in Indiana want to put your kids on a bus and send 'em to Montreal to school, that's fine. But when *I'm* President, not one dime of Federal money will be spent to bus any student anywhere." The crowd is on its feet now, whooping, hollering. ". . . And if any *demon*strator ever lays down in front of *my* car, it'll be the *last* car he'll ever lay down in front of . . ." The noise is deafening. "He's gonna turn this country around," says one graying, shirt-sleeved fan. "It's not that we dislike niggers—we hate 'em." And a carpenter in his 60s fishes under his shirt, pulls out a $100 check and says: "That money's hard-earned, and it's hard to give it. But we need this man."

"The people of the United States are going to take back government into their own hands," Wallace announced last week in his first nationwide TV half-hour (on NBC-TV), and he is in fact a revolutionary—a kind of carnival-mirror Marx waging class war on the way things are. "We gonna show 'em in November that the average American is sick and tired of all these overeducated ivory-tower folks with pointed heads lookin' down their noses at you and me," he thunders. He proposes instead a return to common sense, but it is the common sense of the garrison state. "If we were President today, you wouldn't get stabbed or raped in the shadow of the White House, even if we had to call out 30,000 troops and equip them with 2-foot-long bayonets and station them every few feet apart . . . If you walk out of this hotel tonight and someone knocks you on the head, *he'll* be out of jail before *you're* out of the hospital and on Monday morning they'll try the *police*man instead of the criminal . . . That's right, we gonna have a *police* state for folks who burn the cities down. They aren't gonna burn any more cities."

GEORGE'S ARMY. For a silent America hankering after a simpler, more innocent past that may or may not ever have existed, Wallace is heady brew—and it seems to be selling better than its own drummers ever imagined possible. Out of Montgomery headquarters, currently sprawled over 60,000 square feet of a rent-free building once occupied by the Veterans Administration, big, bearish ex-press secretary Ed Ewing, 36, and a task force of four young lawyers mounted the drive to pilot Wallace and his American Independent Party through a bewildering welter of state electoral regulations and get him on the ballot. "What we started with," says one of the "Mission: Impossible" lawyers, Tom Turnipseed (sic), 32, a converted Republican from South Carolina, "was a list of people in each state who had written letters supporting the governor. We wrote each one of these people letters, calling them to an initial statewide meeting." They got an eye-popping 80 per cent turnout, and soon an amateur army of Wallace people—watched over by George's pros—was out in the precincts collecting signatures, hawking buttons and bumper stickers, planting canned press releases in local papers.

Some of the Wallace people were embarrassments—a motley of wild-eyed right-wing extremists who had to be gently eased out or dealt around. Others, still aboard, are John Birchers or old-line Southern segregationists. Some key elements of Wallace's Tennessee command are indistinguishable from the management of the White Citizens Council, and his man in Georgia, onetime State House Speaker Roy Harris, publishes a white-supremacist weekly newspaper in Augusta. But others, around the country, are raw newcomers to politics—the true believers who may not know much about the art of politicking but who know what they like with all the furious certainty of a Chautauqua revivalist: Among them:

In Pinole, Calif., a workingmen's suburb on San Pablo Bay, Mrs. Mary Marshall, a housewife in her mid-40s, wrote Wallace a fan letter after a "Meet the Press" appearance last year—and suddenly found herself running a campaign outpost out of an abandoned shoe store in El Sobrante. "We worked till 11 at night New Year's Eve registering people," she says, "and all Christmas afternoon. It just seemed to me if we didn't do something to change the trends today, we wouldn't have too many free Christmases. So we worked." She hasn't stopped. Wallace? "He's just our savior, that's all."

In the mountain town of Hendersonville, N.C., Larry Taylor, a 29-year-old gas station operator, got sore when Gulf sent him a load of Democratic and Republican tiepins to give away to customers—but none from the American Independent Party. So he plastered his station with Wallace signs, laid in a stock of Wallace bumper stickers, ties, hats and tiepins, tithed 10 per cent of his profits to the Wallace campaign—and reports that business has doubled since. "I'm for Wallace," he says, "because he's for states' rights, he's honest, he won't back down. If New York wants blacks to go to school with whites, let them have it. If North Carolina wants separate but equal schools, let them have it. Wallace is for the black man, but I don't think he wants black and white to live side by side."

In Detroit, insurance man Larry Lee, a political novice, joined up early, now figures he spends 1 per cent of his time on insurance, 99 per cent on Wallace—mainly running a cadre of 200 to 300 volunteers drawn chiefly from the white-collar suburbs and the blue-collar union rank and file. There, law and order is the catalytic issue—and it has sprung Pandora's box. "It's just fabulous," exults Lee. "Our mail contributions have risen from $50 to $60 a week to $600 to $800 a week. Humphrey doesn't even seem to be in it. It's a Wallace-Nixon race."

In Memphis, pretty Mrs. Linda Wright, 26, the wife of a Green Beret lieutenant recently wounded in Vietnam, stopped by a Wallace storefront to collect a stack of literature for him. "My husband," she said, "is going to set up a Wallace 'headquarters' in Nha Trang . . . He's so upset over the war policy—he says they won't let them fight over there because there's so much politics, and people are getting killed for nothing. But we've always been for Governor Wallace—he's for the little people."

'BY THE PEOPLE.' They are the silent America, and no one knows their number because no national politician has ever taken their census at the polls. But they are unmistakably there. A day's mail at Montgomery GHQ brings in 5,000 letters, most of them written in laborious longhand, many on ruled dime-store tablet sheets—and $25,000 in the small donations of the faithful. In only a few states can Wallace be said to have an authentic organization. Far more typical is Georgia, where headquarters is a single, underfurnished meeting room at Atlanta's Henry Grady Hotel; or Los Angeles, where the American Independent Party calls a made-over tacos stand home; or Florida, where state chairman Jake Wallace Purvis, George's cousin, cheerily confesses, "We don't organize on the county or precinct level and we don't really set up county chairmen. I tell everybody who wants to work for Wallace he's a chairman." But Florida headquarters drummed up 226,000 Wallace signatures in a single day, Georgia simply quit collecting at 180,000 and California generated 107,263 petitioners— 41,204 more than enough for a ballot spot. Across the U.S., staffers figure 2.3 million voters have signed up for Wallace. "He is," boasts a chief campaign aide, "the only candidate being nominated by the people."

And rarely in memory have the people seemed so volatile to the political pros. The national parties are panicked, Wallace gloats, and he is mistaken only in degree. Democratic regulars in the South despair of stopping him; a Georgia party loyalist toured the state, came home to Atlanta looking haunted and told an acquaintance, "You know how many people I've found for Humphrey?" His eyes darted up and down the street to see if anyone was listening; then he closed his thumb and forefinger into an eloquent zero. In Texas, Democratic precinct workers have taken to agreeing with Wallace people on the Presidency and urging them only to support the state Democratic ticket. In border Maryland, well-placed polls today predict a Nixon-Wallace-Humphrey finish in that order—with Nixon first only because he tapped Gov. Spiro Agnew for Veep.

NEW MATH. In the North, private polls have shaken the calculations of both major parties. One in Iowa, another in Michigan show Wallace has doubled his holdings over the summer. In Connecticut, the state labor council polled union members and found 30 per cent for Wallace. In Granite City, Ill., a traditionally Democratic industrial satellite of St. Louis, the Jaycees set out voting booths around town—and logged 597 votes for George, 480 for Nixon and 380 for Humphrey. In Washington, a Midwestern congressman's staffer called on Alabama Rep. William Nichols's office to ask if there wasn't some way he could run with Wallace without publicly declaring for him. In New York, a city official stood in a ticket of blue-collar workers watching a Labor Day parade up Fifth Avenue led by the hierarchs of the trade-union establishment flashing Humphrey buttons. "Those guys may be for Humphrey," growled one, to the nods of his pals, "but we're for Wallace."

For all the odds against him, Wallace stands an excellent chance of sweeping at least the Deep South. And the Deep South alone could be enough, in a close race, to deprive either Nixon or Humphrey of a majority in the Electoral College and thus throw the election into the House. There, each of the 50 states would have one vote, with an absolute majority of 26 required to win—and Wallace's strategy is pinned to the belief that neither national party will be able to put together 26 votes. In that event, barring some stop-Wallace compact by the big parties, the Alabaman believes he will pick the President. And the President he picks would be the man who entered a "covenant" to turn the destiny of the blacks back to the states, roll back fair housing and reapportionment and repopulate the courts. He might even want to find a job for an unemployed former governor of Alabama.

'USIN' MY WORDS.' Even that turn of events seems remote. Yet neither party feels confident in its assessment of whom Wallace will hurt and precisely how badly. Particularly in the South, Republicans are nervously spreading the word that a vote for Wallace amounts to a vote for Humphrey, since Dixie could well be the difference between victory and defeat for Nixon. Humphrey's agents figure that, if Wallace gets 10 per cent of the total Presidential vote, it will be mainly at Nixon's expense—but that anything over 10 per cent will start hurting Hubert. By no accident, both major parties picked stolid, hyphenated Americans for Veep—thus aiming at holding down the appeal of Wallace to the ethnic vote. Neither was either party ignoring the plain appeal of Wallace's simplistic sloganeering about law and order. "They're both usin' my words and my philosophy," said Wallace, half gloating, half irritated—and if his campaign ended now it would indeed have made its mark on the politics of 1968.

The last, best hope of the major parties is that Wallace's movement—like almost every third-party effort in U.S. history—will fade in the homestretch as his supporters break to one or the other of the big-league candidates. Yet Wallace, even in his private moments, is not beyond dreaming that "Mission: Impossible" will have a happy ending after all. Restlessly prowling his suite at the Fontainebleau one day last week, he snatched up a phone book, flipped it open as though it were a battle chart and shrugged off a question about what he will do in 1972 should he fail this time around. "I ain't got time to talk about losin'," he huffed, picking up the phone. "Hello, operator?"

Now and again, alone with his pals, he has been known to mutter: "Godamightydamn—wouldn't it be sump'n if I were to actually win this thing?" He won't, of course, but the very fact of his candidacy seems destined to cheapen the prize for whoever does.

The High Cost of Campaigning

Victor H. Bernstein

The cost of political campaigning imposes on the office seeker a qualification not specified in the Constitution: he must either be rich or have rich friends. Perhaps because he qualified so handsomely on both counts, the late John F. Kennedy showed himself to be more sensitive to this situation than have most of our Presidents, and shortly after taking office he appointed a Commission on Campaign Costs empowered to recommend more democratic ways of gilding the path to public office.

The commission made its report to the White House in April, 1962, where for four years it lay (presumably lightly) on the conscience of Mr. Kennedy's successor. At any rate, at the end of May, 1966 (whether by design or not, probably too late for legislative action this election year), President Johnson laid before Congress a series of proposals which in some respects follow the commission's recommendations, but in others depart from them considerably. His proposals are analyzed in detail elsewhere in this article.

These developments have been stimulated by a steady and staggering rise in the cost of political campaigning. A four-year lease on the White House runs to many millions of dollars. A Senate seat can cost a million or more (a fact which accounts, at least in part, for the current travail of Sen. Thomas E. Dodd). More than $2 million was spent to make John Lindsay mayor of New York; even a House race, if it is in a competitive metropolitan district, may require $50,000 for the nomination campaign, and as much again for election. In 1964, the country's political campaign bills (including all races from the dog catcher to President) totaled an

"The High Cost of Campaigning," *The Nation*, June 27, 1966. Reprinted by permission of the publisher.

estimated $200 million. This year, with the White House lease still unexpired, the bill is likely to be somewhat smaller—say $175 million, with the bulk spent at state levels. Do these formidable sums account for the prevalence of riches among our leading politicians (Rockefeller, Kennedy, Harriman, Romney, Pell, Ottinger, Johnson, et al.), and is this good for democracy? On the other hand, is democracy better served by relatively penurious politicians who owe office to support by the rich? How can a democratic electoral system be divorced from an aristocracy of wealth?

Politically, the rich have always been very much with us. The signers of the Declaration of Independence, and to an even greater extent, the authors of the Constitution, were largely landed gentry or wealthy merchants. Our early Presidents were all patrician—even Andrew Jackson, symbol of the rough frontier. Abraham Lincoln proved nothing except that the exception proves the rule. True, there was a tendency for the post-Civil War new industrialists to run the country from wherever they were making their money, rather than from Washington. But beginning with Teddy Roosevelt, most White House occupants have again been drawn from the upper economic strata of American society.

The influence of affluence has been noticeable in the Congress, too, and especially in the Senate, once known as the "millionaire's club." Donald R. Matthews, in his *U.S. Senators and Their World,* analyzed the personnel of the Senate for the decade 1947–58. Of the 180 individuals studied, the author found only two who were the sons of unskilled workers: Wagner, son of a janitor, and O'Daniel, son of a construction worker. A handful revealed lower-class origins: Margaret Chase Smith, daughter of a barber, and Everett Dirksen, son of a house painter, among others. The "typical" Senator, Matthews found, was white, Protestant, native born of upper-middle-class origins, and college educated for a profession (most often law). "If these are taken as 'requirements,' " he added, "probably less than 5 per cent of Americans have any significant chance of becoming a Senator."

The American democrat who tends to sneer at the British caste system may be astonished to learn that proletarians—miners, steelworkers, carpenters—are a good deal more common in Parliament than in Congress. One reason is that we have no labor party. But more important, perhaps, in an upwardly mobile society such as ours, an individual tends to identify with strata above him, whereas in a more rigidly stratified society he is likely to look to his own class for political representation.

In this country, running for public office is a private enterprise; except in one or two states, tax money does little more than provide boards of elections, polling booths and ballots or voting machines. Like that other waif of the American political system, the political party itself, methods of financing campaigns evolved quite outside the law, and it was not until certain obvious abuses touched the national conscience that regulative legislation was enacted. The first federal statute was adopted in 1867; it protected federal employees against political assessments. Over the next six decades, further laws were passed, and these were finally codified and revised by the Federal Corrupt Practices Act of 1925. This Act as amended, together with the Hatch Act of 1939–40, provides the principal ground rules for the raising and spending of money to attain federal elective office.

Unhappily, the regulations regulate nothing, as is indicated in the boxed summary below of the laws and the loopholes. In the view of many experts, such as Herbert E. Alexander, director of the Citizens' Research Foundation, they make a bad situation worse by encouraging cynical disregard for law, increasing the costs of campaigning, failing to broaden the base of political financing, and leading to so complicated a flow of funds from giver to receiver as to deprive both of any assurance that the money always follows its intended channel.

All advertising, whether to sell soup or win office, entails risk: one never knows whether the results justify the expenditures. In political advertising, there is built-in waste. The multiplicity of committees typical of a candidate's campaign multiplies administrative costs without necessarily increasing income. TV, which is eating up more and more of campaign funds, is more often than not a hugely wasteful medium. At least a dozen times, on my home TV, I watched Richard Hughes campaigning for office in 1964, and he rather won me over. But my admiration, so expensively won, did him no good at all; he was running for governor of New Jersey, while I live in Connecticut.

For a Congressional candidate in a metropolitan district TV is so wasteful that it is rarely used; there are forty or more districts within listening range of the major New York City broadcasting stations. But even without broadcasting costs, a Congressional campaign comes high. "One district-wide mailing," says Robert Price, the deputy mayor of New York and a veteran campaign manager, "will cost at least $20,000, including printing and postage. Two brochures—not too much for a four- or five-month campaign—cost another $20,000. If you are lucky, you minimize paid help by getting volunteers; still, there are office rentals, posters, advertising stationery, phone bills, etc., to pay. The absolute minimum is $50,000." If primary expenses are included, the total may rise to $75,000 or more. That's a lot of money to pay for a $30,000-a-year job with tenure guaranteed for two years only.

How best to spend the money is a big problem; how to raise it is even bigger. "The average Congressional candidate," said Mr. Price, "can expect to get $1,500 from the National Congressional Campaign Committee, another $1,000 from the county committee, and perhaps an additional $1,000 from other party groups. The rest must be raised through solicitation. If he commands a popular following, he can raise a substantial sum from the small contributions of many people through a broadcast or mail appeal. But usually for the bulk of what he needs he must rely on friends, or friends of friends, or labor or business. The biggest givers are likely to be firms with government contracts, or with hopes of getting one; they are what I call the predators—the guys who, if you win, will want something for their money." Mr. Price is on record as stating that, as manager of Lindsay's $2 million-plus mayoralty campaign, he turned down certain large contributions because he thought there were strings attached.

Most campaign managers, and presumably most candidates, are not likely to be that fussy, and the higher and more influential the office sought, the more likely is the contributors' list to be studded with the names of the wealthy. They give directly to party committees, or they buy a page ad in a party pamphlet for $15,000 (until a few months ago, such ads were tax deductible), or they join the President's Club for $1,000, or they pay $100 or more for a "campaign" or "testimonial" dinner (at this writing, Senator Dodd is most anxious to establish before the Senate ethics committee that there is a difference between the two, even if the beneficiary is an incumbent). And not a few are suffused with nonpartisan generosity; in 1964, according to the Citizens' Research Foundation's extensive files, at least eighty individuals gave $500 or more to candidates or committees of both parties.

The real question in all this is not who gives, or how much, but what the giver gets in return. It would be a calumny on our legislators, I trust, and certainly an oversimplification of our politico-economic system, to say that we are governed not so much by the men in office as by the men whose financial support put them there. On any issue, the legislator has many factors to think about other than the interests of his big contributors: his party platform, the wishes of the Administration (particularly if it is of his party), the recommendation of the relevant legislative committee, a voting deal he may have made with a fellow legislator, the rival claims of lobbyists, what he thinks the ordinary people of his constituency want (in the last analysis, their votes put him into office). There may even be times when he votes his best judgment on what's good for the country.

But history reveals many instances of outright legislative corruption and even more of what appears to be legislative subservience to an industry. There are in Congress today legislators known as "oil men," or "cotton men," or "air industry men," et al. When, as frequently happens, the welfare of a constituency is bound up with the welfare of an industry, the legislator is torn by no divided loyalty. The worst that may be said of him is that he may be betraying consumers elsewhere who can't vote for him— an occupational hazard in our political system, based as it is on sectional representation.

Furthermore, one may ask: Did big money shape the politics of these "industry" men, or was it their politics that attracted the big money in the first place? In 1956, with Eisenhower the candidate, the top men of the American Petroleum Institute made contributions of $500 or more, totaling $171,750—all of it to the GOP. In 1964, with an old Texas hand running on the Democratic ticket, GOP receipts from this source dropped to $48,-000, while the Democrats received $24,000. Considering Johnson's regional and economic background, is there any reason to suppose that he would be a less staunch supporter of the oil-depletion allowance if he hadn't received the contribution of $24,000?

None of this means that the big political contributor gets nothing for his money. Is it coincidence that eleven of the nation's top twenty-five defense contractors paid $15,000 each for a page ad in a book put out by the Democrats last year? Is it coincidence that in 1952, of twenty-seven non-career diplomatic appointments made by Truman, half the beneficiaries had contributed $500 or more to the Democratic Party, and all were Democrats; and that a year later, of thirty similar appointments made by Eisenhower, twelve of the appointees had given $500 or more to the

GOP, and all but one were Republican? At the very least, the big contributor gets what Alexander Heard, chancellor of Vanderbilt University, calls "access" to the decision makers.

There is a final consideration: Does money win? From 1932 to 1942, the Democrats, consistently spending less money, won the Presidency. They have done so again since 1960. The 1960 figures will surprise many. Repeated accusations have been made that the Kennedy family "bought" this election; nevertheless, Citizens' Research Foundation statistics show total reported campaign expenditures at the national level as: Republicans, $11,300,000; Democrats, $10,587,000. In 1964, the GOP outspent the Democrats by one of the biggest margins in history—and certainly lost by the biggest margin.

However, this seeming triumph of ideology over crass money ignores several factors. For one thing, the incumbent usually does not have to spend as much money as the challenger; his "image" has already been projected. Secondly, the figures given do not include pre-nomination (primary or convention) costs, which federal law does not require to be reported. "It is in seeking the nomination," says Robert Price, "that wealth, or access to it, counts most for the candidate. Once he wins the nomination, he already has the attraction of a winner, and he has the party apparatus at his disposal; until then, he is more or less on his own." In this context, it was in Kennedy's primary victory over Humphrey in West Virginia, say, that money talked loudest.

The conditions under which political campaigns are financed in this country are indictable on a number of major counts: they (1) breed contempt for law, (2) put a premium on wealth, (3) open the office holder to charges of subservience to his financial backers and (4) fail to encourage widespread citizen participation in the pre-balloting electoral process.

Conditions in the West European democracies are somewhat better, I think. This is not because they have better laws, or their people are more law abiding, but because of the nature of their party structures. All major Left parties are tied to labor; whether you are a Labour candidate in Britain, a Socialist in France, a Social Democrat in Germany or a Communist in Italy, everyone knows that your campaign is being financed by union treasuries. While the Center and Right parties are less well organized, and their fund sources not always so precisely definable, they are equally plainly the creatures of business and industry (and, in some instances, the Church). In Germany and France, various trade and industry organizations have set up central collecting agencies for political funds. In some countries (the Conservative Party in Norway, for example), fixed annual quotas are collected from each business firm or trade association. In any case, membership in a European party, whether of the Right or Left, involves not merely an act of penmanship but some form of financial responsibility.

I do not want to oversimplify the European party system; it has its own complexities. But broadly speaking, party labels on the Continent, at least, mean more than they do here, as regards both politics and the financing thereof.

As long as running for public office in the United States remains a more

DISTRIBUTION OF MEMBERSHIP OF PRESIDENT'S CLUB, BY STATE, 1964

(Reprinted from "Financing the 1964 Election," by
Herbert E. Alexander; published by Citizens'
Research Foundation

This appendix shows approximate distribution of membership, by state, combining state President's Club memberships where separate, and contributions of $1,000 or more by state residents to national-level, non-Congressional Democratic committees. Some duplication may have resulted if an individual contributed to both a state club and to committees at the national level.

State	Number of Contributors of $1,000 or over *	State	Number of Contributors of $1,000 or over *
Alabama	93	Nevada	7
Alaska	2	New Hampshire	9
Arizona	22	New Mexico	3
Arkansas	8	New York * *	1,031
California * *	532	North Carolina	19
Colorado	34	North Dakota	—
Connecticut	23	Ohio	120
Delaware	18	Oklahoma	18
Florida	135	Oregon	7
Georgia	23	Pennsylvania	65
Hawaii	—	Rhode Island	4
Idaho	4	South Carolina	20
Illinois	173	South Dakota	—
Indiana	5	Tennessee	20
Iowa	2	Texas	400
Kansas	8	Utah	1
Kentucky	11	Vermont	1
Louisiana	26	Virginia	98
Maine	—	Washington	40
Maryland	77	West Virginia	6
Massachusetts	57	Wisconsin	20
Michigan	28	Wyoming	—
Minnesota * *	190	District of Columbia	294
Mississippi	21	Puerto Rico	9
Missouri	41	Virgin Islands	4
Montana	7	Canal Zone	—
Nebraska	9	Guam	3
New Jersey	49	TOTAL	3,801

* Husbands and wives counted separately where $2,000 or more was donated.

* * Figures combined for state President's Club memberships and contributions of $1,000 or more by state residents to national-level Democratic committees campaigning for President Johnson. Not included are contributions to Senatorial or Congressional or other non-Presidential committees.

or less private enterprise, it is difficult to see how its financing can be effectively controlled. Teddy Roosevelt saw this in 1907, and as President suggested that election campaigns be subsidized out of the federal treasury. Nobody liked the idea; no doubt it smelled of socialism. In Europe—and elsewhere abroad—the Socialist devil is thoroughly familiar, and no stigma attaches to borrowing from him occasionally. Thus, partial subsidies of the electoral process are quite common there. Where broadcasting is state owned, parties are given a certain amount of free time, usually in proportion to their voting strength. The French Government prints and distributes campaign circulars and sample ballots in behalf of all candidates, and also pays for election posters; Britain underwrites one free mailing for each candidate. Japan publishes an "electoral gazette" containing objective descriptions of all candidates and their platforms, and underwrites two 4 x 5-inch newspaper ads for each office seeker. Some West German states (*Laende*) award small but direct cash subsidies to the state party organizations; in some instances, the law requires that the money must be used for "educational purposes" (it almost never is); in other cases, no strings at all are attached.

It remained for Puerto Rico, however, to go almost the whole hog. Under its Election Fund Act of 1957, initiated by Luis Muñoz Marín to rid the country of vote buying and kickbacks from government employees, the national treasury allots each party $75,000 annually in non-election years and (under a 1964 revision of the law) a minimum of $162,500 in election years. The latter sum may be increased, depending upon the number of "straight-ticket" votes the party receives in an election; it cannot, however, be decreased. The allotments are expected to cover the major share of campaign expenses. The law requires a strict accounting of all receipts and expenditures.

In this country, proposals to reform our systems of political financing fall into two schools. Both seek to broaden the base of citizen involvement, to restore public confidence in and increase public respect for the relevant legal regulations, and to increase the opportunities of the poor man to attain office. The difference is that while one school hopes these objectives can be reached in the framework of our "private enterprise" system of fund raising, the more radical school insists that in this field private enterprise simply won't work, and turns to the direct subsidy as a solution.

Typical of the "conservative" school are President Johnson's recent proposals which, like the recommendations of the Kennedy-appointed Commission on Campaign Costs, seek not to change or broaden present political financing methods in any basic way, but simply to control them more effectively. The commission was somewhat more daring than the President, as can be seen by reference to the boxed analysis of the Johnson proposals. Moreover the commission, aware that its recommendations might not prove adequate, suggested that after a trial period they should be subject to revision, with special attention given to a "matching-incentive" system under which private contributions up to perhaps $10 each would be matched by equal contributions from the national treasury.

Plainly, the commission's report was a compromise; its chairman, Professor Heard, has taken a bolder approach elsewhere. While he subscribes to many of the commission proposals, he also urges (1) consideration of payment of cash subsidies to parties and candidates at both state and national levels; (2) government action to reduce TV and radio costs so as to make broadcast opportunities more available for all; and (3) an underwriting by government of some, at least, of the general communications cost of political campaigns.

A year before the Puerto Rican bill was passed, the late Sen. Richard Neuberger (D., Ore.) offered a measure authorizing direct payments from the federal treasury to the national party committees. In a Presidential year, the amount would be 20c per vote based on the average number of votes cast for President in the preceding two elections; in off years, it would be 15c based on the two preceding votes for Congress. In terms of recent elections, this would mean a subsidy of $10 million to $12 million for each party in a Presidential campaign, and $6 million to $7 million each for an off-year campaign.

Aside from affirming the logical principle that running for public office is properly a public enterprise, and therefore should be publicly financed, the subsidy system offers certain specific advantages. It involves every taxpayer in every election, at least financially; it makes the legislator more (or entirely) independent of private interests, and it increases the political opportunity of men without access to wealth. The tendency toward an undue proliferation of small parties which a subsidy system might encourage could be guarded against by adopting the British practice that requires candidates to post deposits which are refundable only if the candidate garners a stipulated number of votes.

Formidable arguments can be raised against the system. Authority goes where money goes, and allotting the subsidies to the national committees makes the state and local organization subservient to Washington. Local Democratic leaders are already restive over the phenomenal success of the President's Club as a money raiser; they see in it not only a drain of money that ought to remain at home, but also an expansion of Presidential authority over the party. Even if the law mandated the sharing of funds with state and local party organizations, on what basis would the eligibility of these organizations be decided? The New York City Democratic organization is torn by a reform movement; would the reform group be entitled to subsidy funds?

Opponents of subsidies raise two further arguments. Will candidates for nomination be subsidized as well as candidates for election? If so, how do you keep out the crackpots who represent no one but themselves? The British system of demanding deposits might work in states where there are primaries; how could it be adapted to the convention or caucus type of nominating procedure? Finally, the opponents say that subsidies would discourage, rather than encourage, citizen involvement in the electoral process; impersonal tax money should not be allowed to replace the individual, voluntary contribution which gives the voter the feeling that he has a personal stake in the campaign.

Perhaps the most singular aspect of the political finance problem is how few people want to do something about a situation that so many admit to be scandalous (many of the charges against Senator Dodd could be leveled, with equal plausibility, against other legislators). Many politicians agree that the present system is bad; still, the experts' consensus is that even President Johnson's modest reforms will meet with stout Congressional opposition. Legislators who have managed to win office under existing conditions see little reason to make things better for potential rivals. Nor is there any sign that the American voter is pressing hard for change. Most Americans view politics with considerable skepticism anyway; they expect shenanigans, and whether these occur before or after a man reaches office seems of no great moment.

One can argue plausibly that in a country where money, education and broad social outlook tend to be strongly correlated, it is a good thing that wealth should play an important role in politics. In a better ordered society, of course, no such correlation would exist, and there would be no justification for the advantage that wealth now gives the politician. While we wait for the millennium, some form of subsidy would seem to be in order, if only for the reason that the one-third or one-quarter of Americans who are ill fed, ill housed and ill clothed are also ill represented—or not represented at all—in government. And perhaps, as a start, the funds needed for subsidies could be raised by a turnover tax on the broadcasting, advertising, printing and newspaper industries. They are the industries the money would be spent on in any case.

THE LAWS AND THE LOOPHOLES
A Summary of Federal Regulations Affecting the Financing of Political Campaigns—and Why They Don't Work

THE LAW: No political committee can receive contributions or make expenditures of more than $3 million in any one year. *The Loopholes:* The limits apply only to committees operating in two or more states, and therefore state and local committees are exempt; it permits the creation of any number of interstate committees, each of which may receive or spend up to $3 million a year.

THE LAW: Every political committee covered by federal statute must report periodically to the Clerk of the House of Representatives the names of all contributors of $100 or more and the names of all persons to whom at least $10 was distributed, together with the totals of all other expenditures. *The Loopholes:* Nobody checks or audits the reports, and you have to go to Washington to see them. They need be kept on file for only two years.

THE LAW: A candidate for the Senate may spend up to $25,000 and for the House up to $5,000. Each candidate must file, shortly before and again within a month after each election, a statement itemizing each contribution and expenditure made or received by him, or by any person for him, with his knowledge and consent. *The Loopholes:* Note that the law limits expenditures, not contributions receivable. With regard to expenditures, the key phrase is "with his knowledge and consent." The candidate can state that one of his committees put up 100 highway billboards "without his knowledge and consent," and by common consent he can get away with the disclaimer. Since the candidate is entitled to as many committees as he can gather members for, limits to spending disappear entirely. As for reporting, a candidate merely states that all contributions made to him were turned over to a committee for his election. And the committee need not report at all because it is intrastate.

THE LAW: No national bank, corporation or labor union may contribute to the election, primary, pre-nomination convention or caucus campaign of any candidate for federal elective office. *The Loopholes:* The banned organizations contribute in the name of individuals, or form "educational" or "nonpartisan" organizations which may legally contribute for "bipartisan" purposes. But how "bipartisan" is a COPE get-out-the-vote drive?

THE LAW: No government contractor may contribute during the negotiations for, or the life of, the contract. *The Loophole:* The president (or secretary or treasurer) of the firm makes the contribution.

THE LAW: No individual may contribute more than $5,000 to any one candidate or committee during the calendar year. *The Loophole:* But there is nothing to stop the individual from making unlimited $5,000 gifts to as many candidates and committees as he likes.

Note: *No limitations of any kind are placed on the personal receipts or expenditures of candidates for President and Vice President, nor are they required to make any financial report to anyone.*

THE PRESIDENT'S PROPOSALS
An Analysis of His Suggestions for a Federal Election Reform Act

PROPOSAL: All gifts exceeding $100 received by federal legislators, and all income from personal services received by them or on their behalf, are to be reported annually, with appropriate criminal sanctions to be provided for failure to comply. *Critique:* A highly desirable piece of legislation timed, no doubt, to relieve the Democratic Party of some of the pressures upon it generated by the charges against Sen. Thomas E. Dodd (D., Conn.).

PROPOSAL: Every candidate for federal office, as well as every committee—state as well as interstate or national—that supports a candidate would be required to report all contributions and expense items that exceed $100. For the first time, the disclosure provisions would include candidates for the Presidency and Vice Presidency, and also all fund raising and spending in pre-election campaigns (primaries and convention nominations). *Critique:* While plugging many loopholes in present law, the proposal is weakened by two factors. First, its lack of definition of a "committee" would require, presumably, that a handful of high school youngsters who collected $100.29 for a favored candidate would have to report. Under such conditions, disclosures could prove so massive as to be indigestible. The proposal's second weakness aggravates this difficulty: it fails to set up adequate machinery for receiving and processing the reports.

PROPOSAL: Present ceilings on total expenditures by candidates for federal office would be repealed and the total contribution coming from any single source to the campaign of any candidate would be limited to $5,000. *Critique:* All experts would agree on the repeal of present ceilings. Since they are unenforceable, they simply encourage cynical disregard of law. The $5,000 suggested limitation, if adequately enforced, would go a long way toward plugging the scandalous leaks in present law. However, it could not prevent the determined Democrat (or Republican) giver from contributing $5,000 each to as many candidates as he wished.

PROPOSAL: The present law preventing corporations with government contracts from making contributions to federal campaigns should be extended to cover state and local campaigns. *Critique:* A sound broadening of present law, but it leaves untouched a major loophole in the field: corporations, banks and labor unions, all of which are ostensibly barred by present law from political contributions, can still contribute through their individual officers.

PROPOSAL: Individual contributors could deduct from taxable income each year the first $100 of their contributions. *Critique:* As a possible alternative to an income-deduction plan, the Kennedy Commission on Campaign Costs recommended a flat tax credit of half the contribution up to a maximum of $10 a year. As between the two schemes, the flat tax credit is clearly preferable. Under the income-deduction system, the wealthy are favored; i.e., to a person in the 25 per cent income-tax bracket, a $100 contribution would cost $75, while to a richer man in the 75 per cent bracket, it would cost only $25.

PROPOSAL: The only item permitted for sale by a candidate or committee would be campaign souvenirs at no more than $5 each. *Critique:* In 1964, the Democrats charged $15,000 for 1-page ads in their convention publication; if the President's proposal is enacted into law, the Republicans won't be able to follow suit.

Chapter Seven

SUGGESTED QUESTIONS FOR CLASS DISCUSSION.

1. It appears that the idea of direct popular election of the President is favored by a great many people—possibly by a large majority of voters. Why will it be difficult, if not impossible, to amend the Constitution to provide for such direct election? Would it, in fact, drastically alter the bases of power of election as they now exist?
2. Are national conventions for nominating presidential candidates really "pure democracy at work," or are they so subject to control by the parties' leadership that the time has come to replace them with presidential primaries?
3. Did the 1968 presidential election depart from the patterns of the last three decades in terms of (a) party regularity in voting? (b) In holding the old alliances together? (c) In the national support for a third party candidate?
4. Do we need new laws designed to limit the amounts of money spent by parties and candidates? Would shortening the campaign by law be effective? Are the soaring costs of campaigning already imposing a limit?

Chapter Eight

THE CONGRESS

Article 1 of the Constitution states that "All legislative powers herein granted shall be vested in a Congress of the United States. . . ." The Congress is one of the main actors in the drama of American politics and often occupies the center of the stage. It is a focal point of a vast number of political pressures and it participates in the making of virtually all major domestic and international policies.

Many deliberative bodies have fallen on difficult days in the twentieth century, and the Congress is no exception. It is subjected to continuing criticism, well-informed or ill-informed, and is perpetually exhorted to reform itself. Members and observers alike appear to delight in examining and reexamining Congress and in issuing prescriptions for its reform. What are the problems of Congress? Why is it encountering difficulties and what, if anything, should be done? Can it discharge its enormous responsibilities effectively? Can Congress develop an overall program of its own, or is it essentially a headless and uncoordinated body that needs guidance from the President? Can it produce legislation of the quality that is needed in the amount that is needed? Does it appropriate billions of dollars each year in a wise and knowing way, or does it sometimes act spasmodically, arbitrarily, and in ignorance? The cases in this chapter take a look at the world that is the Congress of the United States.

The Extraordinary Power of Freshmen in Congress

Thomas P. Murphy

As usual, public attention in this election year is directed almost entirely to the Presidency—to who the nominees will be and who the eventual winner will be. Comparatively little attention, as usual, is paid to the Congressional race. And yet members of the present House of Representatives may actually determine who the next President will be, and members of the new House may actually determine what the next President can accomplish. In this article, I want to review the history of the past two Houses to show what enormous power these legislators, and in particular the freshman legislators, have accumulated in recent years.

The present, predominantly Republican freshman class in the 90th Congress was swept in during the Democratic debacle of 1966. In that election, the Republicans scored a net gain of 47 seats in the House. Further, the Republicans elected 48 *new* Representatives, while the Democrats elected only 14—and of these 14 Democratic freshmen, 7 were conservatives from the Deep South. To round out the Administration's losses, 23 of the bumper crop of 71 Democratic freshmen who had been elected in the 1964 sweep, and who had helped push President Johnson's Great Society programs through the 89th Congress, were unseated.

The Democratic Congressional defeat in 1966 was almost as severe as Barry Goldwater's Presidential defeat in 1964. The result was that the Democrats are now faced with a very real possibility that was almost unthinkable after the Democratic victory of 1964—that the Republicans may recapture the White House in November. Whether they do or not will depend in part on how effectively the Republican leadership continues to undermine the President's programs by organizing its freshman Congressmen against them.

J.F.K.'S CONGRESSIONAL PROBLEM

Even though John F. Kennedy was elected President in 1960, that year the Democrats lost 20 seats in the House of Representatives. In addition, many Southern Democrats went on to vote with the Republicans on substantive matters, including goals presumably agreed upon in the Democratic party platform. So Kennedy was faced with major obstacles in pushing through the legislation he needed to redeem his campaign pledges.

President Kennedy decided to take steps toward getting Congressional cooperation. He had Larry O'Brien develop the most systematic program for presenting the Administration's view that had been seen on Capitol Hill since the early days of the Roosevelt Administration. Although the power advantage of the Republican-Southern Democratic alliance was such that even a well-organized approach to the 88th Congress could not guarantee legislative success, President Kennedy's odds were vastly improved by O'Brien's work.

First, the Kennedy strategists challenged the old guard in the person of "Judge" Howard Smith of Virginia, the Democratic chairman of the House Rules Committee. For many years, Smith had used his position on the Rules Committee to keep liberal legislation from reaching the floor of the House. If unchecked, he would have demanded amendments that would have weakened the legislation, or might even have prevented much of the Kennedy program from coming to a vote. Kennedy's strategy was to diminish the power of Smith's vote by enlarging the Rules Committee. In this move, the 1960 freshmen Democrats supported the President 13–5, giving him the very narrow margin by which the measure finally passed. This was only the first of several Kennedy "must" measures that were saved by the Democratic freshmen.

Another example was Kennedy's feed grains price-support bill, which won by 209–202: The freshmen voted 14 to 3 in favor of it. The minimum-wage bill, however, despite receiving an 11-vote plurality from the Democratic freshmen, lost by 216 to 203. While the rest of the Republicans had opposed the President by a ratio of below six to one on this issue, the Republican freshmen voted against him 36 to 2. Thus it was the Republican freshmen who torpedoed Kennedy's minimum-wage bill—a lesson that President Johnson has surely had reason to consider in dealing with his own 90th Congress.

The 71 Democratic freshmen helped into office by the heavy vote for President Johnson in 1964 felt that they had a mandate to go "all the way with L.B.J." In the 89th Congress, they provided the full margin of victory on much of President Johnson's key legislation. And they did this knowing that most of them would face extremely difficult reelection campaigns, owing to (1) the absence of the President on the 1966 ticket; (2) the normal off-year attrition suffered by the party in control of the Presidency (an average of 40 seats lost in each of the past seven elections); and (3) the fact that they represented normally Republican, or at best marginal, districts.

These Democratic freshmen were vulnerable to charges of being rubber stamps for the President unless they took some independent stands, but independence was difficult. It was difficult in the face of the barrage of legislation requested of the Congress; the President's own proclivities for making his preferences known directly to individual legislators; and his own use of the O'Brien organization. In addition, and perhaps paramount, most of the Democratic freshmen felt a strong personal commitment to carrying forward the social philosophy of the Kennedy-Johnson program.

The Democratic freshmen of 1964 received more lavish attention from the President than any previous group of freshmen had enjoyed. President Johnson knew that their narrow margins of victory would put the freshmen under great pressure to establish independent voting records in Congress. Yet he also knew that their support was essential to the success of his legislative program. Accordingly, he took steps to solidify their positions with their constituents so that they could, in turn, give full support to him without fear of retaliation at the polls. For example, instead of releasing the Presidential campaign staff after the 1964 election, President Johnson had the Democratic National Commtitee (D.N.C.) retain a large number of specialists to provide services to the Democratic forces in Congress, with special preference for the freshmen. One service enabled a Congressman to phone press releases and statements to the D.N.C. while debates and decisions were still hot. Through its communications network, the D.N.C. was then able to speed these items to radio stations and newspapers in the Congressman's district—and provide him with some instant image-building among his constituents.

Other Administration efforts to provide individual support to the new House Democrats included invitations to visit the White House in small groups, so that the President could become personally acquainted with them and with their problems. These meetings were often followed by press releases and meetings with Administration officials in charge of programs of interest to the Congressmen's districts. And, of course, the Johnson Administration did not fail to impress upon the freshmen the ways in which the Federal Government could aid local projects dear to the hearts of the voters in their home districts.

Early in the first session, Vice-President Humphrey was assigned the task of guiding the new freshmen in the techniques of being Congressmen. The "ombudsman" function in particular was both a burden and an opportunity for the new Democrats who were willing to cooperate with the Administration. As a Senator, Humphrey had loudly complained that the ombudsman function interfered with his legislative functions. Nevertheless, it was the Vice-President who met with the freshmen every three or four weeks early in the 1965 session to help them adjust to Washington, and to the ombudsman role in particular.

The freshmen were also treated very well in terms of committee assignments. The vast majority received their first or second committee choices —owing, in some cases, to direct interventions by the Democratic leadership. Of course, such assignments can have a major impact on a Congressman's reelection possibilities. The right committee assignments give him additional knowledge of problems relevant to his district, access to the administrative officials who deal with these problems, and a chance for some publicity on matters meaningful to his constituents.

The Republicans later charged that the 1964 Democratic freshmen were too successful in obtaining their share of the pork barrel. They alleged that this was possible only because the freshmen "sold" their votes to Lyndon Johnson. But another explanation—advanced by the successful freshmen on their own behalf—was that their success was due to their Republican predecessors' neglect of the matters on which they themselves had been able to get action.

Whatever their motives, the Democratic freshmen—with the exception of the seven Southern Congressmen—may be credited with the successful record of the 89th Congress. Early in the first session of the 89th Congress, the new Democrats again challenged the conservative coalition of Republicans and Southern Democrats that had often stymied the Kennedy legislative program. The Democratic freshmen helped push through a change in the House rules that made it possible to bypass the Rules Committee controlled by "Judge" Smith if it did not grant a ruling within 21 days. This meant that the conservative coalition could no longer keep liberal legislation from reaching the floor of the House by arbitrarily refusing to grant a ruling. The freshman Democrats—including 44 out of the 48 who had taken seats held by Republicans in the 88th Congress—provided President Johnson with a plurality of 55 votes on the rules-change vote, and still the measure passed by only 22 votes.

The Department of Housing and Urban Development was created by a vote of 217 to 184, or a margin of 33 votes. Since the freshman Democrats voted 59 to 10 in favor of it, they again contributed the full margin of victory. And the freshman Democrat votes also made the difference on medicare, rent supplements, repeal of the "right to work" section of the Taft-Hartley Act (a move that later died in a Senate filibuster), the poverty program, and other key legislation of the 1965 session. Without doubt, the Great Society legislative programs passed by the 89th Congress would have been defeated without their support.

SECTIONAL AND PARTY LOYALTY

The Democratic freshmen of 1964 are the largest number of Democrats who have ever taken the seats of senior Republicans. Moreover, what Democratic losses there were in 1964 were almost all sustained in the South, where Goldwater's candidacy created an unusual wave of support for the Republican Party. Since most of the defeated Southern Democrats would have voted the same way as the Republicans elected in their places, that shift had no real effect on the Great Society domestic programs.

To see the extent to which the Republican-Southern bloc was able to override considerations of party discipline, look at the voting patterns on ten of the closest key issues put before the 89th Congress:

Eighteen of the twenty newly elected Republicans did not support the President on a single one of the ten votes; the other two voted the Democratic position one time out of ten.

Seven Southern Democrats—three of them from the President's own Texas delegation—voted against the President on more than half of the ten votes.

Two of the Southern Democrats did not support the President on any of the Great Society programs.

Today's 90th Congress presents a marked contrast to the hyperactive 89th. The 90th Congress, faced with racial conflict of revolutionary dimensions and bitterly divided by the commitment in Vietnam, has concentrated on wielding the ax to trim Administration programs. Particularly in the area of urban legislation, the 48 Republican freshmen have had a controlling voice in dictating cutbacks—and they have been aided by many Democrats reluctant to support a tax increase without some compensatory reductions in Federal spending.

The model-cities appropriation was defeated by 20 votes: The G.O.P. freshmen voted 37–10 for the cutback. The squeeze on rent supplements was approved, with the Republican freshmen voting 41–7 for reducing the appropriation. But President Johnson's Appalachian development bill passed by 21 votes, despite the fact that the G.O.P. freshmen voted against it by 34–14. In this instance, Democratic party discipline—bringing votes of 11–3 from the Democratic freshmen and 31–7 from the Democratic sophomores—saved the Administration.

At the end of September 1967, the Republican-sponsored motion for recommittal of continuing appropriations joined the fiscal battle against the Administration. It was passed by 20 votes: The Republicans, including all 48 freshmen, voted as a bloc for the motion. Just six days later, however, a Democratic motion to prevent further delay of continuing appropriations was passed by eight votes. The Republicans again voted as a solid bloc in opposition, but this time the Administration succeeded in getting nine Democrats, seven from the South (including the influential Wilbur Mills of Arkansas), to switch their votes. Had the Administration been able to peel off 10 votes from the Northern G.O.P. freshman bloc in the *first* place, the original recommittal motion would have been defeated without recourse to soliciting vote-switching from Democratic Southerners. These two votes illustrate the new-found effectiveness, at least in fiscal matters, of G.O.P. party discipline—and the peril to Administration measures presented by Republican bloc voting.

The defeat of the first rat-control measure was accomplished by a solid 41–6 G.O.P. freshman vote against the bill (this vote threatened to immortalize the 90th as the "Rat Congress"). When a second rat-control bill passed by 54 votes, it was because 38 Republicans switched their votes. The Democratic vote was virtually unchanged.

Then, in late September 1967, the fiscal battle began in earnest. Twenty-eight G.O.P. freshmen sent a letter to the House Speaker urging a six-day, extended-hour work week and asking for "some procedural improvements in the House of Representatives." This incident later made national headlines—when Democrat Vanik pointed out that 12 of the petitioners were absent for a roll-call vote on the same day the letter was sent. And on October 10, a package of bills intended to deal with the issue of organized crime was submitted by 23 freshman Republicans. They charged that organized crime was preying on the urban poor.

These events illustrate two significant points. First, members of the freshman bloc, in this case the Republicans, are sufficiently aware of their potential power to take concerted action; and second, the party leadership can take advantage of this potential either to propose or to oppose legislation. In the 90th Congress, the keynote has been opposition.

The Administration, faced with a large deficit stemming from the staggering costs of the Vietnam War, has had enough trouble holding the line on established programs without trying to initiate new ones. As with the rent-supplements and model-cities bills, the Senate has reverted to its traditional role as a court of last appeal for the restoration of House cuts. The House, meanwhile, has acted as an anchor weighing down the entire ship of state. But perhaps this extreme fiscal conservation in the House is logical: All of the members of the House are up for reelection in 1968, whereas only one-third of their Senate colleagues are.

REPUBLICAN AND DEMOCRATIC PROSPECTS

The legislative record that the G.O.P. will put before the voters in 1968 is largely negative. It shows opposition to Administration proposals and few constructive counterproposals. Republican negativism at the Congressional level, however, stands in sharp contrast with the behavior of state and local Republican leaders. Eight Republican governors, headed by Nelson Rockefeller, rather than simply running against Administration programs, have proposed a 60-point program of their own for dealing with the urban crisis.

The voice of moderate Republicanism, stilled in 1964 and sure to be strongly challenged in its comeback attempt this year, is being heard loud and clear at the state and local levels—but, with the exception of a few Senators, it is noticeably silent on Capitol Hill. Of course, the battle for the Republican Party will eventually be decided by the county chairmen who go to Miami in August. But the party's schizophrenia is already clearly visible when one compares its negative Congressional record with the positive public pronouncements of Governors Romney and Rockefeller, or with the vigorous public policies of Republican mayors like New York's John Lindsay.

Some Democratic governors, in contrast with the Republican governors, and beginning with the so-called "Governors' Revolt" after the 1966 election, have tried to exert a more *conservative* influence on their national party leadership. This effort, which has taken the form of pressure for greater Federal dependence on state governments—for example, for Federal-state tax-sharing plans—has had the support of the Democratic freshmen in the 90th Congress. By supporting this move toward conservatism, the new freshmen have come into conflict with the Democratic sophomores —those freshmen from the class of 1964 who were reelected in 1966.

Though reduced in number, the sophomore survivors—who exerted such power as freshmen in the 89th Congress—have continued to be a bulwark of Administration support. The 1966 crop of Democratic freshmen, however, seems to have other ideas. Let us compare the freshman with the sophomore votes on some key issues: Of ten urban issues recorded in Table III, the Democratic freshmen *and* the Republican freshmen voted against the President on three of the ten votes, whereas the 41 Democratic sophomores who first joined the Congress in the 1964 Johnson landslide continued to give the President lopsided support. On only five of the ten votes did the Democratic freshmen vote with the Democratic sophomores. As for the other two votes, the Democratic freshmen split their votes evenly on the ninth, but on the tenth vote (the teacher corps) they opposed the President when both the Democratic sophomores and the *Republican* freshmen supported him—a truly remarkable situation.

This record of apparently growing conservatism among House Democrats is at least partially due to the fact that the 26 Democratic freshmen of 1964 who were defeated in 1966 represented the liberal wing of the party. Had they not been defeated, the record of the 90th Congress might have been far different. Now, it appears that 13 of these former legislators will seek their old House seats again this year. If the Republicans follow their suicidal pattern of 1964 and nominate a far-right Presidential candidate, the Democrats could reelect a large portion of those legislators who shaped the "Fighting 89th." Over one-third of the previously held 26 seats are in just two states—Iowa and Michigan—that could easily swing back to the Democrats.

ALTERNATIVES FOR 1968

The divisions within each party have grown wider during the past year, and the lackluster record of the 90th Congress reflects the domestic and foreign strains facing the nation. What, then, are the prospects for the 1968 elections? One possibility for the Republicans is to run a conservative Presidential nominee and, backed by their negative Congressional record, bank solely on opposition to President Johnson and the Great Society. If it were not for the Vietnam issue, such a strategy would probably be as suicidal as it was in 1964. But Vietnam cannot be ignored—and time is running out for President Johnson.

On the other hand, if a moderate Republican wins the Presidential nomination, the Democrats may well charge that he is only a front cloaking the inherent conservatism of the party regulars. To support this charge, the conservative G.O.P. record in Congress could be cited.

What are the Democratic alternatives for 1968? First, the President can occupy the wide middle of the road as he did in 1964. But running against a moderate, he would be in great trouble. President Johnson's speech to the A.F.L.-C.I.O. suggests that he will likely adopt a Harry Truman stance and point to the record of "Republican obstruction" in the 90th Congress. Even if Republican legislators fail to repair their image in the second session, however, continuing American casualties in Vietnam, or another summer of racial violence, could drown out the President's message.

A moderate Republican could harness both of these emotionally-charged issues, plus the one issue the Republican Congressional performance *has* dramatized—the nation's dangerous financial plight. Romney's handling of the Vietnam question was damaging precisely because he had already gained some credibility in the other two areas. Now only Governor Rockefeller seems to qualify. He has wealth and business experience, he is a strong campaigner, he is a "winner," and he captured the Negro vote in Manhattan in his last race for the governorship. By avoiding a premature candidacy, he has avoided the acid test of declaring himself in detail on Vietnam.

Even so, much of Rockefeller's support is with the independent voter, and this will not necessarily help him accumulate convention delegates. It may be unrealistic to think that the body that tried to shout him down in 1964 will give him the nomination later this year.

In trying to determine how the national pulse will affect the election on the Congressional level, we should remember that, according to voter surveys, people frequently do not know or remember how their Congressmen voted on key issues. A Congressman's record, then, is not always basic to his election. In 1966, the voters seemed to be responding to something more intangible—they were expressing a mood of uneasiness and frustration regarding Vietnam, the economy, and violence in the cities.

In addition, it would have taken a near-miracle to reelect Democratic freshmen from some of the traditionally Republican districts that in 1964 reacted against Barry Goldwater. And there is no question that in 1966 there was much disenchantment with the President personally.

The Democratic freshmen of 1964 responded vigorously to the apparent Great Society mandate, but half of them were nonetheless defeated in 1966. It will be interesting to see whether the voters in 1968 reward or penalize the Republican freshmen for pursuing the apparent mandate of 1966—a tougher approach to Administration programs—or whether their fate, too, will be determined by forces beyond their control.

Last year it seemed that the Democrats might feel properly chastised and, faced with a smaller majority in the House, regroup under the President's leadership in the interests of self-preservation. But this did not occur in the first session of the 90th Congress. In fact, the liberal Democratic Study Group, which had been a major element in the organization and record of the 89th Congress, didn't function at all during the first session. Members of the group couldn't find anyone to accept the chairmanship. This disorganization is typical of what happened to the Democrats when the Republicans closed ranks and began to stretch the President's supporters over the surtax barrel.

If the Republican Party can agree early on a strong candidate to oppose the President, these Republican freshmen will surely fare better in 1968 than the Democratic freshmen did in 1966. But without such a strong Presidential candidate, the Republicans will need a more effective defense than their own legislative record. At present it is hard to see what issue could possibly provide them with such protection, since the dissatisfaction with Vietnam will affect members of both parties.

INCREASED FRESHMAN POWER

Whatever the outcome of the Congressional and Presidential races, several elements are enhancing the power of the freshman Congressmen. Important precedents were set by the freshman delegations of the 89th and 90th Congresses. Both delegations, one heavily Democratic and the other heavily Republican, had the votes to determine the outcome of major issues. This power was due in part to the size of the freshman delegations—71 Democrats in the 89th and 59 Republicans in the 90th—but what is important is that the freshmen mobilized this power with a view to group interest.

This increase in the freshmen's potential power—and the psychological changes making them willing to use it—have allowed them to successfully challenge many House traditions. They have rejected the idea that freshmen should be seen and not heard: Keeping quiet, they argue, is not the way to be reelected. They have supported and even led revolts against prestigious committee chairmen. In short, the House of Representatives will never be the same.

One basic reason for this new aggressiveness among freshman Congressmen is the greater competition for House seats. This greater competition means that winning candidates are probably better qualified than previous winners; and it means that an elected Congressman, to be reelected, may try to achieve more for his constituents and to become better known to them.

This increasing competition for Congressional seats has at least two causes:

1. The growing number of election districts unsafe for either party. In recent House elections, both Republicans and Democrats invaded districts once earmarked for the opposition. These forays, turning safe districts into marginal ones, have further weakened the old-time party machines. The Democratic machine in lower Manhattan and in some parts of the South, for example, can no longer count on electing a listless party regular against a dynamic Republican.

2. The growing political power of the suburbs. The suburbs have been becoming larger and more politically heterogeneous because of liberal middle-class Democrats emigrating from the urban core. They will become even more powerful, politically, because of reapportionment, by gaining representation according to their population.

In short, the spread of the two-party system to some Northern cities, to the South, and to the farm states (once traditionally Republican), together with the new power of the politically divided suburbs, is increasing competition for public office, and this in turn may be breeding a more vigorous type of Congressman.

The higher level of voter education may be another cause of freshman assertiveness. The unqualified Congressional candidate may find it more and more difficult to mislead people into voting for him. This too would increase the level of competence and performance among new Congressmen—and so be another element contributing to the growth of freshman power.

But whatever the origins of the new freshman power, it may still face one major limitation. A new kind of interdependence between Presidential and Congressional elections may be emerging. When large numbers of freshman Congressional candidates upset opposition-party incumbents, these switches usually occur in marginal districts. But the victorious new Congressmen may soon make a jolting discovery: While their votes can make the difference in passing or defeating the President's programs, their own fate at the polls, because of the marginal nature of their districts, may well be in the President's hands. In an age when the mass media have created the cult of the Presidential personality, when the public may identify *all* party candidates with the man who leads the party, the voters—even in a Congressional election—may really be voting for or against the President. If so, the political fortunes of the nation's Congressmen will vary—directly or inversely, depending on party—with the fortunes of the man in the White House.

Russell of Georgia: The Old Guard at Its Shrewdest

Douglas Kiker

If the day ever comes when Lyndon Johnson decides there is no alternative but to withdraw United States forces from Vietnam and leave that troubled land to its own destiny, his most valuable supporter in the Congress will be Senator Richard Brevard Russell of Georgia.

On the other hand, if Johnson orders a further escalation of the war, the most outspoken defender of that decision will be the same Richard Russell, who in fact is also a major backer of the Administration's present limited-war policy.

As more than one Democratic President has learned—and as Lyndon Johnson long has known—this ultraconservative Southerner is a highly knowledgeable, sophisticated politician who can be uniquely useful to Presidents when he chooses.

Of his conservatism there can be no doubt. To civil-rights advocates he is the ultimate legislative enemy, while states' rightists cherish him as their champion. With few exceptions he has opposed the Great Society just as he opposed the New Frontier. During the Cuban missile crisis he urged Kennedy to invade Cuba. He is a "big-bomber" man who has voted against the nuclear-test-ban treaty and foreign aid. Political cartoonists commonly picture him in a Confederate general's uniform or with a committee chairman's gavel in his raised hand—a symbol of domestic conservatism, legislative obstruction, committee rule, and the evils of the seniority system.

He has indeed been all those things. But he is in addition a highly complex personality, feared and respected at both the Pentagon and the CIA as a father figure. And back home he is a high prince of state politics, beyond criticism or meaningful challenge.

Brusque and remote of manner and ascetic in his tastes, he is known also for his kindly, gentle nature and for a monumental sense of honor. At sixty-eight, he has a worrisome cough and a near-photographic memory; he frets at times that his thirty-three years of service in Washington have permitted Georgia voters to forget him.

His Washington home is a small, impersonally furnished apartment. A bachelor who says his one major regret is that he never took a wife, he makes work his whole life and always has done so. He has no social life, no intimate friends, pays meticulous attention to detail, and doesn't like to delegate authority. He is a loner ("He who travels, travels fastest alone," his father once advised him) who keeps his office under his hat and his staff generally in the dark.

His hard work has borne rich reward, however. People come to him. His name would be included today—as twenty years ago—on any list of

"Russell of Georgia: The Old Guard at Its Shrewdest," *Harper's Magazine*, September 1966. Reprinted by permission of the author.

Washington's dozen most powerful men. President Johnson calls him regularly for advice. He is a frequent guest at intimate White House dinners. And he has attained the ultimate mark of prestige in a town where politics is approached as a sport by its fans. For he is one of those special personalities about whom there exists a "theory."

It concerns his past Presidential ambition, the extent of his power in the Senate, and his special relationship with Lyndon Johnson.

According to this theory Russell—in 1952—considered himself a national figure who stood an excellent chance of winning the Democratic Presidential nomination. When the party coldly rejected him as no more than a regional segregationalist, the shock produced two reactions. First, he gave up hope of national office to assume determined leadership of the Senate's Southern bloc. Second, he chose Johnson as a protégé to whom he could transfer his ambition. Now he sits in the Senate, seeing his power slowly fade and watching his protégé turn into a far different President from the one he had in mind.

This is a convenient theory. It may even be partly valid. But it fails to reckon with Russell's complex personality and underestimates the influence he still exercises in national affairs.

When Johnson was Democratic Majority Leader he used to divide his colleagues into the haves and the have-nots of power. There were the "whales," and there were the "minnows," and Russell was "the principal whale." Today Russell is no longer Moby Dick, but he is still a very big fish, using his power, among other things, to lead the fight against the Administration's latest civil-rights bill. He is also quietly guiding a tricky, wartime defense budget through an election-year Congress. And he is becoming increasingly outspoken about Vietnam.

As to the civil-rights bill, Russell's hope this year is to keep it bottled up in the Judiciary Committee. Failing that, he wants it to come to the floor for debate, complete—with its national fair-housing provision which he sees as a valuable shield. Since fair housing would have immediate impact outside the South, Russell anticipates that Northern and Eastern Senators who normally support civil-rights legislation will not be anxious for this one to come out of committee in an election year. If it does they will be in no hurry to end debate, for a vote for fair housing would anger many white constituents while a vote against it would alienate Negroes.

"If they're in good faith, I'll help them hold that in the bill, I certainly will," Russell says, with a gleam in his eye.

Russell senses another advantage in the fact that public pressure for new civil-rights legislation is not as strong as it was in 1964. Although he is not saying so, he seems pretty confident of blocking the passage of the Administration's bill this session. "There is increased feeling over the country that we've got a great many civil-rights laws already, some of them very drastic, and it's well enough to see how these work out," he said in an interview this summer.

Russell's role in fighting civil-rights legislation is an old, familiar one and is attracting less public attention than his views on Vietnam.

"It's the nearest thing to a total national frustration this country has ever encountered," he says. "You can't help anybody who won't help themselves. Without some kind of stability there we're wasting our time." The United States, he proclaims bluntly, should start winning the war—or get out.

These views seem paradoxical. If the war is worth winning, how can we consider withdrawal? Conversely, if we can afford to get out, is not greater escalation foolish? Russell's position is further confused by the fact that he has consistently defended the Administration's present policy. Once "our forces and our flag were committed," there was "no honorable alternative," in his opinion. He says Johnson inherited "a pretty well fixed policy" in Vietnam and has been "exceedingly cautious" in exercising it. "If he had been handed a clear slate, I'd say he'd made some errors. But he didn't get one."

And yet—"I wouldn't fight this kind of one-handed war," he adds. "The only thing to do is punish North Vietnam until they're willing to negotiate. I wouldn't hit the towns, but I'd hit every industry capable of producing any weapons or materials of war."

More than anything else, however, he wants out. Earlier this year he suggested a "survey" to determine if a majority of the South Vietnamese wish the United States to leave. If so, he said, the American presence should be withdrawn immediately. In a more recent private interview in his Senate office, he suggested two other alternatives:

In the event of civil war in South Vietnam, the United States should adopt the "enclave theory" of retired General James Gavin, quit the interior offensive, and pull all American troops back to selected, well-protected coastal sites. If civil war is averted, the United States should request the International Control Commission member nations—Canada, India, and Poland—to conduct and supervise popular elections immediately.

Russell never wanted the United States to become involved in Vietnam. In 1954 he protested an Eisenhower Administration proposal to send U.S. aircraft to aid the French at Dienbienphu. During the past two years he has urged repeatedly that we reevaluate our role, warning that the involvement will prove increasingly costly "in both blood and treasure." And he has belittled the strategic value of South Vietnam. "I don't buy this so-called domino theory," he says. "We don't have to have South Vietnam to hold back the hordes of communism."

Such talk has led to speculation that Russell might eventually break with the Administration, call for unilateral withdrawal, and thus join forces with Sentaors Fulbright and Morse. This forecast is wide of the mark. Russell has achieved a unique position from which he can back up the Administration's present policy, support a stepped-up war, or rise to the President's defense if he should sound the call of frustrated retirement from Vietnam.

WITH A PERMANENT LEASE

The foundation of Russell's power is awesome and unlikely to be matched by any future Senator. For new Senate rules adopted in 1963 prevent new members from attaining such a position of wide influence by specifying that no Senator may serve on more than two major standing committees. An added "grandfather clause," however, allowed those who already were serving on more than two to retain their seats. Russell serves on three—Armed Services, Appropriations, and Space. He is also a member of the Democratic Policy Committee, which reviews all new legislative proposals, and the Democratic Steering Committee, where a Southern bloc under his leadership has a strong voice in committee assignments. As chairman of both the Senate Armed Services Committee and the Defense Appropriations Subcommittee, he is the Capitol Hill boss man of the U.S. military establishment. Similarly, he is chairman of a special Armed Services-Appropriations Subcommittee which supervises the policy and budget of the CIA. He is the number-two Democrat on the main Appropriations Committee, where he is unofficial "president" and Arizona's aged Senator Carl Hayden is "chairman of the board." He leads the Southerners, a cartel of honey-voiced, iron-fisted committee and subcommittee chairmen who are still one of the principal power blocs of national politics.

He is Southern—country Southern—and he loves the old-time ways. His ancestors have lived in the Deep South since Colonial times; in the Civil War Sherman's troops burned his grandfather's cotton mill. His home is in Winder, one of those little red-clay Georgia farm towns which seem to hold a permanent lease on the slow passage of time.

The Russells are a political family. The Senator's father served in the state legislature, ran unsuccessfully both for Governor and U.S. Senator, and eventually became chief justice of the state supreme court. Richard Brevard's own political rise was phenomenal. Elected to the Georgia legislature at twenty-two, he was its Speaker within six years. Three years later he was elected Governor—at thirty-three, the youngest chief executive in the state's history. Three years afterward, he entered the Senate, succeeding Robert La Follette as its youngest member. Within two years he was floor-managing major New Deal legislation; within ten he was leader of the Southern bloc, the region's outstanding political figure, and its favorite Presidential candidate.

He is a segregationist, though he knows he is fighting a losing battle at a time of historic social unrest and change. If it were up to him, the Negro's relative position in American society today would be just what it was thirty years ago, and the United States would remain forever a completely segregated nation of blacks and whites.

Within this framework, he would, of course, support and work hard for equal Negro advancement—for better education and housing and health care, for improved economic opportunity and generally elevated living conditions. He does not hate the black man, nor does he wish him harm; just the opposite. But he does believe he has a special place in America, and that is with other black men. Furthermore, he fails to understand why the Negro does not desire the same thing.

His conservatism was correctly measured by Georgia Republicans who ran big ads during the 1964 Presidential campaign proclaiming, "Russell and Goldwater Vote Alike!" He quotes Washington, who admonished the young Republic in his Farewell Address to "resist with care the spirit of innovation." While he concedes that the modern age poses unprecedented challenge to the conservative philosophy, he insists that the Constitution remains the master mechanic's kit containing all the tools needed to tune up the federal government to run with the times. His is the classic, conservative fear that the historical trend in the U.S. is toward an overwhelmingly powerful central government.

ADAMANT OLD PRO

This was not always his view. When he came to Washington as a New Dealer, he was a Southern agrarian populist from the hard-times, rutroaded cotton country who backed Franklin Roosevelt all the way. The man who charged in 1965 that federal aid to education constituted an intolerable invasion of states' rights was the same who said in 1935, "I trust and believe that the day is not far distant when the federal government will recognize its responsibility . . . and will provide funds to assist in the maintenance of the public schools of this country."

The Southern Beauregard who always seems to shout "Charge!" in international affairs and "Whoa!" in domestic matters, the disillusioned New Dealer, the Old South segregationist, the Congressional lion secure in his bone-littered den, the heartbroken Presidential aspirant determined forever to show 'em, the baron of the legislative branch resisting the pull of the modern tide of the Presidency—he is all of these. But there is also a part of him which New Mexico's Clinton Anderson had in mind when he called Russell "the Senator's Senator." This is the Russell who, according to Washington's Henry Jackson, "has a genius for cutting through confusion to get to the facts and the truth"; who, says North Dakota's Milton Young, "always has come up with the good judgment when we have faced difficult problems"; who is characterized by Connecticut's Abraham Ribicoff as "an outstanding public servant and a great human being."

This is the adamant old segregationist who rushed home to Georgia the moment the 1964 civil-rights bill was signed into law to proclaim publicly, "It is now on the books and it becomes our duty as good citizens to learn to live with it." This is the Senator who was one of Lyndon Johnson's first choices for appointment to the Warren Commission—the wise, thoroughly fair, sympathetic old pro who lends valuable tactical advice to his legislative opponents; the master of the Senate's complicated rules; the one man who can always sense the Senate's mood; the virtuoso of legislative timing; the honest broker of inevitable compromise, whose expertise extends over a dozen different fields.

This Russell is the Senate's (and in some ways, the federal government's) chief boatswain, who has his own opinion about the captain, the crew, and the set course, but has a professional pride in smart seamanship, and is always the first man called when rough weather threatens.

A historic Russell exploit was his conduct of the MacArthur hearings during the Korean War. When President Truman relieved the General of his command in the spring of 1951, the United States was fighting its first frustrating war of containment in Asia. Weary of apparently endless costly stalemate, many Americans were of a mind to agree with the General when he publicly criticized his Commander in Chief's policy of limited war and insisted, "There is no substitute for victory." His dismissal caused a national uproar out of which Republicans were sure they could fashion a valuable issue for the coming Presidential election.

Urged on by other Democratic leaders, who saw a tactical advantage in beating Congressional Republicans to the draw, Russell wired Mac-Arthur immediately, inviting him to testify before the Senate Armed Services Committee. The General accepted.

Russell next fought off a Republican proposal that the General testify before a special joint committee and a subsequent attempt to have the Armed Services hearings televised. He announced that the hearings would be secret for security reasons, unless MacArthur personally requested otherwise, but promised "quick and full public reports" daily. It was a gamble, but a shrewd one based on his familiarity with the military mind, and it paid off. The General agreed to secret hearings, thus denying himself the golden opportunity of stating his case before what surely would have been a vast national TV audience.

The Senator accorded the General all the honors due a hero of the Republic, treated him with elaborate patience and courtesy, but kept firm personal control of the proceedings. He promised MacArthur a full, fair hearing, and he proceeded to give him one. The hearings began as the nation's biggest news story. By the time they ended, nearly two months later, the testimony filled volumes, cartoonists were picturing the two men with long white beards, and public interest had so dwindled that nobody seemed to notice that the committee never issued a final report and never made an official judgment on the merits of the dismissal.

OLDER BROTHER TO THE WHITE HOUSE

If Vietnam eventually causes the President to pick up the phone, it will not be the first time he has called on Russell for help. Their relationship began in the 1930s, when Johnson was a young Congressman representing a Texas district intensely interested in rural electrification. "Every year the House cut REA funds and every year he came to me to get the money restored in the Senate," Russell remembers. "He knew what he was talking about, and I thought to myself, 'That boy's a good Congressman.' We became and have remained good friends."

Johnson fought hard for Russell as Presidential nominee of the 1952 convention. Russell, in turn, taught Johnson his legislative techniques and, in 1953, backed him for election as Majority Leader, although he was still not halfway into his freshman term. Today the Senator, who believes "the President should be the seeker, always," never calls the President, but the President frequently calls the Senator. Russell's role has been described as that of "an older brother who calls them like he sees them."

Though their relationship has become a political legend, it has not been placid. Both are tough, intensely competitive men who don't like to get beaten, especially by the other. A mutual friend calls it a "hate-love relationship between two old horny-handed professionals."

One moment of stress occurred in 1964 when Russell, despite Southern indignation at passage of the civil-rights bill, carefully allowed that he would vote for Johnson "because I am a Democrat." But he arranged to be off inspecting West European defense installations while Johnson campaigned in the South. Yet, one week after the election, he was invited to a deer hunt at the LBJ Ranch. Georgia's young, ambitious Governor Carl

Sanders, who had gone down the line for Johnson in the South, got an invitation, too. It came second-hand, from Russell, who quietly leaked the story to reporters to show Georgians that he still had the pipeline to the White House.

Pure gold gushed from that pipeline last fall, when Russell, for once, seemed to be in political trouble. He had been hospitalized with bronchitis and emphysema, and rumors about his health persisted. In early September authoritative word came that Governor Sanders would oppose him in the Democratic primary. Shortly thereafter, Russell announced that he suddenly was "highly encouraged" that the $2.2 billion C5A jet transport contract would be awarded to the Georgia-Lockheed Company. A wild afternoon of trading in aircraft stocks on the New York market followed. The next day the Pentagon confirmed the report.

The award, ending one of the fiercest struggles in U.S. aircraft manufacturing history, assured the Georgia company of continued high employment into the foreseeable future. Russell, of course, won statewide praise. The night before the announcement he had, in fact, been a guest at an intimate White House dinner. Shortly afterward Sanders withdrew from the race, saying he had become convinced that Russell's health was "excellent." He had also, it is believed, seen polls indicating that Russell would skin him alive in a primary.

As a result, Russell faces no meaningful opposition for renomination this fall, although there is always the chance that some last-minute, off-beat challenge could force him to wage an expensive campaign. But he will be reelected this year and six years hence if he chooses to run again. For he is a Georgia political institution. The businessmen like him; so do the Republicans and the downstate woolhats. To most people, voting for him is a habit. Negro voters, of course, don't like him, but there are too few of them as yet to counteract his solid overall support, based on appreciation of the local gains that flow from his Senate power. For he has always seen to it that the state gets it brimful share of federal spending, especially defense funds. With fifteen major installations, Georgia is one of the top ten states in defense-contract awards.

Today, Russell is second in seniority only to Carl Hayden. Half of his fellow members have been there only eight years and thus are shavetails compared to a man who welcomed Robert Taft to Washington. When he came to town in 1933, Senators still wore morning coats. Today it is not unusual to spot an occasional sports jacket being worn on the floor. But Richard Russell has never been seen in a sports coat on the floor of the Senate, and never will be.

As the Senate is changing, so is his home state. In Georgia at present, one-fifth of the voters are Negro, half the population is urban, and more of the same is in prospect. More and more Negroes are lining up at the registration offices. From places like Villa Rica, Sugar Hill, Ludowici—and Winder—young folk are still on the move to Atlanta and other cities.

Russell will never move. Along with the old people who keep on living at the old home place despite repeated invitations from the children to move into town, he wouldn't feel comfortable there.

Fulbright: 'The Idea Is to Influence You into a Wiser Policy'

Following is a partial transcript of Secretary of State Dean Rusk's testimony before the Senate Foreign Relations Committee on March 12, 1968

SEN. J. W. FULBRIGHT (D.-ARK.): The Committee will come to order. Mr. Secretary, I have a particular aspect of this that interests me and I hope to make a point.

The first thing to me, and the most important, is this question of consultation with the Congress. I wish to make this as clear as I can what I mean by this.

I believe that we in the Senate, and by that I mean all of us, but particularly this Committee and through us, that the Senate should be informed fully about the policy which this Administration intends to follow in the immediate future and before public announcement of this policy is made. In other words, not inform us after the decision is made.

In other words, if you believe, and by you I mean the Administration, that we should send a hundred or two hundred thousand or fifty thousand men, we should be notified and have a reasonable time to discuss the wisdom of such a course.

I believe there is some value in the idea of collective judgment on a matter of this grave importance.

To be very frank about it, our experience during the past four years has not been satisfactory. We have been led gradually into a disastrous situation which I do not believe is in the interests of the country. I believe it is our duty to insist that we and the people generally through our discussions have the opportunity to register our approval or disapproval of your proposals. The Constitution contemplates that the Congress has the right to initiate or declare war. We have been negligent in our insistence upon this right, but it is still not too late to draw back before the full-scale, all-out war, possibly involving nuclear weapons, begins, and that we reassess our present situation.

THE WISEST COURSE

In a word, I do not believe anyone is infallible, and that the wisest course is for all of us to consult together and to discuss these matters before further and significant commitments are made.

So long as we profess to be a democracy under our Constitution, I do not understand why this is not acceptable to the Administration.

SECRETARY RUSK: Mr. Chairman, I said yesterday, and I think the distinguished Majority Leader said recently, that President Johnson has attempted to consult with the Congress more than any recent President

"Fulbright: 'The Idea Is to Influence You into a Wiser Policy,'" *Washington Post*, March 13, 1968. Reprinted by permission of the publisher.

on a great many of these matters. The President is consulting with the Chairmen of Committees, and the Secretary of Defense is meeting on Wednesday with the policy group of the House Armed Services Committee. The Secretary of Defense will be before this Committee, I understand, on Monday in connection with military assistance. I think there is a good deal of consultation going on here, yesterday, this morning. I would think that the views of members of the Committee have been set forth rather clearly.

SEN. FULBRIGHT: Mr. Secretary . . . I don't feel that I learned anything yesterday about what the plans of the Administration are in the immediate future. I fully understood that you declined to discuss that.

What I am talking about now is the exact, precise plans that you have with regard to this matter of escalation. There was a very full statement in the New York Times on Sunday indicating that within the Administration there are differences of view, and so on. This was somewhat encouraging. But when we approach the matter of what is the policy in this regard, I thought you declined to answer.

SECRETARY RUSK: Well, I told the Committee the conversations I had with the President on Sunday, and I have not discussed the matter with him since, that is the net of the matter.

FOR PRESIDENT TO MAKE

I think you, yourself, have pointed out last night in another place that these decisions are basically for the President to make. The Constitution is what it is. I am not in a position to dispose of the Constitution. Congress itself, with two dissenting votes, resolved that the United States is therefore prepared as the President determines, to take all necessary steps, including the use of armed force, to assist any member or protocol state of the Southeast Asia Collective Defense Treaty requesting assistance in defense of its freedom.

SEN. FULBRIGHT: Mr. Secretary, I am sorry you bring up that resolution. I have already spent a good deal of time on it. I think you used that resolution to prevent consultation, to prevent discussion, that was the effect of it. We passed it. We had all of one hour and forty minutes of listening to you, or primarily the Secretary of Defense, on the morning of August 5th, I think it was, and I certainly don't think that is consultation. This is a method of avoiding and preventing both consultation and discussion.

SECRETARY RUSK: Senator, that resolution was the same type resolution that was passed with regard to the Middle East, Formosa, the Cuban situation . . . There was time, if the Congress wanted to take more time. I think the idea of the leadership was that a prompt passage of the resolution would have the maximum deterrent effect upon Hanoi.

SEN. FULBRIGHT: That was your idea. The Administration insisted that that was its purpose and it was not to enlarge the war, and so on . . . We are in very serious difficulty. What I am proposing is that we not follow this old system of just accepting anything the Administration sends down without question, which we have literally done and did in August '64. We had entirely too much confidence, in my opinion, in the wisdom of this or any other Administration, and I am only proposing that the Congress, this Committee, and through us the Congress has a contribution to make on decisions of this importance.

ESSENCE OF OUR SYSTEM

I think that is the very essence of our system. If we don't do that, I would feel very derelict in my duty. After we have had a full discussion, we know what you plan, and if we have an opportunity to express ourselves, and you in spite of that take another decision, of course that is your responsibility. I don't suppose we have any power to prevent you doing it.

But the idea is that we might influence you into a wiser policy, and certainly it is evident that there is not much satisfaction with the present policy.

SECRETARY RUSK: Senator, I understand your view. I would add to the comment that when you get into detailed questions such as whether you are sending additional units of this or that or the other sort at any given time, President Eisenhower remarked to President Johnson the other day that if he were General Giap he would just love to know what we are and are not going to do for months ahead. This is not an easy system of government under which we handle the details of military operations facing an enemy in the field. We didn't do that during the Korean War. The Secretary of State didn't come down during the Korean War for public hearings talking about the military operations going on in the face of the enemy. Secretary Hull didn't come down during World War II and hold public hearings and give the enemy all the information that could be developed in public hearings. There is nothing that would be more valuable to us than if Hanoi or Peking or Moscow were to hold public hearings portraying everything they had in mind, what their plans are for the future.

SEN. FULBRIGHT: Mr. Secretary, I apologize, I don't seem to make clear to you at all what I have in mind. I haven't the slightest interest in the day-to-day tactics of the military, that is not what I am trying to raise. I am trying to raise the question of policy of enlarging this war, to go all-out on the war, so to speak, which I think it would be if you put 200,000 men, which is the current news that we get.

FAILED TO MAKE POINT

I think I failed to make my point, but this is from the Wall Street Journal, which is certainly a very responsible and excellent institution.

"Now stubbornness up to a point is a virtue, but stubbornness could also go beyond the realm of reasonableness. We believe the Administration is duty bound to recognize that no battle and no war is worth any price, no matter how ruinous, and that in the case of Vietnam it may be failing for the simple reason that the whole place and cause is changing from within."

On the next one he says:

"These considerations may be a little subtle for the ill-tempered mood the Foreign Relations Committee currently displays, but underlying the dispute is a point worth supporting. Scrupulous consultation not only serves the interests of the Congress but those of the nation and the Administration itself."

I think that expresses it.

I am not interested in the tactics of this war. I am interested in the policy. Are we, regardless of costs, now going to escalate the war without, apparently, that is what seems to be implied in the recommendation of Westmoreland that he be sent 200,000 more troops—can't we agree that we really ought to be told that maybe this Senate has some contribution to make?

SECRETARY RUSK: Senator, I can't get into speculation about numbers. I have seen some speculative stories that I think are off by a good deal . . . The President has only the men and the money that the Congress makes available. The Congress has the decision as to what men and what money to make available, the last chance to debate it and the last chance to vote on it. This is the nature of our Constitutional system.

A FEEL FOR THE ATTITUDES

These are matters that are primarily for the Secretary of Defense rather than for myself. I am not the best person to get into them. I certainly am not in a position to get into them publicly in advance of any decisions that might be made or required, or disclose here all of the factors that go into judgments on these matters and be examined very carefully.

The President is in touch with the leadership and every Committee Chairman of the appropriate Committees, and I have no doubt at all that he has a good feel for the attitudes of the Congress, including members of this Committee. After all, one can derive a good deal from the expressions that were made here yesterday about attitudes on these questions, regardless of the fact that there were not specific details in front of the Committee.

SEN. FULBRIGHT: I still don't think it is specific details, what I have in mind. But let me read you what you said on April 7, 1965.

"We do not now have a plan to ask for further resolutions on this subject unless there is some substantial development from the other side in the general scale of operations, unless the situation takes quite a different turn."

Now, it seems to me the implications from that in April were if it does take a different turn you would take some move, either a new resolution or take some kind of action that would give us an opportunity to express ourselves. Certainly you will admit, I think, that it has taken a different turn since April 7, 1965. Wouldn't—

SECRETARY RUSK: I would think, sir, although the scale of the effort has been increased, the basic underlying policy has remained the same. That policy, as enumerated by several Presidents in this post-war period, and as declared again by the Congress in August, 1964, is set forth in the Southeast Asia Resolution.

LONG RANGE POLICY

It dealt with the largest long-range policy of the United States towards Southeast Asia, and it stated—and this resolution was drafted, as you remember, in cooperation with the leadership; it was not the resolution in its exact text that was put forward by the Executive. It was changed, and it contained a provision that if the Congress wished to do so it could rescind this resolution by a concurrent vote which does not involve a veto of the President.

Now, I think the policy is a policy that was there before it was in the Southeast Asia Treaty. It has been a longstanding policy of this country in the post-war period under different Administrations, Republican and Democratic; under different Congresses, Republican and Democratic. It is a succinct statement of a national policy.

SEN. FULBRIGHT: Mr. Secretary, I seem unable to keep you on the main question.

Do I understand you saying in a very polite, roundabout way, that you have no intention to consult with this Committee and Congress, you are going to do as you please and we are going to take it or like it, and you think the Tonkin Resolution is full authority? I want to make your answer clear, and I don't intend to get diverted into these secondary issues.

As I have already stated, we listened to the Secretary of Defense and yourself one hour and forty minutes. That was all of the discussion, it really wasn't a discussion, we simply listened to your statement of a set of facts which I think the evidence has clearly proved to have been untrue, clearly proved to be untrue.

WHAT DO WE DO NOW?

Nobody, no reasonable man can say that there wasn't provocation, in my opinion, on the action of those ships. If you will take the trouble to read the documents of your own Defense Department, it is certainly a very equivocal statement at the least that there wasn't what any normal man would call provocation.

But I don't want to argue about that. . . . What are we going to do now?

Are you saying in a very polite way, I guess, that you are not going to take this Senate, this Committee, into your confidence before you announce whatever the decision is in the future? . . . Do you think you will be able or willing, the Administration, to let us know prior to a decision what you intend to do? Because I think it is very important, and it is the equivalent, I think, of in the constitutional sense of asking us to take the initiative in the declaration of a war, even though it doesn't follow that form. Are we or are we not going to be told?

SECRETARY RUSK: Senator, I indicated to you that the President has not reached his conclusions.

SEN. FULBRIGHT: I know.

SECRETARY RUSK: And there is therefore no knowledge, at least as far as I know at the present time as to what action may be required by the Congress, and certainly there would be consultations with the appropriate Committees, depending upon what that action is.

SEN. FULBRIGHT: Which I conclude to mean that you have no intention of consulting with us on the specifics prior to a decision.

In other words, after you have considered the recommendation of Westmoreland and others and made up your mind what you are going to do, then you will tell us, is that a true statement?

SECRETARY RUSK: I think that you know that senior members of this Committee have been consulted on the general situation in Southeast Asia. None of these things are new.

SEN. FULBRIGHT: We have been consulted, but as somebody, I think Senator Carlson made very clear . . . the consultation and information we get from the Executive is not consistent with what we get from the leading members of the press, and frankly, we tend to feel the press is better informed than the Executive.

INTENTION NOT TO INFORM?

But that really isn't what I am asking. You will not say that your present intention is not to inform this Committee or the Congress as to what your plans are. If that is true then we have no business in interesting ourselves in the matter.

SECRETARY RUSK: I have not said that to you, sir.

SEN. FULBRIGHT: That is the way I understand it.

SECRETARY RUSK: I simply haven't gone further than what I have said, which is not a negative. It is simply—

SEN. FULBRIGHT: It is implicit in it. You say he hasn't yet made up his mind. As if I understand it when he has made up his mind and makes decisions then you will tell us. I don't know how else to interpret it. Isn't that what you mean?

SECRETARY RUSK: I think, sir . . . the views of the Members of this Committee are pretty well apparent, not only on the floor of the Senate, but in our hearing yesterday, in appearances made by members of the Committee in other places, on television and otherwise. I don't think there is much mystery about the views of the Members of this Committee on such issues.

SEN. FULBRIGHT: Then your position is you already know what the Committee thinks, therefore, there is no need for consultation?

SECRETARY RUSK: We know a good deal, don't we?

SEN. FULBRIGHT: Well, I don't quite agree and particularly with the Senate. They haven't been confronted with the precise questions to decide upon . . . I agree with you this system is hard to work with. It is a very complex system compared to the orthodox totalitarian system. Nevertheless, I think many of us feel that it has certain values and in spite of its difficulty those values should be retained and the essence of that is the participation of the Congress in the making of decisions which affect the very existence of the country, particularly war, I mean the lives of our citizens and our fortunes.

IF IT WAS JUST THE WAR

My goodness, Mr. Secretary, I need not tell you it is not only the war in Vietnam that bothers us, but it is this international monetary system, domestic monetary system, domestic violence and unrest, all of these, I believe, are affected by Vietnam, and that is why I am so insistent.

If it was just the war in Vietnam and everything else was going along pretty well . . . I don't think I or others would be quite as disturbed as we are.

Now, I think we arrived at that point where a real discussion is justified. I think the whole feeling about this present situation is a turning point, a crucial turning point. We are either going down the road of an all-out war or we are going to pull back and seek a political decision to it. I believe— that is what I mean by policy.

It isn't so much, I am not, and I don't think the Committee wants, to advise you to send 50,000 instead of 50 or 206,000 instead of 200. That is not the point at all. It is the decision of, are we really going down that road to seek a military victory regardless of cost? . . . I think we ought to be allowed to discuss it.

SEN. FRANK LAUSCHE (D.-OHIO): If it is the Senator's opinion that we should send no more troops to Vietnam, why doesn't he offer a resolution declaring it to be the sense of the Senate that no more troops be sent to that land?

SEN. FULBRIGHT: I think you have got the cart before the horse. If they tell us what they have in mind then we can in whatever wisdom we have, take a position for or against it.

SEN. LAUSCHE: Well, based upon what the Senator has said, I don't think that it would make any difference what the Administration would say, his position would remain adamant. I believe it is wrong for us to wait for the Administration to make a proposal solely for the purpose of beating it down.

SEN. MIKE MANSFIELD (D.-MONT.): . . . no President, no President has ever met with more Senators or more groups than President Johnson, and I think that when he presented the Tonkin resolution to us that he was trying to be cooperative and trying to get the Executive and the Legislative to work together. But I would hope that . . . it would be possible, and I would assume it would be, for more consultation between the Executive and the Members of the Senate.

WE'D LIKE TO BE HEARD

We might be able to make proposals which would have some degree of validity. We would like to be heard, because we are representatives of sovereign states, and we do represent, at least we think, the will of our own people as well as our own conscience.

SEN. GEORGE AIKEN (R.-VT.): It would be more of a point if some of those who believe that the President is right and believe in his policy and his decisions in regard to the Vietnamese War, should introduce a resolution so expressing the sense of the Senate that we have full confidence in the decision of the President and believe that he alone should make the decisions relative to the carrying on of our operations in Southeast Asia.

Now, I wouldn't vote for such a resolution, but I think that would be much fairer than it would to introduce a resolution which would later be interpreted as cutting and running on the part of the Congress, because Congress has given to the President everything he has asked for for carrying on the war. He even got the Tonkin Resolution although it was misunderstood at the time. We have given him a renewal of the draft law. We have given him every single dollar he has asked for for carrying on the war over there . . .

SEN. ALBERT GORE (D.-TENN.): I respectfully suggest that a resolution approving the Vietnam policy or a resolution disapproving the Vietnam policy would be fruitless, I doubt if either would pass the Senate.

THE IMPORTANT THING

The important thing is to avoid a catastrophe for the country. A stalemate between the President and the Senate would be no more satisfactory than a military stalemate in Vietnam. What is needed here is the teamwork between the President and the elected representatives of the people to the end of achieving a wise policy. Unfortunately, we haven't had in the past the teamwork which our Constitutional Forefathers envisioned. I am not sure that the Senate could have saved us from this mistake. It has been a horrible mistake, it has been a disastrous policy leading this country already to tragedy, and with further escalation under consideration, a policy which threatens to lead us to catastrophe.

SEN. FULBRIGHT: Well, I think the Senator has expressed very well what I was trying to get at . . .

SEN. LAUSCHE: I concur fully with the words spoken by Senator Gore about the need of teamwork.

Now, my views are that instead of achieving teamwork these meetings are creating a positive division. I suggested in our last meeting that the whole Committee ought to meet with the President, with the view of discussing what course ought to be followed . . . How wonderful it would be for our country and our military leaders and for the morale of our people if Hanoi conducted meetings of this type, if Moscow did likewise and Peking also followed.

Finally, I want to say that the Congress can stop the President. It can refuse to appropriate the moneys which he asks for increased personnel.

SEN. STUART SYMINGTON (D.-MO.): Nearly every month in the (Senate) Preparedness Subcommittee we put out critical reports of our activities. We are short of helicopters. We have too many ships that haven't been unloaded. We haven't called up the Reserves. We haven't given the proper training to draftees. Nobody that I know of attacks the (Senate) Armed Services Committee or the Preparedness Subcommittee as doing something that is against the national interest. I presume that they are doing what perhaps we also, some of us here are doing, trying to find out if there is some way we can stop the killing in North Vietnam and negotiate ourselves out of this unfortunate war . . . I think these hearings do exactly what the military hearings do, and I am for both. I think it is important that the American people fully understand the problems.

SECRETARY RUSK: It is not easy to discuss all of these matters in public sessions and talk about the attitude of other governments and the details of possible negotiating positions and problems arising on the field of battle.

I AM AVAILABLE

But, it seems to me that we can make an effort . . . to search for those elements on which there are agreement, because I think there are a good many . . . and then . . . to find out which the questions are and on which there seems to be some serious divergences.

I am available to the Committee to make that effort and I will do so in the greatest good spirit and candor . . . I would hope that we could proceed and finish up this public session and try to make arrangements for some private meetings from time-to-time in which we could go over such questions as a negotiated solution.

SEN. FRANK CHURCH (D.-IDAHO): We are involved in a war, a very precarious war, in Asia, that could easily grow to the point of a general engagement on the Asian mainland, that could involve China . . . The stakes are so high, Mr. Secretary, the stakes are so very high, that it seems to me that the general question of American policy, the general objective of the necessity to keep this war confined within manageable limits, these are matters of such mortal importance to the American people that the decisions concerning them can't be made behind closed doors.

WORLD LISTENING

SECRETARY RUSK: I think we ought to really also keep in mind that the debate is being listened to all over the world. Of course, we have the great constitutional prerogatives of complete free speech and discussion. That we can never surrender . . .

SEN. CLIFFORD CASE (R.-N.J.): I think that there is no such thing as a right of a country to exist apart from its own willingness and ability to preserve its own existence . . . The primary obligation, the existence of a nation is its ability to exist by itself. This is not a radical statement in history. It is the very basis of relations between countries, and I think it is error on our part to think that there is anything in the status quo at any particular time that we are obliged to enforce, and now this is not the same as saying that we have an interest in the maintenance of a balance which exists. But to say that there is a right of this sort seems to me to be that kind of oversimplification of a problem which leads us into great error and in part is responsible for the very difficulties we face today.

SECRETARY RUSK: Well, Senator, I would call attention to the fact that the right of all nations, large and small, to live as independent nations, free from aggression is fundamental to the United Nations Charter . . . and the fact it was the destruction of small states by overriding powers from without which led directly to the catastrophe of World War II. So I must say I am very much disturbed about the implications of what you say.

SEN. CASE: I want to make a distinction between the question of willingness and ability . . . I think we ought to at least leave open the question whether a state is not viable . . . A fundamental basis of the state's right to exist is its will to exist as a state, and that this cannot be imposed from the outside.

SECRETARY RUSK: I profoundly disagree with what I take to be the implications of what you said . . .

SEN. FULBRIGHT: I am not sure that I understand you, but certainly I would welcome executive sessions if you wished to come and tell us in executive session what you are planning . . . I would just add that I think the consequences of not discussing this kind of a decision or this particular decision with the Congress may only add to the frustration and unease that afflicts the country today. I think it is very profound and very dangerous.

SEN. BOURKE HICKENLOOPER (R.-IOWA): Secretary Rusk . . . Have you ever refused to come before the Foreign Relations Committee in executive session to talk freely, with the idea that the sensitive parts of your testimony could be deleted and the rest of it be immediately released to the public?

SECRETARY RUSK: That was a suggestion that I made to the Committee in connection with the discussions, that we do that as we have done on other occasions . . .

SEN. GORE: Mr. Secretary, I hope I correctly detect a constructive turn of the hearings. You have suggested and the Chairman has responded with respect to closer consultation in executive session. I think this is an accomplishment.

I wish to explore with you the possibility of a settlement based upon a neutral status, a nonaligned status of not only Vietnam, but of the Indo-China Peninsula. That includes, as you know, Cambodia, Laos, North and South Vietnam.

I must say in all candor that I have not thought that we were in essence offering to negotiate without conditions . . . Inherent in our offer is the acceptance of a division of the country of Vietnam, a severing of the country into two. Inherent in our offer of negotiation is acceptance of a constitution prepared under our tutelage.

As long as we insist upon having in South Vietnam something made in our own image, then the war is going to last a very long time.

But this is but background to inquiry of you, if in fact you really mean the point, and if you really mean this thing that you said yesterday, that the United States would be willing to withdraw her 500,000-plus troops if North Vietnam would withdraw her 70-some thousand, coupled with the cessation of hostilities, and whether you really mean . . . that the countries of Southeast Asia can be nonaligned if they so choose.

SECRETARY RUSK: I realize that there are some problems about a public session, but I think that there is enough water under the dam for me to be able to inform the Committee that we have tried to negotiate with Hanoi a common set of points that would be a basis for negotiation . . . as an alternative approach to the question of an agenda and what subjects would be required.

On the matter of neutralization we will have to forget North Vietnam, because North Vietnam has made it very clear that they are not interested in being a neutral, they are a member of what they call the Socialist Camp.

Now, if South Vietnam wants to be nonaligned, if it has assurance that it has that privilege, if it is going to be safe, if it is going to—if its non-alignment is going to be respected by the rest of the world, that will cause us no problems.

PROTECT OTHERS?

SENATOR CHURCH: Despite this massive presence of American troops in South Vietnam you testified yesterday that the North Vietnamese are spreading into Laos, even to Cambodia, into quite possibly into Thailand. . . . If this infiltration continues there does it mean that American troops will be called upon to protect these other countries as we have been called upon to protect South Vietnam.

SECRETARY RUSK: That question has not come up in that form, Senator. It is our hope that in Thailand, for example, and in Cambodia, it will be possible for their own local forces to nip this activity in the bud.

SENATOR CHURCH: Well, I think we all hope that is the case. But on the basis of the testimony so far there is reason for concern that it won't be the case. Another difficulty is that time and time again we have heard from official spokesmen of the Administration one interpretation of the war and we get quite a different interpretation from so many on the scene.

A NEWS PROBLEM

SECRETARY RUSK: There is a little problem here about the nature of the news. Let me just illustrate it in this way: If a reporter comes across an incident in which an American soldier beats up on a Vietnamese in a bar some night and he has a chance to report on any one of 2000 acts of kindness and helpfulness and friendship between American soldiers and local South Vietnamese, which story is likely to be accepted as news? There is the problem that it is controversy, it is violence, it is that kind of thing that is news, and these other things that go on all the time don't get much attention.

I am not blaming the press of this day or the press in Saigon in this respect. I am saying it is in the nature of news that it should come this way.

SENATOR CHURCH: I think that the basic question is not the purity of our motive or the desirability of an objective that we have sought in Vietnam. But it is a sense or proportion.

Now, out in Asia there are vast populations that are waiting to engulf us. We maintain 132 major military bases in foreign countries. . . . We have formal commitments to the defense of 42 nations. We have already spent so lavishly abroad that by the end of this year we will have spent an incredible $100 billion, nearly so in Vietnam alone, and we have seen a half of the gold drained out of our Treasury.

OF CHIEF CONCERN

My chief concern is . . . that we try to find a rational balance between commitment and capacity, and I am fearful that in Asia the policy of sending more and more Americans to fight more and more Asians on the widening Asian front is feeding the crocodile with American lives, and I think these questions are so basic that the time for an agonizing reappraisal of American policy is at hand. Perhaps out of the agony in Vietnam we can learn some lessons and apply them against the future, and that, I hope, will be a part of the contribution that this Committee can make.

SEN. KARL MUNDT (R.-S.D.): This has been a war in which we have an unusual and unprecedented amount of dissent in this country.

I think one reason is because we are waging two wars at the same time in Vietnam, an economic war and a political war. (Second) even after five years the Administration is unwilling to place a priority on whether or not we should concentrate on getting it over with successfully, or whether we should put it on the same level as the economic problems at home. Third, I think that it is unusual because it is an undeclared war. (Fourth) it is the first time I can ever think of where the Administration at high levels has said in so many words that they encouraged discussion and dissent. Perhaps this has resulted in a little bit more dissent than was anticipated.

SUPPLIES TO THE U.S.S.R.
Fifth, it is the first war in American history in which we have encouraged our American fabricators and exporters and manufacturers to sell and ship supplies to the U.S.S.R. at the time that all of the sophisticated weapons, all of the petroleum being used by Hanoi, comes to it from Russia.

The sixth one is because we have failed somehow or other to bring into this picture on our side sentiment wise, economic wise, diplomacy wise, the great important free countries of the world.

Is it possible, therefore, if we pull out of Vietnam that we set in motion another chain of miscalculations by would-be aggressors and tyrants that having failed in our effort to resist Communist aggression there we would not again attempt to stop it some place else so that we might encourage, therefore our Nation and before the world, other area of the world?

SECRETARY RUSK: Senator, this is one of the most fundamental questions before our Nation and before the world. I don't want to appear dramatic, but let's go back to that conversation in June 1961 between President Kennedy and Chairman Khrushchev. In effect Chairman Khrushchev said to this young President of ours, "Mr. President, take your troops out of Berlin or there will be war."

THE REPLY IN KIND
It was necessary for this young President to say, "Then, Mr. Chairman, there will be war. It is going to be a very cold winter." And with that remark the two shook hands and took their departure.

Now, suppose Chairman Khrushchev had thought or had said, "Don't kid me, Mr. President, because I know that your people will collapse or draw back when I put on the pressure." That is a very easy way to get into war. This is why in shorthand I have tried to emphasize the overwhelming importance of the fidelity of the United States, and the necessity for people to understand that at the end of the day we will meet our commitments.

SENATOR MUNDT: We had some discussion yesterday that you got beat up a little bit by one or two of my colleagues for saying something about containing Red China, and by containing Red China I suppose you mean, at least that is what I interpret that to mean, that you are trying to maintain some kind of organization for peace which will not permit or encourage the Red Chinese when they get a delivery system early in 1970 for the bombs which they already have stockpiled, it will not really make, it seems to me it is a good bet, for them to use the bombs in a war of aggression, that is what I think about containing the Chinese. If we can't help contain them who can, Mr. Secretary? What other countries can contain them? Or do we pull out the plug and let the water pour in?

SECRETARY RUSK: I think this is something that the free nations of Asia are very much concerned about. Now, we can hope that when the Chinese fully understand, as they develop their own weapons, what these weapons are and what they can do, that the weapons themselves will carry with them some prudence.

SEN. MUNDT: I would like to recommend once more that this situation of divisive necessity in this country has reached a serious spot. You can see it manifested in this Committee and in the House, among the great newspapers of this country, and if this is important to our peace, and important to our survival, and important to our security, somebody ought to show some leadership in trying to convey the facts in a convincing manner to a public which is bewildered and confused, and I gave you six reasons why I thought they were confused. How can it be done? It could be done by a white paper setting out, as governments have done before, not only for our own people but for the countries of the free world, who should come to recognize that they ought to give some diplomatic support to our efforts to negotiate, that they ought to discontinue trading with the enemy.

If you don't want to do that, it can be done through a presidential message to a joint session of Congress in a dignified formal way where he can present the evidence. He doesn't have to ask for a new resolution, he doesn't have to ask for more manpower. He doesn't have to vacate any of his cherished administrative prerogatives, but he can at least take the people into his confidence, with these major reasons while discussing the issues with the Congress.

CAREFULLY NOTED

SECRETARY RUSK: Thank you, Senator, I have taken careful notes of what you said.

SEN. SYMINGTON: Last October, I proposed this Government announce as of a certain date the cessation of all offensive military action in South Vietnam, as well as over North Vietnam, and also announce that there would be no reinforcements into the theater.

The Government would also announce that these policies were being undertaken in earnest hope that their adoption would result in prompt and meaningful negotiations in the interest of a just peace.

At the same time the United States should also announce that . . . if the North Vietnamese and Vietcong nevertheless continued hostilities, then the United States would feel free to pursue this war in any manner of its own choosing.

Concurrently with the above proposed announcement of United States policy, I suggested that the Government of South Vietnam should announce its willingness to negotiate with anybody and offer amnesty to members of the Vietcong.

I made that statement in the floor talk, and not a person in the Administration ever brought this suggestion up with me, although I did bring it up with some members of the Administration. But I would like to ask you this morning, what do you think of the suggestion?

SECRETARY RUSK: Well, Senator, although it might not have been discussed with you in detail, it was examined in detail. We continue to examine all possibilities and all variations and I would be be glad to go into certain aspects of this in private session. But let me say some elements in your program have already been tried in one way or another.

SEN. CLARK: I have reluctantly come to the conclusion from your testimony and particularly your answers to Senator Mundt that it is more likely than not . . . that if a decision will shortly be made to send substantial additional combat troops to Vietnam, we on this Committee are more apt than not to read about it in the newspapers. I say again I hope I am wrong, but I think what might be called the eyeball philosophy seems to have a considerable appeal to the Administration.

I would like to shift now and read to you, Mr. Secretary, a brief summary of my own conclusions.

"The war in Vietnam is at a stalemate which neither side can convert into a military victory without leaving the country—and perhaps the world—in ruins.

A DEVOURING CANCER

"Vietnam is a cancer which is devouring our youth, our morals, our national wealth, and the energies of our leadership. The casualty list from this war only begins on the battlefield. As victims we must also count the programs of the Great Society, the balance of payments, a sound budget, a stable dollar, the world's good will, detente with the Soviet Union, and hopes for a durable world peace. The toll of this war can never be measured in terms of lives lost and dollars spent—they are only the tip of a vast iceberg whose bulk can never be accurately measured.

"We are not likely to end the war by a military victory. This has been amply demonstrated by the recent VC offensive. This is primarily a political war, a war which cannot be won by bullets and bombs short of annihilation of both the enemy and the people for whom we fight.

"Nor can we get out by unilateral withdrawal and I stress that because my position in that, as some of my colleagues, has been so grossly misrepresented in the press and elsewhere, I have never been for scuttle and run.

"Nor is the only alternative to do more of what we are doing on both the political and the military side."

Barenblatt v. United States: A Tactical Retreat?

It has long been recognized that the power of Congress to conduct investigations is implicit in the legislative process and that this power is so broad as to encompass inquiries concerning the administration of existing laws as well as proposed or possible needed statutes. Still, Congress is not a court or law enforcement agency; every inquiry must be related to its legitimate legislative function. Does this legitimate function include the right to expose past activities of persons solely for the sake of exposure? In Watkins v. United States *the Court said No. In this case, a labor union official appearing before the House Un-American Activities Committee refused to answer Committee questions about the associations and activities of others with whom he had associated but who had "long since removed themselves from the Communist movement." The Court sustained Watkins' right of refusal to make such exposures.*

This and other decisions like it greatly antagonized many members of Congress and some highly vocal constituents. In 1957–58, the Congress mounted a determined effort to curb the Court. This threat appears to have caused the Court to take a somewhat more restrained position on investigations of alleged subversive activities.

Lloyd Barenblatt was convicted for contempt of Congress for refusing to tell a subcommittee of HUAC whether or not he had been a member of the Communist Party from 1947 to 1950, while a graduate student at the Universtiy of Michigan, or anything about his current associations with the Party. He was sentenced to six months in prison and fined $250. A court of appeals affirmed the decision. After remanding the case once, the Supreme Court granted certiorari a second time.

Mr. Justice Harlan delivered the opinion of the Court.

Once more the Court is required to resolve the conflicting constitutional claims of congressional power and of an individual's right to resist its exercise. The congressional power in question concerns the internal process of Congress in moving within its legislative domain; it involves the utilization of its committees to secure "testimony needed to enable it efficiently to exercise a legislative function belonging to it under the Constitution. . . ." The power of inquiry has been employed by Congress throughout our history, over the whole range of the national interests concerning which Congress might legislate or decide upon due investigation not to legislate; it has similarly been utilized in determining what to appropriate from the national purse, or whether to appropriate. The scope of the power of inquiry, in short, is as penetrating and far-reaching as the potential power to enact and appropriate under the Constitution.

Broad as it is, the power is not, however, without limitations. Since Congress may only investigate into those areas in which it may potentially legislate or appropriate, it cannot inquire into matters which are within

Barenblatt v. United States, 360 U.S. 109; 79 Sup. Ct. 1081; 3 L. Ed. 2d 115 (1959).

the exclusive province of one or the other branch of the Government. Lacking the judicial power given to the Judiciary, it cannot inquire into matters that are exclusively the concern of the Judiciary. Neither can it supplant the Executive in what exclusively belongs to the Executive. And the Congress, in common with all branches of the Government, must exercise its powers subject to the limitations placed by the Constitution on governmental action, more particularly in the context of this case the relevant limitations of the Bill of Rights. . . .

Our function, at this point, is purely one of constitutional adjudication in the particular case and upon the particular record before us, not to pass judgment upon the general wisdom or efficacy of the activities of this Committee in a vexing and complicated field.

The precise constitutional issue confronting us is whether the Subcommittee's inquiry into petitioner's past or present membership in the Communist Party transgressed the provisions of the First Amendment, which of course reach and limit congressional investigations. . . .

The Court's past cases establish sure guides to decision. Undeniably, the First Amendment in some circumstances protects an individual from being compelled to disclose his associational relationships. However, the protections of the First Amendment, unlike a proper claim of the privilege against self-incrimination under the Fifth Amendment, do not afford a witness the right to resist inquiry in all circumstances. Where First Amendment rights are asserted to bar governmental interrogation resolution of the issue always involves a balancing by the courts of the competing private and public interests at stake in the particular circumstances shown. These principles were recognized in the Watkins case, where, in speaking of the First Amendment in relation to congressional inquiries, we said . . . : "It is manifest that despite the adverse effects which follow upon compelled disclosure of private matters, not all such inquiries are barred. . . . The critical element is the existence of, and the weight to be ascribed to, the interest of the Congress in demanding disclosures from an unwilling witness. . . ."

The first question is whether this investigation was related to a valid legislative purpose, for Congress may not constitutionally require an individual to disclose his political relationships or other private affairs except in relation to such a purpose. . . .

That Congress has wide power to legislate in the field of Communist activity in this Country, and to conduct appropriate investigations in aid thereof, is hardly debatable. The existence of such power has never been questioned by this Court, and it is sufficient to say, without particularization, that Congress has enacted or considered in this field a wide range of legislative measures, not a few of which have stemmed from recommendations of the very Committee whose actions have been drawn in question here. In the last analysis this power rests on the right of self-preservation, "the ultimate value of any society. . . ." Justification for its exercise in turn rests on the long and widely accepted view that the tenets of the Communist Party include the ultimate overthrow of the Government of the United States by force and violence, a view which has been given formal expression by the Congress.

On these premises, this Court in its constitutional adjudications has consistently refused to view the Communist Party as an ordinary political party, and has upheld federal legislation aimed at the Communist problem which in a different context would certainly have raised constitutional issues of the gravest character. . . . To suggest that because the Communist Party may also sponsor peaceable political reforms the constitutional issues before us should now be judged as if that Party were just an ordinary political party from the standpoint of national security, is to ask this Court to blind itself to world affairs which have determined the whole course of our national policy since the close of World War II. . . .

We think that investigatory power in this domain is not to be denied Congress solely because the field of education is involved. . . . Indeed we do not understand petitioner here to suggest that Congress in no circumstances may inquire into Communist activity in the field of education. Rather, his position is in effect that this particular investgation was aimed not at the revolutionary aspects but at the theoretical classroom discussion of communism.

In our opinion this position rests on a too constricted view of the nature of the investigatory process, and is not supported by a fair assessment of the record before us. An investigation of advocacy of or preparation for overthrow certainly embraces the right to identify a witness as a member of the Communist Party . . . and to inquire into the various manifestations of the Party's tenets. The strict requirements of a prosecution under the Smith Act . . . are not the measure of the permissible scope of a congressional investigation into "overthrow," for of necessity the investigatory process must proceed step by step. Nor can it fairly be concluded that this investigation was directed at controlling what is being taught at our universities rather than at overthrow. The statement of the Subcommittee Chairman at the opening of the investigation evinces no such intention, and so far as this record reveals nothing thereafter transpired which would justify our holding that the thrust of the investigation later changed. The record discloses considerable testimony concerning the foreign domination and revolutionary purposes and efforts of the Communist Party. That there was also testimony on the abstract philosophical level does not detract from the dominant theme of this investigation—Communist infiltration furthering the alleged ultimate purpose of overthrow. And certainly the conclusion would not be justified that the questioning of petitioner would have exceeded permissible bounds had he not shut off the Subcommittee at the threshold.

Nor can we accept the further contention that this investigation should not be deemed to have been in furtherance of a legislative purpose because the true objective of the Committee and of the Congress was purely "exposure." So long as Congress acts in pursuance of its constitutional power, the judiciary lacks authority to intervene on the basis of the motives which spurred the exercise of that power. . . . [I]n stating in the Watkins case . . . that "there is no congressional power to expose for the sake of exposure," we at the same time declined to inquire into the "motives of committee members," and recognized that their "motives alone would not vitiate an investigation which had been instituted by a House of Congress if that assembly's legislative purpose is being served." Having scrutinized this record we cannot say that the unanimous panel of the Court of Appeals which first considered this case was wrong in concluding that "the primary purposes of the inquiry were in aid of legislative processes. . . ." Certainly this is not a case like *Kilbourn* v. *Thompson* . . . where "the House of Representatives not only exceeded the limit of its own authority, but assumed a power which could only be properly exercised by another branch of the government, because it was in its nature clearly judicial. . . ." The constitutional legislative power of Congress in this instance is beyond question.

Finally, the record is barren of other factors which in themselves might sometimes lead to the conclusion that the individual interests at stake were not subordinate to those of the state. There is no indication in this record that the Subcommittee was attempting to pillory witnesses. Nor did petitioner's appearance as a witness follow from indiscriminate dragnet procedures, lacking in probable cause for belief that he possessed information which might be helpful to the Subcommittee. And the relevancy of the questions put to him by the Subcommittee is not open to doubt.

We conclude that the balance between the individual and the governmental interests here at stake must be struck in favor of the latter, and that therefore the provisions of the First Amendment have not been offended.

We hold that petitioner's conviction for contempt of Congress discloses no infirmity, and that the judgment of the Court of Appeals must be

Affirmed.

Mr. Justice Black, with whom The Chief Justice, and Mr. Justice Douglas concur, dissenting.

The First Amendment says in no equivocal language that Congress shall pass no law abridging freedom of speech, press, assembly or petition. The activities of this Committee, authorized by Congress, do precisely that, through exposure, obloquy and public scorn. . . . The Court does not really deny this fact but relies on a combination of three reasons for permitting the infringement: (A) The notion that despite the First Amendment's command Congress can abridge speech and association if this Court decides that the governmental interest in abridging speech is greater than an individual's interest in exercising that freedom, (B) The Government's right to "preserve itself," (C) The fact that the Committee is only after Communists or suspected Communists in this investigation.

(A) I do not agree that laws directly abridging First Amendment freedoms can be justified by a congressional or judicial balancing process. There are, of course, cases suggesting that a law which primarily regulates conduct but which might also indirectly affect speech can be upheld if the effect on speech is minor in relation to the need for control of the conduct. . . .

To apply the Court's balancing test under such circumstances is to read the First Amendment to say "Congress shall pass no law abridging freedom of speech, press, assembly and petition, unless Congress and the Supreme

Court reach the joint conclusion that on balance the interests of the Government in stifling these freedoms is greater than the interest of the people in having them exercised." This is closely akin to the notion that neither the First Amendment nor any other provision of the Bill of Rights should be enforced unless the Court believes it is reasonable to do so. Not only does this violate the genius of our written Constitution, but it runs expressly counter to the injunction to Court and Congress made by Madison when he introduced the Bill of Rights. "If they [the first ten amendments] are incorporated into the Constitution, independent tribunals of justice will consider themselves in a peculiar manner the guardians of those rights; they will be an impenetrable bulwark against every assumption of power in the Legislative or Executive; they will be naturally led to resist every encroachment upon rights expressly stipulated for in the Constitution by the declaration of rights." Unless we return to this view of our judicial function, unless we once again accept the notion that the Bill of Rights means what it says and that this Court must enforce that meaning, I am of the opinion that our great charter of liberty will be more honored in the breach than in the observance.

But even assuming what I cannot assume, that some balancing is proper in this case, I feel that the Court after stating the test ignores it completely. At most it balances the right of the Government to preserve itself, against Barenblatt's right to refrain from revealing Communist affiliations. Such a balance, however, mistakes the factors to be weighed. In the first place, it completely leaves out the real interest in Barenblatt's silence, the interest of the people as a whole in being able to join organizations, advocate causes and make political "mistakes" without later being subjected to governmental penalties for having dared to think for themselves. It is this right, the right to err politically, which keeps us strong as a Nation. For no number of laws against communism can have as much effect as the personal conviction which comes from having heard its arguments and rejected them, or from having once accepted its tenets and later recognized their worthlessness. Instead, the obloquy which results from investigations such as this not only stifles "mistakes" but prevents all but the most courageous from hazarding any views which might at some later time become disfavored. This result, whose importance cannot be overestimated, is doubly crucial when it affects the universities, on which we must largely rely for the experimentation and development of new ideas essential to our country's welfare. It is these interests of society, rather than Barenblatt's own right to silence, which I think the Court should put on the balance against the demands of the Government, if any balancing process is to be tolerated. Instead they are not mentioned, while on the other side the demands of the Government are vastly overstated and called "self preservation." . . . Such a result reduces "balancing" to a mere play on words and is completely inconsistent with the rules this Court has previously given for applying a "balancing test," where it is proper: "[T]he courts should be astute to examine the effect of the challenged legislation. Mere legislative preferences or beliefs . . . may well support regulation directed at other personal activities, but be insufficient

to justify such as diminishes the exercise of rights so vital to the maintenance of democratic institutions. . . ."

(B) Moreover, I cannot agree with the Court's notion that First Amendment freedoms must be abridged in order to "preserve" our country. That
notion rests on the unarticulated premise that this Nation's security hangs
upon its power to punish people because of what they think, speak or
write about, or because of those with whom they associate for political
purposes. The Government, in its brief, virtually admits this position
when it speaks of the "communication of unlawful ideas." I challenge this
premise, and deny that ideas can be proscribed under our Constitution.
I agree that despotic governments cannot exist without stifling the voice
of opposition to their oppressive practices. The First Amendment means
to me, however, that the only constitutional way our government can preserve itself is to leave its people the fullest possible freedom to praise,
criticize or discuss, as they see fit, all governmental policies and to suggest, if they desire, that even its most fundamental postulates are bad
and should be changed: "Therein lies the security of the Republic, the
very foundation of constitutional government." On that premise this land
was created, and on that premise it has grown to greatness. Our Constitution assumes that the common sense of the people and their attachment
to our country will enable them, after free discussion, to withstand ideas
that are wrong. To say that our patriotism must be protected against false
ideas by means other than these is, I think, to make a baseless charge.
Unless we can rely on these qualities—if, in short, we begin to punish
speech—we cannot honestly proclaim ourselves to be a free Nation and
we have lost what the Founders of this land risked their lives and their
sacred honors to defend.

(C) The Court implies, however, that the ordinary rules and requirements of the Constitution do not apply because the Committee is merely
after Communists and they do not constitute a political party but only a
criminal gang. "[T]he long and widely accepted view," the Court says, is
"that the tenets of the Communist Party include the ultimate overthrow
of the Government of the United States by force and violence." This justifies the investigation undertaken. By accepting this charge and allowing
it to support treatment of the Communist Party and its members which
would violate the Constitution if applied to other groups, the Court, in
effect, declares that Party outlawed. It has been only a few years since
there was a practically unanimous feeling throughout the country and in
our courts that this could not be done in our free land. Of course it has
always been recognized that members of the Party who, either individually
or in combination, commit acts in violation of valid laws can be prosecuted.
But the Party as a whole and innocent members of it could not be attainted
merely because it had some illegal aims and because some of its members
were lawbreakers. . . .

[N]o matter how often or how quickly we repeat the claim that the
Communist Party is not a political party, we cannot outlaw it, as a group,
without endangering the liberty of all of us. The reason is not hard to find,
for mixed among those aims of communism which are illegal are perfectly

normal political and social goals. And muddled with its revolutionary tenets is a drive to achieve power through the ballot, if it can be done. These things necessarily make it a political party whatever other, illegal, aims it may have. . . . Significantly until recently the Communist Party was on the ballot in many States. When that was so, many Communists undoubtedly hoped to accomplish its lawful goals through support of Communist candidates. Even now some such may still remain. To attribute to them, and to those who have left the Party, the taint of the group is to ignore both our traditions that guilt like belief is "personal and not a matter of mere association" and the obvious fact that "men adhering to a political party or other organization notoriously do not subscribe unqualifiedly to all of its platforms or asserted principles. . . ."

The fact is that once we allow any group which has some political aims or ideas to be driven from the ballot and from the battle for men's minds because some of its members are bad and some of its tenets are illegal, no group is safe. Today we deal with Communists or suspected Communists. In 1920, instead, the New York Assembly suspended duly elected legislators on the ground that, being Socialists, they were disloyal to the country's principles. In the 1830's the Masons were hunted as outlaws and subversives, and abolitionists were considered revolutionaries of the most dangerous kind in both North and South. Earlier still, at the time of the universally unlamented alien and sedition laws, Thomas Jefferson's party was attacked and its members were derisively called "Jacobins." Fisher Ames described the party as a "French faction" guilty of "subversion" and "officered, regimented and formed to subordination." Its members, he claimed, intended to "take arms aginst the laws as soon as they dare." History should teach us, then, that in times of high emotional excitement minority parties and groups which advocate extremely unpopular social or governmental innovations will always be typed as criminal gangs and attempts will always be made to drive them out. It was knowledge of this fact, and of its great dangers, that caused the Founders of our land to enact the First Amendment as a guarantee that neither Congress nor the people would do anything to hinder or destroy the capacity of individuals and groups to seek converts and votes for any cause, however radical or unpalatable their principles might seem under the accepted notions of the time. Whatever the States were left free to do, the First Amendment sought to leave Congress devoid of any kind or quality of power to direct any type of national laws against the freedom of individuals to think what they please, advocate whatever policy they choose, and join with others to bring about the social, religious, political and governmental changes which seem best to them. Today's holding, in my judgment, marks another major step in the progressively increasing retreat from the safeguards of the First Amendment. . . .

Finally, I think Barenblatt's conviction violates the Constitution because the chief aim, purpose and practice of the House Un-American Activities Committee, as disclosed by its many reports, is to try witnesses and punish them because they are or have been Communists or because they refuse to admit or deny Communist affiliations. The punishment imposed is generally punishment by humiliation and public shame. There is nothing strange or novel about this kind of punishment. It is in fact one of the oldest forms of governmental punishment known to mankind; branding, the pillory, ostracism and subjection to public hatred being but a few examples of it. . . .

I do not question the Committee's patriotism and sincerity in doing all this. I merely feel that it cannot be done by Congress under our Constitution. For, even assuming that the Federal Government can compel witnesses to testify as to Communist affiliations in order to subject them to ridicule and social and economic retaliation, I cannot agree that this is a legislative function. Such publicity is clearly punishment, and the Constitution allows only one way in which people can be convicted and punished. . . [I]f communism is to be made a crime, and Communists are to be subjected to "pains and penalties," I would still hold this conviction bad, for the crime of communism, like all others, can be punished only by court and jury after a trial with all judicial safeguards.

It is no answer to all this to suggest that legislative committees should be allowed to punish if they grant the accused some rules of courtesy or allow him counsel. For the Constitution proscribes all bills of attainder by State or Nation, not merely those which lack counsel or courtesy. It does this because the Founders believed that punishment was too serious a matter to be entrusted to any group other than an independent judiciary and a jury of twelve men acting on previously passed, unambiguous laws, with all the procedural safeguards they put in the Constitution as essential to a fair trial—safeguards which included the right to counsel, compulsory process for witnesses, specific indictments, confrontation of accusers, as well as protection against self-incrimination, double jeopardy and cruel and unusual punishment—in short due process of law. . . . They believed this because not long before worthy men had been deprived of their liberties, and indeed their lives, through parliamentary trials without these safeguards. . . . It is the protection from arbitrary punishments through the right to a judicial trial with all these safeguards which over the years has distinguished America from lands where drum-head courts and other similar "tribunals" deprive the weak and the unorthodox of life, liberty and property without due process of law. It is this same right which is denied to Barenblatt, because the Court today fails to see what is here for all to see—that exposure and punishment is the aim of this Committee and the reason for its existence. To deny this aim is to ignore the Committee's own claims and the reports it has issued ever since it was established. I cannot believe that the nature of our judicial office requires us to be so blind, and must conclude that the Un-American Activities Committee's "identification" and "exposure" of Communists and suspected Communists . . . amount to an encroachment on the judiciary which bodes ill for the liberties of the people of this land.

Ultimately all the questions in this case really boil down to one—whether we as a people will try fearfully and futilely to preserve Democracy by adopting totalitarian methods, or whether in accordance with our traditions and our Constitution we will have the confidence and courage to be free.

I would reverse this conviction.

Mr. Justice Brennan, dissenting.

I would reverse this conviction. It is sufficient that I state my complete agreement with my Brother Black that no purpose for the investigation of Barenblatt is revealed by the Record except exposure purely for the sake of exposure. This is not a purpose to which Barenblatt's rights under the First Amendment can validily be subordinated. An investigation in which the processes of lawmaking and law-evaluating are submerged entirely in exposure of individual behavior—in adjudication, of a sort, through the exposure process—is outside the constitutional pale of congressional inquiry. . . .

Joe Pool of HUAC

Larry L. King

Until a certain hectic week in August, Joe Pool was just another junior Congressman. His pet legislative scheme would have turned a Texas mountaintop into a National Park—provided, Pool made clear, that a major oil company retain drilling and mineral rights. True, he had got his name in the paper a few months previously when the House Un-American Activities Committee investigated the inner tickings of the Ku Klux Klan. He also had been the subject of Page One stories when his $30,000 fund-raising "Appreciation Dinner" in Washington coincided with Drew Pearson's revelations in the Dodd Case, causing suspicious reporters to show up and count the lobbyists, contractors, and professional glad-handers among Pool's official appreciators. But roly-poly Joe Pool remained, until late this summer, slightly less anonymous than the Unknown Soldier. He was also having reelection troubles from a Republican in his new Dallas district.

Then came his House Un-American Activities Committee hearings. A week after the storm broke he proudly told a cheering Dallas crowd, "Little Joe has been catapulted into a very prominent spot in American history overnight." The Dallas *Morning News* rhapsodized: "The [House Un-American Activities] Committee, since the day of Texas' Martin Dies, has been the people's last resort against those in Washington who are lenient on rats in our midst. In protecting the function of this Committee, Mr. Pool is protecting the voice of the people." A woman wired: "AN AMERICAN HERO WAS BORN TODAY." A Grand Prairie, Texas, man resorted to special delivery and a special form of Latin to advise: "NON CARBORUNDUM ILLEGITIMI!" ("Don't Let the Bastards Grind You Down!"). The Veterans of Foreign Wars told Pool that if he would get up to their national convention in the New York Hilton, they'd lay a special award on him.

"Joe Pool of HUAC," *Harper's Magazine*, November 1966. Reprinted by permission of the author.

When Congressman Pool flew home for the weekend, some three hundred Dallas boosters jammed a hotel ballroom to sing "For He's a Jolly Good Fellow." Placards said, "Give 'Em Hell, Joe!" Spokesmen for the Jewish War Veterans, the American Legion, and the VFW variously gave Joe the nod in impromptu eulogies over Davy Crockett, Sam Houston, and Douglas MacArthur. An ancient warrior represented as being eighty-eight years old and a veteran of San Juan Hill, garbed in a Rough Rider's outfit, paused to give the Congressman a palsied salute. A woman shouted, "You're my next President, Joe Baby!" Others took it up.

It was too much. Joe Pool wandered around the ballroom shaking hands, as he told me, "bawling like a baby." "When all that happened it—well, it just got to me. I felt *humble,* you know whatta mean?" Pool recovered from his attack of humility long enough to tell the throng, "Most Americans live for the day when they can do something for their country that will go down in history. I feel like I did exactly that last week." That started them singing again.

Writing in a national magazine recently, historian Arthur Schlesinger, Jr. suggested the approach of a new "McCarthy Era." Pointing out that witch-hunting traditionally reaches its peak during wars, Schlesinger wrote, "If history repeats itself—and history sometimes does—the war in Vietnam ought to produce something roughly comparable to the McCarthy phenomenon. The Vietnamese war is just as frustrating as the Korean war and a good deal harder for most people to understand. . . . As the war increasingly dominates and obsesses our national life, we can look for the appearance of associated symptoms: the oversimplification of issues, the exchange of invective, the questioning of motives and loyalties, and the degradation of debate."

If we are to have a new McCarthy Era we must, by a small extension of logic, have a new McCarthy. Does Joe Pool qualify? What manner of cat is he?

"YEW OLE LIBERAL THANG"

It was World War II that opened Pool's eyes to the joys of "investigative work." His biographical sketch notes that he served as "special investigator with Air Corps Intelligence." Pool says that "when a plane crashed we'd cordon off the area and try to reconstruct what happened, figure out what went wrong." For a time he was a Provost Marshal's gumshoe, looking into thefts, frauds, larcenies, and crooked crap games in a half-dozen Southwestern states.

He was elected to the Texas Legislature in 1952, and in time became Chairman of the House Investigating Committee. During this period the state government was rocked by major scandals involving insurance companies, loan sharks, real-estate schemes, and the Veterans' land program. Attendant explosions sent a few folks to jail (including the Texas Land Commissioner and a State Representative), inspired at least one prominent suicide, and caused another public figure to seek the better climate of Brazil. Joe Pool's Investigating Committee had nothing to do with any of this. It did, however, war on lewd and horror comic books.

To this day Joe is intrigued by intrigue. Some months ago I chanced upon the Congressman in a Capitol corridor. Perhaps I eyed him a bit warily, for I had just written in the *Texas Observer* of his votes, and in less than complimentary terms.

Pool jovially hailed me in the thick accent of our common habitat. "Yew ole Liberal thang, yew! Lemme buy yew a cuppa coffee. Ah wanta talk *turkey* to yew."

What Joe wanted to talk turkey about was the upcoming HUAC hearings into operations of the Ku Klux Klan. Joe had a scheme. We would go, the two of us, in tandem and incognito, into the seedier traps of deepest Dixie—into snooker parlors, roadside honky-tonks, cheap hotels, stock-car race tracks, hillbilly dance joints, fishing and hunting clubs—there to infiltrate the Klan, during the annual adjournment of Congress, until we knew its spookiest secrets by heart. "You gotta have undercover work to get anywhere on a thang like this," Joe assured me. "We'll wear ole clothes. Khaki britches and short-sleeved sports shirts and thangs like that. I betcha we can crack 'em."

"Godamighty, Joe," I said. "We'd probably get killed!"

Pool acted as if he hadn't heard. He said, "We can get the evidence. I don't have any doubts about that. You can get you some good stories that'll sell, and as far as I'm concerned you can keep all the money. All I want is the publicity." He stared at me over his coffee cup there in the hushed splendor of the House Restaurant. "A-course," he said, thoughtfully, "you'll have to shave that shaggy ole beard off."

A BARSTOOL KIND OF FRANKNESS

As Harry Truman once said of Stalin in an unguarded moment, "I like Ole Joe." He is a jovial companion at libations, quick to pick up the tab for his table, and maybe the neighboring one as well. He is good to his employees, paying them well and smiling away mistakes. He makes easy jokes on himself. Only five feet, six inches tall and admitting to 235 pounds, he likes to tell of being introduced as the Congressman-at-Large to a lady who cracked, "Well, you durn sure look like you qualify!"

Somebody over at *The New Republic* wrote that Joe would have to be seen to be believed, that he looks like "a frog on a lily pad," and that "he is not very bright." It *is* true that you can relax beside Pool without feeling like he may steal your girl. He may not be much prettier than Elizabeth, New Jersey, and he will never bore you with a lot of small talk about Dostoevski or the later plays of T. S. Eliot or prevailing economic conditions in Peru. One should not deduce from this, however, that Joe Pool is without resources.

Some months ago I was in Pool's office when a staff member told him of a Dallas newspaper story to the effect that his GOP opponent was having trouble gaining meaningful financial backing from the Republican National Committee. Pool looked up from signing his mail and drawled, "I thought that never *would* get printed. Planted that rumor nearly two weeks ago." He led the laughter.

There is sometimes a sort of blurted, barstool frankness about him that makes you wonder whether he ever kept a secret. Asked why he was the only member of the House to vote against the Wilderness Bill (to preserve certain wooded areas in their native state) when it passed 388 to 1, he said, "Well, I figured I could throw my conservative friends an anti-Lyndon vote and at the same time not do much damage." In the summer of 1963, Pool rather curiously announced to the world that he would sleep in his Congressional office "until the demonstrators disperse." He did, for one night, which was the announced duration of the March on Washington anyway. Two years later, when I pressed him for an explanation of what he had expected to accomplish by the theatrical act, Pool said candidly, "Tell you the truth, I'm not sure I could explain it to myself. It just seemed like a good idea at the time."

Perhaps Pool is most appreciated in professional circles for his ability to walk the political chalk line well enough to keep the President's goodwill even while voting against most of the President's programs. There is nothing especially mystic about why Joe Pool has so much unexpended coin in Lyndon Johnson's piggy bank.

A few years ago LBJ wanted to appear on the Texas ballot both as a candidate for U.S. Senator *and* on the national ticket. This required a May, rather than a July Democratic Primary (as was customary) if Johnson hoped to go to the July Democratic National Convention in 1960 with his Senatorial renomination locked up. Technical points were involved, some requiring an amendment to the Texas Constitution, but the main goal was to allow Johnson to hedge his political bet. It was Joe Pool, then a member of the Texas Legislature, who rushed forward to sponsor the necessary bill and gain its enactment.

Having served his political apprenticeship in the boondocks, Pool was elected to Congress in a manner that seems to have been preordained. He was one of two dozen candidates, all so obscure they might have profitably robbed liquor stores without wearing masks, to vie for the Congressman-at-Large seat vacated by Martin Dies. An El Paso County judge led the first primary from here to Iwo Jima, Pool barely qualifying for the showdown runoff thirty days later. Within a week the leading candidate had been indicted (and was ultimately convicted) of income-tax evasion; he had not filed an income tax in ten years. Pool got to Washington virtually by default. He immediately asked for his seat on the House Un-American Activities Committee.

LIVE MEN AND DEAD WOMEN

I called on Congressman Pool in Washington the Monday following his hero's welcome in Dallas. A uniformed Capitol Hill policeman, eying my beard, asked what he could do for me. Jean Jones, Pool's executive secretary, the sight of whom will almost automatically make you think of Girls, has suffered everything on Capitol Hill from bearded prophets to cocktail-hour proposals of marriage. She spoke to the nervous cop in tones meant to assure him that I carried no bombs.

The walls were covered with Washington Wallpaper: autographed photos of the mighty (HST, JFK, LBJ) and the obscure (booted Texas oil barons, a 4-H Club champion who had probably raised the fattest hog, mink-clad matrons giving Pool, or perhaps receiving from him, some certificate or scroll of special merit). There were oil paintings by student Rembrandts at Southern Methodist or Texas Christian. Just inside the Congressman's private chamber is a partition shielding him from a view of the sink where his staffers brew mildly vile pots of coffee. The partition was festooned with colorful record jackets advertising the triumphs of certain hillbilly or rock-'n'-roll music men. A neat, hand-lettered sign said, "These Records Made in Texas!"

Behind his executive desk Joe Pool came off like the lean, loose-jointed Texan of legend the same way R. C. Cola comes off as Châteauneuf du Pape. He filled the padded chair, horizontally speaking, though you had the notion that maybe under the desk his feet didn't quite reach the floor. "Come on in," he said, grinning. "Hail, I put up with lots worse than you, lately."

We both enthused over his new prominence. Pool lovingly described his Dallas homecoming, and how the salute of the old Rough Rider had moved him to tears. Art Cameron, a young Capitol Hill lawyer assisting Pool with "Constitutional questions," relaxed on the couch with a fat *Constitution Annotated*. Behind the partition Jean Jones ran water and clanked a coffee pot.

"You're a writer," Pool accused me, suddenly. "Tell me somethin'. Few days ago I was interviewed by a kid from the school paper up at Harvard. You know, Harvard College?" I said I knew. "Anyway, he promised he'd call back today," Pool said, "to let me check my direct quotes out. But he didn't call. You reckon he will?"

I said I had no way of knowing.

"I doubt it," Joe judged. "He tole me he didn't see eye-to-eye with me. Which didn't come as too big a surprise. He probably went off and wrote it like he wanted to." He toyed with an ashtray. "A-course," he said, elaborately casual, "I had Art here, and Jean, with me all the time *he* was here. They can be my witnesses . . . if I need 'em."

The prospective witnesses went with us to the Capitol Hill Democratic Club across the street when I volunteered to buy post-work drinks. "The thing about this man," Art Cameron said, once we'd claimed a table, "is that he handled himself so *beautifully* during all those outbursts. He had to make quick decisions time after time after time. And he *always* made the right one." Pool dropped his head and said modestly that, well, *some* people might not agree with that, but he'd done the best he could and he knew *one* thing about it: he'd sure earned his money *that* particular week. Miss Jones said, "It was a real education. I learned that a reporter can paint any picture he wants just by being selective—by writing *some* things and leaving out *other* things. That damn Washington *Post!* You read the actual transcripts and you'll find a different hearing than the one you read about in the papers." Pool said, philosophically, that well, you can't fight City Hall, and Art Cameron said that was for sure.

I remarked that Pool's GOP opponent, who a few weeks earlier had been judged capable of winning, must have suddenly felt as if the moon and the stars had dropped on him.

Pool grinned. "I dunno. . . . He jumped on me in the papers. Said I'd did the same thing as all those street rioters when I ignored that court order. I don't think anybody very smart's gonna see it like that. A-course, you never can tell . . ."

"Hell," I said, "the only way you can lose this election, Joe, is to get caught in bed with a live man or a dead woman."

Pool boomed with laughter. He poked his finger at me in a stabbing motion, gasping mirth: "*You* . . . said . . . that! *I* didn't."

A Congressional staffer in a bow tie paused to wring Pool's hand. "You really got after those nuts," he said. "I'm proud of you Congressman." Pool thanked him and noted that "they really got after *me*, for a while there, didn't they?" He offered to buy his admirer a drink but the fellow explained about a waiting wife and dinner.

John Saylor, an affable Pennsylvania Republican long a fixture in the House, who gets along so well with his Democratic colleagues that he feels as much at home in their private club as he does in the GOP's Capitol Hill Club around the corner, ambled by and gave Pool a friendly wink. "You want to know why I get along on both sides of the aisle?" Art Cameron asked me, bipartisanly. He tugged at Saylor's elbow and introduced us. He told me that Saylor had stayed at his grandmother's funeral an hour and a half longer than any other Congressman had. We chatted for a while with Saylor. Then he wandered off in search of bigger game.

JOE TAKES SOME BOWS

Two or three other people stopped to congratulate Pool as he sat basking in his new glory, smilingly mumbling something about how "the Commonists" probably didn't agree but *he* sure as heck did appreciate it. Pool stopped Arizona Democrat Morris "Mo" Udall, who happened by with three constituents in tow, and through gasps of laughter, his broad belly shaking uncontrollably, he repeated my crack about being "caught in bed with a live man or a dead woman." Udall smiled as if his feet hurt and moved on.

Soon the crowd thinned, shuffling away to the bar or in search of dinner. I asked Pool what he thought the HUAC hearings had proved. "I think," he said, "it proves the Commonists are behind all this treason. They showed their true colors. Lot of 'em admitted being Commonists, or Marxist-Leninists or Progressive Labor, or whatever it is." Suddenly, he beamed, turning to Jean Jones: "Say, Jean, my opponent says he's a *Progressive* Republican. Think we can make anything out of that?" They laughed like winners who own the dice.

Why, I asked Joe, had he abruptly ended the hearings—even when two witnesses, who had been officially called, clamored to testify?

Pool said, "We thought we'd proved what we set out to prove. They *said* they was Commonists! And then, too, we wanted to be sure we gave those two boys—the ones who didn't testify—their Constitutional rights. Give 'em time to prepare their defenses. Get lawyers." He explained that the two had been represented by Arthur Kinoy, the American Civil Liberties Union attorney who had been bodily carried to jail. "You know," Joe confided, leaning across the table, "that Kinoy thang had me worried for a while. If that judge had found him *not guilty*—Lord God! Well, I'da been *in* for it!" (Kinoy was fined $50 on disturbance charges by a judge in the District of Columbia.) Pool felt another seizure of confidential information coming on. He said in a conspiratorial tone. "You know the luckiest thang we ever done? Hold those Klan hearings! Yessir! Now we can say we got the Klan and the Commonists after us at the same time!" His eyes twinkled over such twin good fortune.

I said there was a rumor that the White House, as well as the Congressional leadership, had soured on the stormy HUAC hearings and had instructed Pool to stop them. Anything to it?

"Not a thang in the world," Pool said, heatedly. "A-course, I guess a lot of people might like to think so!"

I mentioned the Johnson Administration's opposition to the bill. The Administration had taken the position, I said, that no new legislation is needed; that the demonstrations are a long way from treason; that since Vietnam isn't officially "a war," Congress must move slow in legislating punitively against dissenters. Could Pool account for the Administration's logic?

Pool said that maybe I'd better ask the President; he couldn't tell *him* what to do, either. Then he added, "Some of those Administration witnesses didn't stand up to well to the Committee. That Army General—the one that testified that all them demonstrations don't hurt our troop morale? Well, when we pinned him down he admitted it might help the *Vietcong's* morale! That's the same thing, now, don't you think?"

Art Cameron said, "Oh, Congressman Ichord got that out of the General *so* beautifully. It was just . . . well, *beautiful!*"

Pool said that you sure couldn't put much past ole Dick Ichord. Then he told Cameron, "We got ole Ramsey Clark comin' up here to testify tomorrow."

"He'll be pretty tough," Cameron predicted.

"I dunno," Pool said. "I heard he said he wouldn't hurt us much."

"He's an Administration witness."

"Well . . . I *heard* that, anyway."

"You just wait," Cameron warned. "I'll bet he throws you some real Constitutional toughies."

"That right?" Pool asked. He gazed into his glass, discouraged.

"Joe," I said, "some people see you as 'the New McCarthy.' You have any comment?"

Pool's laugh seemed genuine. "Boy! If I ever heard one to quit on, that's *it!* Waiter, brang me the check for this table!" While he signed the check, dismissing my halfhearted efforts to pay, he shook his head: "Yew ole Liberals! I dunno. . . ."

I told the Congressman I hoped to see him later in the week. "Make it before Thursday," he said. "I'm goin' to Vietnam."

To Vietnam?

"Yeah," he said, offhandedly. Then he grinned. "Reckon what my Republican opponent's gonna say about that?"

I mumbled that I didn't even know what to say. When had this come about? And for what purpose?

"I'm on the Post Office and Civil Service Committee, too," Pool reminded me. "Chairman's asked me to go over and investigate our boys' mail service. We've had a lotta complaints that the mail's been slow gettin' there, and things like that." He added quickly that the assignment had been given him "before all this notoriety."

Would he talk to the troops about their morale, or whether antiwar demonstrations hurt their cause?

"You betcha! You just betcha! And I'm takin' a whole shoebox full of letters people have give me since this thang come up. I'm gonna show those boys over there fightin' Commonism that America's backin' 'em up! And that all these dadgummed Vietniks and beatniks and whatnot with their beards—" He trailed off, momentarily abashed.

I said, "Joe, you sure do make it sound personal."

"Aw," Pool said, "I didn't mean *you!*"

Joe told me to take it easy, moving away. Somebody at the bar yelled, "Hey there, Statesman!" as he walked by. Somebody else called, where was his police escort? Another barstool comedian asked didn't he know that the Communists might be waiting for him out there in the dark, right out there in front of the Congressional Hotel? Joe Pool waved and laughed and performed a little series of bobbing half-bows, thinking, maybe, what a friendly bunch of guys hung around Washington once you got to know 'em and the notion struck you that maybe you were catching the world premiere of McCarthy in the Round. He pushed against the thick glass door and bounced energetically down the hall that, if you just followed it far enough and made all the right turns at the right places, would take you straight to Vietnam.

Chapter Eight

SUGGESTED QUESTIONS FOR CLASS DISCUSSION.

1. The folkways of the Congress have long held that freshmen members are to be seen and not heard. Is the "coat-tail effect" of Presidential power, especially in a Presidential election year, changing some of the established norms?

2. Does great individual power of a member of Congress tend to weaken or strengthen the power of the body itself vis-à-vis the wishes of the majority? Or does the nature of a legislative body require a few leaders of great power?

3. Since 1900 the President has occupied such a paramount position in foreign relations that this position has seldom been challenged. Such challenges have usually come in a war situation. What can the Congress, and especially the Senate, really do in checking Presidential policy?

4. Should the investigating powers of Congress be more restricted or even broader than they now are? Does exposure by committees really serve a useful, and legitimate purpose?

THE PRESIDENT AND THE EXECUTIVE BRANCH

The President of the United States occupies the most important and powerful elective office in the world. He operates at the center of a vast executive establishment that generates a continuing flow of decisions and recommendations affecting the people of the United States and, directly or indirectly, the people of almost every other nation in the world. He does not play one role alone but many roles: chief executive, commander-in-chief of the armed forces, chief legislator (in that a great deal of draft legislation is prepared in the Executive Branch), director of American foreign policy, ceremonial head of state, leader of his political party, moral and ideological leader of the nation, and elected representative of all Americans. The burdens on the President are enormous and may be expected to grow. No man can be a "good President" in every sense of that term for the job has become too big—yet the political system never lacks for men eager to occupy the White House.

Lyndon Johnson and the Paradox of the Presidency

C. Peter Magrath

During the Presidential campaign of 1964 Lyndon Johnson's opponents questioned the sincerity of his desire to be President of "all the people" (not just Democrats), but today none would deny the effectiveness of this appeal. Johnson's election victory was enormous: he captured 61 per cent of the vote, the greatest percentage of the total presidential vote in history. The decisive outcome of his contest with Barry Goldwater tells us much about Lyndon Johnson's political acumen; it also reveals much about the American people and what they expect of the presidency.

They want their President to be a great nonpartisan leader, a fact that Johnson had marked well in the early 1950's. As Senate Democratic Leader he was deeply impressed by the strength of Eisenhower's "above politics" appeal. Johnson concluded that the best politics was nonpartisan politics, and he bent every effort to making the Senate Democrats appear as a constructive opposition, cooperating with President Eisenhower whenever possible. Ever since then, as both President and candidate, Johnson has spoken the language of national unity with unvarying monotony. He has also sought to camouflage his Democratic ties, presenting himself as a President under whose broad nonpartisan umbrella all Americans can comfortably stand. His success in winning votes with these tactics (and the failure of Barry Goldwater's openly divisive and partisan approach) is now undoubted.

But the Johnson brand of nonpartisanship has a significance that extends far beyond the winning of elections. His performance since becoming President—particularly his virtuoso combination of politics with nonpartisanship—suggests that he may have found the key to solving one of the fundamental paradoxes of the American presidential office. To understand how Johnson has shaped the modern presidency, we must first appreciate the full dimensions of the paradox that has bedeviled every President since George Washington: the President is chief of state, but he is a partisan political leader as well. On the one hand he represents the *entire* nation and embodies many of its highest ideals. On the other, he is a politician elected at the head of a partisan ticket and often identified with particular interest groups.

In parliamentary systems, like the British, there is no such confusion of roles. The monarch (or president in parliamentary republics) is chief of state—an uncontroversial figure around whom the nation can unite—and the prime minister serves as political leader. Everyone expects the prime minister to govern as an avowed party leader, and this division of labor simplifies life for the citizen. If a good British Tory roundly curses Harold

"Lyndon Johnson and the Paradox of the Presidency," *Yale Review*, Vol. LIV, No. 4, June 1965. Copyright 1965 Yale University. Reprinted by permission of the author and publisher.

Wilson, he can all the while proclaim his undying loyalty to Elizabeth Regina—the permanent human symbol of the British nation.

At times the ambivalent position of the American President works to his advantage. To take but one of the many examples from recent history, the Cuban missile crisis of 1962 occurred in the midst of a hot political campaign in which President Kennedy had stumped for a Democratic Congress. Once the serious nature of the Soviet-American confrontation became evident, Kennedy left the campaign trail and gave his undivided attention to the Cuban problem. Former President Eisenhower, who was campaigning for Republican candidates, found it necessary to draw a distinction between John F. Kennedy, the nation's President, and John F. Kennedy the Democratic Party leader. First, he asked all Americans "to stand behind our constitutional Commander in Chief" with all "the vigor of our minds and hearts." But in the next breath Eisenhower said, "Of course, we support the President in foreign affairs, but we must make sure that we defeat his recent efforts to get in Washington a virtually one-party Congress."

Since Kennedy was a single person, not a separate "constitutional Commander in Chief" and a separate "party leader," the effort to rally around him and in the same instant to repudiate him politically broke down. The public mind is not that subtle. It sees but one President, and the missile crisis increased Kennedy's public prestige and probably contributed to his party's success in the 1962 congressional elections. Republicans claimed they had been "Cubanized"; they might more accurately have said they were "Presidentized."

If the President's position as chief of state strengthens him in times of national crisis, making him a difficult target for his opponents, it also weakens his effectiveness as a political leader. And this is a serious matter, for the presidency is our most vital political institution. We look to the President for domestic leadership and we entrust him with awesome international responsibilities in an age of missiles and thermonuclear bombs. But to lead effectively he must be an adept practitioner of the political arts, a politician of the highest skill.

Yet, the very fact that the President is our sole national leader paradoxically confines his political freedom. When large segments of the public perceive him as overly "political," either in the sense that he is too much a party man or too much a partisan of special interests, he forfeits his claim to being the sole representative of the entire American community. Politics, for many Americans, is synonymous with "dirt" and there is ample evidence that a powerful strain in our popular culture equates it with crooked manipulation of the worst sort. The presidency, however, is a venerated office. Any man who sits in the White House profits by being a successor to George Washington, Thomas Jefferson, and Abraham Lincoln. Because in the public view the office is to a degree sacred, its occupant demeans it when his behavior appears too partisan.

There is, in short, an acute tension between the desires of the general public and the inescapably political role of the President. But the President cannot serve just as a venerable chief of state, for he holds an elective office won in the rough and tumble of party politics. If he hopes to govern men and to influence public measures—instead of being governed by

others and helplessly buffeted by events—the President must be a prac-
ticing politician of the highest order. If he is to be the nation's political
leader, he must constantly fight for his policy objectives. He must do so
in the face of conflicting pressures from Congress, from state governors,
from bureaucrats within his own executive branch, and from hundreds of
interest groups, not to mention foreign nations. There is, too, the resistance
of the opposition party, and, very often, the apathy of the public as influential factors with which a President must reckon.

The consequence of this schizophrenic role that we demand of our Chief
Executive is plain: only a superb behind-the-scenes politician whose *public*
appearance is nonpartisan can be a really successful President. The experiences of every President since the Second World War are highly
instructive on this point, and they show why Lyndon Johnson's accomplishments have been so remarkable. Harry S. Truman's ripping, "give-the-
Republicans-hell" campaign in 1948 carried him to a narrow victory
against an overconfident opponent; it also left him a politically marked
man. Not only was his public image that of a Democratic partisan, but
he also acquired the coloration of a "group partisan" who one-sidedly did
the bidding of organized labor. In the eyes of many millions of Americans,
President Truman was the White House Agent of William Green of the
AFL and Philip Murray of the CIO in their bitter disputes with management. Nor was the image wholly inaccurate. Truman, after all, had vetoed
the Taft-Hartley Act and he lustily campaigned against it. In 1952 he
took the union side in his controversial (and almost unanimously condemned) seizure of the steel industry.

The President's difficulties were in large part due to the political mood
of the country. There was a strong national desire for a period of postwar
"normalcy," and it expressed itself in the essential conservatism of Congress. But Truman compounded his domestic problems by behavior that
much of the population thought too partisan. He needlessly lowered his
public stature and weakened his presidential powers. The Fair Deal never
became more than a high-sounding campaign slogan.

By contrast, Truman's greatest achievements were in foreign affairs,
the one area in which he largely avoided partisan politics. There, by an
explicit understanding with the Republican congressional leadership, he
wisely practiced bipartisanship—that is, nonpartisanship. The results were
impressive. They included the "Truman Doctrine," the Marshall Plan, the
"Point Four" program, and the North Atlantic Treaty Organization.

How, one asks, was all this possible? The answer is not simple. Constitutionally, the President is the nation's undisputed leader in foreign
affairs; his discretionary powers are greatest when he turns to international problems. Since Soviet imperialism in the late 'forties was so obviously menacing, it made Truman's international leadership easier. The
Republican congressional leadership, moreover, recognized the foreign
dangers as fully as Truman. Convinced—until November 1948—that the
next President would be Republican, they felt the burden of responsibility
that comes with power. As Richard Neustadt wrote in his brilliant study
of *Presidential Leadership,* "The war was over, Roosevelt dead, Truman a
caretaker, theirs the trust."

During his second term, however, Truman stumbled badly, even in foreign affairs. At first his decision to repel the Communist invasion of South Korea with American arms won wide approval. But he committed a serious mistake in failing to ask Congress for what it certainly would have granted, a bipartisan resolution supporting the intervention. Instead of a decision to go into Korea reached by a Democratic President and ratified in part by the congressional Republicans, the American involvement in Korea became a purely presidential decision. Once the Chinese crossed the Yalu and the war became a frustrating stalemate on the 38th parallel, the way was open for it to become a partisan issue. The Korean War became "Truman's War."

By 1951 the President's foreign policy, no less than his domestic policy, had become envenomed in partisanship. The removal of the insubordinate General MacArthur, though essential if Truman was to remain Commander in Chief, brought an almost unprecedented storm of partisan fury upon the President's head. His national popularity stood at a record low: there is no reason to doubt the Gallup polls that reported less than 33 per cent of the population approving of Truman's performance. In many ways Truman was a remarkably able President, but his presidency foundered on the rock of partisanship.

Significantly, the enormous appeal of Truman's successor, Dwight D. Eisenhower, was based on his sharply nonpartisan public image. A man held in the greatest personal respect by the vast majority of Americans, Eisenhower was both to himself and to most Americans a great national healer. His general objectives were surely laudable. He proposed to unify the nation after the abrasive discord of the New and Fair Deals and, while checking Communist aggression, to seek ways of promoting international peace.

Eisenhower's conception of the presidency was not an expansive one, but he was no Buchanan or Harding. In international affairs, certainly, there could be no doubt that Eisenhower sought to lead the nation. His record of accomplishments in foreign affairs was mixed. The presidential candidate had talked bravely of "rolling back the Iron Curtain"; the President refused to risk nuclear war in order to aid the Hungarian rebels in 1956. There were also some terrible blunders, most notably the U-2 affair and the humiliation of Eisenhower by Khrushchev at the Paris Conference in 1960. In general, however, it seems fair to say that the President successfully continued the Truman-Acheson policies of containing international Communism. He cautiously sought to negotiate with the Soviet Union, and, in a rather cumbersome fashion, adjusted American foreign policy to the new political realities in Asia and Africa.

In domestic affairs, however, the President's performance was poor. His leadership on some of the urgent political questions of the 'fifties—civil rights, public education, and McCarthyism—is best described as temporizing. In fact, one of Eisenhower's most serious flaws was his uncertainty about his domestic policy objectives. For example, what appeared as weakness when he repudiated his generally liberal budget in 1957 was less weakness than a personal uncertainty over the budget's social welfare features and a growing dislike for heavy federal expenditures. In 1958 and 1959, when Eisenhower submitted more conservative budgets that harmonized with what had become his settled conviction on the need to reduce federal spending, he emerged as a strong leader on the subject of balanced budgets. As a politician a President is entitled, indeed, often required, to compromise his objectives. But if he is unsure of them in the first place, he cannot be an effective political leader.

Ironically, it was the image of a beloved Ike "above politics," his greatest political asset, which was also his greatest liability. It is true that Eisenhower's well-publicized distaste for politics was itself good politics, bringing him landslide election victories in 1952 and 1956 and keeping his popularity high. Still, there is no reason to doubt his ingrained distaste for what he—in company with many of his fellow citizens—contemptuously dismissed as "politics." "I have no great liking for that," he would say, and he meant it.

He was often insensitive to the nuances of political power and to the ways in which politicians think and act. He never, for example, really seemed to understand the threat which Joe McCarthy posed to the executive branch and, specifically, to his own political power. McCarthy's subsequent fall was a fortunate consequence of the Wisconsin demagogue's excesses; it owed little to Eisenhower's policy of nonintervention. Similarly, the astute Orval Faubus ran rings around the President during the Little Rock school crisis. Not until Faubus had the Arkansas National Guard out in the streets where, in effect, it was defying the federal government, did Eisenhower belatedly rise to the challenge.

In Eisenhower's defense it needs be said that his broad goals, which were to foster a spirit of compromise and of national unity, necessarily took on a quality of over-generality and imprecision. Vagueness and imprecision, of course, are no handicap to an experienced politician. But Eisenhower was not an experienced politician—and not a particularly successful President. The terse judgment of the late Sam Rayburn seems correct: "No, won't do. Good man. Wrong profession."

The presidency of John F. Kennedy was short but revealing. Unlike Eisenhower, Kennedy was at ease in the world of politics and, as he showed in the 1962 fight with Big Steel, fully understood the nature of political power. Intellectually, he was the best prepared man to sit in the White House since Woodrow Wilson. His personal popularity, at least until the civil rights demonstrations of 1963, was high. Yet, continuing a pattern evident since the Truman presidency, Kennedy's major successes were largely confined to international affairs. His Administration launched the widely praised Peace Corps. Kennedy erred grievously in the ill-conceived Bay of Pigs invasion, but recouped with a brilliant exercise in cold war politics during the Cuban missile crisis. In the summer of 1963 he eased Soviet-American tensions by negotiating a nuclear test-ban treaty and then winning its approval in the Senate.

In domestic affairs the Kennedy record was mediocre. He obtained the Trade Expansion Act of 1962, and he achieved some minor reforms in social and economic welfare legislation. There were many setbacks also: Congress rejected his "must" program for federal aid to education, medicare, and reform of the antiquated tax laws.

Kennedy, a polished intellectual, was often ineffective in articulating his programs in such a way as to win public support. His rhetoric, while captivating to college professors, lacked the flair for popular dramatization. He did not, for instance, have the touch of a Roosevelt who in 1940 sold a wary country his controversial Lend Lease program by arguing that it was no more than the act of one neighbor lending "a length of garden hose" to another whose home had caught fire. In addition, though Kennedy came to the White House from the Senate, he frequently misjudged congressional sentiment. He was almost too deferential to Congress. Kennedy, as John P. Roche has wryly noted, "always treated Congress with elaborate solicitude, but it was that of a kindergarten teacher who suspects that one of the children has secreted a hand grenade on the premises."

In part, of course, Kennedy's problems were caused by the political environment that confronted him. He sought liberal legislation at a time when much of the nation was largely indifferent to his reformist urgings. Although the Democrats controlled Congress, many of them were conservatively inclined. When, as often happened, Southern Democrats allied themselves with the strong Republican opposition, the President was left with something less than a majority.

Negro demands for their full civil rights further complicated his task. Kennedys' political, not to mention his personal, commitments led him to espouse the Negro cause. Far more than the Eisenhower Administration, the Kennedy Administration enforced civil rights legislation. It intervened vigorously to suppress segregationist resistance to the decrees of federal courts in Alabama and Mississippi. In the summer of 1963 the rising tide of Negro protests spurred Kennedy into sending Congress the bill that eventually became the Civil Rights Act of 1964. But in taking these actions Kennedy, like Truman before him, began to be identified as a partisan President—a biased political ally of the civil rights groups. Increasingly, much of the public perceived him as a servant of Martin Luther King and Roy Wilkins, and in the months preceding his assassination surveys conducted by the American Institute of Public Opinion showed a sharp decline in Kennedy's national popularity. In such a political climate, even a Roosevelt would have had difficulties in getting his programs through Congress.

Lyndon B. Johnson came to the presidency with a background of over twenty years in Congress. His experience included six years as the Senate's Democratic Majority Leader, where he established a reputation as one of the ablest Senate politicians in modern history. By succeeding to the presidency at a moment of national shock over Kennedy's assassination, he obtained a strong momentum of popular support. His skilful leadership during the gray days of the winter of 1963–64 brought the nation to a high peak of unity, thus avoiding a period of acrimony and confusion which very easily could have been the result of the sensational events that occurred in Dallas. At the same time, Johnson developed national confidence in himself, and he ably cultivated a broad and diverse collection of interest groups during the "honeymoon" phase of his term.

President Johnson's political orientation and his international and domestic objectives are similar to Kennedy's; his legislative effectiveness seems markedly greater. Johnson was a "congressman's congressman," and he is a master of behind-the-scenes persuasion. Within its first year the Johnson Administration scored an impressive number of legislative successes: it won enactment of the landmark Civil Rights Act of 1964; with the Anti-Poverty Program it began the first step of a coordinated national effort to curb the human and economic plight of what Michael Harrington has called "the other America"; and it gained significant legislation aimed at such important problems as public housing, social security income, urban mass transportation, and wilderness conservation.

In international affairs, where the American President must contend with political forces largely beyond his control, Johnson's record is more mixed. NATO's woes are still serious; the Congo and Castro's Cuba continue to trouble American policy makers. Soviet-American relations, however, appear to be stabilizing, and there is a possibility that the test-ban treaty may be followed by new agreements intended to defuse the explosive tension between the two super powers. South Vietnam remains, as it was under Eisenhower and Kennedy, a mess. Almost any move (whether a decision to expand the war, maintain the same level of United States involvement, or negotiate for neutralization) is likely to be wrong from some point of view.

Vietnam, though, has tested Johnson's political aplomb under fire. The attack during the summer of 1964 on American destroyers in the Gulf of Tonkin by Communist North Vietnamese PT boats presented him with his major international crisis. Johnson's reaction, which was to order a potent but limited single air strike against the PT bases, was a masterful exercise in the use of power with restraint. He also put to good use a tactic developed by President Eisenhower during the Formosa and Lebanon crises of the 1950's, asking Congress for a resolution approving his action. The ensuing Southeast Asia Resolution that Congress speedily passed by an almost unanimous vote supported the President's determination "to take all necessary measures to repel any armed attack against the forces of the United States and to prevent further aggression."

With one stroke Johnson had demonstrated American firmness in Southeast Asia, partly blunted the criticisms of Administration vacillation made by the Goldwater Republicans, and obtained bipartisan support for a significant foreign affairs decision. Most important of all, the congressional resolution gave him a protective cover against domestic political criticism of any *future* military action he might take in that troubled part of the world. Johnson is not likely to repeat the political error of President Truman.

Although the judgment must be tentative, Lyndon Johnson gives indications of becoming one of the superb politician-Presidents of all time. His Southernness, combined with his Northern political support and his presidential commitment to civil rights, puts him in a unique position to interpret the North and South to each other. Like Kennedy, he too faces the distinct danger of being publicly labeled as the partisan of a special interest. So far, however, he has been able to avoid excessive identification with the civil rights groups. From a purely political point of view he has had one advantage not available to Kennedy: Johnson has had Negro riots—a sort of political equivalent to the lawless defiance of white Southern extremists—to denounce. The urban disorders of the summer of 1964 gave the President a natural opportunity to condemn Negro violence, thereby strengthening his public image of general independence from narrow group ties.

In personal terms Lyndon Johnson exudes a homey tone that for many Americans is appealing. His talk of a "Great Society" has elemental popular appeal, and his political touch seems deft. In two weeks during the spring of 1964, for example, Johnson subtly united persuasion, pressure, and public appeals in such a way as to get the railroad industry and the operating brotherhoods to settle a five-year-old dispute that threatened a major breakdown in the nation's transportation system. Within minutes of the final agreement between the negotiators the President was on national television announcing the settlement and reading a letter from "a little girl named Cathy May." Cathy May had feared that if the railroads stopped running her grandmother would be unable to come and see her first Holy Communion. But now, the President told the nation, "Cathy's grandmother can go to see her and all of my fellow Americans can be proud that the railroad management and the railroad brotherhoods came, labored, worked and reasoned together and in the American way found an answer." The language was pure corn, but it brilliantly communicated the country's dependence on its transportation system in a way that John Kennedy's elegant messages could never do. It was also shrewd politics in the best nonpartisan style.

Lyndon Johnson's great opportunity is to become an Eisenhower with political skill, or, to put it another way, a Roosevelt whose public image is nonpartisan. His public personality is good, his presidential prestige is high, and his main national appeal—like Eisenhower's—is that of a nonpartisan unifier, a consensus President. Unlike Eisenhower, he is political to his fingertips. So much is this the case that the most serious danger Johnson faces is that his skill and zest for political manipulation could be turned against him. This in fact was one of Goldwater's strategies during the 1964 presidential campaign, the attempt to brand Johnson as a political trickster who was nothing but an amoral tactician of power. The accusation, made in the context of the unsavory Bobby Baker affair, undoubtedly tarnished Johnson's presidential lustre. But Goldwater's own political image was so negative that a majority of the American people, with varying degrees of enthusiasm, preferred Johnson. Today, with the advantage of an endorsement as President in his own right by over forty-two million citizens, he enjoys an even stronger base from which to apply his political magic in making himself appear as a nonpartisan President of "all the people."

Johnson's performance since the November election victory demonstrates that he intends to play to the hilt his favorite role as a consensus leader. He is a Democrat who, according to the American Institute of Public Opinion, received 20 per cent of the normally Republican vote and 56 per cent of the Independent vote. He is for economy, yet favors an expansion of social welfare. He supports full integration of the American Negro into the Great Society, yet he continues to collaborate politically with segregationist politicians in the South. He is a friend to organized labor—his 1965 State of the Union message, for instance, proposed changes in the controversial section of the Taft-Hartley Act which permits state right-to-work laws—yet he enjoys the confidence of business.

The experience of past Presidents suggests that eventually Johnson will have to make unpleasant choices that may cost him some of his broad-based support. He is a master of the political balancing act, but, for an activist President, there are limits to the politics of harmony—and Johnson, on the basis of his record, not to mention his restless temperament, is clearly an activist President. Moreover, no President elected on a party ticket and dependent on the support of interest groups can wholly escape a partisan identity.

But the public will to have a nonpartisan President is very strong. As Elmer E. Cornwell, Jr., has observed in his important recent study of presidential leadership of public opinion, the mass media operate continually to cast him in that role, and "the more the public comes to see the President as the personification of the *nation*, irrespective of party, the less willing it is to accept the partisan side of his office." Obviously, at least in this era of American history, the task of a President is to fuse shrewd presidential politics with a nonpartisan public image. By temperament, by experience, by the circumstances of his first coming to the presidential office, and by the nature of the election that confirmed him there, President Johnson seems to be unusually alert both to the need and to the possibility of reconciling the two contradictory roles incorporated in his office.

State of the Union

Lyndon B. Johnson,

PRESIDENT, UNITED STATES OF AMERICA
DELIVERED TO THE 90TH CONGRESS OF THE
UNITED STATES, JANUARY 10, 1967

Mr. Speaker, Mr. Vice President, distinguished members of the Congress.

I share with all of you the grief that you feel at the death today of one of the most beloved and respected and effective members of this body, the distinguished Representative of Rhode Island, Mr. Fogarty.

I have come here tonight to report to you that this is a time of testing for our nation.

At home, the question is whether we will continue working for better opportunities for all Americans, when most Americans are already living better than any people in history.

Abroad, the question is whether we have the staying power to fight a very costly war, when the objective is limited and the danger to us is seemingly remote.

So, our test is not whether we shrink from our country's cause when the dangers to us are obvious and close at hand, but rather whether we carry

"State of the Union," *Vital Speeches of the Day*, Vol. XXXIII, No. 8, February 1, 1967. Reprinted by permission of the publisher.

on when they seem obscure and distant—and some think that it is safe to lay down our burdens.

I have come tonight to ask this Congress and this nation to resolve that issue: To meet our committments at home and abroad, to continue to build a better America, and to reaffirm this nation's allegiance to freedom.

As President Abraham Lincoln said, we must ask "where we are and whither we are tending."

The last three years bear witness to our determination to make this a better country.

We have struck down legal barriers to equality.

We have improved the education of seven million deprived children, and this year alone we have enabled almost one million students to go to college.

We have brought medical care to older people that were unable to afford it. Three and one-half million Americans have already received treatment under Medicare since July.

We have built a strong economy that has put almost three million more Americans on the payrolls in the last year alone. We have included more than nine million new workers under a higher minimum wage. We have launched new training programs to provide job skills for almost one million Americans.

We have helped more than a thousand local communities to attack poverty in the neighborhoods of the poor.

We have set out to rebuild our cities on a scale that's never been attempted before.

We have begun to rescue our waters from the menace of pollution and to restore the beauty of our land and our countryside, and our cities and our towns.

We have given one million young Americans a chance to earn through the Neighborhood Youth Corps, or through Head Start a chance to learn.

So, together, we have tried to meet the needs of our people and we have succeeded in creating a better life for the many as well as the few. And now we must answer whether our gains shall be the foundations of further progress, or whether they shall be only monuments to what might have been—abandoned now by people who lacked the will to see their great work through.

I believe that our people do not want to quit—though the task is great, the work hard, often frustrating, and success is a matter of days or months, or years—sometimes it may be even decades.

But I have come here tonight to discuss with you five ways of carrying forward the progress of these last three years. And these five ways concern programs and partnerships and priorities and prosperity and peace.

First, programs. We must see to it, I think, that these new programs that we have passed work effectively and are administered in the best possible way.

Three years ago we set out to create these new instruments of social progress. This required trial and error, and it has produced both. But as we learn through success and failure we are changing our strategy and we are trying to improve our tactics. In the long run, these starts, some rewarding, others inadequate and disappointing, are crucial to success. One example is the struggle to make life better for the less fortunate among us.

On a similar occasion, at this rostrum in 1949, I heard a great American President, Harry S. Truman, declare this: and I quote, "The American people have decided that poverty is just as wasteful and just as unnecessary as preventable disease." Unquote.

Many listened to President Truman that day here in this chamber but few understood what was required and did anything about it. The executive branch and the Congress waited 15 long years before ever taking any action on that challenge, as it did on many other challenges that great President presented.

And when three years ago you here in the Congress joined with me in a declaration of war on poverty, then I warned—and I quote: "It will not be a short or easy struggle. No single weapon will suffice. But we shall not rest until that war is won."

And I have come here to renew that pledge tonight.

I recommend that we intensify our effort to give the poor a chance to enjoy and to join in this nation's progress.

I shall propose certain administrative changes suggested by the Congress as well as some that we have learned from our own trial and error.

I shall urge special methods and special funds to reach the hundreds of thousands of Americans that are now trapped in the ghettos of our big cities, and through Head Start to try to reach out to our very young little children.

The chance to learn is their brightest hope and must command our full determination, for learning brings skills, and skills bring jobs, and jobs bring responsibility and dignity as well as taxes.

This war, like the war in Vietnam, is not a simple one. There is no single battle line which you can plot each day on a chart. The enemy is not easy to perceive or to isolate or to destroy. There are mistakes and there are setbacks, but we are moving, and our direction is forward.

This is true of other programs that are making and breaking new ground.

Some do not yet have the capacity to absorb well or wisely all the money that could be put into them. Administrative skills and trained manpower are just as vital to their success as dollars. And I believe those skills will come, but it will take time and patience and hard work.

Success cannot be forced at a single stroke. So, we must continue to strengthen the administration of every program if that success is to come, as we know that it must.

We have done much in the space of two short years, working together.

I have recommended and you, the Congress, have approved 10 different reorganization plans combining and consolidating many bureaus of this Government and creating two entirely new Cabinet departments.

And I have come tonight to propose that we establish a new department, a Department of Business and Labor.

By combining the Department of Commerce with the Department of Labor and other related agencies, I think that we can create a more economical, efficient and streamlined instrument that will better serve a growing nation.

This is our goal throughout the entire Federal Government. Every program will be thoroughly evaluated. Grant-in-aid programs will be improved and simplified as desired by many of our local administrators and our Governors.

Where there have been mistakes, we will try very hard to correct them.

Where there has been progress, we will try to build upon it.

Our second objective is partnership—to create an effective partnership at all levels of government. And I should treasure nothing more than to have that partnership again between the Executive and the Congress.

The 88th and 89th Congresses passed more social and economical legislation than any single two Congresses in American history. Most of you who were members of those Congresses voted to pass most of those measures. But your effort will come to nothing unless it reaches the people.

Federal energy is essential. But it is not enough. Only a total working partnership among Federal, state and local governments can succeed. The test of that partnership will be the concern of each public organization, each private institution and each responsible citizen.

Each state and county and city needs to examine its capacity for government in today's world, as we are examining ours in the executive department and as I see you are examining yours. Some will need to reorganize and reshape their methods of administration, as we are doing. Others will need to revise their constitutions and their laws to bring them up to date, as we are doing. Above all, I think we must work together and find ways in which the multitudes of small jurisdictions can be brought together more efficiently.

During the past three years we have returned to state and local governments about $40-billion in grants-in-aid. This year alone 70 per cent of our Federal expenditure for domestic programs will be distributed through the state and the local governments. With Federal assistance, state and local governments by 1970 will be spending close to $110-billion annually. These enormous sums must be used wisely, honestly and effectively.

We intend to work closely with the states and the localities to do exactly that.

Our third objective is priorities—to move ahead on the priorities that we have established within the resources that are available.

I wish, of course, that we could do all that should be done, and that we could do it now, but the nation has many commitments and responsibilities which make heavy demand upon our total resources. No Administration would more eagerly utilize for these programs all the resources they require than the Administration that started them.

So, let us resolve now to do all that we can with what we have, knowing that it is far, far more than we have ever done before, and far, far less than our problems will ultimately require.

Let us create new opportunities for our children and our young Americans who need special help.

We should strengthen the Head Start program, begin it for children 3 years old and maintain its educational momentum by following through in the early years.

We should try new methods of child development and care from the earliest years before it's too late to correct them. And I will propose these measures to the 90th Congress.

Let us ensure that older Americans, and neglected Americans, share in their nation's progress.

We should raise Social Security payments by an overall average of 20 per cent. That will add $4.1-billion to Social Security payments in the first year. I will recommend that each of the 23 million Americans now receiving payments get an increase of at least 15 per cent. I will ask that you raise the minimum payment by 59 per cent, from $44 to $70 a month, and to guarantee a minimum benefit of $100 a month for those with a total of 25 years of coverage.

We must raise the limit that retired workers can earn without losing Social Security income.

We must eliminate by law unjust discrimination in employment because of age.

We should embark upon a major effort to provide self-help assistance to the forgotten in our midst—the American Indians and the migratory farm workers.

And we should reach with the hand of understanding to help those who live in rural poverty. And I will propose these measures to the 90th Congress.

So let us keep on improving the quality of life and enlarging the meaning of justice for all of our fellow Americans. We should transform our decaying slums into places of decency through the landmark model cities program.

I intend to seek for this effort this year the full amount that you in Congress authorized last year.

We should call upon the genius of private industry and the most advanced technology to help rebuild our great cities.

We should vastly expand the fight for clean air with a total attack on pollution at its sources, and—because air, like water, does not respect manmade boundaries—we shall set up "regional airsheds" throughout this great land.

We should continue to carry to every corner of the nation our campaign for a beautiful America—to clean up our towns to make them more beautiful, our cities, our countryside by creating more parks and more seashores and more open spaces for our children to play in and for the generations that come after us to enjoy.

We should continue to seek equality and justice for each citizen before a jury, in seeking a job, in exercising his civil rights. We should find a solution to fair housing so that every American, regardless of color, has a decent home of his choice.

We should modernize our Selective Service system. The National Commission on Selective Service will shortly submit its report. I will send you new recommendations to meet our military manpower needs, but let us resolve that this is to be the Congress that made our draft laws as fair and as effective as possible.

We should protect what Justice Brandeis called the "right most valued by civilized men"—the right to privacy. We should outlaw all wiretapping, public and private, wherever and whenever it occurs except when the security of this nation itself is at stake—and only then with the strictest governmental safeguards. And we should exercise the full reach of our constitutional powers to outlaw electronic bugging and snooping.

I hope this Congress will try to help me do more for the consumer. We should demand that the cost of credit be clearly and honesty expressed so our average citizen can understand it.

We should immediately take steps to prevent massive power failures, to safeguard the home against hazardous household products and to assure safety in the pipelines that carry natural gas across our nation.

We should extend Medicare benefits that are now denied to 1,300,000 permanently and totally disabled Americans under 65 years of age.

We should improve the process of democracy by passing our election reform and financing proposals, by tightening our laws regulating lobbying, and by restoring a reasonable franchise to Americans who move their residences.

We should develop educational television into a vital public resource to enrich our homes, educate our families and to provide assistance in our classrooms. And we should insist that the public interest be fully served through the public's airways.

And I will propose these measures to the 90th Congress.

And now we come to a question that weighs very heavily on all of our minds, on yours and mine.

This nation must make an all-out effort to combat crime.

The 89th Congress gave us a new start in the attack on crime by passing the Law Enforcement Assistance Act that I recommended. We appointed the National Crime Commission to study crime in America and to recommend the best way to carry that attack forward.

And, while we do not have all the answers, on the basis of its preliminary recommendation we are ready to move.

This is not a war that Washington alone can win. The idea of a national police force is repugnant to the American people. Crime must be rooted out in local communities by local authorities, and our policemen must be better trained and must be better paid and must be better supported by the local citizens that they try to serve and to protect.

And the national Government can and expects to help.

So, I recommend to the 90th Congress the Safe Streets and Crime Control Act of 1967. It will enable us to assist those states and cities that try to make their streets and their homes safer and their police forces better and their correction systems more effective and their courts more efficient.

And when the Congress approves, the Federal Government will be able to provide a substantial percentage of the cost:

90 per cent of the cost for developing the state and local plan—master plan—to combat crime in their area.

60 per cent of the cost of training new tactical units and developing instant communications and special alarm systems, and introducing the latest equipment and techniques so that they can become weapons in the war on crime.

And 50 per cent of the cost of building crime laboratories and police academy-type centers so that our citizens can be protected by the best-trained and served by the best-equipped police to be found anywhere.

We will also recommend new methods to prevent juvenile delinquents from becoming adult delinquents. And we'll seek new partnerships with states and cities in order to deal with this hideous narcotics problem. And we'll recommend strict control on the sale of firearms.

At the heart of this attack on crime must be the conviction that a free American—as Abraham Lincoln once said—must, and I quote, "let reverence for the laws become the political religion of nation," unquote.

Our country's laws must be respected. Order must be maintained and I will support with all the constitutional powers the President possesses our nation's law enforcement officials in their attempt to control the crime and the violence that tear the fabric of our communities.

Many of these priority proposals will be built on foundations that have already been laid. Some will necessarily be small at first but every beginning is a consequence. And if we postpone this urgent work now, it will simply have to be done later and later we'll pay a much higher price.

Our fourth objective is prosperity, to keep our economy moving ahead, moving ahead steadily and safely.

We have now enjoyed six years of unprecedented and rewarding prosperity.

Last year, 1966:

Wages were the highest in history, and the unemployment rate, announced yesterday, reached the lowest point in 13 years.

The total after-tax income of the American families after taxes rose nearly 5 per cent.

The corporate profits after taxes rose a little more than 5 per cent.

Our gross national product advanced 5½ per cent to about $740-billion.

Income per farm went up 6 per cent.

Now we have been greatly concerned because consumer prices rose 4½ per cent over the 18 months since we decided to send troops to Vietnam. This was more than we had expected, and the Government tried to do everything that we knew how to do to hold it down. Yet, we were not as successful as we wished to be.

In the 18 months after we entered World War II, prices rose not 4½ per cent, but 13½ per cent. In the first 18 months after Korea—conflict broke out there—prices rose not 4½ per cent, but 11 per cent.

Now during those two periods we had O.P.A. price controls that the Congress gave us, War Labor Board and wage controls. Since Vietnam we have not asked for those controls and we have tried to avoid imposing them. We believe that we have done better, but we make no pretense of having been successful or done as well as we wished.

Our greatest disappointment in the economy during 1966 was the excessive rise in interest rates and the tightening of credit. They imposed very severe and very unfair burdens on our home buyers and on our home builders and all those associated with the home industry.

Last January and again last September I recommended fiscal and moderate tax measures to try to restrain the unbalanced pace of economic expansion. Legislatively and administratively we took several billions out of the economy and with these measures, in both instances, the Congress approved most of the recommendations rather promptly.

As 1966 ended, price stability was seemingly being restored. Wholesale prices are lower tonight than they were in August. So are retail food prices.

Monetary conditions are also easing. Most interest rates have retreated from their earlier peaks. More money now seems to be available, and, given the cooperation of the Federal Reserve System, which I so earnestly seek, I'm confident that this movement can continue, and I pledge to the American people that I will do everything in the President's power to lower interest rates and to ease money in this country.

The Federal Home Loan Bank Board tomorrow morning will announce that it will make immediately available to savings and loans associations an additional $1-billion and will lower from 6 per cent to 5¾ per cent the interest rate charged on those loans.

We shall continue on a sensible course of fiscal and budgetary policy that we believe will keep our economy growing without new inflationary spirals; that will finance responsibly the needs of our men in Vietnam and the progress of our people at home; that will support a significant movement in our export surplus, and will press forward toward easier credit and toward lower interest rates.

I recommend to the Congress a surcharge of 6 per cent on both corporate and individual income taxes to last for two years or for so long as the unusual expenditures associated with our efforts in Vietnam continue. I will promptly recommend an earlier termination date if a reduction in these expenditures permit it. This surcharge will raise revenues by some $4.5-billion in the first year.

For example, a person whose income tax, whose tax payment, the tax he owes, is $1,000—he will pay under this proposal an extra $60 over the 12-month period, or $5 a month. The overwhelming majority of Americans who pay taxes today are below that figure and they will pay substantially less than $5 a month. Married couples with two children, with incomes up to $5,000 per year, will be exempt from this tax—as will single people with an income of up to $1,900 a year.

Now, if the Americans today still paid the income and excise tax rates in effect when I came into the Presidency in the year 1964, their annual taxes would have been over $20-billion more than at present tax rates. So, this proposal is that while—while we have this problem and this emergency in Vietnam, while we're trying to meet the needs of our people at home, your government asks for slightly more than one-fourth of that tax cut each year in order to try to hold our budget deficit in fiscal 1968 within prudent limits and to give our country and to give our fighting men the help they need in this hour of trial.

For fiscal 1967 we estimate the budget expenditures to be $126.7-billion —126.7—and revenues of $117-billion. That will leave us a deficit this year of $9.7-billion.

For fiscal 1968 we estimate the budget expenditures of $135-billion and, with the tax measures recommended and a continuing strong economy, we estimate revenues will be $126.9-billion. The deficit then will be $8.1-billion.

I will very soon forward all of my recommendations to the Congress. Yours is the responsibility to discuss and to debate, to approve or modify or reject. I welcome your views as I have welcomed working with you 30 years as a colleague and as Vice President and President.

I should like to say to the members of the opposition, whose numbers, if I am not mistaken, seem to have increased somewhat, that the genius of the American political system has always been best expressed through creative debate that offers choices and reasonable alternatives.

Throughout our history, great Republicans and Democrats have seemed to understand this. So let there be light and reason in our relations. That is the way to a responsible session and a responsible government.

Let us be remembered as a President and a Congress who tried to improve the quality of life for every American—not just the rich, not just the poor but every man, woman and child in this great nation of ours.

We all go to school—to good schools or bad schools. We all take air into our lungs—clean air or polluted air. We all drink water—pure water or polluted water. We all face sickness some day, some more often than we wish, and old age as well. We all have a stake in this Great Society, in its economic growth, in reduction of civil strife—a great stake in good government.

And we just must not arrest the pace of progress we've established in this country in these years. So our children's children will pay the price if we are not wise enough, and courageous enough, and determined enough to stand up and meet the nation's needs as well as we can in the time allotted us.

Abroad, as at home, there is also a risk in change. But abroad, as at home, there is a greater risk in standing still. No part of our foreign policy is so sacred that it ever remains beyond review. We shall be flexible where conditions in the world change, and where man's efforts can change them for the better.

We are in the midst of a great transition, a transition from narrow nationalism to international partnership; from the harsh spirit of the cold war to the hopeful spirit of common humanity on a troubled and a threatened planet.

In Latin America, the American chiefs of state will be meeting very shortly to give our hemispheric policies new direction.

We've come a long way in this hemisphere since the inter-American effort in economic and social development was launched with the conference at Bogota in 1960 under the leadership of President Eisenhower. The Alliance for Progress moved dramatically forward under President Kennedy.

There is new confidence that the voice of the people is being heard, that the dignity of the individual is stronger than ever in this hemisphere. And we're facing up to and meeting the meaning of the hemisphere problem together—in this hemisphere that reform under democracy can be made to happen because it has happened.

So, together, I think, we must now move to strike down the barriers to full coopration among the American nations, to free the energies and the resources of two great continents on behalf of all of our citizens.

Africa stands at an earlier stage of development than Latin America. It has yet to develop the transportation and communications and agriculture and, above all, the trained men and women without which growth is impossible. There, too, the job will best be done if the nations and the people of Africa cooperate on a regional basis.

More and more our programs for Africa are going to be directed toward self-help.

The future of Africa is shadowed by unsolved racial conflicts. Our policy will continue to reflect our basic commitments as a people to support those that are prepared to work toward cooperation and harmony between races, to help those who demand change but reject the fool's gold of violence.

In the Middle East the spirit of goodwill toward all unfortunately has not yet taken hold. An already tortured peace seems to be constantly threatened. We shall try to use our influence to increase the possibilities of improved relations among the nations of that region, and we are working hard at that task.

In the great subcontinent of South Asia live more than a sixth of the earth's population. Over the years we and others have invested very heavily in capital and food for the economic development of India and Pakistan.

We are not prepared to see our assistance wasted, however, in conflict. It must strengthen their capacity to help themselves. It must help these two nations, who are both our friends, to overcome poverty and to emerge as self-reliant leaders and find terms for reconciliation and cooperation.

In Western Europe we shall maintain in NATO an integrated common defense. But we also look forward to the time when greater security can be achieved through measures of arms control and disarmament and through other forms of practical agreement.

We are shaping a new future of enlarged partnership in nuclear affairs, in economic and technical cooperation, in trade negotiations, in political consultation, and in working together with the governments and peoples of Eastern Europe and the Soviet Union.

The emerging spirit of confidence is precisely what we hoped to achieve when we went to work a generation ago to put our shoulder to the wheel and try to help rebuild Europe. We faced new challenges and opportunities then and there, and we faced, also, some dangers. But I believe that the peoples on both sides of the Atlantic, as well as both sides of this chamber, wanted to face them together.

Our relations with the Soviet Union, Eastern Europe are also in transition. We have avoided both the acts and the rhetoric of the cold war. When we have differed with the Soviet Union, or other nations for that matter, I tried to differ quietly and with courtesy and without venom. Our objective is not to continue the cold war, but to end it.

We have signed an agreement at the United Nations on the peaceful uses of outer space.

We have agreed to open direct air flights with the Soviet Union.

We have removed more than 400 nonstrategic items from export control.

—determine that the Export-Import Bank can allow commercial credits to Poland and Hungary and Bulgaria and Czechoslovakia as well as to Rumania and Yugoslavia.

We have entered into a cultural agreement with the Soviet Union for another two years.

We have agreed with Bulgaria and Hungary to upgrade our legations to embassies.

We have started discussions with international agencies on ways of increasing contacts with Eastern European countries.

This administration has taken these steps even as duty compelled us to fulfill and execute alliances and treaty obligations throughout the world that were entered into before I became President.

So, tonight I now ask and urge this Congress to help our foreign and our commercial trade policies by passing an East-West trade bill and by approving our consular convention with the Soviet Union.

The Soviet Union has in the past year increased its long-range missile capabilities. It has begun to place near Moscow a limited antimissile defense. My first responsibility to our people is to assure that no nation can ever find it rational to launch a nuclear attack or to use its nuclear power as a credible threat against us or against our allies.

And I would emphasize that that is why an important link between Russia and the United States is in our common interest in arms control and in disarmament. We have the solemn duty to slow down the arms race between us, if that is at all possible, in both conventional and nuclear weapons and defenses. And I thought we were making some progress in that direction the first few months I was in office. And I realized that any additional race would impose on our peoples, and on all mankind, for that matter, an additional waste of resources with no gain in security to either side.

And I expect in the days ahead to closely consult and seek the advice of the Congress about the possibilities of international agreements bearing directly upon this problem.

Next to the pursuit of peace, the really greatest challenge to the human family is the race between food supply and population increase. That race tonight is being lost. The time for rhetoric has clearly passed. The time for concerted action is here, and we must get on with the job.

We believe that three principles must prevail if our policy is to succeed:

First, the developing nations must give high priority to food production, including the use of technology and the capital of private enterprise.

Second, nations with food deficits must put more of their resources into voluntary family planning programs.

Third, the developed nations must all assist other nations to avoid starvation in the short run and to move rapidly towards the ability to feed themselves.

Every member of the world community now bears a direct responsibility to help bring our most basic human account into balance.

I come now finally to Southeast Asia, and to Vietnam in particular. Soon I will submit to the Congress a detailed report on that situation. Tonight I want to just review the essential points as briefly as I can.

We are in Vietnam because the United States of America and our allies are committed by the SEATO Treaty to "act to meet the common danger of aggression in Southeast Asia."

We are in Vietnam because an international agreement signed by the United States, North Vietnam and others in 1962 is being systematically violated by the Communists.

That violation threatens the independence of all the small nations in Southeast Asia and threatens the peace of the entire region and, perhaps, the world.

We are there because the people of South Vietnam have as much right to remain non-Communist, if that is what they choose, as North Vietnam has to remain Communist.

We are there because the Congress has pledged by solemn vote to take all necessary measures to prevent further aggression. No better words could describe our present course than those once spoken by the great Thomas Jefferson.

"It is the melancholy law of human societies to be compelled sometimes to choose a great evil in order to ward off a greater evil."

We have chosen to fight a limited war, in Vietnam in an attempt to prevent a larger war—a war that's almost certain to follow, I believe, if the Communists succeeded in over-running and taking over South Vietnam by aggression and by force. I believe, and I am supported by some authority, that if they are not checked now the world can expect to pay a greater price to check them later. That's what our statesmen said when they debated this treaty, and that's why it was ratified 82 to 1 by the Senate many years ago.

You will remember that we stood in Western Europe 20 years ago. Is there anyone in this chamber tonight who doubts that the course of freedom was not changed for the better because of the courage of that stand?

Sixteen years ago we and others stopped another kind of aggression. This time it was in Korea. And imagine how different Asia might be today if we had failed to act when the Communist army of North Korea marched south. The Asia of tomorrow will be far different because we have said in Vietnam as we said 16 years ago in Korea—"this far, and no further."

I think I tell you I reveal no secret when I tell you that we are dealing with a stubborn adversary that's committed to the use of force and terror to settle political questions.

I wish I could report to you that the conflict is almost over. This I cannot do. We face more cost, more loss and more agony. For the end is not yet.

I cannot promise you that it will come this year or come next year. Our adversary still believes, I think tonight, that he can go on fighting longer than we can and longer than we and our allies will be prepared to stand up and resist.

Our men in that area—there are nearly 500,000 now—have borne well the burden and the heat of the day. Their efforts have deprived the Communist enemy of the victory that he sought and that he expected a year ago. We have steadily frustrated his main forces.

General Westmoreland reports that the enemy can no longer succeed on the battlefield.

I must say to you that our pressure must be sustained, and will be sustained, until he realizes the war he started is costing him more than he can ever gain.

I know of no strategy more likely to attain that end than the strategy of accumulating slowly but inexorably every kind of material resource, of laboriously teaching troops the very elements of their trade. That, and patience I mean a great deal of patience.

Our South Vietnamese allies are also being tested tonight because they must provide real security to the people that are living in the countryside. And this means reducing the terrorism and the armed attacks which kidnaped and killed 26,900 civilians in the last 32 months to levels where they can be successfully controlled by the regular South Vietnamese security forces.

It means bringing to the villagers an effective civilian government that they can respect and that they can rely upon and that they can participate in and that they can have a personal stake in their government.

We hope that government is now beginning to emerge.

While I cannot report the desired progress in the pacification effort, the very distinguished and able Ambassador Henry Cabot Lodge reports that South Vietnam is turning to this task with a new sense of urgency. And we can help, but only they can win this part of the war. Their task is to build and protect a new life in each rural province.

One result of our stand in Vietnam is already clear.

It is this: The peoples of Asia now know that the door to independence is not going to be slammed shut. They know that it is possible for them to choose their own national destinies—without coercion.

The performance of our men in Vietnam, backed by the American people, has created a feeling of confidence and unity among the independent nations of Asia and the Pacific. I saw it in their faces in the 19 days that I spent in their homes and in their countries. Fear of external Communist conquest in many Asian nations is already subsiding, and with this the spirit of hope is rising. For the first time in history, a common outlook and common institutions are already emerging.

This forward movement is rooted in the ambitions and the interests of Asian nations themselves. It was precisely this movement that we hoped to accelerate when I spoke at Johns Hopkins in Baltimore in April 1965, and I pledged "a much more massive effort to improve the life of man" in that part of the world in the hope that we could take some of the funds that we were spending on bullets and bombs and spend on schools and production.

Twenty months later our efforts have produced a new reality. The doors of the billion-dollar Asian Bank that I recommended to the Congress and you endorsed almost unanimously, I am proud to tell you, are already open.

Asians are engaged tonight in regional efforts in a dozen new directions; their hopes are high; their faith is strong; their confidence is deep.

And even as the war continues, we shall play our part in carrying forward this constructive historic development. As recommended by the Eugene Black mission, and if other nations will join us, I will seek a special authorization from the Congress of $200-million for east Asian regional programs.

Because we're eager to turn our resources to peace, our efforts in behalf of humanity, I think, need not be restricted by any parallel or by any boundary line. The moment that peace comes—as I pledged in Baltimore —I will ask the Congress for funds to join in an international program of reconstruction and development for all the people of Vietnam and their deserving neighbors who wish our help.

We shall continue to hope for a reconciliation between the people of mainland China and the world community—including working together in all the tasks of arms control, and security, and progress on which the fate of the Chinese people, like their fellow men elsewhere, depends.

We would be the first to welcome a China which decided to respect her neighbor's rights. We would be the first to applaud her were she to apply her great energies and intelligence to improving the welfare of her people. And we have no intention of trying to deny her her legitimate needs for security and friendly relations with her neighboring countries.

Our hope that all of this will someday happen rests on the conviction that we, the American people and our allies, will and are going to see Vietnam through to an honorable peace.

We will support all appropriate initiatives by the United Nations and others which can bring the several parties together for unconditional discussion of peace, anywhere, any time. And we will continue to take every possible initiative ourselves to constantly probe for peace.

And until such efforts succeed, or until the infiltration ceases, or until the conflict subsides, I think the course of wisdom for this country is that we just must firmly pursue our present course. We will stand firm in Vietnam.

I think you know that our fighting men there tonight bear the heaviest burden of all. With their lives they serve this nation, and we must give them nothing less than our full support—and we have given them that— nothing less than the determination that Americans have always given their fighting men. Whatever our sacrifice here, even if it's more than $5 a month, it's small compared to their own.

How long it will take, I cannot prophesy. I only know that the will— the will of the American people, I think—is tonight being tested.

Whether we can fight a war of limited objectives over a period of time and keep alive the hope of independence and stability for people other than ourselves; whether we can continue to act with restraint when the temptation to get it over with is inviting, but dangerous; whether we can accept the necessity of choosing a great evil in order to ward off a greater one.

Whether we can do these without arousing the hatreds and the passions that are ordinarily loosed in time of war—on all these questions, so much turns.

The answers will determine not only where we are, but "whither we are tending."

A time of testing—yes. And a time of transition. The transition is sometimes slow; sometimes unpopular; almost always very painful—and often quite dangerous.

But we have lived with danger for a long time before, and we shall live with it for a long time yet to come. We know that "man is born unto trouble." We also know that this nation was not forged and did not survive and grow and prosper without a great deal of sacrifice from a great many men.

And for all the disorders that we must deal with, and all the frustrations that concern us, and all the anxieties that we are called upon to resolve, for all the issues we must face with the agony that attends them, let us remember that those who expect to reap the blessings of freedom, must, like men, undergo fatigues of supporting it.

But let us also count not only our burdens but our blessings—for they are many.

And let us give thanks to the One who governs us all.

Let us draw encouragement from the signs of hope, for they, too, are many.

Let us remember that we've been tested before, and America has never been found wanting.

So, with your understanding, and with both your confidence and your support, we are going to persist and we are going to succeed.

The Dangerous World of Walt Rostow

J. Robert Moskin

"I've never had a man in whom I have more confidence than Walt," the President of the United States said. He sat tall in his rocker and fingered his glasses: "He's one of the finest counselors I've ever had around me."

Lyndon Johnson was talking about the problems of Presidential decision-making: "Nearly everything that comes in here is 50–50—and just as dangerous as hell. If it is 60–40, Rusk or McNamara has already decided it."

He got out of his chair, crossed the big, white, sunny office, and from his desk, picked up a single sheet of paper. He read aloud the top line: "Bombing of the Port of Haiphong." He went down a numbered list of reasons for bombing the North Vietnamese port and an equally long list against. He dropped the paper on the top of his desk. This, he said, is the kind of problem he has to decide.

The man who prepared that paper—and many others on which the President bases his decisions—is Walt Whitman Rostow, special assistant to the President for national security affairs and his most intimate adviser on foreign policy. Walt Rostow, although totally unknown to millions of Americans, is a highly important and controversial man.

This chunky 51-year-old ex-professor of economic history, whom the President lauds and listens to, has a key voice in American foreign policy. Frequently, the President is on the phone to him for 20 minutes, talking out ideas, listening to his advice. Johnson often writes "See me" on a Rostow memo, and they chew over the problem face-to-face. Rostow hears more of the President's views than any Cabinet officer. He is one of the four regulars—along with Secretary of State Dean Rusk and Secretary of Defense Robert S. McNamara—at the President's decision-making Tuesday lunch. There, the question repeatedly comes: "What do you think, Walt?" And Rostow usually knows precisely what he thinks: he has a thought-out vision of the world and America's place in it. U.S. foreign policy parallels that vision surprisingly.

Rostow is universally accepted as one of the architects of our Vietnam policy. His critics—and he has many—call him the top "hawk" in the White House. Some accuse him of running a "filtration system" that screens from Johnson opinions about the war that conflict with Rostow's. Others hold him primarily responsible for our bombing of North Vietnam and claim he is a crusader for "pain bombing," to exact a price in devastation and casualties. One former associate of both the Kennedy and Johnson administrations charges that without Rostow in the White House, the bombing would stop. He calls Rostow "the most dangerous man in America."

But his biggest fan is LBJ, who says, "His detractors raise him in my estimation every day." Johnson adds, "I have more confidence in his character, in his diligence. If somebody has to pick up a bucket, he goes to get it. He's just a hell of a good man. I'm glad I got him. When called upon, he's a man of conviction who doesn't try to play President."

After the Tuesday lunch, Rostow dashes back to his office, a onetime coal bin in the White House basement. He grabs cables red-flagged for action, throws his jacket over a chair, summons his long-serving secretary, Lois Nivens, and Bromley K. Smith, the extraordinary civil servant who is executive secretary of the National Security Council, and fires off directives and telephone calls. He ends a call with: "It will be done," hits the phone button with the eraser on a yellow pencil and picks up the next call without time for a "Good-bye." When the paroxysm is over, he sits back and lifts his bifocals high on his head. His light-gray eyes smile easily as he explains, "I've just debriefed 'the Town.' We transmit out to the Town the President's decisions. They count on me to let them know the President's view as well as tell him their view." The Town—official Washington—knows this is the President's man, reporting precisely what The Man wants done.

Rostow's job, he says, is to "live with problems filled with razor blades." He forces the pace throughout the Government. He sucks in information the President, imprisoned in the White House, needs for his decisions. He's a man whose word the President feels he can trust precisely.

Precision is a battle Rostow fights every day. When he moved to the White House in April, 1966, from the chairmanship of the State Department's Policy Planning Council, a lot of people around Washington figured LBJ wouldn't long have the patience for his full, professorial reports. Replacing McGeorge Bundy, now president of the Ford Foundation, he followed a sharp, snapping-turtle mind into the White House slot.

Rostow has learned to produce the concise memos LBJ likes. The President says: "This man states it out for you as you want to hear it, and to give you both sides of it. And then you ask him his judgment, and he'll give it to you without trying to market or sell it."

Precision is more than brevity. Rostow must make sure the President knows precisely: a) what the issue is that he will have to consider; b) what everyone's views are about it, and c) what are the President's choices for decision and action. Says Rusk, "Bob McNamara and I can't go running over there every ten minutes of the day with papers in our hand." And he adds of Rostow's job, "He helps frame the questions and clarify the issues that need determination." *When* an issue is brought to the President and *how* it is framed can be vital.

"They scream about a Little State Department here. We would be one man and a motorcycle if they did their job," says one White House official. Rostow must dish up not only the bureaucracy's recommendations but "crank in" the President's own political interests and give him *all* the options. Under Secretary of State Nicholas deB. Katzenbach, chairman of the new Senior Interdepartmental Group, says, "Part of the job Walt is doing ought to be done here. I'd like to do him out of a hunk of his job, and I think my strongest supporter would be Walt."

The need for precision gets even more urgent when the man in Rostow's position has his own strong views. And Rostow does. He has unending opportunities to flesh out his arguments in person with the President. As Bundy says, "The guy who carries that kind of traffic is either good enough so you want his advice or he's not good enough to carry the traffic." In this post, Bundy knows, "You don's screen out the views of people with responsibility. It gets more complicated when you volunteer information to the President. You get awfully steamed up about a problem, and it seems more important to be right than fair. Nobody's perfect at that. Nobody."

Rostow is acutely aware that his usefulness would be finished if key men felt that he was too often getting between them and the President. Some do, of course, but with Secretary Rusk, for one example, Rostow has designed a smooth way of working. He always shoots over to Rusk a copy of any memo he sends up to the President giving his views about a State Department report. "I have to put a personal recommendation on it," Rostow says. But, "There's no paper I send up to the President that I wouldn't have my colleagues in the Cabinet see."

Rusk and Rostow have been in this business together for nearly seven years. When they both came to Washington in 1961, Rostow was earmarked to go to the State Department as head of policy planning, but Rusk chose George C. McGhee. Rostow caught on as Bundy's deputy in the White House, with special responsibility for Southeast Asia.

Recently, Rostow's name made headlines when a dismissed State Department security officer was reported as blaming his discharge on his refusal to clear Rostow at the beginning of JFK's term without a field investigation. Bundy says, "I read that file in 1961, and there was nothing in it that raised any question at all about Walt's loyalty, security or other qualifications." He says he accepted Rostow with "three cheers."

Kennedy continued to think of Rostow as a brain. In "The Great Shake-up of November 1961," when Chester Bowles was moved out as Under Secretary of State, McGhee moved up, and Rostow landed in the policy-planning job he had missed first time around. He stayed there until Johnson, reportedly turning aside men like Bill Moyers or Robert Komer, either of whom the press might call a second Secretary of State, brought Rostow back.

At that time, insiders recall, Rusk's initial wariness had worn off, and he strongly recommended Rostow for the White House assignment. Rusk says, "It was not unfamiliar country to him. He was already entirely familiar with the flow of foreign policy business." Says Rostow of Rusk, "After we'd been in a lot of foxholes together, we became good friends."

Last June, during the Middle East war, Bundy was brought back to head a special committee in the White House and manage the continuing crisis through Rostow. There were many reasons for the special committee. Most important, Rostow had the war in Vietnam and a dozen other problems to follow; he couldn't pile this one on too. In addition, the President needed a center for quick reactions. Says Rusk, "It was important to have a top full-time man on this crisis." In some minds, there was also the realization that the President's representative in the U.N., Arthur J. Goldberg, White House foreign policy adviser Walt Rostow and his brother, Under Secretary of State for Political Affairs Eugene V. Rostow, in charge of the Interdepartmental Control Group on the crisis, are all Jews. And finally, some people wanted to prevent pro-Arab officials in the State Department from getting control of the problem. In all, as Bundy recalls, "The President had a very hot potato there—one more hot potato than the system needed."

The roots of the LBJ-Rostow relationship go back to 1961, when they both made trips to Vietnam for Kennedy—Johnson in May and Rostow in October as deputy to Gen. Maxwell D. Taylor. Even before going, Rostow advocated that we use counterforce in Vietnam.

His trip fortified Rostow's conviction. He concurred in Taylor's report, which said: "the time may come . . . when we must declare our intention to attack the source of guerrilla aggression in North Vietnam and impose on the Hanoi Government a price for participating in the current war which is commensurate with the damage being inflicted on its neighbors to the South."

Ever since, and especially after North Vietnam violated the 1962 agreements on Laos, Rostow has favored imposing a price on the North. His faith in systematic bombing goes back to World War II, when he joined the OSS and worked in London and France as secretary of the U.S.-British "Jockey Committee," which was charged with planning the bomber targeting of oil supplies, factories, bridges and rail lines.

General Taylor's 1961 recommendations to put more American troops on the ground in Vietnam and to counter-attack the North became U.S. policy. It has led to a land war on the mainland of Asia. Rostow still strongly supports the policy he helped design.

This conviction is based on Rostow's special vision of the world. Although no one can separate out how much his thought has influenced other men's minds directly, it supplies the understructure on which are raised the President's policies.

Rostow has been constructing his view of the world all his thinking life. His father, who came to New York from Russia in 1905 to study metallurgical chemistry, was an anti-Communist Socialist. At home in Irvington, N.J., and New Haven, Conn., the three Rostow boys were taught to be concerned with social problems and seek non-Communist answers. These same leanings led their parents, who had met at a Socialist Sunday school in Brooklyn, to name their Flatbush-born middle son after the American poet. His older brother, who became dean of the Yale Law School and is now No. 3 man in the State Department, was named after labor leader Eugene V. Debs, and his younger brother, now in business in Ann Arbor, Mich., was named after philosopher Ralph Waldo Emerson. Says Eugene Rostow, "It was a very talkative family, a very good family to grow up in."

At the age of 17, Walt Rostow vowed to find an answer to Marxism. As a Phi Beta Kappa scholarship student in Yale's class of 1936—and later as a Rhodes Scholar at Oxford—he remembers: "I read Marx and said these are great questions and bad answers. I said I would do better. I waited 24 years and finally did it, and it is better." In an influential little book called *The Stages of Economic Growth,* he worked out a non-Communist explanation of how underdeveloped nations come to "economic maturity." Communism, he decided, is "a disease of the transition to modernization," and Communists are "scavengers of the modernization process."

He says, "I start by assuming this is an incredibly dangerous time, and crises will be endemic. Any damn fool can see this is an extraordinarily dangerous period of history."

He sees the United States standing "in mortal peril"—a comfortable, democratic island in a world where the strength of Eurasia exceeds ours. The turbulence in the world, he warns, threatens our ability to survive as a free and open society. A totalitarian, Communist world would force us into a "fortress mentality." He has written, "the American interest demands, in a sense, that Americans be crusaders. . . ."

The greatest threat, he says, would be realized if a hostile power or group of powers were able to dominate either Europe or Asia. He has long made the recently emphasized argument that our national interest is at stake in Vietnam. "I don't think the nation would sit by and see all of Asia pass to Communist control. This is a prediction," he says. "If we pulled out of Vietnam and saw the dominance of Asia by a single power, we would react and probably have a bigger war.

"There are people in the country, and always have been—notably when your commitments are put to the test—who turn out to be isolationists in the sense that they believe at least they would rather face the consequences of the loss of Asia or Europe than fight a war. My judgment about my country is it would not actually accept the full consequences of our pulling out of Vietnam and letting Asia go."

He calls the war in Vietnam a Chinese-inspired War of Liberation, "an important test of . . . Mao's method." He says, "The problem of Communist China is its actively encouraging other groups to engage in aggression: and it itself has overt expansionist ambitions. The whole shape of Asia is involved. Asians know this." In his eyes, our essential conflict is with an expansive Chinese communism.

He denies that he is preaching an anti-Communist crusade: "We haven't used ideological convictions as reason for war. We are concerned with the attempt to extend power across international frontiers." He insists the war in Vietnam is the result of such an attempt: "The whole thing from the beginning was completely managed from the North. The general staff is in the North. This is a thoroughly organized aggression from the North. A mass of intelligence and captured documents makes this judgment sure."

He even suggests that the Communist leaders in Hanoi should welcome the American presence in South Vietnam as a counterforce to Communist China: "I have no doubt the men in Hanoi cherish their independence. I do not regard them in any simple way as puppets. On the other hand, if we left the Asian mainland, they would themselves be hard put to maintain their independence. . . . What made Tito possible? There was very close to him American power in Europe."

His opponents, including some important Democrats, regard Rostow as both arrogant and wrong. They argue that war pressures are forcing North Vietnam to become increasingly dependent on Communist China, that

China is not expansive and that the Communist powers are too splintered to overrun Asia.

Rostow is convinced we can win the war in the South by reducing the percentage of the population under Vietcong control. He says it is already down from 40 per cent to "well under 30." At the present rate of decline, it would reach 20 per cent by March, but, he adds, "No one can tell where the break-over point is." At some stage, he expects, the enemy will not control enough people to support their soldiers in the South.

He has a reputation as an incurable optimist, and he does hold out great hope. He believes we are at a watershed where men can shape history. If we keep South Vietnam free from Communist domination, he predicts, "the struggle in Vietnam might be the last great confrontation of the post-war era. You can expect a lot of trouble, but if the Wars of Liberation fail where [they] had the maximum opportunity, it's not going to be very attractive to start elsewhere."

He is completely convinced we must stay and fight. "The bombing in the North is having an important attritional effect. They're under tremendous manpower strain. Their casualties are going up at a rate they cannot sustain," he says. "I honestly believe we are on a rising curve. I see light at the end of the tunnel. I can't tell when." He says the North can no longer hope to win on the battlefield; it hopes to win here in the U.S.: "The war now is about the United States. It's not about Vietnam any longer from their point of view."

Although "doves" would not agree with Rostow's thesis, he doesn't like to be labeled a "hawk." He explains: "We cannot deal with the world effectively unless we are prepared to acknowledge the reality of force. My view of force is that there are tragic occasions when it is the best alternative available." He says he spends more time on the problems of the economic development of Vietnam than on the uses of force there. "If 'dove' means using your imagination to find ways the war might be brought to an end in an honorable way without force, then I'm a dove." But faced with force, "then you damn well use force."

In facing the fact of force in the world, Rostow also insists we cannot regard nuclear war as unthinkable. "Nuclear deterrence is not just a matter of hardware but of will," he says. "The essence of deterrence is that the other side will not act because of fear that the act will lead to nuclear engagement. To make that conviction credible is the hardest task ever laid on a human being. From the crises I've seen—Cuba in 1962 and Berlin—the only way that conviction can be conveyed is if the President of the United States is prepared to contemplate nuclear war, if in fact the President has stared down this route."

Talking of the dangers he sees and today's younger generation, he says thoughtfully, "They may think of it as seeing Hitlers or Stalins under every bed. I only hope they perceive that the task is a long task. We certainly, in our time, are not going to achieve, totally, world order. That will remain central to our agenda and theirs."

Rostow's world is studded with crises, but it hasn't always been that way. He started out as an academician and is one of the few Americans to be a professor of both Cambridge and Oxford. He once played semipro baseball in New Haven and now hits an intense game of tennis at 7:30

every other morning before going to the White House. On "no tennis" days, he is in his office by 7:25. He played clarinet and piano in a high school band and still writes music for popular songs. He proudly lays claim to the only song ever written on Air Force One—with words by James Symington, U.S. chief of protocol.

In 1937, he received a fellowship to a summer school in Geneva and met Elspeth Davies, a student leader from Barnard College. They bicycled a lot that summer and after the war were married. In addition to rearing Ann, 12, and Peter, 15, she teaches full-time at American University, and occasionally at the Foreign Service Institute and the National War College.

Of their life in Washington, Rostow says, "We try to do our job and keep out of debt, and it's a hard thing." On his wife's checkbook is pasted a gentle reminder: "You don't have to work for the Federal Government." President Johnson expresses a special regard for Elspeth Rostow, calling her "a stimulating, very intelligent, very wise woman."

After World War II, Rostow worked as an economist in the State Department and then for Gunnar Myrdal in Geneva. He evolved a strong faith in regionalism to stimulate economic development across national boundaries.

Rostow spent most of the 1950's at MIT, teaching and studying the economics of the underdeveloped and the Communist nations. He evolved the theories of economic growth that are his most important intellectual contribution to date. On the side, he advised President Eisenhower on a variety of problems. When he leaves government, he hopes to do parallel research on the growth of political democracy in these same underdeveloped nations. In the 1960 campaign, Rostow worked on Kennedy's foreign and military policies. He gave JFK the phrase "get the country moving again," and Kennedy credited him with originating the "New Frontier" slogan. The invitation to join the Administration in Washington followed. He's been there on the inside ever since.

Rostow carried to Washington with him a book called *The Green Curve Omnibus* by Sir Ernest Swinton. It deals with a paradox that intrigues him. Rostow says, "You have two contrary imperatives in government: one to keep options open and the other to make sure decisions are made in time." The book contains a story that tells how British authorities in London, by failing to face a problem soon enough, caused disaster. If they had decided early enough to ship food to the garrison in the story, it could have survived. Says Rostow, "Sometimes by making decisions you widen the options."

"I'm the first person ever to call the President and tell him the hot line from Moscow is up," says Walt Rostow with a wry smile. He figures this gives him a spot in the record book of history.

The "hot line" is a teletype hookup between Moscow and Washington. We presume the Moscow terminal is in the Kremlin; no American has ever seen it.

Deep in the bowels of the White House is the Situation Room, a one-time bowling alley that is a shabby, overcrowded imitation of the Pentagon War Rooms where the Big Brass gather in moments of crisis. The Situation Room, directed by Rostow, actually consists of two rooms. The inner one is dominated by a long table on which sits a dial-less tan telephone with the legend: "Private Line President." This windowless Conference Room is where the action is.

Next door is the Situation Room itself, where a small group of panic-proof men attempt to keep tabs, instantly, on what is happening in the world. It is usual for the President to call in here about 3 a.m. and ask, "What do you have for me?" Says one of the men who work there, "He has a built-in alarm. He wants to know about the situation in Vietnam: mortar attacks, downed fliers and what's being done to rescue them."

Most of the tools are surprisingly old-fashioned. "We operate like the YMCA," says one aide. There are four teletype machines: AP, UPI, Reuters and one with information monitored from foreign broadcasts and newspapers. Connecting the "Sit Room" with the White House Communications Center, where the modern equipment is, are pneumatic tubes, like the ones that have whooshed money across department stores for generations. On one wall are four clocks—Washington time, GMT, Saigon and Presidential time, which follows the President wherever he may be. On a shelf sits a "three-eyed monster"—three small TV sets mounted together for watching the three networks. In a corner stand waist-high brown "burn bags," where messages are disposed of, and 27-inch-high red-and-white candy-striped bags for burning the most sensitive classified material.

At 0238 last June 5, a Monday, Duty Officer Ray Wotring in the Sit Room spotted an item on the monitor teletype that fighting had broken out in the Middle East. Wotring immediately called Walt Rostow at his home, where he has three direct White House phones. By 0300, confirming information was pouring in, and Wotring called Rostow again: War. "I'm coming right in," Rostow said.

At 0325, Rostow was on the scene. He called Secretary Rusk, who was already informed of the crisis. Bromley Smith, Arthur McCafferty in charge of the Situation Room and Harold Saunders, the staff man who has the Middle East "account," arrived in the next ten minutes. They studied the messages from Tel Aviv and Cairo, and at 0435, Rostow decided to awaken the President. Col. Robert N. Ginsburgh, White House liaison from the Chairman of the Joint Chiefs of Staff, was pulled in. The log adds: "0500 All hell broke loose."

At 0759, the Communications Center rang the Situation Room: the hot line was coming up. This had never happened before. The message was heard first over a secure telephone from the Pentagon, then from State. Almost simultaneously, a pneumatic tube spit out a canister with the message on yellow paper in Russian. McCafferty translated it for Rostow. Another canister brought a translation from the Communications Center. The message said: "Chairman of the Council of Ministers Kosygin would like to know whether or not President Johnson is at your terminal."

Before a reply could be framed saying the President was on his way or Rostow—now with White House Press Secretary George Christian in Rostow's office—could call the President in his bedroom, the next message started: "Please give President Johnson the following message. . . ."

By 0815, Johnson was in the inner Conference Room. He ordered coffee and four hot rolls from the White House mess. Rusk, McNamara, Ambassador to Moscow Llewellyn Thompson, Rostow and the President started preparing a reply. It was filed at 0847, one hour to the minute after Kosygin's first message had been sent.

Rostow says of that first morning, "It was a crisis the end of which certainly couldn't be seen the first day." He remembers, "The first day was air day. We had a tolerably clear picture of what was going on by breakfast." Once the Israelis gained air superiority, the critical questions were how to bring the war to a halt and keep the United States and the Soviet Union at peace.

Rostow's staff men manned the Sit Room around the clock: Smith and Saunders took one 12-hour shift, and McCafferty and Ginsburgh, the other. During the next two days, three messages arrived from Moscow, and three replies went out signed Johnson. Then, on Thursday morning at 1100, the first U.S.-initiated message was sent. We told the Russians that the U.S.S. *Liberty* had been attacked, and our planes were scrambling to assist her; we were not going to war. Says one man very close to the action: "This was the best use of the hot line."

During the crisis, 20 messages went back and forth between Moscow and Washington, keeping communications open and reducing the chances of a terrible mistake. The hot line worked.

The Truth About LBJ's Credibility

Warren Rogers

A mean little story is going the rounds in Washington these days: "Do you know how to tell when Lyndon Johnson is not telling the truth on television? Well, when he goes like this"—finger aside nose—"he's telling the truth. When he goes like this"—pulling an earlobe—"he's telling the truth. When he goes like this"—stroking chin—"he's telling the truth. But when he starts moving his lips, he's *not* telling the truth."

It always gets a big, knowing laugh. What that story and the reaction to it signify is that "the credibility gap" has become the hallmark of the Johnson Administration, just as nonintellectualism was for Dwight D. Eisenhower's and cronyism was for Harry S. Truman's. It doesn't matter that the joke isn't very fair, that it touches on only a minuscule part of Johnson's stewardship. There is just enough truth in it to make it funny. As imagery, it has crowded out all the old Texas-oriented gags about LBJ's baggy-pants tailoring, folksy twang and "Big Possum" machinations.

There is no easier way to start a conversation than to ask the first person you see, "What do you think of the credibility gap?" No matter who it is—senator, shopgirl, hostess with the mostes', cabby with a commentator-philosopher status to protect—they all know what and whom you are talking about.

If the person is informed, if he understands how the Government actually works, instead of only how it is supposed to, he is apt to be tolerant. He knows that all Presidents suffer from a credibility gap—Eisenhower and the U-2, for example, and Kennedy and "the missile gap," from which term we borrowed the gap tag. He may even recall Thomas Jefferson's report of George Washington's reaction to newspaper attacks accusing him of monarchical tendencies:

"The President was much inflamed, got into one of those passions when he cannot command himself, ran on much on the personal abuse which has been bestowed on him, defied any man on earth to produce one single act of his since he had been in the government which was not done on the purest motives . . . that by God he had rather be on his farm than to be made emperor of the world—and yet they were charging him with wanting to be king. . . ."

But if the person has little more than a civics-book comprehension of government, coupled with the ingrained American suspicion of all who wield power, the comment is usually a sweeping generality. He watches TV, listens to radio and reads, and what he sees is an apparent gap between what the President says he does and what the newsmen report he does. The louder the Johnson apologists protest the Presidential innocence, the more ordinary citizens are likely to agree with St. John's First Epistle General: "If we say that we have no sin, we deceive ourselves, and the truth is not in us."

A POTENTIAL ISSUE FOR 1968

These are the people who make up the mass of voters. They respond to polls about the credibility gap, and the response in turn influences others who vote. And so, as the cycle gains momentum, the political opponents of the President—Democrats as well as Republicans—begin to pay attention and maybe nudge it along a little. Gaps of any kind make good campaign issues, and credibility, which everyone can understand because it seems as basic as the Ten Commandments, is an especially good campaign issue. Wily Senate Republican Leader Everett M. Dirksen of Illinois had this in mind when he intoned last year, "We're going to use it a little," and did, in the November elections. Rep. Melvin R. Laird of Wisconsin, chairman of the House Republican Conference, hopes it will be a big campaign issue in 1968, particularly when it comes to the way President Johnson compiles and presents his defense budget—what Laird calls "fiscal gimmickry." Credibility is at least implicit in Sen. Robert F. Kennedy's criticisms of our Vietnam policy.

None of this is lost on President Johnson. The first President in history to go around regularly with the results of polls stuffed into his jacket pocket, he sets great store by public opinion, as reflected in his favorite surveys. Intimates say he grinds his teeth when he hears the phrase "credibility gap" because he believes it carries connotations of deliberate lying. But he is above all a politician, and therefore a realist. He knows that "this credibility thing" is a force to be reckoned with. It interferes with the daily business of being President. It may even prolong the Vietnam war. And it threatens to cost him votes, if not reelection, in 1968.

So what is he going to do about it? He's already done it. In a kind of

New Year's resolution, he began 1967 with a vow to conduct himself with less flamboyance in public. He talked it over with Lady Bird and others whose advice he esteems and decided that if his manner and tone and choice of words were irritants, it was time for a change. The "soft-sell Lyndon" debuted with the State of the Union address in January.

As with any such pledge, he expects to break it now and then. But in the main, we will be seeing a more subdued man, a return to the Lyndon Johnson of 1963 and 1964, when he was appealing to the nation for support—"let us continue"—and struggling to establish himself as President of all the people.

His heady victory in the 1964 election, with the biggest plurality ever, was at least a catalyst in unleashing all his pent-up natural exuberance. As the next election approaches, the leash goes back on. Even his tailoring, some say, will tighten up.

THE HEAT FALLS ON THE PRESIDENT

The Presidential overhaul has gone beyond just the public personality of LBJ. George Christian, the President's new soft-spoken, low-key press secretary, has been instructed to get a better hold on the Government-wide public-information system. This really comes under the heading of more news management, in its legitimate sense. There has been too little of it in the Johnson Administration. Routine news that ought to flow freely and uneventfully sometimes gets so botched up, because of inept handling within the Government, that it widens the credibility gap.

A case in point is what happened when tear gas was first used in Vietnam in late March, 1965. Somehow, first reports neglected to point out that the chemical was not the death-dealing kind of World War I infamy. By the time U.S. Government spokesmen caught up with the truth and put it out, the Communists had posted a major propaganda score, and Johnson's credibility was down another notch. Similarly, when Harrison Salisbury reported in the New York *Times* on bomb damage in Hanoi, U.S. officials knew immediately that some of his statistics were taken from old Communist propaganda. But it was three days before they got around to saying so.

In trying to shield the President from such bobbles by others, Christian has borrowed from the practices of a Republican predecessor, James C. Hagerty, who was Eisenhower's press secretary. Hagerty believed firmly that Ike's Administration should "speak with one voice." He maintained close touch with other press officers, particularly at the State and Defense Departments. There were regular meetings to keep everybody up to date and frequent round-robin telephone conferences.

"Christian is building a lot more coordination among the other PIO's [public information officers] and his office here," one White House man says. "For one thing, he is trying to get them to handle more of their own business. If the Agriculture Department has a good story, it ought to be put out by Agriculture, not by the White House. A reporter on that beat is a specialist, a lot better equipped to deal with it than a White House reporter, who is more of a generalist. If the story is put out here, and there is a mix-up causing controversy, the heat falls on the President no matter who made the mistake."

The big problem Christian faces in this approach is that he is working with LBJ, not Ike. After Eisenhower won the nomination in 1952, he played a get-acquainted round of 18 holes of golf with Hagerty at Denver. "As my press secretary, you will know everything I am doing at all times," he told Hagerty. For eight years, he kept his word. When Hagerty was not present at important meetings, Eisenhower would ask his conferees to "drop into Jim's office before you leave the White House and tell him what happened." Thus, Hagerty could speak with complete assurance about the President's thinking and activities. But, if there was any flare-back, the onus was on him, not the President, and Hagerty took the rap.

LBJ had no such complete rapport with his first press secretary, George E. Reedy, nor all the time with his second, Bill D. Moyers. It seems unlikely he will establish it with Christian. And so, for lack of a buffer, a lightning rod, a whipping boy, all the criticism and incredulity home in on him. It is ironic that when Moyers stepped out as press secretary, he was roundly applauded by the Washington press corps, and yet he left behind him, seemingly through no fault of his own, a growing credibility gap beleaguering his old boss.

How did the President get into this fix? Overwhelmingly, it is because of the kind of person he is—bigger than life in both faults and virtues, the personification of Texas bigness that scoffs at rules made and observed by lesser men. He is the restless dreamer and activist with a papa-knows-best zest for power that he hates to share. He is the one-man army simultaneously blowing the bugles, raising the flag, loading and firing all the muskets, charging, holding off Santa Anna's legions at The Alamo and too self-assured and proud to call in the U.S. cavalry waiting just over the hill. As the most authoritarian President since Franklin D. Roosevelt, he has no time for anything else but being the President. "Remember this," sighs one longtime Johnson-watcher, "in this White House, the President is LBJ, the press secretary is LBJ, the special assistant for national security affairs is LBJ. No White House staff photograph of him is released without his personal okay. He has no talk but shoptalk. He has no hobby. Being President is his hobby."

THE VIRTUES OF DEVIOUSNESS

And he loves surprises. More than a quarter century on Capitol Hill, with its crouch-and-spring parliamentary maneuvers, taught him the virtues of deviousness. But in the White House, the President of all the people is expected by the people to move publicly and with dignity, straight as an arrow, all open and aboveboard, the center of all eyes. A wheeler-dealer who plays his cards close to his chest, checks and then raises, makes a wonderful Senate majority leader, as indeed he was. But no matter how great his actual accomplishments as President, he inspires uneasiness because he violates the symbolism of the office. He will have to wait until after he leaves for history's accolades, just as Harry Truman did for different reasons.

"The 'gap' in President Johnson's credibility," wrote Philip Potter, rough-and-bright Washington bureau chief for Baltimore's *The Sun*, "derives primarily from his penchant for keeping newspapermen and the public in the dark until he is ready to turn on the light."

This obsession with secrecy is what Johnson calls "keeping all my options open." Whenever confronted with a problem, the first thing he wants to know is, "What are my options?" He searches them out, to study them like a poker hand, and he goes to extraordinary lengths to collect ideas—even asking tourists peering through the White House's iron picket fence: "What would y'all do about Vietnam, if you were President?"

"Premature disclosure reduces his options," Moyers has said. "Fundamental to his operations and way of life is surprise, which keeps his foes off-balance. He wants to retain the advantage of calling his own signals and deciding on his own timing."

Keeping his foes off-balance keeps everybody off-balance. The President pursues his policy relentlessly, even in trivial matters. He can't abide having his travel plans publicized until the last moment, although they may be for only a trip to his ranch in Texas. This pokerism plays hob with the famliy lives of White House reporters, who rarely know in advance when they have to go charging off in pursuit of the flapping Presidential coattails. The mutual resentment this creates flared to vendetta proportions last November in the celebrated case of the "Boston-to-Austin" campaign that was ballyhooed but never took place after the President's journey to the Far East.

Presidential aides alerted newsmen that Johnson would make the swing into perhaps 15 states in four days. Moyers telephoned from Southeast Asia to give California Democrats a specific date for the Presidential appearance. Other party leaders elsewhere were similarly advised. Advance men and Secret Service agents scurried to some of the intended stops.

Upon his return, however, the President blandly announced that his next trip was to the ranch, to rest up for surgery. At a press conference on November 4, he conceded he had been asked to campaign and had sent agents around to look over certain areas. But then he caustically denied ever having made a decision, putting all the blame on reporters and columnists: "First, we don't have any plans. So when you don't have plans, you don't cancel plans. We get invited to come. . . . But we have not accepted those invitations. . . . The people in this country ought to know that all these canceled plans primarily involve the imagination of people who phrase sentences and write columns and have to report what they hope or what they imagine. . . ."

It was not the first time the White House press corps was stung like that. Lately, newsmen attending Presidential backgrounders have sometimes come away without writing a line, either because he doesn't tell them anything or they don't trust what he says to hold up.

The Presidential zeal for open options shows, too, in Johnson's way with appointments to key jobs. Moyers says the President discourages advance speculation because "it dispels some element of surprise and makes the announcement, when it comes, less startling and dramatic," thereby reducing the newspaper space and TV time accorded it. Moyers denies Johnson ever canceled an appointment because news of it "leaked" in advance, but he admits that names under consideration sometimes were dropped when it became known they were on the list.

Philip Potter, in his analysis of the credibility gap, told of a personal experience with the President's ire over news leaks:

"After days of hard digging and talks with many responsible people a year. ago, this correspondent disclosed that the President was prepared at a Cabinet meeting to announce a new Food for Peace program. . . .

"On reading the article, the President directed that the mimeographed handouts officially disclosing the plan be burned; the plans for public announcement were canceled. The steps were eventually taken, but in a piecemeal fashion. Thus, it could never be said that *The Sun*'s article was an accurate forecast. The President felt that an option had been foreclosed and he had been betrayed. An inquiry was launched to find out who had talked to this correspondent. A person of Cabinet rank, wholly innocent of having done so, informed this correspondent later he was picked as the culprit and given 'unshirted hell.' "

As tender as he is about criticism, the President can't seem to keep himself from fingering the bruises. And he is quick to holler when they hurt, particularly in the extremely sensitive area of news about Vietnam. He keeps banks of three small television sets, each tuned to a different network, scattered about the White House, so he can watch all the major news shows at the same time, clicking on the sound at will with a remote-control button selector held in his hand.

He devours newspapers and wire-service ticker reports. "He reacts too much to what is said about Vietnam," sighed one official intimately concerned with the problem, "and every time he sneezes, there is pneumonia in Vietnam."

HE HAS A LONG MEMORY

Johnson's cold war with the news media extends long past publication. There is the story of how he blew up over a wire-service dispatch that reported a businessman, while listening to a Presidential lecture on the economy at the White House, let loose a skeptical "Ha!" Some time later, Johnson confided he had checked a tape recording of the meeting, and there was no such "Ha!" on it.

Apart from such personal characteristics and the scarcity of good news managers who could narrow the credibility gap to Johnson himself, there is another big reason for the difficulties. He inherited them. But although the Eisenhower and Kennedy Administrations had credibility gaps, the results were different. The late John Foster Dulles, Eisenhower's Secretary of State, was a brilliant international lawyer who could spin all kinds of marvelous confusions with words. Secretary of Defense Robert S. McNamara, from the beginning under Kennedy, performed the same sort of dipsy doodle, relying mostly on elastic statistics. The difference is that the critical barbs were then aimed at Dulles and McNamara, and their Presidents' plumes were unsullied. With Johnson, only the biggest target is allowed to be visible.

Another Kennedy-Johnson man, UN Ambassador Arthur J. Goldberg, is generally credited, or saddled, with helping the term "credibility gap" to catch on. "We have a great problem here maintaining our credibility with our own people," Goldberg told television viewers on December 19, 1965, in explaining why certain State Department documents were made public. The papers showed the Johnson Administration had considered a peace feeler of sorts from the North Vietnamese Government, contradicting press reports that it had been rejected out of hand.

Nearly seven months earlier, however, the New York *Herald Tribune* was one of the first, if not the first, to talk gap. On May 23, 1965, under the headline, "Dilemma in Credibility Gap," the paper's Washington bureau chief, David Wise, wrote: "The Administration is discovering . . . as other administrations have in the past, that when the gap between a government's actions and its words becomes discernible, it is in trouble." Wise's immediate point was that while LBJ spokesmen were loudly insisting U.S. forces in the Dominican Republic were strictly neutral, reporters eyeballing their activities knew otherwise—and so did millions of TV watchers who heard a U.S. marine refer to the rebels as "the enemy."

Secretary McNamara, a pioneer in credibility gap, has done little to endanger his homesteading rights. In his early days, he confused with peekaboo statements, clamped down on the flow of information from the Pentagon, set security men to tailing newsmen and their sources and even created a system of watchbirds—third parties required to sit in and record conversations between reporters and Pentagon officials. More recently, he has abolished the general press conference—he held none in all of 1966 —and there are no regular daily briefings by the Defense Department, as at State. Like the President, he prefers talking directly to the people through the television camera, with no pesky questions from reporters.

THE SYLVESTER DOCTRINE

McNamara's press aide until this year, Arthur Sylvester, may be remembered chiefly as the man who enunciated the doctrine of a government's right to lie. Shortly after the Cuba missile crisis subsided, Sylvester was challenged at a dinner meeting of Sigma Delta Chi, the national journalistic society, to explain the smoke screen of lies, half-truths and fibs pumped out by the Government during those harrowing days. He replied that a government had an inherent "right, if necessary, to lie to save itself from its going up into a nuclear war. This seems to me basic." Clarifying his remarks for Congress later, he said he meant that "any nation has the right of survival, self-preservation, particularly in this time when it can be faced almost overnight with a nuclear holocaust" and that "in times of extreme peril it is incumbent upon the United States Government, through its chosen representatives, to protect the people it serves from destruction by the enemy."

Sylvester established himself later as a boon to newsmen writing about the Vietnam war. He installed a system of almost instantaneous transmission of news from Saigon to the Pentagon. And he cut through red tape to make it possible for any reporter, with the will and the daring, to go into the thick of the fighting. But discrepancies still plague Pentagon efforts to plug the Vietnam credibility gap, which is the widest of all. Often, the problem is uninformed or deliberately false statements by low-level "spokesmen."

It has not been unheard-of, until recently, for correspondents to attend the daily 5 p.m. briefings in Saigon—so little believed they are called "the five o'clock funnies"—and hear that the American unit they just saw chopped up in a merciless ambush had suffered only "light casualties."

It may be that lying is inevitable in the confrontations of natural enemies like the press and men of power. It may be that Eric Hoffer, the longshoreman-philosopher, has said all there is to say about why President Johnson is in this fix, struggling to bridge the credibility gap and win back his lost popularity points:

"History is made by men who have the restlessness, impressionability, credulity, capacity for make-believe, ruthlessness and self-righteousness of children. It is made by men who set their hearts on toys. All leaders strive to turn their followers into children."

Still, perhaps the voters will say next year of Johnson's stewardship what Huckleberry Finn said of Mark Twain's reportage in *The Adventures of Tom Sawyer:* "There was things which he stretched, but mainly he told the truth."

What Price Federal Aid?

Leo Pfeffer

President Johnson's success in obtaining enactment of the Elementary and Secondary Education Act of 1965 was an exercise in political astuteness bordering upon genius. For at least twenty years the public education establishment, represented chiefly by the National Education Association, and the Protestant establishment—chiefly the National Council of Churches of Christ—had been able to prevent enactment of any measure for federal aid to education which included parochial schools as permissible beneficiaries, while during the same period the Roman Catholic Church, through the National Catholic Welfare Conference, effectively resisted any measure which did not. The President was able to get agreement on and acceptance of a single measure by the NEA, whose battle cry had always been public funds for public schools only; the NCC, traditional guardian of the separation of church and state; and the NCWC, which had never retreated from its oft-repeated position that it would never settle for anything less than a full partner's share in federal funds. This was a truly remarkable achievement, and it may be useful to consider how this came about.

Why did the NEA accept the bill? I think because it felt that the need for federal funds for public education had become desperate and that no bill could pass unless it contained some provision to satisfy the demands of the Catholic Church. This is the proposition that NCWC had been promoting for years and the NEA finally accepted it. I think the NEA was mistaken. At the 1965 meeting of the American Political Science Association, held in Washington shortly after the act was adopted, Dr. Samuel Halpern, legislative draftsman and Congressional liaison man at the Office of Education, stated that before the 1965 bill was drafted, Presi-

"What Price Federal Aid?" *Saturday Review,* January 21, 1967. Reprinted by permission of the author and publisher.

dent Johnson was assured by the legislative leaders of both houses that the Administration had enough votes to pass any federal education bill it wished, including one limited to public schools only.

Why, then, did President Johnson propose the present bill? My guess is that he was then afflicted with the consensus obsession and preferred a bill which the Catholic Church would accept to one pushed through over its opposition.

The National Council of Churches accepted the bill for a number of reasons. One undoubtedly was the ecumenical spirit, which impelled American Protestantism to make some gesture of accommodation to the Catholic Church. Another reason may have been the avoidance of use of the fighting words "parochial schools"; the Act speaks throughout of private and nonpublic schools, as if Exeter and Groton had been clamoring for federal funds. Finally, and perhaps most important, the purpose of the law was asserted to be not to aid private and parochial schools but the poor and educationally disadvantaged children enrolled in both public and nonpublic schools. This is the "child benefit" theory, which American Protestantism long rejected but finally accepted.

The truth is that the law is not unconstitutional on its face and can be administered without violating the First Amendment to the Constitution. The most important part of the law is Title I, which provides more than a billion dollars annually for special services in elementary and secondary schools. In order, however, to qualify for federal funds, a school board must satisfy the Commissioner of Education "that, to the extent consistent with the number of educationally deprived children in the school district . . . who are enrolled in private elementary and secondary schools" provision has been made "for including educational services and arrangements (such as dual enrollment, educational radio and television, and mobile educational services and equipment) in which such children can participate."

But there is nothing in the law requiring that special services be provided within the parochial schools. As alleged in the complaints in two parallel suits instituted in the federal and state courts of New York in December, there are many programs qualifying under Title I which may be carried out for the benefit of children attending private and parochial schools without violating the First Amendment—for example, programs for special or remedial instruction on publicly owned premises after regular school hours, open equally to children attending public and private schools. (The suits challenge the constitutionality of the administration of certain programs under the Act, not the Act itself.)

Why did the Catholic Church accept the measure? First, it may have realized that it was the most that could be hoped for now and that if it were rejected the result might be an all-public school bill. Second, the law leaves a great deal of discretion to local communities, and the Church may well have assumed that whatever the law says on its face, the influence of the Church in the major cities would be sufficiently strong to achieve through administration what the express terms of the law withhold. Finally, the Church realized the potentialities of the child-benefit principle and saw in it a practicable means for the ultimate achievement of its goal of partnership in education financing. This is indicated by the following extract from an editorial which appeared in the April 24, 1965, issue of *America,* the national Jesuit weekly:

> Now, the new federal law does nothing at all to help private schools directly. It gives them no money; it vests no property in them. Every benefit conferred on their pupils comes to them through the public school system. Even the textbooks that will be put into their pupils' hands will remain the property of public school districts.
>
> But the law at least recognizes that these schools exist and are educating children. In a variety of ways, it proposes to assist and improve the education of these children. The aid is, in every instance, directly to the child rather than to the school he attends. But it is aid, and it holds a promise for the future of a truly pluralistic school system.
>
> The "child benefit" principle is capable of being extended to every phase of education other than the directly religious. It could well justify tuition grants to the parents of children in any nonprofit school that the state recognizes as giving an acceptable general education. Here, as with federal aid to public schools, the Elementary and Secondary Education Act is a beginning rather than an end.

The essential fictitiousness of the child benefit principle is evidenced by an incident that occurred in Brooklyn in 1966. A special program was instituted after school hours in a public school located near a Jewish parochial school so that the children of both schools could participate. The parochial school authorities boycotted the program and the public school officials decided that they had no alternative to sending public school teachers into the parochial school during regular school hours to conduct the program exclusively for children enrolled there.

Those who opposed the aid bill unless the provisions were tightened to prevent its administration in violation of the principle of church-state separation warned of the dangerous consequences of such unconstitutional administration. The law has now been in operation for not much more than a year, but enough has already happened to show the validity of these warnings. Among other consequences are the following:

LAWLESSNESS. The sectarian groups are impatient with constitutional restrictions in the administration of the law and exert often irresistible pressure on public school authorities to disregard such restrictions. Msgr. Eugene J. Molloy, chairman of the Committee of Nonpublic School Officials, called the institution of the law suits in New York "a genuine tragedy," clearly implying that it were better that the law should be administered in violation of the Constitution than that its administration be subjected to judicial scrutiny. How can public school authorities teach children to respect the Constitution if they themselves act unconstitutionally? (Before the New York suits were started, U.S. Commissioner of Education Harold Howe II stated that the courts would have to spell out which federally financed services could be provided in church-related schools, and that without such rulings federal and state educational agencies would continue to face serious problems. It remains to be seen whether, now that litigation has been started seeking such rulings, Commissioner Howe will permit it to proceed to judgment, or will try to evade a decision by asserting such technical objections as that the plaintiffs lack standing to bring the suit because they are merely taxpayers.)

DISCRIMINATION. Private interests always have stronger lobbies than the public, and the results show this. When the Hill-Burton Act to aid hospitals was adopted in 1946, most of the funds went to public hospitals. Today the major part goes to private hospitals, and the gap increases steadily. In administering the Education Act in New York, the authorities have adopted as a standard for a disadvantaged private school, to qualify it for aid, the receipt of free lunches under the federal program by 10 per cent of the children; substantially higher requirements are imposed for public schools, in some districts as much as 40 per cent. A public school must be located in an officially designated disadvantaged area to qualify for Title I funds; a private school need not be. Remedial or special reading teachers are assigned to parochial schools at the ratio of one for every 157 eligible pupils; in public schools the ratio is one for every 230 pupils. Title I funds are used to provide remedial arithmetic programs in parochial schools; there are no such programs in the public schools. Public school teachers are sent into parochial schools at a time when the public schools are experiencing a critical shortage of teachers and, the complaint in the New York suit alleges, pressures are exercised and special inducements are offered by public school authorities to get the teachers to accept assignment to parochial schools.

DISINTEGRATION. The prophecy in the *America* editorial of a "pluralistic" school system may well be realized in a way neither anticipated nor desired by the Church. The pressure on the part of the Negro community for public school integration in Northern cities is accelerating an exodus from the public schools to private white schools, the great majority of which are parochial schools. The Catholic Church is aware of the danger and is greatly troubled by it; it has announced plans to investigate the matter and see what can be done about it. But if federal and state funds are poured into private schools, it cannot but make probable an even more accelerated exodus of the middle class white and a few middle class Negro children to the private schools, leaving the public school as a center for society's rejects.

These are some of the dangers that loom ahead. If the present trend in the administration of the Elementary and Secondary Education Act of 1965 is not checked, either by public opinion or judicial action, we may find tragically that we have paid a prohibitive price for federal aid.

If Anything Happens to a President—

U.S. News & World Report

If something now happens to a President that brings disability or death, the handling of the resulting emergency for the Government will be different than in the past.

This is because of a new Amendment to the Constitution—the 25th, ratified February 10.

President Johnson, now 58 years old, suffered a severe heart attack in 1955 while still a Senator. More than three years ago, President John Kennedy was assassinated. Former President Dwight Eisenhower was struck by a heart attack while in office in 1955 and saw practically nobody but doctors and his wife for nearly a week, then was partially incapacitated for several months.

FOR CLARITY. These are among actual events of the past that influenced Congress and the States to change the Constitution. The aim was to clarify the way in which presidential power can be transferred, temporarily or permanently, to the President's successor when the elected Chief Executive is incapacitated or taken by death.

In the hypothetical case of something happening to President Johnson— being carried off by an unexpected illness or accident, for example—then Vice President Hubert Humphrey would become President of the U.S.

This would be the same as in the past. The 25th Amendment, however, makes the Vice President's succession explicit, confirming precedent.

Far more important is the following change in procedure, now required by the 25th Amendment: President Humphrey, succeeding Lyndon Johnson under the imagined circumstance of the President's death, would himself name a new Vice President.

Under previous law there was no Vice President until the next election, a situation that has occurred 16 times in American history. In 1947 the Speaker of the House was made next in line for the Presidency.

Thus, from the time of President Kennedy's death until the 1964 election, Speaker John McCormack of Massachusetts, now aged 75, would have been President if something had happened to Lyndon Johnson.

Then if something had happened to Mr. McCormack, the Presidency would have gone to Senator Carl Hayden of Arizona, as President pro tem of the Senate, Mr. Hayden is 89 years old.

Speaker McCormack would still become President now, if both President Johnson and Vice President Humphrey died in a common disaster. Such a double tragedy is regarded as too remote a possibility to provide for.

CONGRESSIONAL CHECK. Should Mr. Humphrey succeeed to the Presidency, he could name his choice for Vice President, who would serve until the next presidential election. There is only one restraint: His nominee would have to be confirmed by a majority vote of both the House and Senate. In effect this means the choice would almost certainly be a Democrat and a leader in Congress, the Cabinet, or a State Governor.

Less well-defined are the changes in procedure required by the 25th Amendment in case the President becomes "unable to discharge the powers and duties of his office."

If Mr. Johnson, as a hypothetical example, suffered a stroke such as the one that paralyzed Woodrow Wilson in 1919, this sequence would occur:

Assuming President Johnson wanted to do so, he could notify Speaker McCormack and Senator Hayden, in writing, that he was unable to carry out his duties. Vice President Humphrey would then take over all presidential powers and duties as Acting President. This is an entirely new office and title in the American Government.

Suppose, however, that President Johnson's imaginary illness left him incapable of knowing his own limitations.

This crisis, the one most dreaded by constitutional authorities, was a real possibility to insiders when Mr. Eisenhower was stricken by what turned out to be a mild stroke in 1957.

In a much starker form the same crisis would have loomed, if President Kennedy had lingered after his fatal head wound. President Garfield lived for 80 days after being fatally wounded by an assassin, and President Wilson was disabled from 1919 to the end of his term, a period of 17 months.

Under the 25th Amendment, Vice President Humphrey and a majority of the Cabinet could in such circumstances make a finding that the President was unable to perform his duties.

Then Mr. Humphrey would take over as Acting President until the President himself informed Congress that "no disability exists."

SEAT OF DECISION. If a dispute ever arose, with the President seeking to keep or recover his power and the Acting President opposing him, Congress would decide the issue. A two-thirds vote of both Houses is required to uphold the Acting President. "Otherwise, the President shall resume the powers and duties of his office," says the 25th Amendment.

One thing is clear: The Vice President, once the forgotten man of the Constitution, has new stature, a wider role, much potential power.

Chapter Nine

SUGGESTED QUESTIONS FOR CLASS DISCUSSION.

1. Should a President be a strong leader of his political party or should he attempt to "stand above" politics? If he chooses the nonpartisan position, does this weaken his position with his party and make his task as chief legislator even more difficult? How does this affect the off-year elections of his party's congressional candidates?
2. The President's State of the Union address constitutes his recommendations for a legislative program for the next year. Why does Congress rely so heavily on the President's program when the legislative power is constitutionally vested in the Congress?
3. Every modern President has had "a man behind the throne" upon whom he relied heavily. These men have, for many purposes, been the executive himself. Is there any way the system could be altered to insure that no appointed person could wield this much power? Should we try?
4. How much information about the affairs of state should the President furnish the public? Is he justified in sometimes not being entirely candid?

Chapter Ten

JUDGES, LAW, AND THE COURTS

The Constitution is the supreme law of the land. As such it serves as a symbol of law itself—fixed and timeless. However attractive the ideal of an unchanging law, in fact the law must change if it is to govern the affairs of men in a time of change. The Supreme Court is the instrument that adapts the fundamental law to those changing needs while, at the same time, satisfying symbolically the traditional desire for a law that is fixed and unchanging.

The Court, as the agency that interprets the Constitution, has occupied a strategic position in American life. Laws must be tested for their conformity with the supreme law, and the decision as to whether they conform or not is vested in the Supreme Court.

While the Supreme Court has occupied a strategic position, this position has also been a precarious one for it is the only undemocratic institution in a democratic society. Those who have disagreed strongly with the decisions of the Court have almost inevitably been drawn toward a criticism, not only of particular decisions, but of the position of the Court itself. Was not the Court, while presumably making nothing more than expert legal decisions, actually making broad-ranging policy decisions concerning political, social and economic matters? And if this was the case, ought not such decisions be left to elective bodies? Should a handful of judges be allowed to undo the work of hundreds of legislators representing millions of Americans? Or is there a real danger of rash and extreme legislative action that the Court must guard against?

The cases included in this section raise a number of issues relating to judicial review, the functioning of the courts, and the behavior of the police.

Marbury v. Madison: Birth of Judicial Review

The most celebrated case in Constitutional history has never been quite able to outlive the charge of partisan politics and the usurpation of power by the Supreme Court to "supervise" both legislative and executive functions.

Fearing the excesses of the new Jeffersonian Republicans, the Federalists suddenly found great virtues in the nonelective branch of government and made a number of "midnight" judicial appointments to hold the fort until the Federalists could regain control of the government. Marbury, one of the midnight appointees, went directly to the Supreme Court to secure a commission that John Marshall, then Secretary of State and at the time of the suit, Chief Justice, had neglected to deliver.

The Court was faced with a serious dilemma: If it issued the order Jefferson was certain to ignore it. On the other hand, an admission by the Court that it could not interfere in executive matters would be a surrender to what Marshall called "speculative theorists and absolute terrorists" and might set a precedent for the supremacy of elective government. The stakes were high. What Marshall succeeded in doing was (1) to condemn his political opponent, (2) to declare the power of the court to set aside legislative acts (and by implication executive as well) all the while admitting that the Court had no jurisdiction!

Mr. Justice Marshall delivered the opinion of the Court.

At the last term, on the affidavits then read and filed with the clerk, a rule was granted in this case, requiring the Secretary of State to show cause why a mandamus should not issue, directing him to deliver to William Marbury his commission as a justice of the peace for the county of Washington, in the District of Columbia.

No cause has been shown, and the present motion is for a mandamus. The peculiar delicacy of this case, the novelty of some of its circumstances, and the real difficulty attending the points which occur in it, require a complete exposition of the principles on which the opinion to be given by the court is founded.

These principles have been, on the side of the applicant, very ably argued at the bar. In rendering the opinion of the court, there will be some departure in form, though not in substance, from the points stated in that argument.

In the order in which the court has viewed this subject, the following questions have been considered and decided.

1. Has the applicant a right to the commission he demands?

2. If he has a right, and that right has been violated, do the laws of his country afford him a remedy?

3. If they do afford him a remedy, is it a *mandamus* issuing from this court?

William Marbury v. *James Madison,* Secretary of State of the United States 1 Cranch 137; 2 L. Ed. 60 (1803).

. . . It is . . . the opinion of the court,

1. That, by signing the commission of Mr. Marbury, the President of the United States appointed him a justice of peace, for the county of Washington in the District of Columbia; and that the seal of the United States, affixed thereto by the Secretary of State, is conclusive testimony of the verity of the signature, and of the completion of the appointment; and that the appointment conferred on him a legal right to the office for the space of five years.

2. That, having this legal title to the office, he has a consequent right to the commission; a refusal to deliver which, is a plain violation of that right, for which the laws of his country afford him a remedy.

It remains to be enquired whether,

3. He is entitled to the remedy for which he applies. This depends on,

1. The nature of the writ applied for, and,

2. The power of this court.

. . . This, then, is a plain case for a mandamus, either to deliver the commission, or a copy of it from the record; and it only remains to be enquired, whether it can issue from this court.

The act to establish the judicial courts of the United States authorizes the Supreme Court "to issue writs of mandamus in cases warranted by the principles and usages of law, to any courts appointed, or persons holding office, under the authority of the United States."

The Secretary of State, being a person holding an office under the authority of the United States, is precisely within the letter of the description, and if this court is not authorized to issue a writ of mandamus to such an officer, it must be because the law is unconstitutional, and therefore absolutely incapable of conferring the authority, and assigning the duties which its words purport to confer and assign.

The Constitution vests the whole judicial power of the United States in one supreme court, and such inferior courts as Congress shall, from time to time, ordain and establish. This power is expressly extended to all cases arising under the laws of the United States; and, consequently, in some form, may be exercised over the present case; because the right claimed is given by a law of the United States.

In the distribution of this power it is declared that "the Supreme Court shall have original jurisdiction in all cases affecting ambassadors, other public ministers and consuls, and those in which a state shall be a party. In all other cases, the Supreme Court shall have appellate jurisdiction."

It has been insisted, at the bar, that, as the original grant of jurisdiction to the supreme and inferior courts, is general, and the clause assigning original jurisdiction to the Supreme Court contains no negative or restrictive words, the power remains to the legislature to assign original jurisdiction to that court in other cases than those specified in the article which has been recited; provided those cases belong to the judicial power of the United States.

If it had been intended to leave it in the discretion of the legislature to apportion the judicial power between the supreme and inferior courts according to the will of that body, it would certainly have been useless to have proceeded further than to have defined the judicial power, and the tribunals in which it should be vested. The subsequent part of the section is mere surplusage, is entirely without meaning, if such is to be the construction. If Congress remains at liberty to give this court appellate jurisdiction, where the Constitution has declared their jurisdiction shall be original; and original jurisdiction where the Constitution has declared it shall be appellate, the distribution of jurisdiction made in the Constitution is form without substance.

Affirmative words are often, in their operation, negative of other objects than those affirmed; and in this case, a negative or exclusive sense must be given to them, or they have no operation at all.

It cannot be presumed that any clause in the Constitution is intended to be without effect; and, therefore, such a construction is inadmissible unless the words require it.

. . . To enable this court, then, to issue a mandamus, it must be shown to be an exercise of appellate jurisdiction, or to be necessary to enable them to exercise appellate jurisdiction.

It has been stated at the bar that the appellate jurisdiction may be exercised in a variety of forms, and that, if it be the will of the legislature that a mandamus should be used for that purpose, that will must be obeyed. This is true, yet the jurisdiction must be appellate, not original.

It is the essential criterion of appellate jurisdiction that it revises and corrects the proceedings in a cause already instituted, and does not create that cause. Although, therefore, a mandamus may be directed to courts, yet to issue such a writ to an officer for the delivery of a paper is in effect the same as to sustain original action for that paper, and, therefore, seems not to belong to appellate, but to original jurisdiction. Neither is it necessary, in such a case as this, to enable the court to exercise its appellate jurisdiction.

The authority, therefore, given to the Supreme Court by the act establishing the judicial courts of the United States, to issue writs of mandamus to public officers, appears not to be warranted by the Constitution; and it becomes necessary to inquire whether a jurisdiction so conferred can be exercised.

The question, whether an act repugnant to the Constitution can become the law of the land, is a question deeply interesting to the United States; but, happily, not of an intricacy proportioned to its interest. It seems only necessary to recognize certain principles, supposed to have been long and well established, to decide it.

That the people have an original right to establish, for their future government, such principles as, in their opinion, shall most conduce to their own happiness is the basis on which the whole American fabric had been erected. The exercise of this original right is a very great exertion; nor can it, nor ought it, to be frequently repeated. The principles, therefore, so established, are deemed fundamental. And as the authority from which they proceed is supreme, and can seldom act, they are designed to be permanent.

This original and supreme will organizes the government, and assigns to different departments their respective powers. It may either stop here, or establish certain limits not to be transcended by those departments.

The government of the United States is of the latter description. The powers of the legislature are defined and limited; and that those limits may not be mistaken, or forgotten, the Constitution is written. To what purpose are powers limited, and to what purpose is that limitation committed to writing, if these limits may, at any time, be passed by those intended to be restrained? The distinction between a government with limited and un-limited powers is abolished if those limits do not confine the persons on whom they are imposed, and if acts prohibited and acts allowed are of equal obligation. It is a proposition too plain to be contested, that the Constitution controls any legislative act repugnant to it; or, that the legis-lature may alter the Constitution by an ordinary act.

Between these alternatives there is no middle ground. The Constitution is either a superior paramount law, unchangeable by ordinary means, or it is on a level with ordinary legislative acts, and, like other acts, is alterable when the legislature shall please to alter it.

If the former part of the alternative be true, then a legislative act con-trary to the Constitution is not law: if the latter part be true, then written constitutions are absurd attempts on the part of the people to limit a power in its own nature illimitable.

Certainly all those who have framed written constitutions contemplate them as forming the fundamental and paramount law of the nation, and consequently, the theory of every such government must be, that an act of the legislature, repugnant to the Constitution, is void.

This theory is essentially attached to a written constitution, and is, con-sequently, to be considered by this court as one of the fundamental prin-ciples of our society. It is not therefore to be lost sight of in the further consideration of this subject.

If an act of the legislature, repugnant to the Constitution, is void, does it, notwithstanding its invalidity, bind the courts, and oblige them to give it effect? Or, in other words, though it be not law, does it constitute a rule as operative as if it was a law? This would be to overthrow in fact what was established in theory; and would seem, at first view, an absurdity too gross to be insisted on. It shall, however, receive a more attentive consideration.

It is emphatically the province and duty of the judicial department to say what the law is. Those who apply the rule to particular cases must, of necessity, expound and interpret that rule. If two laws conflict with each other, the courts must decide on the operation of each.

So if a law be in opposition to the Constitution; if both the law and the Constitution apply to a particular case, so that the court must either decide that case conformably to the law, disregarding the Constitution; or con-formably to the Constitution, disregarding the law; the court must deter-mine which of these conflicting rules governs the case. This is of the very essence of judicial duty.

If, then, the courts are to regard the Constitution, and the Constitution is superior to any ordinary act of the legislature, the Constitution, and not such ordinary act, must govern the case to which they both apply.

Those, then, who controvert the principle that the Constitution is to be considered, in court, as a paramount law, are reduced to the necessity of maintaining that courts must close their eyes on the Constitution, and see only the law.

This doctrine would subvert the very foundation of all written constitutions. It would declare that an act which, according to the principles and theory of our government, is entirely void, is yet, in practice, completely obligatory. It would declare that if the legislature shall do what is expressly forbidden, such act, notwithstanding the express prohibition, is in reality effectual. It would be giving to the legislature a practical and real omnipotence, with the same breath which professes to restrict their powers within narrow limits. It is prescribing limits and declaring that those limits may be passed at pleasure.

That it thus reduces to nothing what we have deemed the greatest improvement on political institutions—a written Constitution—would of itself be sufficient, in America, where written Constitutions have been viewed with so much reverence, for rejecting the construction. But the peculiar expressions of the Constitution of the United States furnish additional arguments in favour of its rejection.

The judicial power of the United States is extended to all cases arising under the Constitution.

Could it be the intention of those who gave this power to say that, in using it, the Constitution should not be looked into? That a case arising under the Constitution should be decided without examining the instrument under which it rises?

This is too extravagant to be maintained.

In some cases, then, the Constitution must be looked into by the judges.

The Role of the Courts: Conscience of a Sovereign People

J. Skelly Wright

There is abroad in this country a major debate concerning the role of the courts in expanding individual freedom and in increasing respect for human rights.

One school of thought, known as the advocates of judicial restraint, has advised the judges to move cautiously. Judges cannot give the people more freedom than the people themselves want or deserve, they tell us. And whatever freedom the people want or deserve cannot be kept from them by the judges. So from this point of view, it is useless for the judges to concern themselves with expanding the sphere of human freedom. It may be worse than useless, for judicial protection of individual rights may

"The Role of the Courts: Conscience of a Sovereign People," *The Reporter*, September 26, 1963. Reprinted by permission of the author and publisher.

well encroach on the powers and prerogatives of other branches of our government, thereby upsetting our Constitutional system of checks and balances. Thus, it is said, it is to state legislatures and to Congress, rather than to the courts, that the people must look for the protection of their rights. Moreover, if the judges take the burden of defending and expanding freedom upon their own shoulders, then the people may grow lazy and less vigilant, and neglect their own duties in protecting freedom. It is the efforts of the people themselves, expressed through the election of their chosen representatives, which underlie whatever freedom exists in our nation. Or so the advocates of judicial restraint would have it.

But the rival school of thought, derisively called the judicial activists, has taken quite a different view. For them, it is the duty of the courts to do all in their power to protect those freedoms which our Constitution grants. The courts will not be able to do all that is necessary by themselves. The courts have no army like the President, nor can the judiciary declare war as Congress can. But the courts can act as the collective conscience of a sovereign people—just as once nations had chancellors to act as conscience to the king. With courts performing their duty of proclaiming the eternal rights and liberties of the people, the people will not be slow to defend the banners raised by the courts. And the President and Congress will fall in line. This judges must do, according to the judicial activist, in deciding the cases and controversies involving the rights of human beings.

Moreover, freedom under our Constitution is not subject to any elections, state or Federal. The fundamental freedoms announced in the Bill of Rights are inalienable, and the protection of those rights, by the Constitution itself, is consigned to the courts. With the late Justice Robert H. Jackson the activists say:

"The very purpose of a Bill of Rights was to withdraw certain subjects from the vicissitudes of political controversy, to place them beyond the reach of majorities and officials and to establish them as legal principles to be applied by the courts. One's right to life, liberty, and property, to free speech, a free press, freedom of worship and assembly, and other fundamental rights may not be submitted to vote; they depend on the outcome of no elections."

WITNESSES AND THE FLAG

Perhaps the most dramatic demonstration of the difference between these two schools of thought occurred during the Second World War, when the Jehovah's Witnesses experienced a wave of persecution in our country because of their unusual religious beliefs and practices. Matters reached a climax when a number of local school boards required that schoolchildren—including Jehovah's Witnesses—give a daily pledge of allegiance to the flag. The Jehovah's Witnesses refused to do this, for they felt that such an act was contrary to the Bible's command "Thou shalt have no other gods before me." As a consequence of this refusal, Jehovah's Witnesses across the country faced the prospect of having their children expelled from school, arrested as truants, taken from their parents, and sent to reform schools.

Eventually this problem arrived at our highest tribunal, the Supreme Court, as it seems almost every major social problem does today. In a straightforward statement of the views of the advocates of judicial restraint, the Supreme Court announced that it would not interfere with the requirement of the pledge of allegiance. It recognized a major conflict between the freedom of belief of the individual child and his parents versus the power of the state to command allegiance. But, said the court, the reconciliation of that conflict must be left to the people and their elected representatives—this could not be done for them by judges. If the responsibility for protecting the freedom of the individual were left to the people, said the court, the people would rise to that responsibility.

But without guidance from the Supreme Court, the people misread their responsibilities. From the standpoint of religious freedom and respect for human rights, the effect of that Supreme Court decision in the first flag-salute case was disastrous. School board after school board adopted new requirements commanding the flag salute, on pain of expulsion or other penalties. And often the school boards would quote the very words of the Supreme Court opinion in justification of their action. In many cases the salute to the flag was used simply as a device to expel the unpopular Jehovah's Witnesses. The words of the Supreme Court, that the protection of freedom could best be left the responsibility of local authorities, were perverted and used as an excuse for what was in effect religious persecution by the local school boards.

At the same time, and worse than the official action against the Jehovah's Witnesses, was the nation-wide wave of mob violence, attempts at lynching, and physical brutality against the Witnesses—all in the name of patriotism and support for the Supreme Court's opinion. Conditions were such that within three years after the first flag-salute case was decided, a second one reached the Supreme Court. In a dramatic reversal, the court ruled that no authority, state or Federal, could dictate the religious beliefs of any citizen. Schoolchildren could not be coerced into reciting pledges of allegiance when to do so would violate their freedom of religion. Specifically, the children of Jehovah's Witnesses could not be expelled from school because their religious beliefs prevented them from giving the flag salute.

The Supreme Court decision was honored by the local boards. Much of the official persecution of the Jehovah's Witnesses diminished. The new Civil Rights Section of the Department of Justice—founded by the former Attorney General, later Mr. Justice Frank Murphy—helped communicate the Supreme Court ruling to local authorities, and to the people, explaining that the freedom of belief of the Witnesses was protected by law. The rest is history. The Jehovah's Witnesses have been let alone. At least they have been allowed to practice their religion.

Thus, in the very midst of the Second World War, a court defended—indeed expanded upon—Constitutional freedoms. It did so despite the opposition of political authorities. It did so in behalf of a very small and very unpopular minority. And it did so in behalf of one of the most unpopular of freedoms—especially in wartime—the freedom *not* to salute the flag.

The Supreme Court's defense of freedom of religion did not cease with the war. The school-prayer cases of the very recent past demonstrate once again that the Court is alert to even minor abridgments of fundamental freedoms. Once again the apostles of judicial restraint have been critical. But religious freedom in this country is safer today because the Supreme Court has shown the people why even a minor inroad on religious freedom cannot be tolerated.

PROTECTION FOR THE POOR

The courts have also been expanding the sphere of human freedom in the field of criminal law. It has often been said that "History will judge the quality of a civilization by the manner in which it enforces its criminal laws." The Supreme Court has taken the lead in ensuring that our enforcement of criminal law receives the approbation of history. In decision after decision it has sought to upgrade and civilize the manner in which our criminal laws, state and Federal, have been enforced.

The court has demonstrated a determination to diminish the part that poverty plays in the administration of criminal justice—the type of trial a man gets must not depend on whether he is rich or poor. Following this thesis, the court has recognized the right to counsel in both Federal and state criminal trials and has required the state and the national governments to supply a lawyer for the indigent person. More than this, the Supreme Court has required the state and Federal governments to provide a proper appeal for indigents by paying the costs thereof, including a transcript of the testimony taken at the trial. Thus the court has sought to remove the handicap of poverty so that the indigent, too, may receive a fair trial under our law.

Coerced confessions have also received the condemnation of the current court. Under the Anglo-Saxon system of criminal justice, as distinguished from the Continental system, a defendant has a right to remain silent, not only at the time of trial but, most importantly, after his arrest before trial. The Supreme Court has been at pains to condemn, as uncivilized and as a reproach to our system of criminal justice, not only physical pressure, but psychological pressure as well, designed to force an accused to confess.

Perhaps the keynote case on the subject of coerced confessions and third degree is *Chambers* v. *Florida*. There a young Negro was accused of committing a heinous crime that had excited a large number of the white citizens of Florida. Without access to a lawyer or even to members of his family, young Chambers was questioned by the police for days on end while a mob bent on his destruction roamed outside the jail. Under these circumstances, it was said that he confessed to the crime. After his conviction in the state courts of Florida, the Supreme Court heard the case. In reversing that conviction and in denouncing the conditions under which a confession was extracted from Chambers, Mr. Justice Hugo L. Black sounded what has come to be the new creed for the court:

"Under our constitutional system, courts stand against any winds that blow as havens of refuge for those who might otherwise suffer because they are helpless, weak, outnumbered, or because they are nonconforming victims of prejudice and public excitement. . . . No higher duty, no more solemn responsibility, rests upon this Court, than that of translating into living law and maintaining this constitutional shield deliberately planned and inscribed for the benefit of every human being subject to our Constitution—of whatever race, creed or persuasion."

The Supreme Court has not satisfied itself with merely outlawing confessions that are demonstrably involuntary. Taking cognizance of the fact that most confessions are obtained while the accused is alone in police custody immediately after arrest and before being transferred to judicial custody by a committing magistrate, the court has held that where there is unnecessary delay in bringing the accused before the committing magistrate, any confession made during this period of unnecessary delay shall not be received in evidence. Thus the court has sought to outlaw not only coerced confessions but also confessions obtained under circumstances presumptively coercive.

In the protection of rights under the Fourth Amendment against unreasonable searches and seizures, the Supreme Court has also been active. The midnight knock on the door, the hallmark of the totalitarian police, does not pass muster in this country. The court not only has outlawed evidence obtained from unreasonable searches and illegal arrests. By an application of the so-called fruit-of-the-poisoned-tree doctrine, it has ordered excluded from the trial of a criminal case all evidence derived from the evidence illegally obtained. "Knowledge gained by the government's own wrong cannot be used by it," says the court.

Through its decisions in criminal law, the court has given rich meaning to our ideal of equal justice under law. Persons accused of crime, as a class, have little claim to sympathy with the public or to influence with political authorities. It would be easy, even popular, to construct the rights of those who stand at the bar of justice. But the courts have reminded us that the rights of all citizens are safe only to the extent that the rights of each accused person are protected. The phrase "It's his Constitutional right" has entered the common language as a link between the ideals of our civilization and the recognition of the rights of the lowliest offender.

Of course, these civilizing advances in the manner of enforcing criminal justice have also been the subject of criticism. The court itself has been condemned for recognizing the rights of "criminals." What the detractors fail to recognize, of course, is that the Bill of Rights outlined in the first eight Amendments to the United States Constitution are the rights of all citizens of the United States, and until an accused is proved guilty beyond a reasonable doubt after a fair trial, he also, as a citizen, is entitled to those rights.

EQUAL VOTES

The reapportionment cases mark another important area in which the Supreme Court has affected our freedom. When we say "This is a free country," one of the things we mean is that we are a free people who govern ourselves. In order for us to govern ourselves, we require fair apportionment. If, for practical purposes, it were primarily the farmers and small-town residents who voted, and the votes of city people hardly counted at all, then to that extent we would be less a free country.

Reapportionment cases highlight the debate on the role of judges in preserving freedom. And these cases point out the importance of general acceptance, of popular support, of aid from Executive and legislature, and of reaffirmation by the national conscience. For many years, judges would not decide reapportionment cases—no matter how unfair the apportionment, no matter what laws or Constitutional provisions were violated, no matter how many people were denied an effective right to vote. Judges would not decide such cases because, as some of them saw it, a court decision about legislative apportionment could have no effect unless the legislature and the people accepted the decision. And no one could count on, or predict, whether there would be legislative or popular support. And so, though as a matter of law the courts had the power to decide apportionment cases, as a matter of judicial wisdom they generally abstained from these issues. Reapportionment was held to be a political issue that addressed itself to the people.

But the Supreme Court has now declared that such cases are proper for judicial decision. The court has now found that in many areas the political system restrained the people from acting, that there was developing in this country a condition in some respects similar to the rotten-borough system that disgraced England two centuries ago. So the court, in effect, authorized the courts in each state to hear apportionment cases as they came up and to apply to voting the principle of equal protection our Constitution ordains. Some people predicted that the court's decree would be ignored or mocked, that the legislatures and the people would resist to the end the court's efforts in this field, and that the nation's refusal to accept the challenge and rise to the responsibility given them by the courts would become a national disgrace. But the results have been quite different, and the response to the judicial spark has been broader and stronger than anyone could have predicted. In state after state, citizens' groups have stepped forward, swiftly and effectively, to demand enforcement of the Constitutional principles of equality of which the Supreme Court had reminded them. Soon local courts took up the matter of reapportionment. And in some states, even before the question came before the local courts, legislators and governors have supported reapportionment proposals of their own. Now, by and large, citizens generally—from the man in the street to newspapers and preachers—have said "at long last" to the principle that a state's apportionment must conform to the standards of equality required by our Constitution.

MAKING A TRUISM TRUE

Of the areas in which courts, particularly the Supreme Court, have been active in promoting the freedom of us all, the one of first concern to us today is racial justice. The Supreme Court decisions in the field of racial equality have attempted to secure an actual freedom for the Negro from the bonds of discrimination and bigotry—and a freedom for the white from having to live in a society where such injustices occur. That these freedoms belong to the white and to the Negro is solid Constitutional law— nothing could be more clear than that the Thirteenth, Fourteenth, and Fifteenth Amendments to the Constitution were adopted exactly for the purpose of raising the former slave to the level of first-class citizen. The court decisions of our day are but long-delayed steps forward in giving actual effect to that Constitutional law.

The question remains, Will these decisions receive the support of the people, or will they remain only words in the mouths of the judges? Will the other branches of the Federal government, the Executive and Congress —and the state and local governments—respond to the challenge of these Supreme Court decisions and make a reality today the promise of a hundred years ago?

In pleading for passage of the Civil Rights Act of 1963, the Attorney General of the United States began his remarks to the Congress with this statement:

"For generations, Americans have prided themselves on being a people with democratic ideals—a people who pay no attention to a man's race, creed, or color. This very phrase has become a truism. But it is a truism with a fundamental defect: it has not been true." Is there an honest person in this country today who will deny this statement? Are there enough people in this country today so depraved that the Supreme Court's efforts in behalf of racial justice shall be in vain?

In answering these questions, we should first take notice that the landmark 1954 school-desegregation case has received both more support and more opposition than any other case in our century. The support it has received is tremendous. Organizations sprang up to implement its philosophy, people who had been apathetic to all things public suddenly took a new interest in the commonwealth, a wave of idealism swept the country—especially among college youth—to see the old Constitutional principle of equal justice given effect in the problems of the day. Even foreign nations looked at us with new respect as we began to practice what for so long we had merely preached.

But the civil-rights cases also provoked opposition. Men whose positions had been entrenched upon the foundation of old injustices resisted the righting of wrongs. Unthinking men, men used to old customs and old thoughts, refused to alter their ways. And many others were fearful; being unused to change, they were not ready to accept what was for them a revolution in their lives.

And so these court decisions that have inspired such enthusiasm from many of our citizens stand in need of even further support. The voices of the judges have struck a note of conscience in the breast of America, and America has been stirred to new efforts in behalf of an old idealism. But so entrenched an evil is not so easily overcome. The rock of selfishness, the hard core of racial injustice, is not so easily dissolved. Idealism alone is not enough. There must be a recognition by all our people that we have been wrong, morally wrong, in our treatment of the Negro. There must be a day of repentance. There must be a determination to redress the injustice of the past and a firm resolve by all branches of the government, and by the people, that the long suffering of the Negro shall not have been in vain.

Thus we see that in the areas of religious freedom, criminal law, reapportionment, and racial justice the courts have indeed played a leading role in expanding human freedom in our time. And for this they, particularly the Supreme Court, have been subjected to a barrage of calumny and vilification in some parts of our country. Even some thinking men, men of good will whose roots in the fight for human freedom go very deep, deplore the leadership the current Supreme Court has given in the fight for social and political justice. They say they fear the rule of judges. I say their fears are foolish fancies. In expanding human freedom, the judges have nothing to enforce their rule but the conscience of America. And as long as we are ruled by the informed and challenged conscience of America, we have nothing to fear.

A Note on Felix Frankfurter

James Grossman

Felix Frankfurter, in 1894 at the age of twelve, was brought from Vienna to an America in the midst of a great depression. He watched the people of New York hiss the President of the United States at a ceremonial occasion, the dedication of Grant's Tomb. At his first school his teacher believed in corporal punishment. His father did not prosper. And yet apparently to the young boy this was—as it was to be for the man through his long life—the Promised Land. Just as his teacher was one of his greatest benefactors—she taught him English by threatening the other boys with "gentle uppercuts" if they spoke to him in German—everything that happened to him was always for the best. His best piece of luck, he seems to have believed, was the series of accidents that kept him out of Columbia Law School and caused him to go to Harvard. While on his way to Morningside Heights to matriculate, he was induced by a friend to go to Coney Island for the day; later, when he was ill he was advised not to go to a city law school and chose Harvard because he thought Cambridge was in the country.

His career as a student in Harvard Law School has something of the legendary quality of Brandeis's there. He was first in his class each year. For some time after he graduated, and before he was famous, Professor Smith read to the class in torts a brilliant passage from Frankfurter's first-year examination. The letters of recommendation that the Dean, who was given to understatement, wrote for him were so glowing that one lawyer was surprised on studying the signature to see that it was genuine.

Frankfurter obtained a job in one of the best law firms in New York; it was an office that he wanted to be in not only because of its excellence but also because he had heard that "they had never taken a Jew and wouldn't take a Jew." A friendly junior partner suggested that this was a good time to change his name: ". . . there's nothing the matter with it, but it's odd, fun-making." He refused, as Jews often have, to give up a name that must have been in the family for only a relatively short period of time. His refusal did not hurt his prospects, for when he left to join the staff of the new United States Attorney, Henry L. Stimson, he was told that he could come back if he wanted to.

He never returned to private practice in an office or to the chance of making a fortune. His only problem in giving up his job had been whether he was being fair to his employers in not staying with them longer. Characteristically, it was a solace to him that with public service went a reduction in pay, from $1,000 to $750 a year. He seems always to have felt that there was something wrong with being well paid for doing what one likes to do and was never paid for his advocacy in the causes he served in private life. At law school the great John Chipman Gray had asked him, "How would you like to work a month with me on . . . my casebook on Property?" To Frankfurter, as he has told us, this was, "How would you like to enter the Elysian Fields?" and when Gray sent him a check for $100 for his work Frankfurter returned it twice until finally a note came, "Dear Frankfurter, Don't be a damn fool. Yours Cordially, John C. Gray." Years later, Frankfurter would say to his wife when she brushed aside compliments on her beauty, "Marion, you must learn to face the truth even when it's pleasant." One feels that Frankfurter himself could never quite see that in refusing money there was possibly something pleasant that he was refusing to face.

The young Frankfurter was in government service for almost eight years, first in the United States Attorney's office in New York and then in Washington when Stimson became Secretary of War under President Taft. The War Department was probably one of the most interesting branches of the government to work in. It was in effect the colonial office and the ministry of public works, and Frankfurter's faith in government as an instrument of public welfare may have come not only from books but in part from his experience in a conservative Republican administration. Frankfurter was so successful in his work that Taft kept him on although he supported Theodore Roosevelt in 1912, and when Wilson became President he stayed on under the new administration.

His greatest success was social. His friendships ranged from the young Lord Eustace Percy, the seventh son of the seventh Duke of Northumberland, to the aging Justice Holmes. He was one of the first of the great judge's young Jewish friends who made him happy in his last years by celebrating his greatness on every occasion. Frankfurter met everyone, a practice he continued through his entire life. He seems early to have hit on the rule of life that he formulated for Ella Winter at the Peace Conference: ". . . use every chance to make personal contacts. They are what count in life. You never know when one may become important." Put bluntly, this sounds embarrassing, the calculating advice of a Babbitt. But it is the calculation of a man who really enjoyed meeting people, as perhaps Babbitt did also. His open joy in meeting and knowing the great of this world was probably the source of what Holmes amusedly called his "unimaginable gift of wiggling in wherever he wants to." It was not a weakness, but, as with Proust, his strength.

In 1914 he joined the faculty of Harvard Law School. He was as surprised at being asked as if he had an invitation from an East Indian princess to marry her. He found it a difficult offer to accept. Stimson was against it; he thought Frankfurter particularly fitted for public life. Holmes, who as a young man had attacked Plato, warned him of the dangers of the academic life as against thinking under fire, the irresponsibility of running the universe on paper. It was, however, something like the Platonic vision that in the end decided Frankfurter; Harvard would give him time to think, to know what he really thought about things.

He was able, as he had hoped, to combine teaching with work for social welfare, in fact literally, if we accept an unfriendly account in the pre-Villard *Nation* of his argument in the Supreme Court in 1917 for the constitutionality of Oregon's minimum wages and hours laws: "Professor Felix Frankfurter . . . had merely exchanged one group of pupils for another. He lectured the court quietly, . . . and . . . was becomingly tolerant when the gray-haired learners asked questions which seemed to him unnecessary, and gentle when he had to correct a mistaken assumption."

When we entered World War I, Frankfurter returned to government service, working chiefly on labor problems. At President Wilson's request he investigated several ugly situations. His report on the Mooney Case emphasized that the labor leader had been convicted on perjured testimony, and his report on the Bisbee deportations told how members of the I.W.W. had been forcibly removed from Bisbee to New Mexico and left to suffer in a desert town. His old hero, Theodore Roosevelt, much changed in the last few years, denounced him for failing to point out that the I.W.W. were revolutionaries as dangerous as the Bolsheviks. Even before Frankfurter returned to Harvard—he was at the Peace Conference as a Zionist—there was a movement to oust him. It failed, but it had seemed serious enough to Holmes to cause him to write to President Lowell in praise of Frankfurter.

Frankfurter took up teaching again in the fall of 1919, as popular with his students as ever, despite the Red Scare, and despite it as busy as ever in what were then considered radical causes: spending his Easter vacation fighting a labor injunction against the Amalgamated Clothing Workers, briefing at a federal judge's request the rights of aliens who were being deported as revolutionaries, presiding at a meeting for the recognition of Russia. Of an illiberal decision by Taft invalidating Arizona's labor injunction statute, Frankfurter complained in an unsigned *New Republic* editorial, "For all the regard that the Chief Justice of the United States pays to the facts of industrial life, he might as well have written this opinion as the Chief Justice of the Fiji Islands." In the England that Frankfurter so loved this statement might have sent him to jail, but it turned out to be an utterly safe one to be made in the United States, even by a lawyer who argued before the Supreme Court; for the next year, when Frankfurter lost the District of Columbia minimum wage case, not only his friend Holmes but Taft as well was on Frankfurter's side in dissent.

It was inevitable that Frankfurter should come to the aid of Sacco and Vanzetti when he learned of the misleading character of Captain Proctor's testimony as a ballistics expert for the Commonwealth. Trained as a prosecutor under Henry Stimson, a man so scrupulously honorable that later as

Secretary of State he was to abolish spying as a State Department function, Frankfurter could only be outraged—as the highest court of Massachusetts and the Lowell committee were not—by what was most likely routine shabby unfairness on the part of a prosecutor. Frankfurter's powerful argument in the March 1927 *Atlantic Monthly* failed to save the two men but shook opinion outside of Massachusetts; published as a book and used as the basis of the account of the case in *The Letters of Sacco and Vanzetti*, it seems to have been one of the important sources of the belief that not only were the two men unfairly tried but also that they were innocent, a matter on which Frankfurter had expressed no opinion.

With the coming of the New Deal, Frankfurter moved from a position on the edge of power to its very center. He had known Roosevelt when they had both been in Washington, and Roosevelt when Governor of New York had asked his advice on occasion. Frankfurter refused Roosevelt's offer of the post of Solicitor General of the United States, although it was likely to lead to the Supreme Court, just as he had recently refused to go on the highest court of Massachusetts, another possible road to the Supreme Court. It may be that the prospect of a year at Oxford as Eastman Professor was irresistible. After his year in England, one of the happiest in his life, he continued teaching at Harvard, but he was in Washington often, frequently as a guest at the White House.

It is easy to exaggerate Frankfurter's role. The First New Deal was, after all, much more of a Columbia than a Harvard intellectual product. Frankfurter seems to have had little to do with the grand improvisations that were to control economic life; he was much more concerned with achieving some of the limited objectives of traditional liberalism, like the Securities Act that was intended to make Wall Street truthful, and the Public Utilities Holding Company Act, a Brandeisian kind of attack on bigness. His greatest personal success in legislation, writing the ideas in his book *The Labor Injunction* into law, the Norris-LaGuardia Act, had actually been effected in the Hoover administration, during which he had never stayed in the White House. But just because he held no position under Roosevelt and denied that he exercised any power and was discreet —writers still disagree whether this talkative man who indulged in reminiscences freely was for or against the Court-packing plan—he seemed to be Roosevelt's grey eminence, acting effectively behind the scenes like the Court Jew of some benevolent despotism, a sinister or saintly figure, depending on one's view of Jews and despots.

If there is any truth to Hugh Johnson's celebrated characterization of Frankfurter as "the most influential single individual in the United States," it lay in the fact that the country was feeling not so much the direct influence of Frankfurter the advisor as the indirect influence of the great teacher of law. For years Frankfurter had been choosing law clerks for Holmes and Brandeis from the graduating class at Harvard Law School and had been recommending other bright young graduates for positions with some of the largest New York law firms. Now, with its huge expansion of activities under the New Deal, the government became the chief employer of young lawyers. For work in new fields whose nature was not quite known, young men with fresh open minds were wanted, and inevitably Frankfurter was called on to supply many of them. The Happy Hot Dogs, to use the phrase Frankfurter disliked, were by no means all of one kind, for many of them had been taught or had learned to think for themselves, some even to think their way into the closed world of Communism, a risk peculiar in the 30's to intellectuals of open mind.

When Holmes resigned in 1932, Benjamin Cardozo was so much his logical successor that President Hoover appointed him to the Court even though he was a Democrat and even though this gave a single state, New York, three judges. When Cardozo himself died early in July 1938, Frankfurter seeemed to many the logical successor to both Cardozo and Holmes; he was exactly the kind of liberal that they were. For some reason Roosevelt was reluctant to accept the obvious. He said that he wanted someone from west of the Mississippi and had Frankfurter report to him on the qualifications of many men, but none would do.

While the search went on, Roosevelt found himself subjected to a mounting, and at times annoying, pressure from almost everyone whose opinion he respected to appoint Frankfurter. Justice Stone told the President that to form a distinguished court he would have to ignore geography. Ickes and Hopkins, disagreeing on so much, agreed on Frankfurter. Even the Chief Justice of Australia while on a visit to Washington wrote a memorandum urging his appointment. Rich Jews, according to Tom Corcoran, had convinced Roosevelt not to make the appointment. Presumably they were afraid that in a world in which Hitler was daily growing more powerful, Frankfurter's appointment would increase anti-Semitism. Roosevelt may have shared this feeling for he seems at one time to have hoped to wait until Brandeis retired, and Harold Laski even urged Brandeis to quit—or at least he told Ickes that he did—to make room for their friend. Brandeis stayed on, and Roosevelt finally, in January 1939, gave in. A fortnight after Frankfurter took his seat on the Court, Brandeis retired.

By the time of Frankfurter's appointment, the Court that Roosevelt had threatened to pack in 1937 was reduced to a hopeless minority. In part the Court had reformed itself, in part it had been reformed by Roosevelt. Without any change in its personnel it had melodramatically reversed its trend immediately after the Court-packing plan was announced, and in addition Roosevelt had already made two appointments and was to make two more within a year of Frankfurter's. There was no longer a majority on the Court who would declare that economic or welfare legislation would "deprive any person of life, liberty or property without due process of law" or violate any other clause of the Constitution. The battle that Frankfurter was so well equipped to fight as Holmes's follower was already won.

Roosevelt's appointees by and large seem to have come on the Court with the view that their chief duty was to protect legislation from judges— that is, from themselves. As the old majority had been quick to find liberty infringed by welfare laws, the new majority was at first slow to act in the name of liberty, even in the case of regulations interfering with speech, religion, or the rights of Negroes. Frankfurter in the 20's had refused to be impressed by the occasional Supreme Court decisions against intolerant statutes. The Supreme Court could not guarantee toleration, he asserted, for much that was illiberal would still be constitutional and could be stopped not by a liberal court but only by a liberal community which would elect liberal legislators.

True to his views on constitutionality, Frankfurter eary in June 1940 held that school authorities could expel two children who for religious reasons—their parents were Jehovah's Witnesses—refused to take part in the daily ceremony of saluting the flag. What astonishes us, if we do not keep in mind the date of the opinion and Frankfurter's personal background, is the issue that he sees involved in the case. It is no less than national unity, which is the basis of national security, and in its interest the school authorities had the right to determine that the compulsory flag salute was an appropriate means "to evoke that unifying sentiment without which there can ultimately be no liberties, civil or religious." While Frankfurter was delivering his opinion, German armies were sweeping through France; our survival seemed to him to be threatened. (Frankfurter, Ickes wrote in his diary at this very time, "is really not rational these days on the European situation.") In his opinion he never mentioned his own school days, but in his careful description of the flag ceremony one is aware of the earnest immigrant child to whom the daily ceremony must have been part of the natural way to become an American. It is as if he were willing to permit the state to try Pascal's method: if lighting a few candles and saying a few prayers every day, even without faith, can in the end make a man religious, perhaps saluting the flag daily, even against one's beliefs, may in the end bring one to the religion of the flag, patriotism.

Frankfurter's friends were shocked by his decision, although it was completely in accord with his prior views and even in fact with theirs. For a few weeks there was an outbreak of illegal compulsory flag-saluting; people entered other people's houses carrying a flag and demanding that it be saluted. Moscow, Idaho adopted a regulation that to obtain a license to distribute circulars the applicant would have to salute the flag, a requirement that would of course keep Jehovah's Witnesses away. It was perhaps these unfortunate but unnecessary consequences of the case that caused Black and two other Roosevelt appointees to announce that they regretted their vote. A little over three years after Frankfurter's opinion, the Court reversed itself and held that school authorities could not compel a child who was a Jehovah's Witness to salute the flag. In the midst of a great war the Court found unconstitutional a compulsory ceremony of allegiance that it had upheld while we were still at peace.

Frankfurter stood fast. The most interesting part of his opinion is not his plea for self-restraint, which dissenting judges often address to the majority, but his warning on the logical implications of the decision. If not saluting the flag could be a matter of religious right protected by the Constitution, many questions that had always been left to local authorities for decision—free lunches or free transportation for children in parochial schools, compulsory reading of the King James version of the Bible in public schools—would become troublesome constitutional issues for the Court. One would assume that he meant that these were matters in which the Court should not interfere, yet when they did come before the Court he was on the side of interference, even to a more radical extent than the liberal majority. He voted with a minority to hold unconstitutional free transportation for parochial school children and the New York system of released time for off-premise religious instruction.

On the whole, however, Frankfurter was consistent in his career on the Court. As a liberal critic he had attacked a conservative Court for its seizure of power in outlawing legislation and was self-consciously determined not to be guilty of this offense. Generally, he practised the self-restraint he had preached and tried to be guided by those famous words of Cromwell that he had once as a lawyer urged on the Court as a guide. "Brethren . . . by the bowels of Christ I suffer ye to conceive it possible that ye may be wrong." But his judicial humility rarely sat easily on him. At times he almost glories in the unpleasantness of the legislation that it is his judicial duty to uphold: ". . . whether immigration laws have been crude and cruel, whether they may have reflected xenophobia in general or anti-Semitism or anti-Catholicism, the responsibility belongs to Congress. . . ." There is a traditional view that the true greatness of a judge is most clearly shown when he acts against his deepest feelings; the ideal of this high impartiality is the elder Brutus condemning his sons to death and sitting sternly amid their mangled bodies.

If Frankfurter was to be faithful to Holmes and Brandeis, he had to uphold, as he did, the constitutionality of the Smith Act. Whether wisely or foolishly dealt with by the Smith Act, the Communist Party in the United States during the Cold War of the late 40's was surely more of a threat to national welfare than the small group of radicals whose conviction in the 20's under the California Criminal Syndicalism Act was upheld by Holmes and Brandeis. Frankfurter, with the majority in upholding the conviction of the Communist leaders was also with the majority in reversing the conviction of second-string Communists for reasons difficult to understand if one pays attention only to what the Court said. Justice Harlan, who has great gifts of clarity of expression, wrote with incredible obscurity on this occasion, and Frankfurter, who so often wrote concurring opinions to clarify what the Court was deciding, was silent. If the Court's verbal logic was weak, its unexpressed strategic logic was probably sound; it left the Smith Act standing, but only for a possible serious crisis and not for use every day.

Similarly, the Court tended not to stand up boldly to Congress on the question of the powers of its investigating committees. The Court seemed reluctant to define clearly the forbidden areas of Congressional inquiry infringing on freedom of speech and thought, but contented itself and Frankfurter with *ad hoc* decisions aiding Congressional committee victims by announcing rules not suspected before and not always followed consistently thereafter. The Congressional power of inquiry, one surmises, is too important an instrument of government to be seriously cut down, and the best the Court can do apparently is to try occasional evasive action. Freedom's victories are sometimes better won by unedifying devious means than by direct onslaughts of admirable, magnificent rhetoric.

Other judges, Black particularly, were for stronger action and a more open stand for freedom. One can, with a reasonable amount of distortion, see much of the history of the Court in Frankfurter's time as a slowly emerging struggle between a group of judges allied with Black and a group allied with Frankfurter, with Black's group the victor, expanding due process and extending the Court's power. The victorious group has found in the unchanging words of the Constitution a new set of prohibitions on government action, limiting police activities, overturning long-established modes of trial and traditional ways of electing legislatures. Misreading history creatively, Black has asserted that whatever the Bill of Rights forbids the federal government to do, it forbids also to the states. Frankfurter and other first-rate scholars have demolished the historical basis of Black's claim and have shown it to be a distortion of history, but this has not prevented the adoption by the Court of a considerable part of Black's position; possibly all that the scholars have demonstrated is that here, as with Magna Carta, bad history can make good law.

In the first of the reapportionment cases that was to lead ultimately to the rule, "One man, one vote," Frankfurter unashamedly urged the Court's weakness as a reason against its bold new course and unashamedly used the logic and language of the 18th century ("The Court's authority—possessed of neither the purse nor the sword . . .") to prove its weakness. Many students of the Court's history agreed with Frankfurter that only ill could come of the new venture. It appears, however, to have succeeded, and today it does not seem revolutionary to hold that if gerrymandering against Negroes and in favor of whites is unconstitutional, gerrymandering in favor of rural districts and against large cities—even when disguised as Jeffersonian political theory—deprives city folk of the equal protection of the laws.

The Court in the reapportionment cases, as in the desegregation cases, has of course done more than merely veto unconstitutional laws. It has had to govern, to supervise, with the aid of the lower federal courts, educational policies and plans of reapportionment. If the Court has moved into fields in which it would be theoretically more appropriate for others to act, they are fields in which as a practical matter no one would act but the Court. Perhaps the Court has come through its recent crises so well because it is felt that it has by and large seized power only where others have abandoned their duties.

A Congress for more than two decades illiberal and inactive, as far as the public welfare was concerned, may have made the liberal active Court appear so necessary. Liberal opinion thirty years ago, when the Court was obstructing Congress, was certain that a constitutional amendment was needed to curb the Court, which as long ago as the days of John Marshall had usurped power over acts of Congress. In recent years liberals, if they criticized the Court, have complained that it has not sufficiently curbed Congress, and John Marshall is now recognized as our greatest judicial statesman for having made the Court strong. It may be that if Congress continues to be as active for the public welfare as it was in the last session, our scale of values and our view of the role of the Court may change again.

If our sense of the eternal verities which are the Court's business shifts again, our appraisal of its members is likely to shift with it. At the moment, Felix Frankfurter may seem not to have measured up to the great expectations held out for him on his appointment. No one appeared then so likely to be one of the greatest judges in our history as he. His entire life since he had entered Harvard Law School, a number of careers fine in themselves, could be regarded as training for his final career on the Court. As a student of the Court he was fully aware of the organic nature of the Constitution as a living instrument of government. Severe as his criticism of the Court was at times, he was deeply respectful of its traditions, especially as they were embodied in the work of his idol, Holmes.

And yet, perhaps he may have been the victim of his splendid training, unfitted by it for the work that the Court was actually called on to do. If he fell short of greatness it may be because he had been prepared by life for an era that was already past and was not to come again, at least in his lifetime. Holmes had said in speaking of John Marshall, "A great man represents a great ganglion in the nerves of society, or, to vary the figure, a strategic point in the campaign of history, and part of his greatness consists of his being *there*." Holmes himself had the good luck to have this part of greatness, and if Frankfurter did not, it may be just because he thought Holmes a great man. One sometimes has to deny a hero his stature to free oneself of his influence, and this Frankfurter, with his deep loyalty to Holmes, could never do.

If Frankfurter turns out ultimately to have failed of greatness, it will be probably because, like Holmes, he respected power in others and tried to refuse it for the Court on which he sat. Pleased as Frankfurter had always been with the sense of power, he lacked the ruthlessness necessary to those who would possess it; if this turns out to have been a fault, it will always be deemed, whatever else history says of him, to have been a most attractive failing.

Confession and the Court

Isidore Silver

If a legal philosopher were asked to create a system of criminal procedure for a "modern" totalitarian state—i.e., one not characterized by overt brutality—he would probably include certain features. Trial could be secret, without an attorney or jury, and with no stenographic transcript. The sole purpose of the trial would be to induce a confession. The defendant would not be apprised of any right to remain silent and to be represented by counsel. If he is convicted, he can only argue to a suspicious appeals court that such conviction was based upon a confession wrung from him under these circumstances. Since he cannot submit a record of the proceedings, he is reduced to arguing that his word is better than that of his judges. The American mind obviously recoils at such a star-chamber proceeding. Yet, much of our criminal procedure involves this very process,

"Confession and the Court." *Commonweal,* July 8, 1966. Reprinted by permission of Commonweal Publishing Co., Inc.

and that is what the Supreme Court's June 13th decision in the four interrogation cases is all about.

Theoretically, a criminal trial is an adversary (or "accusatory") proceeding in which the prosecution must prove that "x" committed a crime. "X" cannot be compelled to testify against himself. Practically, the system doesn't quite work that way. The police often obtain some evidence of a suspect's guilt, but believe it to be insufficient to permit conviction. At that point, they often arrest the suspect, bring him to a station house for "booking" and conduct an extensive interrogation to induce a confession. This interrogation is generally conducted under the circumstances depicted in the opening paragraph. When a confession—preferably a written one has been obtained, the defendant is then taken before a judge for arraignment. Although there will be no police questioning after the arraignment, this is meaningless. The police have their confession, it is always introduced into evidence at trial, it is often ineffectively contested and it frequently forms the basis for a conviction.

In a sense, the trial is a review—and an ineffective one—of the confession proceeding. Nowhere else in American jurisprudence does a trial depend upon such "weak" evidence. There may be documentary evidence in the form of a signed confession, but it is obviously tenuous. As Chief Justice Warren stated on June 13, the cases questioning the use of such evidence presented "questions which go to the roots of our concepts of American criminal jurisprudence."

Until 1964, the Supreme Court resolved the problems presented by police interrogations by requiring that any resulting confessions be shown to be voluntary and not coerced. At no time—with perhaps one exception —was the mere fact that the accused was held incommunicado and not informed of his right to remain silent sufficient to constitute coercion. In 1964, in Escobedo v. Illinois, the Court held that an accused was denied due process of law. Escobedo, after his request to see a lawyer had been denied, confessed during questioning at a station house. Although the decision was limited to these somewhat unusual facts, for various reasons it caused much consternation in police circles. The Court had decided that, at some point during Escobedo's interrogation, he had become an accused, "and the purpose of the interrogation was to 'get him' to confess his guilt despite his constitutional right not to do so." This meant that his right to counsel came into existence. Since Escobedo had, "for all practical purposes, already been charged with murder," he was entitled to see his lawyer.

Justice Goldberg's cautious and fuzzy opinion evoked a sharp dissent from Justice White. "It would be naive to believe that the new constitutional right announced will depend upon whether the accused has retained his own counsel . . . or has asked to consult with counsel during the course of interrogation." The Justice also discerned what he thought to be a trend in the majority's thinking. "The decision is thus another major step in the direction of the goal which the court seemingly has in mind— to bar from evidence all admissions obtained from an individual suspected of crime, whether involuntarily made or not."

Since *Escobedo* involved a set of peculiar facts, and the court's decision was vague, state courts found substantial room for maneuver in applying the holding of their own reviews of police practices. Since most lower-court judges are notably reluctant to exclude customarily accepted and relevant evidence (and to free "known" criminals in the process), they tended to apply *Escobedo* narrowly. A few courts, such as the California Supreme Court, promulgated rules which required police warnings of defendants' rights whenever an investigation had become an accusatory proceeding and questioning designed to induce defendant to confess had commenced. The confusion in application of *Escobedo* caused the Supreme Court to decide "further to explore some facets of the problem."

THE CHOICES

The Court was faced with several choices. It could have decided that all station house confessions were illegal. First, the atmosphere within which questioning occurred could be deemed coercive, so that no confession could be truly voluntary. Second, if our system is indeed accusatory, then nothing to convict a defendant should come from his own mouth. Third, there are simply too many instances recorded of brutality or psychological pressures; the likelihood of any particular confession's being coerced is substantial, so the practice should be terminated. It could also have held that any confession made during a period of prolonged interrogation was inadmissible. This is the rule promulgated by the Court for lower federal courts; it is not (yet) based upon Constitutional factors.

On the other hand, it could have rigorously limited *Escobedo* (a) to situations where defendant had asked for counsel, or (b) to require that police only inform him of his right to counsel but of no other rights. Or, the Court could have compromised, as it often does when heavily attacked.

The decision was a compromise—an interesting and provocative one. Initially, Justice Warren's lengthy opinion posited certain vital Constitutional truths: police interrogation during a period of incommunicado custody is inherently coercive; the right to remain silent exists at that moment, and not merely after one is formally charged with a crime (a point not avidly contested by the dissenters); a "voluntary" statement requires not only the lack of overt coercion, but also full knowledge of all Constitutional rights. These premises form the intellectual underpinnings of the decision of June 13.

Although the Constitution marched bravely into the police station, once inside, it sat rather quietly. The majority opinion stated that, despite the aforemenioned factors, a confession could still be legal even if made during interrogation and in the absence of counsel, provided that certain standards were met. These standards required, as a minimum, a clear warning to a suspect of his right to remain silent, of the use to which any evidence to be obtained from him could be put, and of his right to counsel. These warnings, said the Court, were absolutely required before any questioning can occur. After such warnings are "effectively" given, the suspect may "waive" (relinquish) these rights, "provided the waiver is made voluntarily, knowingly and intelligently." If he indicates "in any manner" and "at any stage of the process" that he wants to consult with an attorney, questioning must cease. If an attorney is consulted, he has the right to be present during the interrogation and advise the suspect. Thus, the Court paradoxically held that (a) the situation was inherently coercive but that (b) its coercive features could be overcome by following proper procedures.

The decision evoked the displeasure of four Justices and the predictable wrath of police officials. Yet, the storm came, blew over, and the house was still standing. Undoubtedly, many had expected worse; the police were bothered by some of the language in *Escobedo* indicating that a system of criminal justice that, in large part, depended upon confessions was not a healthy system at all. As a result, they were braced for a stringent ruling now. But the decision left some loopholes. Indeed, as Justice Harlan caustically noted, "Those who use third degree tactics and deny them in court are equally able and destined to lie as skillfully about warnings and waivers." James Vorenberg, Executive Director of the National Crime Commission (and a prominent *Escobedo* critic) said that the decision "just moves the battleground from the voluntariness of the confession back to the voluntariness of the waiver."

For the moment, the Constitution stands silently behind the suspect as he is interrogated. Presumably, the police will discover ways of complying with the Court's requirement that warnings must be "effective" (some ambiguity there), that the burden of proof is on the State to show waiver and that such burden is especially high where the interrogation has been lengthy. Apart from the fact that the battleground has shifted, nothing much may have really changed.

Yet, the portents are there. The Court has lit the pyre and Supreme Courtologists may divine the auguries. What are we to make of the Court's reliance on certain foreign legal systems which exclude pre-arraignment confessions altogether? What about the following statement? "The presence of counsel, in all the cases before us today, would be the adequate protective device necessary to make the process of police interrogation conform to the dictates of the privilege (against self-incrimination). His presence would insure that statements made in the government-established atmosphere are not the product of compulsion."

These and other statements indicate that the "new" safeguards established by these cases may not be fully adequate to insure protection of fundamental constitutional rights. The Court, as usual, has left open the possibility of further study, if the state courts do not fully supervise the police.

At least two areas of potential additional requirements are suggested in the decision and the dissents. The paragraph quoted above indicates that the Court is unhappy with any questioning in the absence of counsel. Thus, it might one day decide that a truly effective waiver cannot be accomplished in the inherently coercive atmosphere of the squad room, especially where the person giving the warning is also the one pressing to obtain the waiver. Thus, perhaps we shall see a requirement that an effective waiver can only occur where counsel is present to inform defendant of his rights and to consult with him about the exercise of those rights.

Justice White testily suggested that the Court's concern for what really happens in squad rooms might be alleviated by the use of recording devices, so that all can know whether proper warnings, waivers, and lack of coercion have occurred. The idea is not a bad one, but it would not solve the problem of whether the waiver was knowing and intelligent. Since the Court meticulously investigates the state and quality of defendants' minds in determining existence of true waiver in other types of cases, it surely will do no less here. Besides, will the Court's present majority accept even this "evidence" in the face of a claim that the suspect was "softened up" on the way to the station house? Also, and this may be the most weighty argument, will a recording, even a television tape recording be sufficient to accurately depict the degree of fear and coercion actually *felt*? Ultimately, it is the suspect's, not the police officer's, state of mind and conduct that concern the Court.

In the light of the Court's definition of "voluntary," it appears as if the Court is "planting" quotes to justify later, further-reaching decisions. Just as the Court blandly stated that its decision was "not an innovation," a future Court may, by a similar non-innovation, rule out all confessions entirely.

Chapter Ten

SUGGESTED QUESTIONS FOR CLASS DISCUSSION.

1. Critics of the Court, among them members of Congress, frequently accuse the present Court of "political" activism and usurping the powers of Congress by legislating. How "legal" was the Marshall decision in *Marbury*? What were the implications of the short news story that the Court was being pressed to rule on federal aid to church-related schools and that a U.S. Senator was one of those appearing before the Court in the case? Is this the kind of buck-passing which has made the Court the "storm-center of American politics"?
2. It has for many years been an accepted idea that the Court is an essentially undemocratic institution functioning in a democracy. Is this necessarily true? Is the fact that the Justices are not elected make the Court undemocratic? Is it possible that its record as the defender of minority rights makes it the most democratic institution?
3. When the Court is aware that basic freedoms are being denied persons by the state governments, should it still rely on the legislatures to correct the evil? If they do not, should the Court close its eyes?
4. Does the career of Justice Frankfurter appear to mirror the adaptation of the Court itself to the requirements of a changing society? He went on the Court as the great "liberal"; he retired as the great "conservative." Did he change during this period?

Chapter Eleven

CIVIL RIGHTS
AND LIBERTIES

*It is essential to the functioning of a democracy that the proper claims
of the community be recognized. It is equally important that the majority,
in ruling, not ride roughshod over the rights of individuals and minorities.
Conversely, although the rights of individuals must be recognized, these
rights must not be viewed as absolute and unchallengeable, lest they interfere with the legitimate needs of the community. In short, while each is
essential, each is also modified by the other.*

*When two principles—majority rule and minority rights—conflict in
this way, no final solution of the conflict is possible. Only "proximate"
solutions are possible, and no compromise formula is likely to be stable
for very long. The locus of day-to-day decisions will need to shift gradually,
over a period of time, in response to changing conditions and needs—now
inclining slightly more in the direction of individual rights and later in the
direction of community needs. At any given moment the nature of the
pragmatic solutions are likely to be subject to attack from either side or
from both sides, for the partisans of neither approach will be fully satisfied.
This means that there are no final solutions to most civil rights issues but
only new issues and disputes with solutions that will continue to define
and redefine the proper sphere of the competing principles.*

*Civil rights problems, difficult at best, are aggravated by the way that
the federal system sometimes operates in practice. Those denying basic
rights to others are likely to justify their action on the basis of the principle of states' rights. What are the obligations of the federal government
in such circumstances, and what should be the practical limitations on its*

339

capacity to enforce the rights of individuals against the states? Shall it try to preserve the liberties of the individual citizen at the risk of infringing upon the federal principle; or shall it allow the states to go their separate ways even if it means that the principle of individual rights is infringed upon?

Mapp v. Ohio: A Case for Selective Inclusion

It comes as a shock to most Americans to learn for the first time that the Bill of Rights is a restraint on the federal government only. Relying upon the history of the ratification of the amendments that make up the Bill of Rights, Chief Justice John Marshall, speaking for the Supreme Court in Barron v. Baltimore *(1833) said, in part, "These amendments demanded security against apprehended encroachments by the general government—not against those of the local governments. . . ." Whenever a Constitutional provision was meant to affect the states ". . . words are employed which directly express that intent. . . . These (first eight) amendments contain no expression indicating an intention to apply them to state governments. This Court cannot so apply them." This interpretation has been fully incorporated into American Constitutional development.*

But one of the strongest motives in drafting the post Civil War protective amendments, and especially the Fourteenth, with its prohibitions on the states against denial of due process and equal protection of the laws, was to liquidate the effects of the Barron decision.

Despite a number of narrow interpretations of the scope of protections afforded by the Fourteenth Amendment, since the middle 1920's the Court has proceeded toward "nationalization" of the Bill of Rights by incorporating many of its protections as prohibitions against state's denials of due process and equal protection as commanded by the Fourteenth Amendment.

As a result of the Court's decision in the case which follows, the protection against illegal search and seizure afforded by the Fourth Amendment is now imposed upon the states. In reaching its decision the Court followed the principle of incorporation provided in Palko v. Connecticut *by concluding that this liberty is one of those which are ". . . implicit in the concepts of ordered liberty which lie at the base of all of our civil and political institutions."*

Miss Dollree Mapp was convicted in Ohio of having obscene materials in her possession in violation of state statute. After the Ohio Supreme Court upheld the conviction, Miss Mapp brought an appeal to the Supreme Court.

Mr. Justice Clark Delivered the Opinion of the Court.

. . . On May 23, 1957, three Cleveland police officers arrived at appellant's residence in that city pursuant to information that "a person [*was*] hiding out in the home who was wanted for questioning in connection with a recent bombing, and that there was a large amount of policy paraphernalia being hidden in the home." Miss Mapp and her daughter by a former marriage lived on the top floor of the two-family dwelling. Upon their arrival at that house, the officers knocked on the door and demanded entrance but appellant, after telephoning her attorney, refused to admit

Mapp v. Ohio, 367 U.S. 643; 81 Sup. Ct. 1684; 6 L. Ed. 2d (1961).

them without a search warrant. They advised their headquarters of the situation and undertook a surveillance of the house.

The officers again sought entrance some three hours later when four or more additional officers arrived on the scene. When Miss Mapp did not come to the door immediately, at least one of the several doors to the house was forcibly opened and the policemen gained admittance. Meanwhile Miss Mapp's attorney arrived, but the officers, having secured their own entry, and continuing in their defiance of the law, would permit him neither to see Miss Mapp nor to enter the house. It appears that Miss Mapp was halfway down the stairs from the upper floor to the front door when the officers, in this highhanded manner, broke into the hall. She demanded to see the search warrant. A paper, claimed to be a warrant, was held up by one of the officers. She grabbed the "warrant" and placed it in her bosom. A struggle ensued in which the officers recovered the piece of paper and as a result of which they handcuffed appellant because she had been "belligerent" in resisting their official rescue of the "warrant" from her person. Running roughshod over appellant, a policeman "grabbed" her, "twisted [her] hand," and she "yelled [and] pleaded with him" because "it was hurting." Appellant, in handcuffs, was then forcibly taken upstairs to her bedroom where the officers searched a dresser, a chest of drawers, a closet and some suitcases. They also looked into a photo album and through personal papers belonging to the appellant. The search spread to the rest of the second floor including the child's bedroom, the living room, the kitchen and a dinette. The basement of the building and a trunk found therein were also searched. The obscene materials for possession of which she was ultimately convicted were discovered in the course of that widespread search.

At the trial no search warrant was produced by the prosecution, nor was the failure to produce one explained or accounted for. At best, "there is, in the record, considerable doubt as to whether there ever was any warrant for the search of defendant's home." . . .

The State says that even if the search were made without authority, or otherwise unreasonably, it is not prevented from using the unconstitutionally seized evidence at trial, citing *Wolf* v. *Colorado*, 338 U.S. 25 (1949), in which this Court did indeed hold "that in a prosecution in a State court for a State crime the Fourteenth Amendment does not forbid the admission of evidence obtained by an unreasonable search and seizure." . . .

I

Seventy-five years ago, in *Boyd* v. *United States*, 116 U.S. 616, 630 (1886), considering the Fourth and Fifth Amendments as running "almost into each other" on the facts before it, this Court held the doctrines of those Amendments

> apply to all invasions on the part of the government and its employees of the sanctity of a man's home and the privacies of life. It is not the breaking of his doors, and the rummaging of his drawers, that constitutes the essence of the offense; but it is the invasion of his indefeasible right of personal security, personal liberty and private property. . . . Breaking into a house and opening boxes and drawers are circumstances of aggravation; but any

forcible and compulsory extortion of a man's own testimony or of his private papers to be used as evidence to convict him of crime or to forfeit his goods, is within the condemnation . . . [of those Amendments]. . . .

Less than 30 years after Boyd, this Court, in *Weeks* v. *United States,* 232 U.S. 383 (1914), stated that

the Fourth Amendment . . . put the courts of the United States and Federal officials, in the exercise of their power and authority, under limitations and restraints [*and*] . . . forever secure[*d*] the people, their persons, houses, papers and effects against all unreasonable searches and seizures under the guise of law . . . and the duty of giving to it force and effect is obligatory upon all entrusted under our Federal system with the enforcement of the laws. . . .

Specifically dealing with the use of the evidence unconstitutionally seized, the Court concluded:

If letters and private documents can thus be seized and held and used in evidence against a citizen accused of an offense, the protection of the Fourth Amendment declaring his right to be secure against such searches and seizures is of no value, and, so far as those thus placed are concerned, might as well be stricken from the Constitution. The efforts of the courts and their officials to bring the guilty to punishment, praiseworthy as they are, are not to be aided by the sacrifice of those great principles established by years of endeavor and suffering which have resulted in their embodiment in the fundamental law of the land. . . .

Finally, the Court in that case clearly stated that use of the seized evidence involved "a denial of the constitutional rights of the accused." . . . Thus, in the year 1914, in the Weeks case, this Court "for the first time" held that "in a federal prosecution the Fourth Amendment barred the use of evidence secured through an illegal search and seizure." . . . This Court has ever since required of federal law officers a strict adherence to that command which this Court has held to be a clear, specific, and constitutionally required—even if judicially implied—deterrent safeguard without insistence upon which the Fourth Amendment would have been reduced to "a form of words." . . . It meant, quite simply, that "conviction by means of unlawful seizures and enforced confessions . . . should find no sanction in the judgments of the courts. . . ."

There are in the cases of this Court some passing references to the Weeks rule as being one of evidence. But the plain and unequivocal language of Weeks—and its later paraphrase in Wolf—to the effect that the Weeks rule is of constitutional origin, remains entirely undisturbed. . . .

II

In 1949, 35 years after Weeks was announced, this Court, in *Wolf* v. *Colorado,* supra, again for the first time, discussed the effect of the Fourth Amendment upon the States through the operation of the Due Process Clause of the Fourteenth Amendment. It said:

[W]e have no hesitation in saying that were a State affirmatively to sanction such police incursion into privacy it would run counter to the guaranty of the Fourteenth Amendment. . . .

Nevertheless, after declaring that the "security of one's privacy against arbitrary intrusion by the police" is "implicit in the 'concept of ordered liberty' and as such enforceable against the States through the Due Process Clause," *cf. Palko* v. *Connecticut*, 302 U.S. 319 (1937), and announcing that it "stoutly adhere[d]" to the Weeks decision, the Court decided that the Weeks exclusionary rule would not then be imposed upon the States as "an essential ingredient of the right." . . .

III

Some five years after Wolf, in answer to a plea made here Term after Term that we overturn its doctrine on applicability of the Weeks exclusionary rule, this Court indicated that such should not be done until the States had "adequate opportunity to adopt or reject the [*Weeks*] rule." . . .

Today we once again examine Wolf's constitutional documentation of the right to privacy free from unreasonable state intrusion, and, after its dozen years on our books, are led by it to close the only courtroom door remaining open to evidence secured by official lawlessness in flagrant abuse of that basic right, reserved to all persons as a specific guarantee against that very same unlawful conduct. We hold that all evidence obtained by searches and seizures in violation of the Constitution is, by that same authority, inadmissible in a state court.

IV

Since the Fourth Amendment's right of privacy has been declared enforceable against the States through the Due Process Clause of the Fourteenth, it is enforceable against them by the same sanction of exclusion as is used against the Federal Government. Were it otherwise, then just as without the Weeks rule the assurance against unreasonable federal searches and seizures would be "a form of words," valueless and undeserving of mention in a perpetual charter of inestimable human liberties, so too, without that rule the freedom from state invasions of privacy would be so ephemeral and so neatly severed from its conceptual nexus with the freedom from all brutish means of coercing evidence as not to merit this Court's high regard as a freedom "implicit in the concept of ordered liberty." At the time that the Court held in Wolf that the Amendment was applicable to the States through the Due Process Clause, the cases of this Court, as we have seen, had steadfastly held that as to federal officers the Fourth Amendment included the exclusion of the evidence seized in violation of its provisions. . . . [T]he admission of the new constitutional right by Wolf could not consistently tolerate denial of its most important constitutional privilege, namely, the exclusion of the evidence which an accused had been forced to give by reason of the unlawful seizure. To hold otherwise is to grant the right but in reality to withhold its privilege and enjoyment. Only last year the Court itself recognized that the purpose of the exclusionary rule "is to deter—to compel respect for the constitutional guaranty in the only effectively available way—by removing the incentive to disregard it." . . .

Indeed, we are aware of no restraint, similar to that rejected today, conditioning the enforcement of any other basic constitutional right. The right to privacy, no less important than any other right carefully and particularly reserved to the people, would stand in marked contrast to all other rights declared as "basic to a free society." . . . The Court has not hesitated to enforce as strictly against the States as it does against the Federal Government the rights of free speech and of a free press, the rights to notice and to a fair, public trial, including, as it does, the right not to be convicted by use of a coerced confession, however logically relevant it be, and without regard to its reliability. . . . We find that, as to the Federal Government, the Fourth and Fifth Amendment and, as to the States, the freedom from unconscionable invasions of privacy and the freedom from convictions based upon coerced confessions do enjoy an "intimate relation" in their perpetuation of "principles of humanity and civil liberty [*secured*] . . . only after years of struggle." . . .

V

Moreover, our holding that the exclusionary rule is an essential part of both the Fourth and Fourteenth Amendments is not only the logical dictate of prior cases, but it also makes very good sense. There is no war between the Constitution and common sense. Presently, a federal prosecutor may make no use of evidence illegally seized, but a State's attorney across the street may, although he supposedly is operating under the enforceable prohibitions of the same Amendment. Thus the State, by admitting evidence unlawfully seized, serves to encourage disobedience to the Federal Constitution which it is bound to uphold. . . . In nonexclusionary States, federal officers, being human, were by it invited to and did, as our cases indicate, step across the street to the State's attorney with their unconstitutionally seized evidence. Prosecution on the basis of that evidence was then had in a state court in utter disregard of the enforceable Fourth Amendment. If the fruits of an unconstitutional search had been inadmissible in both state and federal courts, this inducement to evasion would have been sooner eliminated. . . .

Federal-state cooperation in the solution of crime under constitutional standards will be promoted, if only by recognition of their now mutual obligation to respect the same fundamental criteria in their approaches. "However much in a particular case insistence upon such rules may appear as a technicality that inures to the benefit of a guilty person, the history of the criminal law proves that tolerance of shortcut methods in law enforcement impairs its enduring effectiveness." . . . Denying shortcuts to only one of two cooperating law enforcement agencies tends naturally to breed legitimate suspicion of "working arrangements" whose results are equally tainted. . . .

The ignoble shortcut to conviction left open to the State tends to destroy the entire system of constitutional restraints on which the liberties of the people rest. Having once recognized that the right to privacy embodied in the Fourth Amendment is enforceable against the States, and that the right to be secure against rude invasions of privacy by state officers is, therefore, constitutional in origin, we can no longer permit that right to remain an empty promise. Because it is enforceable in the same manner and to like effect as other basic rights secured by the Due Process Clause, we can no longer permit it to be revocable at the whim of any police officer who, in the name of law enforcement itself, chooses to suspend its enjoyment. Our decision, founded on reason and truth, gives to the individual no more than that which the Constitution guarantees him, to the police officer no less than that to which honest law enforcement is entitled, and to the courts, that judicial integrity so necessary in the true administration of justice.

The judgment of the Supreme Court of Ohio is reversed and the cause remanded for further proceedings not inconsistent with this opinion.

Reversed and remanded.

Mr. Justice Black, Concurring.

I am still not persuaded that the Fourteenth Amendment, standing alone, would be enough to bar the introduction into evidence against an accused of papers and effects seized from him in violation of its commands. For the Fourth Amendment does not itself contain any provision expressly precluding the use of such evidence, and I am extremely doubtful that such a provision could properly be inferred from nothing more than the basic command against unreasonable searches and seizures. Reflection on the problem, however, in the light of cases coming before the Court since *Wolf*, has led me to conclude that when the Fourth Amendment's ban against unreasonable searches and seizures is considered together with the Fifth Amendment's ban against compelled self-incrimination, a constitutional basis emerges which not only justifies but actually requires the exclusionary rule.

The close interrelationship between the Fourth and Fifth Amendments, as they apply to this problem, has long been recognized and, indeed, was expressly made the ground for this Court's holding in *Boyd* v. *United States*. There the Court fully discussed this relationship and declared itself "unable to perceive that the seizure of a man's private books and papers to be used in evidence against him is substantially different from compelling him to be a witness against himself." It was upon this ground that Mr. Justice Rutledge largely relied in his dissenting opinion in the *Wolf* case. And, although I rejected the argument at that time, its force has, for me at least, become compelling with the more thorough understanding of the problem brought on by recent cases. In the final analysis, it seems to be that the Boyd doctrine, though perhaps not required by the express language of the Constitution strictly construed, is amply justified from an historical standpoint, soundly based in reason, and entirely consistent with what I regard to be the proper approach to interpretation of our Bill of Rights. . . .

The Court's opinion, in my judgment, dissipates the doubt and uncertainty in this field of constitutional law and I am persuaded, for this and other reasons stated, to depart from my prior views, to accept the Boyd doctrine as controlling in this state case and to join the Court's judgment and opinion which are in accordance with that constitutional doctrine.

Mr. Justice Douglas, Concurring.

. . . *Wolf* v. *Colorado* . . . was decided in 1949. The immediate result was a storm of constitutional controversy which only today finds its end.

I believe that this is an appropriate case in which to put an end to the asymmetry which *Wolf* imported into the law. . . . It is an appropriate case because the facts it presents show—as would few other cases—the casual arrogance of those who have the untrammelled power to invade one's home and to seize one's person. . . .

Memorandum of Mr. Justice Stewart.

Agreeing fully with Part I of Mr. Justice Harlan's dissenting opinion, I express no view as to the merits of the constitutional issue which the Court today decides. I would, however, reverse the judgment in this case, because I am persuaded that the provision of Section 2905.34 of the Ohio Revised Code, upon which the petitioner's conviction was based, is, in the words of Mr. Justice Harlan, not "consistent with the rights of free thought and expression assured against state action by the Fourteenth Amendment."

Mr. Justice Harlan, whom Mr. Justice Frankfurter and Mr. Justice Whittaker Join, Dissenting.

In overruling the *Wolf* case the Court, in my opinion, has forgotten the sense of judicial restraint which, with due regard for stare decisis, is one element that should enter into deciding whether a past decision of this Court should be overruled. Apart from that I also believe that the *Wolf* rule represents sounder Constitutional doctrine than the new rule which now replaces it.

I

From the Court's statement of the case one would gather that the central, if not controlling, issue on this appeal is whether illegally state-seized evidence is Constitutionally admissible in a state prosecution, an issue which would of course face us with the need for re-examining *Wolf*. However, such is not the situation. For, although that question was indeed raised here and below among appellant's subordinate points, the new and pivotal issue brought to the Court by this appeal is whether Section 2905.34 of the Ohio Revised Code making criminal the mere knowing possession or control of obscene material, and under which appellant has been convicted, is consistent with the rights of free thought and expression assured against state action by the Fourteenth Amendment. That was the principal issue which was decided by the Ohio Supreme Court, which was tendered by appellant's Jurisdictional Statement, and which was briefed and argued in this Court.

In this posture of things, I think it fair to say that five members of this Court have simply "reached out" to overrule *Wolf*. With all respect for the views of the majority, and recognizing that stare decisis carries different weight in Constitutional adjudication than it does in nonconstitutional decision, I can perceive no justification for regarding this case as an appropriate occasion for re-examining *Wolf*.

The action of the Court finds no support in the rule that decision of Constitutional issues should be avoided wherever possible. For in overruling *Wolf* the Court, instead of passing upon the validity of Ohio's

Section 2905.34, has simply chosen between two Constitutional questions. . . .

The occasion which the Court has taken here is in the context of a case where the question was briefed not at all and argued only extremely tangentially. The unwisdom of overruling *Wolf* without full-dress argument is aggravated by the circumstances that that decision is a comparatively recent one (1949) to which three members of the present majority have at one time or other expressly subscribed, one to be sure with explicit misgivings. I would think that our obligation to the States, on whom we impose this new rule, as well as the obligation of orderly adherence to our own processes would demand that we seek that aid which adequate briefing and argument lends to the determination of an important issue. It certainly has never been a postulate of judicial power that mere altered disposition, or subsequent membership on the Court, is sufficient warrant for overturning a deliberately decided rule of Constitutional law.

Thus, if the Court was bent on reconsidering *Wolf*, I think that there would soon have presented itself an appropriate opportunity in which we could have had the benefit of full briefing and argument. In any event, at the very least, the present case should have been set down for reargument, in view of the inadequate briefing and argument we have received on the *Wolf* point. To all intents and purposes the Court's present action amounts to a summary reversal of *Wolf*, without argument.

I am bound to say that what has been done is not likely to promote respect either for the Court's adjudicatory process or for the stability of its decisions. Having been unable, however, to persuade any of the majority to a different procedural course, I now turn to the merits of the present decision.

II

I would not impose upon the States this federal exclusionary remedy. The reasons given by the majority for now suddenly turning its back on *Wolf* seem to me notably unconvincing. . . .

Our concern here, as it was in *Wolf*, is not with the desirability of that rule but only with the question whether the States are constitutionally free to follow it or not as they may themselves determine, and the relevance of the disparity of views among the States on this point lies simply in the fact that the judgment involved is a debatable one. . . .

The preservation of a proper balance between state and federal responsibility in the administration of criminal justice demands patience on the part of those who might like to see things move faster among the States in this respect. Problems of criminal law enforcement vary widely from State to State. One State, in considering the totality of its legal picture, may conclude that the need for embracing the Weeks rule is pressing because other remedies are unavailable or inadequate to secure compliance with the substantive Constitutional principle involved. Another, though equally solicitous of Constitutional rights, may choose to pursue one purpose at a time, allowing all evidence relevant to guilt to be brought into a criminal trial, and dealing with Constitutional infractions by other means. Still another may consider the exclusionary rule too rough and ready a remedy, in that it reaches only unconstitutional intrusions which eventuate in criminal prosecution of the victims. Further, a State after experimenting with the Weeks rule for a time may, because of unsatisfactory experience with it, decide to revert to a nonexclusionary rule. And so on. . . . For us the question remains, as it has always been, one of state power, not one of passing judgment on the wisdom of one state course or another. In my view this Court should continue to forebear from fettering the States with an adamant rule which may embarrass them in coping with their own peculiar problems in criminal law enforcement. . . .

Our role in promulgating the Weeks rule and its extensions . . . was quite a different one than it is here. There, in implementing the Fourth Amendment, we occupied the position of a tribunal having the ultimate responsibility for developing the standards and procedures of judicial administration within the judicial system over which it presides. Here we review State procedures whose measure is to be taken not against the specific substantive commands of the Fourth Amendment but under the flexible contours of the Due Process Clause. I do not believe that the Fourteenth Amendment empowers this Court to mould state remedies effectuating the right to freedom from "arbitrary intrusion by the police" to suit its own notions of how things should be done. . . .

A state conviction comes to us as the complete product of a sovereign judicial system. Typically a case will have been tried in a trial court, tested in some final appellate court, and will go no further. In the comparatively rare instance when a conviction is reviewed by us on due process grounds we deal then with a finished product in the creation of which we are allowed no hand, and our task, far from being one of overall supervision, is, speaking generally, restricted to a determination of whether the prosecution was contitutionally fair. The specifics of trial procedure, which in every mature legal system will vary greatly in detail, are within the sole competence of the States. I do not see how it can be said that a trial becomes unfair simply because a State determines that evidence may be considered by the trier of fact, regardless of how it was obtained, if it is relevant to the one issue with which the trial is concerned, the guilt or innocence of the accused. Of course, a court may use its procedures as an incidental means of pursuing other ends than the correct resolution of the controversies before it. Such indeed is the Weeks rule, but if a State does not choose to use its courts in this way, I do not believe that this Court is empowered to impose this much-debated procedure on local courts, however efficacious we may consider the Weeks rule to be as a means of securing Constitutional rights. . . .

I regret that I find so unwise in principle and so inexpedient in policy a decision motivated by the high purpose of increasing respect for Constitutional rights. But in the last analysis I think this Court can increase respect for the Constitution only if it rigidly respects the limitations which the Constitution places upon it, and respects as well the principles inherent in its own processes. In the present case I think we exceed both, and that our voice becomes only a voice of power, not of reason.

Congress Shall Make No Law...

William B. Ball

Jaime and Maria Perez were startled to hear, in early December, that their children, Tommy and Lisa, had been unlawfully receiving benefits from the government of the United States.

The Perez parents live in the squalid Bedford-Stuyvesant section of Brooklyn, with its fifty-fifty Puerto Rican-Negro population. Jaime and Maria do not look forward to prosperity and a home in the suburbs. Their equity in America's great society is in Tommy and Lisa, and at this moment that equity hinges mainly on one thing: education. Tommy and Lisa go to a school in the neighborhood whose facilities are reasonably good and whose staff is highly capable. Moreover, the school is a model of successful racial and ethnic integration. Education there has been much aided lately by programing paid for by the federal government, under the Elementary and Secondary Education Act of 1965 (ESEA). The charge of unlawfulness relates to one thing: The school is St. Teresa of Avila School —run by sisters of the Roman Catholic Church.

Early in December suits were filed in state and federal courts in New York charging that the financing by the federal government of instruction in reading, arithmetic, and other subjects in New York City parochial schools, as well as guidance counseling, is unconstitutional. The suits charged that the lending of textbooks and instructional materials under ESEA, for the benefit of children in these schools, is also unconstitutional. A *New York Times* headline of December 2 contained the gravamen of the complaint: The suits, it said, were over CHURCH-STATE SEPARATION.

Some greeted these juridical accusations with shock. Parents like Jaime and Maria, though uneducated, had nevertheless begun to share in an awareness now pervading the "other America" of an opening society in which rigid nineteenth-century racial and religious classifications were at last in bad odor. They could not begin to understand that through the programs in question their government had done something bad. Some other, more sophisticated observers, however, saw the lawsuits in two broader perspectives—first, as part of a much wider campaign to dramatize what they believed to be an extremist view of the principle of church-state separation; second, as a disturbing survival of America's long history of religious prejudice.

The campaign represents a fascinating alliance of secularist liberals and Bible-thumping conservatives. It is spearheaded nationally by the ebullient, litigious American Jewish Congress and an organization grandly calling itself "Americans United"—an image-wise evolution of its meandering formal title, "Protestants and Other Americans United for the Separation of Church and State." These groups get aid and comfort in their

"Congress Shall Make No Law," Saturday Review, January 21, 1967. Reprinted by permission of the author and publisher.

campaign for "absolute separation of church and state" from old-style liberals in a growingly divided (on religious issues) American Civil Liberties Union, and from some elements in public school associations whose ideal is "every child in a public school."

The emphasis of the campaign is fear, and the stressed object of that fear is the Roman Catholic Church (with a sometimes lingering emphasis on the word Roman). A number of subsidiary fears are exploited: fear that public education will be eroded by virtue of the demands of the Roman Catholic Church for public funds for its schools, fear that the separate religious education of children is socially divisive, fear that religious liberty itself is threatened by government programs providing educational benefits to children in parochial schools.

Rowing frantically in the shallows, the campaigners have not thus far managed to get themselves into the mainstream of modern American attitudes—nor have they yet been able to divert the mainstream to their own direction. Hearing their shrill accusations of "divisiveness," many are coming to feel that it is the campaigners who are divisive, while others also see in the campaign very serious threats to educational freedom and community peace. Numerous Jews, for example, were profoundly disturbed over the carefully prepared press conference which Leo Pfeffer, special counsel to the American Jewish Congress, used as the means of launching the New York lawsuits. Said Rabbi Morris Sherer, executive vice president at Agudath Israel of America: "We deplore the distorted image that the American public receives about the Jewish view on federal aid to nonpublic schools as a result of the primary role played by the American Jewish Congress in its latest attempt to nullify the intent of the education law passed overwhelmingly by the United States Congress in 1965."

Clear it is that the campaign, with its lawsuits (but two of a dozen major test cases being promoted in the United States) and a very extensive public relations campaign accompanying them, will drive rough wedges between group and group at a time when new endeavors in ecumenism and brotherhood, for the relief of poverty and for better education of children, have been gaining strength in the American society. The second perspective which I have mentioned—the historical—brings home some of the reasons why the campaign may result in great civil harm to the nation.

I have spoken of this campaign as a "survival." To American Catholics it presents all too vivid a reminder of an ugly past—a past which witnessed a shockingly extensive bigotry in the elections of 1928 and 1960—a past in which, in 1923 as many as 10 per cent of the adult males of Pennsylvania were members of the Ku Klux Klan. Disturbingly, the campaign bears close resemblance, in its pronouncements on education, to the campaign of the American Protective Association (1887–1908) to marshal all children into a single educational mold, where only those values acknowledged by the state may be expressed. The APA's statement of principles in 1894, plumping militantly on behalf of a state educational monopoly, focused on the Catholic Peril. Barely gulping down a recital that it was "tolerant of all creeds," it proceeded to disgorge paragraphs of imprecation against an "un-American ecclesiastical power" (which the APA was quick to identify as the Roman Catholic Church). The APA diligently deflected public attention away from educational needs and the freedom to choose a church-related school by sowing fear that any expenditure of tax funds in support of the education of children in such schools would "weaken our public schools" and "enrich the coffers" of the churches sponsoring these schools. Reading the Constitution to suit its own predilections, the APA propagandized the view that the Constitution commands an "*absolute* separation of church and state." The APA eventually foundered on internal problems relating to finances and organization and upon popular revulsion against its fulminating bias.

While the campaign today is no phalanx of bigots, and avoids, on the whole, appeals to hatred, its message to the American people amounts to no lesser charge than that the Catholic Church today promotes violation of the American Constitution, raiding of the public treasury, crippling of the public schools, and dividing of the American society. That such a charge, especially when made by religious groups, should stir prejudice in the uninformed is understandable. That it should wound the sensibilities of millions of Catholic citizens now, as a class, no longer servants or dock hands, but contributors at all levels of our society—should also be understandable. The charge, it is to be hoped, will fall on deaf ears, for reasons of law, education, and liberty.

If a supposed constitutional dogma of "absolute" church-state separation was a make-weight argument for the APA in its fight against public aid to the church schools, it comes close to being the present campaign's whole case. The raiding, crippling, and dividing charges in large part depend upon a basic charge that the the aid Catholics and others have sought for children attending religious schools is unlawful. Focusing on the First Amendment's cryptic prohibition against "an establishment of religion," opponents of such aid are fond of pointing out that the Supreme Court has said that this means that government may not support religious objectives. Then the opponents (in a remarkable feat of private interpretation which they pass off as the Court's interpretation) say that that means that government may not support *public* objectives—if these are carried out in church-related institutions.

Under this view—constrictive not merely of religious freedom but of governmental freedom—not only would much of the present ESEA program, which today aids millions of young citizens in parochial schools, have to be scrapped, but a host of other public benefit programs would have to go with it. Banned, for example, by such a doctrine of "absolute separation" would be a federal loan to build a Presbyterian home for the aged, or a government grant to install a physics lab in a Methodist college. If separation is to be absolute, tax exemption of churches and synagogues must go. And separation, let it be noted, cannot be absolute against things we dislike and relative to things we like.

For almost a century after the founding of the nation, the "absolute separation" doctrine was a stranger to American constitutional law. Even the phrase, "separation of church and state," does not appear in any Supreme Court decision until 1879—and then only to indicate that a person's religious beliefs did not exempt him from an enactment of Congress making polygamy a crime. The idea of an absolute separation of church and state was carefully ignored during a century and a half of Protestant political and cultural hegemony in the United States, when little dissent was audible over the use of public schools for the encouragement of Protestant religious attitudes or the use of public funds for the support of Protestant institutions of welfare and education. Absolutist thinking on the separation question comes to us with no reliable historical credentials whatsoever.

That principled pragmatist of the American society, the Supreme Court, has subscribed to precious few absolutes, and it has never subscribed to the doctrine of an absolute separation of church and state. Brittle legalism on church-state issues was exploded by the Court in the memorable statement of Justice William O. Douglas in *Zorach v. Clausen,* in 1952. The Constitution, said Douglas, "does not say that in every and all respects there shall be a separation of Church and State. Rather, it studiously defines the manner, the specific ways, in which there shall be no concert or union or dependency one on the other. That is the common sense of the matter. Otherwise the state and religion would be aliens to each other— hostile, suspicious, and even unfriendly."

In 1963, the Court was specific. Citing its own prior decision upholding publicly financed busing for parochial school children, it said that if a piece of legislation serves a "secular legislative purpose" and has a "primary effect that neither advances nor inhibits religion," the legislation does not offend church-state separation and is constitutionally acceptable. Government's providing, under ESEA, of secular-subject textbooks and instruction—according to governmental standards—is certainly another example of legislation whose primary effect is secular.

If the absolutists' case against all programs aiding strictly secular educational objectives for children in church-related schools is weak, the case for such aid is compelling. One-seventh of the nation's educational effort takes place in church-related schools at an annual saving to the nation's taxpayers of about $2.1 billion. Pressures to "phase out" these schools invoke fantasy. A *New York Times* article of December 17 is headed: HUNDREDS APPEAL FOR NEW SCHOOLS, and records the New York City Board of Education's request for $284 million for forty-six new school construction projects. The education of 26 per cent of all school children in the City of New York is being afforded by Catholic parochial schools; total present annual saving to taxpayers is $423 million. Phase out the parochial schools? *Into what* would even 10 per cent of this huge school population be phased? The answer is simple: into chaos for everybody.

It is to be hoped that the courts and the public, sensitive to religious liberty and conscious of the public contribution of the nation's church schools, will spurn present pleas to make an "unhallowed perversion" (in the words of James Madison) of the vital principle of separation of church and state.

Civil Rights:
The Continuing Revolution

Everett C. Ladd, Jr.

Throughout our history the relations of Negro and white have been caught up in change. In *The Strange Career of Jim Crow* C. Vann Woodward reminds us that the "traditional" Southern solution—the "Jim Crow" system which required segregation and gross exclusion—had in fact a rather short life. Implemented in the late 1890's, it had experienced substantial modification by the end of the Second World War. A series of periods can be identified, each with its own definition or competing definitions of "correct" race relations. And though in each period those speaking for Negro Americans have disagreed over many specific approaches and objectives, in each there has been general agreement both on the content of the racially just society and on the broad outlines of a program for realizing it.

The Supreme Court decisions of May 17, 1954, define the beginning of one such period, a period of revolutionary assault on the Jim Crow system. We are concerned here, of course, with a flow of history, and history rarely stops abruptly only to move on in another direction. The beginning and ending of historical periods usually is blurred over months and years. But the Court action against school segregation does indicate in a general way the beginning of a significant departure in American race relations. And in the same way, it will be argued here, the civil rights legislation of 1964 and 1965 points to the ending of this period and to a charting of a new course for the civil rights movement. The breadth of the assault on Jim Crow in the last decade and the intensity of the struggle for leadership within the civil rights movement might create doubt that any unifying theme—beyond agreement that second-class citizenship must go—existed. But now as this period ends, we become aware that it was a *period*, with its own visions and hopes and a distinctive approach. The changes in objectives, orientation and techniques that herald movement into a new period will be described here, for together they define a dramatically new direction for what is a continuing revolution.

The civil rights movement during the period that is ending as throughout our history looked South. This is hardly surprising. The problems confronting Negro Americans in the South were of a radically different—and far more deplorable—dimension than in the North. It was not wrong to see the North as a purgatory to which Negroes could flee from a Southern hell. Civil rights organizations like the NAACP were founded as *Northern-based* instruments for changing conditions *in the South*. But race advancement is being nationalized and we find ourselves in the mid 1960's at last pushed to a realization that the struggle is not regional. The period

"Civil Rights: The Continuing Revolution," *The Yale Review*, Vol. LV, No. 1, October 1965. Copyright 1965 Yale University. Reprinted by permission of the author and publisher.

into which we are moving is identified first of all, then, by the inadequacy of a "Southern strategy."

The vast migration of Negro Americans in the last half century forms the backdrop for the nationalizing of the politics of race advancement. In 1830 about 93 per cent of all Negro Americans lived in the South, and the figure had dropped only to 85 per cent ninety years later. But during the First World War Negroes began moving in large numbers from the South, and this migration continued in the 'twenties and speeded up greatly in the 'thirties and 'forties. In the mid-'sixties, for the first time in our history, a majority of Negro Americans (51 per cent) were recorded living outside the eleven states of the old Confederacy. And this migration from the rural South to cities South and North continues. So in the first instance the great regional differences historically associated with the race advancement struggle have been blurred because Negroes now are living in large numbers in major cities throughout the country.

But the nationalizing of the politics of race means more than this. The political position of the Southern Negro has been strengthened enormously while that of his Northern counterpart has remained essentially static. In 1954 the North and the South still were two different worlds when measured in terms of Negro political power. In the North Negroes were part of the old New Deal coalition and were able to reap benefits from this. Far from being denied the vote, they were carefully cultivated. But in the South the Negro was powerless. Few white politicians would make any concession to his interests because to do so was to commit political suicide. Today, Northern Negroes remain part of the Democratic coalition, but some of their partners in that coalition are becoming increasingly restive as the civil rights movement pushes for objectives well beyond those of the limited welfare state—those, that is, that the coalition initially was built to achieve. In contrast, there has been a dramatic expansion of Negro political power in the South, well illustrated by developments in electoral politics. Two and a half decades ago fewer than 250,000 Negroes were registered in Dixie, about 5 per cent of those of voting age. Spurred by such landmark decisions as *Smith v. Allwright* (1944), which ended the white primary, Negro registration climbed slowly, and stood at about a million for the 1952 presidential election. Over the next ten years the number increased by 400,000. But in the two years preceding the 1964 presidential election, nearly 900,000 additional Negro voters were added to the lists in the South, and the total registration—2,250,000—represented 45 per cent of all voting-age Negroes in the region.

In some rim-South cities Negro electoral power is even more impressive than the South-wide data would indicate. In Winston-Salem, North Carolina, for example, 14,300 Negroes are registered. Almost one registered voter in three is a Negro. In all the major rim-South cities Negroes have unrestricted access to the ballot box. The relatively high socio-economic position of the Negro population has meant the development of a Negro middle class sufficiently large to give effective political leadership. In general, a pattern of race relations has developed which regards Negro participation in electoral politics as legitimate. In many of these cities Negroes are now holding elective office and positions in the Democratic

Party organization as well as on city boards and commissions. The Negro vote frequently is highly cohesive, going by overwhelming margins to the favored candidate. It is no longer the kiss of death for white politicians to receive and even solicit formal Negro support. In mayoralty elections in Winston-Salem in 1957, 1959, and 1961, the victorious Democratic candidates received substantially less than half of the white vote. They were elected on the basis of smashing 95 to 5 per cent margins from Negro voters. In the 1963 mayoralty race the Democratic candidate made very substantial and specific commitments to Negroes (that the city's swimming pools would remain open on an integrated basis, that a biracial committee would be appointed, and that two additional Negroes would be appointed to the city-county school board) and he was rewarded with 93 per cent of the Negro vote. His margin of victory was about 4600 votes; 4100 of these came from Negroes. Negroes could have defeated him and he knew it. He fulfilled his promises.

This is not to say that the South has become a haven for the oppressed Negro. And a Piedmont North Carolina city like Winston is a quite different place from Selma, Alabama. But it is important to recognize that the Southern Negro is no longer powerless, no longer a blank. The revolution in race relations in the American South can be understood in many ways, but above all as a revolution in political power. The power position of Negro Americans North and South has become increasingly similar, and now in the mid 1960's we have reached a point at which it makes no sense, except for a section of the deep South, to distinguish between the efficacy of the sanctions available. This contributes importantly to the nationalizing of the struggle for racial advancement.

The "Southern strategy" of the civil rights movement in the past has been made necessary as well by the central preoccupation of the movement—the destruction of the Jim Crow system. "Jim Crow must go!" A decade ago Southern Negroes were just beginning to win an occasional battle against Jim Crow. The system still stood. *Brown v. Board of Education of Topeka* sounded a call to arms. The North had discrimination but never the Jim Crow system, so in racial terms North and South were different worlds. But in the last decade gross exclusion barriers have fallen throughout the South, and in the problems beyond gross exclusion North and South are markedly alike.

The great civil rights battles of the last decade were battles against Jim Crow: the Brown decision; Montgomery; Little Rock; the sit-ins which began January 31, 1960, at a Woolworth's in Greensboro; Oxford, Mississippi; Birmingham. And we must add to this list the battle of Washington, culminating in the enactment of major civil rights legislation. For the 1964 and 1965 civil rights legislation was directed primarily at ending gross exclusion in the South. This legislation represents the culmination of the Southern strategy. It is hardly surprising that the legislation in a sense followed the fact, coming as mop-up action—still vitally important —after the Jim Crow system had been toppled.

Negro Americans still face gross exclusion barriers, as Selma so clearly showed; but Selma has become the exception. (I found it striking to read in North Carolina newspapers editorials lecturing Mississippi and Alabama in terms almost identical to those used by Northern papers against North

Carolina half a decade ago.) Large parts of the South are now "open," most major public facilities admitting Negroes. The dramatic gains of spring and summer, 1963, have been extended by the substantial compliance which followed the 1964 legislation.

But the demise of Jim Crow has not brought the racially just society, and Negro leaders North and South have turned their attention increasingly to the problems which remain after gross exclusion has been ended. A new world of racial problems has been opened. These problems have always been present, of course, but now they have been thrust to the forefront by the collapse of gross exclusion.

Much was heard in 1964 about a "civil rights backlash": the strong showing of George Wallace in the Democratic presidential primaries in Wisconsin, Indiana, and Maryland; the overwhelming defeat of open housing ordinances in a number of cities including Seattle and Tacoma, Washington; the repeal of the Rumford Fair Housing Act by California voters. But the term backlash was an inaccurate one. Whites did not draw back, but rather refused to move forward with Negroes to the objectives which the latter are now seeking. The attack on Jim Crow was carried out in a manner consonant with the demands of what Gunnar Myrdal calls the American Creed. "Treat Negroes like any other citizen," the movement insisted. It was the white Southerner who was denying the American Creed, not the Negro. It does seem doubtful that many whites had difficulty justifying to themselves the Jim Crow system, but it is still true that the Negro attack readily found support within American ideology.

Today, however, civil rights leaders are beginning to recognize publicly that "treating Negroes like everyone else," while infinitely better than treating them as inferiors, is not enough. Paul Parks, Education Secretary of the Boston NAACP, spoke for many in the movement when he argued that the end of a formal discriminatory policy in pupil assignment is only part of the answer: "The real problem is that kids (Negro and white) are growing up in Boston separated. If we want to talk about the social structure of tomorrow, then we must have children growing up in competition with no real feeling of race, with a teacher standing in front of the class who understands the situation, one who will batter down feelings of inferiority which the Negro may have, one who will overcome the condition of the child's home and eliminate feelings of race. Otherwise we will stay on the same carousel. . . . We can't start in the home. The Negro is immersed in a culture imposed upon him by a white majority. He accepts the way he is trained to act. This is the best way to gain acceptance. From morning to night the Negro lives in an adult white world, apart from that world." What is argued here for education is being advanced for other areas such as housing and employment. One of the most forceful and cogent general statements of the need for compensatory treatment can be found in a recently published book, *Equality*, by Robert L. Carter, Dorothy Kenyon, Peter Marcuse, and Loren Miller. Remedial action is necessary. It is not enough after three centuries of discriminatory treatment to decide suddenly to treat Negroes "like everyone else."

When the movement asks for compensatory treatment of the kind it must seek, it will encounter strong opposition from "friendly" whites as well as from racists. The American Creed—which is, after all, primarily unreconstructed Liberalism—makes no provision for such demands. The freedom envisioned by the Creed is "negative" freedom, freedom from formal restriction of the individual's pursuit of happiness. Jim Crow imposed this type of restriction, but the problems beyond gross exclusion typically do not. Most white Americans, North and South, will not see that the simple removal of gross exclusion barriers is insufficient in view of the experience of Negro Americans over the last three centuries. Their response to Negroes' demands for compensatory treatments, and it is the Creed's response, will be, "Help yourselves, the opportunity is there." Indeed, this response can already be heard. Witness the hostility to the campaign led by the Rev. Milton Galamison against de facto segregration in the New York school system. In the November, 1964, issue of *Commentary*, Nathan Glazer found fault in the "almost Talmudic arguments about *how many* Negro students make a school 'de facto' segregated. . . ." What Glazer is so easily dismissing here is the growing recognition of the crushing legacy of the ghetto school, and the absolute imperative of ending it. Many liberal whites recently have been discovering self-help when confronted with Negro demands for compensatory treatment. No one, of course, should question the desirability of activity designed to increase race pride, to provide higher motivation, to encourage hard work. But when self-help is posed *as an alternative* to compensatory treatment, it can only indicate how ill-equipped we are intellectually to meet the problems beyond gross exclusion.

This lack of awareness of the depth of our race problem, and hence of a political will for solution, confronts the civil rights movement at precisely the time it is beginning to demand an infinitely greater commitment of the country's resources for the eradication of problems more involved and deep-rooted than those of the past period. The old gross exclusion problems, however agonizing, were straightforward. Discrimination in the economic sphere meant such things as the refusal of Hanes Hosiery Company in Winston-Salem, North Carolina, to hire a Negro in any other than a janitorial capacity. The abuse was flagrant and a remedy was at hand. Hire qualified people without regard to race. This is not to make light of the resistance that Negroes and their white allies faced. Still, any man of the most modest intelligence could understand the problem and its solution. When Negroes are excluded from good jobs, however, because of insufficient training, training which they lack because of problems of education and motivation which go to the very core of what it has meant to be black in white America, then simple solutions are not to be found. We can no longer avoid the full enormity of the economic difficulties of Negro Americans. In 1964 when the median income for white families was over $6800, the median income for Negro families was about $3800, 55 per cent as great. Moreover, the gulf separating Negroes and whites has been widening in dollar, though not in percentage, terms. Between 1959 and 1964, the median income for white families was raised by $1023 while that for Negro families was increasing by only $597. Fewer than 37 per cent of our Negro families earned over $5000 in 1964, a level reached by 69 per cent of the white families. Negroes are victimized by an unemployment rate higher today than it was a decade and a half ago, despite some improvement in the last 24 months. Negro Americans suffer an unemployment rate more than twice as high as the rate for white Americans.

Mechanization and automation continue to eliminate jobs in the unskilled and semi-skilled categories. It is now estimated that there are fewer than half as many such positions as there are high school dropouts. This presents a particular problem for Negro Americans, since the 1960 census found 78 per cent of those twenty-five years of age and older with less than a high school education, and 47 per cent with less than an eighth grade education.

Our economy is producing new jobs, but the increase has been greater in white collar employment. In the last eight years, we have added 5.4 million white collar positions while only one million blue collar jobs. Sometime around 1955, we became a nation with more white collar than blue collar workers. Boeing Aircraft illustrates the rapidity and extent of this employment trend: In 1940 it employed three blue collar workers for every one in a white collar, but today there are three in white collars for every two in blue. Many of the new white collar positions are of a routine nature, to be sure, and are not necessarily beyond the reach of the American poor, white or Negro. But these positions often do present an added hurdle in requiring, in varying degrees, interpersonal manipulation. The mechanics of operating a cash register can be taught with relative ease, but the handling of customers may take much longer.

And even more important, we lack objective and external standards for evaluating performance in many white collar positions. One's success in manipulating people necessarily involves *their evaluation of him* rather than of some act performed. He must be accepted as legitimate. The plumber does his job if the sink does not leak. The client's reaction to him is distinctly secondary. The initiate in a corporation bureaucracy lacks such tangible testimony to his work. He must sell himself. Prejudice toward Negroes presents a somewhat more formidable barrier, then, in white collar than in blue collar employment.

It is problems such as these that the civil rights movement must now face. As long as attention was directed largely to gross discriminations in the economic sphere, the lack of training, the generally poor educational background and that crippling of motivation that is a legacy of the American racial way of life could be partly ignored. The demand could be simply to admit those who could qualify, to take down the big keep-out signs that confronted all Negroes. But as those who have somehow overcome the enormous burdens of American racism are able to achieve positions roughly commensurate with their talents—and we still have a long way to go even here, of course—the problems of the mass become inescapably central. For it is the shocking but unavoidable fact that if all employers began today to hire solely on the basis of merit, the vast majority of Negro Americans would remain trapped at the bottom of our economic ladder. A growing awareness of this contributes a distinctly new flavor to the period into which we are now moving.

How well are we equipped for meeting the economic problems of Negro Americans that remain beyond gross exclusion? Few whites seem ready to endorse preferential hiring policies for Negroes. Few corporations appear ready to commit a portion of their enormous resources to a resolution of the economic difficulties of Negroes through remedial training programs. To be sure, some corporation leaders have had much to say about the joining of corporate power with social responsibility. The pages of *Fortune* and other business journals are filled regularly with discussions of how corporations can justify their enormous economic, social and political power by submitting to the guide of moral conscience, by using the power to promote values which transcend production and profits. Russell Davenport wrote somewhat poetically about the "greatest opportunity on earth" opening here for the corporation:

> It was the belief of the founders of this country, well-substantiated until the rise of the corporation, that men and women could be relied upon to keep the state at arm's length. It is now time for the business community to show that corporate action, which is still private action, and which emanates from individuals, can achieve the same result: that the Rights of Man can be made as safe in corporate hands as they were in individual hands. . . . Indeed, the vista will become immeasurable, once American enterprise awakes to the realization that in the "social problem" it is in fact faced with the greatest opportunity on earth.

But practice usually has been quite different. Andrew Hacker, a thoughtful student of the corporation, concluded that "corporations have the power to enforce the principle of equality in hiring and upgrading, but with one or two exceptions they have decided to play along with white supremacy. . . ."

> Since the end of World War II northern based corporations have been opening branch plants in the South. In return for tax concessions and a docile labor force, these companies have agreed to accept the racial patterns of the region. In some areas the branch plants of corporations do not hire Negroes at all, in others they are kept in custodial positions. . . . To be sure, as in the case of civil liberties, company policies guaranteeing civil rights would encounter local opposition. But if, as Mr. Gossett of Ford [William T. Gossett] claimed, a large corporation "holds power in trust for the whole community" then it is reasonable to expect that such power will be used to promote the values inherent in the nation's Constitution. However, the rhetoric is vapid, and there is some suspicion that the men who utter the aristocratic words know that this is the case. A corporation is, by construction and temperament, unfitted to represent the fundamental values of a free society.

Paul H. Norgren and Samuel E. Hill agree that those corporations who have in fact implemented fair employment practices have had little difficulty in overriding opposition. They found that in the South as well as in the North, when employees are confronted with the choice of accepting fair employment practices or quitting, they invariably have chosen to withdraw their initial objections and to keep their jobs. Nor has there been a shortage of new white applicants.

Some spokesmen deny emphatically that the corporation should be expected to resolve our racial difficulties. A colleague not long ago toured a large and highly mechanized oil refinery and, noting the absence of Negroes, inquired why of the personnel executive who was his host. He was told that jobs at the refinery were highly desirable, that applications far exceeded openings, and hence that candidates had to meet unusually high standards. "Most Negro applicants simply do not score high enough," the executive concluded. "We would be more than happy if they did, and we would most certainly hire them." My colleague then suggested that perhaps the company should take into its training programs Negroes not scoring as well and should give them compensatory training, as its contribution to redressing long-standing injustices. "That's not our job," he was told. Perhaps it isn't. Perhaps one should not expect corporations to do more than produce goods and services for a profit. But this does mean, since the private corporation is our central economic institution, that progress will come slowly. And we cannot expect the corporation to pioneer as we move toward economic advancement for Negro Americans.

Similarly, the civil rights movement must now grapple with facets of educational and residential segregation that are of a more frustrating complexity than the gross exclusion of Jim Crow; that require, if they are to be resolved, a far greater commitment of the nation's resources; and that cannot be resolved simply by treating Negro Americans "like everyone else," but only through remedial action of a more extensive kind than we have envisioned. It was still possible in the 1950's to think of school segregation primarily in terms of policies deliberately designed to maintain rigid school segregation. This is no longer possible. To be sure, school officials continue to discriminate in assigning students. Even when proximity to the school is a guide faithfully followed, the "neighborhood" frequently is defined in a way minimizing integration. The Rev. Robert F. Drinan, Dean of the Boston College Law School and Chairman of the Massachusetts Advisory Committee to the United States Commission on Civil Rights, maintains that "very simple rezoning" would help measurably in promoting racial balance in the Boston schools; and this is probably valid for others as well. But given the extent of residential segregation, North and South, a residential assignment policy will invariably mean—regardless of how the lines are drawn—a continuation of marked racial imbalance, and specifically of the ghetto school. The civil rights movement in this next period will be primarily concerned with achieving integrated schools *in the face of segregated residential areas.*

We are not lacking in testimony to the disastrous results of keeping Negro youths in ghetto schools. The Rev. Milton Galamison, who heads the City-Wide Committee for Integrated Schools in New York, argues forcefully that the low expectations of both teacher and student necessarily produce poor education. "You just can't lump together 800 children who differ from the national norms and standards in almost every way and manufacture a graduating class that matches national or city-wide norms," Mr. Galamison has said. Awareness of this has given intensity to the search for programs to overcome de facto segregation, and a host of proposals have been advanced: busing, "Princeton Plans," innumerable variations in grouping, zoning, and pairing. More will be offered. All will require a commitment of resources far greater than did the attack on Jim Crow in education. And all will generate strong resistance, North and South.

Paradoxically, at the very time the civil rights movement is turning its attention to solutions for school segregation produced by the existence of the ghetto, solution is being pushed further and further from reach by increased residential segregation and the increasing size of the ghetto. The proposals now being offered could have been implemented far more easily, from a technical standpoint, two decades ago than today in most cities.

The United States has been built on waves of immigration and migration, and the continuing movement of Negro Americans from the rural South to cities South and North is one of the most important of these waves. The flight of Negroes to the cities is occurring in the midst of the suburbanization of white America, and the two together have had an enormous impact on residential segregation. Negroes have found themselves concentrated in central city ghettos, geographically more divorced from the white population than ever before. Between 1950 and 1960, New York City lost 450,000 white residents while gaining 300,000 non-whites. Washington's Negro population increased from 35 per cent to 54 per cent of the total in this same decade. Negroes have found themselves barred from suburban living not only by their economic plight but as well by the frequently strong opposition of suburban dwellers to even the most limited residential integration. The resistance of one prosperous suburb, Deerfield, Illinois, is described in an excellent little volume by Harry and David Rosen, *But Not Next Door.*

Before the Second World War, Negroes and whites lived in fairly close proximity in many Southern cities. Old-South cities like Charleston had a "backyard" pattern, with the Negro population scattered fairly uniformly throughout. The homes of Negro servants, indentured and then free, were located in the backyards of the wealthy whites for whom they worked. The more common pattern in the prewar South was one which Charles Johnson calls "urban clusters." Most Negroes residing in the city lived in one to three large clusters, but significant numbers were in smaller clusters—as many as twenty—scattered throughout the city. Although neighborhoods were segregated, substantial numbers of whites lived close to Negroes. These patterns persist today, but there clearly is movement toward further separation of white and Negro residential areas. Clusters are expanding, merging, forming nuclear ghettos. As the South urbanizes, newer residential areas are constructed around the older central cities; and these areas are lily-white, like the suburbs that ring the central cities in the North. When the urban white in the South goes home at night, it typically is to a home further removed from Negro residential areas than at any time in the past.

Poverty and gross racial oppression continue to drive Negroes from the rural South. Low income and opposition to residential integration keep them restricted to physically declining sections of central cities, North and South. The urban Negro population continues its rapid expansion. The central fact of the expanding ghetto confronts the civil rights movement, and will preoccupy it in the period into which we are moving. To paraphrase the Rev. Mr. Galamison, "You just can't lump together thousands of people who differ from national norms and standards in a number of very important ways and manufacture a group that matches national norms." The ghetto feeds on itself. It compounds the disadvantages of a disadvantaged people. It perpetuates the very elements of the legacy of the last three centuries that we are working to eliminate. It kills hope. The riots that have occurred in Northern cities and in Los Angeles were not—as has often been pointed out—race riots. They did not bring gangs of whites and Negroes together in sections where white and Negro residential areas meet. All these riots occurred in the heart of the ghettos, and the only whites around were policemen. They were essentially spontaneous expressions of the very discontents and frustrations of ghetto life, of what we euphemistically call severe social dislocation. Bayard Rustin observed pointedly that the riots were "outbursts of class aggression in a society where class and color definitions are converging disastrously."

The problems of Harlem, and of every other large ghetto, will not be solved as long as the ghettos exist. For the problems cannot be solved within the ghetto context; not by anti-poverty programs, or by more public housing, or by Princeton Plans. The solution lies in ending the process that herds more and more thousands of Negro Americans into urban slums.

The civil rights movement in the period which is ending mobilized growing resources for an attack on the gross denials of the old biracial system: the big keep-out signs that barred Negroes from theatres, schools, restaurants, hotels, playgrounds, and other public accommodations and facilities. War was waged on a system that was obviously and unabashedly discriminatory, that was founded on the assumption of basic inequality. The movement has had great success. The old biracial system has collapsed.

The central objectives in the attack on Jim Crow were status objectives, of the greatest importance to individuals frequently and deeply humiliated. These status goals can be readily seen and understood, and permit solutions that are direct and rapidly achieved. Moreover, the solutions can often be realized through the activity of individuals with no resources but courage.

The goals of the new period, in contrast, blend status and welfare into a complex whole. The enemies in the new period frequently will seem benevolent, a gloved hand extended rather than a mailed fist raised. For the central problems will involve inaction or insufficient action in the face of the bitter fruits of discrimination, rather than action that is obviously anti-Negro. The task of assuring substantial equality of opportunity for Negro Americans will tax our ingenuity, and no direct or immediate solutions will be found. The new period will be one of endless experimentation. Individual frustration may increase because the individual, while able to integrate a lunch counter, cannot abolish a ghetto, cannot substantially affect the conditions that keep Negro family income nearly 50 per cent below that of whites. The objectives of the new period will require the commitment of massive resources.

The end of the Southern strategy through the nationalizing of the race advancement struggle; the infinitely greater complexity of the goals that will preoccupy the civil rights movement beyond gross exclusion; the different and generally expanded commitment of resources required by these goals; the new definition of the racially just society which makes necessary compensatory treatment and hence which comes into conflict with the American Creed; and in general the inability and/or the unwillingness of most white Americans, liberals included, to recognize even the legitimacy of the kinds of programs and policies that the civil rights movement must now demand and which it will demand with greater urgency in the next years: these changes are ushering in a new period in American race relations.

The new period, even more than the old, will teach Americans how demanding "equality of opportunity" is. White America could glory in being swept along by the tide of egalitarianism which in the eighteenth century was ridden by the middle class over the nobility, and in the nineteenth and early twentieth centuries by the white working class over the middle class. But it is more likely that we will hang our heads and lament that what once was a quite straightforward Southern problem is now one confronting the entire nation with all its enormity and complexity.

After the "Agitators" Left Greensboro

James K. Batten

GREENSBORO, ALABAMA

When the tumultuous summer of 1965 was finally over, the exasperated white people of this country town were enormously relieved. They heartily agreed with Hamner Cobbs, editor of the weekly Greensboro *Watchman,* when he wrote on September 16: "It is a remarkable thing, this peace which has settled over the Greensboro community since those little college whelps left us. . . . For no visible reason, this quiet old community was selected by the advocates of racial discord for a real scorching. . . . These people have been here since spring, working day and night in trying to stir up a revolution, if not a civil war."

Like scores of other Deep South communities, Greensboro had just collided with the civil-rights movement. Dozens of college-age volunteers had poured in from all over the country. There had been marches, demonstrations, and boycotts. Some 470 demonstrators had been shipped off to prison camps. On one memorable day in July, outside the old yellow-brick Hale County Courthouse, furious whites had waded into a crowd of demonstrators and had sent several of them to the hospital.

SHIFTING FORCES

That was two years ago. Today, in Greensboro and elsewhere in the rural South, professional civil-rights organizers from the outside are rarely seen. The "black power" controversy has discouraged contributions to civil-rights organizations, and those same organizations have shifted much of their remaining resources and energies from the Southern backwaters to the Negro slums of the North or to protests against the war in Vietnam. Now that the "outside agitators" are gone, are the Negroes they came to help any better off? Has white supremacy been seriously shaken? Or has life in the small-town South simply returned to normal?

Greensboro, a sleepy town of less than four thousand citizens in west central Alabama, seems a good place to explore these questions. With its handsome ante-bellum mansions and its squalid "nigger houses," it is typical of the many Southern communities where the soil is black and rich and the majority of the people are black and poor. In Greensboro and Hale County in the summer of 1965, nearly seventy per cent of the nineteen thousand residents were Negro. Yet the white minority was dominant in every sphere of community life, owning the land, dispensing the jobs, enforcing the law, and running the local government. Editor Cobbs liked to remind his readers: "It is not a case of a white democracy or a black democracy. It is a case of white democracy or none at all."

At the end of 1964, only about 230 Negroes were registered to vote. No Negro had sat on a jury in modern times. And ten years after the Supreme Court's school-desegregation decision, not one Negro youngster had ever sat in a classroom with white children.

When local Negroes, cautiously at first and then more openly, began to heed the call of civil-rights organizers in the spring of 1965, white people were genuinely surprised. But soon many reacted with indignation and cold fury. Cooks were fired. Sharecroppers were evicted from land they had tended for years. Credit was cut off overnight. And when the tension was at its height in July, two Negro churches burned mysteriously in a single week.

Nevertheless, that September six Negro girls broke the color line in Hale County's public schools. Under Federal pressure, county officials began calling an occasional Negro for jury duty. And most significant of all, more and more of the county's Negroes were registered to vote. By the spring of 1966, Negro registration had soared to more than three thousand, thanks primarily to the Voting Rights Act of 1965. Exact comparisons of white and Negro voting strength were never possible, mainly because Hale County for years had failed to purge its voter lists. A tabulation by the Southern Regional Council's Voter Education Project last summer showed an official white registration of 4,515, though the estimated white voting-age population was only 3,594.

Greensboro has not returned to the tranquillity it took for granted before 1965. Under local leaders who came to the fore in the last two or three years, Hale County's Negroes have taken up the fight where the outsiders left it.

In February, 1966, to the dismay of the white community, a group of activists decided to back a Negro preacher, Henry McCaskill, for sheriff. With three white opponents splitting the white vote, McCaskill finished first in the May primary. But in the runoff a few weeks later, the white electorate united behind Ben Kizziah, a former Alabama highway patrolman. Kizziah won, 3,601 to 2,650.

Hundreds of Negroes also voted for Kizziah, and their votes may have been pivotal. Whites and Negroes in Hale County offer sharply conflicting theories to explain those votes. Lewis J. Lawson, president of the Peoples Bank in Greensboro and one of the town's most resolute segregationists, declared, "A lot of colored people still don't trust the other colored man.

He [the Negro] would rather trust his white friend than an untried colored man." But forty-two-year-old Lewis Black, who is now the county's most important Negro leader, insisted that many Negroes feared economic reprisals if they voted for McCaskill.

This June, continuing the civil-rights struggle, a group of ten Negroes attempted a "swim-in" at a pool formerly operated by the municipality and now ostensibly under private control. They were turned away. At the same time, Negro pickets marched outside two variety stores in downtown Greensboro, demanding that Negro salespeople be hired. And at the Negroes' request, an investigator from the U.S. Equal Employment Opportunity Commission visited Greensboro.

Most Monday nights, fifty to seventy-five people turn up at St. Luke's African Methodist Episcopal Zion Church for meetings of the Hale County Improvement Association. Its prime movers are Lewis Black, who once taught music at the Negro high school, and Theresa Burroughs, a beautician who was one of the demonstrators shipped off to prison in the summer of 1965. Although voter registration and school desegregation are still important topics at these meetings, in recent months there has been a greater emphasis on plans to provide economic security for the county's hard-pressed Negroes. Local bakery and sewing co-operatives are to be set up. More than twenty Hale County farmers are already participating in a ten-county vegetable-growing co-operative, approved by the U.S. Office of Economic Opportunity over Governor Lurleen Wallace's veto. A credit union and a nonprofit grocery store also are in operation.

THE WHITE REACTION

The response of most Greensboro white people, at least on the surface, has been an increased rigidity on racial matters. "You've got to be more careful what you do or say," James Key, principal of Greensboro's public schools, told me. "Somebody is seen shaking hands with a Negro, they say he's gone over to the other side—nigger lover, integrationist, or something like that." The Reverend David Carter, the young pastor at the white Greensboro Methodist Church, recalls the time he shook hands with Black at a PTA meeting. "Everybody in town knew about it by six the next morning."

Many whites seem to be withdrawing from all contact with Negroes wherever possible. One Greensboro housewife, sitting on her front porch, remarked, "They pass by here continually asking for work—little boys and girls. But I don't want any Negro help. There are too many emotional problems."

White paternalism also has waned. The Negro who needs to be bailed out of jail or to pay a big hospital bill is less likely now to find a white man ready to advance the money. That is particularly true if the Negro has any record of civil-rights activity. "The white man has done everything for the Negro in this area," one white Greensboro leader declared. "I mean everything—even including his thinking. But there's not much of that paternal feeling now."

Many white residents are more convinced than ever that the only long-range solution to "the nigger problem" is to persuade more Negroes to move away. The goal, of course, is to hasten the day when whites will become the majority in Hale County. Cobbs has espoused this idea in his editorial columns. "I want to spread 'em all over the country," he explained. "If they congregate, who in hell wants 'em? It [moving Negroes out] is just basic civic policy among white folks. If a nigger man really wants to leave—and will stay gone—then he can get a free ride to Cleveland."

As white men withdraw their land, their credit, and their paternalistic support, many Negroes are being forced to struggle for economic independence. Albert Turner, one of the few remaining organizers for Dr. Martin Luther King's Southern Christian Leadership Conference in rural Alabama, explained the situation this way:

"In one sense, the Negro is worse off than before. But in another sense, he's better off. This may mean some temporary suffering, but otherwise he'd have been in that condition for the rest of his life. We're in a transition period. You'd be surprised how many people came off the plantation and bought themselves a house, sometimes the house they'd been living in, for a hundred dollars. They tear it down and build it back. They sell a cow and a pig and all the chickens they've got to scrape up the money and buy an acre of land. And it's theirs, instead of somebody else's. They would never have stepped out and become independent people if they hadn't gotten kicked off."

Sixty-year-old Eugene Garrett spent fifty-two years sharecropping on the plantation of a prominent Hale County farmer-politician. In 1965, Garrett began attending civil-rights meetings at St. Matthew's African Methodist Episcopal Church in Greensboro. He was asked to lend a hand in the voter-registration campaign, but he begged off. "I told them I was on another man's land, and I had nowhere to go."

Garrett's caution was of no avail. In the fall of 1965, shortly after Negro cottonpickers had boycotted Garrett's landlord at harvest time, the landowner announced that he was finished with sharecropping. Garrett was out of a job, the only one he had ever known.

For months he remained in his old cabin rent-free, subsisting primarily on the skimpy income from a few rented acres of farmland. But this spring, thanks to financial help from sons living in Detroit, Racine, and Birmingham, he moved into a modest new bungalow nine miles west of Greensboro on an unpaved farm road. In his last twenty-three years of sharecropping, Garrett had cultivated his crops with his landlord's tractors. Now he uses a horse to tend his ten rented acres. "It's pretty hard," he told me. "I get home some evenings and can't get no further than the steps. But I wouldn't take nothing for it. If you're doing something for me, I'm always afraid I'll do wrong and you're going to scorn me for it. I might even do wrong trying to do right."

ROADS TO IMPROVEMENT

While working out ideas to better the Negroes' economic conditions, leaders of the Hale County Improvement Association are opening tenuous lines of communication to key white officials. And these officials, while proceeding with extreme caution, are beginning to respond to Negro overtures—not from any change of heart, it appears, but largely because of the big and still growing Negro vote.

"If I call the county commissioners about a road or a street light, they get out and do it right fast," Black said. "I know they don't give a hoot for me, but they respect me." Black added that one white officeholder "tries to be square with me because he don't want me to march a thousand people down there and raise hell."

One day last fall, Mrs. Burroughs phoned all five members of the Board of Revenue, the county governing board, urging them on behalf of herself and her neighbors to build a road to serve about fifteen houses at the western edge of Greensboro. The following Monday, Mrs. Burroughs and a delegation of neighbors—most of them recently registered to vote—appeared at the courthouse to press their request; that same day a county road-building crew began work. Mrs. Burroughs is not ready to claim that the new votes made the difference. "We had been trying to get that road for eight or nine years," she said. "The only thing I can say is that they didn't do it before, but they did do it this time."

Probate Judge Hal Knight, chairman of the Board of Revenue and one of the most powerful men in Hale County politics, shrugged off suggestions that the increased Negro registration was affecting the board's decisions. "It's not that I don't want all the votes I can get," he admitted. "But that's not what motivated me. . . . A lot of niggers should have had roads that didn't have roads. When I got to be probate judge [in 1964], I built 'em some roads. If you do things like that, you'll have better relations."

Knight is anxious to avoid the impression that he is courting the Negro vote. He said that he would not "bootlick" anybody when he seeks re-election in 1970. "We've got some good sound niggers, and they'll vote for me, I believe. Old-line niggers will see what Mr. Hal says about it."

Some of Knight's old friends, however, insist that he is quietly adjusting his political behavior to meet the new realities. "Hal Knight is perfectly aware that these Negroes have to be taken care of," one of them said. "He's going to pick up some of those Negro votes. Hal is more reasonable than he used to be."

Perhaps the white official who speaks most bluntly about the need for a realistic approach is James Key, the school principal. Key incurred the wrath of some white citizens last fall when he agreed to become chairman of the Hale County anti-poverty program, of which Black is vice-chairman. Key told me: "Some people said, 'Let them [the Negroes] have it and blow it all to pieces. They'll misappropriate the funds and then we'll have them in the penitentiary.' But that's completely unrealistic."

Key believes that Hale County's white people will make a grave mistake if they refuse to recognize any potential leadership in the Negro community. Without naming Black, Key argued that although white people may not like the Negroes' leader, "If he's the leader, he's the one you've got to deal with. We're past the day when we can ignore all of them. There's been a strong shift toward the meeting and discussing of this thing. We're going to have to do it, or the political power of the county is going to shift." What he meant was that if the Negro leaders' overtures for co-operation are continually rebuffed, all-black government might well become their top-priority goal.

From the Negroes' point of view, the gains made so far may seem minuscule. Whites and Negroes sit down occasionally to talk about poverty, but the anti-poverty program shows few indications of getting past the talking stage. Greensboro merchants are still reluctant to hire Negroes for other than menial jobs. Restaurants and motels may be theoretically desegregated under the 1964 Civil Rights Act, but Negroes are most emphatically not welcome, so they stay away. In the public schools, despite gradually increasing desegregation, the overwhelming majority of Negro children still receive inferior, segregated education.

All this has inevitably produced some disillusion after the excitement generated by the civil-rights movement in the summer of 1965. "It has ruint the children," one old Negro complained. "It had 'em built up so high. They believed they would be governor of the state and President of the country. Everything clipped out from under 'em, and down they come."

But Mrs. Burroughs insists that the disillusion has passed. "We realize now that things don't happen overnight. People thought we had an Aladdin's lamp. But they realize now it takes work. We haven't let up one bit. We wouldn't want our children to come up under the oppression we've had to live under. It [the civil-rights movement] is the best thing I've ever participated in. I wouldn't have wanted to live without its coming."

A Mississippi Mayor Fights the Klan

Arlie Schardt

When the new mayor of Laurel, Mississippi, launched an attack against the Ku Klux Klan last fall, optimists called it the dawn of a new day for the entire state and cynics called it an opportunistic gesture. Although neither group has been proved correct, there are signs that progress of a sort is being made in Mississippi.

Mayor William Henry Bucklew, a forty-year-old Mississippian, is not exactly the kind of man one expects to find leading drives against the KKK. He was a director of George Wallace's 1964 Presidential campaign in Maryland, North Carolina, and Virginia; he is a member of the speakers' bureau of the Mississippi State Sovereignty Commission, an arm of the state government created to perpetuate segregation. (Its funds have since been cut off by Governor Paul Johnson.) Bucklew ran unsuccessfully for lieutenant governor in 1959 with a campaign that, one Negro leader said, "gave us a real hot time." Bucklew, a fundamentalist Baptist, is also the founder of a Boys Town that provides a home and education for 263 boys, and is a civic doer with a long list of accomplishments.

Laurel is also the home of Sam Bower, a vending-machine dealer who is Grand Dragon of the White Knights of the Ku Klux Klan, a Mississippi-based group that has a reputation as the most covert and vicious of all the

"A Mississippi Mayor Fights the Klan," *The Reporter,* January 27, 1966. Copyright 1966 by The Reporter Magazine Company. Reprinted by permission of the author and publisher.

Klans. Police estimate that the White Knights in Laurel have from fifty to a hundred active members backed by many sympathizers. When Bucklew became mayor last July, the city's most pressing problem was a series of unsolved terrorist bombings and shootings. The violence was part of a KKK design, begun in May, 1964, with the bombing of the Laurel *Leader-Call*, to establish an unofficial control of the city of 28,000. Though the *Leader-Call's* editor-publisher, J. W. West, was himself a segregationist, the Klan had decided that "the press" must be silenced. In the thirty-four bombings and shootings that followed, including some in which the Klan apparently hit the wrong victims, Negroes and whites alike were terrorized. As the violence increased with the terrorists still unapprehended, fear captured Laurel. "We had a very defeated attitude," says Bucklew. "Most folks were ashamed. Laurel was drying up. People knew it was happening but they wouldn't say why." The townsmen were afraid to serve on juries, enabling the Klan to assure its terrorists immunity from punishment.

BUCKLEW'S DECISION

The more powerful the Klan grew, the more members it attracted. "We're gettin' some big shots in our organization now," a Klansman boasted to the new mayor last summer. When three major firms canceled plans to come to Laurel because of the wave of unchecked violence, Bucklew recognized that continued violence would kill the town economically. He decided that the only way to stop the Klan was to marshal public opinion against it and to expose the night riders.

Mayor Bucklew is short and a bit overweight, and his conversation is laced with fundamentalist homilies; from the breast pocket of his black suit protrude the tips of a three-pronged handkerchief—red, white, and blue. He does not have the appearance of a crusader. But when there are no voters within earshot, he reveals himself as a shrewd man capable of transforming ideas into deeds. Moreover, his decision to fight the Klan took courage.

Bucklew began by assembling every leading law-enforcement official of Laurel and Jones County—the police chief, sheriff, and prosecuting attorneys—and asking them to sign a statement condemning the actions of the Klan. On Friday, October 15, the statement appeared under a massive banner headline on the front page of the *Leader-Call*, accompanied by a photograph of the signing at Bucklew's desk. It listed all thirty-five acts of terrorism, complete with the names of victims, dates, and places. It described the Klan structure and the Klan's effort to interfere with the jury-selection system.

On the same page appeared another statement written by James A. Wheeler, a Laurel civic leader and insurance executive, which described the difficulty in attracting new industry: "It is . . . extremely difficult, if not impossible, to explain the recent bombings, shootings and burnings. . . ." Noting that Mississippi had asked the nation to let the state handle its own problems, Wheeler said this was as it should be, provided the state met its responsibilities, among them the maintenance of law and order. He pointedly reminded those who might be inclined to tolerate the bombings that such acts ". . . serve as an open invitation to all types and sorts of people to descend on us."

TWENTY-THREE VITAL MINUTES

Three days later, on October 18, Bucklew delivered a twenty-three-minute talk on WDAM-TV that was broadcast throughout most of south-eastern Mississippi: "I must honestly confess I have waited many months in hopes that someone else might sound the alarm," he began. He then delivered an aside that politicians apparently still find *de rigueur* in the rural South: a eulogy of Mississippi and Dixie, followed by the inevitable blast at "biased newsmen" who somehow have caused all the trouble. He went on to say that his greatest fear was of "the flood of scum, degenerates, free-lovers, night riders, church burners, home bombers and hooded thugs running loose," a phrasing that neatly eased the Klan into the same category as the despised civil-rights workers.

"You ninety-nine out of one hundred who do not believe in bombings, shooting into homes, calling and threatening life and property, you who do not believe in writing smear letters without signing your name, I now will speak for you who prefer to remain silent. This is my state and your state. I'm ashamed, aren't you? No, we did not take part. We shudder, we blush, we deny when possible. We even excuse or try to justify these acts. But they continue and, in some areas, increase. We no longer laugh because some of our citizens want to be judge, jury, and executioner as they try, in secret places in the dark of night, to decide which laws they will obey and which laws they will break. You, or your family, or mine might well be their next target.

"Many of these fanatics talk so much about God," he added, displaying a charred cross and a Molotov cocktail. "Can you imagine a loving, merciful, forgiving God blessing the act of any creep who would burn a home or a house of worship? Those who create such acts of violence are not only Godless, they are traitors. These mob fiends who are infecting our city and state are actually demanding that the Federal government move in and take over every phase of our existence." He concluded by pledging $1,000 of his own money as a reward for information leading to arrest and conviction of the terrorists, and urged everyone to tell his friends to get out of the Klan.

The Laurel police would not let Bucklew drive home that night without an escort, and they have guarded his house every night since. But Governor Johnson sent him a warm letter of praise, and most Laurel residents responded favorably. "This town was afraid and apathetic before," said a white businessman. "Everybody knew what should be done but was afraid to start it off." A minister apologized for having been afraid to speak out from his pulpit and promised to do so the next Sunday. The Jones County Baptist Association, numbering forty-six churches, passed a resolution of support.

But, as Bucklew was fully aware, brave speeches have a way of being forgotten. He decided to have petitions circulated throughout the county; people were asked to sign a statement of principles opposing violence, pledging to serve on juries when called, and endorsing the right of every citizen to security from molestation, "regardless of race, color or creed." Signers' names were to be published in the *Leader-Call*. Bucklew hoped there would be so many signatures that nonsigners would be conspicuous by their absence and eventually go along.

It did not quite work out that way. Almost immediately the White Citizens Council protested Bucklew's action with the sort of logic that is clear only to other Citizens Council minds: Bucklew, they said, had made Laurel look like "a lawless jungle" with his TV address. (No mention was made of the fact that thirty-five news dispatches from Laurel reporting bombings and shootings had already effectively portrayed the town.) Klan officials demanded and got equal TV time, using it to deny the Klan's advocacy of violence. And many residents received phone calls warning them not to sign the petition, saying signers would be "singled out" and reprisals would follow. Klan pressure eased considerably after churches began turning in lists of signers, and banking and business leaders, including official representatives of Masonite, Laurel's primary industry, expressed full support for Bucklew. Finally a full page of names—about five hundred—was published. But enough minor harassment to signers resulted to cause Bucklew to withhold further names, although he has at least five hundred more in hand.

If his follow-up drive to cripple the Klan has not been an overwhelming success, at least the primary purpose of Bucklew's strategy has been. Since his speech, there have been no more bombings in Laurel. But though the bombings have stopped, no one has been punished for the crimes already committed. And though Laurel's Negroes may be in less danger of being shot, their lives have not changed in other respects. White-collar jobs are still closed to them, their schools are still segregated and substandard, and most of them are still afraid to join the civil-rights movement.

The small local chapter of NAACP is headed by Dr. B. E. Murph, a forty-seven-year-old dentist whose own house has been shot into twice. It has led a registration drive that has raised the total of Negro voters from six hundred to nearly three thousand. But with only about a dozen active helpers, Murph has not had time to deal with the pressing problem of segregated schools. These schools, taught by teachers who are themselves products of the same system, are ill equipped to prepare Negroes for better jobs, even if opportunities were offered them. As a result, the brightest young Negroes leave town as soon as they can, partly to get better jobs than Laurel offers, and partly because, in Murph's words, "they don't appreciate the violence. They go to safer places."

'WE DON'T HAVE TO LIKE IT'

Today, however, there is hope that Laurel itself may become one of those safer places. The white leaders of the community appear to have survived a near-disaster, and possibly they have learned a lesson. Recently a group of them gathered in Mayor Bucklew's office to study a copy someone had obtained of the forty-page constitution of the White Knights of the KKK, plus a written plan of harassment. More than a few found new significance in the familiar words of Barry M. Goldwater printed on the back cover: "Extremism in the cause of liberty is not a vice. Moderation in the pursuit of justice is no virtue."

As for Mayor Bucklew, he continues to steer Laurel in a new direction. His private feelings may be correctly analyzed by the Mississippi Negro leader who said: "A few years ago he was with George Wallace. A man his age doesn't change this much. I can see political aspirations lingering there." But it is a hopeful sign that Bucklew is honest about his own limitations: "I am a segregationist but I'm not a criminal. For that reason I'm going to accept the law. We can't do anything but lose, fighting the Federal government with the authority it has. So the truth is, we must adjust to the things that are inevitable. We don't have to like it. We just have to do it."

Lawless Lawmen

Alan Barth

For the first time in his 42-year tenure as Director of the Federal Bureau of Investigation, J. Edgar Hoover is in trouble. He is in trouble with the law because FBI agents have been charged with violating state and federal prohibitions against eavesdropping. He is in political trouble because the asserted violations of law by his subordinates may prove painfully embarrassing to the Administration, prejudicing some politically important prosecutions—the Bobby Baker case among them. He is in trouble because recent disclosures of eavesdropping by the FBI call into question the reliability of his own statements.

On May 24 of this year, the Solicitor General of the United States, Thurgood Marshall, made an astonishing admission to the Supreme Court in connection with the case of Fred B. Black, Jr., convicted two years earlier of income tax evasion:

> On April 21, 1966, attorneys of the Tax Division of the Department of Justice—which was responsible for the prosecution of the tax evasion charges against petitioner—were advised by attorneys of the Criminal Division that, in the preparation of an unrelated matter, the latter had learned that conversations between petitioner and other persons at about the time of petitioner's indictment had been overheard by government agents using a listening device installed in petitioner's hotel suite.

The "device" had been installed, Mr. Marshall went on to say, by the Federal Bureau of Investigation in connection with a different inquiry. It was in operation between February and April 1963. "During that time," the Marshall memorandum declared, "the monitoring agents overheard, among other conversations, exchanges between petitioner and the attorney who was then representing him in connection with the tax-evasion charges."

The Solicitor General then made two interesting assertions: The monitoring of Black's conversations had no effect upon his conviction or the fairness of his trial; and, "during the preparation and trial of petitioner's case, no attorney involved in its presentation (or, so far as appears, any other attorney of the Department of Justice) knew that a listening device had been installed in petitioner's suite." Mr. Marshall reported in a Supplemental Memorandum on July 13 that the "device" was "a tubular microphone which was installed through the common wall of a room adjoining the suite occupied by petitioner at the Sheraton-Carlton Hotel in Washington, D.C. The microphone extended through the six-inch common wall and one-fourth of an inch into the one-half inch moulding of petitioner's suite."

This is precisely the kind of penetration of private premises which the Supreme Court unanimously held to be an unlawful trespass and a breach of the Fourth Amendment in the *Silverman* case in 1959. Evidence obtained in this way is inadmissible in any American court. Nevertheless, as the Solicitor General acknowledged, Mr. Hoover was authorized to engage in such eavesdropping. "Under Departmental practice in effect for a period of years prior to 1963, and continuing into 1965, the Director of the Federal Bureau of Investigation was given authority to approve the installation of devices such as that in question for intelligence (and not evidentiary) purposes when required in the interest of internal security or national safety, including organized crime, kidnappings and matters wherein human life might be at stake. Acting on the basis of the aforementioned Departmental authorization, the Director approved the installation of the device involved in the instant case."

Other allegations of FBI eavesdropping have recently come to light in connection with an investigation of gambling activities in Las Vegas. On June 30, Edward G. Marshall, District Attorney of Clark County, Nevada, announced that he will prosecute FBI agents for violation of Nevada's laws which forbid any form of electronic eavesdropping.

The Las Vegas story is stuff for the movies. FBI agents stationed in that city of chance and joy came one day, in the winter of 1960–61, to the president of the local telephone company and told him that they wished to lease 25 private telephone lines in the name of the Henderson Novelty Company—a fictional enterprise—to run to the FBI office in Las Vegas. The lines were to run in the other direction to the Fremont Hotel, the Sands Hotel, the Dunes Hotel, the Stardust Hotel, the Desert Inn and one or two other places in Las Vegas, for the purpose of listening in on the conversations of a collection of gambling operators during 1961, 1962 and 1963. A concealed microphone, or "bug," had to be installed to make this eavesdropping feasible.

One of them was placed in the base of a telephone in the private office of Edward Levinson, president and major owner of the Fremont Hotel, a prominent Las Vegas casino. The way it was done was described in an affidavit of Marvin E. Barr, a special service supervisor for Central Telephone:

> My conversations with telephone company employes revealed that the following procedure was followed for installing the lines of the Henderson Novelty Company. . . . If the intended destination of the new leased line was the Fremont Hotel, for example, John Zacker would then induce trouble on the Fremont Hotel telephone lines down at the central office. When the

Fremont Hotel called in to complain of its disrupted service, John Mallory would be sent out to make the repairs. Under the pretext of making the repairs, Mallory would install the new leased line on behalf of the Henderson Novelty Company at its intended destination within the hotel in accord with his directions from Bob Lee [an FBI agent]. After installation of the line, John Zacker would correct the trouble he had induced on the Fremont Hotel lines.

One day in 1963, however, Mr. Levinson decided to redecorate his office, and incidentally change the location of his telephone. The telephone company installer who did this job became aware of the bug hidden inside the instrument and told Levinson about it. The result was a general search and discovery among the big-time casino operators of Las Vegas and a sudden end to the operations of the Henderson Novelty Company. Levinson filed a $2 million damage suit against the FBI agents and the Central Telephone Company for conspiracy to violate his privacy.

Las Vegas was not the only scene of FBI eavesdropping in this period. A security supervisor for the Southwestern Bell Telephone Company in Kansas City testified under oath before Senator Edward V. Long's Senate subcommittee on administrative practice and procedure that the FBI leased lines to tap or bug a number of office and residence telephones in Kansas City between 1961 and 1965. Another supervisor for the company gave an account of the methods by which it was done. His task was to run the extra lines in accordance with FBI instructions, leaving it to the FBI men themselves to install the requisite listening device. Senator Long wanted to know about the destination of the cable: "Do you suspect that it went to the FBI office here in Kansas City?" The supervisor replied: "I know that it went to the FBI office, yes, sir."

Finally, the account of an FBI agent himself in a matter related to the Las Vegas gambling operations sheds some light on the way in which he and fellow-agents worked. The testimony was given in a federal court in Denver by Special Agent R. Burns Toolson, in charge of the Desert Inn case.

Q. You were conducting—and when I say "you," Mr. Toolson, I am referring to the Federal Bureau. You were conducting an investigation as pertains to certain matters at the Desert Inn, were you not, sir?

A. That is right.

Q. Now, directing your attention to the device itself. We have had considerable testimony of the manner in which the device transmitted the sounds from the executive office to the FBI headquarters. Would you tell us what your function was in connection—in this connection and what you did in connection with the material gotten from this device during the year 1962?

A. Well, I was generally responsible for it. They had various clerks who would record any conversations coming over this device. I would subsequently play these back and I would make a summary of them; either verbatim or a summary of any pertinent information.

Q. In other words—Let me ask you, first. Was every sound recorded to your knowledge that took place in the executive suite during 1962?

A. Not every sound. There was cleaning people in there and things of that nature that was never recorded. No.

Q. That's the purpose of bugging it, wasn't it?

A. Yes, that's correct.

Q. Well, would you tell us what instructions if any that you gave as pertains to what the clerks and the agents sitting on the recorder devices should record?

A. They were instructed to record any information of a pertinent nature that may relate to criminal intelligence activities; these people's movements; their associates. We tried to identify any unknown contacts; what people we didn't know who they were in contact with. We were interested in their business activities, to determine whether this money was being invested and how much it was being invested. We were interested in all phases of their activities. We were interested in any mention of any division of skimmed funds in that room.

Whatever was said in the executive suite, whether it related to personal and supposedly private affairs or to thoroughly ligitimate business dealings —and it should be remembered that gambling is legal in Nevada and that the men under investigation were not then charged with any crime—the snoopers sifted and filed away for possible use.

It should be noted that this eavesdropping, whether it involved a telephone interception within the meaning of the Federal Communications Act or not, violated the laws of Nevada; and some of it at least could have been accomplished only through a trespass which was in itself a violation of law and, which when done by a law enforcement agency in pursuit of evidence amounted to a plain and gross violation of the Fourth and Fifth Amendments.

Fred Black, Jr. had business relations with Edward Levinson in Las Vegas. So did Bobby Baker. Attorneys for Bobby Baker have already protested that the charges of tax evasion, theft and conspiracy for which he is under indictment were based upon information obtained through wiretapping or bugging or both. If they succeed in showing this to be the case, the entire prosecution will be tainted.

Attorney General Katzenbach summed it up in an appearance before the Long subcommittee on July 13, 1965: "As I have said repeatedly, once you put a wiretap on or use an illegal device of any kind, the possibilities of prosecution are gone. It is just like a grant of immunity . . . and I have dismissed cases or failed to bring cases within that area [he was discussing the area of national security] because some of the information did come from wiretaps. But there we feel that the intelligence and preventive aspects outweigh the desirability of prosecution in rare and exceptional instances."

But of course the Bobby Baker case has nothing to do with national security, and the country is extremely unlikely to feel that its "intelligence and preventive aspects outweigh the desirability of prosecution." The country—or critics of the Administration, at any rate—is much more likely to feel, if the prosecution of Bobby Baker should be dropped or thrown out of court, that the reason is to be found in his former close personal relations with President Johnson. And, although this is an imputation for which there is no discernible justification, it remains, nevertheless, a serious political hazard.

This is no doubt why, for the first time, there appears to be some serious conflict between Mr. Hoover and his political superiors. The FBI Director might understandably have felt some exasperation at having the Solicitor General go before the Supreme Court and absolve everybody else in the Department of Justice of responsibility for bugging Fred Black's hotel room. He could not have been pleased either by Robert Kennedy's response on June 26, in an interview on the American Broadcasting Company's television program, "Issues and Answers" to the question: "Did you authorize the FBI wiretaps of gamblers' telephones in Las Vegas in '62 and '63?" Senator Kennedy was Attorney General in '62 and '63. His answer was succinct: "No, I did not." He added that he had never authorized any wiretaps except in national security cases.

Richard Harwood, an investigative reporter for *The Washington Post*, reported in that newspaper that a Justice Department figure "knowledgeable in these affairs" had said: "Anyone who claims that Hoover had no authority for what he did in Las Vegas is just not telling the truth. And anyone who says Bill Rogers, Bobby Kennedy and Nick Katzenbach didn't know what he was doing doesn't know the facts. 'Whizzer' White knew a lot about this himself when he was working for Bobby."

When he appeared before a House Appropriations subcommittee on February 1, 1963 to justify the 1964 appropriation request of the FBI, Mr. Hoover said:

We have throughout the entire country at the present time less than 100 telephone taps. As a matter of fact the actual number today is 95. All are in security cases. In accordance with policy of many years' standing telephone taps are utilized only in cases where the internal security of the country is involved, or where kidnapping and extortion may bring about the jeopardy of a human life. The FBI does not have authority to authorize any wiretap. Each one must be authorized in advance and in writing by the Attorney General.

Mr. Hoover has made this statement, in almost the exact words, every year at appropriation time for almost a decade. The number of wiretaps acknowledged varies slightly from year to year, but that is about all; in 1959 it was 74, in 1965 it was down to 44. Mr. Hoover is always indignant at suggestions that the FBI taps telephones profligately; he was particularly so at the 1965 hearing. "You will hear statements publicly that the FBI has thousands of telephones tapped throughout the country," he told the subcommittee. "That is absolutely untrue."

Mr. Hoover's declarations have been backed up repeatedly by a succession of Attorneys General. Testifying before the Senate Judiciary Committee on March 22, 1966, Attorney General Katzenbach said, for example: "Within the federal government, wiretapping is strictly regulated. The FBI uses wiretaps only for intelligence purposes in national security matters, and then only with the express approval of the Attorney General. This has been true since 1940. President Johnson has extended this rule to all agencies of the federal government."

Now, it is perfectly plain that the eavesdropping in Las Vegas and in Kansas City did not involve internal security, kidnapping or extortion. And according to Senator Kennedy, it did not have authorization from him, in advance or in writing or in any other form. How, then, can the facts be squared with Mr. Hoover's strong disclaimer?

Perhaps the FBI will assert that what was done at Las Vegas and at Kansas City was not wiretapping in the strict legal sense of the term but simply a form of bugging, entailing not an interception within the meaning of the Federal Communications Act but a mere reproduction of all voices heard within the bugged room, by telephone or otherwise. The distinction is technical and obscure. A listening device installed within a telephone or attached to a telephone line—and installed with the connivance of a telephone company—looks like a telephone tap. Calling it anything else seems disingenuous.

But the truth is that the whole record of the Department of Justice in regard to wiretapping for the past 30 years has been disingenuous in the extreme.

Section 605 of the Federal Communications Act of 1934 contains the following provision:

> No person not being authorized by the sender shall intercept any communication and divulge or publish the existence, contents, substance, purport, effect, or meaning of such intercepted communication to any person; and no person not being entitled thereto shall receive or assist in receiving any interstate or foreign communication by wire or radio and use the same or any information therein contained for his own benefit or the benefit of another not entitled thereto. . . .

It is quite true, however, as Attorney General Katzenbach acknowledged, that "since 1940, every Attorney General has construed the act as not prohibiting wiretapping as such, but as prohibiting the interception and disclosure or use for personal benefit of the information so obtained. Because of the prohibition on disclosure, information obtained as a result of a wiretap cannot be used by state or federal authorities for the purpose of prosecution."

What a deceptive gloss this puts upon the law! The words plainly forbid use of intercepted information, not alone for personal benefit but for any benefit! And they preclude use by state or federal authorities, not only for the purpose of prosecution but for any purpose, including intelligence.

The Supreme Court has tried repeatedly to explain this to the Department of Justice. It could scarcely have found clearer language in which to do so than Justice Roberts' in the *Nardone* case in 1937:

> The plain words of Sec. 605 forbid anyone, unless authorized by the sender, to intercept a telephone message, and direct in equally clear language that "*no person*" shall divulge or publish the message or its substance to "*any person.*" . . .

What this says, inescapably and at the very least, is that no FBI agent who taps a telephone may disclose the substance of what he hears to any other agent, including J. Edgar Hoover himself. Nor may he make any use of what he hears for his own benefit or the benefit of anyone else. If wiretappers really make no use of the information they glean—if they really keep it secret even from their colleagues—there cannot be much point in tapping at all.

Ever since 1940, bills have been introduced to authorize wiretapping by the FBI under the supervision of the Attorney General. Congress after

Congress has debated these proposals—and rejected them. Yet Justice has persisted in pretending that it already has power to do what it keeps begging Congress to permit.

Mr. Hoover—with the consistent support of Attorneys General, it must be said—has developed a most ingenious justification for disregarding the law of the land. He has in his possession, he says, a confidential memorandum from President Franklin D. Roosevelt dated May 21, 1940 which, according to Mr. Hoover, "authorized the Attorney General to approve wiretapping when necessary in situations involving the defense of the nation."

The idea that an activity specifically forbidden by an Act of Congress can nevertheless be authorized by a confidential memorandum from a President—and from a President dead these 20 years and more—is an idea repugnant to the concept of a government of laws. There is not a syllable in the Federal Communications Act which makes an exception for kidnapping or extortion or internal security. There is not a clause in the Constitution that allows an Attorney General to authorize a violation of law by his subordinates, even with the support of a living President.

It was in that great dissenting opinion which he wrote nearly 40 years ago in the first wiretapping case to come to the Supreme Court that Mr. Justice Brandeis warned against lawless law enforcement:

> If the Government becomes a lawbreaker, it breeds contempt for law; it invites every man be a law unto himself; it invites anarchy. To declare that in the administration of the criminal law, the end justifies the means—to declare that the Government may commit crimes in order to secure the conviction of a private criminal—would bring terrible retribution.

Chapter Eleven

SUGGESTED QUESTIONS FOR CLASS DISCUSSION.

1. Some of the Justices of the Supreme Court have been urging that the Court, at the next opportunity, move all the protections of the Bill of Rights under the 14th Amendment and thereby secure these liberties against encroachment by all governments. Do you agree with this position? Should state governments be free to do what the national government cannot do? What would be some objections to this procedure?
2. What constitutes an "establishment of religion" prohibited by the First Amendment? Can there be a "child benefit" without benefitting the church which supports his school?
3. For many years we have been told that the problem of racial discrimination is one of attitude, and not a legal or political one at all. It is a problem whose solution can only be hurt rather than helped by legislation. Do you agree? Do you think protest marches and demonstrations have helped or hurt the cause of minorities?
4. How much influence have economic interests had in securing greater freedom for Negroes? Do you think this might be the ultimate solution?
5. Should governments be free to violate their own laws concerning the protection of individual liberties in the name of protecting themselves from subversion? in the name of necessity to identify and apprehend criminals?

THE POLITICS OF POVERTY

Because the United States is a rich nation and the signs of this wealth are to be found on all sides, many Americans have found it easy to over-look, and almost to forget, the poverty that is to be found in the country alongside its wealth. Once eyes are opened to it, poverty is to be found North, South, East, and West. It can be found as easily in lonely rural areas as in teeming cities.

Its impact is not narrowly restricted but affects almost every aspect of the life of the poor. Minds as well as bodies may suffer from malnutrition. Poverty shapes the social, cultural, political, economic, educational, and personal lives of the poor. The "discovery" of poverty and its effects does not automatically point the way toward a solution of the problem. Is there a key that will unlock the door to the problem and, if so, what is it? Jobs? Education? Alteration of the physical environment? Family planning and improved medical care? Guaranteed higher incomes, or what? And, if there is no single problem, and hence no one key that will unlock the entire thing, how are the various approaches to be combined most fruitfully?

Notes on Instant Urban Renewal

Roger Montgomery

Last year in Cleveland they called it "instant urban renewal." This year Molotov cocktails in Detroit confirm the message from Cleveland. The ghetto slums remain largely unaffected by the several billion federal dollars ostensibly directed at their eradication.

Despite repressive efforts on behalf of "law and order," the riots presumably will continue as long as a part of the American population feels hopelessly walled up in the slums. An eventual positive response is inevitable. Even now, when Presidential priorities put the hunt for scapegoats and the engineering of more effective law enforcement ahead of the search for remedies, the need for continued and intensified efforts on behalf of slum dwellers seems generally recognized.

The President and most of those who recognize this need indicate that they believe the response must take the form of pumping more money into existing programs. Johnson has stated that his plans are already before Congress—the only thing wanting is Congressional action to fund them. But the riots should warn us that current welfare services, poverty programs, and urban renewal may not do the trick. They suggest that our present social welfare strategy may have basic internal problems. More money in support of this strategy may not solve the problems of the urban lower class. If this is true, the current drift in welfare policy risks continued failure.

We must reexamine our efforts to deal with the problems of lower class people caught in the slums to see why these efforts have been so ineffective. This reassessment can begin with an analysis of slum clearance, housing, and urban renewal programs. Extrapolation from our experience with these may provide clues to the whole bundle of urban welfare needs. The following findings bear review, then, not so much for their specific content as for their cumulative implications about the general direction of successful social welfare efforts.

Beginning about ten years ago, a number of social scientists began to research the urban renewal program. Their findings, which were received so defensively by the federal renewal establishment, were not an attack on the bureaucrats so much as attack on the assumptions underlying our whole welfare strategy. If anyone was being criticized, it was Congress and the President's Budget Bureau which set the tasks for the housing and urban renewal bureaucracy.

URBANIZATION VERSUS LOCAL POLITICS. No aspect of the current American urban scene has received more study and documentation than the crippling mismatch between the structure of local government and the metropolitan-regional character of urbanization phenomena. The social and economic aspects of urbanized areas in no way fit the random geographic boundaries that limit local political organization. Consequently the solutions to urban problems which are so largely social and economic exist outside the limits of local political responsibility. The solution space and the political space simply do not coincide. Renewal planning in Newark has proceeded as though Newark were an isolated place, not a small piece of the New York metropolitan region. When Newark tried to face its low income housing needs, it was forced to seek solutions within its own political boundaries. This began a circular process: As services such as subsidized low-rent housing were provided, people in need of such services were attracted. At the same time, upwardly mobile working class and lower middle class people chose to move out of Newark in order to move up the status ladder. This produced a dynamically unstable situation which Newark was powerless to combat.

The institutional responses of the federal urban renewal assistance people have taken two directions. They have attempted to require "metropolitan planning" as a condition for federal aid; and they have made believe that every locality can somehow behave as a complete urban unit. In Detroit, for instance, the federal renewal agency has contributed to a metropolitan planning effort that can supposedly synchronize operations throughout the metropolitan area. Some slight success can be registered in the coordination of the relatively apolitical programs like the federal interstate highways. But hot issues like low-income housing get little consideration from upper class suburbs. The center city goes it alone, just as if no regional planning were involved. The other idea, that each political subdivision can work as a complete urban unit, shows up as the nonsense it is in such extreme cases as the all-Negro suburbs of Kinloch, Missouri, and Robbins, Illinois, with their hopeless little renewal programs struggling to attract new industry as if they were full-fledged cities.

Slum problems exist in a metropolitan context. Solutions which depend upon the vagaries of local political organizations seem to be precluded.

PROBLEM AVOIDANCE BY LOCAL GOVERNMENT. The present services approach to such welfare problems as slum improvement has been channeled through local government. This reflects the ideology which still dominates conventional thinking; it does not reflect the insights of social studies on the nature of local government in present-day America. With rare unanimity, political scientists who have examined the way decisions are reached at the local level agree that the practice is more one of problem-avoiding than of problem-solving. Their evidence clearly indicates that services which must flow through local government will flow haltingly if at all because of the local units' predisposition to avoid decisions.

INTERDEPENDENCE. Analysis of renewal operations shows a thicket of overlapping responsibilities, each with a veto power. In Detroit, for instance, the split between land planning responsibilities lodged with the public authority and development investment decisions help by private entrepreneurs stymied development of their first renewal project so that it stretched out over twenty years—a long time to devote to somewhat over one hundred acres of slum to be transformed into a few hundred units of middle class housing. The same split in the same project forced the public agency to abandon its 1947 objective of building decent low-cost housing and accept the private developers' need to build only for upper income families. When complex, interdependent responsibilities place the veto in many hands, only a miracle permits anything at all to be done.

ENTERPRISE EFFECT. Social research into the decision-making processes surrounding urban renewal has identified an enterprise effect: Local renewal agencies become devoted to protecting and advancing their interests as institutions in a way more and more unconnected with the urban problem issues that called such agencies into existence. They become progressively detached from their functional role with respect to the overall public interest or the needs of low-income people. Harold Kaplan's study of Newark and the Mowitz-Wright papers on Detroit emphasize this point. The enterprise effect blooms because of the peculiar federal-local relationship characteristic of renewal and welfare programs in general. Federal aid programs require localities to establish special purpose agencies to use the funds. As time goes by, these local agencies become more and more dedicated to pleasing the federal bureaucracy. It is easier that way, and that is where the money is. An informal pattern of vertical organization grows up, isolated from the needs of welfare recipients and chiefly concerned with satisfying a higher level bureaucratic market for local bureaucratic routines.

As a side effect of the enterprise phenomenon, citizen participation becomes practically impossible in planning renewal and housing projects. Kaplan and others have shown vividly how the dynamics of the system prevent this. Next to income problems the inability of slum dwellers to participate in decisions about their own lives may be the most pressing problem in the ghetto.

DEFINITIONAL PROBLEMS. To make complex bureaucracies work in providing services aimed at slum clearance and housing problems, elaborate rule systems must be evolved. These depend upon definitions. But even such a basic and seemingly simple item as a minimum housing standard has defied definition. On housing quality, for instance, Scott Greer observes, ". . . the terms 'blight' and 'nonblight' will not be mutually exclusive. Thus, one man's blight may be another man's nonblight, depending upon how important he thinks a given condition of characteristic to be. Yet people's homes are condemned and destroyed because they fall in the blight category, and billions of dollars are spent in blight removal."

DESIGN NORMS. Professional public housers and urban renewalists decide what kind of homes low-income people will get as a result of present public programs. Evidence shows that these professionals develop their own standards, which may or may not match up with those of the users. Housing gets designed in the way that will advance the designer through the ranks of the design bureaucracy, whether that of a public agency or a private firm. Whether or not the design satisfies the consumer becomes secondary if it is considered at all.

MONITORING PROBLEMS. A similar process perverts the indices necessary to make modern social accounting meaningful for the slum clearance and housing field. Instead of measuring the impact of renewal on the low-cost housing supply, federal statistics measure bureaucratic workload indicators like project approvals and acreage assignments in prospective renewal plans. This has made the comparative assessment of program benefits so central to contemporary management techniques terribly difficult. Worse, it has diverted attention from the slum problem. In Detroit and Newark federal figures give at a glance the number of projects and the procedural status of planinng in each, but they give no indication of the overall state of the city's housing.

RELOCATION. Few features of urban renewal have received more attention from social researchers than the forced move from the slum in the face of the federal bulldozer. Considerable literature documents the apparently damaging psychological and social effects of the move. In a society which so strongly supports the sovereignty of the individual in making consumer choices, forced relocation can never be a good thing.

Some economists who have studied renewal argue that, if renewal must force people to move, the houses they want to continue occupying must still be useful. It follows that these dwellings should not be torn down until suitable alternatives exist. Such logic suggests, then, that a slum house ought to be vacant before it can be legitimately removed from the available housing stock.

WORKLOAD PROBLEMS. Even the modest funds available to renewal and housing agencies get tied up in the internal processes of bureaucracy. Sometimes it seems they never get spent at all. For example, Detroit invented a large part of what is now called the model cities program. President Johnson has picked it up and announced it as the major new feature of his slum-eradication strategy. Congress approved modest planning grants for the fiscal year 1966–67 which ended on June 30. Yet when the riots broke out in Detroit in July, it still had not received approval of its model cities planning grant application.

Nearly all programs experience such delays. They do not stem from ill will on the part of the administrators, nor from ineptitude. The reason that even today's modest renewal workload chokes the pipelines of the system is federal bureaucratic involvement in a mass of details that defy streamlining.

Medical Ghettos

Anselm L. Strauss

In President Johnson's budget message to Congress this year he proposed a quadrupling of federal spending on health care and medical assistance for the poor to $4.2 billion in fiscal 1968:

The 1968 budget maintains the forward thrust of federal programs designed to improve health care in the nation, to combat poverty, and assist the needy. . . . The rise reflects the federal government's role in bringing quality medical care, particularly to aged and indigent persons.

Three years earlier in a special message to Congress the President had prefaced reintroduction of the medicare bill by saying:

We can—and we must—strive now to assure the availability of and accessibility to the best health care for all Americans, regardless of age or geography or economic status. . . . Nowhere are the needs greater than for the 15 million children of families who live in poverty.

Then, after decades of debate and massive professional and political opposition, the medicare program was passed. It promised to lift the poorest of our aged out of the medical ghetto of charity and into private and voluntary hospital care. In addition, legislation for heart disease and cancer centers was quickly enacted. It was said that such facilities would increase life expectancy by five years and bring a 20 per cent reduction in heart disease and cancer by 1975.

Is the medical millennium, then, on its way? The President, on the day before sending the 1968 budget to Congress said: "Medicare is an unqualified success."

"Nevertheless," he added, "there are improvements which can be made and shortcomings which need prompt attention." The message also noted that there might be some obstacles on the highroad to health. The rising cost of medical care, President Johnson stated, "requires an expanded and better organized effort by the federal government in research and studies of the organization and delivery of health care." If the President's proposals are adopted, the states will spend $1.9 billion and the federal government $1 billion in a "Partnership for Health" under the Medicaid program.

Considering the costs to the poor—and to the taxpayers—why don't the disadvantaged get better care? In all the lively debate on that matter, it is striking how little attention is paid to the mismatch between the current organization of American medicine and the life styles of the lower class. The major emphasis is always on how the *present* systems can be a little better supported or a trifle altered to produce better results.

I contend that the poor will never have anything approaching equal care until our present medical organization undergoes profound reform. Nothing in current legislation or planning will accomplish this. My arguments, in brief, are these:

The emphasis in all current legislation is on extending and improving a basically sound system of medical organization.

This assumes that all those without adequate medical services—especially the poor—can be reached with minor reforms, without radical transformation of the systems of care.

This assumption is false. The reason the medical systems have not reached the poor is because they were never designed to do so. The way the poor think and respond, the way they live and operate, has hardly ever (if ever) been considered in the scheduling, paperwork, organization, and mores of clinics, hospitals, and doctors' offices. The life styles of the poor are different; they must be specifically taken into account. Professionals have not been trained and are not now being trained in the special skills and procedures necessary to do this.

These faults result in a vicious cycle which drives the poor away from the medical care they need.

Major reforms in medical organizations must come, or the current great inequities will continue, and perhaps grow.

I have some recommendations designed specifically to break up that vicious cycle at various points. These recommendations are built directly upon aspects of the life styles of the poor. They do not necessarily require new money or resources, but they do require rearrangement, reorganization, reallocation—the kind of change and reform which are often much harder to attain than new funds or facilities.

HOW TO BE HEALTHY THOUGH POOR

In elaborating these arguments, one point must be nailed down first: *The poor definitely get second-rate medical care.* This is self-evident to anyone who has worked either with them or in public medical facilities; but there is a good deal of folklore to the effect that the very poor share with the very rich the best doctors and services—the poor getting free in the clinics what only the rich can afford to buy.

The documented statistics of the Department of Health, Education, and Welfare tell a very different story. As of 1964, those families with annual incomes under $2,000 average 2.8 visits per person to a physician each year, compared to 3.8 for those above $7,000. (For children during the crucial years under 15, the ratio is 1.6 to 5.7. The poor tend to have larger families; needless to add, their child mortality rate is also higher.) People with higher incomes (and $7,000 per year can hardly be considered wealthy) have a tremendous advantage in the use of medical specialists— 27.5 per cent see at least one of them annually, compared to about 13 per cent of the poor.

Health insurance is supposed to equalize the burden; but here, too, money purchases better care. Hospital or surgical insurance coverage is closely related to family income, ranging from 34 per cent among those with family income of less than $2,000 to almost 90 per cent for persons in families of $7,000 or more annual income. At the same time, the poor, when hospitalized, are much more apt to have more than one disorder— and more apt to exhaust their coverage before discharge.

Among persons who were hospitalized, insurance paid for some part of the bill for about 40 per cent of patients with less than $2,000 family income, for 60 per cent of patients with $2,000–$3,999 family income, and for 80 per cent of patients with higher incomes. Insurance paid three-fourths or more of the bill for approximately 27 per cent, 44 per cent, and 61 per cent of these respective income groups. Preliminary data from the 1964 survey year showed, for surgery or delivery bills paid by insurance, an even more marked association of insurance with income.

Similar figures can be marshaled for chronic illness, dental care, and days of work lost.

Strangely enough, however, *cash* difference (money actually spent for care) is not nearly so great. The under $2,000 per year group spent $112 per person per year, those families earning about three times as much ($4,000–$7,000) paid $119 per person, and those above $7,000, $153. Clearly, the poor not only get poorer health services but less for their money.

As a result, the poor suffer much more chronic illness and many more working days lost—troubles they are peculiarly ill-equipped to endure. Almost 60 per cent of the poor have more than one disabling condition compared to about 24 per cent of other Americans. Poor men lose 10.2 days of work annually compared to 4.9 for the others. Even medical research seems to favor the affluent—its major triumphs have been over acute, not chronic, disorders.

WHAT'S WRONG WITH MEDICAL ORGANIZATION?

Medical care, as we know it now, is closely linked with the advancing organization, complexity, and maturity of our society and the increasing education, urbanization, and need for care of our people. Among the results: Medicine is increasingly practiced in hospitals in metropolitan areas.

The relatively few dispensaries for the poor of yesteryear have been supplanted by great numbers of outpatient hospital clinics. These clinics and services are still not adequate—which is why the continuing cry for reform is "more and better." But even when medical services *are* readily available to the poor, they are not used as much as they could and should be. The reasons fall into two categories:

—factors in the present organization of medical care that act as a brake on giving quality care to everyone;

—the life styles of the poor that present obstacles even when the brakes are released.

The very massiveness of modern medical organization is itself a hindrance to health care for the poor. Large buildings and departments, specialization, division of labor, complexity, and bureaucracy lead to an impersonality and an overpowering and often grim atmosphere of hugeness. The poor, with their meager experience in organizational life, their insecurity in the middle class world, and their dependence on personal contacts, are especially vulnerable to this impersonalization.

Hospitals and clinics are organized for "getting work done" from the staff point of view; only infrequently are they set up to minimize the patient's confusion. He fends for himself and sometimes may even get lost when sent "just down the corridor." Patients are often sent for diagnostic tests from one service to another with no explanations, with inadequate directions, with brusque tones. This may make them exceedingly anxious and affect their symptoms and diagnosis. After siting for hours in waiting rooms, they become angry to find themselves passed over for latecomers—but nobody explains about emergencies or priorities. They complain they cannot find doctors they really like or trust.

When middle class patients find themselves in similar situations, they can usually work out some methods of "beating the system" or gaining understanding that may raise staff tempers but will lower their own anxieties. The poor do not know how to beat the system. And only very seldom do they have that special agent, the private doctor, to smooth their paths.

Another organizational barrier is the increasing professionalism of health workers. The more training and experience it takes to make the various kinds of doctors, nurses, technicians, and social workers, the more they become oriented around professional standards and approaches, and the more the patient must take their knowledge and abilities on trust. The gaps of communications, understanding, and status grow. To the poor, professional procedures may seem senseless or even dangerous—especially when not explained—and professional manners impersonal or brutal, even when professionals are genuinely anxious to help.

Many patients complain about not getting enough information; but the poor are especially helpless. They don't know the ropes. Fred Davis quotes from a typical poor parent, the mother of a polio-stricken child:

> Well they don't tell you anything hardly. They don't seem to want to. I mean you start asking questions and they say, "Well, I only have about three minutes to talk to you." And then the things that you ask, they don't seem to want to answer you. So I don't ask them anything any more. . . .

For contrast, we witnessed an instance of a highly educated woman who found her physician evasive. Suddenly she shot a question: "Come now, Doctor, don't I have the same cancerous condition that killed my sister?" His astonished reaction confirmed her suspicion.

Discrimination also expresses itself in subtle ways. As Frank Riessman and Sylvia Scribner note (for pychiatric care), "Middle class patients are preferred by most treatment agents, and are seen as more treatable. . . . Diagnoses are more hopeful. . . ." Those who understand, follow, respond to, and are grateful for treatment are good patients; and that describes the middle class.

Professional health workers are themselves middle class, represent and defend its values, and show its biases. They assume that the poor (like themselves) have regular meals, lead regular lives, try to support families, keep healthy, plan for the future. They prescribe the same treatment for the same diseases to all, not realizing that their words do not mean the same things to all. (What does "take with each meal" mean to a family that eats irregularly, seldom together, and usually less than three times a day?)

And there is, of course, some open bias. A welfare case worker in a large Midwestern city, trying to discover why her clients did not use a large, nearby municipal clinic more, described what she found:

> Aside from the long waits (8 a.m. to about 1 p.m. just to make the appointment), which perhaps are unavoidable, there is the treatment of patients by hospital personnel. This is at the clinic level. People are shouted at, ridiculed, abused, pushed around, called "Niggers," told to stand "with the rest of the herd," and in many instances made to feel terribly inferior if not inadequate. . . . This . . . was indulged in by personnel other than doctors and nurses. . . .

Even when no bias is intended, the hustle, impersonality, and abstraction of the mostly white staff tend to create this feeling among sensitive and insecure people: "And I do think the treatment would have been different if Albert had been white."

The poor especially suffer in that vague area we call "care," which includes nursing, instructions about regimens, and post-hospital treatment generally. What happens to the lower class patient once released? Middle class patients report regularly to their doctors who check on progress and exert some control. But the poor are far more likely to go to the great, busy clinics where they seldom see the same doctor twice. Once out they are usually on their own.

DISTANCE AND DISUSE

Will the poor get better care if "more and better" facilities are made available? I doubt it. The fact is that they underutilize those available now. For instance, some 1963 figures from the Director of the Division of Health Services, Children's Bureau:

> In Atlanta, 23 percent of women delivered at the Grady Hospital had had no prenatal care; in Dallas, approximately one-third of low-income patients receive no prenatal care; at the Los Angeles County Hospital in 1958, it was 20 percent; at the D.C. General Hospital in Washington, it is 45 percent; and in the Bedford Stuyvesant section of Brooklyn, New York, it is 41 percent with no or little prenatal care.

Distances are also important. Hospitals and clinics are usually far away. The poor tend to organize their lives around their immediate neighborhoods, to shut out the rest of the city. Some can hardly afford bus fare (much less cab fare for emergencies). Other obstacles include unrealistic eligibility rules and the requirement by some hospitals that clinic patients arrange a blood donation to the blood bank as a prerequisite for prenatal care.

Medical organization tends to assume a patient who is educated and well-motivated, who is interested in ensuring a reasonable level of bodily functioning and generally in preserving his own health. But health professionals themselves complain that the poor come to the clinic or hospital with advanced symptoms, that parents don't pay attention to children's symptoms early enough, that they don't follow up treatments or regimens, and delay too long in returning. But is it really the fault of whole sections of the American population if they don't follow what professionals expect of them?

THE CRISIS LIFE OF THE POOR

What are the poor really like? In our country they are distinctive. They live strictly, and wholeheartedly, in the present; their lives are uncertain, dominated by recurring crises (as S. M. Miller puts it, theirs "is a crisis-life constantly trying to make do with string where rope is needed"). To them a careful concern about health is unreal—they face more pressing troubles daily, just getting by. Bad health is just one more condition they must try to cope—or live—with.

Their households are understaffed. There are no servants, few reliable adults. There is little time or energy to care for the sick. If the mother is ill, who will care for her or take her to the clinic—or care for the children if she goes? It is easier to live with illness than use up your few resources doing something about it.

> As Daniel Rosenblatt and Edward Suchman have noted: The body can be seen as simply another class of objects to be worked out but not repaired. Thus, teeth are left without dental care. . . . Corrective eye examinations, even for those who wear glasses, are often neglected. . . . It is as though . . . blue-collar groups think of the body as having a limited span of utility; to be enjoyed in youth and then to suffer with and to endure stoically with age and decrepitude.

They are characterized by low self-esteem. Lee Rainwater remarks that low-income people develop "a sense of being unworthy; they do not uphold the sacredness of their persons in the same way that middle-class people do. Their tendency to think of themselves as of little account is . . . readily generalized to their bodies." And this attitude is transferred to their children.

They seek medical treatment only when practically forced to it. As Rosenblatt and Suchman put it: "Symptoms that do not incapacitate are often ignored." In clinics and hospitals they are shy, frustrated, passively submissive, prey to brooding, depressed anxiety. They reply with guarded hostility, evasiveness, and withdrawal. They believe, of their treatment, that "what is free is not much good." As a result, the professionals tend to turn away. Julius Roth describes how the staff in a rehabilitation ward gets discouraged with its apparently unrehabilitatable patients and gives up and concentrates on the few who seem hopeful. The staffs who must deal with the poor in such wards either have rapid turnover or retreat into "enclaves of research, administration, and teaching."

The situation must get worse. More of the poor will come to the hospitals and clinics. Also, with the increasing use of health insurance and programs by unions and employers, more will come as paying patients into the private hospitals, mixing with middle class patients and staff, upsetting routines, perhaps lowering quality—a frightening prospect as many administrators see it. As things are going now, relations between lower-income patients and hospital staff must become more frequent, intense, and exacerbated.

It is evident that the vicious cycle that characterizes medical care for the poor must be broken before anything can be accomplished.

In the first part of this cycle, the poor come into the hospitals later than they should, often delaying until their disorders are difficult to relieve, until they are actual emergency cases. The experiences they have there encourage them to try to stay out even longer the next time—and to cut the visits necessary for treatment to a minimum.

Second, they require, if anything, even more effective communication and understanding with the professionals than the middle class patient. They don't get it; and the treatment is often undone once they leave.

What to do? The conventional remedies do help some. More money and insurance will tend to bring the poor to medical help sooner; increased staff and facilities can cut down the waits, the rush, the tenseness, and allow for more individual and efficient treatment and diagnosis.

But much more is required. If the cycle is to be *broken*, the following set of recommendations must be adopted:

Speed up the initial visit. Get them there sooner.

Improve patient experiences.

Improve communication, given and received, about regimens and treatment to be followed.

Work to make it more likely that the patient or his family will follow through at home.

Make it more likely that the patient will return when necessary.

Decrease the time between necessary visits.

This general list is not meant to be the whole formula. Any experienced doctor or nurse, once he recognizes the need, can add to or modify it. An experience of mine illustrates this well. A physician in charge of an adolescent clinic for lower-income patients, finding that my ideas fitted into his own daily experience, invited me to address his staff. In discussion afterward good ideas quickly emerged:

Since teen-age acne and late teen-age menstrual pain were frequent complaints and the diagnoses and medications not very complicated, why not let nurses make them? Menstruating girls would be more willing to talk to a woman than a man.

Patients spend many hours sitting around waiting. Why not have nursing assistants, trained by the social worker and doctor and drawn from the patients' social class, interview and visit with them during this period, collecting relevant information?

Note two things about these suggestions: Though they do involve some new duties and some shifting around, they do not call for any appreciable increase of money, personnel, or resources; and such recommendations, once the need is pointed out, can arise from the initiative and experience of the staff themselves.

A Cold Shoulder for the Poverty Program

James K. Batten

NEW BERN, NORTH CAROLINA

During this state's Ku Klux Klan revival in the mid-1960's, the cow-pasture oratory usually included one standard line guaranteed to catch the mood of the milling crowds. It went like this: "The niggers got the NAACP, the Jews got the B'nai B'rith, the Catholics got the Knights of Columbus. What in the hell has the poor white man got but the Ku Klux Klan?"

"A Cold Shoulder for the Poverty Program," *The Reporter*, May 30, 1968. Reprinted by permission of the author.

In much of the rural South, one is tempted to concede, "Not very much." The great social programs launched by Washington in the last five years, while bringing new hope to thousands of Negroes, have frequently by-passed the poor whites. Nobody intended that result, of course, and Federal agencies like the Office of Economic Opportunity have worked hard to combat it. But often they have failed. Consequently, many Southern poor whites are, in one sense, even more deeply alienated today from the national mainstream than are their Negro neighbors. At least the civil-rights movement and the poverty program have buoyed the spirits of large segments of the South's Negro population. But poor whites have watched both developments with mounting hostility, convinced that nobody was leading any grand crusades for them.

Here in Craven County, set in the fertile agricultural heartland of eastern North Carolina, this pattern can be seen with great clarity. Craven in many ways is typical of the rural and small-town South where white and Negro poor live side by side in substantial numbers. Of Craven's poor families enumerated by the 1960 census, 2,772 were white and 2,360 were Negro.

Except for the huge Marine Corps base at Cherry Point, the county's economy has remained predominantly agricultural. New Bern (population 18,000), once the colonial capital of North Carolina and now an overnight stop for tourists following Route 17 along the coast, is the county seat and the principal town. The remainder of the county's 55,500 civilian residents are scattered through a few small towns and across the rural countryside.

PRIDE MISAPPLIED

The war on poverty came to Craven County in late 1964. Within a year, Craven Operation Progress was being acclaimed by the OEO as one of the nation's most promising rural poverty programs. Part of this strong beginning was due to the agency's original sponsorship by the North Carolina Fund, created by the then Governor Terry Sanford in 1963 to help improve social conditions in the state. Another factor in the early success was the agency's first director, James J. Hearn, an aggressive young lawyer whose experience on Capitol Hill taught him how to wheedle money out of the Federal bureaucracy.

Today, more than three years later, Craven Operation Progress has given way to a successor, Coastal Progress, Inc., which brought neighboring Jones and Pamlico Counties into a joint enterprise with Craven. The tri-county program, now under a new director, James Godwin, is still regarded as one of OEO's best rural projects.

But for all its accomplishments, Coastal Progress, Inc., has failed in its attempts to reach the thousands of poor whites who need help almost as badly as do their poor Negro neighbors. Negroes have flocked in to take advantage of the new programs, but the whites have kept their sullen distance.

There are several reasons, including the whites' refusal to acknowledge their poverty and a stubborn pride that prevents them from seeking help. "I know a lot of white people who need help," one backwoods grocer explained, "but they feel embarrassed to ask for it. They've got too much pride. A person hates to say he's desperate, down and out." Director Godwin agreed: "They just don't see themselves as being in poverty, and yet some of them are so poor it's pathetic."

All this is undoubtedly important, but there is a more fundamental explanation for the whites' aloofness, and it has to do with racial prejudice. Most poor whites in Craven County shun the poverty program primarily because they regard it almost universally as "something for the niggers."

Godwin, an outgoing, hard-driving former insurance executive and a native of rural South Carolina, readily admits that racial feelings lie at the heart of the CPI's failure to reach poor whites. He observes gloomily that neither he nor anybody else, in Washington or elsewhere, knows how to solve the problem.

Last summer, he recalled, two energetic community organizers, white natives of Craven County, were trained for the task of reaching the poor whites. They got nowhere. "These people were carefully selected from the poor themselves," Godwin told me, "and we trained them carefully. But after a while, both workers gave up and asked if they couldn't try something else." Craven's poor whites were simply not accepting CPI's ideas of community organization.

CPI's other programs have not fared much better. The Neighborhood Youth Corps in Craven County, for example, includes 104 Negroes and only twenty-two whites. The county's year-round Head Start program has twenty-nine Negro children and sixteen whites. In Jones County, only three of twenty-seven Head Start children are white; in Pamlico, only three of fifteen.

One of CPI's proudest successes has been a strawberry-marketing cooperative, through which low-income farmers under pressure from dwindling Federal tobacco allotments are able to add $1,000 to their farm profits by tending an acre of strawberries. But here again, Negroes have jumped in enthusiastically, while white farmers have hung back. Only eight of the co-op's seventy-six low-income farmers are white.

When a visitor inquires about the reasons underlying the poor whites' virtual boycott of programs so potentially valuable to them, conversation quickly turns back to the early days of Craven Operation Progress in late 1964 and 1965. From all accounts, the poverty program was branded almost immediately by the white community as a program for Negroes. Larry Pate, a well-to-do farmer who was chairman of the original board of Craven Operation Progress, insists even now that the description was accurate. "It seems they're just trying to help the Negro," Pate told me. "They say that's not true, but it is true."

Pate and other prominent white people in Craven County tend to place part of the blame on James Hearn, the first director. Hearn, a New Yorker and a man of firm equalitarian views, was determined to run the new agency on a strictly nondiscriminatory basis. This came as a shock in a community where segregation remained the accepted social pattern. Local whites still talk in horrified tones of how Hearn "ordered" white and Negro staff members to lunch together in New Bern's restaurants.

Now on OEO's regional staff in Kansas City, Hearn insists that his policy was not to flout Craven's racial customs unnecessarily. "But people who work together as a staff have to be together all the way, they have to be Americans together." Hearn added that his own views were irrelevant, since OEO policies left little room for adjusting to Southern racial traditions.

Looking back, he concedes that in a setting like Craven County, the unapologetic practice of racial equality by a new social agency would almost automatically frighten away race-conscious poor whites. And so, perhaps inevitably, Craven Operation Progress, in the words of Larry Pate, "got to be known as a program for integration. And that reputation doesn't die very fast."

Hearn had hoped that men like Pate would use their influence to persuade Craven's poor whites to swallow their racial qualms and seek help from the poverty program. But few of them did. In fact, the suspicion and hostility of the conservative white middle class undoubtedly was a crucial ingredient in shaping the poor whites' own reluctance to participate. "People follow the thinking of their leaders, let's face it," one CPI staff member told me. "And the leaders here say it [the poverty program] encourages shiftlessness and the like." During the program's early days the slogan "I Fight Poverty, I Work," confined to bumper stickers in most parts of the country, blossomed on billboards in Craven County.

The example set by the white leadership was particularly important because in the rural South poor whites traditionally have prized their free-and-easy relationship with the white gentry. It has served to console them for their hardships and reinforce their pride in being white—and thus superior to "the niggers."

"The poor white man," one local politician explained, "can go into the restaurant and buy a cup of coffee and shoot the breeze with the big farmers. I know the largest tobacco farmer in Craven County, and his white tenants go out to his house and play gin rummy. They cuss him in public, they argue with him in public, and there's a certain genuine social equality here."

This status clearly is a valuable possession for a man who has little else. And he naturally is determined to avoid any behavior that might conceivably cast doubt on his standing as a right-thinking white man. In Craven County, many poor whites concluded that the quickest way to jeopardize that standing was to get involved with the poverty program.

STAYING IN PLACE

When OEO decreed that one-third of each local anti-poverty board must be representatives of the poor, Craven Operation Progress scoured the county to find a few suitable poor whites. One woman, a welfare client, was appointed because her caseworker detected in her a streak of native resourcefulness. But the woman never attended a meeting of the board. Asked why, she replied, "You want to know the truth? There were just too many colored people associated with it. I get along with colored people all right, but I don't want to rub elbows with 'em, you know? I want them to stay where they are and me stay where I am."

The same spirit was more vehemently reflected in a stocky, florid-faced man named Wyatt Holton, who runs a filling station a few miles east of

New Bern across the Neuse River. Until a year ago, he was the Exalted Cyclops (president) of the Craven County Klavern of the Ku Klux Klan. Not long ago, Holton was thinking of opening a small wholesale and retail seafood business. He mentioned his need for a $5,000 loan to a member of the Craven Operation Progress board. Holton still bristles when he recalls the answer he got. "He referred me to Tom Wallace—he's a nigger from Greensboro. He wears Bermuda shorts and he's a damn wheel. [Wallace is CPI's deputy director.] I just knew I wasn't going over there and ask that nigger to help me. I wouldn't ask him, by God, if I had to crawl on my belly. If I couldn't get a white man that had enough interest to see into it for me, I just wouldn't have gone over there. There's never been a nigger good as I am, I tell you."

A few poor whites, of course, have overcome their misgivings and reluctantly sought help from the poverty program. Usually it has been a case of pride being overwhelmed by a desperate need for assistance. In a rented farmhouse near Vanceboro, a hotbed of Klan activity, a white mother hesitantly explained why she permitted her sixteen-year-old daughter to join the Neighborhood Youth Corps. The girl earns $12.50 a week by doing odd jobs at nearby Farm Life High School.

"I certainly don't want my children to chop and tie tobacco all their lives," she murmured, savoring a dip of snuff. "There ain't nothing in labor—fifty or sixty cents an hour. That ain't nothing." The conversation soon made it clear that the girl's income from the Neighborhood Youth Corps was helping her stay in school. A high-school diploma, in the girl's mind, was her only possible ticket out of her family's dreary world in Craven County. "She wants to be a secretary in a business office," her mother said. "She don't want to wind up in a sewing room like her sister did."

The woman was asked about her neighbors' reaction to the girl's involvement in the poverty program. "They hain't throwed off on me," she said. "I've always treated colored people right, but I've always been taught to go with my color. But if you're poor, you can't help that."

Poor whites who reason that way, however, remain a distinct minority. And because their overtures to whites are usually rebuffed, CPI staff members seem increasingly resigned to serving the Negroes who clamor for help and forgetting the seemingly unreachable poor whites. The new twenty-three-member CPI board is symptomatic of this outlook. Poor Negroes are well represented; poor whites have no representatives at all.

"We haven't knocked ourselves out, to tell you the truth," one Head Start official admitted when asked about attempts to recruit white children. "There are so many Negro kids who want to come." When a staff member in Pamlico County was pressed to discuss his efforts to reach poor whites, he shrugged apologetically. "Can I plead negligence?" he asked. "It's just hopeless."

The same resignation apparently has overtaken OEO headquarters in Washington. "They don't press us like they used to," one CPI administrator, a Negro, confided. "We tried so hard to satisfy them [on involvement of whites] that we were jeopardizing what we had here. It gave certain people in the Negro community the impression that we were trying harder to get whites than Negroes, and they felt that was discrimination in reverse. We were in a pinch between D.C. and the local citizens."

The poor whites' aloofness, it should be noted, extends beyond the confines of the poverty program. Anything thought to carry any social or racial stigma is avoided whenever possible. Some Craven County welfare officials, for example, concede that some poor whites probably fail to claim benefits for fear of lowering themselves in the eyes of friends and neighbors.

At New Bern's three-year-old Craven Technical Institute, Director Thurman Brock complained that of about three hundred adults learning to read, write, and do arithmetic in a basic education program, only ten are white. Those ten are employed at Cherry Point and attend classes on the base. The Institute's more advanced classes in such subjects as electrical circuitry and blueprint reading are integrated without any problems. "The only white people whom integration scares off in Craven County," Brock said sadly, "are those in need of this basic education."

ROUGH JUSTICE

The full implications of the poor whites' stubborn avoidance of programs designed to aid all the nation's poor can only be guessed at. But it is worth observing that poor white people, inside and outside the South, are prime carriers of the white racism regarded by the Kerner Commission as the root of the nation's racial troubles. Unless these people can be helped out of their own economic and psychological deprivation, then this particular source of racist sentiment will not be diminished. Indeed, as resentful poor whites watch their black neighbors partake of benefits they themselves refuse, their bitterness may become even deeper.

The only consolation is that in Negroes' acceptance and whites' rejection of the new governmental largesse, the result is an unintended equalizing of the benefits received by blacks and whites from the American economic and political system. Poor whites, unburdened by black skin, have had some opportunity to rise through the normal workings of the system, while Negroes generally have not. So in places like Craven County, the poverty program and similar government enterprises have given Negroes a compensatory boost.

As Godwin of CPI put it, "The exploitation of the poor whites has been the same, in some ways, as the exploitation of poor Negroes. But the poor whites have a hope of breaking out, while it's only very recently that any such spark has been kindled in the blacks. The poor white always got the road-grader job, while the Negro was assigned to dig ditches."

An executive of the North Carolina Fund agreed. It is too bad, he said, that poor whites are shunning the help they badly need. "But the Negroes," he pointed out, "still have a long way to go to get the same fruits of the system that poor whites have always gotten, just because they're white."

Appalachia: Again the Forgotten Land

Peter Schrag

Once again Appalachia is becoming America's forgotten land. Seven years and more than seven billion federal dollars after John F. Kennedy brought the region to national attention, grand solutions have soured into new problems, the exploitation of land and people continues, and even the best and most hopeful efforts are jeopardized by a war 10,000 miles away and by ugly political machines all too close to home.

Because of the work of a handful of dedicated people—VISTA workers, Appalachian volunteers, and local residents—some hope has returned with the mounting welfare checks, and some sense of the possible is growing even in the most remote creeks and hollows. But now the programs that have been most effective—many of them aimed at giving the poor a measure of choice and control—are threatened by the politicians' response to local commercial pressures and by the rapacious demands of the strip-mine operators. Efforts at regional development are being directed by distant planners and small-town chambers of commerce, while individuals trying to organize the poor are called agitators and Communists, and are driven from the region under agreements between state politicians and national poverty officials who have become politically too weak to resist.

Appalachia, the original American frontier, extends from southern Pennsylvania to northern Alabama, covering 182,000 square miles of land rich in coal, timber, sandstone, natural gas, water, and some of the most magnificent scenery on the continent. In 1966, nearly 100 million tons of coal worth close to $400 million were mined in Kentucky alone. Where the strip mines have spared the hillsides, the folded mountains, covered by white oak, pine, walnut, beech, and other trees, extend in all directions to the blue-gray horizon. But in the half-abandoned coal camps that adjoin the sulphur-polluted creeks, on the streets of the little towns, and in the welfare offices, the poverty of the people stands in brutal contrast to the wealth of the land. Along the winding roads, the rotting carcasses of abandoned automobiles lie alongside smoldering coal dumps and the decaying tipples of exhausted mines, and in the brown and yellow streams, once rich with fish, the sad trash of poverty accumulates in rusty piles.

Appalachia, now growing its third welfare generation, has counties where more than a third of the population is unemployed, where the government check—social security, welfare, aid to dependent children—is the prime source of income, and where some men are so far from their last job that it cannot properly be said that they have a trade at all. Here the average adult has a sixth-grade education, three-fourths of the children who start school drop out before they complete the twelfth grade, and the

"Appalachia: Again the Forgotten Land," *Saturday Review,* January 27, 1968. Reprinted by permission of the publisher.

statistics of human pathology—tuberculosis, silicosis, infant mortality—are so high that they do not belong in the Western world at all.

Everything has eroded: The best of the resources flow forever downstream and toward the industrial cities of the North. Heavy rains wash the topsoil from the hills and turn the rivers into muddy torrents, the coal fires the mills of the North and the generators of the TVA (which is the prime buyer of Appalachian fuel), while the most skilled and ambitious of the young leave the hills and hollows to find work in Cleveland, Chicago, or Detroit. "We've been the great pool of manpower for the Northeast," said a poverty worker in eastern Tennesseee. "And the pool has been turned on and off at will. The rest of the country gets automobiles and the gadgets of affluence. All this region gets is silicosis."

Appalachia's coal regions enjoyed a brief, uncertain moment of prosperity during and immediately after World War II, when the war economy and the pressure of John L. Lewis's United Mine Workers brought decent wages, hospitals, and pension plans. But when the war boom ended, many of the mines closed, leaving the survivors of a single-product economy without resources or useful skills. The coal industry ultimately returned to prosperity with a rising demand for fuel, but it did so as a highly efficient, mechanized enterprise. Using modern equipment, 140,000 men can now dig more coal than 700,000 did twenty years ago. And while many of the deep mines continue to operate, frequently under enlightened management, a substantial part of the industry is now stripping the mountains, cutting or blasting away the topsoil and vegetation—which spills down the slopes—to get at the coal beneath. Each year the strip mines of Kentucky scar some 12,000 acres of land, leaving the bare cliffs of the high wall above and the sliding spoil banks on the hills below.

The legal basis for this damage rests in the so-called broad form deed: Before strip mining became prevalent, thousands of mountaineers sold their mineral rights to coal and land companies for a few cents an acre, entitling the companies to remove minerals and holding them harmless for any damage except that incurred through malice. The courts have held that this immunity extends even to the uprooting of graves and the destruction of the homes and gardens that are occasionally covered by slides. Under the broad form deed, said a mountaineer, "they've dug up the dead and buried the living." Although several states have enacted strip-mine laws requiring operators to restore the land, and although many companies are diligently trying to comply, enforcement is often difficult or ineffective.

In West Virginia, a new statute now entitles property owners to collect triple damages from the coal companies, but in the mountains of eastern Kentucky that state's law has had little effect. Kentucky's new governor, Louie B. Nunn, received support from the strip-mine interests in the 1967 election, and it is unlikely that he will be overzealous in enforcing or strengthening it. Under his predecessor, Edward T. Breathitt, state officials experimented with techniques of restoring the hillsides, but even they admitted privately that where the slopes are steep, there is no possible way of eliminating slides and reclaiming the land. In the mountains of eastern Kentucky, the only effective hope for conservation appears to be the elimination of the strip mine altogether. (Last month, the day Breathitt's term expired, he approved a set of tough regulations, limiting strip mines to slopes of less than 28 degrees; if those regulations stand, they will severely restrict strip mining and will represent a major victory for conservation in the region.)

In this sad economy of food stamps and subsistence, the coal company is no longer the great employer—and hence the paternalistic provider—it used to be. Gone are the days when the company owned the buildings, ran the store, and furnished the services, and even the most naïve have now abandoned the hope that some day "the mines will open up again." What remains is the condition of dependency: Through a half-century of rural industrialization, the once-independent mountaineer was reduced to reliance on a single enterprise, and, when it no longer required his labor, to nothing except the dole. The public payroll, and most notably the public schools, now furnish the prime source of employment. In Appalachia, schools mean jobs for bus drivers, clerks, lunchroom employees, coaches, and teachers, and hence they represent the most important source of political power at hand. In the isolated mountain counties, where kinship and tribal loyalties overshadow the abstractions of political ethics, the school superintendent is often a political boss who controls contracts for insurance, construction, and fuel, appointment to other offices, and employment in the system.

In Breathitt County, Kentucky, for example, Marie Turner or her husband have held the school superintendency for more than forty years, and thus they also control most of the other offices the county has to offer. There are similar machines in other areas, and although many people feel that people like the Turners have been benevolent bosses—Breathitt County, someone said, would have fallen apart without the Turners—they have been bosses nevertheless. At a time when Appalachia was out of the national consciousness and the mountaineer was a figure for mythology and amusement, the Turners did what they could for their people. The *quid pro quo* was patronage and power.

The American romance with the happy hillbilly came to an end in the early Sixties. Prompted by Mr. Kennedy's concern with Appalachian poverty—which he saw first hand in the 1960 West Virginia primary—Americans began to discover the misery behind the moonshine. Television crews and magazine writers swarmed to the hills in such numbers that one Kentucky motel owner began to conduct photographic safaris to hollows that he promised "ain't been worked yet." While bands of hungry, desperate miners roamed the coal regions dynamiting trains and bridges, Congress passed the Manpower Development and Training Act, the Appalachia Redevelopment Act, and a variety of other measures designed to bring the heretofore invisible poor some share of the affluence that most Americans took for granted.

Although the federal poverty program was aimed at all indigent Americans, Appalachia came to symbolize, along with the urban ghetto, the most pressing item on the nation's social agenda. As a consequence, special funds have been appropriated for the construction of Appalachian highways, water facilities, and hospitals; the distribution of surplus food has been augmented through a food stamp program which enables the poor to purchase more groceries than their welfare checks would otherwise permit; unemployed fathers have been given jobs, at $1.25 an hour, in a "work experience and training" program (they are generally called "happy pappies"); young men and women have been enrolled in the Job Corps and the Neighborhood Youth Corps; vocational education has received increased support, and large sums have been made available for the education of the disadvantaged, which, in the mountain counties, means almost everybody.

To anyone visiting Appalachia now, these programs have clearly had an effect: new roads and vocational schools are under construction or already in use; the happy pappies have planted trees on hillsides that had been covered by strip-mine spoil banks; medical facilities are more accessible; the school dropout rate has been reduced (partly because federal funds are keyed to enrollment); and there appear to be fewer obvious signs of malnutrition than there were three years ago. In some families, the money earned by adolescents in the Youth Corps has become the most important source of income. It has also become a source of pride and respect. "After those kids received their first pay check," said Don Roarke, the director of a four-county Youth Corps in eastern Kentucky, "they were dressed better, they held their heads higher. You could see the difference." At the same time, the graduates of many vocational programs are finding jobs as heavy-machine operators and mine technicians, a few of them in the mountains, others in Northern cities.

For many more, however, the existing programs serve only to hide the misery: The new highways are beginning to make it possible to cross large portions of Appalachia without seeing a tarpaper shack or a coal dump; the food stamps run out before the end of the month, and the schools, though far better than they used to be, still remain a blind alley, graduating children who are approximately two years behind the national average on standardized tests. "The bare gut essentials are now being met," said Tom Gish, the editor of the Whitesburg, Kentucky, *Mountain Eagle,* who is undoubtedly the most outspoken and dedicated journalist in the region. "By and large people are getting fed and getting coal for the winter. If you go back to the early Sixties when there was mass hunger and violence, then you can say there's been improvement. Peace has been restored."

But the peace is shaky, and the economy remains dependent on the federal government. President Johnson's recent declaration that "the dole is dead" was, to say it mildly, premature. Poverty remains endemic: Median family income in eastern Kentucky is $3,505, and Gish predicts that if poverty funds are reduced there will be more violence. In the county seats, the prosperous get roads and water lines and sewers, but only a few miles away the privies stand alongside the dirty creeks from which people draw their water, rain turns the unpaved roads into muddy ruts, and the youngsters can't go to school because they have no shoes.

The prime beneficiaries of government funds appear to be the swelling banks, which are afraid to invest their deposits in anything but government bonds; the small businesses; and the politicians. For all their ignorance and isolation, the economic and political interests of Appalachia have a highly developed knack for using outside help to perpetuate the existing structure and the conditions of dependency. In Perry County, Kentucky, a political enemy of a former county school superintendent used his influence as director of a poverty project to help elect a new school board and oust the superintendent; the new administration then rewarded him with the directorship of another federally financed program administered by the schools. In other areas, the directors of happy pappy programs discourage their charges from participating in community action groups that threaten local political machines, and in almost every community the traditions of nepotism are so powerful that many people still regard the poverty program as a source of employment rather than as a means of upgrading the skills of human beings and the social health of the community. "Jobs are coveted so much, and loyalties to kin are so strong," said a poverty worker in Kentucky, "that it's pretty hard to persuade anyone that you have to pick people on merit."

Although some training programs have brought new skills and confidence, and although many children who had once gone hungry through the school day are now receiving hot lunches (sometimes even in the most remote one-room schools), many school officials have refused to appoint outsiders, preferring to promote politically faithful employees to the uncertainties of new blood and new ideas. In one community, a group of men who were enrolled for training in construction and maintenance composed a letter to Washington:

> We were in the building and maintainence class under MDTA that took up on April 10 and ended September 29. They told us each day we would have 2 hours of electricity, pluming, carpentry and painting but for the most of it all we did was paint school buildings and repair and cover the roofs of the schools. When some of the men bucked on painting so much they was told if they didn't like it they could leave. To start we was told the government would buy around a thousand dollars of lumber a month for us to work with we unloaded plenty new lumber and racked it up on the racks. For awhile we used some then we was told we could buy it for 25 cents a foot and then they said it wasnt for sale but it still got missing. In electricity all we had were 9 days, on our certificate of training it says we got 320 hours. They just didn't care much if we learned a thing or not we was just putting in time. Now we are in worse shape than when we started and we got knocked off the food stamps for 30 days. We didn't get the training they said or the permanent jobs they promised at the start. The only jobs we have heard about are temporary and a long way off. A man with a family in school cant just leave out at the promise of a job.

Given these conditions, the most promising idea for Appalachia has been community action—training individuals to organize local groups for social improvement, community welfare, and self-help. As originally conceived, the Community Action Program (CAP) of the Office of Economic Opportunity was to include "maximum feasible participation" of the poor: Community action agencies were, if possible, to be free from domination by local politicians. In some areas of Appalachia, the program worked effectively, despite the suspicions of county officials: Community centers have been built, small marketing cooperatives (selling quilts and other local products) have been organized, and new leadership has developed.

In the eastern Kentucky counties of Leslie, Knott, Letcher, and Perry, a four-county Community Action Program (LKLP), which includes poor people as well as sympathetic county judges, has established a network of depots to inform people of their welfare rights, of new training programs, and of the availability of medical facilities. Among other things, LKLP operated a transportation system to bring the sick from the hollows to the area clinics, it is training local people in welfare work and social service, and it has prompted a number of projects to clear the region of decaying bridges and abandoned coal tipples.

Despite such successes, however—and there are others—many CAP agencies have been captured by established interests or abandoned after local battles destroyed embryonic organizations before they had a chance to function. Many of those that survive must straddle an uncertain line between ineffectiveness and the dangerous course of challenging the established order. Recent Congressional action, moreover, indicates that control for all local CAP agencies will be given to local elected officials, thus making CAP—in Appalachia, at least—the biggest potential pork barrel since the invention of rivers and harbors.

Because of the limitations of the Community Action Program, some of the most effective community work has been done by VISTA (Volunteers in Service to America—the domestic Peace Corps); by the Appalachian Committee to Save the Land and People, which has been fighting the strip mines; by the long-standing Council of the Southern Mountains; and by the Appalachian Volunteers, a private organization which originated among students at Berea College, but which is now fully autonomous. Originally, the Appalachian Volunteers (AVs) concentrated on the repair of schoolhouses, the distribution of books—more than a million were collected and placed in mountain schools—and on other community work. The AVs and VISTAs, who often work together, have moved into isolated mountain communities—places named Marrowbone and Cave Ridge, Clover Fork and Horse Creek—have come to know the inhabitants, and are helping to create new organizations and a new sense of confidence: adult education groups, nursery schools, community centers, craft shops, and, most significantly, a belief that choices are available and collective action possible. "These are the first people," said a woman in the mountains, "who promised to do something, and then did."

What they have done, among other things, is to arouse the suspicions and fears of the established interests. In the past year, the AVs have become increasingly involved in the strip-mine issue and in tax reform, helping to organize protests, transport people to meetings, and warn affected property owners when the strip-mine bulldozers were coming. In their zealousness, some have talked, none too privately, about overturning local political structures and establishing some vague new order; a few were poorly trained or offensive in dress or manners. As a consequence, they have been labeled Communists and agitators (though many are natives of the region), and they are now threatened with the suspension of all federal support.

The precipitating incident took place in the summer of 1967 when a small Pike County, Kentucky, farmer named Jink Ray, supported by his neighbors (and, later, by Appalachian Volunteers), stood in front of the bulldozers of the Puritan Coal Company, which had come to strip his land. Within a few days the matter had become a regional *cause célèbre* and threatened to develop into a mountain shoot-out. Under the new Kentucky strip-mine law, Governor Breathitt lifted the company's permit, ordering the state's Department of Natural Resources to determine whether the slopes to be mined exceed the statutory limits. Two weeks later, after several conferences among Pike County officials, the county sheriff, in a midnight raid, arrested an AV fieldworker named Joe Mulloy and two organizers for the Southern Conference Education Fund on charges of violating a Kentucky sedition law. (The man charged with the prosecution was a former president of the Independent Coal Operators Association who was then a candidate for state office.)

In indicting the three, the Pike County grand jury concluded that "a well organized and well financed effort is being made to promote and spread the communistic theory of the violent and forceful overthrow of the government of Pike County" and that "the employees of the Appalachian Volunteers and other federally financed antipoverty programs have collaborated and cooperated with known communist organizers to help them organize and promote the violent overthrow of the constitutional government of Pike County." The grand jury, said Harry M. Caudill, the Whitesburg attorney who is probably the most eloquent spokesman for the mountains, "was certain that the revolution was about to begin in Pike County, and that the neighboring counties, in domino fashion, would then fall to the enemy."

Although the sedition law was quickly declared unconstitutional by a federal court, the Pike County affair reinforced suspicions not only about the Appalachian Volunteers, but about everything that smacked of community action.

In many eastern Kentucky counties VISTA workers are no longer welcome. In West Virginia, Governor Hulett Smith, while praising the VISTA program in mental health, charged the AVs with "misconduct" and demanded an OEO investigation. In Kentucky, Governor Breathitt (who could not succeed himself as governor but was nonetheless involved in the political campaign) demanded and received assurances from OEO Director Sargent Shriver that some current OEO grants to the Appalachian Volunteers would not be renewed, and that the cancellation of other federal support for AV activities would receive "most serious consideration." In Hazard, Kentucky, a few months later, an exasperated staff member of the Community Action agency declared that "we're still trying to beat this Red rap. People in the Work Experience and Training Program have been told that if they had anything to do with us they'd be off the rolls."

What is most in jeopardy now is not merely the budget of the Appalachian Volunteers (who are trying to find private funds to replace their uncertain federal support), but the principle of independent community action itself. The efforts of the past three years have (in some areas at least) generated a degree of independence that will be difficult to arrest: Even before the poverty program began, the Appalachian Group to Save the Land and People, composed entirely of mountaineers, had begun to campaign for stricter strip-mine laws and for the imposition of a severance tax on the minerals that now flow untaxed from the region. In the creeks and hollows, residents have stopped bulldozers, sometimes with their bodies, sometimes with shotguns and dynamite. When Youth Corps funds ran out during the 1967 Congressional debate on the poverty program, the staff members in many Appalachian communities came to work anyway, and when Shriver announced the curtailment of AV support, the residents of a number of mountain communities signed letters and telegrams of protest. This fall, for the first time in history, teachers in an eastern Kentucky county went on strike for higher pay. Nevertheless, if prime responsibility for the Appalachian portion of the war on poverty is delegated to the established regimes, the basic political arrangements will remain unchanged: Every dollar in federal funds will make the politicians that much stronger.

And yet, even if Appalachia's poor achieve greater political power and independence, the problems will persist. "You can't have real community action," said a Kentucky CAP director, "until you have economic choice." To date, regional development has meant a few highways and hospitals, not jobs. The area's topography and its unskilled population make it unattractive to industry, leading to the desperate suggestion that the best program is training people so they can move away. "They want to regard these towns as breeding grounds," said Robert Cornett, who was Breathitt's director of area development. "I'm losing faith in the planners. They're always looking for big solutions. You have to do it slowly with roads and health and small businesses, woodworking industries, or maybe poultry."

People like Cornett hope to encourage the construction of new housing (which is desperately needed) through the pooling of public and private resources, and to foster greater local concern for development. "You have to use what's here, to improve the power structure, not tear it down." So far, the results have been meager. In some of the county seats, even the most proper people are still unpersuaded that poverty really exists, or that it would persist if the unemployed just had enough character to work. "I grew up here in Hazard," said a staff member of the local CAP, "but I never noticed the poverty until I went outside. I never saw it."

Perhaps the chief consequence of the recent programs in Appalachia is the realization that poverty and exploitation, isolation and ignorance, are not susceptible to left-handed solutions, that they are linked to the general affluence, and that they raise moral questions which strike at the very heart of America's willingness to bring a decent life to all its citizens. What do the Combs and Caudills, the Napiers and Brashears of eastern Kentucky think, after the food stamps run out in the third week of the month, when they hear the President declare that the "dole is dead"? What kind of judgment does one make about a nation that can spend close to $500,000 to kill a Vietcong but less than $150 a month to support the family of an unemployed miner who lives in a place called Stinking Creek? How great is a society that permits the systematic, mechanized defacing of its hillsides while it encourages the natives of these same hills to move into the slums of Detroit? "People expected this thing to be solved in six months," said Perley F. Ayer, the chairman of the Council of the Southern Mountains. "But in education alone we're 5,000,000 years behind."

It is difficult to cheer the results of Appalachian development or the war on poverty: The harmonious interplay of poverty, politics, and the welfare mind combine to frustrate even the most valiant effort. But it is even more difficult to criticize the intent of these programs or the officials who are charged with running them. They have been forced to live with a limited and reluctant mandate that prohibits them from anything more than making poverty bearable and, if possible, invisible. The vested Appalachian interests in the status quo—coal companies, railroads, banks, local bar associations, insurance agencies, politicians—are so vast that they represent a fair cross section of American society itself. Their stockholders and beneficiaries live all over the nation; they help sustain our affluence. If Appalachia hasn't changed, it may be in part because too many are dependent on it as it now is. "The reason little has happened," said Ayer, "is that America doesn't have its heart in it."

Can the Southern Negro Exodus Be Stemmed?

Paul Clancy

KINGSTREE, SOUTH CAROLINA

The South is experiencing the most explosive economic growth of any area in the nation. South Carolina alone took in more than a billion dollars in new and expanded industry during the past two years. But, according to a report called "The Advancing South: Manpower Prospects and Problems" which has just been released by the Twentieth Century Fund, the Southern Negro has little chance of sharing in the prosperity as long as he remains poorly educated, lacking in industrial experience, and the victim of discrimination. By 1975, Negro unemployment may still be more than double that of Southern whites.

During the last decade, more than a million Negroes in the South abandoned their homes and migrated by car, bus, and train to what they thought was a promised land: the cities of the North and West. Many of them were illiterate, and most of them were unskilled and unprepared for the violence and loneliness of life in the city. South Carolina contributed its share. More than twenty per cent of its Negro population took a chance on getting a better break, even in the city slums.

THE HUMAN APPROACH

Williamsburg County, the poorest in South Carolina and one of the poorest in the nation, lost 14,636 Negroes between 1950 and 1960, more than half its Negro population. They left for Baltimore, Philadelphia, New

York, Rochester, and a dozen other cities with the hope of finding work or at least better conditions for their children. They left a rural setting where the average Negro family earned $916 a year, where 90.9 per cent had family incomes of less than $3,000, where the average dependent child received $21.43 a month for his welfare. The majority were share-croppers, forced off the land by machines that can do the job faster and more cheaply and by acreage controls that benefited the farmowner but not the sharecropper.

Williamsburg, once a land of sprawling wealthy cotton plantations, lies neglected in the center of South Carolina's wide coastal plain, some seventy miles southeast of Columbia, the state capital. Its chief product is tobacco, a tightly controlled crop that brings good profits for the big land-owner who happens to have a large allotment. Its leaders believe that the Negro is lazy, and they feel little responsibility for his decision to leave. The county achieved brief national attention earlier this year when those same leaders refused to put up the administrative costs of the Federal food-stamp program and the poor raised the money among themselves. It made the news again in September, when Governor George Romney of Michigan came to investigate what causes Negroes to migrate to the slums of the North. Local politicians bristled at the implication that they were indirectly responsible for Northern urban uprisings. "We treat our niggers as human beings, not machines," State Senator LaNue Floyd said. "Rom-ney'd better straighten out his troubles in Detroit before coming down here and telling us what to do."

Floyd was elected in 1966 after defeating a Negro funeral-home director, Virgil Dimery, in the Democratic primary. (No Negro has been elected to the General Assembly since Reconstruction.) As might be expected, there was a total polarization of votes, with whites, even though they make up only a third of the population, still able to outvote the Negroes. But it was the first serious challenge. Four years ago there were a mere 250 Negroes registered in the county; today there are about six thousand.

Although whites did not plan it that way, the Negro migration gives them a political advantage because the vast majority of those who leave are just approaching voting age. Dimery, who is registration chairman of the Williamsburg County Voters' League, estimates that only ten thousand of the 27,000 Negroes left in the county are old enough to vote. He believes that more than ninety per cent of the Negro high-school graduates leave the county for good.

The family of Leroy Davis offers a good example. Davis owns a grocery-filling station in Hemingway, on the northeast edge of the county. He raised seven children and was able to send each one at least part of the way through college. But when the time came for them to find jobs, there were none. One by one, Davis's four sons and three daughters packed up and left for New York. "I would rather for them to have stayed, but there wasn't anything I could do for them here," he told me.

At the other edge of the county, in Greeleyville, Jeanette Henryhand, a young girl who finished fourth in her high-school class, is still looking for a job. She spent a summer working in a garment factory in New York City, where her older brother and sister live. But "Things are better here.

If I find something to do, I prefer staying." She applied for a job at a small garment factory near Kingstree, the county seat, but so far has had no success. Most of her friends are gone. Out of a graduating class of fifty-two, she said, only four have stayed. All four have been unable to find steady jobs.

There are few alternatives to flight from the blighted areas of the South. "Toughing it out," as one Negro farmer put it, "requires a lot of land and not many mouths to feed." Learning a trade or getting a college education doesn't help much here because there simply aren't enough jobs.

A group of young Negroes can be found most days of the week lolling about in front of the county courthouse in Kingstree. One youth, a graduate of all-Negro Tomlinson High last June, had been able to find work picking tobacco, "a real drag," at a dollar an hour. Now the leaf season is over and there is no more work for him. He wants to attend college next year but would need nearly $1,000—more than he could save in many years. Negro leaders claim that local banks are reluctant to provide Federally guaranteed loans for Negroes to attend college. He has been able to save only $30, about enough for a one-way bus ticket to Rochester. He is going.

GREENER PASTURES

There are many state policies in the South that tend to drive Negroes away in large numbers. Williamsburg's unwillingness to take part in the food-stamp program is indicative of an attitude toward "handout" programs that is region-wide. Local leaders want to drop the program because, they feel, it removes the incentive to work. They blame the stamp program for the inability of the farmer to get in his tobacco and of the white family to obtain $3-a-day domestic help. South Carolina is the only state in the Southeast with no commodity-distribution program, and food stamps are used in only thirteen of forty-six counties. However, Governor Robert E. McNair announced in mid-October that a state-wide food-stamp program is being considered.

Most states in the region regularly forgo millions of Federal welfare dollars for Aid to Dependent Children by refusing to put up sufficient state funds. South Carolina pays in the neighborhood of $20 a month for each dependent child, up to a maximum of $99 for a family. Mississippi pays under $10 a month for each child. It is no wonder that New York's over $50 per child acts like a magnet for the desperate rural mother with several children to care for.

Most white leaders say that Williamsburg County has "excellent race relations," although the two races have rarely sat down and talked out their problems. Negroes complain that they are still victims of a dual standard of justice. But if relations are better, said E. I. Lawrence, a farmer, it is because the Negroes have begun asserting themselves.

Lawrence, fifty-six, said he taught school for twenty years but, because he was outspoken and a member of the NAACP, he was blackballed by the county board of education. He went back to farming with his father and became president of the Voters' League. His father, E. W. Lawrence, is about eighty years old, the son of a slave; he has been able to hold onto 415 acres of land, the largest Negro landholding in the county.

"You can sum it up," the son told me, "by saying there's not enough net income on the farm to maintain a sizable family. So when a man reaches adult age, he usually tries to find greener pastures. I was an only son and I was able to stick it out. But because I stayed and realized we were not getting our share of the better jobs, I started fighting. Everywhere where we were receiving injustice, especially since Kennedy and Johnson had given us something to fight with, we started pushing and pulling. Everything we got we had to fight for. When we first started to register, we were not even able to go in the courthouse. They just didn't think Negroes had the right to be in there."

The father told me: "The sharecropper today is always in debt. He is just existing. I get to thinking that in my way back yonder we made a better living of it. You can't live like we used to, on twelve or fifteen cents a day. Our standard of living was not so high. Back then a man starved but he lived. Now his mind is not set on perishing. His mind is up and he's down, trying to stay up with the rest of the world."

"What are our needs?" the son asked. "Jobs and better schools. If we have those, I think we will make it."

In 1954, the year the Supreme Court ruled that separate-but-equal schools were unconstitutional, 1,959 Negro children entered the first grade in the segregated schools in Williamsburg County; twelve years later, only 485 of them finished high school (twenty-five per cent, compared with sixty-one per cent for their white counterparts). Many of them never got past the fifth grade. It has been estimated that about sixty-six per cent of the adult Negro population in the county are functional illiterates (those with five years of school or less).

Many Negro children in Williamsburg never go to school at all since they are not forced to by law. (A bill passed by the 1967 General Assembly will require school attendance by 1974.) Hundreds of them stay home to take care of their younger brothers and sisters so their mothers can work. By the age of ten or twelve, the children begin working on the farm.

Williamsburg County, like most Southern school districts where Negroes constitute a majority of the student enrollment, has experienced a minimum of desegregation and a minimum of pressure from Washington. While seventy-one per cent of the enrollment is Negro, only three per cent are attending desegregated schools. There is not a single Negro on the county board of education or any of the six area trustee boards, so the majority racial group in the county has virtually no voice in determining the educational policies that affect its children.

Like most of the rural areas of the state, Williamsburg is caught in the transition between an agricultural and an industrial age. But the departure of one does not guarantee the arrival of the other. Although South Carolina shares the South's economic boom, industry has been slow to reach rural counties despite the availability of cheap labor, the right-to-work law, and tempting tax advantages. "The most important job," state technical education director Wade Martin said at recent budget hearings, "is to convince industry of the advantages of rural work attitudes, rather than low wages."

Once trained, rural workers in the South have been shown to "outperform" workers in other parts of the country by as much as thirty-five per cent, Martin said.

WHAT'S BEING DONE?

There are hundreds of Federal programs aimed at rural development, many designed to keep people on the farms long enough for industrial development to bring job opportunities. The Farmers Home Administration loaned almost a million dollars to Williamsburg farmers last year and provided homebuilders' loans to 475 families at low interest rates. The Economic Development Administration tries to gear its programs toward industrial development in areas of unemployment and high migration rates. The Small Business Administration sank $14 million into small towns in the state last year for the development of job-producing industries. A notable example, highly praised by Secretary of Agriculture Orville Freeman on a recent trip to Columbia, is the Congaree Iron and Steel Company. Founded nine years ago with SBA loans, the firm employs four hundred persons, eighty per cent of them Negro.

Project T-Square (Training for Tomorrow) is an experimental South Carolina program sponsored by OEW, HEW, and the Department of Labor that actually goes out and recruits the hard-core unemployed, provides them with up to an eighth-grade education, and equips them with a trade. The job skills are based on the greatest needs of the community and the communities chosen are the poorest in each area. The related labor Mobility Demonstration Project, under the Manpower Development and Training Act, moves rural families to industrial growth centers. The T-Square program represents an effort at co-ordination between state agencies: employment security, education, health, anti-poverty, welfare, vocational rehabilitation; all are combining to put the jobless back on their feet. Begun in May, the program is expected to reach 22,500 persons by the end of its second year. Of three centers opened so far, the nearest to Williamsburg is forty miles away and will take only thirty-three students this year.

A group of Williamsburg Negro farmers has banded together with farmers in two other counties to form a vegetable-marketing co-operative that will handle the produce of at least five hundred low-income farmers. They are working closely with the State Development Board to attract a vegetable-processing plant. If things go their way, it will mean an economic breakthrough for the Negro farmer who now subsists on less than $100 a month.

The most important long-range planning will perhaps come out of the new Coastal Plains Regional Commission, which will concentrate on the economic uplift of 156 counties in North Carolina, South Carolina, and Georgia. This Appalachia-type project, funded by the Department of Commerce, will direct Federal dollars at the development of local potential, but it is still in the planning stage.

How much these programs can do to counteract the great surge of rural families to the cities remains to be seen. Meanwhile, generations of Negroes have torn up their roots from the Southern soil and gone to the crowded and cold urban centers. Some who have the qualifications and the right contacts can find a new life in the city, but others find only frustration in their inability to break employment barriers and rigid housing patterns. According to a report released in June by the Brandeis University Center for the Study of Violence, "A high proportion of Southern Negroes living in the ghetto increases the possibility that a city will have a riot," especially where the Negro has been rejected and broken by the city.

The Negro in the South has endured unbelievable hardship, much of it a reflection of the general poverty of the region. But prosperity has begun arriving and, with it, a wealth of new attitudes and ideas such as "creative federalism" and special attention to Negro colleges. These attitudes may be slow in filtering down to the rural Negro family, but there is every indication that they will. Although the exodus continues at a rapid rate, there are signs that it is beginning to level off. Stopping it will take a major effort by the South and by the Federal government to provide jobs, education, and decent homes for the rural Negro.

Chapter Twelve

SUGGESTED QUESTIONS FOR CLASS DISCUSSION.

1. How effective can the old-time virtues of self-reliance, ambition, hard work, and thrift be in helping solve the problems of poverty in today's society?
2. How efficient can an antipoverty program be if authority and funds are channeled through existing local governmental offices and agencies?
3. What kinds of programs might be effective in restoring the illiterate and unskilled to the labor markets? Where might objections to such programs come from?
4. Has the welfare program become a way of life preferred by those who depend upon it for subsistence? Is it conceivable that there may be reasons for insuring that these people stay on relief?
5. Is there any reason to think that there are racial overtones in the reluctance of both Congress and the states in refusing to come to grips with the problems of poverty?

Chapter Thirteen

THE POLITICS OF
VIOLENCE

A major strand woven into the American political tradition involves respect for law and order and a belief that individuals and groups should operate within the legal framework in the pursuit of their objectives. Underlying this conviction is the assumption that the political system is responsive to felt needs and that it adjusts fairly readily when pressing needs are expressed through normal political channels.

There is an area of American life in which the political system, for various reasons, has been insufficiently responsive—that having to do with the way in which blacks and whites are to live together in the United States. Over a long period of time, the system has been unresponsive to the legitimate demands and needs of a significant proportion of the American population.

In such circumstances, what course of action is open to the perpetually disadvantaged? Patience and legal recourse? They feel that course has been tried and has been found wanting. Civil Disobedience? There is a minor strand in the American political tradition that justifies civil disobedience. (A selection from Thoreau's "Essay on Civil Disobedience" is included in the chapter.) Civil disobedience has certain advantages, but it has limitations as well. A serious shortcoming is that it is not psychologically satisfying to the disadvantaged. It is natural for those who feel abused and wronged to want to strike back not bow to the unilateral use of force.

If respect for law and order is a major strand in the American political tradition there is a second strand that is scarcely less prominent; the resort

411

to violence as a response to felt injustice. If one may paraphrase the German military strategist Clausewitz, the resort to violence is a continuation of politics by other means. When groups of Americans have felt that the system was rigged against them, they have not been slow to take matters into their own hands from the time of the Boston Tea Party and Shay's Rebellion to the present. Many forms of popular culture continue to celebrate an era in the West when violence was an accepted means of settling public and private disputes.

However much one may deplore the eruption of violence into politics, it is not convincing to argue that resort to violence has invariably been counterproductive for those resorting to it. The riots during the long hot summers of 1966 and 1967, for example, did a great deal to focus the attention of the American electorate on the problems of race and the ghetto. What is clear, is that violence has a way of begetting violence. The white violence of the Klan, the vigilantes, and sometimes the police, helped to spawn the black violence of the riots. The riots, in turn, induced fear and further violence, such as the murder of a great American, Dr. Martin Luther King.

The cases in this chapter deal with the problems of race and violence, and they discuss some of the ways in which these problems might be tackled.

From Civil Disobedience (1849)

Henry David Thoreau

THE INDIVIDUAL CONSCIENCE, THE STATE, AND SLAVERY

I heartily accept the motto,—"That government is best which governs least;" and I should like to see it acted up to more rapidly and systematically. Carried out, it finally amounts to this, which I also believe,—"That government is best which governs not at all;" and when men are prepared for it, that will be the kind of government which they will have. Government is at best but an expedient; but most governments are usually, and all governments are sometimes, inexpedient. The objections which have been brought against a standing army, and they are many and weighty, and deserve to prevail, may also at last be brought against a standing government. The standing army is only an arm of the standing government. The government itself, which is only the mode which the people have chosen to execute their will, is equally liable to be abused and perverted before the people can act through it. Witness the present Mexican war, the work of comparatively a few individuals using the standing government as their tool; for, in the outset, the people would not have consented to this measure.

This American government,—what is it but a tradition, though a recent one, endeavoring to transmit itself unimpaired to posterity, but each instant losing some of its integrity? It has not the vitality and force of a single living man; for a single man can bend it to his will. It is a sort of wooden gun to the people themselves. But it is not the less necessary for this; for the people must have some complicated machinery or other, and hear its din, to satisfy that idea of government which they have. Governments show thus how successfully men can be imposed on, even impose on themselves, for their own advantage. It is excellent, we must all allow. Yet this government never of itself furthered any enterprise, but by the alacrity with which it got out of its way. *It* does not keep the country free. *It* does not settle the West. *It* does not educate. The character inherent in the American people has done all that has been accomplished; and it would have done somewhat more, if the government had not sometimes got in its way. For government is an expedient by which men would fain succeed in letting one another alone; and, as has been said, when it is most expedient, the governed are most let alone by it. Trade and commerce, if they were not made of India-rubber, would never manage to bounce over the obstacles which legislators are continually putting in their way; and, if one were to judge these men wholly by the effects of their actions and not partly by their intentions, they would deserve to be classed and punished with those mischievous persons who put obstructions on the railroads.

But, to speak practically and as a citizen, unlike those who call them-

Norman Holmes Pearson, ed. *Walden and Civil Disobedience* (New York: Rinehart Editions, 1948).

selves no-government men, I ask for, not at once no government, but *at once* a better government. Let every man make known what kind of government would command his respect, and that will be one step toward obtaining it.

After all, the practical reason why, when the power is once in the hands of the people, a majority are permitted, and for a long period continue, to rule is not because they are most likely to be in the right, nor because this seems fairest to the minority, but because they are physically the strongest. But a government in which the majority rule in all cases cannot be based on justice, even as far as men understand it. Can there not be a government in which majorities do not virtually decide right and wrong, but conscience?—in which majorities decide only those questions to which the rule of expediency is applicable? Must the citizen ever for a moment, or in the least degree, resign his conscience to the legislator? Why has every man a conscience, then? I think that we should be men first, and subjects afterward. It is not desirable to cultivate a respect for the law, so much as for the right. The only obligation which I have a right to assume is to do at any time what I think right. It is truly enough said, that a corporation has no conscience; but a corporation of conscientious men is a corporation *with* a conscience. Law never made men a whit more just; and, by means of their respect for it, even the well-disposed are daily made the agents of injustice.

.   .   .

How does it become a man to behave toward this American government to-day? I answer, that he cannot without disgrace be associated with it. I cannot for an instant recognize that political organization as *my* government which is the *slave's* government also.

All men recognize the right of revolution; that is, the right to refuse allegiance to, and to resist, the government, when its tyranny or its inefficiency are great and unendurable. But almost all say that such is not the case now. But such was the case, they think, in the Revolution of '75. If one were to tell me that this was a bad government because it taxed certain foreign commodities brought to its ports, it is most probable that I should not make an ado about it, for I can do without them. All machines have their friction; and possibly this does enough good to counterbalance the evil. At any rate, it is a great evil to make a stir about it. But when the friction comes to have its machine, and oppression and robbery are organized, I say, let us not have such a machine any longer. In other words, when a sixth of the population of a nation which has undertaken to be the refuge of liberty are slaves, and a whole country is unjustly overrun and conquered by a foreign army, and subjected to military law, I think that it is not too soon for honest men to rebel and revolutionize. What makes this duty the more urgent is the fact that the country so overrun is not our own, but ours is the invading army.

.   .   .

. . . Practically speaking, the opponents to a reform in Massachusetts are not a hundred thousand politicians at the South, but a hundred thousand merchants and farmers here, who are more interested in commerce and agriculture than they are in humanity, and are not prepared to do justice to the slave and to Mexico, *cost what it may*. I quarrel not with far-off foes, but with those who, near at home, coöperate with, and do the bidding of, those far away, and without whom the latter would be harmless. We are accustomed to say, that the mass of men are unprepared; but improvement is slow, because the few are not materially wiser or better than the many. It is not so important that many should be as good as you, as that there be some absolute goodness somewhere; for that will leaven the whole lump. There are thousands who are *in opinion* opposed to slavery and to the war, who yet in effect do nothing to put an end to them; who, esteeming themselves children of Washington and Franklin, sit down with their hands in their pockets, and say that they know not what to do, and do nothing; who even postpone the question of freedom to the question of free-trade, and quietly read the prices-current along with the latest advices from Mexico, after dinner, and, it may be, fall asleep over them both. What is the price-current of an honest man and patriot to-day? They hesitate, and they regret, and sometimes they petition; but they do nothing in earnest and with effect. They will wait, well disposed, for others to remedy the evil, that they may no longer have it to regret. At most, they give only a cheap vote, and a feeble countenance and God-speed, to the right, as it goes by them. There are nine hundred and ninety-nine patrons of virtue to one virtuous man. But it is easier to deal with the real possessor of a thing than with the temporary guardian of it.

All voting is a sort of gaming, like checkers or backgammon, with a slight moral tinge to it, a playing with right and wrong, with moral questions; and betting naturally accompanies it. The character of the voters is not staked. I cast my vote, perchance, as I think right; but I am not vitally concerned that that right should prevail. I am willing to leave it to the majority. Its obligation, therefore, never exceeds that of expediency. Even voting *for the right* is *doing* nothing for it. It is only expressing to men feebly your desire that it should prevail. A wise man will not leave the right to the mercy of chance, nor wish it to prevail through the power of the majority. There is but little virtue in the action of masses of men. When the majority shall at length vote for the abolition of slavery, it will be because they are indifferent to slavery, or because there is but little slavery left to be abolished by their vote. *They* will then be the only slaves. Only *his* vote can hasten the abolition of slavery who asserts his own freedom by his vote.

· · ·

The broadest and most prevalent error requires the most disinterested virtue to sustain it. The slight reproach to which the virtue of patriotism is commonly liable, the noble are most likely to incur. Those who, while they disapprove of the character and measures of a government, yield to it their allegiance and support are undoubtedly its most conscientious supporters, and so frequently the most serious obstacles to reform. Some are petitioning the state to dissolve the Union, to disregard the requisitions of the President. Why do they not dissolve it themselves,—the union between themselves and the state,—and refuse to pay their quota into its treasury? Do not they stand in the same relation to the state that the state does to the Union? And have not the same reasons prevented the state from resisting the Union which have prevented them from resisting the state?

How can a man be satisfied to entertain an opinion merely, and enjoy *it*? Is there any enjoyment in it, if his opinion is that he is aggrieved? If you are cheated out of a single dollar by your neighbor, you do not rest satisfied with knowing that you are cheated, or with saying that you are cheated, or even with petitioning him to pay you your due; but you take effectual steps at once to obtain the full amount, and see that you are never cheated again. Action from principle, the perception and the performance of right, changes things and relations; it is essentially revolutionary, and does not consist wholly with anything which was. It not only divides states and churches, it divides families; ay, it divides the *individual*, separating the diabolical in him from the divine.

Unjust laws exist: shall we be content to obey them, or shall we endeavor to amend them, and obey them until we have succeeded, or shall we transgress them at once? Men generally, under such a government as this, think that they ought to wait until they have persuaded the majority to alter them. They think that, if they should resist, the remedy would be worse than the evil. But it is the fault of the government itself that the remedy *is* worse than the evil. *It* makes it worse. Why is it not more apt to anticipate and provide for reform? Why does it not cherish its wise minority? Why does it cry and resist before it is hurt? Why does it not encourage its citizens to be on the alert to point out its faults, and *do* better than it would have them? Why does it always crucify Christ, and excommunicate Copernicus and Luther, and pronounce Washington and Franklin rebels?

One would think, that a deliberate and practical denial of its authority was the only offense never contemplated by government; else, why has it not assigned its definite, its suitable and proportionate penalty? If a man who has no property refuses but once to earn nine shillings for the state, he is put in prison for a period unlimited by any law that I know, and determined only by the discretion of those who placed him there; but if he should steal ninety times nine shillings from the state, he is soon permitted to go at large again.

If the injustice is part of the necessary friction of the machine of government, let it go, let it go: perchance it will wear smooth,—certainly the machine will wear out. If the injustice has a spring, or a pulley, or a rope, or a crank, exclusively for itself, then perhaps you may consider whether the remedy will not be worse than the evil; but if it is of such a nature that it requires you to be the agent of injustice to another, then, I say, break the law. Let your life be a counter friction to stop the machine. What I have to do is to see, at any rate, that I do not lend myself to the wrong which I condemn.

As for adopting the ways which the state has provided for remedying the evil, I know not of such ways. They take too much time, and a man's life will be gone. I have other affairs to attend to. I came into this world, not chiefly to make this a good place to live in, but to live in it, be it good or bad. A man has not everything to do, but something; and because he cannot do *everything*, it is not necessary that he should do *something* wrong. It is not my business to be petitioning the Governor or the Legislature any more than it is theirs to petition me; and if they should not hear my petition, what should I do then? But in this case the state has provided no way: its very Constitution is the evil. This may seem to be harsh and stubborn and unconciliatory; but it is to treat with the utmost kindness and consideration the only spirit that can appreciate or deserves it. So is all change for the better, like birth and death, which convulse the body.

·   ·   ·

. . . I know this well, that if one thousand, if one hundred, if ten men whom I could name,—if ten *honest* men only,—ay, if *one* HONEST man, in this State of Massachusetts, *ceasing to hold slaves*, were actually to withdraw from this copartnership, and be locked up in the county jail therefor, it would be the abolition of slavery in America. For it matters not how small the beginning may seem to be: what is once well done is done forever. But we love better to talk about it: that we say is our mission. . . .

Under a government which imprisons any unjustly, the true place for a just man is also a prison. The proper place to-day, the only place which Massachusetts has provided for her freer and less desponding spirits, is in her prisons, to be put out and locked out of the State by her own act, as they have already put themselves out by their principles. It is there that the fugitive slave, and the Mexican prisoner on parole, and the Indian come to plead the wrongs of his race should find them; on that separate, but more free and honorable ground, where the State places those who are not *with* her, but *against* her,—the only house in a slave State in which a free man can abide with honor. If any think that their influence would be lost there, and their voices no longer afflict the ear of the State, that they would not be as an enemy within its walls, they do not know by how much truth is stronger than error, nor how much more eloquently and effectively he can combat injustice who has experienced a little in his own person. Cast your whole vote, not a strip of paper merely, but your whole influence. A minority is powerless while it conforms to the majority; it is not even a minority then; but it is irresistible when it clogs by its whole weight. If the alternative is to keep all just men in prison, or give up war and slavery, the State will not hesitate which to choose. If a thousand men were not to pay their tax-bills this year, that would not be a violent and bloody measure, as it would be to pay them, and enable the State to commit violence and shed innocent blood. This is, in fact, the definition of a peaceable revolution, if any such is possible. . . .

·   ·   ·

When I converse with the freest of my neighbors, I perceive that, whatever they may say about the magnitude and seriousness of the question, and their regard for the public tranquillity, the long and the short of the matter is, that they cannot spare the protection of the existing government, and they dread the consequences to their property and families of disobedience to it. For my own part, I should not like to think that I even rely on the protection of the State. But, if I deny the authority of the State when it presents its tax-bill, it will soon take and waste all my property, and so harass me and my children without end. This is hard. This makes it impossible for a man to live honestly, and at the same time comfortably, in outward respects. It will not be worth the while to accumulate property; that would be sure to go again. You must hire or squat somewhere, and raise but a small crop, and eat that soon. You must live within yourself, and depend upon yourself always tucked up and ready for a start, and not have many affairs. A man may grow rich in Turkey even, if he will be in all respects a good subject of the Turkish government. Confucius said: "If a state is governed by the principles of reason, poverty and misery are subjects of shame; if a state is not governed by the principles of reason, riches and honors are the subjects of shame." No: until I want the protection of Massachusetts to be extended to me in some distant Southern port, where my liberty is endangered, or until I am bent solely on building up an estate at home by peaceful enterprise. I can afford to refuse allegiance to Massachusetts, and her right to my property and life. It costs me less in every sense to incur the penalty of disobedience to the State than it would to obey. I should feel as if I were worth less in that case.

Thus the State never intentionally confronts a man's sense, intellectual or moral, but only his body, his senses. It is not armed with superior wit or honesty, but with superior physical strength. I was not born to be forced. I will breathe after my own fashion. Let us see who is the strongest. What force has a multitude? They only can force me who obey a higher law than I. They force me to become like themselves. I do not hear of *men* being *forced* to live this way or that by masses of men. What sort of life were that to live? When I meet a government which says to me, "Your money or your life," why should I be in haste to give it my money? It may be in a great strait, and not know what to do: I cannot help that. It must help itself; do as I do. It is not worth the while to snivel about it. I am not responsible for the successful working of the machinery of society.

The authority of government, even such as I am willing to submit to,— for I will cheerfully obey those who know and can do better than I, and in many things even those who neither know nor can do so well,—is still an impure one: to be strictly just, it must have the sanction and consent of the governed. It can have no pure right over my person and property but what I concede to it. The progress from an absolute to a limited monarchy, from a limited monarchy to a democracy, is a progress toward a true respect for the individual. Even the Chinese philosopher was wise enough to regard the individual as the basis of the empire. Is a democracy, such as we know it, the last improvement possible in government? Is it not possible to take a step further towards recognizing and organizing the rights of man? There will never be a really free and enlightened State until the State comes to recognize the individual as a higher and independent power, from which all its own power and authority are derived, and treats him accordingly. I please myself with imagining a State at last which can afford to be just to all men, and to treat the individual with respect as a neighbor; which even would not think it inconsistent with its own repose if a few were to live aloof from it, not meddling with it, nor embraced by it, who fulfilled all the duties of neighbors and fellow-men. A State which bore this kind of fruit, and suffered it to drop off as fast as it ripened, would prepare the way for a still more perfect and glorious State, which also I have imagined, but not yet anywhere seen.

Civil Disorders

INTRODUCTION

The summer of 1967 again brought racial disorders to American cities, and with them shock, fear and bewilderment to the nation.

The worst came during a two-week period in July, first in Newark and then in Detroit. Each set off a chain reaction in neighboring communities.

On July 28, 1967, the President of the United States established this Commission and directed us to answer three basic questions:

What happened?

Why did it happen?

What can be done to prevent it from happening again?

To respond to these questions, we have undertaken a broad range of studies and investigations. We have visited the riot cities; we have heard many witnesses; we have sought the counsel of experts across the country.

This is our basic conclusion: Our nation is moving toward two societies, one black, one white—separate and unequal.

Reaction to last summer's disorders has quickened the movement and deepened the division. Discrimination and segregation have long permeated much of American life; they now threaten the future of every American.

This deepening racial division is not inevitable. The movement apart can be reversed. Choice is still possible. Our principal task is to define that choice and to press for a national resolution.

To pursue our present course will involve the continuing polarization of the American community and, ultimately, the destruction of basic democratic values.

The alternative is not blind repression or capitulation to lawlessness. It is the realization of common opportunities for all within a single society.

This alternative will require a commitment to national action—compassionate, massive and sustained, backed by the resources of the most powerful and the richest nation on this earth. From every American it will require new attitudes, new understanding, and, above all, new will.

The vital needs of the nation must be met; hard choices must be made, and, if necessary, new taxes enacted.

Violence cannot build a better society. Disruption and disorder nourish repression, not justice. They strike at the freedom of every citizen. The community cannot—it will not—tolerate coercion and mob rule.

Violence and destruction must be ended—in the streets of the ghetto and in the lives of people.

Segregation and poverty have created in the racial ghetto a destructive environment totally unknown to most white Americans.

What white Americans have never fully understood—but what the Negro can never forget—is that white society is deeply implicated in the ghetto. White institutions created it, white institutions maintain it, and white society condones it.

Summary of Report of The National Advisory Commission on Civil Disorders. U.S. Government Printing Office. March 3, 1968.

Our recommendations embrace three basic principles:

- *To mount programs on a scale equal to the dimension of the problems;*
- *To aim these programs for high impact in the immediate future in order to close the gap between promise and performance;*
- *To undertake new initiatives and experiments that can change the system of failure and frustration that now dominates the ghetto and weakens our society.*

These programs will require unprecedented levels of funding and performance, but they neither probe deeper nor demand more than the problems which called them forth. There can be no higher priority for national action and no higher claim on the nation's conscience.

We issue this Report now, four months before the date called for by the President. Much remains that can be learned. Continued study is essential.

It is time now to turn with all the purpose at our command to the major unfinished business of this nation. It is time to adopt strategies for action that will produce quick and visible progress. It is time to make good the promises of American democracy to all citizens—urban and rural, white and black, Spanish-surname, American Indian, and every minority group.

As Commissioners we have worked together with a sense of the greatest urgency and have sought to compose whatever differences exist among us. Some differences remain. But the gravity of the problem and the pressing need for action are too clear to allow further delay in the issuance of this Report.

WHAT HAPPENED?
Profiles of Disorder

The report contains profiles of a selection of the disorders that took place during the summer of 1967. These profiles are designed to indicate how the disorders happened, who participated in them, and how local officials, police forces, and the National Guard responded. Illustrative excerpts follow:

Newark

. . . It was decided to attempt to channel the energies of the people into a nonviolent protest. While Lofton promised the crowd that a full investigation would be made of the Smith incident, the other Negro leaders began urging those on the scene to form a line of march toward the city hall.

Some persons joined the line of march. Others milled about in the narrow street. From the dark grounds of the housing project came a barrage of rocks. Some of them fell among the crowd. Others hit persons in the line of march. Many smashed the windows of the police station. The rock throwing, it was believed, was the work of youngsters; approximately 2,500 children lived in the housing project.

Almost at the same time, an old car was set afire in a parking lot. The line of march began to disintegrate. The police, their heads protected by World War I-type helmets, sallied forth to disperse the crowd. A fire engine, arriving on the scene, was pelted with rocks. As police drove people away from the station, they scattered in all directions.

A few minutes later a nearby liquor store was broken into. Some persons, seeing a caravan of cabs appear at city hall to protest Smith's arrest, interpreted this as evidence that the disturbance had been organized, and generated rumors to that effect.

However, only a few stores were looted. Within a short period of time, the disorder appeared to have run its course.

. . .

. . . On Saturday, July 15, [Director of Police Dominick] Spina received a report of snipers in a housing project. When he arrived he saw approximately 100 National Guardsmen and police officers crouching behind vehicles, hiding in corners and lying on the ground around the edge of the courtyard.

Since everything appeared quiet and it was broad daylight, Spina walked directly down the middle of the street. Nothing happened. As he came to the last building of the complex, he heard a shot. All around him the troopers jumped, believing themselves to be under sniper fire. A moment later a young Guardsman ran from behind a building.

The Director of Police went over and asked him if he had fired the shot. The soldier said yes, he had fired to scare a man away from a window; that his orders were to keep everyone away from windows.

Spina said he told the soldier: "Do you know what you just did? You have now created a state of hysteria. Every Guardsman up and down this street and every state policeman and every city policeman that is present thinks that somebody just fired a shot and that it is probably a sniper."

A short time later more "gunshots" were heard. Investigating, Spina came upon a Puerto Rican sitting on a wall. In reply to a question as to whether he knew "where the firing is coming from?" the man said:

"That's no firing. That's fireworks. If you look up to the fourth floor, you will see the people who are throwing down these cherry bombs."

By this time four truckloads of National Guardsmen and troopers and policemen were again crouched everywhere looking for a sniper. The Director of Police remained at the scene for three hours, and the only shot fired was the one by the Guardsman.

Nevertheless, at six o'clock that evening two columns of National Guardsmen and state troopers were directing mass fire at the Hayes Housing Project in response to what they believed were snipers. . . .

Detroit
. . . A spirit of carefree nihilism was taking hold. To riot and destroy appeared more and more to become ends in themselves. Late Sunday afternoon it appeared to one observer that the young people were "dancing amidst the flames."

A Negro plainclothes officer was standing at an intersection when a man threw a molotov cocktail into a business establishment at the corner. In the heat of the afternoon, fanned by the 20 to 25 m.p.h. winds of both Sunday and Monday, the fire reached the home next door within minutes. As residents uselessly sprayed the flames with garden hoses, the fire jumped from roof to roof of adjacent two- and three-story buildings. Within the hour the entire block was in flames. The ninth house in the burning row belonged to the arsonist who had thrown the molotov cocktail. . . .

. . .

. . . Employed as a private guard, 55-year-old Julius L. Dorsey, a Negro, was standing in front of a market when accosted by two Negro men and a woman. They demanded he permit them to loot the market. He ignored their demands. They began to berate him. He asked a neighbor to call the police. As the argument grew more heated, Dorsey fired three shots from his pistol into the air.

The police radio reported: "Looters, they have rifles." A patrol car driven by a police officer and carrying three National Guardsmen arrived. As the looters fled, the law enforcement personnel opened fire. When the firing ceased, one person lay dead.

He was Julius L. Dorsey . . .

. . .

. . . As the riot alternately waxed and waned, one area of the ghetto remained insulated. On the northeast side the residents of some 150 square blocks inhabited by 21,000 persons had, in 1966, banded together in the Positive Neighborhood Action Committee (PNAC). With professional help from the Institute of Urban Dynamics, they had organized block clubs and made plans for the improvement of the neighborhood. . . .

When the riot broke out, the residents, through the block clubs, were able to organize quickly. Youngsters, agreeing to stay in the neighborhood, participated in detouring traffic. While many persons reportedly sympathized with the idea of a rebellion against the "system," only two small fires were set—one in an empty building.

. . .

. . . According to Lt. Gen. Throckmorton and Col. Bolling, the city, at this time, was saturated with fear. The National Guardsmen were afraid, and the police were afraid. Numerous persons, the majority of them Negroes, were being injured by gunshots of undetermined origin. The general and his staff felt that the major task of the troops was to reduce the fear and restore an air of normalcy.

In order to accomplish this, every effort was made to establish contact and rapport between the troops and the residents. The soldiers—20 per cent of whom were Negro—began helping to clean up the streets, collect garbage, and trace persons who had disappeared in the confusion. Residents in the neighborhood responded with soup and sandwiches for the troops. In areas where the National Guard tried to establish rapport with the citizens, there was a smaller response.

New Brunswick

. . . A short time later, elements of the crowd—an older and rougher one than the night before—appeared in front of the police station. The participants wanted to see the mayor.

Mayor Sheehan went out onto the steps of the station. Using a bullhorn, she talked to the people and asked that she be given an opportunity to correct conditions. The crowd was boisterous. Some persons challenged the mayor. But, finally, the opinion, "She's new! Give her a chance!" prevailed.

A demand was issued by people in the crowd that all persons arrested the previous night be released. Told that this already had been done, the people were suspicious. They asked to be allowed to inspect the jail cells.

It was agreed to permit representatives of the people to look in the cells to satisfy themselves that everyone had been released.

The crowd dispersed. The New Brunswick riot had failed to materialize.

PATTERNS OF DISORDER

The "typical" riot did not take place. The disorders of 1967 were unusual, irregular, complex and unpredictable social processes. Like most human events, they did not unfold in an orderly sequence. However, an analysis of our survey information leads to some conclusions about the riot process.

In general:

- *The civil disorders of 1967 involved Negroes acting against local symbols of white American society, authority and property in Negro neighborhoods—rather than against white persons.*
- *Of 164 disorders reported during the first 9 months of 1967, eight (5 per cent) were major in terms of violence and damage; 33 (20 per cent) were serious but not major; 123 (75 per cent) were minor and undoubtedly would not have received national attention as "riots" had the nation not been sensitized by the more serious outbreaks.*
- *In the 75 disorders studied by a Senate subcommittee, there were 83 deaths. Eighty-two per cent of the deaths and more than half of the injuries occurred in Newark and Detroit. About 10 per cent of the dead and 36 per cent of the injured were public employees, primarily law officers and firemen. The overwhelming majority of the persons killed or injured in all the disorders were Negro civilians.*
- *Initial damage estimates were greatly exaggerated. In Detroit, newspaper damage estimates at first ranged from $200 million to $500 million; the highest recent estimate is $45 million. In Newark, early estimates ranged from $15 to $25 million. A month later damage was estimated at $10.2 million, 80 per cent in inventory losses.*

In the 24 disorders in 23 cities which we surveyed:

- *The final incident before the outbreak of disorder, and the initial violence itself, generally took place in the evening or at night at a place in which it was normal for many people to be on the streets.*
- *Violence usually occurred almost immediately following the occurrence of the final precipitating incident, and then escalated rapidly. With but few exceptions, violence subsided during the day, and flared rapidly again at night. The night-day cycles continued through the early period of the major disorders.*
- *Disorder generally began with rock and bottle throwing and window breaking. Once store windows were broken, looting usually followed.*
- *Disorder did not erupt as a result of a single "triggering" or "precipitating" incident. Instead, it was generated out of an increasingly disturbed social atmosphere, in which typically a series of tension-heightening incidents over a period of weeks or months became linked in the minds of many in the Negro community with a shared network of underlying grievances. At some point in the mounting tension, a further incident—in itself often routine or trivial—became the breaking point and the tension spilled over into violence.*
- *"Prior" incidents, which increased tensions and ultimately led to violence, were police actions in almost half the cases; police actions were "final" incidents before the outbreak of violence in 12 of the 24 surveyed disorders.*
- *No particular control tactic was successful in every situation. The varied effectiveness of control techniques emphasizes the need for*

advance training, planning, adequate intelligence systems, and knowledge of the ghetto community.

- *Negotiations between Negroes—including young militants as well as older Negro leaders—and white officials concerning "terms of peace" occurred during virtually all the disorders surveyed. In many cases, these negotiations involved discussion of underlying grievances as well as the handling of the disorder by control authorities.*

- *The typical rioter was a teenager or young adult, a lifelong resident of the city in which he rioted, a high school dropout; he was, nevertheless, somewhat better educated than his nonrioting Negro neighbor, and was usually underemployed or employed in a menial job. He was proud of his race, extremely hostile to both whites and middle-class Negroes and, although informed about politics, highly distrustful of the political system.*

- *In a survey of Negro males between the ages of 15 and 35 residing in the disturbance area in Newark, about 45 per cent identified themselves as rioters, and about 55 per cent as "noninvolved." But a Detroit survey revealed that only approximately 11 per cent of the total residents of two riot areas participated in the rioting, over 16 per cent identified themselves as "counter-rioters" who urged rioters to "cool it," and about 73 per cent identified themselves as "noninvolved."*

- *Most rioters were young Negro males. Nearly 53 per cent of arrestees were between 15 and 24 years of age; nearly 81 per cent between 15 and 35.*

- *In Detroit and Newark about 74 per cent of the rioters were brought up in the North. In contrast, of the noninvolved, 36 per cent in Detroit and 52 per cent in Newark were brought up in the North.*

- *Numerous Negro counter-rioters walked the streets urging rioters to "cool it." The typical counter-rioter was better educated and had higher income than either the rioter or the noninvolved.*

- *The proportion of Negroes in local government was substantially smaller than the Negro proportion of population. Only three of the 20 cities studied had more than one Negro legislator; none had ever had a Negro mayor or city manager. In only four cities did Negroes hold other important policy-making positions or serve as heads of municipal departments.*

- *Although almost all cities had some sort of formal grievance mechanism for handling citizen complaints, this typically was regarded by Negroes as ineffective and was generally ignored.*

- *Although specific grievances varied from city to city, at least 12 deeply held grievances can be identified and ranked into three levels of relative intensity:*

First Level of Intensity
  1. *Police practices*
  2. *Unemployment and underemployment*
  3. *Inadequate housing*

Second Level of Intensity
  4. *Inadequate education*
  5. *Poor recreation facilities and programs*

6. *Ineffectiveness of the political structure and grievance mechanisms*

Third Level of Intensity

7. *Disrespectful white attitudes*
8. *Discriminatory administration of justice*
9. *Inadequacy of federal programs*
10. *Inadequacy of municipal services*
11. *Discriminatory consumer and credit practices*
12. *Inadequate welfare programs*

- *The results of a three-city survey of various federal programs—manpower, education, housing, welfare and community action—indicate that, despite substantial expenditures, the number of persons assisted constitute only a fraction of those in need.*

The background of disorder is often as complex and difficult to analyze as the disorder itself. But we find that certain general conclusions can be drawn:

- *Social and economic conditions in the riot cities constituted a clear pattern of severe disadvantage for Negroes compared with whites, whether the Negroes lived in the area where the riot took place or outside it. Negroes had completed fewer years of education and fewer had attended high school. Negroes were twice as likely to be unemployed and three times as likely to be in unskilled and service jobs. Negroes averaged 70 per cent of the income earned by whites and were more than twice as likely to be living in poverty. Although housing cost Negroes relatively more, they had worse housing—three times as likely to be overcrowded and substandard. When compared to white suburbs, the relative disadvantage is even more pronounced.*

A study of the aftermath of disorder leads to disturbing conclusions. We find that, despite the institution of some post-riot programs:

- *Little basic change in the conditions underlying the outbreak of disorder has taken place. Actions to ameliorate Negro grievances have been limited and sporadic; with but few exceptions, they have not significantly reduced tensions.*
- *In several cities, the principal official response has been to train and equip the police with more sophisticated weapons.*
- *In several cities, increasing polarization is evident, with continuing breakdown of interracial communication, and growth of white segregationist or black separatist groups.*

ORGANIZED ACTIVITY

The President directed the Commission to investigate "to what extent, if any, there has been planning or organization in any of the riots."

To carry out this part of the President's charge, the Commission established a special investigative staff supplementing the field teams that made the general examination of the riots in 23 cities. The unit examined data collected by federal agencies and congressional committees, including thousands of documents supplied by the Federal Bureau of Investigation, gathered and evaluated information from local and state law enforcement agencies and officials, and conducted its own field investigation in selected cities.

On the basis of all the information collected, the Commission concludes that:

> The urban disorders of the summer of 1967 were not caused by, nor were they the consequence of, any organized plan or "conspiracy."

Specifically, the Commission has found no evidence that all or any of the disorders or the incidents that led to them were planned or directed by any organization or group, international, national or local.

Militant organizations, local and national, and individual agitators, who repeatedly forecast and called for violence, were active in the spring and summer of 1967. We believe that they sought to encourage violence, and that they helped to create an atmosphere that contributed to the outbreak of disorder.

We recognize that the continuation of disorders and the polarization of the races would provide fertile ground for organized exploitation in the future.

Investigations of organized activity are continuing at all levels of government, including committees of Congress. These investigations relate not only to the disorders of 1967 but also to the action of groups and individuals, particularly in schools and colleges, during this last fall and winter. The Commission has cooperated in these investigations. They should continue.

THE BASIC CAUSES

In addressing the question "Why did it happen?" we shift our focus from the local to the national scene, from the particular events of the summer of 1967 to the factors within the society at large that created a mood of violence among many urban Negroes.

These factors are complex and interacting; they vary significantly in their effect from city to city and from year to year; and the consequences of one disorder, generating new grievances and new demands, become the causes of the next. It is this which creates the "thicket of tension, conflicting evidence and extreme opinions" cited by the President.

Despite these complexities, certain fundamental matters are clear. Of these, the most fundamental is the racial attitude and behavior of white Americans toward black Americans.

Race prejudice has shaped our history decisively; it now threatens to affect our future.

White racism is essentially responsible for the explosive mixture which has been accumulating in our cities since the end of World War II. At the base of this mixture are three of the most bitter fruits of white racial attitudes:

- Pervasive discrimination and segregation *in employment, education and housing have resulted in the continuing exclusion of great numbers of Negroes from the benefits of economic progress.*
- Black in-migration and white exodus *have produced the massive and growing concentrations of impoverished Negroes in our major cities,*

creating a growing crisis of deteriorating facilities and services and unmet human needs.

- In the black ghettos *segregation and poverty converge on the young to destroy opportunity and enforce failure. Crime, drug addiction, dependency on welfare, and bitterness and resentment against society in general and white society in particular are the result.*

These three forces have converged on the inner city in recent years and on the people who inhabit it. At the same time, most whites and many Negroes outside the ghetto have prospered to a degree unparalleled in the history of civilization. Through television and other media, this affluence has been endlessly flaunted before the eyes of the Negro poor and the jobless ghetto youth.

Yet these facts alone cannot be said to have caused the disorders. Recently, other powerful ingredients have begun to catalyze the mixture:

- Frustrated hopes *are the residue of the unfulfilled expectations aroused by the great judicial and legislative victories of the Civil Rights Movement and the dramatic struggle for equal rights in the South.*
- A climate that tends toward approval and encouragement of violence *as a form of protest has been created by white terrorism directed against nonviolent protest; by the open defiance of law and federal authority by state and local officials resisting desegregation; and by some protest groups engaging in civil disobedience who turn their backs on nonviolence, go beyond the constitutionally protected rights of petition and free assembly, and resort to violence to attempt to compel alteration of laws and policies with which they disagree.*
- The frustrations of powerlessness *have led some Negroes to the conviction that there is no effective alternative to violence as a means of achieving redress of grievances, and of "moving the system." These frustrations are reflected in alienation and hostility toward the institutions of law and government and the white society which controls them, and in the reach toward racial consciousness and solidarity reflected in the slogan "Black Power."*
- A new mood *has sprung up among Negroes, particularly among the young, in which self-esteem and enhanced racial pride are replacing apathy and submission to "the system."*
- The police are not merely a "spark" factor. *To some Negroes police have come to symbolize white power, white racism and white repression. And the fact is that many police do reflect and express these white attitudes. The atmosphere of hostility and cynicism is reinforced by a widespread belief among Negroes in the existence of police brutality and in a "double standard" of justice and protection—one for Negroes and one for whites.*

.   .   .

To this point, we have attempted only to identify the prime components of the "explosive mixture." In the chapters that follow we seek to analyze them in the perspective of history. Their meaning, however, is already clear:

In the summer of 1967, we have seen in our cities a chain reaction of racial violence. If we are heedless none of us shall escape the consequences.

REJECTION AND PROTEST: AN HISTORICAL SKETCH

The causes of recent racial disorders are embedded in a tangle of issues and circumstances—social, economic, political and psychological—which arise out of the historical pattern of Negro-white relations in America.

In this chapter we trace the pattern, identify the recurrent themes of Negro protest and, most importantly, provide a perspective on the protest activities of the present era.

We describe the Negro's experience in America and the development of slavery as an institution. We show his persistent striving for equality in the face of rigidly maintained social, economic and educational barriers, and repeated mob violence. We portray the ebb and flow of the doctrinal tides—accommodation, separatism, and self-help—and their relationship to the current theme of Black Power. We conclude:

> The Black Power advocates of today consciously feel that they are the most militant group in the Negro protest movement. Yet they have retreated from a direct confrontation with American society on the issue of integration and, by preaching separatism, unconsciously function as an accommodation to white racism. Much of their economic program, as well as their interest in Negro history, self-help, racial solidarity and separation, is reminiscent of Booker T. Washington. The rhetoric is different, but the programs are remarkably similar.

THE FORMATION OF THE RACIAL GHETTOS

Throughout the 20th century the Negro population of the United States has been moving steadily from rural areas to urban and from South to North and West. In 1910, 91 per cent of the nation's 9.8 million Negroes lived in the South and only 27 per cent of American Negroes lived in cities of 2,500 persons or more. Between 1910 and 1966 the total Negro population more than doubled, reaching 21.5 million, and the number living in metropolitan areas rose more than five-fold (from 2.6 million to 14.8 million). The number outside the South rose eleven-fold (from 880,000 to 9.7 million).

Negro migration from the South has resulted from the expectation of thousands of new and highly paid jobs for unskilled workers in the North and the shift to mechanized farming in the South. However, the Negro migration is small when compared to earlier waves of European immigrants. Even between 1960 and 1966, there were 1.8 million immigrants from abroad compared to the 613,000 Negroes who arrived in the North and West from the South.

As a result of the growing number of Negroes in urban areas, natural increase has replaced migration as the primary source of Negro population increase in the cities. Nevertheless, Negro migration from the South will continue unless economic conditions there change dramatically.

Basic data concerning Negro urbanization trends indicate that:

· *Almost all Negro population growth (98 per cent from 1950 to 1966) is*

occurring within metropolitan areas, primarily within central cities.[1]
- *The vast majority of white population growth (78 per cent from 1960 to 1966) is occurring in suburban portions of metropolitan areas. Since 1960, white central-city population has declined by 1.3 million.*
- *As a result, central cities are becoming more heavily Negro while the suburban fringes around them remain almost entirely white.*
- *The twelve largest central cities now contain over two-thirds of the Negro population outside the South, and one-third of the Negro total in the United States.*

Within the cities, Negroes have been excluded from white residential areas through discriminatory practices. Just as significant is the withdrawal of white families from, or their refusal to enter, neighborhoods where Negroes are moving or already residing. About 20 per cent of the residents of average United States neighborhoods move every year. The refusal of whites to move into "changing" areas when vacancies occur means that most vacancies eventually are occupied by Negroes.

The result, according to a recent study, is that in 1960 the average segregation index for 207 of the largest United States cities was 86.2. In other words, to create an unsegregated population distribution an average of over 86 per cent of all Negroes would have to change their place of residence within the city.

UNEMPLOYMENT, FAMILY STRUCTURE, AND SOCIAL DISORGANIZATION

Although there have been gains in Negro income nationally, and a decline in the number of Negroes below the "poverty level," the condition of Negroes in the central city remains in a state of crisis. Between 2 and 2.5 million Negroes—16 to 20 per cent of the total Negro population of all central cities—live in squalor and deprivation in ghetto neighborhoods.

Employment is a key problem. It not only controls the present for the Negro American but, in a most profound way, it is creating the future as well. Yet, despite continuing economic growth and declining national unemployment rates, the unemployment rate for Negroes in 1967 was more than double that for whites.

Equally important is the undesirable nature of many jobs open to Negroes. Negro men are more than three times as likely as white men to be in low-paying, unskilled or service jobs. This concentration of male Negro employment at the lowest end of the occupational scale is the single most important source of poverty among Negroes.

In one study of low-income neighborhoods, the "subemployment rate," including both unemployment and underemployment, was about 33 per cent, or 8.8 times greater than the overall unemployment rate for all United States workers.

Employment problems, aggravated by the constant arrival of new unemployed migrants, many of them from depressed rural areas, create persistent poverty in the ghetto. In 1966, about 11.9 per cent of the nation's

[1] A "central city" is the largest city of a standard metropolitan statistical area, that is, a metropolitan area containing at least one city of at least 50,000 inhabitants.

whites and 40.6 per cent of its nonwhites were below the "poverty level" defined by the Social Security Administration (currently $3,335 per year for an urban family of four). Over 40 per cent of the nonwhites below the poverty level live in the central cities.

Employment problems have drastic social impact in the ghetto. Men who are chronically unemployed or employed in the lowest status jobs are often unable or unwilling to remain with their families. The handicap imposed on children growing up without fathers in an atmosphere of poverty and deprivation is increased as mothers are forced to work to provide support.

The culture of poverty that results from unemployment and family breakup generates a system of ruthless, exploitative relationships within the ghetto. Prostitution, dope addiction, and crime create an environmental "jungle" characterized by personal insecurity and tension. Children growing up under such conditions are likely participants in civil disorder.

CONDITIONS OF LIFE IN THE RACIAL GHETTO

A striking difference in environment from that of white, middle-class Americans profoundly influences the lives of residents of the ghetto.

Crime rates, consistently higher than in other areas, create a pronounced sense of insecurity. For example, in one city one low-income Negro district had 35 times as many serious crimes against persons as did a high-income white district. Unless drastic steps are taken, the crime problems in poverty areas are likely to continue to multiply as the growing youth and rapid urbanization of the population outstrips police resources.

Poor health and sanitation conditions in the ghetto result in higher mortality rates, a higher incidence of major diseases and lower availability and utilization of medical services. The infant mortality rate for nonwhite babies under the age of one month is 58 per cent higher than for whites; for one to 12 months it is almost three times as high. The level of sanitation in the ghetto is far below that in high income areas. Garbage collection is often inadequate. Of an estimated 14,000 cases of rat bite in the United States in 1965, most were in ghetto neighborhoods.

Ghetto residents believe they are "exploited" by local merchants; and evidence substantiates some of these beliefs. A study conducted in one city by the Federal Trade Commission showed that distinctly higher prices were charged for goods sold in ghetto stores than in other areas.

Lack of knowledge regarding credit purchasing creates special pitfalls for the disadvantaged. In many states garnishment practices compound these difficulties by allowing creditors to deprive individuals of their wages without hearing or trial.

COMPARING THE IMMIGRANT AND NEGRO EXPERIENCE

In this chapter, we address ourselves to a fundamental question that many white Americans are asking: why have so many Negroes, unlike the European immigrants, been unable to escape from the ghetto and from poverty. We believe the following factors play a part:

- The Maturing Economy: *When the European immigrants arrived, they gained an economic foothold by providing the unskilled labor needed by industry. Unlike the immigrant, the Negro migrant found little opportunity in the city. The economy, by then matured, had little use for the unskilled labor he had to offer.*

- The Disability of Race: *The structure of discrimination has stringently narrowed opportunities for the Negro and restricted his prospects. European immigrants suffered from discrimination, but never so pervasively.*

- Entry into the Political System: *The immigrants usually settled in rapidly growing cities with powerful and expanding political machines, which traded economic advantages for political support. Ward-level grievance machinery, as well as personal representation, enabled the immigrant to make his voice heard and his power felt.*

  By the time the Negro arrived, these political machines were no longer so powerful or so well equipped to provide jobs or other favors and were unwilling to share their remaining influence with Negroes.

- Cultural Factors: *Coming from societies with a low standard of living and at a time when job aspirations were low, the immigrants sensed little deprivation in being forced to take less desirable and poorly-paid jobs. Their large and cohesive families contributed to total income. Their vision of the future—one that led to a life outside of the ghetto —provided the incentive necessary to endure the present.*

  Although Negro men worked as hard as the immigrants, they were unable to support their families. The entrepreneurial opportunities had vanished. As a result of slavery and long periods of unemployment, the Negro family structure had become matriarchal; the males played a secondary and marginal family role—one which offered little compensation for their hard and unrewarding labor. Above all, segregation denied Negroes access to good jobs and the opportunity to leave the ghetto. For them, the future seemed to lead only to a dead end.

Today, whites tend to exaggerate how well and quickly they escaped from poverty. The fact is that immigrants who came from rural backgrounds, as many Negroes do, are only now, after three generations, finally beginning to move into the middle class.

By contrast, Negroes began concentrating in the city less than two generations ago, and under much less favorable conditions. Although some Negroes have escaped poverty, few have been able to escape the urban ghetto.

THE COMMUNITY RESPONSE

Our investigation of the 1967 riot cities establishes that virtually every major episode of violence was foreshadowed by an accumulation of unresolved grievances and by widespread dissatisfaction among Negroes with the unwillingness and inability of local government to respond.

Overcoming these conditions is essential for community support of law enforcement and civil order. City governments need new and more vital channels of communication to the residents of the ghetto; they need to improve their capacity to respond effectively to community needs before they become community grievances; and they need to provide opportunity for meaningful involvement of ghetto residents in shaping policies and programs which affect the community.

The Commission recommends that local governments:

- *Develop Neighborhood Action Task Forces as joint community-government efforts through which more effective communication can be achieved, and the delivery of city services to ghetto residents improved.*
- *Establish comprehensive grievance-response mechanisms in order to bring all public agencies under public scrutiny.*
- *Bring the institutions of local government closer to the people they serve by establishing neighborhood outlets for local, state and federal administrative and public service agencies.*
- *Expand opportunities for ghetto residents to participate in the formulation of public policy and the implementation of programs affecting them by improved political representation, creation of institutional channels for community action, expansion of legal services, and legislative hearings on ghetto problems.*

In this effort, city governments will require state and federal support. The Commission recommends:

- *State and federal financial assistance for mayors and city councils to support the research, consultants, staff and other resources needed to respond effectively to federal program initiatives.*
- *State cooperation in providing municipalities with the jurisdictional tools needed to deal with their problems; a fuller measure of financial aid to urban areas; and the focusing of the interests of suburban communities on the physical, social and cultural environment of the central city.*

POLICE AND THE COMMUNITY

The abrasive relationship between the police and the ghetto community has been a major—and explosive—source of grievance, tension and disorder. The blame must be shared by the total society.

The police are faced with demands for increased protection and service in the ghetto. Yet the aggressive patrol practices thought necessary to meet these demands themselves create tension and hostility. The resulting grievances have been further aggravated by the lack of effective mechanisms for handling complaints against the police. Special programs for bettering police-community relations have been instituted but these alone are not enough. Police administrators, with the guidance of public officials, and the support of the entire community, must take vigorous action to improve law enforcement and to decrease the potential for disorder.

The Commission recommends that city government and police authorities:

- *Review police operations in the ghetto to ensure proper conduct by police officers, and eliminate abrasive practices.*
- *Provide more adequate police protection to ghetto residents to eliminate their high sense of insecurity, and the belief of many Negro citizens in the existence of a dual standard of law enforcement.*

- *Establish fair and effective mechanisms for the redress of grievances against the police, and other municipal employees.*
- *Develop and adopt policy guidelines to assist officers in making critical decisions in areas where police conduct can create tension.*
- *Develop and use innovative programs to ensure widespread community support for law enforcement.*
- *Recruit more Negroes into the regular police force and review promotion policies to ensure Negro officers full opportunity for fair promotion.*
- *Establish a "Community Service Officer" program to attract ghetto youths between the ages of 17 and 21 to police work. These junior officers would perform duties in ghetto neighborhoods but would not have full police authority. The federal government should provide support equal to 90 per cent of the costs of employing CSOs on the basis of one for every ten regular officers.*

CONTROL OF DISORDER

Preserving civil peace is the first responsibility of government. Unless the rule of law prevails, our society will lack not only order but also the environment essential to social and economic progress.

The maintenance of civil order cannot be left to the police alone. The police need guidance, as well as support, from mayors and other public officials. It is the responsibility of public officials to determine proper police policies, support adequate police standards for personnel and performance, and participate in planning for the control of disorders.

To maintain control of incidents which could lead to disorders, the Commission recommends that local officials:

- *Assign seasoned, well-trained policemen and supervisory officers to patrol ghetto areas, and to respond to disturbances.*
- *Develop plans which will quickly muster maximum police manpower and highly qualified senior commanders at the outbreak of disorders.*
- *Provide special training in the prevention of disorders, and prepare police for riot control and for operation in units, with adequate command and control and field communication for proper discipline and effectiveness.*
- *Develop guidelines governing the use of control equipment and provide alternatives to the use of lethal weapons. Federal support for research in this area is needed.*
- *Establish an intelligence system to provide police and other public officials with reliable information that may help to prevent the outbreak of a disorder and to institute effective control measures in the event a riot erupts.*
- *Develop continuing contacts with ghetto residents to make use of the forces for order which exist within the community.*
- *Provide the machinery for neutralizing rumors, including creation of special rumor details to collect and evaluate rumors that may lead to a civil disorder, and to disseminate effectively the true facts to the ghetto residents and leaders.*

The Commission believes there is a grave danger that some communities may resort to the indiscriminate and excessive use of force. The harmful effects of overreaction are incalculable. The Commission condemns moves to equip police departments with mass destruction weapons, such as automatic rifles, machine guns and tanks. Weapons which are designed to destroy, not to control, have no place in densely populated urban communities.

The Commission recognizes the sound principle of local authority and responsibility in law enforcement, but recommends that the federal government share in the financing of programs for improvement of police forces both in their normal law enforcement activities as well as in their response to civil disorders.

To assist government authorities in planning their response to civil disorder, this report contains a Supplement on Control of Disorder. It deals with specific problems encountered during riot-control operations, and includes:

- *Assessment of the present capabilities of police, National Guard and Army forces to control major riots, and recommendations for improvement;*
- *Recommended means by which the control operations of those forces may be coordinated with the response of other agencies, such as fire departments, and with the community at large;*
- *Recommendations for review and revision of federal, state and local laws needed to provide the framework for control efforts and for the call-up and interrelated action of public safety forces.*

THE ADMINISTRATION OF JUSTICE UNDER EMERGENCY CONDITIONS

In many of the cities which experienced disorders last summer, there were recurring breakdowns in the mechanisms for processing, prosecuting and protecting arrested persons. These resulted mainly from long-standing structural deficiencies in criminal court systems, and from the failure of communities to anticipate and plan for the emergency demands of civil disorders.

In part, because of this, there were few successful prosecutions for serious crimes committed during the riots. In those cities where mass arrests occurred many arrestees were deprived of basic legal rights.

The Commission recommends that the cities and states:

- *Undertake reform of the lower courts so as to improve the quality of justice rendered under normal conditions.*
- *Plan comprehensive measures by which the criminal justice system may be supplemented during civil disorders so that its deliberative functions are protected, and the quality of justice is maintained.*

Such emergency plans require broad community participation and dedicated leadership by the bench and bar. They should include:

- *Laws sufficient to deter and punish riot conduct.*
- *Additional judges, bail and probation officers, and clerical staff.*
- *Arrangements for volunteer lawyers to help prosecutors and to represent riot defendants at every stage of proceedings.*

- *Policies to ensure proper and individual bail, arraignment, pre-trial, trial and sentencing proceedings.*
- *Procedures for processing arrested persons, such as summons and release, and release on personal recognizance, which permit separation of minor offenders from those dangerous to the community, in order that serious offenders may be detained and prosecuted effectively.*
- *Adequate emergency processing and detention facilities.*

DAMAGES: REPAIR AND COMPENSATION

The Commission recommends that the federal government:

- *Amend the Federal Disaster Act—which now applies only to natural disasters—to permit federal emergency food and medical assistance to cities during major civil disorders, and provide long-term economic assistance afterwards.*
- *With the cooperation of the states, create incentives for the private insurance industry to provide more adequate property-insurance coverage in inner-city areas.*

The Commission endorses the report of the National Advisory Panel on Insurance in Riot-Affected Areas: "Meeting the Insurance Crisis of our Cities."

THE NEWS MEDIA AND THE RIOTS

In his charge to the Commission, the President asked: "What effect do the mass media have on the riots?"

The Commission determined that the answer to the President's question did not lie solely in the performance of the press and broadcasters in reporting the riots. Our analysis had to consider also the overall treatment by the media of the Negro ghettos, community relations, racial attitudes, and poverty—day by day and month by month, year in and year out.

A wide range of interviews with government officials, law enforcement authorities, media personnel and other citizens, including ghetto residents, as well as a quantitative analysis of riot coverage and a special conference with industry representatives leads us to conclude that:

- *Despite instances of sensationalism, inaccuracy and distortion, newspapers, radio and television tried on the whole to give a balanced, factual account of the 1967 disorders.*
- *Elements of the news media failed to portray accurately the scale and character of the violence that occurred last summer. The overall effect was, we believe, an exaggeration of both mood and event.*
- *Important segments of the media failed to report adequately on the causes and consequences of civil disorders and on the underlying problems of race relations. They have not communicated to the majority of their audience—which is white—a sense of the degradation, misery and hopelessness of life in the ghetto.*

These failings must be corrected, and the improvement must come from within the industry. Freedom of the press is not the issue. Any effort to impose governmental restrictions would be inconsistent with fundamental constitutional precepts.

We have seen evidence that the news media are becoming aware of and concerned about their performance in this field. As that concern grows, coverage will improve. But much more must be done, and it must be done soon.

The Commission recommends that the media:

- *Expand coverage of the Negro community and of race problems through permanent assignment of reporters familiar with urban and racial affairs, and through establishment of more and better links with the Negro community.*
- *Integrate Negroes and Negro activities into all aspects of coverage and content, including newspaper articles and television program-ming. The news media must publish newspapers and produce pro-grams that recognize the existence and activities of Negroes as a group within the community and as a part of the larger community.*
- *Recruit more Negroes into journalism and broadcasting and promote those who are qualified to positions of significant responsibility. Re-cruitment should begin in high schools and continue through college; where necessary, aid for training should be provided.*
- *Improve coordination with police in reporting riot news through ad-vance planning, and cooperate with the police in the designation of police information officers, establishment of information centers, and development of mutually acceptable guidelines for riot reporting and the conduct of media personnel.*
- *Accelerate efforts to ensure accurate and responsible reporting of riot and racial news, through adoption by all news gathering organiza-tions of stringent internal staff guidelines.*
- *Cooperate in the establishment of a privately organized and funded Institute of Urban Communications to train and educate journalists in urban affairs, recruit and train more Negro journalists, develop methods for improving police-press relations, review coverage of riots and racial issues, and support continuing research in the urban field.*

THE FUTURE OF THE CITIES

By 1985, the Negro population in central cities is expected to increase by 72 per cent to approximately 20.8 million. Coupled with the continued exodus of white families to the suburbs, this growth will produce majority Negro populations in many of the nation's largest cities.

The future of these cities, and of their burgeoning Negro populations, is grim. Most new employment opportunities are being created in suburbs and outlying areas. This trend will continue unless important changes in public policy are made.

In prospect, therefore, is further deterioration of already inadequate municipal tax bases in the face of increasing demands for public services, and continuing unemployment and poverty among the urban Negro popu-lation:

Three choices are open to the nation:

- *We can maintain present policies, continuing both the proportion of the nation's resources now allocated to programs for the unemployed and the disadvantaged, and the inadequate and failing effort to achieve an integrated society.*

- *We can adopt a policy of "enrichment" aimed at improving dramatically the quality of ghetto life while abandoning integration as a goal.*
- *We can pursue integration by combining ghetto "enrichment" with policies which will encourage Negro movement out of central city areas.*

The first choice, continuance of present policies, has ominous consequences for our society. The share of the nation's resources now allocated to programs for the disadvantaged is insufficient to arrest the deterioration of life in central city ghettos. Under such conditions, a rising proportion of Negroes may come to see in the deprivation and segregation they experience, a justification for violent protest, or for extending support to now isolated extremists who advocate civil disruption. Large-scale and continuing violence could result, followed by white retaliation, and, ultimately, the separation of the two communities in a garrison state.

Even if violence does not occur, the consequences are unacceptable. Development of a racially integrated society, extraordinarily difficult today, will be virtually impossible when the present black ghetto population of 12.5 million has grown to almost 21 million.

To continue present policies is to make permanent the division of our country into two societies; one, largely Negro and poor, located in the central cities; the other, predominantly white and affluent, located in the suburbs and in outlying areas.

The second choice, ghetto enrichment coupled with abandonment of integration, is also unacceptable. It is another way of choosing a permanently divided country. Moreover, equality cannot be achieved under conditions of nearly complete separation. In a country where the economy, and particularly the resources of employment, are predominantly white, a policy of separation can only relegate Negroes to a permanently inferior economic status.

We believe that the only possible choice for America is the third—a policy which combines ghetto enrichment with programs designed to encourage integration of substantial numbers of Negroes into the society outside the ghetto.

Enrichment must be an important adjunct to integration, for no matter how ambitious or energetic the program, few Negroes now living in central cities can be quickly integrated. In the meantime, large-scale improvement in the quality of ghetto life is essential.

But this can be no more than an interim strategy. Programs must be developed which will permit substantial Negro movement out of the ghettos. The primary goal must be a single society, in which every citizen will be free to live and work according to his capabilities and desires, not his color.

RECOMMENDATIONS FOR NATIONAL ACTION
Introduction
No American—white or black—can escape the consequences of the continuing social and economic decay of our major cities.

Only a commitment to national action on an unprecedented scale can shape a future compatible with the historic ideals of American society.

The great productivity of our economy, and a federal revenue system which is highly responsive to economic growth, can provide the resources.

The major need is to generate new will—the will to tax ourselves to the extent necessary to meet the vital needs of the nation.

We have set forth goals and proposed strategies to reach those goals. We discuss and recommend programs not to commit each of us to specific parts of such programs but to illustrate the type and dimension of action needed.

The major goal is the creation of a true union—a single society and a single American identity. Toward that goal, we propose the following objectives for national action:

- *Opening up opportunities to those who are restricted by racial segregation and discrimination and eliminating all barriers to their choice of jobs, education and housing.*
- *Removing the frustration of powerlessness among the disadvantaged by providing the means for them to deal with the problems that affect their own lives and by increasing the capacity of our public and private institutions to respond to these problems.*
- *Increasing communication across racial lines to destroy stereotypes, to halt polarization, end distrust and hostility and create common ground for efforts toward public order and social justice.*

We propose these aims to fulfill our pledge of equality and to meet the fundamental needs of a democratic and civilized society—domestic peace and social justice.

EMPLOYMENT

Pervasive unemployment and underemployment are the most persistent and serious grievances in the Negro ghetto. They are inextricably linked to the problem of civil disorder.

Despite growing federal expenditures for manpower development and training programs and sustained general economic prosperity and increasing demands for skilled workers, about two million—white and non-white—are permanently unemployed. About ten million are underemployed, of whom 6.5 million work full time for wages below the poverty line.

The 500,000 "hard-core" unemployed in the central cities who lack a basic education and are unable to hold a steady job are made up in large part of Negro males between the ages of 18 and 25. In the riot cities which we surveyed, Negroes were three times as likely as whites to hold unskilled jobs, which are often part time, seasonal, low-paying and "dead end."

Negro males between the ages of 15 and 25 predominated among the rioters. More than 20 per cent of the rioters were unemployed, and many who were employed held intermittent, low status, unskilled jobs which they regarded as below their education and ability.

The Commission recommends that the federal government:

- *Undertake joint efforts with cities and states to consolidate existing manpower programs to avoid fragmentation and duplication.*

- *Take immediate action to create 2,000,000 new jobs over the next three years—one million in the public sector and one million in the private sector—to absorb the hard-core unemployed and materially reduce the level of underemployment for all workers, black and white. We propose 250,000 public sector and 300,000 private sector jobs in the first year.*
- *Provide on-the-job training by both public and private employers with reimbursement to private employers for the extra costs of training the hard-core unemployed, by contract or by tax credits.*
- *Provide tax and other incentives to investment in rural as well as urban poverty areas in order to offer to the rural poor an alternative to migration to urban centers.*
- *Take new and vigorous action to remove artificial barriers to employment and promotion, including not only racial discrimination but, in certain cases, arrest records or lack of a high school diploma. Strengthen those agencies such as the Equal Employment Opportunity Commission, charged with eliminating discriminatory practices, and provide full support for Title VI of the 1964 Civil Rights Act allowing federal grant-in-aid funds to be withheld from activities which discriminate on grounds of color or race.*

The Commission commends the recent public commitment of the National Council of the Building and Construction Trades Unions, AFL-CIO, to encourage and recruit Negro membership in apprenticeship programs. This commitment should be intensified and implemented.

EDUCATION

Education in a democratic society must equip children to develop their potential and to participate fully in American life. For the community at large, the schools have discharged this responsibility well. But for many minorities, and particularly for the children of the ghetto, the schools have failed to provide the educational experience which could overcome the effects of discrimination and deprivation.

This failure is one of the persistent sources of grievance and resentment within the Negro community. The hostility of Negro parents and students toward the school system is generating increasing conflict and causing disruption within many city school districts. But the most dramatic evidence of the relationship between educational practices and civil disorders lies in the high incidence of riot participation by ghetto youth who have not completed high school.

The bleak record of public education for ghetto children is growing worse. In the critical skills—verbal and reading ability—Negro students are falling farther behind whites with each year of school completed. The high unemployment and underemployment rate for Negro youth is evidence, in part, of the growing educational crisis.

We support integration as the priority education strategy; it is essential to the future of American society. In this last summer's disorders we have seen the consequences of racial isolation at all levels, and of attitudes toward race, on both sides, produced by three centuries of myth, ignorance and bias. It is indispensable that opportunities for interaction between the races be expanded.

We recognize that the growing dominance of city school district populations by disadvantaged minorities will not soon be arrested. No matter how great the effort toward desegregation, many children of the ghetto will not, within their school careers, attend integrated schools.

If existing disadvantages are not to be perpetuated, we must drastically improve the quality of ghetto education. Equality of results with all-white schools must be the goal.

To implement these strategies, the Commission recommends:

- *Sharply increased efforts to eliminate de facto segregation in our schools through substantial federal aid to school systems seeking to desegregate either within the system or in cooperation with neighboring school systems.*
- *Elimination of racial discrimination in Northern as well as Southern schools by vigorous application of Title VI of the Civil Rights Act of 1964.*
- *Extension of quality early childhood education to every disadvantaged child in the country.*
- *Efforts to improve dramatically schools serving disadvantaged children through substantial federal funding of year-round quality compensatory education programs, improved teaching, and expanded experimentation and research.*
- *Elimination of illiteracy through greater federal support for adult basic education.*
- *Enlarged opportunities for parent and community participation in the public schools.*
- *Reoriented vocational education emphasizing work-experience training and the involvement of business and industry.*
- *Expanded opportunities for higher education through increased federal assistance to disadvantaged students.*
- *Revision of state aid formulas to assure more per student aid to districts having a high proportion of disadvantaged school-age children.*

THE WELFARE SYSTEM

Our present system of public welfare is designed to save money instead of people, and tragically ends up doing neither. This system has two critical deficiencies:

First, it excludes large numbers of persons who are in great need, and who, if provided a decent level of support, might be able to become more productive and self-sufficient. No federal funds are available for millions of men and women who are needy but neither aged, handicapped nor the parents of minor children.

Second, for those who are included, the system provides assistance well below the minimum necessary for a decent level of existence, and imposes restrictions that encourage continued dependency on welfare and undermine self-respect.

A welter of statutory requirements and administrative practices and regulations operate to remind recipients that they are considered untrustworthy, promiscuous and lazy. Residence requirements prevent assistance to people in need who are newly arrived in the state. Regular searches of recipients' homes violate privacy. Inadequate social services compound the problems.

The Commission recommends that the federal government, acting with state and local governments where necessary, reform the existing welfare system to:

- *Establish uniform national standards of assistance at least as high as the annual "poverty level" of income, now set by the Social Security Administration at $3,335 for an urban family of four.*
- *Require that all states receiving federal welfare contributions participate in the Aid to Families with Dependent Children-Unemployed Parents program (AFDC-UP) that permits assistance to families with both father and mother in the home, thus aiding the family while it is still intact.*
- *Bear a substantially greater portion of all welfare costs—at least 90 per cent of total payments.*
- *Increase incentives for seeking employment and job training, but remove restrictions recently enacted by the Congress that would compel mothers of young children to work.*
- *Provide more adequate social services through neighborhood centers and through family-planning programs.*
- *Remove the freeze placed by the 1967 welfare amendments on the percentage of children in a state that can be covered by federal assistance.*
- *Eliminate residence requirements.*

As a long-range goal, the Commission recommends that the federal government seek to develop a national system of income supplementation based strictly on need with two broad and basic purposes:

- *To provide, for those who can work or who do work, any necessary supplements in such a way as to develop incentives for fuller employment;*
- *To provide, for those who cannot work and for mothers who decide to remain with their children, a minimum standard of decent living, and aid in saving children from the prison of poverty that has held their parents.*

A broad system of supplementation would involve substantially greater federal expenditures than anything now contemplated. The cost will range widely depending on the standard of need accepted as the "basic allowance" to individuals and families, and on the rate at which additional income above this level is taxed. Yet if the deepening cycle of poverty and dependence on welfare can be broken, if the children of the poor can be given the opportunity to scale the wall that now separates them from the rest of society, the return on this investment will be great indeed.

HOUSING

After more than three decades of fragmented and grossly underfunded federal housing programs, nearly six million substandard housing units remain occupied in the United States.

The housing problem is particularly acute in the Negro ghettos. Nearly two-thirds of all non-white families living in the central cities today live in neighborhoods marked with substandard housing and general urban blight. Two major factors are responsible.

First: Many ghetto residents simply cannot pay the rent necessary to support decent housing. In Detroit, for example, over 40 per cent of the non-white occupied units in 1960 required rent of over 35 per cent of the tenants' income.

Second: Discrimination prevents access to many non-slum areas, particularly the suburbs, where good housing exists. In addition, by creating a "back pressure" in the racial ghettos, it makes it possible for landlords to break up apartments for denser occupancy, and keeps prices and rents of deteriorated ghetto housing higher than they would be in a truly free market.

To date, federal programs have been able to do comparatively little to provide housing for the disadvantaged. In the 31-year history of subsidized federal housing, only about 800,000 units have been constructed, with recent production averaging about 50,000 units a year. By comparison, over a period only three years longer, FHA insurance guarantees have made possible the construction of over ten million middle and upper-income units.

Two points are fundamental to the Commission's recommendations:

First: Federal housing programs must be given a new thrust aimed at overcoming the prevailing patterns of racial segregation. If this is not done, those programs will continue to concentrate the most impoverished and dependent segments of the population into the central-city ghettos where there is already a critical gap between the needs of the population and the public resources to deal with them.

Second: The private sector must be brought into the production and financing of low and moderate rental housing to supply the capabilities and capital necessary to meet the housing needs of the nation.

The Commission recommends that the federal government:

- *Enact a comprehensive and enforceable federal open housing law to cover the sale or rental of all housing, including single family homes.*
- *Reorient federal housing programs to place more low and moderate income housing outside of ghetto areas.*
- *Bring within the reach of low and moderate income families within the next five years, six million new and existing units of decent housing, beginning with 600,000 units in the next year.*

To reach this goal we recommend:

- *Expansion and modification of the rent supplement program to permit use of supplements for existing housing, thus greatly increasing the reach of the program.*
- *Expansion and modification of the below-market interest rate program to enlarge the interest subsidy to all sponsors and provide interest-free loans to nonprofit sponsors to cover pre-construction costs, and permit sale of projects to nonprofit corporations, cooperatives, or condominiums.*
- *Creation of an ownership supplement program similar to present rent*

supplements, to make home ownership possible for low-income families.
- *Federal writedown of interest rates on loans to private builders constructing moderate-rent housing.*
- *Expansion of the public housing program, with emphasis on small units on scattered sites, and leasing and "turnkey" programs.*
- *Expansion of the Model Cities program.*
- *Expansion and reorientation of the urban renewal program to give priority to projects directly assisting low-income households to obtain adequate housing.*

CONCLUSION

One of the first witnesses to be invited to appear before this Commission was Dr. Kenneth B. Clark, a distinguished and perceptive scholar. Referring to the reports of earlier riot commissions, he said:

> I read that report . . . of the 1919 riot in Chicago, and it is as if I were reading the report of the investigating committee on the Harlem riot of '35, the report of the investigating committee on the Harlem riot of '43, the report of the McCone Commission on the Watts riot.

> I must again in candor say to you members of this Commission—it is a kind of Alice in Wonderland—with the same moving picture re-shown over and over again, the same analysis, the same recommendations, and the same inaction.

These words come to our minds as we conclude this Report.

We have provided an honest beginning. We have learned much. But we have uncovered no startling truths, no unique insights, no simple solutions. The destruction and the bitterness of racial disorder, the harsh polemics of black revolt and white repression have been seen and heard before in this country.

It is time now to end the destruction and the violence, not only in the streets of the ghetto but in the lives of people.

Learn and Burn, Brothers

REVOLUTION: A DEFINITION

(Excerpted from a speech Black History: 1940–1967)

Nations are characterized not by what they say, but by what they do. Fascism is defined in part by a standing army. It is defined in part by extreme wealth and extreme poverty. It is defined in part by government support of business. Fascism is defined in part by government support of racism. Fascism is defined in part by oligarchy government. Fascism is defined in part by marching boots, waving flags, and shooting guns. Fascism is defined in part by well planned, well executed coups. Fascism was defined

Antiriot Bill—1967, Hearings Before the Committee on the Judiciary, United States Senate, 90th Cong. 1st Sess., H.R. 421. August 2, 3, 4, 7, 10 and 11, 1967. U.S. Government Printing Office, Washington, D.C., pp. 31–36; 81.

in part by Germany. It has been refined by the United States. We are living in a Fascist nation, ruled by an oligarchy which got its power by a coup. We are living in a nation that has a standing army of mercenaries because the army is the only job available for most poor people—Black and white. We are living in a nation where government is the biggest single consumer and employer. We are living in a nation that distributes its wealth in such a way that some get all and some get none. We are living in a nation where racism was written in its constitution and extermination is in its soul. We are living in a Fascist nation, brothers and sisters and we have got to understand what that means. Germany exterminated the Jews there, or at least made a valiant effort. The United States exterminated native Americans, called Indians by white people, or at least made a valiant effort. The United States will exterminate the Black people here, or at least make a valiant effort. 60 to 80 million died in Middle Passage. The Algonquins, the Iroquois, the native inhabitants of New England, coastal Virginia, Georgia, the majority of the native Floridians were exterminated. The Plains People, the Sioux, the Black Foot, the Apache, the myriad other plain folk now numbered among the many thousand gone. We have got to look at the root to identify the fruit. A bunch of murderers, thieves, gamblers, prostitutes and religious fanatics settled this land 300 years ago. A bunch of slave holder land speculators and petty bourgeoise made up the first government. Vampires, every one of them. Sucking the land for minerals, sucking our blood for labor. Some were just mosquitoes—a little bug spray and they were gone; some were bats, turn the light on them and they were immobilized. But some were real vampires like the ones we read about in scary books. Some we didn't recognize as dangerous. Some when we turned the light on looked like humans and when they crept into our beds at night we didn't realize that they had bitten us—turned us into non-living things that only looked like humans. We didn't know that we too had become vampires sucking the blood of our blood, eating the flesh of our own flesh. But Brother Malcolm knew. He saw that we were becoming non-human; that we were hustling each other; that we were degrading each other—and he told us about it. Kennedy knew. He saw that white people were non-human. He tried to tell his people about it and they lynched him. Malcolm tried to tell us and we lynched him. Just as Frederick Douglas made Lincoln the white statesman of the 19th century, so Malcolm was making Kennedy the white statesman of the 20th. Both were cut down by their own flesh, by their own blood. It does not matter, though it is worth noting, that the same paymaster handled both bills, there should not have been a Black piper to play that tune. Black folk can't afford to dance if the tune is Black Death. And if whitey is calling the tune the rhythm is always Black Death, Black Death, Black Death. We have got to understand that we are living in a country that wants to kill us.

We've heard many people say: Give us our rights or exterminate us. That is not my cry. Move Over or I'll Move Over You. I Will Take My Rights or I Will Destroy You. Isn't that nicer? Doesn't that have a better ring to it? That's what Malcolm was saying. Civil rights are meaningless. You are born with them or you acquire them with naturalization. We were born here. If we don't have Civil Rights by now you can believe we won't ever have them. We must organize for our human rights. We must organize to reorganize this country. This is our land and we must take it. I'm talking about Revolution now. World wide Black Revolution. That's what Malcolm was talking about. He was talking about getting guns from China. That's what we have to talk about. He was talking about learning African languages, African customs. He was talking about knowing the Black nations that make up Asia and refusing to go fight them. He was talking about world wide Black Revolution.

Here in Cincinnati we recently had a rebellion. We fought well. We showed we could rebel. Now we must move to Revolution. Revolution is in part Revelation. The revealing of our sweet Black lives to ourselves. Revolution is the wiping out of all that blocks our revelation. Revolution is the destruction, not blindly but very carefully planned and executed, of all that stands in our way. Procedure, law, order, white folks, Black Anglo-Saxons, our emotions, our fears, our loves, our hates, everything that stands in the way of complete Revolution must be eradicated. The preachers who preach the lie, the teachers who teach it. All must go until the world is encased in a Black Flame of life, liberty and the pursuit of happiness.

Sometimes Revolution is burning a store, sometimes its building one; sometimes Revolution is quitting school, sometimes its enrolling; sometimes its taking a job, sometimes its quitting one; sometimes its love, sometimes its hate, but always Revolution is lonely. Whether leader or led, whether workhouse or Rockdale and Reading, whether you get hostility and rejection or love and understanding you are always alone. Don't start playing with Revolution unless you are prepared to be out in the streets when everyone else says Let's Negotiate. Don't play with Revolution unless you are prepared to sleep alone, eat alone, work alone, cry alone, fight alone, be tired alone, sit in jail alone. Don't play with Revolution unless you are prepared to watch your best friend marry your best girl because you don't have the time to give her, unless you are prepared to watch your wife walk out on you because you don't have time to hold a job, unless you are prepared to watch your mother turn her back on you and your father curse you, unless you are prepared to give all of yourself to a total Revolution. Revolution knows no compromise. Revolution is not a new white toy, it is Black survival and Black survival, brothers and sisters, is no white game. We have got to understand that they aren't playing.

Of all our studies, to quote Brother Malcolm, History is best qualified to reward all research. Our job now is not Revolution, but steps toward it. Learn and burn, brothers. Learn and burn.

NIKKI GIOVANNI.

TESTIMONY OF BRYCE KINNAMON, CHIEF OF POLICE, CAMBRIDGE, MD.

MR. KINNAMON. Yes, sir.

THE CHAIRMAN. You also had incidents on July 28?

MR. KINNAMON. Yes, sir.

THE CHAIRMAN. Speak a little louder, sir.

MR. KINNAMON. Yes, sir.

THE CHAIRMAN. About what area did it cover?

MR. KINNAMON. Well, the actual riot covered about a block.

THE CHAIRMAN. Now, you also had a riot in 1963, is that correct?

MR. KINNAMON. Yes, sir.

SENATOR DIRKSEN. Mr. Chairman, I did not hear.

MR. KINNAMON. The mike doesn't seem to be working.

THE CHAIRMAN. Tell us exactly what happened.

MR. KINNAMON. Well, several weeks prior to this riot there had been an effort made in Cambridge to organize, and we had several incendiary fires set. None of these fires amounted to anything. It was minor, and they were controlled very quickly by the local fire departments. There were various meetings held, but they were unable to organize. I think it would be safe to say that 15 to 25 were in attendance at these meetings, and several of the meetings had to be canceled because of lack of attendance, and there was a splinter group which formed an organization called CAF, that is Cambridge Action Federation. They invited Rap Brown into Cambridge to make a speech on the 24th. This speech was scheduled to begin at 8 p.m. Did not show up in Cambridge until about 9:30.

He made a very inflammatory speech which I have the tape here, and also have a transcript of this speech. When his speech was finished, they gathered at the headquarters of this CAF and Rap Brown led a group of people toward the business district of Cambridge. While they were marching, our intelligence reports that he was instructing them to burn and tear Cambridge down, to shoot any policeman who tried to interfere or any people, policemen regardless of whether they were black or white.

I had my men deployed on the main business district. We had information that this group was traveling toward the main district down Elm Street.

THE CHAIRMAN. You have his speech there?

MR. KINNAMON. Yes, sir.

THE CHAIRMAN. Transcription?

MR. KINNAMON. Yes, sir.

THE CHAIRMAN. Will you play it?

(The complete speech referred to follows:)

A poem went . . . said: "What happens to a dream that were? Does it dry up like a raisin in the sun? Or does it fester like a sore—and then run? Or does it sag like a heavy load? Or does it explode?" Uh . . . that question was never answered. Detroit answers that question. Detroit exploded. New York exploded. Harlem exploded. Dayton exploded. Cincinnati exploded. It's time for Cambridge to explode, ladies and gentlemen!

They say "If Dayton don't come around, we are gonna burn Dayton down." Black folks built America. If America don't come around, we going burn it down, brother. We are going to burn it down if we don't get our share of it.

It's time black folks stopped talking about being non-violent 'cause we ain't non-violent towards each other. Every Friday and Saturday you prove that. You cut up more people among your race than any other race. As for being violent, you don't be violent to your brother. Be non-violent in your communities and let it end right there.

"Take your violence to the honkeys. Take it to the (loud cheering blurred word).

It takes a lot of effort . . . It takes a lot of effort to love black in America. You've been told all your life if you're black, you're wrong. If you're black, there's something wrong with you. They tell you black cows don't give good milk; black hens don't lay eggs. Devil's food cakes. You know, you put on black to go to funerals. When you put on white you go to weddings. They talk about flesh-colored band-aids. You ain't never seen a black-flesh-colored band-aid. So they tell you there's something wrong with being black.

You've got to be proud of being black. You've got to be proud of being black. You can't run around here calling yourself colored. And calling yourself Negroes. That's a word the honkies gave you. You're black, brother, and be proud of it. It's beautiful to be black. Black folks got to understand that. We built this country. They tell you you're lazy. They tell you you stink. Brother, you realize what the state be of this country if we was lazy. We built this country. They captured us in Africa and brought us over here to work for them. Now, who's lazy?

He walks around and tells you: "You lazy." You don't want to work. All you want to do is lay around. Hell! You can't do nothing but lay down after he done work you to death. I tell you what—first thing I'm (   ) representing the change gonna come. Now we got to make the change come, see? 'Cause it's our job. Now, my mother. She worked from kin to kate every day of her life. My old man Tommed so I wouldn't have to. Brother, the streets belong to us. We got to take them.

They ain't gonna give it to us. We got to take 'em. There ain't no reason in the world why on the other side of Race Street the honky pecker-wood owns all the stores. If I can't control my community over here, he ain't gonna control his over there.

They run around and tell you: "Don't start no fight with the honky pecker 'cause he can't win. He outnumber you. Hell! Don't you know they always outnumber us. David was outnumbered when he fought the lions. He was outnumbered. Daniel in the lion's den, when he fought the lion; Moses was outnumbered. All of us is outnumbered. That don't make no difference. 'Cause let me tell you, brother, we work in their houses. They ain't got to leave home. When they want to do work they let us come in their house and that shows you how stupid the honky is. Cause he ain't got to leave home.

And we look at what the man does to black people. A ten-year old boy in Newark is dead! A 19-year old boy shot 39 times, 4 times in the head. It don't take but one bullet to kill you. So they're really trying to tell you something else. How much they hate you. How much they hate black folks. When they shot him 39 times they said: "Die, nigger, die." And they shot him some more. 19-years old—he's dead today. But we go over to Vietnam and fight the races crapper war. We got to be crazy. Something's got to be wrong with black men. Our war is here.

If I can die defending my Mother land, I can die defending my mother. And that's what I'm going to die defending first. See, you are less than a man if you can't defend your mother, your brother and your family. You ain't doing nothing, brother. That war over there in Vietnam is not the war of the black man. This is our war.

You've got to understand what they are doing, though. America has laid out a plan to eliminate all black people who go against them. America is killing people down south by starving them to death in Alabama. Babies die. 500 people die a year for lack of food and nourishment. And yet we got enough money to go to the moon. Think about that. People in New York and Harlem die from rife and bites to death. Big old rats bite them to death and you tell the man about it and the honkey say: "Hell, man, we can't do nothing about them rats." Do you realize this is the same man who exterminated the buffalo? He killed the buffalo. Hell, if he wanted to kill the rats he could do it.

See, all this stuff is called genocide. This is what the Germans did to the Jews. They got black folks minds so they goin' kill you off and you won't rebel. You won't do nothing but sit back and let them kill you off and that's what they're doing. They're killing you off. And they're escalating it. They're moving it up to kill as many black folks as they can. You look at what happens when a brother goes to that war to fight. Do you realize the casualty rate? It's 30% black. That means that 30% of everybody that goes to Vietnam and gets killed is black. They tell us we just 10% of the United States. Something's wrong with their statistics. Something's wrong with their numbers. They say the brother who in Vietnam comprise 22% of that fighting force and we 10% over here. You got to look at they killing you off.

And they killing off the black young men, so ladies, you better get ready. You got to fight them, too. You got no business letting your brother, your sons, your nephews go to that war. That ain't your war. All right, you'd better get you some guns. You's better get you some guns. The man's moving to kill you. And the only thing the honkey respects is force. He proved this up there in Plainfield, New Jersey. Let me tell you what he did in Newark. He killed 24 people. That's too many people to lose. We ain't got no business losing 24 people. But in Plainfield, which is about 12 miles from Newark, the brothers broke in some stores and stole themselves some guns. They stole them some guns. They stole 46 guns. That ain't stealing. How can you steal from a thief? He's done stole everything from us.

He run around and he talks about black people looting. Hell, he the biggest looter in the world. He looted us from Africa. He looted America from the Indians. Man can you tell me about looting? You can't steal from a thief. This is the biggest thief going. So don't you worry about, but look what the brothers did in Plainfield. The brothers got their stuff. They got 46 automatic weapons. So the peckerwood goes down there to take the weapons and they stomp one of them to death. They stomp the cop to death. Good. He's dead! They stomped him to death. They stomped him. You all might think that's brutal, but it ain't no more brutal than killing a pregnant woman. And that's what the honkey does. He kill pregnant black women. They stomped him to death and threw a shopping basket on his head, took his pistol and shot him and then cut him. You know he was hurt. They don't like to hear about niggers cutting. They don't never want to hear about niggers cutting. But they cut. And they went back to their community with their 46 weapons and they told that peckerwood cop, they say: "Don't you come into my community." We going to control our community. And the peckerwood cop says: "Huh, well, we got to come down there and get them weapons." The brothers told him, "Don't come in my community." He didn't come. And the only reason he didn't come is he didn't want to get killed. And the brothers had the material to do it. They had 46 carbines down there. That's what he respects. Power. He respect that kind of power. So, the next day they were looking back across the country, so they say, well, we going to go down there and take them guns. We going to search the houses. So the brothers say, "Cool." And they hid the guns. And they say we'll go down there and look. So, when he went down there he started kicking down doors and tearing up brothers' property. And the brothers saw what was going on and the brothers told him: "If you kick down one more door, I'm going to shoot your leg off." And look what the honky did. He left. That's the kind of force he respects.

Brothers, you've got to get some guns. I don't care if its B-B guns with poisoned B-Bs. He's done declared war on black people. He don't mind killing them. It might be your son he kills next. Or it might be your daughter. Or it might be you. So, wherever you go, brother, take some of them with you. That's what you do, brother. An eye for an eye; a tooth for a tooth. Tit for tat, brother, that's the only kind of war that man knows. That's the only thing he recognizes. Ain't no need in the world for me to come to Cambridge and I see all them stores sitting up there and all them honkies owns them. You got to own some of them stores. I don't care if you have to burn him down and run him out. You'd better take over them stores. The streets are yours. Take 'em. They gave you the streets a long time ago; before they gave you houses. They gave you the streets. So, we own the streets. Take 'em. You've got to take 'em. They ain't going to give them to you.

Freedom is not a welfare commodity. It ain't like that old bad food they give you. They can't give you no freedom. You got to take your freedom. You were born free. You got to exercise that right though, brother, cause the honkey got you where he wants you.

You making money for him. If you make money for that honkey, you don't make money for yourself. You make money for him and then take it back to him. And he takes it to his community. And he lets you live over here amidst your roaches, your rats, and mosquitoes. And he lives over home. Then he comes back. You see that school over there—I don't know whether the honkey burned that school or not but y'all should have burned that school a long time ago. You should have burned it down to the ground. Ain't no need in the world, in 1967, to see a school like that sitting over there. You should have burned it down and then go take over the honkey's school. Go take over his school. He burned down your Elks home because he didn't want you out there doing no dancing and stuff. He wants you to go home and suffer the whole summer. He wants you to sit in them hot houses and say, see what we can do to you when we get ready. He controls you niggers. That's what he's been telling you and you been sitting back there saying, "Yassuh, Yassuh." You been sitting back there telling him: "Yassuh, y'all control us." They gave you 5 nigger cops who can't whip nothing but black heads.

You've got to understand, that's part of that man's trick. Ye ain't making no progress cause them niggers ain't walking but in a car. They think they're making progress, brother. They ain't making no progress. Not when they can't whip no honkeys.

You got to understand. You got to know that, all your enemies ain't white. You got some black enemies, too. And when you find your enemies, brother, you got to get rid of him, just like you get rid of the honkeys. Now if these cops down here, if they ain't doing what you want them to do, they ought to be in their community. If they ain't doing what you want them to, then they shouldn't be in the community. Put 'em out of the community. You got the power. If a black cop whips a black brother and they ain't got not more than one car. I know they ain't going to give him no more than one car. They're supposed to be walking, cause from then on I'm going to burn his car up. I know the white man ain't going to give him no other car so that means he is going to be walking. Every time he walks I'm going to bomb him with some bricks. I'm going to run him out of town cause he ain't got no business here. He ain't nothing but a handkerchief-head nigger. A handkerchief-head nigger! He doing what the honkey wants him to do. And that's what all black people do. You got to fight that man. We ain't behind in terms of manhood, brother; we behind in terms of executing him. If a man runs around and lets a honkey cop, or a black cop, beat his wife * * * and he don't do nothing, when his wife gets out of jail and goes home she oughta beat him. People laughed a few years ago when an organization called the Deacons for Defense came up. Brother, you got to get yourself a whole bunch of Deacons for Defense. Cause if you don't you got to get some sisters and some ushers for defense. Cause the man is moving. He's moving to kill black people. He might be doing it one by one but you look at it. In Newark, they lost 24. Beautiful thing about Detroit, they ain't lost but two and they killed three peckerwoods. Three peckerwoods. That's tit for tat.

They burned down over a hundred million dollars worth of that peckerwood's property and that his god. Money is his god. Don't you let him tell you the church and the Bible is his god. You look at what he do, man. Who leads the prisoner to the electric chair? The preacher, And he say "Thou shalt not kill." A preacher! That's the way the man's mind works. That's the way it works. He don't think nothing of black folks. All you can do for the honkey is work for him, him and spend your money in his stores.

That's all he wants you to do. He don't even want to see you no other time. He don't want to see you. But, brother, he done told you black is bad and he believes it. But he don't know how bad black is until you show him. Black is bad, brother. Get that! Black is bad.

But you ain't knowing how black bad is. Until the brothers get their minds together and start moving on that man. You got to start talking about taking your community and controlling it. You got to control everything in your community from your Elk Hall to your school to your barroom. You got to control that. Cause if you can't control it, you see it's a weapon against you. Anything you don't control in your community is a weapon. Public education is a weapon. Cause they're teaching people how to hate black. They're teaching little children how to hate black. They're putting in their old stinky history books that Columbus discovered America. How in the world is some dumb honkey going to discover a country with people living there? There Indian was here, but he was saying * * * he was saying that the Indian ain't human cause he ain't white. So, the country didn't begin until we discovered it. And Columbus was looking for India. To show you how dumb he was, did you ever look where India was on the map? Columbus was the white Joe Louis. That's who he was. He was the white Joe Louis. He didn't know nothing. He tells you that George Washington is the father of the country and you should celebrate his birthday. And you do. George Washington had slaves. He had your grandfathers, and your great-grandfathers and their great-grandfathers. They were his slaves. How he going to be the father of my country? That's a lot of junk, brother.

He don't mean nothing to me. He just another dumb honkey. Abraham Lincoln. They tell you all niggers should love Abraham Lincoln. Love him for what? The only reason he gave, he declared war against the north, is cause they were losing money. He didn't dig no black folks. He didn't like you. But they got stuff down there in their history books and you read it and you believe it. You run out there and celebrate their birthday. The Fourth of July. Independence Day, and we still in chains. See, ain't no such thing as second-class citizenship, brother; you either free or you slave. Don't run around here telling nobody you citizens. How many black mayors has Cambridge got? None. Not none. How many black councilmen has Cambridge got?

All you got is five nigger cops. Them 5 cops ain't even working for you. If you was to go and march down Race Street tonight, the first one hit you in the head, try to lose all the strength in his stick in your head, is going to be my man. See people running around. Yeah, they got a whole bunch of Uncle Toms and you better watch them. But let me tell you what to do with Uncle Toms. Of course, the white man hates niggers so bad, when he moves he moves against everybody. He moves against everybody,—Uncle Toms included. One day you going to wake up one morning and be an Uncle Tom knocking on your door saying: "Let me in, man." You know what you do? Open your door and give him a gun and tell him to shoot some of them. And if he shoots some of them, he can come in. If he shoots a whole bunch of them, he can come in my house.

But, brother, the man hates everything black. Everything black but black Cadillacs and black shoes. Everything else black he ain't got nothing else to do with.

Now, we're gonna talk about Lyndon Johnson. Lyndon Johnson is the greatest outlaw going. He is a two-gun cracker. He's killing black folks here and he's killing them in Vietnam. Thay's Lyndon Johnson, your President. That's who he is. And they talk about how bad Hitler was. At least before Hitler burned the Jews he killed them with gas. Lyndon Johnson is throwing napalm on human beings in Vietnam. Burning them to death. He's burning babies. He's burning hospitals. He can't be nothing but an outlaw. Any time a man sends a plane full of napalm over a village of children, over school-houses, and blow 'em up, and burn children, believe me, brother, the only reason he do it, brother, is because the Viet Cong is black, too.

You are going to have to start studying your history. You going to have to understand that black folks is not a minority. We got more black folks across the world than we got white people. You got to start looking at China like brothers, because they are yellow people. Viet Cong. Some of the Viet Congs are browner than some of us. They get . . . India. Indians are dark skinned people. These are the colored people of the world. These are the black people of the world. That's the third world they be talking about. Now, the honkey is surrounded. He is surrounded. He don't know what to do. But, brother, be-lieve me, he knows what to do here because you let him do it. See, he done renovated 26 concentration camps across the world. If you don't know what a concentration camp is, let me run it down. You read about all them Jews that got burned up by Hitler. They burned 'em up, they taken them to con-centration camps. And then they took them from the concentration camps to the ovens. Told them they were gonna get showers and then they turned on the gas and took them out to a furnace and burned them.

Now, America done renovated 26 and they ain't for the Indians, cause they on reservations. Now, think who it's for. All right, now that you know who it's for, look at the way we were then four years ago. We were so non-violent it wasn't funny. Cause the white man told us we had to be non-vio-lent and he would love us. And we believe it. All the while he was shooting us, he was telling us to love him to death. And we believed it. A few years ago, if the honkey President had sent out a letter with the President's seal on it saying report to concentration camps at 9 o'clock in the morning, every nigger in America would have been there on time. And to follow that same thing, he'd tell you cause he knows you love religion, see. He'd tell you to go in there and be baptized and he'd turn the gas on you. I mean, don't . . . religion is good.

I met a lady in Alabama once who said: "Prayers is good in prayer meet-ings but it ain't worth a damn in bear meetings." Brother, you need the bear every day. You need the animals. You need the animal every day. He runs around and he tells you how bad you are but how violent that man. He tells you not to be violent. A few weeks ago, in the Bowery—that's where all the poor, poor, trashy, honky peckerwoods live—who ain't got no money they live in the Bowery, but look what happened: Some young honkeys went over and poured gas on these people and set them on fire. Bums, drunkards. They set 'em on fire. That's violence. The white man don't never look at that. Vietnam is violence. But soon as you go out there and burn down a few old filthy stores, that you own anyway, the man say you trying to be violent. We ain't trying to be violent with him. He knows all about violence. He taught us how to be violent. But we been using our violence in the wrong way. We been using violence against each other. Ain't no need in the world for black people have to fight each other. You ain't got no business in the world hating your brother. I don't care if he makes you mad. If my brother makes me mad, I'm going to go look for a honkey.

I'm going to take out 400 years' worth of dues on him, too. Every time you hit one of them take out 400 years' worth of dues, cause that's the dues he owes you for knowing you and owing you. So every time you catch him, brother, you do it to him.

And don't let him come into your community. Ain't got no reason for white folks to be leisurely walking up and down your community. He's got no business coming over, talking about taking black women out of your community. You ain't a man if you let that animal come over here and take a black woman out of your community. To do what he want to do with her. And that's what he's doing. He doing what he want to do with her. Brother, it's up to you to stop that. You don't need God to stop that. You can stop that. See, God gave you two arms, two legs and everything he gave the honkey, but the honkey's been using his. You ain't been using yours.

He's been running around here letting them do everything they want. I mean, don't be trying to love that honkey to death. Shoot him to death. Shoot him to death, brother. 'Cause that's what he's out to do to you. Like I said in the beginning, if this town don't come round, this town should be burned down. It should be burned down, brother. They're going to have to live in the same stuff I live in 'cause I ain't going to make it no better for them. But do this brother—don't burn up your own stuff. Don't tear up your own stuff. Whenever you decide to fight the man, take it to his battleground. It's one thing that man respects. Its money. That's his god. When you tear down his store, you hit his religion. You hit him right where it hurts him on Sunday. In his pocket. That's the only god that man's got. In his pocket. That's his best friend. In his pocket. So, when you move to get him, don't tear up your stuff, don't tear up your brother's stuff, hear?

THE CHAIRMAN. I think the whole text should be put in the record. It was that speech that instigated the riot in your town, was it not, Chief?

MR. KINNAMON. Yes, sir.

THE CHAIRMAN. And Brown there had been charged and arrested and is now out on bond?

MR. KINNAMON. Yes, sir.

. . .

Chapter Thirteen

SUGGESTED QUESTIONS FOR CLASS DISCUSSION.

1. *The Report of the National Advisory Commission on Civil Disorders* has made it clear that violence is now accepted as a form of political action by an alarming number of people. Do you think that rigid enforcement of "law and order" will be able to control such violence in the future?
2. What kind of short-run programs might be effective in forestalling further rioting while long-run programs are being formulated?
3. Do you think that warnings by the Commission and others that more violence is in store will bring about a widespread change in attitude which the Commission believes is essential to efforts to correct the evils of the ghetto?
4. Do you think that most Americans really abhor violence? Are they really deeply concerned if the violence is no immediate threat to their own safety? Do they react more strongly when violence is committed by Negroes than when committed by whites such as the Klan?

Chapter Fourteen

THE MAKING OF FOREIGN AND MILITARY POLICY

There are over 125 nations in the world, scores of international organizations, and various other kinds of actors on the international scene. At any given moment a substantial number of them will be considering actions that the United States must be concerned with and may need to respond to. This means that the machinery that produces American foreign and military policy must generate a continuing flow of decisions—wise decisions, let us hope—on matters great and small. In an era of intercontinental ballistics missiles and thermonuclear warheads, there is little margin for error. A serious failure of judgment on the part of American leadership or a breakdown in its policy-making machinery could have catastrophic consequences.

How is American foreign policy made? To what extent can and should the public be brought into the making of foreign and military policy? What is the role of the press? What is the proper role of Congress? Is it inevitable that the President and Congress be at odds with one another over foreign policy? The cases in this chapter have been selected to throw light on these and other issues.

The Path to Vietnam: A Lesson in Involvement

William P. Bundy,

ASSISTANT SECRETARY OF STATE
FOR EAST ASIAN AND PACIFIC AFFAIRS,
DELIVERED BEFORE THE NATIONAL STUDENT
ASSOCIATION, UNIVERSITY OF MARYLAND,
COLLEGE PARK, MARYLAND, AUGUST 15, 1967

You have asked me to speak this morning on the topic: "The Path to Viet-Nam: A Lesson in Involvement." I welcome this opportunity to review the whole history of United States actions with respect to Viet-Nam—speaking personally as to the period up to 1961, during which I had no policy responsibility, and of course necessarily more officially for the period since January of 1961.

Quite apart from the enormous present importance of South Viet-Nam and our actions there, I have often reflected—as one who was tempted to become a professional historian—that the story of Viet-Nam, of Southeast Asia, and of American policy there forms an etxraordinarily broad case history involving almost all the major problems that have affected the world as a whole in the past 25 years. For the strands of the Viet-Nam history include the characteristics of French colonial control compared to colonial control elsewhere, the end of the colonial period, the inter-relation and competition of nationalism and Communism, our relation to the Soviet Union and Communist China and their relationships with each other, our relation to the European colonial power—France, and—at least since 1954—the relation of Viet-Nam to the wider question of national independence and self-determination in Southeast Asia and indeed throughout Asia.

The Viet-Nam story is above all a product of Vietnamese aspirations and decisions. In the early period, French decisions were crucial. But I am sure you want me to focus on the American policy role, how and why we became involved, and how we reached the present position. This should not be a purely historical discussion, of course, and I know that you have natural and valid concerns that focus particularly on the decisions of the last two years and on the decisions that confront us now and in the future. So I shall touch briefly on these, fully expecting that your questions will be quite largely in this area.

For our mutual convenience in analysis, I have tried to isolate 10 major American decisions, going back to 1945. It is not for me to defend, or necessarily to justify, policy decisions taken before 1961, but it is essential to examine them if one is to understand the present position.

Our first decisions affecting Viet-Nam were in 1945. President Roosevelt deeply believed that French colonial control in Indochina should not be

"The Path to Vietnam," *Vital Speeches of the Day*, Vol. XXXIII, No. 23, September 15, 1967. Reprinted by permission of the publisher.

restored, and this attitude led us, in the closing months of the war against militarist Japan, to adopt what the French have always considered an obstructive attitude toward their return. Separately, we briefly gave modest assistance to Ho Chi Minh as an asset against the Japanese. This story, like so much else in the whole record, is best told in Robert Shaplen's thoughtful "The Lost Revolution."

Second, when the French had returned, we stood aside. In the critical year 1946, and over the next 3–4 years, the French first made the Fontainebleau Agreement and then broke it so that major conflict started. It has often been argued, by Shaplen among others, that we could have exerted greater pressure, perhaps even effective pressure, on the French to go through with the Fontainebleau Agreement and to set Viet-Nam on the path to early independence. The failure to exert such pressure may thus be construed as a negative policy decision on our part.

I myself am skeptical that we could conceivably have affected the unfortunate course that the French followed in this period. If it is argued that our overwhelming Marshall Plan aid to France should have given us leverage, then it must be pointed out at the same time that the Marshall Plan became operative only early in 1948 and that by then the die was largely cast. Moreover, I doubt very much if the proud and bruised French nation would have responded even if we had tried to act to end the colonial era, as we did to a major extent with the Dutch in Indonesia.

In a very real sense, the tragedy of Viet-Nam derives from the fall of France in 1940 and all the understandable emotions aroused by that event among French leaders, including notably de Gaulle himself. Restored control in Indochina was a badge, however mistaken, for a France that meant to be once again a world power. Although it may be argued that we should at least have tried, I doubt if this deep French attitude could have been shaken by anything we did or said, and least of all by anything said or done in connection with the wise and right policy of helping France to get back on her feet.

The third period of American decision began in 1950, just before our involvement in the defense of Korea against Soviet-inspired aggression. The Communists had just taken control in China and entered into the 1950 alliance with the Soviet Union. Communism did then appear to our policy makers as something approaching a monolith, and we came to see the French stand in Indochina as part of a global attempt to repel Communist military adventures. In essence, we acted on two lines of policy between 1950 and 1954—on the one hand, economic and growing military assistance to the French, on the other hand steady urging that the French proceed rapidly to grant real independence to Indochina, both for its own sake and as the best means of preventing Communist control.

Here it has been argued that we did too much assisting or at least too little urging. I find myself sympathetic to this point of view, as indeed it was expressed at the time by such wise men as Edmund Gullion, who served in Viet-Nam and much later became our distinguished Ambassador in the Congo from 1961 to 1963.

Yet, again, I am not sure whether a different United States policy in this period could have brought about the desired result of a France first successfully waging a costly and bloody war to defend Viet-Nam and then granting it independence. Again, French attitudes and actions had deep roots in the still shaky situation of France, and in the combination of a valid concern for the Communist threat and a desire to maintain a major French presence and hold in Indochina. Even if the French had acted wisely in every respect in this period, they might have been able to achieve nothing more than a division of the country into Communist and non-Communist areas. The vital difference might have been that valid non-Communist nationalism in Viet-Nam would have had a chance to stand on its feet and develop respected leaders before 1954, and if this had happened the whole later story might have unfolded in a very different way.

As it was, the spring of 1954 brought French defeat, in spirit if not in military terms, and left non-Communist nationalism in Viet-Nam almost bankrupt.

The period of the Geneva Conference is the fourth period of American decision. That is a complex story, well told from a relatively detached viewpoint by Anthony Eden, now Lord Avon, in his memoirs.

We played a critical backstage role at Geneva. We maintained the possibility of military intervention, which many observers at the time believe played a crucial part in inducing the Soviets and the Communist Chinese alike to urge Hanoi to settle for a temporary division of Viet-Nam at the 17th parallel and for an independent Cambodia and Laos. And we began to lay the groundwork for SEATO, as part of the effort to show strength and to convince Communist China that it would not have a free hand in Southeast Asia.

Yet we were unwilling to participate fully in the framing of the Geneva Accords, apparently because our policy makers did not wish to associate themselves in any way with a loss of territory to Communist control. So the Geneva Accords were framed largely between Hanoi, Communist China and the Soviet Union on the one side and the French, who were under the urgent time pressure of their domestic politics on the other. In the end, we confined ourselves to saying two things:

a. That we would view any aggression in violation of the Accords with grave concern and as seriously threatening international peace and security.

b. That we took the same position on the reunification of Viet-Nam that we took in other "nations now divided against their will"—meaning, then and now, Germany and Korea—and that we would continue to seek unity through free elections supervised by the United Nations. In effect, we thus interpreted the election provision as providing for a free determination by the people of Viet-Nam as to whether they wished reunification, and in that sense endorsed it consistently with the similar positions we had taken in Germany and Korea.

All sorts of things could be said about our decisions in that period. Some are of the view that we should have taken military action and tried to nail down at least a clear military division of Viet-Nam, or even to defeat Ho; I myself think that by the spring of 1954 that course would have been untenable.

It may also be argued—and I do not know the contemporary factors—that, involved as we already were by preceding decisions, we should have participated forthrightly in the making of the Accords and lent our weight to them from the outset, declaring right then that we meant to stand— with the French if possible, but alone if necessary—in supporting non-Communist nationalism in South Viet-Nam. We would then have acted as we had done for non-Communist nationalism in Korea, although without its being necessary or desirable for us to put continuing forces on the ground as we had to do in the face of the conventional threat to Korea.

At any rate, in July 1954 a new national entity came into being in South Viet-Nam with what appeared at the time to be extraordinarily small chances of survival. At the very end, the French, with a degree of American pressure, installed the staunchly nationalist Diem as Prime Minister, hardly thinking that he would survive and looking rather to a short period in which the French could exit with some semblance of grace and let nature take its course.

The fifth set of American decisions came in this setting, and indeed overlapped the period of the Geneva Conference. The first aspect of these decisions was our leading role in the formation of the SEATO Treaty, signed at Manila in September of 1954 and ratified by our Senate in February, 1955, by a vote of 82–1. In the SEATO Treaty, South Viet-Nam and its territory were specifically included as a "protocol state," and the signatories specifically accepted the obligation, if asked by the Government of South Viet-Nam, to take action in response to armed attack against South Viet-Nam and to consult on appropriate measures if South Viet-Nam were subjected to subversive actions. The Geneva Accords had of course already expressly forbidden aggressive acts from either half of Viet-Nam against the other half, but there had been no obligation for action by the Geneva participating nations. SEATO created a new and serious obligation extending to South Viet-Nam and aimed more widely at the security of the Southeast Asian signatories and the successor states of Indochina.

The second aspect of our decisions at this period was an evolving one. In late 1954 President Eisenhower committed us to furnish economic support for the new regime, in which Diem was already showing himself tougher and more able than anyone had supposed possible. And in early 1955, without any formal statement, we began to take over the job of military assistance to South Viet-Nam, acting within the numerical and equipment limitations stated in the Geneva Accords for foreign military aid.

In short, in the 1954–55 period, we moved into a major supporting role and undertook a major treaty commitment involving South Viet-Nam.

These decisions, I repeat, are not mine to defend. In the mood of the period, still deeply affected by a not unjustified view of monolithic Communism, they were accepting with very wide support in the United States, as the vote and the debate in the Senate abundantly proved. And the Senate documents prove conclusively that there was full understanding of the grave implications of the SEATO obligations, particularly as they related to aggression by means of armed attack.

The important point about these decisions—and a point fervently debated within the Administration at the time, according to many participants—is that they reflected a policy not merely toward Viet-Nam but toward the whole of Southeast Asia. In essence, the underlying basic issue was felt, and I think rightly, to be whether the United States should involve itself much more directly in the security of Southeast Asia and the preservation of the largely new nations that had come into being there since World War II.

There could not be the kind of clear-cut policy for Southeast Asia that by then evolved in Northeast Asia, where we had entered into mutual security treaties individually with Japan, Korea, and the Republic of China. Some of the Southeast Asian countries wished no association with an outside power; others—Malaya, Singapore, and the northern areas of Borneo, which were not then independent, continued to rely on the British and the Commonwealth. So the directly affected area in which policy could operate comprised only Thailand, the Philippines, and the non-Communist successor states of Indochina—South Viet-Nam, Laos, and Cambodia.

Yet it was felt at the time that unless the United States participated in a major way in preserving the independence and security of these nations, they would be subject to progressive pressures by the parallel efforts of North Viet-Nam and Communist China.

The judgment that this threat of aggression was real and valid was the first basis of the policy adopted. Two other judgments that lay behind the policy were:

a. That a successful takeover by North Viet-Nam or Communist China of any of the directly affected nations would not only be serious in itself, but would drastically weaken and in a short time destroy the capacity of the other nations of Southeast Asia, whatever their international postures, to maintain their own independence.

b. That, while we ourselves had no wish for a special position in Southeast Asia, the transfer of the area, or large parts of it, to Communist control achieved by subversion and aggression would mean a major addition to the power status of hostile and aggressive Communist Chinese and North Vietnamese regimes. It was believed that such a situation would not only doom the peoples of the area to conditions of domination and virtual servitude over an indefinite period, but would create the very kind of aggressive domination of much of Asia that we had already fought the militarist leaders of Japan to prevent. It was widely and deeply believed that such a situation was profoundly contrary to our national interests.

But there was still a third supporting judgment that, like the others, ran through the calculations of the period. This was that the largely new nations of Southeast Asia were in fact valid national entities and that, while their progress might be halting and imperfect both politically and economically, this progress was worth backing. To put it another way, there was a constructive vision of the kind of Southeast Asia that could evolve, and a sense that this constructive purpose was worth pursuing as a matter of our own ideals, as a matter of our national interest, and as a realistic hope of the possibilities of progress if external aggression and subversion could be held at bay.

These I believe to have been the bedrock reasons for the position we took in Viet-Nam and Southeast Asia at this time. They were overlaid by what may appear to have been emotional factors in our attitude toward Communism in China and Asia. But the degree of support that this major policy undertaking received at the time went far beyond those who held these emotions. And this is why I for one believe that the bedrock reasons I have given were the true and decisive ones.

So the United States became deeply involved in the security of Southeast Asia and, wherever it was welcomed, in the effort to achieve economic progress as well. And the undertaking to support South Viet-Nam economically and militarily and through the Protocol to the SEATO Treaty must be seen as a part of the wide view that the choice was between fairly deep involvement in Southeast Asia, or standing aside in the face of an estimate that to do so would cause Communist Chinese and North Vietnamese power and domination to flow throughout the area.

The unfolding of this policy between 1954 and 1961 is a tangled and difficult story. Mistakes, even serious mistakes, were undoubtedly made then and later. Some of these, many believe, were in our economic and particularly in our military assistance policies in Viet-Nam, and it has been argued—to me persuasively—that we should have at least tried harder to counter the growing authoritarian trends of the Diem regime in the political sphere.

What was not a mistake—but the logical corollary of the basic policy—was the handling of the provision in the Geneva Accords that called for free elections in 1956. It has been argued that this provision, which was certainly badly drafted, called for a single nationwide election, with reunification assumed. Our interpretation—that what was meant was in effect a plebiscite as to whether reunification was desired—has strong support in reason and the recollections of Geneva participants. What cannot be disputed is that the determination was to be free; the word appears three times in the article of the Accords.

Much hindsight nonsense has been written about what took place in 1956 on this issue, and if any of you are planning a thesis subject, I commend to you the examination of the *contemporary* sources and discussion. You will, I think, find clear confirmation that by 1956 two propositions were accepted—first, that South Viet-Nam, contrary to most expectations in 1954, was standing on its own feet and had demonstrated that the makings of a valid non-Communist nationalism existed there, and, second, that North Viet-Nam—which had gone through a period of harsh repression in 1955 and 1956 in which Bernard Fall estimates that nearly 50,000 political opponents were killed outright—would not conceivably have permitted any supervision or any determination that could remotely have been called free.

In the face of these facts, Diem refused to go through with the elections, and we supported him in that refusal. Incidentally, I am told that we urged that he put the monkey on Hanoi's back and force them to refuse supervision or free conditions—as they would surely have done. Diem proudly rejected this advice, which did not change what would have happened, but did leave the elements of a propaganda argument that still rages. It is, I repeat, hindsight nonsense, and I would only quote two contemporary statements—one by the then junior Senator from Massachusetts, John F. Kennedy, the other by Professor Hans Morgenthau.

Kennedy categorically rejected "an election obviously stacked and subverted in advance, urged upon us by those who have already broken their own pledges under the agreement they now seek to enforce."

And Morgenthau referred to the tremendous change between 1954 and 1956 and the "miracle" of what had been accomplished in South Viet-Nam. He went on to say that the conditions for free elections did not exist in either North or South Viet-Nam and concluded:

> "Actually, the provision for free elections which would solve ultimately the problem of Viet-Nam was a device to hide the incompatibility of the Communist and Western positions, neither of which can admit the domination of all of Viet Nam by the other side. It was a device to disguise the fact that the line of military demarcation was bound to be a line of political division as well."

Unfortunately, the promise of South Viet-Nam in 1956 was not realized in the next five years. In the face of Diem's policies, discontent grew— much as it grew in the same period in Korea under Rhee. As in Korea, that discontent might well have led to an internal revolution in a more or less traditional Asian manner. This is not what happened. Despite all that romantics like Lacouture may say, what happened was that Hanoi moved in, from at least 1959 onward (Bernard Fall would say from 1957), and provided a cutting edge of direction, trained men from the North, and supplies that transformed internal discontent into a massive subversive effort guided and supported from the outside in crucial ways.

The realistic view, then and later, has been well summarized by Roger Hilsman in his recent book (with which, incidentally, I have serious factual differences on the period after 1963). Hilsman puts it thus (page 471 of his book):

> "Vietnam, in truth, was in the midst of two struggles, not one. The guerilla warfare was not a spontaneous revolution, as Communist propaganda would have it, but a contrived deliberate campaign directed and managed from Hanoi. But Vietnam was also in the throes of a true revolution, a social and nationalistic revolution very much akin to the 'new nationalisms' that pervaded both the Congo crisis and Indonesia's confrontation with Malaysia. Even while the struggle went on against the Viet Cong, power was in the process of passing from the French-educated mandarin class to representatives of the new nationalism, the Buddhists, the students, and the 'young Turks' in the military. . . ."

This, then was the situation as it confronted the Kennedy Administration in January of 1961. All this is history. Reasonable men can and do differ about what was done. But those who believe that serious mistakes were made, or even that the basic policy was wrong, cannot escape the fact that by 1961 we were, as a practical matter, deeply engaged in Southeast Asia and specifically in the preservation of the independence of South Viet-Nam.

President Kennedy came to office with a subversive effort against South Viet-Nam well under way, and with the situation in Laos deteriorating rapidly. And for a time the decisions on Laos overshadowed Viet-Nam, although of course the two were always intimately related.

In Laos, President Kennedy in the spring of 1961 rejected the idea of strong military action in favor of seeking a settlement that would install a neutralist government under Souvanna Phouma—a solution uniquely appropriate to Laos. Under Governor Harriman's astute handling, the negotiations finally led to the Geneva Accords of 1962 for Laos, and the process—a point not adequately noticed—led the United States to a much more explicit and affirmative endorsement of the Geneva Accords of 1954, a position we have since consistently maintained as the best basis for peace in Viet-Nam.

In Viet-Nam, the situation at first appeared less critical, and the initial actions of the Kennedy Administration were confined to an increase in our military aid and a small increase of a few hundred men in our military training personnel—a breach—it may be argued—to this extent of the limits of the Geneva Accords, but fully justified in response to the scale of North Vietnamese violation of the basic non-interference provisions.

Although the details somewhat obscured the broad pattern, I think any fair historian of the future must conclude that as early as the spring of 1961 President Kennedy had in effect taken a seventh United States policy decision—that we would continue to be deeply engaged in Southeast Asia, in South Viet-Nam, and under new ground rules in Laos as well.

This was *not*—despite the hindsight straw man recently erected by Professor Galbraith—because President Kennedy believed at all in a monolithic Communism. Professor Galbraith forgets a good deal, and notably the Vienna meeting of June 1961 in which President Kennedy set out deliberately to work with the Soviet Union for the Laos settlement—even as at the very same time he dispatched Vice-President Johnson to visit Viet-Nam and Thailand and in effect to reaffirm our courses of action there. The total pattern of United States policy toward Communist countries under both President Johnson and President Kennedy belies the Galbraith thesis.

No, neither President Kennedy nor any senior policy-maker, then or later, believed the Soviet Union was still united with Communist China and North Viet-Nam in a single sweeping Communist threat to the world. But President Kennedy did believe two other things that had, and still have, a vital bearing on our policy.

First, he believed that a weakening in our basic resolve to help in Southeast Asia would tend to encourage separate Soviet pressures in other areas.

James Reston has stated, on the basis of contemporary conversations with the President, that this concern specifically related to Khrushchev's aggressive designs on Berlin, which were pushed hard all through 1961 and not laid to rest till after the Cuban missile crisis of 1962. At any rate, President Kennedy clearly did believe that failure to keep the high degree of commitment we had in Viet-Nam and Southeast Asia had a bearing on the validity of our commitments elsewhere. As Theodore Sorensen has summarized it (page 641 of "Kennedy"), "This nation's commitment (in South Viet-Nam in January, 1961) . . . was not one that President Kennedy felt he could abandon without undesirable consequences throughout Asia and the world."

Secondly, President Kennedy believed that the Communist Chinese *were* a major threat to dominate Southeast Asia, and specifically that a United States "withdrawal in the case of Viet-Nam and the case of Thailand might mean a collapse in the entire area." (Press Conference of June 14, 1962.) Indeed, President Kennedy in one statement expressly supported the "domino theory." (TV appearance, September 9, 1963.)

My own view, based on participation and subsequent discussion with others, is that the underlying view of the relation between Viet-Nam and the threat to Southeast Asia was clear and strongly believed throughout the top levels of the Kennedy Administration. We knew, as we have always known, that the action against South Viet-Nam reflected deeply held ambitions by Hanoi to unify Viet-Nam under Communist control, and that Hanoi needed and wanted only Chinese aid to this end and wished to be its own master. And we knew, as again we always have, that North Viet-Nam would resist any Communist Chinese trespassing on areas it controlled. But these two propositions were not then, as they are now, inconsistent with the belief that the aggressive ambitions of Communist China and North Viet-Nam—largely North Vietnamese in old Indochina, overlapping in Thailand, Chinese in the rest of Southeast Asia—would surely feed on each other. In the eyes of the rest of Southeast Asia, certainly, they were part of a common and parallel threat.

So, in effect, the policy of 1954–61 was reaffirmed in the early months of 1961 by the Kennedy Administration. Let me say right here I do not mean to make this a personal analysis of President Kennedy, nor to imply any view whatever as to what he might or might not have done had he lived beyond November of 1963. But some untrue things have been said about the 1961 period, and I believe the record totally supports the account of policy, and the reasons for it, that I have given.

We then come to the eighth period of decision—the fall of 1961. By then, the "guerrilla aggression" (Hilsman's phrase) had assumed truly serious proportions, and morale in South Viet-Nam had been shaken. It seemed highly doubtful that without major additional United States actions the North Vietnamese threat could be stemmed.

President Kennedy took the decision to raise the ante, through a system of advisers, pilots, and supporting military personnel that rose gradually to the level of 25,000 in the next three years.

I do not think that it is appropriate for me to go into the detail of the discussions that accompanied this decision. Fairly full, but still incomplete, accounts have been given in various of the books on the period. What can be seen, without going into such detail, is that the course of action that was chosen, considered and rejected, at least for the time being, the direct introduction of ground combat troops or the bombing of North Viet-Nam, although there was no doubt even then—as Hilsman again makes clear—that the bombing of North Viet-Nam could have been sustained under any reasonable legal view in the face of what North Viet-Nam was doing. Rather, the course of action which was adopted rightly stressed that the South Vietnamese role must remain crucial and primary.

In effect, it was decided that the United States would take those additional actions that appeared clearly required to meet the situation, not knowing for sure whether these actions would in fact prove to be adequate, trying—despite the obvious and always recognized effect of momentum and inertia—not to cross the bridge of still further action, and hoping strongly that what was being undertaken would prove sufficient.

This was the policy followed from early 1962 right up to February of 1965. Within this period, however, political deterioration in South Viet-

Nam compelled, in the fall of 1963, decisions that I think must be counted as the ninth critical point of United States policy-making. It was decided at that time that, while the United States would do everything necessary to support the war, it would no longer adhere to its posture of all-out support of the Diem regime unless that regime made sweeping changes in its method of operation. The record of this period has been described by Robert Shaplen and now by Hilsman. Undoubtedly, our new posture contributed to the overthrow of Diem in November, 1963.

I do not myself think that we could in the end have done otherwise, but the important historical point is that our actions tended to deepen our involvement in South Viet-Nam and our commitment to the evolution of non-Communist nationalism, always foreseen to be difficult—that would follow the overthrow of Diem.

Unfortunately, the fall of Diem—while it had overwhelming popular support in South Viet-Nam—failed to produce an effective new government. For a year and a half, South Viet-Nam wallowed in political confusion, and power finally passed, with the agreement of civilian political leaders, to the Thieu-Ky, military-led government of June 1965.

This political confusion was disheartening, but it was not surprising. For South Viet-Nam had never been trained by the French to govern itself, and above all it was faced with steadily rising North Vietnamese and Viet Cong terrorist and military action. Intensification of that action began almost at once after the overthrow of Diem and demonstrated, if it needed demonstrating, that the struggle was not over Diem—despite Communist claims and honest liberal qualms—but was an attempt to destroy non-Communist nationalism of any sort in South Viet-Nam.

In early 1964, President Johnson expressly reaffirmed all the essential elements of the Kennedy Administration policies, publicly, through every action, and through firm internal directives. It is simply not true to say that there was any change in policy in this period toward greater military emphasis, much less major new military actions. Further actions were not excluded—as they had not been in 1954 or 1961—but President Johnson's firm object right up to February 1965 was to make the policy adopted in late 1961 work if it could possibly be done, including the fullest possible emphasis on pacification and the whole political and civilian aspect.

The summer of 1964 did bring a new phase, though not a change in policy. The situation was continuing to decline, and North Viet-Nam may have been emboldened by the trend. Certainly, infiltration was rising steadily, and as we now know more clearly, began to include substantial numbers of native North Vietnamese. But, more dramatically, American naval ships on patrol in the Gulf of Tonkin were attacked, and there were two responding United States attacks on North Vietnamese naval bases.

This led President Johnson to seek, and the Congress to approve overwhelmingly on August 7, 1964, a resolution—drafted in collaboration with Congressional leaders—that not only approved such retaliatory attacks but added that:

"The United States regards as vital to its national interest and to world peace the maintenance of international peace and security in Southeast Asia. Consonant with the Constitution of the United States and the Charter of the United Nations and in accordance with its obligations under the Southeast Asia Collective Defense Treaty, the United States is, therefore, prepared, as the President determines, to take all necessary steps, including the use of armed force, to assist any member or protocol state of the Southeast Asia Collective Defense Treaty requesting assistance in defense of its freedom."

So things stood through the election period. But as 1964 drew to a close, the situation was moving steadily downward in every respect, both military and political. A review of policy was undertaken, analyzing three basic choices: to continue the existing policy with every improvement that could be devised within its limits, to take new and major military measures, while adhering to the same basic objectives that had been followed all along, or to move toward withdrawal.

From late November onward, these choices were intensively examined, even as the military threat grew, the political confusion in Saigon deepened, and all the indicators recorded increasingly shaky morale and confidence not only in South Viet-Nam but throughout the deeply concerned countries of Southeast Asia. By late January, it was the clear judgment of *all* those concerned with policy and familiar with the situation that the first choice was rapidly becoming no choice at all—and not, to use the phrase of one commentator, a "constructive alternative." To "muddle through" (that commentator's phrase) was almost certainly to muddle out and to accept that South Viet-Nam would be turned over to Communist control achieved through externally backed subversion and aggression.

This was a straight practical judgment. It ran against the grain of every desire of the President and his advisers. But I myself am sure it was a right judgment—accepted at the time by most sophisticated observers and, in the light of reflective examination, now accepted I believe by virtually everyone who knows the situation at all at first hand.

There were, in short, only two choices—to move toward withdrawal or to do a lot more, both for its military impact and, at the outset, to prevent a collapse of South Vietnamese morale and will to continue.

And, as the deliberations continued within the Administration, the matter was brought to a head by a series of sharp attacks on American installations in particular. These attacks were serious in themselves, but above all they confirmed the over-all analysis that North Viet-Nam was supremely confident and was moving for the kill. And, as they thus moved, it seemed clear that they would in fact succeed and perhaps in a matter of months.

Let me pause here to clear up another current historical inaccuracy. The basis for the successive decisions—in February to start bombing, in March to introduce small numbers of combat forces, and in July to move to major United States combat forces—was as I have stated it. It depended on an over-all view of the situation, and on an over-all view that what had been going on for years was for all practical purposes aggression—and indeed this term dates from late 1961 or early 1962 in the statements of senior Administration spokesmen.

But there is a separate point whether, as has sometimes been asserted, it was the United States alone which unilaterally changed the character of the war in the direction of a conventional conflict. It is alleged that

Hanoi was adhering to a tacit agreement that, so long as we did not bomb North Viet-Nam, Hanoi would not send in its regulars, at least in units.

Multiple and conclusive evidence which became available from the spring of 1965 onward seems to me to refute these contentions. As has been repeatedly made public over the past two years, we know that one North Vietnamese regiment entered South Viet-Nam by December 1964, and we know that several other regiments entered in the spring of 1965 on timetables of infiltration that can only have reflected command decisions taken in Hanoi prior to the beginning of the bombing.

From the standpoint of the basis for U.S. decisions, this evidence simply reinforces the February picture that Hanoi was moving for the kill. Native North Vietnamese, alone or in regular units, were in themselves no more and no less aggressive than the earlier native South Vietnamese who had gone North and become North Vietnamese nationals. The point is that *Hanoi*—as we suspected then and later proved—had taken major steps to raise the level of the war before the bombing began.

As to any tacit agreement, these facts alone seem to disprove that there ever was one. Moreover, students of North Vietnamese behavior, and especially of the recent major captured North Vietnamese documents, would in any event find such an allegation hard to credit. Is it not far more reasonable to conclude that Hanoi preferred to conceal its hand, but was prepared at all times to put in whatever was necessary to bring about military victory—and that the regular units were simply a part of that policy, introduced after they had run out of native Southerners and wanted to maintain and step up the pressure?

But this historical point is less important than the fundamental elements of the situation as it stood at the time. On the one hand, all of what I have earlier described as the bedrock elements still remained—a strong Chinese Communist and North Vietnamese threat to Southeast Asia, a crucial link between the defense of South Viet-Nam and the realization of that threat and the validity of non-Communist nationalism, whatever its imperfections, in South Viet-Nam and in the other nations of Southeast Asia.

Moreover, the wider implications for our commitments elsewhere appeared no less valid than they had ever been. Viet-Nam still constituted a major, perhaps even a decisive, test case of whether the Communist strategy of "wars of national liberation," or "people's wars" could be met and countered even in the extraordinarily difficult circumstances of South Viet-Nam. Then as now, it has been I think rightly judged that a success for Hanoi in South Viet-Nam could only encourage the use of this technique by Hanoi, and over time by the Communist Chinese, and might well have the effect of drawing the Soviets into competition with Peking and Hanoi and away from the otherwise promising trends that have developed in Soviet Policy in the past 10 years.

Finally, it was judged from the outset that stronger action by us in Viet-Nam would not operate to bring the Soviet Union and Communist China closer together, and that the possibility of major Chinese Communist intervention could be kept to a minimum, so long as we made it clear at all times, both by word and deed, that our objective was confined solely to freeing South Viet-Nam from external interference, and that we did not threaten Communist China but rather looked to the ultimate hope of what the Manila Declaration, of last fall, called "reconciliation and peace throughout Asia."

On the other hand, it was recognized from the outset that the taking of these new major military measures involved heavy costs and hazards. The South Vietnamese still had to play the crucial role in military security and above all in political and economic development and stability. A greater American role was bound to complicate South Vietnamese evolution. It was bound to increase the scale of the war and to cost significantly in lives and very heavily in resources. Even though the casualties and damage of the war remain far below what was suffered in Korea, war is never any thing but ugly and brutal.

The balance was struck, after the most careful deliberation, in favor of a course that has since been followed. The key elements in the policy were stated in President Johnson's Baltimore speech of April 1965, and the major combat force commitment was explained in the President's statement of July 28, 1965. These have been the cornerstones of policy, and they have been elaborated and explained repeatedly and at length by all senior Administration spokesmen.

In essence:

a. Our objective remained solely that of protecting the independence of South Viet-Nam from external interference and force. We declined, and still decline, to threaten the regime in North Viet-Nam itself, or the territory and regime of Communist China.

b. We indicated in April of 1965 that we were prepared for discussions or negotiations without condition, and we have relentlessly pursued our own efforts to enter into meaningful discussions as well as following up on a host of peace initiatives by others. Unfortunately Hanoi has clung firmly to the objective of insuring a Communist takeover of South Viet-Nam, and has refused to enter into any fruitful discussions. Indeed, Hanoi has rejected any discussions whatever, initially unless its basic objective was accepted in advance through the so-called "third point," more recently unless we agreed to a complete cessation of the bombing without any responsive action on their part. Hanoi's philosophy toward negotiation has now become authoritatively available, particularly in the section on "fighting while negotiating" in the captured remarks of one of the North Vietnamese leaders, Comrade Vinh.

c. We continued to place every possible emphasis on the crucial non-military aspects of the conflict, greatly strengthening our own contribution to the essentially South Vietnamese task of restoring stability and control in the countryside and working for the welfare of the people.

d. Militarily, our actions were directed to proving to North Viet-Nam that its effort to take over the South by military force must fail, and to extending and enlarging the areas in which the vital business of bringing real security and peace to the countryside could go forward with all the strength we could hope to give it. The total effort in the South remained primary, even as the bombing of military targets in the North was carried on—initially to demonstrate resolve, but always and basically to make Hanoi's infiltration far more difficult and costly and to prevent levels of new men and equipment that could only, in the arithmetic of guerrilla warfare, multiply many times over, for each addition from North Vietnam, the requirement for forces in the South.

e. We encouraged the South Vietnamese in their own resolve to move to a constitutional basis of government, a process set under way formally by Prime Minister Ky in January of 1966 and followed since that time in the face of all the difficulties and dangers of attempting to create such a basis in a country without political experience and ravaged by terrorism and by guerrilla and conventional military action.

f. We encouraged the South Vietnamese at the same time to proceed on the track that has now become reconciliation, the holding out to members of the Viet Cong of the possibility of re-entering the political life of their country under peaceful conditions. In essence, we seek and would accept a fair determination of the will of the people of South Viet-Nam along the lines well summarized by Ambassador Goldberg's Chicago speech of May 12, 1967.

These were the South Vietnamese aspects of our policy. But then, as previously, the policy was seen in the wider context of the future of Southeast Asia. So it was that President Johnson lent our strong support in April of 1965 to the development of regional cooperation and of economic projects created through Asian initiative. By this vital element in our policy, we made clear again that our underlying objective was to do what we could to assist in the constructive task of bringing about a Southeast Asia of cooperative and independent nations, whatever their international postures might be.

We had a security job to do in Viet-Nam, and were joined over time by five other area nations in supplying military forces to do that job. And we are assisting Thailand against a concerted Chinese Communist and North Vietnamese effort at external subversion—an effort begun, to keep the record straight, as early as 1962 and clearly and definitely by December 1964, before our major decisions in Viet-Nam. Our SEATO and ANZUS undertakings remain firm.

But we looked beyond these, and we must still look beyond these, to the whole question of the future of Southeast Asia, and to the role that we can play in assisting the nations of the area to consolidate their national independence and to improve the welfare of their people.

This, then, is a bare-bones account of "The Path to Viet-Nam." Even within its own terms, it may omit what others would include. And, long as it may seem, it is still incomplete in two respects that it would take far too much time to cover.

First, it is plainly inadequate to focus solely on our policies toward Viet-Nam or even toward Southeast Asia as a whole. Those policies are intimately related to the rest of Asia, to the implications of Asian developments for other areas and in the last analysis for our own national security, and to our central world purpose—the creation of an international order of independent states.

Secondly, I have tried to isolate what I consider to have been the major policy decisions. Obviously, policy is not just a matter of single decisions, however fully considered. A vast number of lesser policy decisions have accompanied these basic ones, and the way in which a basic policy is carried out in the end affects its substance. I have not tried to cover, for example, decisions on the balance of effort within South Viet-Nam, decisions on particular negotiating proposals, decisions on the pace and nature of the bombing of North Viet-Nam, or the subtle and difficult problem, over the years, of United States influence toward political progress in the South. I know full well that these are areas in which many of you undoubtedly hold strong views. I welcome discussion of them.

What, then, is "the lesson in involvement?"

Is it that we have been trapped into a difficult situation by a series of lesser decisions taken with no clear view of their implications?

Is it that we should never have become engaged in Southeast Asia?

Is it that we should never have attempted to support South Viet-Nam?

Is it that, having supported South Viet-Nam in certain respects (including a treaty), and having become deeply engaged in Southeast Asia, we should nonetheless have decided—or should now decide—to limit the actions we take, or even to withdraw entirely?

The first question seems to me both separate and difficult. At some point in the history I have recited we became committed, deliberately and by formal constitutional process, to the support of the freedom of South Viet-Nam from external interference. That commitment included a strong treaty obligation, and that is a clear part of the story. But what is perhaps more to the point is that great powers must face two central points:

> a. As Irving Kristol has pointed out in his recent article in *Foreign Affairs,* the very definition of a great power is that not only its actions but the cases in which it declines to act have major consequences. At every stage in the Viet-Nam story, it has seemed clear to the leaders of this country that *not* to act would have the gravest effects. This is the way that successive choices have appeared to four successive Presidents.
>
> b. The second point that a great power cannot escape is that its actions in themselves affect the stakes. When great powers commit themselves—by treaty and by a total course of conduct extending over many years—an element of reliance comes into being, both within the area and within other areas in which commitments have also been undertaken.

Yet, all this being said, I do not think one can conclude that because we said or did A, we must necessarily say or do B—in an old phrase of Bismarck's. So I, for one, do not believe that the "lesson in involvement" is that we are the prisoners of history.

Rather, I think we should be focusing on the second, third, and fourth questions I have listed above.

These are big questions, and if I have tried to do anything today it is to stress that the matter has really been looked at for at least the last 13 years in this kind of larger framework. The policies followed today are, as they must be, the policies of this Administration. No one can say whether another administration would have done the same. What can be said is that the underlying viewpoint and analysis of factors have been largely similar throughout the last 13 years, if not longer.

This does not prove, of course, that this analysis has been correct. The United States has no divine dispensation from error, and the most that your leaders, at any time, can do is to exert the best human judgment and moral sense of which they are capable. I for one am convinced that this has been done at all stages.

In essence, the question is not capable of geometric proof. Like all policy, it is a judgment. Our bet with history has been that Southeast Asia does matter, that the independence of South Viet-Nam crucially affects Southeast Asia, and that non-Communist nationalism in Southeast Asia and in Viet-Nam has in it the seeds of a peaceful, progressive, and stable area that can take its place in a world at peace.

Other factors enter in, as I have tried to summarize, and despite their variations from time to time remain of major general importance. But it is primarily from the standpoint of Southeast Asia that I would like to close my remarks today. How do the bets I have described look today?

Southeast Asia surely matters more than ever. A region which may have held as few as 30 million inhabitants in 1800—and which is carried under the heading of "peripheral areas" in some textbooks on East Asia—now holds more than 250 million people, more than Latin America and almost as much as the population of Western Europe. The resources of this area are large, and its people—while not yet capable of the kind of dramatic progress we have seen in the northern parts of Asia—have great talent, intelligence, and industry. Its geographical location—while it should not be in the path of great power collisions—is crucial for trade routes, and in other respects.

From the standpoint of our own security, and the kind of world in which we wish to live, I believe we must continue to be deeply concerned to do what we can to keep Southeast Asia from falling under external domination and aggression that would contribute to such domination. And I believe also that we have a wider concern in doing what we can, and as we are wanted, to assist sound programs on an individual country or regional basis, and to improve the welfare of the peoples of the area. And I do not think that you can do the latter unless the former is achieved.

The second part of our bet is that the independence of South Viet-Nam critically affects Southeast Asia. South Viet-Nam and its 15 million people are important in themselves, but they assume an additional importance if the judgment is accepted that a success for aggression there would drastically weaken the situation in Southeast Asia and indeed beyond. That judgment cannot be defended solely by reference to the dynamics of major aggressive powers and their prospective victims in the past. I myself believe that those parallels have validity, but the question is always what Justice Holmes called "concrete cases." In this concrete case, I think the underlying judgment has been valid, and remains valid today.

None of us can say categorically that the Communist Chinese would in due course move—if opportunity offered—to dominate wide areas of Southeast Asia through pressure and subversion. But that is what the Chinese and their maps say, and their Communist doctrine appears to add vital additional emphasis. It is what they are doing in Thailand today, and through local Communist allies in Burma, Cambodia, Malaysia, and Singapore. And it is what they would like to do in Indonesia again.

Surely Adlai Stevenson was right that the threat of Communist China is not so fanciful that it should not serve as a valid assumption of policy. And we can be more categorical that Hanoi intends to dominate at least the successor states of Indochina, and would move rapidly to this end if it were to get practical control of South Viet-Nam.

Perhaps the hardest point for some to grasp is the psychological impact of a development such as the fall of South Viet-Nam in this setting. As to Hanoi and Peking, judgment and past experience point to the conclusion that it would greatly encourage them to push further. As to the threatened nations, the view of their leaders is a matter of record. All over Southeast Asia, whatever the posture of the individual nation, the great body of responsible opinion—and I invite you to check this against any first-hand account—accepts the judgment stated only the other day by the independent and nonaligned Prime Minister of Singapore, Mr. Lee Kuan Yew:

> "I feel the fate of Asia—South and Southeast Asia—will be decided in the next few years by what happens out in Viet-Nam."

I could multiply that quotation ten times over in public statements, and ten times more in private statements. As Drew Middleton of the *Times* reported last June after a trip in the area:

> "Despite some misgivings, non-Communist leaders from Tokyo to Tehran largely support United States policies in South and Southeast Asia."

This does not mean that every nation accepts our choice of military actions. Some would have us do more, some less. But it does lead to the clear conclusion that our own view accords with the deep sense in Southeast Asia, and indeed elsewhere in Asia, that the struggle in South Viet-Nam is crucial to the independence and continued ability to work for its people of each and every nation for a wide area.

Lastly, there is the question whether a new Southeast Asia is in fact being built and can be developed. On this point, surely the developments of the last five years, and particularly the last two years, have been vastly encouraging. Where Indonesia in 1965 was drifting rapidly to Communist control and practical alignment with Peking, it now stands on a staunchly nationalist basis, abandoning the threat to its neighbors and seeking to work out the chaotic economic problems left by Sukarno—with the multilateral help of ourselves and others. Regional cooperation within Southeast Asia, and among Asian nations as a whole, has taken great and historic strides. And it is the widely accepted view in the area—which I share—that these developments would have been far less likely if we had not acted as we did in 1965, and if Communist force had thus taken over in South Viet-Nam.

So all over Southeast Asia there is today a sense of confidence—to which Drew Middleton again testified from his trip. Time has been bought and used. But that confidence is not solid or secure for the future. It would surely be disrupted if we were, in President Johnson's words, to permit a Communist takeover in South Viet-Nam either through withdrawal or "under the cloak of a meaningless agreement." If, on the contrary, we proceed on our present course—with measured military actions and with every possible non-military measure, and searching always for an avenue to peace—the prospects for a peaceful and secure Southeast Asia now appear brighter than they have been at any time since the nations of the area were established on an independent basis.

In short, I think the stakes are very grave indeed. The costs are large, and it is clear that we must steel our national capacity and resolve to continue in a tough struggle and still do those things that we must do to meet our problems at home. I find it impossible to believe that we do not have the national capacity and resolve to do both.

The Arrogance of Power

J. William Fulbright

America is the most fortunate of nations—fortunate in its rich territory, fortunate in having had a century of relative peace in which to develop that territory, fortunate in its diverse and talented population, fortunate in the institutions devised by the Founding Fathers and in the wisdom of those who have adapted those institutions to a changing world.

For the most part America has made good use of its blessings, especially in its internal life, but also in its foreign relations. Having done so much and succeeded so well, America is now at that historical point at which a great nation is in danger of losing its perspective on what exactly is within the realm of its power and what is beyond it. Other great nations, reaching this critical juncture, have aspired to too much and, by over-extension of effort, have declined and then fallen.

I do not think for a moment that America, with its deeply rooted democratic traditions, is likely to embark upon a campaign to dominate the world in the manner of a Hitler or Napoleon. What I do fear is that it may be drifting into commitments which, though generous and benevolent in intent, are so universal as to exceed even America's great capacities.

At the same time, it is my hope—and I repeat it here because it is the major point that I wish to convey in these lectures—that America will escape those fatal temptations of power which have ruined other great nations and will instead do only that good in the world which it can do, both by direct effort and by the force of its own example.

The stakes are high indeed: They include not only America's continued greatness, but nothing less than the survival of the human race in an era when, for the first time in human history, one generation has the power of veto over the survival of the next.

In the seventeenth century, a distinguished Frenchman, Jean de La Bruyère, asked a question that remains one of the profound paradoxes of men and nations. "How," he asked, "does it serve the people and add to their happiness if their ruler extend his empire by annexing the provinces of his enemies? . . . How does it help me or my countrymen that my country be successful and covered with glory, that my country be powerful and dreaded, if, sad and worried, I live in oppression and poverty?"

"The Arrogance of Power," excerpts from an address by Senator J. W. Fulbright, chairman of the Senate Committee on Foreign Relations, delivered at the School of Advanced International Studies at Johns Hopkins University in Washington, D.C., May 5, 1966.

The question, phrased somewhat differently, is how and why it happens that the groups into which men organize themselves come to be regarded as ends in themselves, as living organisms with needs and preferences of their own which are separate from and superior to those of the individual, warranting, when necessary, the sacrifice of the hopes, the pleasures and the lives of individual men.

It is a paradox of politics that so great a part of our organized efforts as societies is directed toward abstract and mystic goals—toward propagating an ideology, toward enhancing the pride and power and self-esteem of the nation, as if the nation had a "self" and a "soul" apart from the individuals who compose it, and as if the wishes of individual men, for life and happiness and prosperity, were selfish, dishonorable and unworthy of our best creative efforts.

When all is said and done, when the abstractions and subtleties of political science have been exhausted, there remain the most basic unanswered questions about war and peace and why we contest the issues we contest and why we even care about them.

As Aldous Huxley has written: "There may be arguments about the best way of raising wheat in a cold clmate or of re-afforesting a denuded mountain. But such arguments never lead to organized slaughter. Organized slaughter is the result of arguments about such questions as the following: Which is the best nation? The best religion? The best political theory? The best form of government? Why are other people so stupid and wicked? Why can't they see how good and intelligent we are? Why do they resist our beneficent efforts to bring them under our control and make them like ourselves?"

Many of the wars fought by man—I am tempted to say most—have been fought over such abstractions. The more I puzzle over the great wars of history, the more I am inclined to the view that the causes attributed to them—territory, markets, resources, the defense or perpetuation of great principles—were not the root causes at all, but rather explanations or excuses for certain unfathomable drives of human nature.

For lack of a clear and precise understanding of exactly what these motives are, I refer to them as the "arrogance of power"—as a psychological need that nations seem to have to prove that they are bigger, better or stronger than other nations. Implicit in this drive is the assumption that the proof of superiority is force—that when a nation shows that it has the stronger army, it is also proving that it has better people, better institutions, better principles—and, in general, a better civilization.

The evidence for my proposition is the remarkable discrepancy between the apparent and hidden causes of some modern wars and the discrepancy between their causes and ultimate consequences.

The precipitating cause of the Franco-Prussian War, for example, was a dispute over the succession to the Spanish throne, and the ostensible "underlying" cause was French resistance to the unification of Germany.

The war was followed by German unification—which probably could have been achieved without war—but it was also followed by the loss of Alsace-Lorraine, the humiliation of France and the emergence of Germany as the greatest power in Europe, which could not have been achieved without war. The peace treaty, incidentally, said nothing about the Spanish throne, which everyone apparently had forgotten.

One wonders to what extent the Germans were motivated simply by the desire to cut those haughty Frenchmen down to size and have a good excuse to build another monument in Berlin.

The United States went to war in 1898 for the stated purpose of liberating Cuba from Spanish tyranny, but then, after winning the war—a war which Spain had been willing to pay a high price to avoid—the United States brought the liberated Cubans under an American protectorate, and, incidentally, annexed the Philippines, because, according to President McKinley, the Lord told him it was America's duty "to educate the Filipinos, and uplift and civilize and Christianize them, and by God's grace do the very best we could by them, as our fellowmen for whom Christ also died."

Isn't it interesting that the voice was the voice of God but the words were those of Theodore Roosevelt, Henry Cabot Lodge, Admiral Mahan, those "imperialists of 1898" who wanted America to have an empire just because a big, powerful country like the United States ought to have an empire?

The spirit of the times was expressed by Albert Beveridge who proclaimed Americans to be "a conquering race." "We must obey our blood and occupy new markets and if necessary new lands," he said, because "in the Almighty's infinite plan . . . debased civilizations and decaying races" must disappear "before the higher civilization of the nobler and more virile types of man."

In 1914, all Europe went to war, ostensibly because the heir to the Austrian throne had been assassinated at Sarajevo but really because that murder became the symbolic focus of the incredibly delicate sensibilities of the great nations of Europe.

The events of the summer of 1914 were a melodrama of abnormal psychology: Austria had to humiliate Serbia in order not to be humiliated herself, but Austria's effort to recover self-esteem was profoundly humiliating to Russia. Russia was allied to France, who had been feeling generally humiliated since 1871, and Austria, in turn, was allied to Germany, whose pride required her to support Austria no matter how insanely Austria behaved, and who may, in any case, have felt that it would be fun to give the German Army another swing down the Champs Elysées.

For these ennobling reasons, the world was plunged into a war which took tens of millions of lives, precipitated the Russian Revolution and set in motion the events that led to another world war, a war which took tens of millions' more lives and precipitated the worldwide revolutions of which we spoke last week, revolutions whose consequences are beyond the foresight of any of us now alive.

Both the causes and consequences of war may have more to do with pathology than with politics, more to do with irrational pressures of pride and pain than with rational calculations of advantage and profit.

It has been said that buried in the secret soul of every woman is a drum majorette; it might also be said that there is a bit of the missionary in all of our souls. We all like telling people what to do, but unfortunately they usually don't appreciate it. I myself have given my wife some splendid suggestions on household management, but she is so ungrateful for my advice that I have stopped offering it. The phenomenon is explained by the Canadian psychiatrist and former Director-General of the World Health Organization, Brock Chisholm, who writes:

". . . Man's method of dealing with difficulties in the past has always been to tell everyone else how they should behave. We've all been doing that for centuries.

"It should be clear by now that this no longer does any good. Everybody has by now been told by everybody else how he should behave. The criticism is not effective; it never has been, and it never is going to be. . . ."

Ineffective though it has been, the giving—and enforcement—of all this unsolicited advice has, at least until recently, been compatible with the survival of the human race.

Man is now, however, for the first time, in a situation in which the survival of his species is in jeopardy. Other forms of life have been endangered, and many destroyed, by changes in their natural environment; man is menaced by a change of environment which he himself has wrought by the invention of nuclear weapons and ballistic missiles.

Our power to kill has become universal, creating a radically new situation which, if we are to survive, requires us to adopt some radically new attitudes about the giving and enforcement of advice and, in general, about human and international relations.

The enormity of the danger of extinction of our species is dulled by the frequency with which it is stated, as if a familiar threat of catastrophe were no threat at all. We seem to feel somehow that because the hydrogen bomb has not killed us yet it is never going to kill us.

This is a dangerous assumption because it encourages the retention of traditional attitudes about world politics when our responsibility, in Dr. Chisholm's words, is nothing less than "to re-examine all of the attitudes of our ancestors and to select from those attitudes things which we, on our own authority in these present circumstances, with our knowledge, recognize as still valid in this new kind of world. . . ."

The attitude, above all others, which I feel sure is no longer valid is the arrogance of power, the tendency of great nations to equate power with virtue and major responsibilities with a universal mission. The dilemmas involved are preeminently American dilemmas, not because America has weaknesses that others do not have, but because America is powerful as no nation has ever been before and the discrepancy between its power and the power of others appears to be increasing.

I said in a speech in New York last week that I felt confident that America, with its great resources and democratic traditions, with its diverse and creative population, would find the wisdom to match its power. Perhaps I should have been more cautious and expressed only hope instead of confidence, because the wisdom that is required is greater wisdom than any great nation has ever shown before. It must be rooted, as Dr. Chisholm says, in the re-examination of "all of the attitudes of our ancestors."

It is a tall order. Perhaps one can begin to fill it by an attempt to assess some of the effects of America's great power on some of the small countries whom we have tried to help.

Reflecting on his voyages to Polynesia in the late eighteenth century, Captain Cook later wrote: "It would have been better for these people never to have known us."

In a recently published book on European explorations of the South Pacific, Alan Moorehead relates how the Tahitians and the gentle aborigines of Australia were corrupted by the white man's diseases, alcohol, firearms, laws and concepts of morality, by what Moorehead calls "the long downslide into Western civilization."

The first missionaries to Tahiti, says Moorehead, were "determined to re-create the island in the image of lower-middle-class Protestant England. . . . They kept hammering away at the Tahitian way of life until it crumbled before them, and within two decades they had achieved precisely what they set out to do."

It is said that the first missionaries who went to Hawaii went for the purpose of explaining to the Polynesians that it was sinful to work on Sunday, only to discover that in those bountiful islands nobody worked on any day.

Even when acting with the best of intentions, Americans, like other Western peoples who have carried their civilization abroad, have had something of the same "fatal impact" on smaller nations that European explorers had on the Tahitians and the native Australians.

We have not harmed people because we wished to; on the contrary, more often than not we have wanted to help people and, in some very important respects, we have helped them. Americans have brought medicine and education, manufactures and modern techniques to many places in the world; but they also brought themselves and the condescending attitudes of a people whose very success breeds disdain for other cultures.

Bringing power without understanding, Americans as well as Europeans have had a devastating effect in less advanced areas of the world; without wishing to, without knowing they were doing it, they have shattered traditional societies, disrupted fragile economies, and undermined people's confidence in themselves by the invidious example of their own efficiency. They have done this in many instances simply by being big and strong, by giving good advice, by intruding on people who have not wanted them but could not resist them.

Have you ever noticed how Americans act when they go to foreign countries?

Foreigners frequently comment on the contrast between the behavior of Americans at home and abroad; in our own country, they say, we are hospitable and considerate, but, as soon as we get outside our own borders, something seems to get into us and, wherever we are, we become noisy and demanding and strut around as if we owned the place. The British used to say during the war that the trouble with the Yanks was that they were "overpaid, oversexed and over here."

I recently took a vacation in Mexico and noticed in a small-town airport two groups of students on holiday, both about undergraduate age; one group was Japanese, the other American. The Japanese were neatly dressed and were talking and laughing in a manner that neither annoyed anybody nor particularly called attention to themselves. The Americans, on the other hand, were disporting themselves in a conspicuous and offensive manner, stamping around the waiting room in sloppy clothes, drinking beer and shouting to each other as if no one else were there.

This kind of scene, unfortunately, has become familiar in many parts of the world. I do not wish to exaggerate its significance, but I have the feeling that, just as there was once something special about being a Roman or a Spaniard or an Englishman, there is now something about the consciousness of being an American abroad, something about the consciousness of belonging to the biggest, richest country in the world, that encourages people who are perfectly well behaved at home to become boorish when they are in somebody else's country and to treat the local citizens as if they weren't really there.

One reason why Americans abroad may act as though they "own the place" is that in many places they very nearly do: American companies may dominate large segments of a country's economy; American products are advertised on billboards and displayed in the shop windows; American hotels and snack bars are available to protect American tourists from foreign influence; American soldiers may be stationed in the country and, even if they are not, the population are probably well aware that their very survival depends on the wisdom with which America uses her immense military power.

I think that any American, when he goes abroad, carries an unconscious knowledge of all this power with him, and it affects his behavior just as it once affected the behavior of Greeks and Romans, of Spaniards, Germans and Englishmen, in the brief high noons of their respective ascendancies.

It was the arrogance of their power that led nineteenth-century Englishmen to suppose that if you shouted at a foreigner loud enough in English he was bound to understand you, or that now leads Americans to behave like Mark Twain's "innocents abroad," who reported as follows on their travels in Europe:

"The peoples of those foreign countries are very ignorant. They looked curiously at the costumes that we had brought from the wilds of America. They observed that we talked loudly at table sometimes. . . . In Paris, they just simply opened their eyes and stared when we spoke to them in French! We never did succeed in making these idiots understand their own language."

For all our noble intentions, the countries which have had most of the tutelage in democracy by United States Marines are not particularly democratic. These include Haiti, which is under a brutal and superstitious dictatorship, the Dominican Republic, which is in turmoil, and Cuba, which, as no one needs to be reminded, has replaced its traditional right-wing dictatorships with a Communist dictatorship.

Maybe, in the light of this extraordinary record of accomplishment, it is time for us to reconsider our teaching methods. Maybe we are not really cut out for the job of spreading the gospel of democracy. Maybe it would profit us to concentrate on our own democracy instead of trying to inflict our particular version of it on all those ungrateful Latin Americans who stubbornly oppose their North American benefactors instead of the "real" enemies whom we have so graciously chosen for them.

And maybe—just maybe—if we left our neighbors to make their own judgments and their own mistakes, and confined our assistance to matters of economics and technology instead of philosophy, maybe then they would begin to find the democracy and the dignity that have largely eluded them and we, in turn, might begin to find the love and gratitude that we seem to crave.

Korea is another example. We went to war in 1950 to defend South Korea against the Russian-inspired aggression of North Korea. I think that intervention in that war was justified and necessary. We were defending a country that clearly wanted to be defended: Its army was willing to fight and fought well, and its Government, though dictatorial, was a patriotic Government which commanded the support of the people.

Throughout the war, however, the United States emphasized as one of its war aims the survival of the Republic of Korea as a "free society," something which it was not then or for a long time after the war.

We lost 33,629 American lives in the war and have since spent $5,610,-000,000 on direct military and economic aid and a great deal more on indirect aid to South Korea. The country, nonetheless, remained until recently in a condition of virtual economic stagnation and political instability.

These facts are regrettable, but the truly surprising fact is that, having fought a war for three years to defend the freedom of South Korea, most Americans are probably ignorant of, and almost certainly uninterested in, the current state of the ward for whom they sacrificed so much.

We are now engaged in a war to "defend freedom" in South Vietnam. Unike the Republic of Korea, South Vietnam has an Army which is without notable success and a weak, dictatorial Government which does not command the loyalty of the South Vietnamese people.

The official war aims of the United States Government, as I understand them, are to defeat what is regarded as North Vietnamese aggression, to demonstrate the futility of what the Communists call "wars of national liberation," and to create conditions under which the South Vietnamese people will be able freely to determine their own future.

I have not the slightest doubt of the sincerity of the President and the Vice President and the Secretaries of State and Defense in propounding these aims. What I do doubt—and doubt very much—is the ability of the United States to achieve these aims by the means being used.

I do not question the power of our weapons and the efficiency of our logistics; I cannot say these things delight me as they seem to delight some of our officials, but they are certainly impressive. What I do question is the ability of the United States, or France or any other Western nation, to go into a small, alien, undeveloped Asian nation and create stability where there is chaos, the will to fight where there is defeatism, democracy where there is no tradition of it and honest government where corruption is almost a way of life.

Our handicap is well expressed in the pungent Chinese proverb: "In shallow waters, dragons become the sport of shrimps."

Early last month demonstrators in Saigon burned American Jeeps, tried to assault American soldiers, and marched through the streets shouting, "Down with the American imperialists," while one of the Buddhist leaders made a speech equating the United States with the Communists as a threat to South Vietnamese independence.

Most Americans are understandably shocked and angered to encounter such hostility from people who by now would be under the rule of the Viet Cong but for the sacrifice of American lives and money. Why, we may ask, are they so shockingly ungrateful? Surely they must know that their very right to parade and protest and demonstrate depends on the Americans who are defending them.

The answer, I think, is that "fatal impact" of the rich and strong on the poor and weak. Dependent on it though the Vietnamese are, our very strength is a reproach to their weakness, our wealth a mockery of their poverty, our success a reminder of their failures. What they resent is the disruptive effect of our strong culture upon their fragile one, an effect which we can no more avoid than a man can help being bigger than a child.

What they fear, I think rightly, is that traditional Vietnamese society cannot survive the American economic and cultural impact.

.   .   .

The cause of our difficulties in Southeast Asia is not a deficiency of power, but an excess of the wrong kind of power, which results in a feeling of impotence when it fails to achieve its desired ends.

We are still acting like Boy Scouts dragging reluctant old ladies across streets they do not want to cross. We are trying to remake Vietnamese society, a task which certainly cannot be accomplished by force and which probably cannot be accomplished by any means available to outsiders. The objective may be desirable, but it is not feasible.

There is wisdom, if also malice, in Prince Sihanouk's comparison of American and Chinese aid. "You will note the difference in the ways of giving," he writes. "On one side, we are being humiliated, we are given a lecture, we are required to give something in return. On the other side, not only is our dignity as poor people being preserved, but our self-esteem is being flattered—and human beings have their weaknesses, and it would be futile to try to eradicate [them]."

Or, as Shaw said: "Religion is a great force—the only real motive force in the world; but what you fellows don't understand is that you must get at a man through his own religion and not through yours."

The idea of being responsible for the whole world seems to be flattering to Americans, and I am afraid it is turning our heads, just as the sense of global responsibility turned the heads of ancient Romans and nineteenth-century British.

A prominent American is credited with having said recently that the United States was the "engine of mankind" and the rest of the world was "the train."

A British political writer wrote last summer what he called "A Cheer for American Imperialism." An empire, he said, "has no justification except its own existence." It must never contract; it "wastes treasure and life": its commitments "are without rhyme or reason." Nonetheless, according to the author, the "American empire" is uniquely benevolent, devoted as it is to individual liberty and the rule of law, and having performed such services as getting the author released from a Yugoslav jail simply by his threatening to involve the American consul, a service which he describes as "sublime."

What romantic nonsense this is. And what dangerous nonsense in this age of nuclear weapons. The idea of an "American empire" might be dismissed as the arrant imagining of a British Gunga Din, except for the fact that it surely strikes a responsive chord in at least a corner of the usually sensible and humane American mind. It calls to mind the slogans of the past about the shot fired at Concord being heard round the world, about "manifest destiny" and "making the world safe for democracy" and the demand for "unconditional surrender" in World War II. It calls to mind President McKinley taking counsel with the Supreme Being about his duty to the benighted Filipinos.

The "Blessings-of-Civilization Trust," as Mark Twain called it, may have been a "daisy" in its day, uplifting for the soul and good for business besides, but its day is past.

It is past because the great majority of the human race are demanding dignity and independence, not the honor of a supine role in an American empire.

It is past because whatever claim America may make for the universal domain of its ideas and values is countered by the Communist counterclaim, armed like our own with nuclear weapons.

And, most of all, it is past because it never should have begun, because we are not the "engine of mankind," but only one of its more successful and fortunate branches, endowed by our Creator with about the same capacity for good and evil, no more or less, than the rest of humanity.

An excessive preoccupation with foreign relations over a long period of time is a problem of great importance, because it diverts a nation from the sources of its strength, which are in its domestic life.

A nation immersed in foreign affairs is expending its capital, human as well as material; sooner or later that capital must be renewed by some diversion of creative energies from foreign to domestic pursuits.

I would doubt that any nation has achieved a durable greatness by conducting a "strong" foreign policy, but many have been ruined by expending their energies on foreign adventures while allowing their domestic bases to deteriorate.

The United States emerged as a world power in the twentieth century not because of what it had done in foreign relations, but because it had spent the nineteenth century developing the North American continent; by contrast, the Austrian and Turkish empires collapsed in the twentieth century in large part because they had for so long neglected their internal development and organization.

If America has a service to perform in the world—and I believe it has—it is in large part the service of its own example.

In our excessive involvement in the affairs of other countries, we are not only living off our assets and denying our own people the proper enjoyment of their resources; we are also denying the world the example of a free society enjoying its freedom to the fullest. This is regrettable indeed for a nation that aspires to teach democracy to other nations, because, as Burke said, "Example is the school of mankind, and they will learn at no other."

There is, of course, nothing new about the inversion of values which leads nations to squander their resources on fruitless and extravagant foreign undertakings. What is new is the power of man to destroy his species, which has made the struggles of international politics dangerous as they have never been before and confronted us, as Dr. Chisholm says, with the need to re-examine the attitudes of our ancestors so as to discard those that have ceased to be valid.

We all, as Dr. Chisholm explains, enjoy telling people how they should behave, and the bigger and stronger and richer we are, the more we feel suited to the task, the more, indeed, we consider it our duty. Dr. Chisholm relates the story of an eminent cleric who had been proselyting the Eskimos and said:

"You know, for years we couldn't do anything with those Eskimos at all; they didn't have any sin. We had to teach them sin for years before we could do anything with them."

I am reminded of the three Boy Scouts who reported to their scoutmaster that as their good deed for the day they had helped an old lady cross the street. "That's fine," said the scoutmaster, "but why did it take three of you?" "Well," they explained, "she didn't want to go."

The good deed above all others that Americans feel qualified to perform is the teaching of democracy and the dignity of man. Let us consider the results of some American good deeds in various parts of the world.

Over the years since President Monroe proclaimed his doctrine, Latin Americans have had the advantages of United States tutelage in fiscal responsibility, in collective security and in the techniques of democracy. If they have fallen short in any of these fields, the thought presents itself that the fault may lie as much with the teacher as with the pupils.

When President Theodore Roosevelt announced his "corollary" to the Monroe Doctrine in 1905, he solemnly declared that he regarded the future interventions thus sanctified as a "burden" and a "responsibility" and an obligation to "international equity."

Not once, so far as I know, has the United States regarded itself as intervening in a Latin-American country for selfish or unworthy motives—a view not necessarily shared by the beneficiaries. Whatever reassurance the purity of our motives may give must be shaken a little by the thought that probably no country in all human history has ever intervened in another except for what it regarded as excellent motives.

"The wicked are wicked, no doubt," wrote Thackeray, "and they go astray and they fall, and they come by their deserts; but who can tell the mischief which the very virtuous do?"

Somehow, therefore, if we are to save ourselves, we must find in ourselves the judgment and the will to change the nature of international politics in order to make it at once less dangerous to mankind and more beneficial to individual men.

The Press, the President and Foreign Policy

James B. Reston

The conflict between the men who make and the men who report the news is as old as time. News may be true, but it is not truth, and they never see it the same way. The first great event, or "Man in the News," was Adam, and the accounts of his creation have been the source of controversy ever since. In the old days, the reporters or couriers of bad news were often put to the gallows; now they are given the Pulitzer Prize, but the conflict goes on.

The reasons are plainly that we are changing the world faster than we can change ourselves, and are applying to the present the habits of the past. We are imposing on a transformed world the theories and assumptions that worked in another time at home, and nowhere does this clash of past and present, theory and reality, seem more dramatic than in the application of American constitutional theory to the conduct of American foreign policy.

That theory is that the people know best. The first constitutional principle is that the success of any group of people in dealing with their common problems rests on their knowledge and understanding of the problems to be solved, and on their intelligence, judgment and character in meeting those problems. The conclusion drawn from this is that the intelligence, judgment and character of a majority of the people, if well-informed, will probably produce more satisfactory solutions than any leader or small band of geniuses is likely to produce.

This is undoubtedly sound doctrine for sinking a sewer or building a bridge or a school in a local community, but is it a practical way to conduct foreign policy? Are the people getting adequate information to enable them to reach sound judgments on what to do about South Asia, or the Atlantic, or the balance of payments, or China, or outer space? Is there any such information and any such people? And would enough of them pay attention to sustain a commercial newspaper or radio or television station that concentrated on these fundamental questions? These questions raise the old problem of the people's right to be informed and the government's obligation to govern effectively, which sometimes means governing secretly.

Two contemporary situations illustrate the dilemma. Over 300,000 Americans, many of them conscripts, are now fighting a war in Viet Nam. Most of them do not know how it started, and even many officials are extremely vague about how we got so deeply involved. It cannot be said that the people were well informed before their commitment to the battle, or even that their representatives in the Congress really debated the decision to wage this kind of war. On the other hand, the President is now

"The Press, the President and Foreign Policy," *Foreign Affairs*, Vol. 44, No. 4, July 1966. Reprinted by permission of the publisher.

conducting that war as Commander-in-Chief with television cameras on the battlefield recording daily for vast television audiences the most brutal and agonizing scenes of the struggle.

In the first case, there was so little information and so much executive authority that the President could do about what he pleased; and in the second case, the people have so much information about the violent incidents of the war that it is questionable whether the President of a democratic country can really sustain his policy over a long period of time while the public is being invited to tune in on the eleven o'clock news and see Johnny killed. Something is obviously out of balance.

In analyzing the relationship between public opinion and public policy, it may be useful to try to understand the practical every-day conflict between reporters and officials and how it developed. General Washington went to his grave hating the press, and with good reason. Longfellow said, "This country is not priest-ridden, but press-ridden." I once had an argument about the press with a parson who referred me as penance to the first three verses of the 19th Chapter of the Gospel according to Luke: "And Jesus entered, and passed through Jericho. And behold there was a man named Zacchaeus . . . and he sought to see Jesus . . . and could not for the press. . . ."

The United States had a press before it had a foreign policy. This is a large part of the trouble between its writers and its officials today. The American press was telling the country and the world where to get off before there was a State Department. The eighteenth-century American pamphleteers not only helped write the Constitution but thought—with considerable justification—that they created the union. They believed that government power was potentially if not inevitably wicked and had to be watched, especially when applied in secret and abroad, and they wrote the rules so that the press would be among the watchers. In their more amiable moods, they no doubt conceded that the press should serve the country, but they insisted that the best way to serve it was to criticize its every act and thought, and something of this pugnacious spirit has persisted until now.

The natural and historical differences between the American diplomat and the American reporter are still the main cause of their present trouble. The American diplomat before the Second World War was trained in the days of our isolation to be a silent observer of world affairs. He was as discreet as a priest; he was supposed to know everything and to tell nothing. Even in America, let alone Britain, your ideal State Department man was as handsome as Joseph Grew and as elegant as Dean Acheson, or vice versa. In contrast, the American reporter, circa 1930, was a very gabby and even rakish fellow who was usually trained in the police court, the county courthouse, or, as in my own case, the sports press-box (where, incidentally, you had the consolation of knowing who had won at the end of the day). He was not discreet, but skeptical and often even impertinent. His general view of public officials was that they were probably up to something bad which the Founding Fathers had somehow appointed him personally to expose.

The American reporter of my generation was brought up to believe in the cocky frontier tradition of "publish and be damned," but the American diplomat of the same age quickly came to believe that if he helped you to publish the facts, *he* was likely to be damned, and this was only one of the conflicts that soon developed between the government and the press.

The conduct of foreign policy is a process that never ends; the production of a newspaper or a television news program is a miracle that has to be accomplished somehow on the split second. The Secretary of State must think in generations and continents, but the reporter thinks in "stories," in "minutes" and often in "fragments." One profession is quiet, the other noisy; one slow, the other fast; one precise, the other imprecise. What makes their relationship even more difficult is that they are stuck with one another. They are married without the possibility of divorce, separation or even an occasional period of quiet. The government is always acting and the press is always blabbing and criticizing, and what makes this alliance even more galling is that it is unequal.

There are actually only a few hundred American reporters, editors and commentators dealing primarily with foreign-policy questions all over the world, and those reaching the largest audience are not the well-known commentators but the news agency reporters who serve most daily American newspapers and the radio and television stations as well.

Two points of history and geography are important to an understanding of the American news agency as the primary source of most foreign-policy news. Unlike Reuters in Britain, Havas in France and Wolff in Germany, the original American news agency, the Associated Press, was created not for private profit or government convenience but as a non-profit coöperative association to serve the newspapers that shared the costs. This had some significance, for since it had to serve editors of wholly different and conflicting views on domestic and foreign policy, it had to be as impartial, non-partisan and unbiased as possible. The result was that mutual distrust among American newspapers created the most accurate and trustworthy source of world news the world has ever seen, and with the advent of a second American world-wide news agency, now called United Press International, competition increased both the flow and the accuracy of the news.

The geographical point is more interesting and less encouraging. The American news agencies have to serve a vast continental country covering four different time zones, with some parts facing on the Pacific and some on the Atlantic, some looking north and some south, some living in arctic and some in tropical climates. Accordingly, news had to be written so that a news story on international trade could be filed at length for maritime cities interested in international commerce and briefly for agricultural towns concerned primarily with the price of corn. And vice versa. The news agencies had to devise a technique of writing the news so that each story could be adapted to the diverse needs and interests of widely varied communities.

Accordingly, they invented the "headline" or "all-purpose" agency news story which could be published at length in the large city papers or cut in half for the middle towns or reduced to a paragraph for the very small papers. This solution to a technical problem had results nobody in the A.P. or U.P.I. intended and certainly nobody in the State Department wanted. It tended to sharpen and inflate the news. It created a tradition of putting the most dramatic fact in the story first and then following it with paragraphs of decreasing importance. Thus it encouraged, not a balanced, but a startling presentation of the news, based on what one of my irreverent colleagues calls the "Christ, how the wind blew!" lead. This was fine for the news of wrecks or murders, but was a limiting and distorting device as news of foreign policy became more and more complicated.

II

The conflict between journalists and diplomats is getting worse instead of better for a variety of reasons. The press corps in the major capitals is getting so large that it is often smothering the news rather than covering it. When I started covering the State Department for *The New York Times* in 1941, Secretary of State Hull saw the "regulars" every weekday in his office. He could explain his policies, often in the most vivid Tennessee mountain language, read from the diplomatic cables if he felt like it, and indicate, with full assurance that his confidence would be respected, what was on the record and what had to be off the record. A generation later, the Secretary of State has to meet the reporters in an auditorium where everybody is wired for sound.

The change in the nature of war has also complicated the problem of reconciling the traditions of press and government. The nation is engaged in an underground war, an economic war, an intelligence war, in every continent of the earth. This requires a vast American secret service operation in the armed services and the Central Intelligence Agency. What it costs and all that it does are not disclosed, and this is not only necessary, but it is something comparatively new in American life, at least on the present scale. The old tradition of the American press is that anything a government hides, except in open and declared war, is wrong and should be exposed, but a press demanding unlimited freedom for this principle could in some cases risk the nation's freedom. Yet the problem cannot be solved simply by saying that the operations of the intelligence services of the government are none of the public's business. I knew for over a year that the United States was flying high-altitude planes (the U-2) over the Soviet Union from a base in Pakistan to photograph military and particularly missile activities and bases, but *The New York Times* did not publish this fact until one of the planes was shot down in 1960. Was this a correct judgment? I think it was, but in other circumstances, the press is criticized for not printing intelligence and even military information.

The press, radio and television help create the atmosphere in which the nation lives. It is not an atmosphere that encourages calm reflection or wide perspectives, and it makes little allowance for the limitations of human frailty. We have transferred into the capitals of the world the American police-blotter definition of the news—which is the news of violence and contention, of the unusual rather than the usual—given it the voice of the radio and the eyes of the television camera and added the insistent shouts of the advertiser and the singing commercial.

There are, of course, advantages. The American people are given more information about events that affect their lives than any other people in the world. More Americans now see their public officials and hear them discuss public questions on television than ever before in the history of any sovereign state, but there are disadvantages, too. Casual conversation about delicate diplomatic questions is necessarily imprecise, while the language of diplomacy is supposed above everything else to be precise. Officials find the television interview more dangerous but more alluring than the private interview, for though what is said on television must stand as spoken, they can reach millions by television in no more time than it takes to talk quietly and privately to a single newspaper reporter.

In times of high controversy over policy, this constant public thrust and counter-thrust of criticism and defense, while inevitable in a democracy, has a serious effect on public officials. The more their policies are criticized, the more time they spend on defending their policies, until the words become as important as the acts and the defense of the policy takes on more meaning than the policy itself.

The energy devoted by the President and the Secretaries of State and Defense to the public-relations aspects of foreign policy is almost beyond calculation. When they are being criticized, they seem all the more eager to argue their case in public. If we really knew the cost of all this physical and nervous strain on the principal officers of our government, we would probably be appalled. The pressure merely of being agreeable to critics in the press and the Congress must by itself be a trial, and it certainly leaves little time for reflection on anything except the particular crisis in the headlines at the moment.

The obvious conclusion to be drawn from all this is that neither the press, nor the Congress, nor the Executive Branch has yet adjusted effectively to the new demands of the age. We are all following the procedures that were no doubt adequate when foreign policy was a secondary consideration. At the State Department, the men who are available to most reporters are not informed, and the men who are informed are usually too busy with the crisis to be available. On Capitol Hill, each committee is sovereign and assumes that Cabinet officers have nothing else to do but to repeat the same testimony three or four times to three or four different committees. And in the news-gathering agencies we go on doing more or less what we did a generation ago.

III

Personally, I do not believe that the constitutional assumption that "the people know best" is a very reliable guide to the conduct of American foreign policy today. Similarly even the modern techniques for reporting foreign news are not yet adequate to the subject or to the need, but we should be careful about reaching the conclusion that the remedy lies with a less assertive press. It is not the press that is extending its power to the detriment of a sound balance between public opinion and foreign policy, but the President, whose power in this field is greater than that of any head of government in the modern world.

The question we have to ask is not about the President's interests, but about the public interest. No doubt both President and press will abuse their power from time to time, but where is the greater danger to the public interest—in the present power of the press or in the present power of the President?

I believe the power of the Presidency has been increasing steadily since the Second World War, particularly since the introduction of nuclear weapons, and that the power of the press and even of the Congress to restrain him has declined proportionately during this same period.

The Presidential power in the foreign field is in direct proportion to the size of the issue. The press can still embarrass him by premature disclosure of his plans, and the Congress can still oppose and even defy him on peripheral issues, but on the great acts of foreign policy, especially those involving the risk or even the act of war, he is more powerful in this age than in any other, freer to follow his own bent than any other single political leader in the world—and the larger and more fateful the issue, the greater is his authority to follow his own will.

As the leader of a world-wide coalition of nations engaged in constant contention with hostile forces in scores of different theaters of action or manœuvre, he is virtually assured of support once he proclaims his intentions. The Congress, of course, retains its power to deny him the funds to carry out his plans, but it cannot do so without repudiating him in the face of the enemy and assuming responsibility for the crisis that would surely follow.

President Johnson's use of the so-called Congressional Resolution on Viet Nam illustrates this point. The Congress did not initiate that resolution. It was written in the State Department and sent to Congress for approval on the morning after Communist P.T. boats made an unsuccessful attack on U.S. destroyers patrolling in the Gulf of Tonkin. It was not limited to the specific attack or even to the specific country at war. It asked the Congress to give the President authority to use whatever power "he" deemed necessary, not only in the Gulf of Tonkin or in Viet Nam but anywhere in all of Southeast Asia against any Communist aggression.

Obviously, the Congress complied, with very little debate and with only two dissenting votes. It could scarcely have done otherwise. It followed the procedure initiated by President Eisenhower in the Formosan and Lebanon resolutions of the fifties, and in similar situations in the future it is hard to imagine any Congress—even one dominated by the opposition party—doing otherwise.

The gravity of the issues since the advent of the cold war and atomic weapons has clearly enhanced the power of the President. In fact, I cannot think of a single major foreign-policy move any President wanted to make since the Second World War that he was unable to carry through because of the opposition of the press or of Congress.

President Wilson died believing that the balance of political power in America had swung so far toward the Senate that no President would ever be able to pass another major treaty. Yet President Eisenhower and his Secretary of State, John Foster Dulles, scattered treaty commitments all over the Middle East and South Asia with scarcely a dissenting voice in the Congress or in the press. President Kennedy waged one proxy war against Cuba, and risked a nuclear war with Russia over that same island without even asking the Congress. President Johnson sent more than 300,-000 men to war in Viet Nam despite some sharp criticism from many of the nation's leading newspapers and commentators.

I do not say this is wrong, but merely that it is a fact of the nuclear age. In the Cuban missile crisis of 1962, President Kennedy was free to blockade Cuba, or bomb Havana, or, for that matter, to do nothing, on the excuse that we had missiles in Turkey, so why not Soviet missiles in Cuba? Eisenhower was free to send his bombers to Dien Bien Phu in 1953 to relieve the French, or to refuse to do so, just as he was free to go to the help of Hungary when it was invaded by the Red Army, or to pass by on the other side. President Johnson was obviously free to bomb North Viet Nam or not to bomb it, to negotiate with Hanoi or to blow it up, to mine the harbor of Haiphong or to leave it alone. No sovereign in history ever had such power or responsibility.

The press may report the news but the President makes it. If Senators are dominating the front pages with their protests against his foreign policy, and editors and professors are creating newsworthy disturbances on the university campuses and on the editorial pages, the President has a convenient remedy. He can divert public attention to himself. He can arrange a conference on an island in the Pacific, for example. Within 72 hours, he can bring the leaders of the nations on his side to a meeting that will arrest the interest of the world. Reporters and photographers will converge from all the capitals and fill the front pages with accounts of the proceedings, thereby overwhelming the less dramatic Senatorial mutterings.

This gives the President quite an edge. The reporters and commentators on the scene may see all this as an elaborate camouflage of realities and write their waspish critiques of the proceedings at his conference, but unless the great man is incorrigibly clumsy, which with the help of an experienced civil service he usually is not, the big front-page headlines will have much more effect than the witty chatter on page 32.

The two Roosevelts were the Presidents who first understood the primacy of news over opinion. Teddy Roosevelt used to joke that he "discovered Monday." He recognized that editors had little news on Sunday night and that if he held back his Presidential announcements until then, he got a better display on the front pages on Monday morning, even with secondary news, than he got on Wednesday with really important news. Franklin Roosevelt, who was elected to the Presidency four times against the overwhelming opposition of the American newspapers, was even better at dominating the news. He concentrated on the reporters and the front pages and vilified or scorned the commentators and the editorial pages.

Every President since then has understood the point. Europe has a press that elevates opinion; America has a press, radio and television that emphasize news. The Lippmanns, the Krocks, the Alsops, have their audiences, and the brilliant young American satirists, Russell Baker of *The New York Times* and Art Buchwald of the *Herald Tribune*, tickle the intellectuals and often come nearer to the truth than all the solemn scribblers, but news is more powerful than opinion, and this is the point the politicians have understood.

Thus the President almost always has the initiative over both press and Congress if he chooses to use the instruments of power now at his command. He is no equal partner with the Congress in the conduct of foreign affairs, if he ever was. He and he alone is in constant communication with almost every other leader in the world. He can reach his own countrymen from his television studio in the White House whenever great events justify a request for network time. When the Congress is squabbling in the wings over Rule 22 or the intricacies of repealing Section 14-b of the Taft-Hartley Act, the President is constantly proclaiming the brotherhood of man, progress, generosity toward the weak and the elevation of the poor and underdeveloped.

There is a theory, widely advertised at annual meetings of editors and publishers, that the modern Presidential press conference is a restraining influence on the Chief Executive. According to this notion, the reporters are representatives of the people, like members of the British House of Commons, who have the power to make the great man answer questions, usually about his shortcomings or failures. There is a shred of truth in this, but not much more.

President Johnson demonstrated his command of the press conference in a very simple way. He knew that the Washington press corps was full of specialists, some of whom had devoted most of their careers to the study of foreign affairs, or the federal judiciary, or science or military affairs, and therefore not only knew their subjects, but probably knew more about them than he did. If he announced his news conferences in advance, they would come running with their well-informed and awkward inquiries. So he simply did not announce his news conferences.

He called them when only the White House correspondents were around, and then usually on the weekends when only a few of them were on duty. He held them in his own executive office, where he was not on display before the cameras, but talking intimately with the reporters who travel with him all the time and are not only familiar to him but subject to his system of punishments and rewards, which can be embarrassing to a reporter on a highly competitive beat.

The point here is not that this is wicked, but merely that nobody need grieve too mournfully over the fiction of a poor, defenseless President badgered by a pack of insensitive and irresponsible barbarians. There is nothing in the Constitution that obliges him to conduct his office for the convenience of reporters. If he is experienced enough to get to the White House, he is usually nimble enough to handle the reporters who work there.

Every President develops his own defenses in this situation. Franklin Roosevelt scorned and ridiculed his questioners. He once pinned a Nazi Iron Cross on John O'Donnell of the *New York News* during the Second World War and ordered Robert Post of *The New York Times* to put on a dunce cap and stand in the corner. Asking President Truman a question was like pitching batting practice to the Yankees. He decapitated you and then grinned. President Eisenhower was amiably incomprehensible. President Kennedy, the real master of "the game," was a witty computer. He either overwhelmed you with decimal points, or disarmed you with a smile and a wisecrack. And President Johnson learned early to apply to the press conference the technique of the Senate filibuster.

President Johnson held only nine formal news conferences last year and has had only one this year. This, however, distorts the record and does not clarify his method. No President in the history of the Republic has ever devoted so much time to reporters, editors and commentators. But he thinks of reporters in subjective rather than in objective terms, as individuals rather than as instruments of a free press in a free society; he sees them individually and at such length that the reporters themselves are often embarrassed to intrude so much on his other duties. It was not unusual last year for the President to sit casually in his rocking chair talking steadily to a reporter for a couple of hours, and sometimes even much longer than that.

This, of course, can be very helpful to the reporter concerned, but conversations of this length somehow imply, even if the President does not intend them to do so, a confidential, personal relationship that actually ties the reporter up more than it frees him to do his job. It is very difficult to sit and listen to a President explaining his terrible problems and narrow options without becoming sympathetic to the man and subjective about his policies. It is all the harder to remain detached about the range of topics discussed when he asks you what you would do in his place.

The power of the President to use the free press against itself is very great. If, for example, an influential columnist or commentator criticizes him for landing 25,000 Marines in the Dominican Republic to put down a rebellion, it is very easy for him to call in several other carefully selected commentators and give them the detailed argument for landing the Marines. He has all the vivid facts of the situation, and if he wants to put them out, he does not have to announce them himself. Other reporters will be perfectly willing to accommodate him, even though they know they are being used to knock down the story of another colleague.

The function of criticism itself has changed in an odd way during President Johnson's Administration. In the past, there has been a reasonable expectation among people writing political criticism that if they identified a problem, checked it out thoroughly, and proposed a reasonable remedy, publication of these things would be read within the government in good faith and maybe even considered worthy of executive action.

This is still true today on questions of policy, but if the topic deals with individuals in the Administration, the chances are that the criticism will perpetuate the situation criticized. For example, if you write today that a particular Cabinet member has been exhausted by overwork, and should be liberated for his own and the nation's good, you can be fairly sure that you have condemned that man to stay at his grindstone until everybody has forgotten that you ever mentioned him.

Also, if you learn that the President is going to do something on Friday and print it on Tuesday, this is likely to be regarded as an impertinence and a presumption which the President will punish by changing his plans. I once saw the speech President Johnson was going to make at the twentieth anniversary celebration of the founding of the United Nations and printed his plans for ending the financial crisis that was going on in the U.N. at that time. He was furious. He called in the Secretary of State the very night of publication, ordered the speech rewritten to eliminate the reported plans and made a different speech.

This is fair enough, but behind it there is a philosophic idea that has some disturbing possibilities. Bill Moyers, the White House press secretary, explained the President's view in these terms: "It is very important for a President to maintain up until the moment of decision his options, and for someone to speculate days or weeks in advance that he's going to do thus and thus is to deny to the President the latitude he needs in order to make, in the light of existing circumstances, the best possible decision."

No doubt this is true in many circumstances, but not in all. Is absolutely nothing to be printed about clandestine plans by the President to mount an illegal invasion at the Bay of Pigs in Cuba for fear of interfering with the President's option to humiliate the country? Are the people to be denied information about Presidential options that will involve them in a war they have to finance and fight? If all Presidential options are to be protected from speculation "until the very last minute," what redress will there be the next day after the President has opted to dispatch the Marines or bomb Hanoi, or publish a request to wage war as "he" deems necessary all over Southeast Asia?

These are hard questions, and the answers are not that the Commander-in-Chief must telegraph all his punches in advance. But at the same time, the doctrine of "no speculation" before action, even on non-military matters, is something new in the catalogue of Presidential privilege.

In such a world, no doubt he needs all the advantages and privileges he can get. He has to take responsibility for his actions and we do not. He is the principal actor on the stage, but he did not write the script and may not even like the role. Therefore, he tries constantly to use whatever devices he can to ease the agony. He manages the news, as the heads of all institutions do, by emphasizing his successes and minimizing his losses. He has his own photographers constantly taking his picture and releases those that convey the impression of strong leadership or compassion or whatever other mood he wants to convey at the moment. All this is understandable, but we should not be foooled: the trend of power is running with the President, the danger of excessive use of power lies not in the newspapers but in the White House, and even the most casual look at the influence of reporters and commentators today makes this fairly obvious.

IV

Never have reporters and commentators reached so many people in America with their news and views as they do now, or had so little power to influence the direction of the nation's foreign policy. The television network "stars" reach as many as 26 million viewers a night. They bring in their vivid reports on video tape from all the major capitals and battle-fields of the world and occasionally even bounce them off man-made stars in transoceanic broadcasts, but the reaction of the public is quite different in the foreign field than in the national field.

A fundamental change has occurred in the attitude of the American people toward the government's conduct of foreign policy. In the old days, the people tended to believe the government was wrong until war was actually declared; now, confronted with torrents of ambiguous and often contradictory information about questions that could lead to war, the tendency is to assume the government is right. I believe the American reporters were nearer to the truth than the published government reports during the critical periods that preceded the indirect American invasion of Cuba in 1961 and the large American intervention in South Viet Nam in 1965, but the people paid little attention to those reports and the government was free to use its own judgment, which was not brilliant.

What influence the press has on the conduct of foreign policy often comes indirectly, not through the mass of the people, but mainly through the Congress of the United States. The relations between well-informed reporters in Washington and influential Senators and Congressmen are quite different from the relations between reporters and officials of the Executive Branch of the government. Officials in the White House, the State Department and the Defense Department, though polite and often friendly, almost always regard the reporter with suspicion.

Congressmen are different. Unlike officials of the Executive, they live most of the time in the open. They think the good opinion of the press is important to their reëlection, which interests them, so they see us and some of them even read us. Also, they are always making speeches and, like reporters, looking for mistakes to correct or criticize, especially if they are in the opposition. So the reporter and the Congressman are often natural allies. They exchange information in a discreet way, and sometimes in ways that are not so discreet. When the Administration comes to the Congressmen for its money, it has to answer their questions and justify its programs and in the process it discloses a lot of information which interests the press a great deal. Also reporters gather a great deal of information in foreign embassies from some of the finest diplomats in the world, and when this appears in the press, Congressmen often want to question Cabinet members about it, and can do so much more easily than the reporters who published it in the first place.

This relationship between reporters and diplomats is not only widely misunderstood but under-rated. Even well-informed and sophisticated Americans are often irritated by the toplofty pronouncements of American commentators, who seem to pass judgment on the Buddhists and Catholics in Viet Nam one day, explain the mysteries of Southern Rhodesia, the Congo and South Africa the next, psychoanalyze Senator Fulbright and Secretary of State Rusk on the third, and so on triumphantly through the week, without ever a doubt or a day of rest. It seems an impossibility and a presumption for any one man to know so much about so many things, but that is not the way it is.

Most of us are merely reporters of other men's ideas. Diplomats and reporters have one job in common: they have to report what is going on, the first to his government, the second to his paper or station. All the influential people in Washington may be furious about France but they will be polite to the French Ambassador. They will tell a thoughtful reporter what they really thank about President de Gaulle's policy but they will probably pull their punches with Charles Lucet. Knowing this, the French Ambassador will often talk to a well-informed reporter. He will exchange information, but on one condition, namely that the source of the information is not disclosed.

Therefore, if the reporter is passing on information gathered by the French in Saigon or by the Canadian member of the International Control Commission on Viet Nam, he cannot disclose where he got the information. He must pretend that somehow, in his infinite knowledge and wisdom, this is the way things are, for he is obliged to indulge in "compulsory plagiarism."

In the process a great deal of useful information and political analysis is gathered. The diplomats are the unpaid stringers for the reporters, the reporters the unpaid tipsters for the diplomats. Ideas that professional diplomats might hesitate to mention to the Secretary of State, and information and analysis which the reporter probably would not have gathered in any other way, thus get into the newspapers, hopefully wtihout propaganda, and may sometimes even be read by the President—which may have been what the diplomat had in mind in the first place.

In such ways, reporters and commentators do no doubt have influence. They keep the debate on foreign affairs going. We can irritate the President, divert him from his tasks, stir up his enemies, excite the public and force him to calm things down, and sometimes even make a persuasive point which he may modify a policy to meet. But his power is at the center of action and we are at the edge, and my conclusion from this is fairly plain. We may be a nuisance but we are not a menace. And the way power is running to the President, it would be unwise, I think, to concentrate too much on weakening whatever influence we have left.

V

In the State Department, which is not unduly frivolous, the Foreign Service officers have a fable. The grasshopper, worried about getting through the winter, sought advice from the cockroach, who seemed to thrive on cold weather. The cockroach was sympathetic. On the night of the first frost, he said, find a warm spot back of a radiator in a bakery, turn yourself into a cockroach, and stay there happily until spring. "But how," asked the grasshopper, "do I make myself into a cockroach?" "Look," said the cockroach, "I'm merely giving you policy guidance."

Most critics of the press and government give much the same kind of policy guidance: change and be saved, they say. Transform yourselves into something quite different from what you are. Stop giving the customers just anything they want—any amusement, any violence, anything that sells beer or cosmetics—and give them instead information they need to know to be good citizens in a democracy. You were not protected by the First Amendment in order to be a cheerleader for the status quo or your own social or economic class but to serve the general interest.

We will only fool ourselves if we think we are going to compete effectively for the mass mind against the voice of the hawker, or bring about vast changes in the present ways of making, reporting and listening to the news, but some things might be done in some important places to reach and enlarge what Carlyle called the vital "remnant" of thoughtful citizens.

Newspapers are no longer the first messengers of the spot news, and television has deprived the newspaper of the great "picture" story. As a result, the modern newspaper is searching for a new role, or should be, and that role lies in the field of thoughtful explanation, which tends to make it more of an ally of the official than a competitor. We are no longer in the transmitting business, but in the education business. In fact, the mass communications of this country probably have more effect on the American mind than all the schools and universities combined, and the problem is that neither the officials who run the government, nor the officials who run the newspapers, nor the radio and televsion news programs, have adjusted to that fact.

We are in trouble on the news side for a very simple reason: we have not kept our definition of news up to date. We are pretty good at reporting "happenings," particularly if they are dramatic; we are fascinated by events but not by the things that cause the events. We will send 500 correspondents to Viet Nam after the war breaks out, and fill the front pages with their reports, meanwhile ignoring the rest of the world, but we will not send five reporters there when the danger of war is developing, and even if we do, their reports of the danger will be minimized, by editors and officials alike, as "speculation" and hidden back among the brassiere ads, if they are not hung on the spike.

I believe we in the news business are going to have to twist ourselves around and see these wider perspectives of the news, the causes as well as the effects, what is going to happen in addition to what governments do. It is not governments that are transforming the world today, but the fertility of people, the creativity of scientists, the techniques of engineers and economists and the discoveries of physicians. Almost all governments in the world today are merely rushing around trying to keep up with the consequences of what is happening outside their own official offices. What the Roman Catholic Church does about birth control, for example, is probably going to be bigger news than what the Indian government does about it. The movement toward the unification of Europe did not start with governments but with private citizens like Jean Monnet. And it is being carried on by European businessmen—who like the larger markets and the fluidity of labor across national frontiers—rather than by governments.

Ideas are news, and we are not covering the news of the mind as we should. This is where rebellion, revolution and war start, but we minimize the conflict of ideas and emphasize the conflict in the streets, without relating the second to the first. If the Secretary of Defense says, for the thousandth time, that the United States has enough hydrogen bombs on airplanes and submarines to wipe out both China and the Soviet Union, even after they have destroyed every major city in the United States, he is assured a big boxcar headline on the front page of every big city newspaper in America and a prominent place on the Cronkite and Huntley-Brinkley shows. But if some thoughtful professor makes a speech demonstrating that the destruction of the human race can be avoided, he may easily be ignored even in his home town.

What few practical suggestions can we make that may have some chance of acceptance in a few places? First, we are not likely to get more serious correspondence in the daily newspaper until we stop making analytical articles compete for space with spot news. There is always more spot news, much of it trivial rubbish, than any paper can print. It should not be impossible, however, to get the publishers of the big city newspapers to set aside a few columns of space every day for articles on the big issues. They do not make the recipes or the comics compete for space with spot news. They print them daily "for another reason," for a certain group of their readers, and the same thing could be done for their most thoughtful subscribers.

Second, the networks could do much more than they are now doing if they would put aside an hour each weekend to review the important news of the week and put it into some historical perspective. Congressional hearings which aim not to legislate but to educate have immense possibilities. Let the responsible committees of Congress explore the problems of population, of the Atlantic Alliance, of the balance of payments, of education and poverty—say one great issue every month or so—and let the networks carry the principal parts of the testimony for an hour at the weekend.

Third, much more could be done in the field of adult education on foreign affairs if the right kind of case studies were prepared and made available to study groups in the churches, service clubs and other non-government organizations. Some of this goes on, but the method of study is vital to its success. The problem, I believe, is to present the great issues as a series of practical choices: to let the people look at the alternatives as the President has to look at them and try at the end to decide between the hard and dangerous courses. We need simple case-study outlines containing first a statement of the facts; second, a definition of one course of action, followed by arguments for and arguments against; and so on through definition of a second course, and a third and fourth. The difficulty with the presentation of foreign-policy news to the people today is that it comes out a jumble of important and trivial things and personalities, so that the people cannot quite get the questions for decision clear, and end up either by giving up, or choosing up sides for or against the President. Even the Sunday newspapers might find room in their endless pages and sections for a syndicated case study of the issue of the month, but if not there, the foundations might take the project on.

Fourth, if I may engage in a little heresy, it may be that news and analysis of news in a democracy are too serious to be left to newspapermen. The United States has been involved in the world now for two generations. We have developed in the process a very large company of men and women in the universities, the foundations, international business, communications and the government, who are well-informed on world affairs—some of them better informed on many subjects than any other people in the world. Unfortunately, they are not sharing with their fellow-countrymen a great deal of what they know.

The great opportunity of the daily newspaper is that it reaches people when they are paying attention. Galbraith can write a learned, amusing and provocative book about his diplomatic mission in India, which would probably come out when everybody's mind was on the Congo or the sad decline of the New York Yankees, and if he was lucky, 50,000 people would read it, but if he took a day in the middle of the Indian-Pakistani war to analyze the conflict for the newspapers he could have an attentive audience of easily 20,000,000.

We need more open pages, preferably next to the editorial pages, where the best minds of the world could give their analysis of current developments; where the vivid passages out of the best speeches and periodical articles and editorials of the world could appear; where we could find the philosophers worrying not about the particular bill of the day but the issue of the decade. These could, if edited by thoughtful minds, be among the liveliest pages in the daily newspaper and bring some sense of balance and history to contemporary events. The "Letters to the Editor" columns of most newspapers—this is not true of New York—have been dominated by publicists and crackpots for years. We should be able to do better than that and make them into an exciting forum for the exchange of ideas and even for criticism of the papers themselves.

These modest suggestions for broadening and deepening the flow of serious news in America are not really beyond the capacity of the big papers and stations, and they are not, in my view, against their long-range commercial interest. Also, if we let our reporters use their minds as well as their legs on serious inquiries and then print their findings, we will undoubtedly attract and keep more sensitive and perceptive men and women. At the same time, we should attract more and more of the intelligent young readers who are pouring out of our universities in an ever larger stream and expecting from their newspapers a much more detailed and sophisticated account of world affairs.

On the official side, too, some improvements are desirable and even possible. The attitude of the President toward the reporters is vital. If he regards them primarily as a problem and therefore tries to manipulate them, they eventually convey their suspicion and even hostility to the people. If, on the other hand, he regards them as an opportunity and tries to explain his problems to them, they can be a valuable educational force. It is the President, however, who has the initiative and the capacity to define the rules and set the tone of public discussion. A revival of the calm philosophic talk or the quiet "conversation," as typified by Roosevelt's fireside chat, could help keep the public mind on the larger questions and minimize the capacity of others to divert attention onto narrow personal issues.

There has been a decline, too, in recent years in the relations between the experts in the State Department and the reporters. The reason for this is that the experts know the President likes to dominate public announcements and are afraid that they might disclose something that would detonate his temper. And since the most useful information comes, not from the top leaders, but from the men who brief the leaders, this chokes down a very valuable stream of information.

No government in history ever received such a torrent of information from abroad as the United States Government does at present. Washington is inundated every day with reports on every imaginable problem. A good deal of this information is interesting and unclassified and could help nourish the flow of knowledge into the newspapers and periodicals of the nation, but it is not made available mainly because nobody thinks of making it available or because the idea has grown up that all this "belongs" to the government.

It should be possible for officials and reporters to do much better than they have done in discussing these problems and opportunities together. There is a great deal of chatter about it with the White House Press Secretary on the presidential press plane flying between Washington and Texas, but all suggestions for more formal committees to analyze and correct obvious shortcomings, or alternatively for the press to establish some way of correcting itself, have usually ended in useless vapor.

"If there is ever to be an amelioration of the condition of mankind," John Adams wrote in 1815, "philosophers, theologians, legislators, politicians and moralists will find that the regulation of the press is the most difficult, dangerous and important problem they have to resolve. Mankind cannot now be governed without it, nor at present with it."

I am more hopeful. There is some reason to believe that the old conflict will diminish in time. Powerful forces are working for coexistence. In his own interest, the reporter is having to become an educator, and the more he concentrates upon explaining the news instead of being first with the news, the more the official will want to coöperate with him.

Subversion by Government

Norman Cousins

The CIA was conceived twenty years ago as a specific response to the global subversive activities of communism. It was decided, on the highest levels of government, that what the U.S. needed was a super-secret agency with worldwide capabilities—an agency far more secret than even the FBI.

The CIA was specifically exempted at the start from most of the checks and balances that are indigenous to American Constitutional government. The funds at its disposal might run into billions of dollars, but there was no requirement for open public or legislative debate or review. The agency would be responsible to the President and would operate through a watchdog committee in Congress but even this procedure was at variance with the Constitutional requirements.

The work of the CIA was divided into two broad areas. One area involved the operation of a top-level information-gathering service that would make its reports available to the security centers of government, such as the White House, Department of Defense, Department of State. The second area was an operational branch that would carry out top-secret activities designed to advance the national interests of the United States.

It is now essential, on the basis of available but limited information, to attempt an assessment.

The analyses and reports compiled by the information or intelligence arm of the CIA, according to many competent observers inside and outside government, have been of the highest order.

"Subversion by Government," *Saturday Review,* March 4, 1967. Reprinted by permission of the author and publisher.

It is over the action area, however, that the difficulties and the debates have arisen. The most recent disclosures about the CIA concern secret government funds being channeled into universities, labor unions, and organizations of students, newsmen, and businessmen. CIA officials privately would probably point to such activities as being among their finest achievements. For these were no cloak-and-dagger operations involving thefts of secret documents or underground acts of daring and violence. These activities have been part of an effort to mount an intellectual and cultural counter-offensive against the threat of communist ideology. The CIA was shrewd enough to know that the most effective forces it could recruit and send into the field would come not from the far right but from the center and the non-communist left. In the case of the international meetings of students, newsmen, and labor leaders, the main purpose of the CIA was not to use Americans as agents but to give the United States top-level representation at world intellectual or economic meetings involving opportunities for leadership.

Defenders of these CIA activities say that the nation has been well served by what they describe as a highly sophisticated and knowledgeable counter-offensive against the enemies of cultural and political freedom. It is also said that the CIA, both in Washington and in the field, has maintained the highest standards in the recruiting of its personnel.

But all this is beside the main point. For what is intended as a defense of the CIA actually constitutes its severest indictment. It has now been demonstrated that even the most well-intentioned purposes and projects, when conceived and carried out within the context of undercover operations, carry penalties that far outweigh any good that might be achieved. The abuses of the CIA are not chargeable to poor judgment of its officials. The abuses are inherent in the terrible misconception behind the existence of the CIA.

The secret underwriting by the CIA of activities by the National Student Association is a case in point. Some student leaders who cooperated with the CIA were exempted from the draft. All were required to lie and to sign oaths saying they would not reveal the true state of affairs.

Half the nation's population is under the age of twenty-five. It is always risky to characterize the dominant mood of any generation, but there are many indications that many of the young people of this country today are losing confidence in the ability of their elders to operate a civilization responsibly or to demonstrate the kind of integrity that can provide a moral tone for the society. The discovery that the government itself has played a corrupting role is not likely to have a cleansing effect on the attitudes of the young people toward adult-approved institutions.

The misconception behind the existence of the CIA is a simple one. That misconception is that it is possible and proper to turn over to a group of men the kind of authority and power that the U.S. Constitution was specifically designed to prevent. In fact, the very existence of the CIA is a monument to the failure of the recent and present generation of policymakers in government to take the basic philosophy of this nation seriously. The main point or principle that emerged from the work of the Philadelphia Constitutional Convention was that the biggest danger to human

freedom was represented not just by bad men at the heads of bad governments but by good men who were put in positions where they were able
to operate outside the law. The Founding Fathers didn't have to be told
that extraordinary situations would arise in which extraordinary authority
might be required. What concerned them, however, was that the existence
of such situations might stampede and mislead men into creating a mechanism that in itself would be subversive of Constitutional government.

While the full story of the CIA in practice, as apart from theory, is
known only to a few, enough is now known to underscore the foresight
of the American Founders. Consider Cuba. When President John F. Kennedy came to office, he was confronted by a fully developed plan to equip
and finance an emigré invasion of Cuba. The effort failed, despite extravagant advance assurances to the contrary. The President was urged to bail
out the enterprise by authorizing the use of American troops for invasion
purposes. This the President refused to do—not because the might of the
United States was inadequate for such an objective, but because the President had a sense of history, respect for the moral position of the United
States in the world, and was opposed to the killing of thousands of Cubans.

The Cuban episode revealed one aspect of the grave danger represented
by the CIA. This was that it could set forces in motion which could impel
an American President, governed by considerations of national pride, to
depart from his own basic policies. President Kennedy had the wisdom
and the courage to avoid compounding a national error. It would be a
serious mistake, however, to suppose that such qualities are automatically
built into the Presidency.

President Dwight D. Eisenhower sought to ease world tensions by ex-
ploring with the Soviet Union the possibility of bringing the spiraling
world arms race under control. He wanted to take full advantage of any
genuine change in Soviet leadership following the death of Josef Stalin.
The President's moves in this direction were blocked by the action of the
CIA in penetrating the airspace of the Soviet Union with a spying plane
at precisely the time a Paris summit meeting was about to begin. The
President was persuaded by the head of the CIA to identify himself with
the incident, lest it appear before the world that the President had been
cut off from the nation's own security policies.

General Eisenhower ordered the discontinuation of the spying planes
over Russian territory, but the episode undermined his long-held hope that
he could make a fundamental contribution to the enlargement of world
peace. No one knows whether the summit meeting, if it had been held,
would have altered history, but it is not inconceivable that a dent might
have been made in the arms race, possibly including the signing of a
nuclear test ban and a nonproliferation treaty. In any event, it was demonstrated once again that the CIA had veto power over U.S. policy.

The role of the CIA in Vietnam is a matter of speculation. One of the
sticking points in the Geneva negotiations of 1954 that ended the French
occupation of Indo-China had to do with the provision in the Geneva
Treaty calling for all outside forces to leave the area. Premier Mendès-
France of France has said he was pressed at the negotiations to provide
assurance that the departure of the French would not be the signal for

the arrival of the Americans. Mendès-France replied he had no reason to believe that the United States would not respect the terms of the Geneva Treaty. Shortly after the French left, the United States moved into Laos and Vietnam. The Bao Dai government in South Vietnam was replaced by that of U.S.-backed Ngo Dinh Diem. The countrywide free elections specified in the Geneva agreement were called off by South Vietnam. Shortly thereafter, the Vietcong started its campaign of assassination, terror, and subversion against the South. The Vietcong was backed by North Vietnam but a large part of its total military supplies—at one point it reached an estimated 80 per cent—came from the United States, having been captured or turned over by Vietcong sympathizers.

Eventually, the Diem government was violently overthrown from within and its President killed in a coup in which the United States was a tacit partner, according to former U.S. Ambassador to Vietnam Frederick G. Nolting, Jr. The Ambassador said he believed it was not the CIA but the State Department that gave its approval to the enterprise. Be that as it may, the critical point here is that the government of the United States was involved in the subversion of another government. The overthrow and murder of Diem made a shambles of America's declaration that it came into South Vietnam at the express invitation of that government in order to keep it from being subverted.

As for Laos, this observer has no information about the role of the CIA in the ghastly mistake that led the United States in 1960 to help Phoumi Nosavan stage his military coup against the elected government of Souvanna Phouma. What is known, however, is that the coup touched off a civil war, with the United States in the incredible position of supplying arms to both sides and paying the salaries of both armies.

Eventually, the United States helped to restore the government of Souvanna Phouma, but the incredible misadventure had meanwhile taken the lives of thousands of civilians and soldiers.

While in Vientiane, Laos, in 1960, I met a pilot from the Tom Dooley Hospital who told me he had just turned down an offer of $3,000 a month from the CIA to fly arms secretly to a corner of Burma where remnants of the Chinese Nationalist Army had settled after the revolution. Several weeks after my encounter with the pilot, I read newspaper reports about demonstrations outside the U.S. Embassy in Rangoon when it became known that the United States had violated Burmese sovereignty and had jeopardized Burma's security vis-à-vis its powerful neighbor to the north. If one aspect of the work of the CIA is to make friends for the United States, this particular aim was not furthered in Burma.

The Secretary of State has justified these activities by describing them as an inevitable concomitant of international life in the world today. The United States, he has said, should not be the only country to stand aloof from such undertakings.

This remarkable statement misses the main points at issue. One point is that one of the characteristics that distinguishes the United States from totalitarian countries is the trust that it can inspire both in its own people and in other peoples throughout the world. How do we weaken the communist conspiracy or any other conspiracy when we make other nations uncertain and suspicious about the depth and range of our secret activities inside their countries? Is it established that the only effective way of dealing with totalitarians is to imitate them?

A second point has to do with the concept of a free society held by those who are now acting in its name. When did the American people give their representatives in government the right to engage in the subversion of other governments or to decide arbitrarily and outside Constitutional processes how their money is to be spent, or to involve its own citizens in secret oaths, or to give some citizens special privileges for playing the game?

The third point is that there is no more pathetic fallacy than the notion that such enterprises can be carried out without corrupting those who are part of them. Those who believe that it is possible to mount a CIA in a free society and keep its operations sanitary are poor students of history. Moreover, the notion that it is possible to keep these operations totally secret is a species of naïveté.

Nothing would be easier than to attempt to pin the blame on a few government officials. The blame must reach into the society as a whole. Nothing as large as this could have come this far without the involvement of large elements of the American community.

A government now exists within a government. That interior government has not been elected. It cannot easily be replaced or recalled. But neither is it beyond the reach of the American people. It will be said that the nation's security requires that further debate over the CIA be closed. But it is precisely in the name of national security that the debate must be pursued—that is, if the national security bears any relationship to what the nation is all about.

Chapter Fourteen

SUGGESTED QUESTIONS FOR CLASS DISCUSSION.

1. Do you agree that it was in the interest of the United States to involve itself directly in the affairs of Southeast Asia, even to the point of committing American combat troops in Vietnam? Do you think our position is imperialistic?

2. Do you agree with Senator Fulbright's assessment that our involvement in Southeast Asia has been a tragic mistake and now poses a threat to both our internal and external safety? Could Fulbright's position be called isolationist?

3. What do you think the responsibility of the press is in reporting events in the sometimes delicate area of international relations? Should it sometimes become a partner in suppressing news?

4. Do you think an organization like the CIA really poses a threat to American democracy, or are our roots in the democratic process so deeply embedded that the system can tolerate a secret agency wielding power which at times is in conflict with Constitutional prohibitions? What difficulties do you see in the conflict between the necessity for an agency which operates in secrecy and the demands of public government so essential for a democracy?